Economic Integration in Central America

William R. Cline and Enrique Delgado, Editors

*A study sponsored jointly by the Brookings Institution
and the Secretariat of Economic Integration of Central America*

THE BROOKINGS INSTITUTION / WASHINGTON, D.C.

THE BROOKINGS INSTITUTION is an independent organization devoted to nonpartisan research, education, and publication in economics, government, foreign policy, and the social sciences generally. Its principal purposes are to aid in the development of sound public policies and to promote public understanding of issues of national importance.

The Institution was founded on December 8, 1927, to merge the activities of the Institute for Government Research, founded in 1916, the Institute of Economics, founded in 1922, and the Robert Brookings Graduate School of Economics and Government, founded in 1924.

The Board of Trustees is responsible for the general administration of the Institution, while the immediate direction of the policies, program, and staff is vested in the President, assisted by an advisory committee of the officers and staff. The by-laws of the Institution state: "It is the function of the Trustees to make possible the conduct of scientific research, and publication, under the most favorable conditions, and to safeguard the independence of the research staff in the pursuit of their studies and in the publication of the results of such studies. It is not a part of their function to determine, control, or influence the conduct of particular investigations or the conclusions reached."

The President bears final responsibility for the decision to publish a manuscript as a Brookings book. In reaching his judgment on the competence, accuracy, and objectivity of each study, the President is advised by the director of the appropriate research program and weighs the views of a panel of expert outside readers who report to him in confidence on the quality of the work. Publication of a work signifies that it is deemed a competent treatment worthy of public consideration but does not imply endorsement of conclusions or recommendations.

The Institution maintains its position of neutrality on issues of public policy in order to safeguard the intellectual freedom of the staff. Hence interpretations or conclusions in Brookings publications should be understood to be solely those of the authors and should not be attributed to the Institution, to its trustees, officers, or other staff members, or to the organizations that support its research.

Foreword

Economic integration represents an important policy option for developing countries faced with choices among economic development strategies. At a time when international economic disturbances have raised new questions about the reliability of alternative trade and development regimes, it is appropriate to review the experience of perhaps the most successful integration effort among developing countries, the Central American Common Market (CACM). That experience contains many lessons about the possibilities, as well as the limitations, of economic and social development through integration.

Created in 1960 after many years of regional cooperation, the CACM was an almost immediate success. Trade among the member countries (Costa Rica, El Salvador, Guatemala, Honduras, and Nicaragua) multiplied severalfold in the early 1960s, as member countries eliminated their mutual tariffs on most industrial goods. In the years that followed, growth within the region was rapid. Industrial development surged ahead as the newly widened market permitted exploiting economies of scale. Goods formerly imported were produced within the region, easing balance of payments constraints on growth. External investment increased as foreign investors perceived new opportunities within the enlarged regional market.

By the late 1960s, the issue of unequal distribution of the benefits of integration among member countries, so often a dilemma within integration movements among developing countries, had reached serious proportions. In 1968, the integration effort received a heavy blow when a brief war broke out between Honduras and El Salvador, largely over the issue of migration. Since then, the CACM has not returned to full operation, although growth and trade have continued briskly within a four-member CACM that no longer includes Honduras. Bilateral trade agreements have maintained some trade ties between Honduras and CACM members other than El Salvador.

If integration succeeded in stimulating growth and industrialization despite the unequal distribution of its benefits among member countries, its success was limited in generating employment and fostering a more equitable distribution of income. Moreover, integration has scarcely affected the agricultural sector, where protection remains the norm. Questions about basic development strategy for the region remain unanswered, as the CACM looks beyond the initial phase of import substitution in those sectors most easily adapted to regional production.

This book presents the results of research on these issues sponsored jointly by the Brookings Institution and the Secretariat of Economic Integration of Central America (SIECA). The studies review the course of integration in the region, and evaluate its economic effects quantitatively. They address employment, income distribution, and integration in the agricultural sector, as well as the issues of comparative advantage and development strategy.

Editors William R. Cline and Enrique Delgado are, respectively, senior fellow in the Brookings Foreign Policy Studies program and director of Central American Studies of Integration and Development in the Secretariat of Economic Integration of Central America in Guatemala City. Sr. Delgado is also a member of the Brookings associated staff.

The project was financed by the U.S. Agency for International Development through its Regional Office for Central America and Panama (ROCAP). In addition to those whose assistance is acknowledged in the various chapters, many institutions and individuals made this study possible. The initial organizing and guiding influences of SIECA Secretary General Roberto Mayorga-Cortés, Irving Tragen, former director of ROCAP, and Kermit Gordon, late president of Brookings, made possible the program of joint SIECA-Brookings research, which spanned a five-year period beginning in 1973. The collaboration of various divisions within SIECA, especially the statistics division, was invaluable, as was the cooperation of the central banks of the region. The editors are particularly grateful to the Development Research Center of the World Bank for its contribution to the chapter on the agricultural sector programming model. Jere Behrman, Mordechai Kreinin, William Miernyk, Ishaq Nadiri, and Paul Strassman provided expert advice at various stages in the program of SIECA-Brookings research. Eileen Dripchak, Karen Nurick, and Carmen Pipino provided research assistance; Delores Burton and Marie Hanks typed the manuscript.

The views presented in this book are those of the authors and should not be ascribed to the persons or organizations whose assistance is acknowledged above, or to the trustees, officers, or other staff members of the Brookings Institution.

Bruce K. MacLaury
President

June 1978
Washington, D.C.

Contents

List of Tables

Chapter 3 (Continued)

Chapter 4

Chapter 5

Chapter 7 (Continued)

Chapter 8

Appendix C (Continued)

Appendix D

Appendix D (Continued)

Appendix E

Appendix F

Appendix F (Continued)

Appendix G

Appendix H

Appendix H (Continued)

Appendix I

Appendix J

Appendix K

CHAPTER I

Introduction

William R. Cline and Enrique Delgado

A. The Integration Experience

The idea of economic and political integration of Central America has
been a part of the region's heritage since the days of its political
fragmentation after independence from Spain. In the 1950s, leaders from
the five countries of the region--Guatemala, El Salvador, Honduras,
Nicaragua, and Costa Rica (from north to south in sequence) began to
take serious steps toward realizing the objectives of economic integration. The first measures were bilateral trade agreements among individual countries. Toward the end of the decade, with the assistance and
encouragement of the United Nations Economic Commission for Latin America
(ECLA), concrete plans for economic integration were emerging. The plans
emphasized cooperation in the allocation of new industries for the purpose
of implementing on a regional basis industrialization projects too large
for any individual country's market.

After nearly a decade of doubts about the idea of integration, U.S.
policymakers involved in the region moved vigorously to support a Common
Market based on free trade within the region while in practice downgrad-
ing the prospects for region-wide "integration industries" (especially
insofar as these would involve local monopoly, as under the previous ECLA
thinking). Soon after an initial pact along these lines among Guatemala,
El Salvador, and Honduras, the two remaining countries joined in the formation in 1960 of the Central American Common Market (CACM). Panama,
mainly because of its special status based on the existence of the canal,
remained outside the plan. Nevertheless, Panama has maintained a continuing interest in association, under special conditions, with the countries
of the region. This interest has led to limited treaties of free trade
with the countries of the region, as well as participation in various institutions of regional cooperation.

The CACM provided for free trade within the region (except for a
list of exempted items, mainly agricultural) and the harmonization of
tariff rates to a common external tariff schedule. Although it also provided for harmonized tax policies (but only after a ratification delay
of several years), the Market's chief feature was free intraregional trade
with its resulting regional stimulus to production of goods formerly purchased from outside, especially industrial goods.

From a period of euphoria in the face of burgeoning regional trade
in the early 1960s, the Common Market moved into a stage of contention

among partners. Especially Honduras, and to some extent Nicaragua and Costa Rica, felt that free trade was favoring the countries with the largest industrial bases--Guatemala and El Salvador. Honduras argued that although it had joined the integration effort to industrialize, its former pattern of exporting traditional raw materials while importing industrial goods appeared to be repeating itself on a regional scale. The dissident countries cited their trade deficits with the region as evidence of failure to obtain a fair share of the benefits of integration; the dissidents demanded a return to emphasis on the allocation of new industries among members.

Even as negotiations were underway in 1969 to address these problems, the acrimony between El Salvador and Honduras growing out of migration from the former to the latter exploded into a war between the two countries. Though brief, the war ruptured the Common Market, both through the resulting withdrawal of Honduras and through the disruption of regional trade caused by the still-unresolved physical interdiction of the flow of Salvadorian goods intended for the Honduran market or for transshipment to Nicaragua and Costa Rica to the south.

In the years after the war, negotiations proceeded toward the reentry of Honduras into the Common Market, at times coming close to success (especially the Modus Operandi proposals of 1970). However, the negotiations foundered on two fundamental points: first, the exact location of the border between Honduras and El Salvador, which led to a continuing dispute; and second, the issue of special arrangements in the Common Market to provide for balanced growth of the member countries in general and for special advantages for Honduras in particular.

Despite the blow to the CACM caused by the withdrawal of Honduras, Central American success with economic integration remains considerable. Among the other four countries a free trade area continues. Even Honduras still participates in economic integration to a limited degree through a series of bilateral trade agreements negotiated since 1969. Furthermore, there are prospects of the reestablishment of full Honduran participation in the CACM as the result of intensive negotiations conducted by the "High Level Committee" established in 1973. In March 1976 the High Level Committee presented a draft treaty (Tradado Marco) prepared with the help of the Permanent Secretariat of the General Treaty of Central American Economic Integration (SIECA). The draft treaty provided for reintegration of Honduras as well as modalities for much more thoroughgoing integration than in the past. The prospects for such changes are discussed in the concluding chapter of this book. Briefly, the direction of the CACM at present appears to be toward a revitalized and more profound integration effort rather than toward retrogression from the degree of integration already achieved.

By all accounts the CACM must be judged as one of the most successful efforts of integration among developing countries. The elimination of tariffs on most products represented a remarkable achievement, as did the rapid expansion of intraregional trade that followed. By contrast, trade liberalization under the Latin American Free Trade Association (LAFTA) has proved to be extremely limited. (Lafta began in 1960, as did the CACM.)

LAFTA includes Mexico and all of the South American countries except the Guianas. Thus, it contains countries with a wider range of
size and levels of development (from relatively undeveloped Bolivia
and Paraguay to relatively developed Argentina, Brazil, Mexico) than
does the CACM. This greater range poses greater problems of unbalanced
benefits from free trade. Furthermore, in several LAFTA countries
industrialization had gone beyond that in Central America at the beginning of the 1960s. As a result, the strength of vested industrial interests opposing competition from other countries appears to have been
greater in LAFTA than in the CACM.[1] Indeed, one school of thought has
been that because industries are already established in the area, LAFTA
should avoid jeopardizing many of them through trade liberalization and,
instead, should concentrate its efforts on joint programs for investment
in new industries.[2]

Impatience with the slow pace of integration within LAFTA led Bolivia, Colombia, Chile, Ecuador, and Peru to establish the Andean Pact in
May 1969. Venezuela joined the Andean Group in 1973.

The Andean Group represented a brighter opportunity than LAFTA for
rapid integration achievements. The member countries constituted a narrower range of variation in level of development. The members saw the
group as a way to achieve economic size comparable with that of the largest individual economies in Latin America (those of Brazil, Argentina,
and Mexico). From the start, the Andean Group provided for measures to
deal with the sources of conflict that had emerged within LAFTA. These
measures included special tariff treatment for the poorest members, the
elaboration of sectoral programs of industrial development (as opposed
to reliance on free trade alone), and the common treatment of foreign capital.[3] The latter, providing for a relatively strict treatment of foreign
capital,[4] generally regarded as a hallmark of the Andean Group, was designed to counter what some have seen as the Achilles heel of economic
integration--that integration provides the vehicle for multinational cor-
porations to enter regional markets duty-free, diverting market-widening
benefits from Latin American interests to U.S., European, and Japanese
firms.

After a dynamic start characterized by a surge in intra-Andean trade,
the Andean Group passed into a phase of uncertain status by the mid-1970s.
By late 1975 there were serious disagreements within the Group over the
set of common external tariffs to be adopted, sectoral development plans,
and even on the election of authorities.[5] In October 1976, Chile withdrew from the Andean Group, leaving only four members.[6] Chile's withdrawal represented the culmination of disagreement over the Group's economic
policies, particularly in the area of foreign investment, following the
advent of the economically orthodox military regime in Chile.

Experience with economic integration among developing countries in
Asia and Africa also provides interesting contrasts with the Central
American case. Outside of Latin America probably the most significant
effort has been that of the East African Community.[7] The East African
experience represents a unique case in which integration began under

---

NOTE: Footnotes appear at the end of each chapter.

4

the auspices of British colonial rule of the territories that, in the early 1960s, became the independent countries of Kenya, Uganda, and Tanzania. Dating from the 1920s, economic integration of the three areas was far reaching. It included a customs union in which not only was intraregional trade duty free but external tariff receipts were pooled and allocated among countries on the basis of product destination.[8] The three areas had a single currency (the East African shilling). Efforts in regional transportation and other segments of infrastructure were pooled through a Common Services Organization (established in 1961).

Economic antagonisms existed within the region. Uganda and Tanzania resented what appeared to be greater economic advantages gained from integration by the more developed Kenya. Intraregional trade balances, persistently in surplus for Kenya and in deficit for the other two countries, were taken as evidence of the Kenyan advantage even when the other two countries were experiencing more rapid economic growth overall than was Kenya.

After independence, growing economic differences and the departure from a common currency threatened continued East African integration, but because of a political commitment to integration--especially as a sign of African unity among newly independent countries--a new Treaty for East African Cooperation was signed in 1967. The treaty provided for a customs union in the trade of manufactured goods. It had two mechanisms designed to favor the poorer members: a transfer tax that could be levied by a deficit member on imports from a surplus member; and the East African Development Bank, constituted with specific lending shares favoring Uganda and Tanzania relative to Kenya (with specified shares of 38 3/4 percent, 38 3/4 percent, and 22 1/2 percent, respectively).

The revitalized Community functioned well for three years. Beginning in 1970, however, it faced serious political and economic difficulties. A military coup in Uganda initiated a period of protracted political differences among members. The "Authority" of the Community, composed of the three heads of state, failed to meet after 1970. On the economic side, serious foreign exchange shortages led to more and more frequent imposition of quotas on imports from partners, and by mid-1975, "the common market provisions of the treaty were virtually a dead letter."[9] Transportation services began to break down as Tanzania imposed restrictions on trucks carrying Kenyan goods to Zambia, and as the Railways Corporation discontinued passenger service between Kenya and Uganda because of disputes over the transfer of revenues among countries. More fundamentally, by the mid-1970s political directions were extremely divergent among the three countries, with capitalist ideology dominant in Kenya, socialism in Tanzania, and a personalist military regime in Uganda openly in extreme opposition to the regimes in Kenya and Tanzania. In this situation a renewed political commitment to restore meaningful economic integration was out of the question. Indeed, a central lesson of the East African experience would appear to be that nongermane political divergences among members can destroy even an integration effort with a long historical tradition and with relatively well-developed institutions for the equitable sharing of economic benefits arising from integration.

In Asia, economic integration has progressed even less than in Latin America and Africa. The Association of South-East Asian Nations (ASEAN) formed in 1967 by Malaysia, the Philippines, Thailand, Indonesia, and Singapore constitutes a loose organization for economic cooperation without even a planned elimination of intragroup trade barriers. An expanded version of the Association of South-East Asia formed in 1961 by Malaysia, the Philippines, and Thailand, the ASEAN group has experienced recurrent difficulties associated with political disputes between Malaysia and the Philippines.[10]

Another Asian integration effort is the Regional Cooperation for Development (RCD) established in July 1974 by Iran, Pakistan, and Turkey. The RCD does not pursue the elimination of intragroup trade barriers but has concentrated on cooperation in specific areas such as transportation and communications and joint industrial planning with the goal of allocation of industries among members.[11]

In qualitative terms, a review of integration efforts among developing countries leads to the conclusion that the Central American Common Market (CACM) is one of the most successful. That the CACM is perhaps at the forefront among integration movements is also borne out quantitatively by international trade statistics. Table 1 shows the percentage of total exports that are directed to partner countries within several integration groupings in the developing countries.

By 1974 the Central American Common Market stood at the head of the list of integration efforts when measured by this criterion for integration success. Approximately 26 percent of exports by Central American countries went to CACM partners (here including Honduras). The next area was the East African Community, with only about half as large a regional share of exports. Within Latin America, the Latin American Free Trade Association (LAFTA) area was far behind, with only about 10 percent of exports going to partners, and the Andean Group was still further behind, representing only 3.4 percent of the export market for member countries. The record of the CACM was all the more impressive when viewed over the period since its inception; the region's share in partners' exports rose almost fourfold from a 1960 base that stood far behind comparable trade shares for the Association of South-East Asian Nations and behind even LAFTA.[12] The comparison with LAFTA in particular shows that intragroup exports rose only marginally above historical shares in LAFTA while those for the CACM rose dramatically, indicating near absence of any effect of LAFTA, but a strong impact of the CACM on partner trade patterns.

In view of the above considerations on international experience with economic integration among developing countries, the CACM may be seen as a success case that should provide important evidence on the potential for economic benefits of such integration. The empirical studies presented in this book therefore carry policy implications not only for Central America but also for other integration movements among developing countries.

B. Nature of the Study

Despite its relative success in international terms, the CACM has faced periodic difficulties associated with divergent perceptions of the

6

Table 1. Intratrade of Economic Groupings of
Developing Countries, Selected Years

Regional Groupings	Intratrade as Percent of Total Exports of Each Group			
	1960	1970	1972	1974
Latin American Free Trade Association	7.7	10.2	10.7	9.7
Andean Group	1.5	2.7	3.6	3.4
Central American Common Market	7.5	26.9	22.5	25.6
Caribbean Community	4.8	8.1	10.2	7.1
Permanent Consultative Committee of the Maghreb	4.7	2.2	2.1	1.8
East African Community	14.1	16.9	13.7	13.9
Central African Customs and Economic Union	1.7	7.5	8.9	7.4
West African Economic Community	2.4	9.1	8.4	4.3
Association of South-East Asian Nations	21.7	14.8	14.5	11.3
Council of Arab Economic Unity	3.3	3.6	2.4	1.4
Arab Common Market	3.5	4.1	3.1	1.5
Regional Cooperation for Development	2.2	1.1	0.6	0.5

SOURCE: UNCTAD, Handbook of International Trade and Development Statistics (New York, 1976), p. 52.

degree of fairness in a country's distribution of economic benefits arising from integration. Beginning in the mid-1960s, dispute over the factual basis for claims of inequitable member country participation in the benefits of integration, and a general need for diagnosis of the economic problems and future development strategy of the region, set the stage for a major economic research effort. Indeed, economic analyses periodically reviewing the region's progress in integration had already become an accepted practice. The U.N. Economic Commission for Latin America had carried out evaluations of this type in 1954 and 1965. In 1972, in response to the severe disturbances to the Common Market from the war and the failure of negotiations to resolve them, the Permanent Secretariat of the General Treaty of Central American Economic Integration (SIECA) carried out a massive study, Integrated Development of Central America in the Present Decade,[13] with the participation of experts from international organizations. One of the results of that study was the conclusion that an institutionalized research effort was required. The outgrowth of the conclusion was the SIECA/Brookings research project and, therefore, this volume. This joint research effort involved highly qualified Central American professionals at SIECA and a methodologically focused input by researchers at the Brookings Institution.

Initial planning of the joint effort, in early 1973, identified three main areas for research. The first was the subject of benefits and costs of economic integration in Central America. This topic was crucial in view of unresolved questions on appropriate policy measures to foster balanced growth in the Common Market. Only the development of more reliable economic measurements of the level and country distribution of the benefits and costs of integration could provide an impartial, objective basis for reforms necessary to strengthen the cohesion of the CACM (such as special provisions for less-developed countries or for countries not enjoying a full share of the economic benefits of integration).

An assessment of the costs and benefits of economic integration required both a political-economic review of the Central American experience, and a quantitative effort of economic analysis conceptualizing and then measuring the economic effects. The corresponding studies that resulted are respectively chapters 2 and 3 of this volume. Chapter 2 examines the political and economic evolution of the CACM. The chapter reviews the early dynamics of the Common Market and explains the later surfacing of disagreements among some of the member countries about the means of achieving balanced growth among the countries. Chapter 3 develops a new methodology for measuring static and dynamic welfare effects of economic integration among developing countries. It then applies the remarkably rich data base available for Central America to obtain empirical estimates of the economic effects of integration. The chapter gives special attention to detailed estimation by country, so that policy conclusions may be drawn about appropriate steps for achieving equitable distribution of benefits among members. The chapter also seeks to obtain a complete accounting of the various economic effects of integration and to arrive at an overall judgment on whether the benefits have been sufficiently large to warrant the considerable political efforts that have been required to achieve integration.

A second broad area identified as one of priority for SIECA/Brookings research was the subject of employment. A persistent policy problem throughout the developing world has been the need to accelerate the growth of employment opportunities, both as a means of making fuller use of the one abundant factor, labor, and of attenuating social problems associated with what frequently appears to be a pattern of increasing income inequality in the course of economic development.[14] This volume examines the employment problem through two approaches. The first, presented in chapter 4, involves econometric estimates of employment and production functions for manufacturing industry. The central policy issue addressed in that approach is whether industrial employment can be encouraged through changes in the relative prices of capital and labor. The empirical estimates of the degree of substitutability between labor and capital, in response to varying relative prices of these two factors of production, permit an evaluation of this policy question. The second approach, presented in chapter 5, examines a broader spectrum of employment issues, including increases in labor supply from demographic growth, the distribution of income, the evolution of labor demand in the light of productivity trends, and the structure of wages. Together, the two approaches provide the basis for an overview of the employment problem in Central America and of possible policy measures for accelerating employment growth.

The third main area identified for research was that of comparative prices in Central America. This area of research represented a natural extension of similar previous work in other Latin American countries coordinated at the Brookings Institution under the program "ECIEL," the Spanish language acronym for Joint Studies on Economic Integration in

Latin America. Application of ECIEL methodologies to the case of Central America represented an opportunity for collaborative work by national statistical agencies in the execution of a consumer price survey applying standardized procedures and sample periods in all five Central American countries. The price study therefore served as a vehicle for institution building as well as for basic research on the question of price patterns within a customs union. With the sharp acceleration of world and regional inflation in the period 1973-76, the reliability of national price survey methods took on new importance, and the SIECA/Brookings price studies thereby helped lay the foundation for a more accurate tracking of inflation through future repetitions of the standardized consumer price survey. Chapter 8 presents the research results in the area of price comparisons.

Midway through the three-year span originally projected for SIECA/ Brookings research, two additional research areas were included in the program: the assessment of sectoral comparative advantage, and the development of agricultural sector policy models. The study on present and future comparative advantage by country and industrial sector, presented in chapter 6, was one with high priority for short-term as well as longer-term policy purposes. In the near term, SIECA was soon to design a new set of common external tariffs. Tariff reform ideally should reflect analysis of the prospects for future comparative advantage of each productive sector. The same type of information was relevant for industrial tax incentive policies. Thus, in the revision of tariff and incentive policies, a sector showing extremely high protection and incentives but low current and future comparative advantage would be an appropriate candidate for reduced protection and tax incentives. Conversely, sectors identified as having high future comparative advantage might legitimately be encouraged by higher than average protection, at least over an interim period. In addition to the near-term purpose of reforming the structure of tariffs and incentives, the longer-term objective of balanced growth among member countries represented a policy area requiring analysis of comparative advantage. In any future programs seeking to allocate industries by country in order to insure at least a minimum level of participation of lesser-developed members in industrial expansion, the design of an efficient allocational pattern would require information on the sectoral comparative advantage of each country relative to the other members. The study of comparative advantage presented in chapter 6 addresses these policy issues. In order to carry out the study, it was also necessary to prepare estimates of sectoral rates of "effective protection" (tariff protection on value added by activity). These estimates, representing a useful byproduct, appear as appendix K.

Our final study, on agricultural sector planning, represented a meeting of heightened policy need with recent developments in methodology. On the side of policy needs, upheaval in world grains markets in 1972-73 highlighted the susceptibility of the region to external shocks in grains prices and to uncertain availability of supply. The ministers of agriculture of the five Central American countries responded with an energetic program seeking (i) to establish regional self-sufficiency in basic grains by 1980, (ii) to expand the integration process to include the agricultural sector (largely omitted from intraregional trade liberalization), and (iii) to establish a more effective program of agricultural prices for stimulating output.[15]

Methodological tools capable of providing invaluable analysis of the issues raised by this program had recently been developed by researchers dealing with agricultural sector planning models. In particular, such research efforts had led to the successful establishment of an agricultural sector planning model in Mexico, used for ongoing policy analysis.[16] It was therefore natural to add to the SIECA/Brookings program of joint research a project to prepare an agricultural sector policy model for Central America similar to those recently established in Mexico and several other developing countries. In this effort the SIECA/Brookings program had the extreme good fortune to enlist the participation of the Development Research Center of the World Bank, the center that had originally led the development of the CHAC agricultural model for Mexico. The World Bank generously contributed the time of key professionals and computer support in a joint project involving Brookings, World Bank, and SIECA personnel.

Chapter 7 presents the study of the agricultural sector, based on a sectoral programming model. The objective of the modeling effort is to explore a series of policy questions, including the following: (i) What would be the trade, welfare, and employment effects of liberalization of agricultural trade within the CACM? (ii) What producer response may be expected from alternative minimum price policies for basic grains? (iii) What policies are required in order to achieve the target of regional self-sufficiency in basic grains by 1980? What are the implications of the target for the costs of supplying regional needs? In addition to providing answers to these policy questions, the agricultural sector effort seeks to provide the institution-building function of installing in Central America an ongoing agricultural sector modeling capability for use in future policy analysis.

C. A Preview of Findings

The concluding chapter of this volume provides a detailed review of its findings. To enhance an integrated reading of the individual studies contained in the following chapters, however, it may be helpful to consider their principal conclusions at the outset.

The survey of the institutional evolution of the Common Market in chapter 2 first recalls the original objectives of integration. Unwilling to keep their economies dependent upon the uncertain base of exporting raw materials, policymakers in the 1950s turned to economic integration as a means of achieving a sufficiently large market to allow efficient industrialization within Central America. Under the early tutelage of the Economic Commission for Latin America (ECLA), integration efforts centered on a prospective scheme of "integration industries" that would be allocated among member countries. By 1960, however, the focus of integration had turned to free trade members, prompted by the positions of the more industrialized countries (Guatemala and El Salvador) and encouraged by U.S. policymakers, who feared that the ECLA approach would establish a series of regional monopolies.

The formation of the Common Market in 1960 was followed by early success as intraregional trade mushroomed to unexpected levels. The resulting atmosphere of euphoria gave way to one of contention by the mid-

1960s, however, as the poorest member country, Honduras, and to some extent Nicaragua and Costa Rica, protested an unjust concentration of integration's benefits in the other countries. It then became clear that the modality of free trade as the chief theme of integration had omitted any effective mechanism for redistributing benefits among partners. The war between El Salvador and Honduras in 1969, caused in part by heavy migration from the former to the latter, served to dramatize the divisions growing between Honduras and the Common Market on economic grounds. Honduras left the Market, posing an institutional crisis that remains unresolved today.

It is in this policy context that chapter 3 attempts to measure the economic benefits and costs of Central American integration. The results are relevant to the very existence of the CACM: Have its benefits justified the political effort required? The analysis also addresses the distributional question: What has been the distribution of measurable economic benefits and costs among member countries? Using a methodology that starts with traditional concepts of trade creation and diversion but develops new measurements of effects particularly relevant to developing countries (employment, economies of scale, foreign exchange savings, structural transformation, and investment), the chapter concludes that integration had a large net positive effect on the economies of the region. It raised their gross national products by 3 to 4 percent above levels they otherwise might have reached. And except for Honduras, the distribution across members was relatively equitable. Honduras did show a relatively low share in benefits, but even its net economic effects were positive, and as a result Honduras probably suffered economically by its decision to withdraw from the CACM. Chapter 3 concludes with estimates of the amount of transfers to Honduras that would be required to achieve a fair distribution of the benefits of integration, and a concrete proposal for mechanisms to accomplish these transfers if Honduras were to reenter the Market.

Chapter 4 examines employment in the manufacturing industry. Inadequate growth of employment is a persistent policy problem in the region, and the chapter conducts a detailed statistical analysis of the scope for greater labor absorption in manufacturing. Contrary to what is often supposed, it is determined that there exists a considerable degree of flexibility in the combination of labor and capital; policies that affect relative prices of capital and labor will influence employment opportunities. The chapter explores a number of these policies, such as tariffs on capital goods, interest rate policy, and tax policy. The study finds statistical evidence to the effect that technology change over time is biased against the use of labor, suggesting the need for increased efforts at insuring the adoption of appropriate technology. The chapter also estimates the employment effects of economic integration, using the sectoral output changes attributed to integration in chapter 3. The estimates show an important contribution of integration to the solution of the employment problem, but one that is too limited to constitute a complete solution to a problem that is essentially one of overall development strategy of the individual national economies.

Chapter 5 expands upon the theme of employment. The low degree of unionization in the region is noted and a growing "employment gap" on the basis of estimates of labor supply and demand is identified. The chapter suggests that increasing capitalization contributed to this gap (and, correspondingly, that if output per worker had not risen so rapidly in the 1960s, the demand for labor could have kept pace with its supply). The chapter documents the highly uneven distributions of income in the region and draws inferences from the differences among countries. It proposes a model of rent distribution in the export economy whereby a considerable portion of national income amounts to rent available for division among classes. The conditions of labor and the equity of income distribution depend upon the way this rent is shared. In support of the model the chapter presents calculations indicating that wages to labor and receipts of owners covering imputed capital costs exhaust only a fraction of total value added, leaving a margin to be distributed by relative bargaining strength and social factors. In essence the chapter advocates employment-stimulating measures that will improve the bargaining position of labor. As a caveat on the potential of integration as one such measure, the chapter presents "worst case" estimates (again based on output composition effects measured in chapter 3) indicating that integration might even have reduced employment by shifting the weight of the economies from labor-intensive agriculture to capital-intensive industry.

Optimal sectoral strategy within the CACM is the theme of chapters 6 and 7. Chapter 6 examines sectoral comparative advantage in the industrial sector, among the member countries and for the group as a whole relative to the rest of the world. It ranks industries by measures of comparative advantage that incorporate both static and dynamic considerations. Labor intensity weighs heavily in these measures, so that implicitly the comparative advantage criterion relates to the policy objective of stimulating the growth of employment. And the designation of sectoral comparative advantage among the five countries bears directly upon the issue of the equitable distribution of integration benefits. That is, programs designed to stimulate industries in a particular country for purposes of equity should consider the underlying comparative advantage by country. The chapter also examines the relationship of tariff and tax incentives to sectoral comparative advantage, singling out those sectors that enjoy high incentives but show poor prospects for comparative advantage (as well as the reverse).

Chapter 7 uses a mathematical programming model to examine the prospects for further integration in agriculture. Free trade still does not exist in key agricultural products, and the CACM could achieve higher welfare gains through trade liberalization in this sector. The chapter considers the distributional implications, by country and rural class, of liberalizing agricultural trade in the region. It also provides measures of the responsiveness of output to prices, an important tool for assessing policy in the area of minimum prices.

Finally, the study of comparative prices in chapter 8 finds a great similarity in the level and structure of prices among the five Central American countries, especially in the traded goods sectors. The exception is the case of Nicaragua, where prices are found to be about 15 percent above the regional average. These results help clarify the comparative level of real income among the five countries, a subject of the discussion on balanced growth in chapter 2. In particular, adjustments of

national accounts data for price differences leave unchanged the conclusion that Honduras has the lowest income per capita in the region (and
thus is a prime candidate for redistribution on welfare criteria as
well as on grounds of participation in benefits of the Common Market).

The relatively close adherence of sectoral price levels among member countries, especially in traded goods, suggests that integration is
effective in harmonizing prices (although a more complete test would
require measures for preintegration periods). The finding of abnormally
high prices in Nicaragua, on the other hand, may reflect a temporary
situation associated with the Managua earthquake, as well as a possibly
overvalued exchange rate.

The chapters of this book are divided into three broad groups:
part I, analysis of the integration experience; part II, examination of
the employment problem; and part III, sectoral studies on industrial comparative advantage, agricultural policies, and comparative prices. The
studies in the third group have in common a bearing on the analysis of
comparative advantage among the five countries of the region. All of the
studies, with the exception of the institutional background study presented
in chapter 2, have in common the application of quantitative techniques and
empirical information to the analysis of policy problems of economic integration and development in Central America. Although no claim is laid
that these chapters represent an exhaustive set of policy studies (considering that some important issues are addressed only tangentially, including controversial subjects such as the role of foreign investment
and land reform), the research results presented do address a large
spectrum of critical economic policy issues facing the CACM, in the
tradition of policy research already so well established by SIECA in
the past. Furthermore, the methodologies developed in this study and
the policy conclusions derived should be of relevance to the issue of
economic integration among developing countries generally.

In addition to these main chapter studies, special studies appear
as appendices. They include a review of past literature on Central
American economic integration, studies of industrial concentration and
effective protection, estimates of the scarcity price of foreign exchange
derived from an econometric model, and various methodological and statistical studies.

Chapter 1

NOTES

1. For a presentation of this assessment and an overview of economic integration in Latin America, see Joseph Grunwald, Miguel S. Wionczek, and Martin Carnoy, Latin American Economic Integration and U.S. Policy (Washington, D.C.: Brookings Institution, 1972).

2. A viewpoint reported, and criticized, by Bela Balassa, "Regional Integration and Trade Liberalization in Latin America," Journal of Common Market Studies 10(1) (September 1971): 65.

3. See, for example, Inter-American Development Bank, Institute for Latin American Integration, The Latin American Integration Process in 1973 (Washington, D.C., n.d.).

4. The Andean Pact ruled out foreign investment in banking, domestic trade, and most service activities, and stipulated that within fifteen to twenty years all foreign-owned enterprises would be transformed into joint ventures having domestic majority control. Grunwald, Wionczek, and Carnoy, Latin American Economic Integration and U.S. Policy, p. 59.

5. Carlos F. Diaz-Alejandro, Journal of Development Economics 3(3) (September 1976): 304-5. Book review of David Morawetz, The Andean Group: A Case Study in Economic Integration Among Developing Countries (Cambridge, Mass.: M.I.T., 1974).

6. "The Lima Protocol and Chile's Withdrawal," Latin American Free Trade Association Newsletter, no. 38 (September-October 1976).

7. From Arthur Hazlewood, Economic Integration: The East African Experience (London: Heinemann, 1975).

8. Part of the motivation for the pooling was that Uganda is a landlocked country; for administrative ease, its external tariffs came to be collected at the port cities in Kenya and Tanzania.

9. Hazlewood, East African Experience, p. 173.

10. OECD, Regional Cooperation in Asia (Paris, 1970), pp. 39-40.

11. F. Kahnert, P. Richards, E. Stoutjesdijk, and P. Thomopoulos, Economic Integration among Developing Countries (Paris: OECD, 1969), pp. 77-78.

12. The high intragroup trade share of the ASEAN group in 1960 appears to reflect historical and geographical patterns for Malaysia, the Philippines, and Thailand, rather than any institutional accomplishment. The intragroup trade share fell markedly by 1974.

13. SIECA, El Desarrollo Integrado de Centroamerica en la Presente Década: Bases y Propuestas para el Perfecionamiento del Mercado Común

Centroamericano, 12 vols. (Guatemala City: SIECA, 1972). Many of the findings of this study are reported in appendix B of this book.

14. See, for example, William R. Cline, "Distribution and Development: A Survey of Literature," Journal of Development Economics 1 (1975): 359-400; and Montek Ahluwalia, "Inequality, Poverty, and Development," Journal of Development Economics 3 (1976): 307-42.

15. SIECA, Acuerdo de San José Aprobado en la Segunda Reunión de Ministros de Agricultura de Centroamerica (San José Costa Rica, 25 and 26 October 1974).

16. As reported in Louis M. Goreux and Alan S. Manne, eds., Multilevel Planning: Case Studies in Mexico (Amsterdam: North-Holland, 1973), part IV.

Part I

THE INTEGRATION EXPERIENCE

Institutional Evolution of the Central American Common Market and the Principle of Balanced Development

Enrique Delgado

A.   Introduction

This chapter reviews Central American experience with the application of the concept of balanced development among the five countries in the Central American Common Market: Costa Rica, El Salvador, Guatemala, Honduras, and Nicaragua. After an examination of the general political and economic dynamics of integration among developing countries, the chapter traces the history of the Central American case over the past twenty-five years. The principal focus of the discussion is on the problem of achieving balanced development. Accordingly, the discussion concludes with a special examination of the difficulties in measuring the comparative levels of development of the countries, and with an assessment of alternative concepts of "balance" in the distribution of integration's benefits.

The Central American countries have maintained an active program of economic integration since 1950. That program witnessed the formation of a Common Market in 1960, and since 1972 the member countries have considered seriously the eventual evolution of an economic union.

During the twenty-five years of the Integration Program, there have been numerous successes as well as crises. Perhaps none of the guiding principles of integration has caused more concern, nor more open conflicts among the five countries, than the concept of "balanced development."

NOTES: (i) The author wishes to thank Dr. Roberto Mayorga-Cortes for his useful observations on the first draft of this chapter, and Gabriel Siri for his assistance in performing the factoral analysis of relative levels of development.

(ii) Footnotes and a glossary of terms appear at the end of the chapter. The glossary contains a brief description of the principal agreements (designated A1, A2, and so on) and of institutional organizations (designated B1, B2, and so on) mentioned in the text.

Despite difficulties of definition and implementation, the broad aspiration for balanced development has been present throughout the integration process.   The concept has evolved from a general expression of
"reciprocity in the program benefits" that prevailed in the 1950s to a
more ambitious concept of balanced development beginning in the mid-
1960s and continuing to date.   The new draft General Treaty for the
creation of the Central American Economic and Social Community prepared
by the Permanent Secretariat (SIECA)[B4] and recently submitted to the five
governments for consideration, contains a special chapter covering the
principle of balanced development.

As this principle implies the existence of different degrees of
development among the member nations, and its application requires actions to reduce current disparities, the integration scheme necessarily
requires methods for "measuring" differences in the degrees of relative
economic and social development among the nations as well as the effect
of economic integration upon the economies of each of the Central American countries.

SIECA therefore considered it advisable to devote special effort to
the search for these methods of measurement. With this purpose in mind,
it contracted the services of the Brookings Institution, with the support of the Regional Office for Central America and Panama (ROCAP) of
the U.S. Agency for International Development. Since the middle of
1973, the joint SIECA/Brookings Project has been working in this field
of research, among others, and this chapter represents the result of
related studies.[1]

B.   Integration Dynamics

Political motivations combined with economic objectives form the
basis for economic integration movements.   The political framework,
including considerations of common defense, contributes to the continuity
of integration movement over time.   Economic objectives affect the different schemes of integration and shape their historical course.   The
combined ultimate objectives of such movements may include more advanced
degrees of political cooperation among the member countries, including
their future alignment into a single state after passing through the
formation of a free trade zone, a customs union, a Common Market, or
other intermediate stages.

The official documents formally constituting schemes of integration
form only a part of the integration commitment. The movement also includes informal commitments, such as those contained in public declarations of the goals of parties within the movement. These supplementary
understandings constitute a tacit agreement that sometimes supersedes
the formal one and makes the general commitment more comprehensive and
meaningful.

The formal associative pact usually contains two different sets of
obligations: those that set forth the ultimate purpose of the parties,
such as the evolution over time of an economic union; and those that
represent binding actions related to the fulfillment of a concrete phase
of association (free trade, and so on) which may change an early stage

but do not necessarily continue to the proposed final stage of the association. Consequently, these agreements are inherently transitory. It
is assumed that once the stage of integration explicitly referred to in
the agreement is reached, the agreement will be replaced by a new treaty.
Moreover, a current agreement may eventually encounter practical difficulties because the stated objectives may be modified in the course
of time, the anticipated means for the attainment of the latter may
prove to be inadequate, or the observance and support of objectives by
the member countries may not live up to expectations.

Instability of the basic agreements and, at times, their limited
practical application have often led to hasty conclusions that the integration process is in a stage of dissolution. Instead, it may be more
appropriate to conclude that what actually occurs is a divergence between the letter of the treaty and the real situation involved in the
relations between the states. The divergence may be occasioned by overly ambitious objectives set by the basic agreement, by unequal willingness of the parties to achieve objectives simultaneously, or by tacit
expectations of the various member countries which transcend the formal
commitment of the agreement.

1. Balanced Development

Because the integration commitment is subject to many differing
interpretations, at any one time any of the members may claim that the
others are not fulfilling their obligations. Consequently, there is
likely to be difficulty in attaining agreement on the method or methods
required to achieve one of the fundamental objectives of integration--
balanced development.

In groups of underdeveloped countries involved in a process of economic integration, the concept of balanced development implies recognition of the existence of significant differences among member countries
in their degree of relative economic development, and the need for adopting mechanisms which will favor to a greater extent the lesser-developed
members.

Such mechanisms must be closely related to the explicit and tacit
agreements. If the expectations of the member countries include a unified economy as a prelude to political unity, powerful instruments for
achieving balanced development will be required. However, if the commitment is restricted to seeking economic gain while member countries retain their own structures and systems, the possibilities for application
of the principle of balanced development will be minimal.

Furthermore, the objective of balanced development faces practical
difficulties of quantification in order to (i) determine the real differences in development levels of the member states; (ii) assess the
costs and benefits of economic integration; and (iii) select suitable
devices for applying corrective measures to the uneven economic growth
among the members.

The necessary political foundations for economic integration require certain similarities between the members, in particular their geographical proximity and the existence of common goals and interests.

On the other hand, homogeneity in the degree of relative development of the participants in an integration scheme does not necessarily require equal levels of development among members. In fact, all known and existing integration processes show differences in the degree of development and in the size of the participating countries. Although these differences may lead to elements of friction and the need to adopt formulas of compromise among the members, they also stimulate development within the group. That is, to the extent that equal levels of development of member countries reflect similar resource endowments, the possibilities for intercountry complementarity would tend to be low. By contrast, the more dissimilar the composition of resources of the nations, the greater should be the complementarity of their economic relations.

Indeed, the ideal situation for integration would be that member countries have equal relative development and a high degree of unevenness in the composition of their resources. In this hypothetical case a distinction must be made between human and material resources. Whereas ideally material resources would diverge, human resources would be equal among member countries, reflecting their equal levels of development.

2. Political Aspects

Economic development of the members attained through the operating integration commitment reinforces the commitment of parties and fosters more advanced stages of integration, provided that any disruptive forces of the group continue to remain weaker than the binding links that are developed by integration in the course of time. Associative tendencies are developed whenever the benefits of integration are universally perceived. Underlying objectives may also include greater degrees of political and economic independence and of prestige in the relations of the group with the rest of the world.

Experience shows that the dynamic factors of integration are intensive during the formative period of the free trade zone. It becomes less so as the integration process advances toward new and higher levels of interaction. The reason for this is that the greater the degree of integration attained at a given time, the greater is the resulting resistance which must be overcome to move past the current stage.

This resistance tests the will of the members and may give rise to stagnation and even dissolution of the integration process. Resistance results both from the passive force of inertia and the active opposition of vested interests from within and outside the region. These interests consider themselves adversely affected by integration, and involve local political leaders who often regard integration as gradually shrinking their sphere of influence.

On the other hand, the integration process brings about the formation of bonds of interest among sectors of the population, especially at the managerial level and among technocrats, who counteract the disruptive forces. The degree of dynamism and endurance of the process ultimately depends on the unstable equilibrium between these forces.

Internal equilibrium between the members is frequently influenced by external factors, especially by the group's position relative to the principal competing actors on the international stage. External forces can be decisive if internal equilibrium becomes precarious, and they can tilt the balance one way or the other. Furthermore, if the association of countries is motivated by the need to insure a desirable degree of political and economic independence vis-a-vis other nations, it is to be expected that pressures will be exerted to dissolve the association, or else to mold it along acceptable lines.

Prediction of the future behavior of the integration process, as Professor Hass points out, would require full knowledge of the conditioning variables of the process.[2] Until now studies of integration processes rely solely on a wealth of information or empirical generalizations which do not suffice to formulate a theory.

3. Economic Framework

Literature on customs unions has dwelt mainly on measuring commercial activity generated by the creation and operation of the European Common Market. It refers both to the increase in trade between the members and to the decrease, by substitution, in the flow of goods and services from the rest of the world, which traditionally had supplied the domestic markets of the community.

The theory of customs unions, since the initial studies by J. Viner,[3] has considered the creation of trade as a positive welfare element, and the diversion of trade as a negative element (the latter resulting from a substitution of less-expensive imports by higher priced goods provided by members of the customs union). However, the negative effects may be overcome if the customs union allows for a more accelerated economic development of the integrating states.

It is noteworthy that the latter concept has been incorporated into integration models when applied to groupings of underdeveloped countries. In the European case, it has been of less interest to refer to the possible effects upon development of their respective members, for these countries are generally classified as highly developed. Nevertheless, the European Economic Community and customs unions in underdeveloped countries share the common feature of gaining economic benefits through economies of scale attainable by means of an enlarged domestic market.

In the case of underdeveloped countries, the main economic motivation has been the pursuance of more diverse objectives than in the European case. Through integration the developing countries seek to establish an internal market which permits them to: (i) diversify production and reduce their extreme dependence on the exportation of a few primary commodities; (ii) accelerate their rates of economic growth in order to raise living standards and curtail chronic unemployment; and (iii) modify or modernize their productive sector and exploit natural resources to greater advantage. Therefore, underlying every process of economic integration among underdeveloped countries is the conviction that the size of domestic markets is a significant limitation to economic growth, for there exist serious obstacles to economic expansion through sole reliance on expanded international trade.

These obstacles involve the established order of international trade whereby the industrial countries, although potential buyers of manufactured goods from the underdeveloped countries, protect their market by means of tariffs and other artificial barriers. Another obstacle is the fact that the brands of industrial products from underdeveloped countries are unknown; that these products lack distribution systems in the industrial countries; or if manufactured by multinational concerns, the products are part of market allocation schemes which exclude exportation to other countries.

The extreme dependence of the developing countries on a few export commodities deeply influences their production patterns and social structures. Sudden price rises for major export products are not fully exploited by underdeveloped countries because these increases are unforeseen, the cycle is brief, and domestic producers are slow to respond. Thus, the larger part of the price increase obtained in the rising phase of the cycle translates into price rises for factors, especially land; increases in income of the wealthy minority of the population; and an increase in imports, especially luxury items corresponding to the distribution resulting from the additional income. Only a fraction of the higher price is exploited through increased fiscal revenue and through the spillover into other sectors of the population, which results in a moderate increase in the consumption of domestic goods and services, and in private investment which, unfortunately, is repeatedly poured into traditional activities.

When prices fall, the economy must adjust to the decline of the over-accelerated activity at the end of the rising phase, with serious consequences for employment and for private investment generated during the previous period, especially in areas of marginal production. Such periods have regularly coincided with strong social pressures and with a decline in the growth rate of the GNP.

One of the implications of this phenomenon is that these countries are constantly suffering inflationary effects of external origin. During a price rise, inflation stems from the increasing costs of production factors, and during a price decline, from an excess in the domestic money supply, until it is curtailed by means of restrictive fiscal and credit policies.

In view of these distortions caused by cyclical behavior in export prices, it is reasonable to assume that the real growth achieved by such economies over an extended period of time is less than that which would correspond to average prices in that period, but with smaller fluctuations around the average. In this sense, if economic integration contributes to diversification of production and to making the growth of the economy less dependent on price fluctuations of a few export products, then benefits will have been achieved in terms of the fundamental objectives of the integration program.

These objectives are considered attainable through increased trade of new goods, especially manufactured goods, among the countries in the area. To the extent that the Common Market would increase industrial production aimed at the enlarged internal market, it would gradually fulfill the dual purpose of diversifying the productive apparatus and reducing the extreme dependence of the whole area on the external sector.

To be relevant for underdeveloped countries, the theory of economic integration necessarily rests on the more general theory of economic development. Since there is no universal formula which explains the conditions necessary for economic development, the Central American experience, as well as that of other groups of underdeveloped countries, is a subject of interest to those who study the interaction of integration and development.

Economic development is a process which is characterized not only by a sustained and significant growth in the production of goods and services but also by qualitative changes in the economic and social structures. These changes tend to spread the benefits of growth to the population as a whole. On the other hand, when this broad concept is applied to relations between states, within the framework of economic integration, it follows that the commitment to deal with the balanced economic development of members will involve not only an interaction which transcends the simple movement of merchandise and production factors by virtue of free trade but also structural changes in property and income flows, which will lead to a better distribution of wealth at both the national and regional levels.

It is well known that all underdeveloped countries suffer in varying degrees from outdated structures of property ownership, the roots of which date back to the colonial period. Nevertheless, the problem lies in transferring to the regional level those decisions of economic policy which fall into the internal field of action of the states, and over which the integration entities have very little jurisdiction. Therefore, the effective application of the principle of balanced economic development requires a clear distinction between what this principle represents within the respective fields of national and regional action.

C. The Central American Commitment

1. The Principle of Reciprocity

During the course of the Central American integration process, the concept of balanced development gradually emerged as an aspiration of the nations which considered themselves less developed than the other members. At the outset, a concept of much lesser scope prevailed, involving only mutual cooperation and reciprocity in sharing the benefits and burdens of integration.

At the first meeting of the Committee for Economic Cooperation[B1] held in Tegucigalpa, Honduras (1952), emphasis was placed on the desirability of upholding the principle of reciprocity "according to which development of different productive activities in any integration program should be carried out in a manner such that, with participation of the various countries, the resulting trade will be achieved on the basis of reciprocal interest."[4] Reciprocity in benefits (and costs) was in fact embodied in each project of interest to two or more countries in the group. The mere fact of their joining in the project demonstrated antici- pated usefulness for the participants. Moreover, the principle of reci- procity was envisioned as equally applicable to commercial relations among the countries of the area. An increase in trade was expected to be the result of the execution of specific projects; any agreement to establish an industry in a participating country would imply free access to the Central American market for its products and inputs.

A parallel movement, the gradual creation of a free trade zone among the member states, developed concurrently with the specific plans for eco- nomic development within the economic integration scheme. Historically, the free trade movement was not motivated by the same considerations as the integration program conceived and executed within the Committee for Economic Cooperation with the assistance of the Economic Commission for Latin America (ECLA). The initial signing of bilateral treaties by El Salvador and Nicaragua (1951)[5] followed principles which at times did not coincide with the plan of gradual and progressive economic integration. In the initial stages of the program the establishment of a free trade zone was considered an objective to be attained by the expansion of common development plans. However, this implicit understanding was not generally shared by all countries in the area, whereas the expansion of trade through liberalizing agreements was unanimously accepted, and no conflict between the two schemes was foreseen at that time.

During the first phase of the integration program, application of the principle of reciprocity of benefits centered on the possibility of establishing a regional complex of primarily industrial enterprises hav- ing the double characteristic of being new and of regional interest. The Committee, at its first extraordinary meeting held in San Salvador (1955), requested the Secretariat (ECLA) to carry out a general evaluation of possible industries for this purpose.

The Secretariat submitted ten industries for consideration.[6] At the same time, evaluation studies on forest resources, prepared by FAO experts, were examined to determine the possibility of manufacturing pulp and paper and other subsidiary activities of the wood industry. Other reports prepared by FAO covered the cattle, fats and oils, and cotton industries. The Technical Assistance Council of the United Nations and its specialized agencies carried out other studies, especially on regional infrastructure,[7] statistical coordination, and intrazonal trade.[8] The scope and variety of the studies conducted in this period were impressive, and they provided a wealth of previously unavailable information on the region.

The studies embodied the concept that to attain the desired aims it was necessary to develop "long-range planning of a positive nature, a careful study of available resources, and the promotion of new activi- ties," with the recognition that the mere signing of free trade agree- ments between the nations would not suffice to foster integration, let alone to achieve economic reciprocity. It was also recognized that the mere application of fiscal incentives to industrial development would not be enough to stimulate the new capital investments required to fulfill the dual purposes of economic growth and balanced development.

The integration program placed emphasis on those two sectors which allowed the easiest assessment of integration benefits: physical infrastructure and industrial development. Expansion of these sectors was intended to have a favorable effect on the general development of the region and to benefit each member nation by the location of the different projects, seeking to attain a dynamic equilibrium among countries by the constant addition of new projects. The Committee gave particular importance to the formulation of projects which would: (i) link development of agricultural activities to industrial development; (ii) foster trade and economic complementarity in Central America; and (iii) achieve reciprocity in distribution (including both purely economic considerations and those of spatial distribution of projects among and within the countries in the area). In the case of existing industries the concept of reciprocity meant their expansion to meet the needs of the regional market, especially when this expansion involved technological advances and projection complementarity among the countries.

2. Balanced Development

The integration program hinged on the principle of economic reciprocity during the entire period of the bilateral treaties (1950-56)[A1], [A2]. It is important to note again the coexistence in Central America of two courses of action, not always parallel: the signing of the free trade agreements and the efforts to achieve a gradual and progressive economic integration on the basis of coordinated projects of regional interest. One of the first occasions of conflict in these courses of action came when the governments decided to lay the ground for a new instrument to improve upon and replace the existing bilateral agreements.

During the Committee's third meeting in Managua (1956), the possibility of signing a multilateral treaty was considered. Such a treaty was to consolidate the partial zones created by the bilateral agreements into a single zone of free trade. The Committee anticipated (i) the establishment of a free trade zone limited to a list of items; (ii) the equalization of external tariffs for the articles on the list and their raw materials; (iii) duration of ten years for the new instrument; (iv) the promotion and protection of regional industries; and (v) the creation of a Central American Trade Commission for administration of the treaty.

Within the Ad hoc Commission for the proposed treaty, a conflict arose about whether the list of free trade goods annexed to the proposed treaty should also include new industrial products of regional interest. Another problem was how to insure, on a long-term basis, the "permanency" of the commitment for the establishment or expansion of regional industries and the coordination of industrial development in Central America; such a long-term commitment was intended to avoid uneconomic duplication of investments. The thesis favoring limitation of free trade for new products until the adoption of the integration rules to which they would be subject was supported by Nicaragua and Costa Rica but opposed by Guatemala and El Salvador.[9]

The conflict regarding the treatment of new products (regional industries), which arose at the third meeting of the Committee and at its

Ad hoc Commission, marked the beginning of an institutional crisis that persists today. Disagreement hinged on a substantial discrepancy between objectives and policy instrumentation. The countries with broader industrial bases favored the establishment of an unrestricted free trade zone, while those of lesser industrial potential advocated programmed industrialization aimed at balanced levels of development among members, in which case free trade would become merely a means to attain this objective. For the latter countries the gradual opening of their markets represented a bargaining instrument, a stance difficult to reconcile with the aims of the nations advocating free trade. For their part, the countries of greater industrial potential argued that the establishment of free trade was a necessary condition for the achievement of higher levels of development for the entire group. They admitted that the concern of the other states was valid but maintained that the problem should be solved by complementary agreements that would not affect the purity of the principle of unrestricted free trade.

3. The Regime of Integration Industries: 1956

At this third meeting of the Committee, eleven industrial branches were declared to be of regional interest. Certain privileges were to be granted to these branches. To this effect the Secretariat (ECLA) was requested to prepare draft legislation. The Secretariat therefore presented a preliminary version of the Regime for Central American Integration Industries (the Regime),[A4] in the form of a multinational agreement.

Discussion within the group of experts turned once again on the positions of Nicaragua and Honduras, on the one hand, and Guatemala and El Salvador, on the other. A subject of debate over which no agreement could be reached was whether free trade for the proposed integration industries was an exclusive privilege of the plants that would be protected by the Regime, or if this treatment could be extended to all plants producing the same goods. The first group of countries argued that free trade "was decidedly the most important privilege of the Regime," and that if this privilege were granted to the product itself and not to the producing plants, the integration industries would not be guaranteed a sufficiently adequate market, especially when the industries had "made substantial investments aimed at covering the entire Central American market." Contrarily, the other group argued that privileges could not be legally granted to specific firms, and that such treatment would definitely set up and consolidate a monopolistic situation which was against the spirit of competition set by the proposed treaty.

A new term, "approximate equality," gradually evolved with regard to balanced development in the distribution of the program's economic benefits and corresponding sacrifices. On broaching the subject, the experts stated for the first time the need for periodical assessment of the benefits of the new integration scheme, in order to assess its effects on the region and on each country in particular. On the assumption that a precise method for measuring such benefits was not possible, the group proposed that an acceptable evaluation procedure should be based not on the net balance of trade pertaining to the products of the "integration industries" but instead on the total value of exports.

To this were added the effects of investments made in the export country to establish or expand integration industries plus other effects (possibly indirect) derived from the program. With regard to the sacrifices of the program (social costs), fiscal losses would be considered, albeit as partial elements, using as a basis the minimum duties fixed by the agreement.

In order to insure approximately equal benefits over time, high priority was given to the mechanism of spatial distribution of the integration industries. To this end, in addition to technical and economic location factors leading to optimal benefits for the entire region, a clear distinction was to be made between immobile factors of production (e.g., geographic location of natural resources) and those which could be modified (such as capital resources and physical infrastructure) by means of positive actions. After assessment of all elements involved in locating plants, it was recommended that those industries "whose plants could supply the Central American market with equal or similar efficiency, regardless of the Central American country in which they were built, should be established in those countries which had obtained the least benefits from the Central American economic integration program."

In short, the integration process has been conceptually dominated by two broad lines of action: (i) the agreement to create a common market with free mobility of goods, services, and factors of production; and (ii) the pursuance by the countries of efforts fostering their individual economic development, but pursuance in the context of the new dimensions afforded by the regional market, taking into account that the responsibilities and benefits of integration would be shared equally by the countries of the region. Essentially, the integration benefits consisted of the new industrial activities which, by mutual agreement, would be established on the basis of adequate spatial distribution.

After a two-year gestation period, the projects of the Multilateral Treaty[A3] and the Regime[A4] culminated in important debates at the fifth meeting of the Committee (1958). At this meeting Guatemala and El Salvador supported the signing of the Multilateral Treaty and a postponement of the Regime for further study, while Nicaragua and Costa Rica advocated simultaneous signing of both agreements, adducing that the Regime was the core of both instruments and the cornerstone of the integration scheme. Guatemala maintained that the Regime violated the spirit of free enterprise by granting exclusive benefits to industries that it protected, and that spatial allocation of industries should be conditioned by market forces. The Guatemalan representative argued that the creation of a larger consumer market would provide by itself a sufficient stimulus for development of the five countries of the area.

Nicaragua argued that the Regime was the only effective vehicle for equitable distribution of costs and benefits of integration among the less-developed countries. That without it, the new industries would be concentrated in those countries having larger industrial bases. And that the smaller countries would be left with the role of supplying raw materials, a role that would not even allow regional trade balance, let alone upgrade their economics through the stimulus of an expanded market. The delegation from Nicaragua also rejected the application of the pejorative term "monopoly" to regional industries, since the Regime would qualify "integration industries" as whole industrial branches composed of one or more related plants, which could be located in different countries under strict price and competition surveillance by the Regime.

In the course of the deliberations, the concept of "balanced development" was used for the first time as one of the fundamental objectives of the program. This objective would be achieved through the interaction of the Regime and the Multilateral Treaty. The treaty would contain a list of traditional goods for free exchange and would be enlarged by successive additions of products coming from new integration industries. The program would lead to a perfected Common Market in the future, in which all goods would be subject to free trade, but during the transitional period the double purpose of expanding the market and protecting the position of the relatively less developed countries would be retained.

Although at the end of the meeting the simultaneous signing of both agreements was generally advocated, signature was accomplished through a compromise formula. In that compromise, the proposed Regime was modified so that the determination of the specific protection conditions for each qualifying industry would be left to protocols.[10] Thus each protocol remained subject to unanimous approval by the countries and to the observance of the same legal procedures as the main agreement.

Lacking a sufficient number of specific projects ready for implementation to allow a relatively satisfactory spatial distribution, the Regime could not withstand the opposing forces, namely, the ideological resistance maintained by the larger countries and the difficulties of practical application. In fact, only one industry was then established under the protection of this agreement, a caustic soda complex in Nicaragua.[11]

4.   Import Substitution

The policy of import substitution, a term applied after the fact to define a nation's aspirations to industrialize with protective external barriers, did not play the principal role in the 1950s that has been assigned to it in more recent times. Rather, the concept prevailing in the Committee was that the countries were separately embarked upon industrial development policies supported by national laws, recognizing at the same time that the dimensions of the domestic market considerably limited their possibilities for industrialization. Moreover, the sudden opening of the regional market provided a greater impetus to development of the countries, especially in the industrial sector.

In this period, the emphasis placed on industrial development as the most effective way to attain the objectives of economic growth and balanced development gave the integration program an external image which has often confused those attempting to evaluate it solely from the standpoint of industrialization. Moreover, it has been assumed that industrialization in Central America is being pushed at all costs, with excessive increases in external tariff barriers, following patterns set by other Latin American countries. These appraisals have little basis in fact. The tariffs established in the years following integration were generally no higher than the average of those existing in the area

prior to equalization. Similarly, the principle of import substitution was not adopted as completely as it was in some other underdeveloped regions. With the rare exception of some tariffs that were
raised disproportionately and unnecessarily, import substitution has been
effected by liberalization of duties on imported machinery, equipment,
raw materials, and intermediate goods which are used in locally manufactured products. In fact, aside from providing a broader market, the
integration program has exerted scant direct influence in this area,
for its action has been geared primarily toward harmonizing the national
laws on industrial development. In the long run, the competition that
evolved among the countries themselves to attract new industries contributed to lower external tariffs via tax exemptions granted by national
authorities.

Industrialization gains attributable to the integration program
independent of the autonomous effects of the expanded market are few.
This is probably the source of the dissatisfaction of some member countries who feel that it has not been possible to advance by coordinate
action toward a more rational and fruitful use of the resources of the
area.

D.   Creation of the Common Market

1.   General Treaty on Economic Integration

The integration scheme prepared at great effort by the Committee
in the 1950s was suddenly modified by the signing of the "Treaty of
Economic Association"[A6] by Guatemala, El Salvador, and Honduras in
February 1960. This treaty, known also as the "Northern Tripartite,"
had multiple motivations. At the beginning of 1959, discussions began
between El Salvador and Honduras on matters pertaining to the revision
of their old bilateral treaty on free trade, a treaty that antedated
the integration movement (1914). Toward the middle of 1959, Guatemala
was included in the discussions. In January 1960 the "Declaration of
El Poy" emerged from the meeting in that border town of the three Presi-
dents. During the months that preceded the declaration, Nicaragua and
Costa Rica were neither informed of the contents of these discussions
nor of the motives of the participants.

In addition to political reasons not discussed here the Tripartite
emerged in part as a result of the discontent of these countries (es-
pecially Guatemala and El Salvador) with the existing integration scheme.
In particular, there was dissatisfaction with the Regime for Central
American Integration Industries, and with the slow process of incorpor-
ating new products into the list of free trade items in the Multilateral
Treaty. (It is noteworthy that neither the Multilateral Treaty nor the
Regime had been put into effect by all five countries.)

By the signing of this Treaty of Economic Association, the Economic
Integration Program suffered one of its most serious setbacks. On the
one hand, the agreement substantially altered the foundations of the program by rendering the Regime for Central American Integration Industries

inoperative by including at once in free trade all products from participating countries. On the other hand, it virtually excluded two Central
American countries, Nicaragua and Costa Rica, from the plan.

Faced with this new situation, the integration process was com-
pelled to shape a new institutional scheme aimed at restoring the unity
of the integration commitment. It involved drawing up a new general
treaty, necessarily influenced by the recent events and attuned to the
largely divergent aspirations of the members. A regional finance mechanism would be incorporated into it, as had been considered by the Committee since 1953 and agreed upon at its sixth meeting in 1959.

A "Development and Assistance Fund" was established by the Tripartite.
The rationale for such a fund would be a matter for consideration; and
to a large extent, all positive action to iron out existing or future
disagreements among the member states regarding balanced development would
be transferred to this financial mechanism.

The new general treaty was initially discussed by the Committee at
San José, Costa Rica, in April 1960, without the participation of the
host country. Costa Rica wanted a prudential waiting period to examine
its position in the integration program. So the new project was negotiated
by the three signers of the Treaty of Economic Association, constituting
a bloc, with Nicaragua placed clearly in a weak position.

It is worth mentioning that in the deliberations of the treaty's
working group the problems of reciprocity and balanced development were
not discussed again. Nicaragua's proposal that would have permitted the
temporary suspension of "imports when they threatened to cause serious
damage to domestic production" was rejected by the group, which considered
that "escape clauses in the General Treaty weakened its objectives."
Another Nicaraguan motion that would have authorized each state to raise
tariffs unilaterally above the agreed uniform minimum in order to cope
with unforeseen balance of payments difficulties suffered the same fate.
The group held that "modification of the uniform tariff could only be
effected by unanimous decision."

The inconsistency pointed out by the Economic Commission for Latin
America (ECLA) between the Regime for Central American Integration Industries and the plan established by the Tripartite Treaty at the beginning of the year apparently was not studied by the group, which did
not adopt any formal decision on this matter. Nevertheless, the same
group stipulated in the draft of the General Treaty that the Regime
would take effect for the countries that had already ratified it no later
than the date on which the General Treaty would become effective.

At the seventh meeting of the Committee held in Managua in December
1960, two important agreements were finally considered and approved,
which shaped the basic integration scheme that has prevailed up to the
present. They are the General Treaty on Economic Integration[A7] and
the Constitutive Agreement on the Central American Bank for Economic
Integration (CABEI).[A8]

It is noteworthy that chapter 7 of the General Treaty sets forth the creation of the bank as "a finance and promotion instrument for integrated economic growth on the basis of regional equilibrium," and stipulates that those countries not previously ratifying the Multilateral Treaty, the Regime for Central American Integration Industries, and the Agreement on Collection of Import Duties [A5] (the former two were signed in June 1958 and the latter, in September 1959), would not be entitled to secure loans or guarantees from the bank. This provision made compulsory the immediate enforcement of the three agreements by the four signers of the treaty, and thus notified Costa Rica of the obligation to sign them as a prerequisite to becoming a member of the bank.

It is clear that, with the exception of the formal adoption of the Regime, but without the modifications that the new situation demanded, the question of balanced development was transferred to the Central American Bank for Economic Integration. The treaty did not anticipate the maladjustments that the Common Market could bring about. In fact, the problem was set aside at this stage of the integration program. As could be seen, the applicability of the Regime of Integration Industries was limited to those products on a temporary list of exceptions to free trade, and among those, only to goods explicitly subject to special procedures prior to their inclusion into the general system of free trade.

If nonmanufactured products were excluded from the list of exceptions to free trade, very few articles remained which could be considered in a possible protocol for the Regime for Central American Integration Industries. Furthermore, since the list was negotiated bilaterally, no single product was left which could be uniformly negotiated between all the members in accordance with the characteristics demanded by the Regime. In other words, inclusion of the Regime in the General Treaty was apparently done to retain the possibility of using a system for distribution of industries among countries, but without the means or mechanisms for practical implementation of such a system.

In the context of the turn taken by the economic integration politics, it is useful to recall that the General Treaty was negotiated and approved in the absence of Costa Rica, which on previous occasions had supported the position of Nicaragua. The latter country appeared to have withdrawn its support of the distribution system. The fact is that Nicaragua was left to choose between two alternatives, namely, remaining excluded from the Integration Program or accepting the form decided upon by the other three countries. This was also the case when Costa Rica was again incorporated into the Program, two years after the signing of the General Treaty.

The Central American Bank was now responsible for maintaining a balanced level of development among the countries. During the first years of its institutional life, the available means and resources to accomplish that task were very limited, especially in the absence of a general policy and a set of regional instruments consistent with the aims of balanced development.

Summing up the evolution of the Program during this critical stage, the signing of the General Treaty in 1960 represented a considerable advance toward a Common Market, but it also sacrificed the mechanisms required to correct imbalances that might occur in the relative economic development of the member countries.

2. Period of Normality

During the first years after the General Treaty for Economic Integration became effective, the Common Market established free trade within the region and uniform external tariff regulations for 94 percent of the customs categories. Concurrently, spectacular growth occurred in intraregional trade. These combined to maintain high expectations of the program, so that numerous sectors of public opinion began to consider the program "irreversible."

During this period, the new institutional organization of the program was established, differing from the former in that it was composed of regionally based organizations, represented especially by the Permanent Secretariat of the Treaty (SIECA). Also, the Central American Bank for Economic Integration was organized and initiated its operations with the public in September 1961.

The major part of this period of normality was dedicated to the problems of standardizing legislation, such as that referring to the Agreement on Uniform Fiscal Incentives for Industrial Development[A10] or to other measures that could facilitate the free movement of merchandise within the member nations.

In March 1963, the Executive Council[B3] declared the production of caustic soda and chlorine, and of vehicle tires and tubes, to be integration industries, and incorporated the corresponding manufacturing plants located in Nicaragua and Guatemala into the Regime of Integration Industries. Simultaneously, the Council considered a proposal by El Salvador that would tend to establish a permanent system of customs incentives for the promotion of new industries that was different from that contemplated by the Regime.

This new instrument, called the "Special System for the Promotion of Industrial Activities,"[A9] was approved by the Council. It consisted of the establishment of protective tariffs for certain articles whose production was considered to be of particular interest to the economic development of Central America; it set protective tariffs governing the production of plate glass, glass containers, electric light bulbs, bodies and chassis for buses and trucks, and refrigeration units. The condition necessary for its application was that the plants would fill at least 50 percent of regional demand.

The principal argument in favor of the new system was that a large number of activities existed which could not be classified as "integration industries" within the Regime because they did not fulfill its more strict qualifications. It should be noted that the new system made no provision for dealing with the problem of spatial distribution of plants and did not require a minimum level of Central American ownership in capital stock, as did the Regime.

With the new system, the Regime ceased to be operative even for new industrial activities. Private investment, especially foreign, which had feared the state intervention implied by the Regime, found a broad entry for activity in the new system. Various plants were established which until then had remained in the stage of negotiation. Some of the industries, originally earmarked for installation in the less-developed countries, were established in those which had a larger domestic market and a broader base for industrial development.

The object of this discussion is not to weigh the merits or disadvantages of industrial concentration for the region as a whole but only to indicate that the relatively less-developed countries of the area gradually lost the means of implementing the principle of balanced development. In fact, the General Treaty without the Regime contained no viable mechanism for the application of this principle.

The earlier defenders of the "programmed" integration system ceased to insist that other similar mechanisms be established to replace the Regime. The climate of general optimism prevailing in all the countries of the region over the spectacular gains in the integration process (especially in the field of intraregional trade) drowned out the voices which clamored for a process of greater balance in the economic relations between the member countries.

3. Efforts at Economic Programming

In 1962 the Economic Council[B2] established the Joint Programming Mission[B5] with the participation of representatives of the SIECA, the Central American Bank for Economic Integration, the Economic Commission for Latin America, the Organization of American States, and the Inter-American Development Bank. The main task of the Mission was to identify economic sectors which could be the objects of both regional and long-term global development. In spite of the elaboration of development strategies for the region, the intensive work carried out by the Mission did not have the unanimous and continuous support of the member countries. In fact, since no regional mechanism existed which could put the Mission's recommendations and plans into effect, its main result was to provide technical assistance to the national planning offices. These offices in turn had a precarious existence, and their own plans, with few exceptions, scarcely influenced the course of investment and development policies in the Central American countries.

Furthermore, far from coordinating their individual programs of industrial development, the countries in the area openly competed to attract plants, engendering a proliferation of similar projects and an excess of installed capacity for most of the traditional industries. In other kinds of activities, intraregional competition was suppressed through agreements between manufacturers which allowed the demarcation of territories for supply of their products.

On the positive side, the spectacular growth in intraregional trade has been noted. To this must be added the intense work undertaken in the field of regional physical infrastructure in the implementation of the Central American road plan. Its first stage involved the Regional Highway Program, scheduled to be carried out in four years at an approximate cost of $80 million.[12] Also, within the same sector, the system of Central American communication by microwaves was established to connect the Central American capitals with each other and the rest of the world.

In this sector, as in others, it was the intention to apply the principle of balanced development by indirect measures. The latter would be aimed at reducing existing disparities in infrastructure projects which would be unfavorable to the location of industries in relatively less developed countries, but also basically seeking to provide the area as a whole with a common network of transportation and communication facilities.

4. The Years of Great Expectations

By 1964 the integration program had generated great optimism. This was expressed in enthusiastic declarations by the ministers of economy at the sixth meeting of the Economic Council (although the Minister of Economy of El Salvador noted permanent obstacles to the free movement of labor in the region). At that time there was no indication that the Common Market would shortly enter a critical period. From time to time the existing problems of the less-developed countries, due to the persistent deficit in their balance of trade, were discussed, but the general climate for the integration effort was favorable.

It was also noted that differences in reciprocal trade could be corrected by the dynamic effects of the Common Market. It was taken for granted that industrial concentration was a phenomenon not resolved even by the larger Latin American countries, which had no more than one or two centers of industrial growth. On the other hand, Nicaragua had succeeded in establishing some major industries oriented toward intraregional trade, Honduras maintained great expectations for developing significant industries based on the exploitation of natural resources, and Costa Rica and Nicaragua participated more and more in regional trade.

In addition to domestic growth factors, prices of traditional export products showed a substantial recovery from the low levels to which they had fallen in the late 1950s. Financing by the Central American Bank and other international institutions expedited industrial growth, highway construction, generation and distribution of electricity, and port improvements.

E. The Emergence of the Crisis

1. First Indications

Despite optimistic expectations for the future development of the integration program, toward the middle of 1964 concerned voices were

heard regarding the scant attention paid to the application of the principle of balanced development. At the ninth meeting of the Economic
Council held in Guatemala (August 1964), the Honduran Minister of Economy referred to "his concern about the extent which balanced development
was taken into account in the implementation of the program." In his
judgement, this was an essential factor, for he himself came from an
area where progress required that principle to be fully in effect. The
Honduran minister mentioned his particular concern about "the lack of
major industrial projects which could be located within his borders. . . ."
On the other hand, at a previous meeting, the Council expressed concern
over a series of Central American agreements that had not been approved
by the governments, a fact that motivated the national associations of
industrialists to issue a statement pressing the governments to "deposit
immediately the pending legal instruments, or else state the reason for
not doing so as soon as possible, and to propose the revisions they consider necessary." In the same statement the representatives of these
associations indicated the following:

> Considering that resistance on the part of some Central
> American countries to deposit the legal instruments of
> integration is largely due to the fear that one region
> may prosper at the expense of another, we suggest . . .
> that a regime be studied for the solution of the temporary
> problems which may arise, in order that the Program may
> avoid dismemberment caused by extremely adverse circum-
> stances for one of the members.

In effect, the negotiating positions of the countries had been gradually transferred from the discussion of the content of the integration
instruments to a more subtle plane of ratifying and/or depositing only
those already approved agreements that most benefited the immediate interests of the individual states. A reason for special concern was the
confusing status of enterprises assumed to be protected by the Regime
for Central American Integration Industries, by the Special System for
Promotion of Industrial Activities and its complementary agreements, by
national laws for incentives to industrial development, or by the incipient Central American Agreement on Uniform Fiscal Incentives to Industrial
Development,[A10] which would replace the national laws.

With regard to the problem of balanced development, the Joint Programming Mission expressed the opinion that differences in the levels of
development among Central American countries were of minor importance,
but that Honduras nevertheless presented an obvious problem whose solution
would demand a united effort. For its part, the Economic Commission for
Latin America (ECLA) also stressed the need for greater efforts toward
application of the principle of balanced development in its document,
"Evaluation of Economic Integration in Central America," requested by
the Economic Council. This document exposed the slow development of the
integration industries and the limited related activity of the Central
American Bank. Prophetically, the document anticipated the possibility
that the less-developed countries might withdraw from the Common Market
and concluded that "such action would be against the interest of the lagging members themselves."

The search for formulae for the application of the principle of balanced development, especially in the case of Honduras, continued to occupy the attention of the integration agencies. These efforts concentrated on the preferential treatment that could be granted to Honduras in the Central American Agreement on Uniform Fiscal Incentives for Industrial Development.[A10]

2. The Discontented Countries

Together with the evaluation submitted for consideration to the Committee for Economic Cooperation, ECLA presented a special study on the Honduran situation. Noting that the existing imbalance was an expression of differences created previously and linked to historical development, the study judged that, if left to the free and spontaneous forces of the Common Market, integration could increase the existing inequalities.

Concerning development policy, ECLA cited two immediate goals: strengthening of economic infrastructure (electricity, transportation, and communications); and implementation of a more diversified productive system, including the establishment of several industries, in particular, major plants for glass sheets, pulp and paper, metallurgy, and chemicals. To accomplish these goals the report recommended:

(i) that the Central American Bank give priority to Honduran investment projects; and

(ii) that within the Regime of Integration Industries the possibility of granting Honduras a minimum of industries be considered.

At the same time the Honduran delegation submitted a document to the Committee[13] that reflected its concern over the neglect of the principle of balanced development observed in recent years (since the signing of the General Treaty), and the substitution of that principle for "equal treatment" for all member countries. The document noted:

(i) a structural tendency of Honduras toward a balance of payments deficit with the other Central American countries;

(ii) unfavorable prospects for the growth of the Honduran economy without a regional policy to correct the imbalance; and

(iii) the absence of corrective measures in the integration industries scheme.

The Honduran representative claimed that preferential treatment for the country had been lacking in the application of industrial development policies, tariff harmonization, fiscal incentives, promotion and financing, and in technical assistance. He also noted that the revisions made to the Regime for Central American Integration Industries were detrimental to the less-developed countries, and that the signing of the Special System was in fact an "antithesis to the basis of reciprocity and Central American equity." He maintained that the elimination of tariff barriers between member countries should have been contemplated for a longer period to allow adjustments in the Honduran economy. He indicated that the Agreement on the Central American Bank was more limited than that originally contemplated for the Development and Assistance Fund referred to in the Treaty of Economic Association. Finally, he pointed out that the Central American Agreement on Uniform Fiscal Incentives granted preference to intermediate and capital goods industries, assuming that all countries had an equal industrial base and thus ignoring the reality of the Honduran industrial structure.

Notwithstanding the Honduran position, the Committee, upon reviewing the state of the Common Market, affirmed that the specific goals for the first stage of the program had been attained satisfactorily. In effect, the phase of tariff harmonization scheduled to finish in 1966 had already been completed; the intraregional trade figures had surpassed the most optimistic expectations; and in all countries increases in overall growth had been achieved, especially in the industrial sector. Nevertheless, the Committee also recognized "that all countries have not been able to exploit to the same degree as others the opportunities afforded by the expansion of the market."

The Committee therefore indicated the need "to define industrial policy with greater precision and to determine the necessary measures for the immediate use of financial and promotional instruments, in order to locate industrial activities among the countries on the basis of efficiency and equitable participation in the benefits of integration." The Committee recommended that the Economic Council determine specific integration industries to be assigned to Honduras in order to accelerate that country's industrial development.

After the presentation of Honduras was dealt with, the Nicaraguan delegate posed the need to conduct studies to "clarify the situation of his country with respect to its participation in the Common Market, from the standpoint of its relative development." This last statement spurred the other countries to express the existence "of imbalances in specific fields of their economic activity."

It is important to note that in spite of the Honduran and Nicaraguan presentations, the ninth meeting of the Committee ended with good prospects for the future, and on the whole, it was dominated by a spirit of complacency regarding the past achievements of the integration program. With respect to the problems posed over balanced development, it was assumed that the coordinated action of the integration agencies, using the instruments at their disposal, would produce the desired results. The Economic Council would formulate industrial policy, determine the list of basic industries feasible for installation in Central America, and assign industries by countries, on the basis of the principle of balanced development, indicating also the applicable legal instruments. The Central American Bank would promote through financing and other means the establishment and operation of specific projects worked out by the Council. The Central American Institute for Industrial and Technical Research (ICAITI)[B6] would advise regional and national agencies in all phases of project feasibility studies and plant design. The Central American Superior School for Public Administration (ESAPAC)[B7] would collaborate in the area of administrative personnel.

In these terms, the wealth of instruments available to the program for formulating and applying the strategy of integrated and balanced development to the Common Market countries seemed to be impressive. Nevertheless, as shall be seen later, events remained unchanged and the corrective measures were not applied until it was too late, and the measures lacked the necessary depth to restore the balance of integration. Threats of crisis increased in the years that followed.

By the twelfth meeting (February 1966), Honduras still had not ratified the Central American Agreement on Uniform Fiscal Incentives to Industrial Development, a situation which had given rise to complaints by the other countries. These complaints were the object of a new presentation by the Honduran delegation.[14] In it Honduras reiterated the lack of application of the principle of balanced development in this instrument, as well as in the rest of the agreements and protocols derived from the General Treaty which adversely affected that country. The Honduran delegation argued that the agreement to establish uniform norms of treatment for industrial development favored an advantageous position for those countries with broader industrial bases. That being the case, preferential treatment to Honduras should go well beyond the mere right to extend exemptions of income and assets taxes for a period of two years.[15] Such a right was weak and practically ineffective, "because in any event those industrial enterprises which in the past obtained substantial fiscal exemptions under national laws in the more-developed countries would continue competing advantageously." The treatment called for by Honduras was a harmonized body of domestic laws which would permit that country to authorize a different treatment to enterprises rather than have a series of partial exceptions. Under such laws Honduras would follow individual criteria of classification in accord with its relative degree of development.[16]

Notwithstanding the general recognition on the part of the other members that Honduras should enjoy preferential treatment, the problem was complicated by the fact that the Agreement on Uniform Fiscal Incentives had already been approved and ratified by all the other countries except Honduras. Aside from this formal difficulty, which apparently was not the object of debate, the significant obstacle stemmed from the urgent need to implement this agreement so that some order could be imposed on the competition for concessions under the national laws of fiscal incentives. All countries were increasing the exemptions and each of them extended treatment automatically equal to that granted the same industries by the other countries in order to attract that industry to their countries. The only beneficiaries of this competition were the business firms, especially foreign enterprises. In addition, most of the national laws had been adopted in the 1950s and contained such broad fiscal exemptions that they left little room for further exonerations. Therefore, any preferential treatment for Honduras in all probability would have had little impact on investment decisions. Meaningful preferential treatment, as requested by Honduras, could have been obtained only through a revision of the agreement in order to reduce substantially the incentives granted by the other countries. Even this alternative was seriously limited by the position of industries already enjoying the privileges, both because of their economic power and because reduction of incentives would have represented a violation of acquired legal rights.

When the Economic Council considered the terms of the Honduran request, the delegations from other countries maintained that it would not be convenient to have different criteria for classification of industries coexist within the Common Market. On the other hand, the countries agreed that Honduras could grant greater benefits in the fields of income and property taxes and in tariff exemptions in the importation of machinery and the necessary equipment for plant installation. In addition, Honduras could authorize a 20 percent differential on tariff exonerations for importation of raw materials, intermediate products, and containers. The Council approved those terms in the Protocol of Preferential Treatment for Honduras, which was signed in September 1966.

On this occasion the Nicaraguan Minister of Economy proposed that the Economic Council grant his country the same preferential treatment given to Honduras, backing his request with an analysis of the Nicaraguan position in relation to the other member states.[17] He pointed out that with the Central American economic integration the balance of payments situation in Nicaragua had deteriorated and threatened to worsen in the future. He argued that the persistent deficit resulted from the lower level of industrial development in Nicaragua relative to that of the other countries in the region. In addition, traditional exports had declined in recent years, and measures were urgently needed to prevent the further deterioration of Nicaragua's position.

The representative from El Salvador pointed out that the limited territorial extension and high population density in his country "placed it in a very special situation, and therefore requested that inherent problems of its national economy be taken into account." He indicated that for the time being he could not support Nicaragua's request because he believed the problem to be more complex than suggested by the Nicaraguan delegation and that it did not stem exclusively from the Common Market operations.

In spite of continuous efforts undertaken shortly afterward, it was impossible to agree on a plan that would solve the special problems posed by Honduras and Nicaragua. Moreover, the growth in intraregional trade brought about repeated disagreements among the member countries on the interpretation of the origin of certain tradable goods. Those disagreements should have been ironed out expeditiously by the integration bodies. The very nature of the previously unforeseen situations demanded a search for immediate solutions. Also, as the pace of the integration process increased and the countries faced a growing deterioration in their foreign trade with the rest of the world, the regional agencies were increasingly being asked to consider matters formerly within the jurisdiction of national authorities. These cumbersome tasks contributed to a relative stagnation of the integration process because of the time and efforts required to search for solutions to the basic problems that the two countries posed to the regional organizations.

3.   Open Conflict

The year 1969 was one full of difficulties for the Central American countries in many respects. These difficulties culminated on July 14 in armed conflict between the republics of El Salvador and Honduras.

Serious limitations on intraregional trade had evolved from the beginning of the year. The growing discontent of Nicaragua over continuous deterioration in its balance of payments prompted the imposition of a domestic consumption tax on a series of goods. The tax decree (Decree No. 3 MEIC) evoked adverse reaction from the rest of the countries, which alleged it to be in clear violation of the General Treaty. Resulting retaliatory measures paralyzed commercial exchange between Nicaragua and the other four countries.

At the seventeenth meeting of the Economic Council (March 20-22), in the face of double pressure from the countries in the region and from local industrialists, the Nicaraguan Minister of Economy reported to the Council that "his government had decided to circumscribe Executive Decree No. 3 MEIC within the legal bounds on internal taxes specified by the General Treaty."[18] The Nicaraguan decision complied with the conditions of the four remaining governments for the suspension of retaliatory measures, which had included the requirement of a customs bond for imports from Nicaragua.

The Honduran delegation reiterated the point made on previous occasions that the industrialization process in the area carried out under the protection of excessive fiscal measures had created a major flow of regional trade in manufacturing products with a high content of imported raw materials. This represented not only higher prices for the Central American consumer but also considerably decreased fiscal receipts.

In the opinion of the Honduran delegate, the fiscal problem had different effects on each country. In fact, those countries with larger industrial production aimed at the Common Market not only benefited by the income effect but also collected taxes imposed upon the imported components that were definitely transferred almost totally to the consumers in the importing countries. In this sense an inequitable financial flow was running from the importing country toward the exporting country. This situation became more serious when the "protocol of San José"[A11] was signed, for it added tariffs of 30 percent to raw materials imported from outside the area. This new surcharge would result in a price rise on final manufacturing products with a bias against Honduras and with corresponding increases in net transfer of domestic resources to other exporting member countries.

To overcome these serious problems the Minister of Economy of Honduras suggested the following courses of action:

(i) A more rigorous determination of the national origin of free tradable merchandise.

(ii) Centralization into a common fund of fiscal collections derived from the application of a list of goods included in the Agreement on Fiscal Incentives, plus the amounts collected from the 30 percent tariff surcharge on raw materials from outside the region. The assets of the fund would be distributed among the five countries, using as criteria the final destination of the manufactured goods produced with these raw materials.

(iii) Establishment of a system of compensation credits to be granted by countries with a surplus in their regional trade to those in deficit, with long-term conditions, nominal rates of interest, and with credits up to the amounts equivalent to consumer's sacrifices (differentials in relative prices) to be earmarked for the promotion of regional exports of characteristically importing countries.

(iv) Adaptation of the Agreement on Uniform Fiscal Incentives to the present conditions of industrial development.

The resolutions actually adopted by the Economic Council at the seventeenth meeting were perhaps the most comprehensive attempts made to date to find an answer to the increasing problems of integration. It was within this spirit of joint effort that the solutions to the overall problems posed appeared to be imminent when, on 14 July 1969, armed conflict broke out between those two Central American countries most united by commercial, social, and historical ties. Actual combat hostilities were brief. However, since that time Central Americans have waited anxiously for the resumption of full relations between El Salvador and Honduras, and a return, with the required modifications, to a new legal and institutional order in the region's economic integration, so unexpectedly and violently disrupted by war.

Developments subsequent to the war were dominated by several short-lived efforts on the part of the governments to save the remnants of the commitments, especially in the brief but intense phases in the second half of 1970 that saw the proposed adoption of a Modus Operandi, and from the middle of 1971 to August 1973, when the Normalizing Commission of the Central American Common Market was established.

The Modus Operandi was proposed by Honduras after the outbreak of open conflict with El Salvador in order to establish a transitory system of commercial relations with the other three countries and to solve, by several measures, the aggravated situation of imbalances faced by that country relative to the other member countries.

Unfortunately the Modus Operandi did not succeed, and on 31 December 1970 Honduras adopted Decree No. 97 which imposed the same external tariff to all imports from Central America that applied to the rest of the world.[19] The decree also expressed the intentions of Honduras to enter into bilateral trade agreements with the other Central American countries and to promote economic development by intensive use of monetary and credit policies and the establishment of selective import controls.

As a consequence of this decree, Honduras was practically isolated from the other Central American countries until the first bilateral trade agreement was signed with Nicaragua (September 1971), the second one with Guatemala (February 1973), and the last one with Costa Rica (May 1973). These agreements were initially opposed by leading sectors of the other parties but were finally accepted as a means to restore--though partially--their trade relations with Honduras. The agreements followed the pattern of the bilateral treaties established in Central America early in the 1950s, but with clear expressions concerning (i) the fact that they were put into effect because of the extremely abnormal conditions existing within the Common Market, recognizing therefore their transitory nature, and (ii) the need to resume regular trade relations as soon as a new scheme of integration could be agreed upon and implemented.

The bilateral treaties were limited to a list of freely traded goods and to another list of goods that were subject to the payment of preferential import taxes levied by the Honduran authorities. Notwithstanding the plans of Honduras to join this transitory regime, that country began again to incur new trade deficits with the other partner countries.

The "Normalizing Commission" referred to above proved unsatisfactory and this led to the initiative taken by SIECA to submit an overall plan for restructuring the Integration Program. This plan was submitted to the governments in October 1972.

F. Development and Integration

1. The Institutional Organization

Economic disparities among nations involved in an integration process have diverse origins and differing degrees of intensity. The most obvious source of disparity is in the levels of economic development of the nations at the time that the integration movement begins. Such differences cannot be alleviated simply by the creation of a Common Market without decisive complementary action. Indeed, it had been argued that if free market forces are allowed to prevail, the initial disparities tend to intensify rather than to correct themselves.

At various times during the economic integration process of Central America the representatives of those nations considered to be relatively less developed stated that they deemed preferential treatment necessary for their respective countries. This would permit them to recover the fiscal and other losses occasioned by their relations with other member countries. Preferential treatment would also allow them greater flexibility in adopting internal policy measures in fiscal incentives and tariffs, where the integration agreement leads to uniformity of national legislation that tends to restrict the action of the adversely affected states.

Despite such proposals for action within the Central American integration movement, a considerable gap has existed between them and the means available for their implementation. Moreover, because of the lack of effective development plans at national levels and because of the impossibility of integrating such plans into a single regional model, proposals for the formulation of an integrated development plan still remain in the realm of good intentions. In addition, despite the fact that the principle of equitable distribution of the benefits (and costs) of integration has persisted throughout the history of the Integration Program, it has been impossible until now to make an adequate study of the effects of integration upon the regional economy, and even less upon the individual economies of the five nations.[20]

The elaboration of a regional development plan that takes into consideration the principle of equitable distribution among the member nations will require a substantial improvement in national programming systems, and this in turn will entail political decision by the governments involved. Regional planning will require a careful separation between those measures of strictly local nature and those that can or should be applied at the regional level. In fact, the regional plan itself could be the sum of these latter types of measures, preferentially based in those areas or sectors of the national economies that have a direct relationship with the integration program, and in accordance with the level of development of these areas or sectors at a given time.

The regional organizations responsible for the conceptual framework of the regional plan should possess extensive analytical instruments for designing proposals and influencing national plans so that they are compatible at the regional level. Measures for insuring balanced development in particular will be the responsibility of the regional organizations, as will the assessment of the degree of balance achieved. Detailed and current regional information based on the situations in all of the member nations are necessary, and the benefits and costs of the regional program should be evaluated periodically for the region as a whole and for each individual nation.

To support these activities, the parties need to have generally accepted methods to measure (i) differences in the relative development of the member nations, and (ii) the social benefits and costs of the integration program for each member nation and for the entire region. In fact, the possible practical application of the principle of balanced development depends essentially upon the standards adopted for these measurements.

2.   The Measurement of Development

The need to "measure" the degree of relative development of the member nations has become evident during the course of the economic integration process. In other groups of nations where the relative levels of development are clearly dissimilar, the nations considered by consensus to be of lesser relative development are clearly identified in the group. That approach establishes immediately the direction in which the measures for redistributing the benefits of integration should be applied, either through preferential treatment in commercial relations, the location of productive activities, the transfer of financial resources, or a combination of these.

However, in the case of Central America, the differences in the relative development of the five countries are not marked. In fact there are more indications of similarity than of discrepancies, not only because of their small size in terms of population and territory but also because all are in the category of countries with an incipient level of industrialization and all are dependent on exporting a few agricultural products. In other words, all of them fall into an intermediate stage between the poorest nations of the Third World and the majority of the nations considered to be developed or industrialized.

Therefore it is difficult to catalog the five nations of the area in the order of their relative degree of development. No indicator exists that is representative enough of a degree of development that it can be used as a unit of measurement in such a comparative listing of these nations.

Although a single indicator, for example, the GDP per capita frequently employed to catalog nations, is useful when large differences exist, it loses its value as these differences are reduced. Nevertheless, the GDP per capita remains the most important indicator among a variety of alternatives, particularly if the usual deficiencies in the calculation of the national product can be avoided. Even so, the GDP per capita does not distinguish the degree of concentration or relative distribution of assets and income among the population strata, nor among the geographical zones of the nations under study.

In underdeveloped countries, wealth and income are concentrated in a very small percentage of the population. Also, in these nations, areas of high development--particularly in the capital cities--coexist with extremely backward areas where the population barely supports itself at subsistence levels. This dualistic phenomenon is repeated in all levels of activity, including those considered modern sectors, such as the transformation industries which include not only manufacturing plants with high capital and technology levels but also shops operated by artisans with primitive production methods.

Therefore, the more accentuated the dualistic nature of the economy, the less representative the GDP per capita as a measure of the degree of development of the nation. Since this indicator is an average of the combined income flows, its validity loses significance as the variances increase. Therefore, in a comparison of relative developmental levels of nations through use of the GDP per capita, account should be taken of the fact that each country is being measured through the use of an abstract figure that only coincides with the average level for the whole range of income groups.

Considering the dualistic nature of the economies, the ideal comparisons should refer to similar regions located in the five nations. For example, it would be desirable to initiate the comparisons between the capital cities of the five countries and gradually incorporate other secondary cities into the analysis until the entire urban sector had been covered, following this with comparisons in the agricultural sector, and continuing progressively in this manner, maintaining comparisons between sectors as homogeneous as possible until a total comparison has been achieved of the more significant elements of the respective productive structures. Obviously, the comparison should also include social fields as far as possible. Nevertheless, the limitations of any comparative method should be recognized, as well as the fact there are nonmeasurable elements of human behavior.

Among the nonmeasurable elements, human attitudes regarding change and managerial capacity are perhaps the most important in relation to

stimulation of economic growth. The only way to overcome the human element obstacle is to assume that the imponderables become gradually embodied in the analysis through their interaction with the specific indicators that have been selected.

A multivariable comparison is inhibited by the lack of comparable
statistical information for the Central American nations, and even more
so if the nations are segregated by sector to evaluate behavioral differences within those sectors from country to country, taking into account
the period of time required to estimate the changes taking place in each
one, both in absolute and relative terms. Nevertheless, even an approximate comparison of this kind is useful since it serves to identify bottlenecks that prevent development and to demonstrate the effects of an integration program upon the growth of the group as a whole and on the
individual member nations.

Throughout the integration process in Central America, it has been
generally accepted that some of the member nations, particularly Honduras,
show a lesser degree of development than the other three members. This
classification is based not upon data corresponding to any one aspect of
the respective economies but rather upon the combined factors involved
in the economic and social development of the countries. A more formal
evaluation is necessarily very complex. On the other hand, although a
single indicator such as GDP per capita is insufficient, it can serve as
a starting point to guide us in the right direction.

In figure 1a, the GDP per capita of the five Central American countries and Panama is represented for the years 1960, 1965, and 1972 (at
constant 1962 prices). This graph is highly significant as an indication
of the relative positions of the countries concerned. The accelerated
growth of Panama is particularly remarkable and separates this nation
from the other five area countries throughout the period. Between 1960
and 1965, the highest rate of growth was Nicaragua's and had it been
maintained, that country would have reached the level of Costa Rica.
Nevertheless, Nicaragua's growth rate decreased between 1965 and 1972,
thereby producing an even greater gap than that between the two nations
in 1960. The GDP per capita of Guatemala was greater than that of Nicaragua in 1960. Guatemala's GDP per capita was surpassed by that of
Nicaragua in 1965, but by 1972 Guatemala was once again at a higher
income level. Of the five Central American nations, El Salvador and
Honduras show the least dynamic growth rates. These two countries were
adversely affected in the last period by the 1969 conflict that inhibited
their development prospects. This conflict undoubtedly affected the rest
of the countries too, but to a lesser degree, and their relative positions
would probably have been different if the rupture of the Common Market
had not occurred. In any case, it is interesting to note that the gap
between El Salvador and Honduras, in terms of GDP per capita, was maintained without any great change during the 1965-72 period.

Although the graph is useful in providing a preliminary appreciation of the relative positions of the six nations of the Central American Isthmus, the GDP indicator--besides having the limitations already
noted--fails to capture the effects of different internal prices used
to value the product. In effect, the same goods can be valued differently if price variations exist from country to country. For this reason,

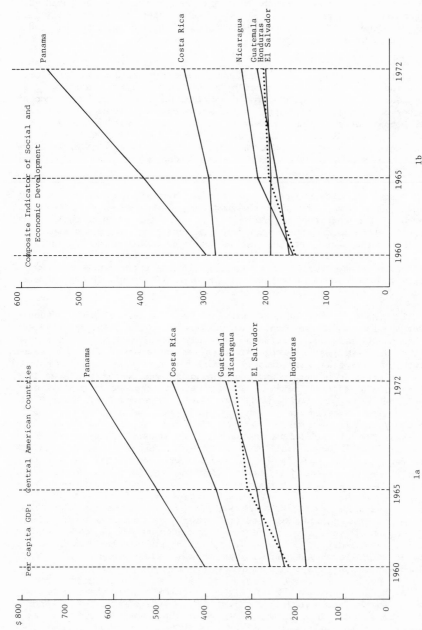

Figure 1. Comparative Relative Economic Development, Central America and Panama

the GDP per capita in order to be effectively comparable should be normalized through use of real price indexes.

In table 1 the figures corresponding to the GDP per capita in 1973
are presented in two columns; in the first the figures are as they appear
in official publications, while the second shows the same figures adjusted
in accordance with the preliminary results of the comparative price study
conducted under the SIECA/Brookings Project.

Table 1. Comparison of 1973 GDP per Capita, According to Official
National Figures and in Terms of Real Value

GDP Ranking	Country	National Figure	GDP Ranking	Country	Real Value
1	Costa Rica	700	1	Costa Rica	720
2	Nicaragua	522	2	Guatemala	451
3	Guatemala	451	3	Nicaragua	442
4	El Salvador	349	4	El Salvador	391
5	Honduras	314	5	Honduras	304

SOURCE: Table 16, chapter 8.

As shown in the table, in the second column the relative positions
of Guatemala and Nicaragua are reversed. This result is due to a reduction of approximately 20 percent in the GDP per capita of Nicaragua because of the difference in price levels between the two countries, as
computed in November 1973. Guatemala maintains the same GDP per capita
in both columns since it is the country used as a base for comparisons.
The gap between the two extremes (Costa Rica and Honduras) is even greater
in the second column, while the differences between the other three nations have diminished.

It is worth noting that in neither column does Nicaragua rank at
the lowest position of economic development in the region, as has been
assumed historically. On the other hand, the real income estimates confirm Honduras as the least advanced country of the region during the
entire period.

Various attempts have been made in the past to correct the deficiencies associated with the simple use of the GDP per capita for purposes of such comparisons. In the study conducted by the United Nations
Conference on Trade and Development (UNCTAD) in 1969,[21] six indicators
of social and economic development were combined and, through factorial
analysis, a "combined index" was developed which was used to catalog
90 developing nations.[22]

According to this system, the six nations of the Central American
Isthmus were ranked in the following descending order of relative de-
velopment: Panama, Costa Rica, El Salvador, Nicaragua, Guatemala, and
Honduras.

The system chosen by UNCTAD permits the determination, at any given time, of the relative positions of the nations as a function of a limited number of factors that reflect the principal development characteristics. No elements corresponding to growth rates or tendencies are included.

The UNCTAD experience prompted SIECA to engage in an effort in the same direction, but differing by (i) increasing the number of variables to cover a wider range of regional, social, and economic objectives; and (ii) selecting three historical points corresponding to the years 1960, 1965, and 1972.[23]

As a result of the comparative analysis undertaken based on the twelve indicators selected and the method of "principal factors,"[24] the level of range corresponding to each country during the years 1960, 1965, and 1972 were determined. The results are shown in figure 1b.

A comparison of figures 1a and 1b show that the use of the combined index does not significantly change the relative positions of Panama, Costa Rica, and Nicaragua, but it produces a striking regrouping of Guatemala, El Salvador, and Honduras. This is probably due to a greater degree of dualism in the latter countries. The influence of dualism is better understood when considering that the municipal area that includes Guatemala City had a population in 1972 of close to 700,000 inhabitants (the largest in Central America), with a total estimated income of approximately $802.5 million. These figures indicate a per capita income of $1,140, while in the rest of the republic—including the other urban centers—income reached a level of only $170 per capita. At the other extreme, Costa Rica presents a more homogeneous level of development throughout its territory, which tends to explain its relative position of greater development which is more pronounced when the combined index is used. The other nations tend to form a group with fewer obvious differences relative to their development.

Regardless of the differences between methods of relative comparison and their interpretation, it can be seen that all of the analyses undertaken display an order for the Central American nations characterized by extremes occupied by Costa Rica at the top and Honduras generally at the bottom.

It is worth noting that the use of a combined index does not necessarily clarify the relative position of the five Central American countries. In this respect, the combined index only shows that real differences among the countries are not significant, except for the case of Costa Rica. In spite of the need for further attempts in this direction, particularly by including estimates of income distribution, the clearest distinction results from the use of the GDP per capita, particularly once the national accounts are properly revised and this indicator is normalized by the existing levels of prices in the five countries.

3.   Distribution of the Benefits of Integration

One of the most important objectives in the Central American integration process is to achieve balanced development. Frequently this concept has been confused with the concept of an equitable distribution of benefits of integration. Therefore it is important to establish the fact that these two concepts are different. Balanced development generally refers to the whole of the national economies and to the measures that should be adopted to eliminate, or mitigate in time, the differences in the levels of development between member countries. Integration benefits, on the other hand, refer to the contribution of economic integration to the economic development of the group. The distribution among countries of the incremental income resulting from the integration process should involve two principles: (i) the assurance of voluntary participation by all members; and (ii) insofar as is compatible with the first principle, the use of the integration benefits to reduce imbalance in developmental levels.

The Secretary General of SIECA stated in this respect that "the equitable distribution of the benefits and costs is perhaps the element of greatest conceptual weight in any integration process, since, in the last instance, it tends to determine the voluntary and permanent participation of the member States, thereby guaranteeing the continuity of the integration process."[25]

Despite the fundamental differences between the two concepts, they tend to interlock as integration develops and becomes increasingly important in the development of the partners, and as it affects those productive sectors that are considered the most dynamic and promising for increasing the rate of development. This latter situation presents itself especially in the case of manufacturing industry, the evolution of which has been more closely tied to integration than has that of the agricultural sector. Thus, the principles of balanced development and equitable distribution of the benefits of integration both enter into programs for the better geographical distribution of industries among the member nations. The establishment of industries in the countries of lesser relative development can act (i) as a way to promote a more accelerated development of the economies, lessening the gap with respect to the relatively more industrialized nations of the group; and (ii) as a way to achieve a better distribution of the integration benefits. It is worth noting that the economic integration movement has been strongly motivated by the expectations of the member nations that related structural changes in production can result in a larger manufacturing sector input to the GNP.

The development of intrazonal commerce has tended to confirm that a relationship exists between the level of industrialization and the capacity of the nations to export to the Common Market. In 1973, almost 90 percent of the interzonal commerce was in manufactured goods. Also, those countries with a greater industrial base have maintained a surplus in their trade balances with the other member countries. Since the integration benefits for a given country are closely related to the volume of its intrazonal commerce, the interest of these nations in increasing their industrial production can be readily understood.

Now, if economic integration represents benefits to the group through a greater individual economic growth, it is necessary to determine whether the distribution of these benefits tends to correct observed disparities in development, to maintain them unaltered, or to increase them. That is, it is necessary to evaluate the net effects of integration upon the relative level of development of the nations, and to incorporate this assessment into planning for balanced development.

The standard meaning that balanced development has in the context of Central American integration, and achievement of that balance, therefore, are influenced by three elements: (i) the degree of relative development of the nations; (ii) the importance of the net integration benefits to their economic growth; and (iii) the means available to correct or mitigate observed disparities in the development of the nations when the benefits of the integration program are insufficient to make such adjustments.

It is obvious that if a situation arises in which a nation receives negative or no benefits from the integration program, the amount of resources redistributed by the group as a whole for the productive development of that nation should be, at least, equivalent to that required to cover that portion of the group's total net benefits considered to be the minimum necessary for continued participation of that nation. In such a case, however, the "usefulness" of that nation to the other partners should be considered, as well as whether the sacrifice of resources that the community proposes to designate for assistance to the nation of relatively less development approximates the total benefit that the other partners receive from the integration program. Whenever the integration process results in scant benefits for the group of nations, the efforts made to maintain the community are reduced as are the options for correcting growth inequalities. It should also be remembered that only a portion of the total benefits can be considered as available for distribution purposes. Assuming that a minimum level of benefits is required for each nation to remain in the program, these minimum amounts should be subtracted from the total of the benefits to determine the amount available for redistribution. It is necessary, therefore, to define those minimum benefits to which each nation aspires. It is also necessary to estimate the distribution of the benefits among nations. Ideally the benefits to be considered should include those that could have been achieved if the limitations imposed by the imperfections in actual agreements were surpassed through transition to more complete integration.

As discussed in chapter 3, probably the most difficult measurement problems involve the dynamic benefits of integration. And within these, measurement may be possible only for that component that has already been realized, leaving open the question of the size of dynamic benefits expected to accrue in the future.

Chapter 3 presents the measurement of benefits and costs of Central American economic integration developed in the SIECA/Brookings research program. These new measurements, and the methodology on which they are based, should provide a new analytical base for policy measures addressing the question of distributional equity within the Central American Common Market.

G.   Conclusions

This chapter has attempted to explain Central American economic integration in terms of its proximate objectives, ultimate goals, depth of commitment, and as a function of the historical evolution of the concept of balanced development of the member nations. The commitment of the members includes two important components: (i) the formal legal pact; and (ii) the tacit pact, consisting of the long-range purposes of the association. The tacit pact embraces the expectations of the parties concerning the general development of the program; these expectations are frequently only mentioned in the agreement but not spelled out in binding terms.

The normative concept of balanced development among the member states requires the corresponding concept of less relative development, which is a simple expression of the comparative levels of development among the nations on the basis of conventional indicators. In the case of Central America, the use of indicators is made difficult by the degree of similarity that characterizes the five nations, both in their productive structures and in their general level of development.

Until now the principle of balanced development has manifested itself in a series of proposals and resolutions of the integration institutions, and in accessory instruments to the principal commitment, without having been included explicitly in the General Treaty of 1960. An explanation of this omission lies in the fact that the principle has been evolving gradually during the course of the integration process. An adequate and satisfactory expression of the principle has not yet been developed so that it could be included in a formal commitment by the members; however the proposed new general treaty, presently under consideration by the governments involved, deals with it for the first time.

Although the principle of balanced development has its roots in the general theory of economic development, its application to the field of economic integration should be considered in a more restricted sense than would be required at the national level. That is, while national economic policy must contemplate all factors involved in the development of the nation, the concept of balanced economic development among the nations of the group includes those factors (or sectors) that are more closely related to the integration process. Otherwise, the obligation of the member nations would remain ill defined and, in most cases, would exceed the available means of application of the principle at the regional level.

The means available to adjust the relative development of the member nations are determined by the progress of the integration movement and are influenced simultaneously by the final objectives of the formal and the tacit commitment of the parties. In the stage of simple formation of a free trade zone, the means available are insignificant. As the process advances toward economic union, these means are increased in depth and in diversity.

Unfortunately, the Central American integration process in the last eight years entered into a critical stage before having perfected the stage of the Common Market envisioned in the General Treaty. For this reason the means necessary for adjustment of the relative development positions of the member nations have been lacking. Nevertheless, it is to be hoped that once the governments agree upon a new integration scheme the dynamic thrust of the process will be regained. When this occurs, the community organizations should concentrate upon the elaboration of an integral plan that permits not only the coordination of national poli- cies as a function of the common objectives but also the adoption of appropriate means of application of the principle of balanced development.

For purposes of achieving balanced development it is necessary to prepare national development plans that are compatible with a regional plan.[26] Sufficient information about national plans has not been avail- able. Overcoming that lack of information is a necessary condition for effective regional planning, since the regional plan is simply the coor- dinated expression of the national plans with the addition of regional measures.

In Central America it has been generally agreed that the lesser rel- ative development of a given member nation adversely affects the economic development of the group. Nevertheless, analytical mechanisms have been lacking to define the appropriate sizes and types of measures required to mitigate the relative backwardness of one country with respect to the others. In this respect it is necessary to distinguish between concerted action to promote the development of an individual member nation and the more restricted measures directed toward compensation for the adverse effects of the integration process upon the economy of the nation in question.

Among the compensatory measures for adverse integration effects, the following can be considered: transfer of fiscal income contemplated in the customs union schemes; establishment of tariffs for exports from the member nations to the less-developed country; preferential treatment measures that this country can use for the inducement of new investments in its territory; and all other measures that have as an objective the redistribution of integration benefits.

Because available means for achieving balanced development are scarce, community action within the plan should be highly selective. That is, all nations cannot be dealt with in accordance with the range of greater or lesser development that they present at any given time, since this approach would result in a dispersion of efforts. Instead, massive action should be taken to correct the position of the lowest nation on the comparative scale as indicated by (i) a lower level of development compared with that of the other member nations, and (ii) lowest relative participation in the net benefits of the integration. Although these two criteria would not necessarily coincide, in the Cen- tral American case they do (as discussed in chapter 3), making it unambiguous which member country is the appropriate one to receive redistributive benefits. Regional plans should, of course, take into consideration the particular problems and obstacles that impede the development of each and every nation of the area. However, a special and preferential plan should exist for the country of least relative development.

Finally, the actions to correct the differences in the levels of relative development of the member nations, and especially of the coun- try that shows obvious backwardness with respect to the others, are not free concessions when they are interpreted in the sense of maximizing integration benefits through "regionalizing" the most difficult problems that confront the members of the group.

GLOSSARY OF TERMS

A. Principal Agreements

1. Central American Integration Program (the Program). A general term to express the concerted efforts for economic integration among the five countries: Guatemala, El Salvador, Honduras, Nicaragua, and Costa Rica. Efforts began in 1950 and evolved in 1960 as the Central American Common Market (CACM).

2. Bilateral Free Trade Treaties. Treaties for limited free traded goods that were signed between pairs of Central American countries from 1950 to 1956, maintaining a common pattern.

3. "Multilateral Free Trade Treaty." Signed in 1958 by all five countries, it established a limited free trade zone covering the territories of these countries and therefore superseding the existing bilateral treaties.

4. "Regime for Central American Integration Industries" (the Regime). Signed in 1958 simultaneously with the "Multilateral Free Trade Treaty," it dealt with spatial distribution of "basic industries" among the five countries.

5. "Agreement on Collection of Import Duties." This agreement, signed in 1959, equalized the external tariffs by adopting a common list of immediate application and a system of gradual harmonization of the remaining customs categories to be completed within a period of five years.

6. "Treaty of Economic Association" (the Tripartite). This treaty between Guatemala, El Salvador, and Honduras was signed in February 1960 establishing a broad free trade zone among these countries. It was superseded by the "General Treaty" of 1960.

7. "General Treaty on Economic Integration." Signed on 13 December 1960 by Guatemala, El Salvador, Honduras, and Nicaragua, it established the Central American Common Market (CACM) as it exists today. Costa Rica joined the treaty in August 1962.

8. "Constitutive Agreement on the Central American Bank for Economic Integration." Signed at the same time as the "General Treaty" on 13 December 1960, it established the bank as the main financial institution of the CACM scheme.

9. "Special System for the Promotion of Industrial Activities." Adopted on 29 January 1963, this system practically replaced the "Regime."

10. "The Central American Agreement on Uniform Fiscal Incentives for Industrial Development." Discussed since 1962, the agreement established uniform treatment for all industries to be established in the area. It divided industries into three categories (A, B, C), according to their importance to economic development.

11. "The Protocol of San José." Formally called the "Agreement for the Defense of the Balance of Payments." Signed in 1965, it allowed the countries to impose an extra charge equivalent to 30 percent of the existing common external import tariff. It also allowed the imposition of internal consumer taxes on a list of goods, departing in certain ways from the general provision contained in Article VI of the General Treaty. This protocol was supposed to be transitory.

B. Institutional Organizations

1. The Committee for Economic Cooperation of the Central American Isthmus (the Committee). Established in 1952, it was formed by the ministers of economy of the five Central American countries and Panama as a subregional organization of the U.N. Economic Commission for Latin America (ECLA). This committee was responsible for the development of the Integration Program, especially prior to the signing of the General Treaty in 1960. It still convenes on special occasions and has ECLA's Secretariat as its main supporting body.

2. The Central American Economic Council. Established in 1960 as the principal regional organization of the General Treaty, the council is made up by the five Central American ministers of economy.

3. The Central American Executive Council. Made up of representatives of the ministers of economy (Economic Council), it deals with current problems of the Common Market and refers matters to the attention of the council.

4. The Permanent Secretariat of the General Treaty of Central American Economic Integration (SIECA). Acts as Secretariat of the two councils mentioned above, as well as of other ministerial committees or technical subcommittees established within the actual Integration Program. It is represented by the General Secretary.

5. The "Joint Programing Mission." Established in 1962 in response to the need for introducing the practical conception of regional development in Central America, it was staffed by Central Americans and guided by a board of representatives of the following agencies: the Permanent Secretariat (SIECA), Central American Bank (CABEI), Economic Commission for Latin America (ECLA), Organization of American States (OAS), and the Inter-American Development Bank (IDB).

6. "The Central American Institute for Industrial and Technical Research" (ICAITI). The institute was created in 1956 as one of the first specialized regional institutions to promote industrial development.

7. "The Central American Superior School for Public Administration" (ESAPAC). The first regional institution, created in 1954 to train government officials in matters related to the administration of the Integration Program. Currently known as the "Central American Institute of Public Administration" (ICAP).

Chapter 2

NOTES

1. The unabridged version of this study was formerly distributed by SIECA in E. Delgado, "Significado y Alcance de los Conceptos de Desarrollo Equilibrado y de Paises de Menor Desarrollo Relativo," Guatemala, SIECA/CAN-VII/D. T. 1., 11 November 1974.

2. Ernest D. Hass, "Reflections on the Joy and Anguish of Pretheorizing," in Regional Integration Theory and Research, eds. L. N. Lindberg and S. A. Scheingold (Cambridge, Mass.: Harvard University Press, 1971).

3. Jacob Viner, "The Customs Union Issue" (New York: Carnegie Endowment for International Peace, 1950).

4. See Raul Prebisch, "Informe Preliminar del Director Principal de la Secretaria Ejecutiva de la Comisión Económica para América Latina, sobre Integración y Reciprocidad Económica en el Istmo Centroamericano" (E/CN/AC.17/3), 1 August 1952.

5. The first bilateral treaty that had features of economic integration was signed by El Salvador and Nicaragua on 9 March 1951, four months before the ECLA meeting in Mexico where Resolution 9, which prompted the Integration Program, was adopted.

6. "Evaluation of the Central American Economic Integration Program and Some New Industrial Possibilities" (E/CN.12/CCE/33).

7. Roads, electric energy, international traffic for highways, maritime transport, and so on.

8. See "Commercial Policy and Free Trade in Central America" (E/CN. 12/CCE/12).

9. See "Informe de la Comisión Ad-Hoc para el Proyecto de Tratado Multilateral de Libre Comercio Integración Económica," Mexico D.F. (E/CN. 12/CCE/ACI/2), 19-24 March 1956.

10. It also directed that protection authorized for integration industries be automatically decreased by an annual 10 percent reduction in the tariff.

11. The other plant protected by the Regime in Guatemala was already in the process of being installed when the agreement was signed.

12. The Regional Highway Program was designed jointly by ECLA, the Central American Bank and SIECA, with the help of the Joint Mission for Central American Planning.

13. "Exposición sobre la Participación de Honduras en el Proceso de Integración Económica Centroamericana" (Document prepared by the Honduran delegation) (CCE/LX/D.T.2), 21 January 1966.

14. "Exposición de Honduras referente al Convenio Centroamericano de Incentivos Fiscales al Desarrollo Industrial," Tegucigalpa, D.C., 11 January 1966, incorporated as Appendix 2 of Act No. 17 of the Central American Economic Council.

15. The preferential treatment granted to Honduras allowed this country to extend the terms of exemptions for two additional years.

16. It is important to mention that the classification favored capital industries, whereas consumer industries were predominant in Honduras.

17. "Efectos del Mercado Común Centroamericano sobre la Economia Nicaraguense," Managua, D.N., 16 September 1966, incorporated as Annex 2 to the Act No. 19 of the Central American Economic Council.

18. Decree 3 MEIC was issued by the Nicaraguan government on 26 February 1969. It established a "compensatory tax for consumption" which was applied (minus the list of exceptions) to products from the rest of Central America, equivalent to the ad valorem component of the tariff in effect in Nicaragua on 1 July 1955.

19. The tariff was unilaterally reduced for food products, raw materials, and capital goods.

20. Brewster in 1972 and Nugent in 1973 independently prepared models for the overall evaluation of the effects of integration; however, the usefulness of the models to correct imbalances is very limited because of their high level of aggregation. SIECA, in 1972, prepared an exploratory model to measure the impact of integration. The methodology consisted of estimation of a series of functions relative to the different sectors of the national economies (investment, consumption, and so on) for the periods 1950-61 and 1962-68. Based on these series, the effect of integration on Central American economies and upon that of the combined group was inferred in terms of percent relative to the observed growth of the GNP, for the periods under consideration and in accordance with various behavior hypotheses. See: Study No. 1 "El Desarrollo Integrado Centroamericano en la Presente Década," SIECA, October 1972.

21. "Special Measures in Favor of the Least Developed Among the Developing Countries. Identification of the Least Developed among the Developing Countries" (UNCTAD TD/13/269), 11 July 1969.

22. The indicators used were: (i) GDP per capita at factor cost; (ii) percentage of the GDP generated by the manufacturing industry; (iii) consumption of energy per capita; (iv) relation between the sum of total enrollment in primary and secondary schools and the amount of population between five and nineteen years of age; (v) number of doctors per 100,000 inhabitants; and (vi) percentage of manufactured goods in total exports.

23. The objectives and indicators were: (i) income level--GDP/capita, and energy consumption/capita; (ii) national integration--paved highways/population and telephones/population; (iii) productivity--agricultural GDP/agricultural employment and skilled labor/employed population; (iv) diversification--industrial GDP/total GDP and percent

manufactured goods/total exports; (v) institutional level--direct taxes/
total taxes and numeraire in public hands/population; (vi) social devel-
opment--sum of enrollment in primary and secondary schools/population of
seven to nineteen years, and total of doctors, nurses, and aides/
population.

24. The calculation of the principal factors was accomplished using
a computational program for the calculation of the correlation matrices,
the characteristic roots and vectors, the factor matrices and, when necessary, the orthogonal rotation "Varimax."

25. Inaugural speech of Dr. Roberto Mayorga-Cortes, Secretary General of the Secretaria Permanente del Tratado General de Integración
Económica Centroamericana (SIECA), in the Seminar on Distribution of the
Costs and Benefits of Economic Integration among Developing Nations," a
joint meeting of UNCTAD and SIECA in Guatemala in December 1973. See
seminar report (TAD/EI/SEM.2/5), 18 April 1974.

26. This means a continuous system of formulation and feedback of
national and regional plans. The national plans are coordinated at regional level by adding new elements of a regional nature in order to develop a common plan. This, in turn, influences the formulation of the
national plans.

Benefits and Costs of Economic Integration in Central America

William R. Cline

During the decade ending in 1968 the five Central American countries freed intraregional trade and harmonized their protection to common external tariffs for most products. Regional trade catapulted from $33 million in 1960 to $258 million in 1968, or to one-fourth of the area's total trade. Thereafter the integration movement suffered setbacks associated primarily with political difficulties between El Salvador and Honduras. This chapter examines the costs and benefits of the integration effort as of 1968 and 1972. The effects are quantified not only for the region as a whole but also for each country, permitting evaluation of the politically sensitive issue of distribution of the Common Market's benefits among its members.

The policy issues addressed in this study include the following:

(i) How large have the net benefits from integration been for Central America as a whole? In view of the political difficulties of achieving cooperation in a Common Market, with its implications of the subordination of national autonomy to at least a limited degree, it is important to determine the magnitude of net welfare gains in order to illuminate the economic benefits purchased with the political effort required.

(ii) What has been the distribution among the five Central American countries of the net gains from integration? The sensitivity of this issue has been explored in the previous chapter, which chronicles the increasingly divisive forces within the CACM caused by the perception by some members that their benefits were inequitably small relative to those of the others.

(iii) Did the withdrawal of Honduras from the CACM in 1969 injure or benefit Honduras, and to what extent did it injure or benefit the remaining four members?

(iv) What would be the nature and magnitude of redistributive mechanisms which would have to be introduced into the CACM in order to

---

NOTE: I am indebted to Bela Balassa and Mordechai Kreinin for comments and to Robert Williams and Molly Wainer for massive and imaginative research assistance as well as suggestions on methodology.

have a distribution of integration's benefits that would be both more equitable and capable of providing sufficient incentives to insure the continued participation of each member, and the renewed participation of Honduras?

A. Background

Before turning to the methodology and results of this chapter's central analysis, it is important to consider certain general economic indicators bearing on the magnitude and distribution of the benefits of integration. One indicator is simply the behavior of growth rates during the periods before and after economic integration. The perceptions of policymakers and the public are influenced by the overall growth record, even without refined analysis of the specific economic effects of integration.

Table 1 presents data on average growth rates of real gross domestic product (GDP) in three periods: 1950-60, before the Common Market was formed; 1961-68, the period of development to full operation of the Common Market; and 1969-73, the period after disruption of the CACM by the war between El Salvador and Honduras and by the withdrawal of Honduras from the free trade arrangement of the Market. It is evident from the table that growth rates in all five countries substantially increased during the period of integration in comparison with those in the period before integration. This fact no doubt is responsible for the generalized perception that the formation of the Common Market did contribute to accelerated growth, even in the absence of analysis of the impact of integration as opposed to that of other factors on the overall growth results.

One of the factors which probably contributed to the increased growth rates during the 1961-68 period was the more favorable evolution of prices for traditional raw materials exports than during the earlier period. During the preintegration years, prices for coffee, cotton, bananas, and sugar were retreating substantially from their peaks in the years of the Korean War.[1] Because of this and additional influences other than integration, the simple comparison of growth rates between the preintegration and integration periods tells little about the net growth effect of the Common Market. Nevertheless, the comparison may be said at least to be consistent with the hypothesis that integration had an important positive effect on on the region's economic growth.

The growth rates reported for the period 1969-73 are equal on average to those of the period 1961-68, although the order among the five countries changes between the two periods. It is noteworthy that for both El Salvador and Honduras the growth rate declines by about one percentage point, probably reflecting the impact of the war between the two countries in 1969 and subsequent disruptions in their trade.

A second type of informal analysis which has been popular in the assessment of the distribution of economic gains from the CACM is examination of the trade balances of the members. Indeed, in discussions on the Modus Operandi in 1970, which attempted to resolve the conditions under which Honduras could be reintegrated into the Common Market, the Honduran Minister of Economy and Finance proposed that each country's contributions to a

Table 1. Annual Growth Rates of Real GDP, Central America

(percent)

Country	Growth Rates[a]		
	(A) 1950-51 to 1959-60	(B) 1961-62 to 1967-68	(C) 1969-70 to 1972-73
Guatemala	4.4	6.6	9.7
El Salvador	4.9	7.8	6.7
Honduras	4.1	7.0	5.9
Nicaragua	6.1	9.8	6.4
Costa Rica	7.3	8.7	7.2
Central America	5.2	7.7	7.8

[a]Calculated by comparing a two-year average of the base period with a two-year average of the terminal period.

SOURCES: Column (A): Calculated from United Nations, Evaluación de la Interfración Económica en Centroamérica (E/CN.12/75, Rev. 1; E/CN.12/762).

Columns (B), (C): Calculated from SIECA, VI Compendio Estadístico Centroamericano, 1975 (Guatemala City: SIECA, 1975).

proposed Fund for Industrial and Agricultural Development be proportional to the country's exports to the region in the previous year.[2]

The prevalent notion is that countries with more favorable trade balances vis-à-vis the other countries of the region are benefiting the most from integration. It will be shown in the model developed below that the benefits do depend importantly on the net impact of integration on the country's trade balance. However, this net impact certainly cannot be determined by mere consideration of actual trade balances with CACM partners; a comprehensive model of changes in trade propensities attributable to integration must be used for this purpose.

Data on trade balances of the five Central American countries are presented in table 2. The data show that Guatemala and El Salvador have enjoyed persistent trade balance surpluses with the CACM, while Honduras, Nicaragua, and Costa Rica have had consistent deficits. These patterns have undoubtedly contributed to a generalized impression among analysts of the CACM that the first two countries have benefited relatively more from the Common Market while the other three have benefited relatively less. While this conclusion may not be drawn from the data, one important fact is evident even in the simple data on trade balances--of the three countries consistently in deficit to the region, only Honduras appears to have the main part of its overall trade deficit associated with a regional deficit. In fact in the period 1966-68, the total trade deficit for Honduras was smaller than its regional deficit--its favorable trade balance with the rest of the world was more than offset by an unfavorable

Table 2. Merchandise Trade Balances, Central America, 1961-72
(annual average, thousand U.S. dollars)

Country	Trade Balances[a]			
	1961-65	1966-68	1969-70	1971-73
Guatemala				
CACM	n.a.	20,157	34,832[b]	31,987[b]
Total	-28,938	-17,592	5,549	4,863
El Salvador				
CACM	n.a.	16,992	13,891[b]	18,486[b]
Total	- 177	-16,527	3,797	-10,767
Honduras				
CACM	n.a.	-16,738	29,338	-16,589
Total	- 3,725	- 8,641	-34,670	-13,553
Nicaragua				
CACM	n.a.	-20,383	- 7,245[b]	-13,457[b]
Total	- 8,252	-38,096	-19,183	-14,188
Costa Rica				
CACM	n.a.	- 5,977	-18,020[b]	-23,645[b]
Total	-32,662	-44,328	-70,478	-110,974

[a]Exports f.o.b. less imports c.i.f.
[b]Includes Honduras.

SOURCE: Calculated from SIECA, VI Compendio Estadístico Centroamericano, 1975 (Guatemala City: SIECA, 1975).

balance with the region. By contrast, Nicaragua and especially Costa Rica appear to have had large overall trade deficits with the rest of the world as well, so that their deficits with the region were more the result of overall deficit positions in their foreign trade than the effect of any structural disadvantage vis-a-vis the CACM. A final inference which may be drawn from the table is that the Honduran deficit with the region was not solely due to the country's participation in the free trade area. This fact may be seen in the figures for 1969-73, which indicate a continuation of Honduras' regional deficit despite withdrawal from the free trade arrangements.

Although these informal analyses of growth rates and trade balances provide useful background information, an accurate evaluation of the benefits and costs of integration requires a comprehensive model of the type developed below.

B. The Welfare Effects of Integration: Overview

The traditional welfare effects of integration are "trade creation" and "trade diversion." By elimination of tariffs on imports from partners, a member will increase total imports. This "trade creation" will have a welfare benefit related to the degree of protection formerly in place. At the same time, the country may switch purchases away from the world market toward the Common Market partner in view of the elimination of tariffs on the partner's goods. This substitution, "trade diversion," causes a welfare cost to the country as it replaces low-cost world market supply with higher priced partner supply. The cost depends on the difference between the partner's price and the world price.

In addition to these two traditional static welfare effects, this chapter quantifies three others:

(i) labor opportunity cost effect;

(ii) economies of scale effect;

(iii) foreign exchange scarcity effect.

Integration causes the country to export more (or new) goods to its partners. The resulting increase in output will bring a windfall gain insofar as (i) labor costs contained in the final price of this output exceed labor's "social" or "scarcity" cost, and (ii) the increment in output may be achieved with less than proportional increase in inputs due to the exploitation of economies of scale. Finally, if the country increases its exports to partners at no expense to its exports to the rest of the world, and at the same time increases by a smaller amount (or even holds constant) its total ceteris paribus imports (although replacing world supply with partner supply), the country will enjoy a relaxation of its foreign exchange constraint. While ex-post total imports will rise to equal the new higher availability of foreign exchange, in the process the additional scarce imported inputs necessary to raise GNP will have been provided; the resulting increase in GNP constitutes the "foreign exchange scarcity" welfare gain.

These five effects are "static" in that they all represent once-for-all outward shifts in the production possibility frontier attainable to the country, given its resources. In addition there are dynamic effects, the most important of which are: (i) structural transformation of the economy (e.g., a shift from traditional exports to industrial production); (ii) the "investment effect"--the inflow of foreign investment, and the stimulus of domestic investment, which would not have occurred in the absence of the market stimulus provided by formation of the Common Market; and (iii) competition: the efficiency-prodding influence of freeing imports for at least the goods of partners.

C. Methodology

In this section the methodology for measuring the static welfare gains from integration is presented, in the following sequence:

(i) The measurement proposed for the traditional concepts of trade creation and diversion and their welfare effects is examined first; followed by

(ii) Treatment of cases where measured trade creation or diversion is negative--and computation of "trade suppression" and "external trade augmentation" and their corresponding welfare effects, for some of these cases;

(iii) Calculations for increased trade balance and output attributable to integration are then discussed; on the basis of which

(iv) The computations are developed for benefits associated with increased use of labor with low opportunity cost, increased exploitation of economies of scale, and foreign exchange savings.

(v) Next, the feedback due to intermediate demand effects of these various integration impacts is incorporated; and

(vi) Finally the special application of the methodology for 1972 when Honduras was no longer a member of the Common Market is addressed.

All of these economic effects are static; the dynamic effects of integration are discussed after the presentation of empirical results for the static effects.

The discussion which follows treats the methodology in a nonmathematical form. The formal algebraic statement of the methodology appears in appendix C.

1.   Trade Diversion and Trade Creation

The traditional economic literature on customs unions identifies trade diversion and trade creation as the two basic effects of integration. This study estimates these traditional effects, and then uses them as the basis for a series of additional estimations relevant for developing countries.

Trade creation occurs when, as the result of the elimination of tariffs on imports from partners in a common market, a country increases its total imports. Trade diversion occurs to the extent that duty-free entry for partner goods merely prompts substitution from imports formerly bought from the rest of the world to purchases from partner countries.

This chapter obtains a concrete measure of trade creation in the following way. A preintegration base year of 1958 is used as the benchmark for trade patterns that could have been expected to prevail in the absence of integration. The pattern of trade during integration (in 1968 and 1972, as two alternative terminal years) is then examined to determine the changes in imports attributable to economic integration. In particular, the total import propensity (imports as a fraction of consumption) will have risen if there exists trade creation in the sector being examined. (All measurements are carried out at the level of twenty-nine industrial sectors—three digits of the International Standard Industrial Classification—and seven raw materials sectors.) The measure of the amount of trade "created" is therefore the increase in the total import propensity, multiplied by the level of consumption in the terminal period.

The magnitude of trade diversion is also estimated on the basis of changes in import propensities. If trade diversion has occurred, the propensity to import from the rest of the world (that is, excluding partners) will have fallen. The size of trade diversion will therefore be the reduction in the propensity to import from the rest of the world, multiplied by the terminal level of consumption.

The welfare benefits and costs for the economy will depend not only upon the absolute sizes of trade creation and diversion but also upon the unit benefit or cost per unit of trade creation or diversion. In the case of trade creation, the unit benefit will be higher, the greater the height of the original tariff. That is, tariffs cause high prices to consumers as well as excess and inefficient domestic production. The higher the tariff, the greater these costs, and therefore the greater the welfare benefits once the tariff is removed for supplies coming from partners. In general terms, the welfare benefit of trade creation will be approximately one-half of the original tariff multiplied by the amount of trade creation itself.[3]

The welfare cost of trade diversion will depend on the excess unit cost of buying from partners rather than from the rest of the world. For each sector an index of common market partner price relative to the world price is constructed on the basis of highly detailed import unit values, as discussed below. The percentage excess price of regional supply relative to world supply is then applied to the estimate of trade diversion in order to calculate the welfare cost of trade diversion.

At this point the basic building blocks of the analysis are complete--the estimates of trade creation and diversion and their corresponding welfare benefits and costs. Before turning to the nontraditional elements of the analysis, it is important to clarify the assumptions lying behind the use of changes in import propensities to identify effects of integration.

In any analysis of the effects of a common market, it is necessary to postulate the anti-monde--the situation that would have existed in the absence of the Common Market. The impact of integration is then measured as the difference between actual experience and conditions that would have occurred in the anti-monde. The crucial feature in the analysis here is the assumption that in the absence of integration (that is, in the anti-monde), trade patterns would have remained unchanged; sectoral propensities to import (total, and from the rest of the world in particular) would have remained at their preintegration levels (1958).

The use of changes in sectoral trade propensities to assess the impact of integration obviously avoids some of the grosser errors associated with a simplistic assignment to integration of all differences in GNP growth rates before and after the formation of the Common Market. Nevertheless, the approach does raise some questions. The most profound question is whether the entire strategy of import-substituting industrialization would have been adopted by the individual countries even in the absence of a common market. If so, then their preintegration import propensities would have changed in any case, moving away from imports of industrial goods based on exports of raw materials, and it would be erroneous to attribute change in the import propensities to the Common Market.

It is unlikely, however, that Central America would have moved in the direction of import-substituting industrialization in the absence of integration. Indeed, the perception of policymakers in the region in the 1950s was precisely that industrialization would be unacceptably inefficient without the broader market and the corresponding economies of scale offered by a common market. This perception was one of the chief forces behind the integration movement. Moreover, the implementation of compart-mentalized industrialization within each national economy and without a common market would have required some new mechanism such as higher national tariffs and, correspondingly, higher costs. In contrast, the Common Market stimulated industrial expansion by increasing the demand for regional production even without an increase in the common external tariffs compared with the preintegration averages among countries. In short, the most reasonable anti-monde is one in which Central America would have continued its production and trade patterns of the 1950s, based on raw material exports and industrial imports, in the absence of integration.

A more technical question is whether the particular sectoral import propensities would have changed over time (without integration) even with no fundamental change in development strategy. For example, if imports are income-elastic goods, the overall import level might be expected to rise relative to GNP. This problem should be adequately dealt with here, since the analysis is product specific; hence, a rise in the weight of income-elastic goods will be captured by the path of consumption of the good, and application of the preintegration import propensities should accurately register the rise of expected imports due to the evolution of demand composition. Nevertheless, studies of common market effects fre-quently attempt to forecast the "natural" tendencies of preintegration propensities, either by projecting past trends (as in a study by the European Free Trade Association, EFTA) or by observing trends in a "control group" of third countries not participating in the union (as in a study on the trade effects of the European Economic Community).[4] In the case of the CACM, neither of these options seems preferable to direct use of preinte-gration propensities. Historical data that would allow assessment of pre-1958 trends are not available. Control group countries do not exist (with the possible exception of Panama, and the assessment of integration effects based on a single such control case would be precarious indeed). Attempts to correct preintegration import propensities to what they would have become in the absence of integration seem more likely to introduce additional biases into the analysis than to remove existing biases.[5]

2. Trade Suppression and External Trade Augmentation

If tariffs remain unchanged for outsiders when a common market is formed, the total import propensity should rise (because imports from part-ners become duty free) and the propensity to import from the rest of the world should fall (as demand shifts to partner sources). In these normal cases, trade creation and diversion are both positive. But if the observed total import propensity actually declines instead of rising, measured trade creation will be negative. This case occurs with some frequency in the estimates here. It is treated in the following way. If the country raised the tariff on the product when moving to the common external tariff, then integration could have caused the observed decline in the total import pro-pensity. In this case the effect is identified as relevant and is named "trade suppression." If instead the tariff remained constant or declined, then there is no reason why integration would have caused the total import propensity to decline, and any observed decline is omitted from the analysis as a nongermane change in the economy unrelated to integration. The germane case where trade suppression is measured includes the more general phenomenon of import-substituting industrialization based on increased tariffs.

Similarly, an observed increase in the propensity to import from the outside world is only consistent with a reduction in the country's tariff in the move to a common external tariff. If the tariff did decline, such a case of negative trade diversion is accepted as germane to integration and is named "external trade augmentation." Otherwise, a measured result of negative trade diversion is omitted from the analysis as a nongermane factor unrelated to integration.

The welfare cost of "trade suppression" is similar to the welfare gain of trade creation. It is measured as one-half the change in the tariff multiplied by the size of trade suppression. Therefore the greater the rise in the tariff, the higher the welfare cost of trade suppression. The welfare benefit of external trade augmentation is comparable with that of trade creation, and it is measured as one-half the change in tariff multiplied by the amount of external trade augmentation.

3.   Nontraditional Static Welfare Effects

In the context of developing countries there are important additional static welfare effects that are not conventionally included in the analysis of customs unions. These are: the use of labor with low opportunity cost; the achievement of economies of scale; and the saving of foreign exchange.

4.   Opportunity Cost of Labor

It is generally accepted that in the developing economy the "shadow price" or social opportunity cost of unskilled labor is below the wage rate. In the surplus labor model of W. Arthur Lewis,[6] labor can be withdrawn from the traditional sectors of family farm agriculture and unorganized urban services at little or even no cost to production in these sectors (as the workers remaining in the sector utilize their own time more fully to make up for the labor withdrawal). In this situation the expansion of output confers a social gain equal to the excess of the labor cost embedded in output price over the social cost of that labor. Thus, if the shadow price of labor is zero, the "opportunity cost of labor" gain is equal to the full fraction of unskilled wages in output value, as applied to the change in gross output. If the shadow price equals the wage rate, the gain falls to zero.

Because integration increases production by raising demand for exports to partners, it will generate an economic benefit by raising employment of workers whose social opportunity cost is low. If the "output effect" of integration is first identified, then for each sector there will be a welfare gain equal to the rise in output value multiplied by the fraction of total output value represented by the excess of labor costs over the social opportunity cost of labor.

Given the high rural unemployment rates found in Central America according to a recent F.A.O. study,[7] it might be reasonable to argue that rural workers could be withdrawn at zero social cost. The calculations here use a more conservative concept. It is assumed that the opportunity cost of labor equals the rural wage as adjusted downward for the probability that the worker will be unable to find a job. For example, if rural unemployment is 40 percent, the shadow price would equal only 60 percent of the wage rate, because the worker would have only a 60 percent chance of finding a rural job. This approach should give an upper bound of the shadow price of labor (considering that workers might be withdrawn with no loss of rural output given high rural unemployment), and as a result the estimates of welfare gain within the "labor opportunity cost" effect will tend to be understated.

The estimate of labor's shadow price uses data on the rural wage rate and on rural underemployment. The F.A.O. study on Central American agriculture[8] has estimated the degree of rural underemployment in each country. The study uses technical coefficients of labor input per crop output to determine the amount of labor which should be required to produce observed agricultural production. The excess of rural labor force availability over the required labor force is then identified as underemployment. The same study reports the average wage for full-time agricultural work in 1970. These data are shown in table 3. The final column reports the estimated shadow price of labor, based on the method discussed above.

Table 3.   Shadow Price of Labor, 1970

Country	Rural Underemployment (percent)	Average Agricultural Wage, 1970 ($ CA/yr)	Shadow Price of Labor ($ CA/yr)
	(A)	(B)	(C)
Guatemala	52.3	224	107
El Salvador	58.3	224	93
Honduras	42.5	162	93
Nicaragua	21.5	258	202
Costa Rica	14.7	398	340

SOURCES: Column A: SIECA, El Desarrollo Integrado de Centroamérica en la Presente Década, Study no. 6, La Política Social y el Desarrollo Integrado (Guatemala City: SIECA, 1972), table 21.

Column B: Grupo Asesor de la F.A.O. para la Integración Económica Centroamericana (GAFICA), "Plan Perspectivo Para el Desarrollo y la Integración de la Agricultura en Centroamérica," mimeographed (Guatemala City: GAFICA, 1972), table J-4.

The "output effect" of integration, for its part, is calculated at the sectoral level on the basis of increased exports to partners. Specifically, in a given sector the imports of partners from the common market will have risen by the sum of trade creation (more imports) and trade diversion (replacement of external by regional supply). By applying a country's share in its partners' imports from the common market to the trade diversion and creation of the respective partners, and summing the result over all partners, it is possible to estimate the increase in exports for a country resulting from integration. The country's output in the sector will have risen by the amount required to meet this additional export demand. In addition, output will have increased to meet import substitution demand as measured by "trade suppression." These increases will be partially offset by reduction in domestic demand caused by the country's trade creation and its external trade augmentation. The net increase in output is then attributed to integration and multiplied by the parameter for low opportunity cost of labor in order to estimate this source of welfare gain. (See appendix C for a more complete description of these calculations.)

5. Economies of Scale

When economies of scale are present, an increase in output value can be accomplished by a less than proportional increase in inputs of labor, capital, and raw materials. If the degree of returns to scale (sum of factor production elasticities) is 1.1, for example, a 100 percent rise in output will require only a 91 percent rise in inputs, and therefore a windfall gain will have occurred, equal to the difference of 9 percent of output (and input) value.

The same sectoral estimates of increased output attributable to integration in each country are used to determine welfare gains from increased exploitation of economies of scale. As discussed below, production function estimates for each sector provide the economies of scale parameters which are applied to the estimates of output change, to calculate the resulting welfare gains from economies of scale.

6. Foreign Exchange Savings

The final nontraditional static welfare effect analyzed in this study is that arising from the saving of foreign exchange. When countries form a common market, they will tend to have a trade balance increase vis-à-vis the rest of the world.[9] In essence, the members' exports to partners will rise by the sum of trade diversion plus trade creation, whereas their total imports will rise by the amount of trade creation only. The group as a whole will experience a trade balance increase equal to trade diversion, as long as the supply elasticities for exports are relatively high and increased exports to partners do not come at the expense of reduced exports to the outside world. When trade suppression and external trade augmentation are present, there will be an additional increase in the trade balance equal to trade suppression (which reduces import requirements) minus external trade augmentation (which raises imports).

In conventional customs union literature, no particular welfare gain stems from this positive trade balance effect because the value of increased exports will be fully offset by the opportunity cost of the factors of production required for export expansion. But in the case of developing countries, the social opportunity cost of foreign exchange is often considerably higher than that indicated by the market exchange rate. As a result, there can be a sizable welfare benefit from the saving of foreign exchange made possible by integration.

The importance of the availability of foreign exchange to economic growth in developing countries was postulated in the well-known two-gap model of Chenery and Strout,[10] which maintained that in addition to the traditional savings constraint there could be a foreign exchange constraint on growth and the latter could frequently be the more limiting, especially at intermediate stages of growth.

It is widely recognized that in developing countries the social opportunity cost of foreign exchange usually exceeds the market exchange rate. That is, although the exchange rate may be one peso to the dollar, the real value of an extra dollar in foreign exchange availability to the economy may be 1.5 pesos. The need for using an accounting price or shadow price for foreign exchange in order to reflect this fact is a standard element in cost-benefit analysis as applied in developing countries.[11]

Behind the consensus on a need for shadow pricing foreign exchange, there are really two schools of thought. The first maintains that a discrepancy exists between the opportunity cost of foreign exchange and the market exchange rate only because tariff and nontariff barriers impede free trade. In this viewpoint, the elimination of protection would cause demand for imports to rise, depreciating the market rate to the point where it would accurately reflect the opportunity cost of foreign exchange. According to this approach, it would be ideal to eliminate protection in the first place; but so long as it exists, a "second best" solution is to evaluate policies and projects by applying a scarcity premium to foreign exchange earned or saved.

A second school of thought is more structuralist in nature. It contends that even the elimination of protection would not necessarily remove the scarcity premium on the opportunity cost of foreign exchange (although the premium might fall). In this approach, foreign exchange is viewed as a specific factor of production, with little substitutability between imports (such as raw materials and machinery) and domestic resources. Conceived in this manner as a specific factor of production, foreign exchange has a specific marginal product (or shadow price in programming terminology). This marginal product typically will exceed the market exchange rate; furthermore, in this second approach, it could well continue to do so even if protection were eliminated and the exchange rate depreciated. For example, with respect to price (as may be the case with fixed market shares for traditional exports having inelastic aggregate world demand and in the absence of a marketing capacity for nontraditional, manufactured exports), then even the exchange rate which maximizes the total receipts of foreign exchange might still fail to capture the full scarcity of foreign exchange measured by its marginal product as a factor input into the economy.

Another theme within this second school of thought is that some stimulus to certain sectors (often industrial) is desirable for "infant industry" purposes, because comparative advantage is expected to change over time; and, given fiscal limits precluding direct production subsidies, import protection is a rational strategy. In this case an accounting price for evaluating foreign exchange will also be appropriate, because

as long as protection exists, a divergence will exist between the opportunity cost of foreign exchange and the market exchange rate; and, according to this approach, protection itself is required in order to
achieve the industrial transformation toward long-run comparative
advantage.

This chapter draws from both of these broad schools of thought to
estimate the shadow price of foreign exchange. Following the first school,
the shadow price may be estimated on the basis of the level of tariff
protection. One measure within this approach, proposed by Harberger[12]
and others, uses the average tariff itself as the shadow price premium
for foreign exchange. (The term "tariff" includes the tariff equivalent
of nontariff barriers, but in the Central American cases the latter are
infrequent so that tariffs themselves form the basis for the measure.)
This procedure derives from the argument that the level of the tariff is precisely the amount of the distortion introduced by the tariff
and therefore the amount of correction needed when judging the scarcity value of foreign exchange.[13]

An alternative tariff-based approach, advocated by Bacha and Taylor,[14]
asks what the equilibrium exchange rate would be in the absence of all
tariffs and export subsidies. Whereas the Harberger approach concerns
an "ex-ante marginal" scarcity price for foreign exchange, the Bacha-
Taylor approach refers to an "ex-post equilibrium" value which would
be the exchange rate after adjustment to a new equilibrium in the event
that all tariffs were eliminated. Under most circumstances this equilibrium approach yields a lower scarcity premium, as would be expected in
view of the fact that under distortion the ex-ante marginal scarcity
value of the thing which is in short supply (in this case, foreign exchange) will generally be greater than the value to which it would settle after elimination of the distortion and supply and demand adjustment
in the markets determining its price.

Between the approaches of Harberger and Bacha-Taylor, the former
appears to be generally the more useful for practical policy evaluations;
the total elimination of tariffs usually is not a realistic prospect, so
that the more relevant shadow price is the current or ex-ante one rather
than that which would prevail under equilibrium without protection.

However, neither of the approaches based on tariffs is sufficient
for dealing with the fact that there may be a high scarcity value of foreign exchange even if tariffs are zero. Even without protection, a decline in exports can cause a multiple decline in GNP because authorities
repress the economy to reestablish balance of payments equilibrium, and
because the required reductions in imports reduce capital stock formation and utilization of existing capacity. Therefore the tariff-based
shadow price should be considered to be a lower-bound estimate.[15]

The second, structuralist, school provides the basis for a conceptually more satisfactory measure of the shadow price of foreign exchange, by means of a programming or econometric model. Using such a
model, the shadow price may be estimated as the change in GNP per unit
of change in the availability of foreign exchange. Appendix J presents
this type of estimation using an econometric model for El Salvador,
prepared by Gabriel Siri of SIECA. The model simulates the impact of

a decrease in exports. The present discounted value of the resulting decrease in GNP in the first and following years is then calculated by finding the change in the equilibrium values of GNP over time. The model indicates a shadow price of foreign exchange of 1.6 times the market rate. That is, a loss of exports of $1.00 reduces the present value of current and future GNP by $1.60 at the market exchange rate.

The model operates basically through the reduction of activity caused by demand reduction from an initial decline in exports. This approach represents the reality of economic policy in Central America, where the standard policy response to a deterioration in the balance of payments is the imposition of restraints on demand. Moreover, the model's estimates are conservative in the sense that they exclude secondary effects on the supply side. In particular, the reduction in exports would require a reduction in imports, which would reduce the the supply of capital goods and therefore reduce investment, future capital stock, and future GNP. Similarly the forced reduction in imports could reduce importation of intermediate inputs and cause the idling of existing productive capacity. Nevertheless, despite this source of bias toward an underestimation of the shadow price of foreign exchange, the model's estimate would appear to be somewhat overstated. A scarcity premium of 60 percent for foreign exchange seems high. Therefore the result may be viewed with some caution, in part because econometric modeling and linear programming approaches to the problem are known to give estimates for the shadow price of foreign exchange that can be extreme.[16]

With respect to empirical estimates using the tariff-based approach, average industrial tariffs for Central America are shown later in the chapter in table 4. When these averages (on the import-weighted basis) are combined with the weighted average tariff for agricultural goods and minerals, and aggregated over the five countries according to the weight of each country's imports from the rest of the world, the result is an overall weighted average legal tariff of 27.3 percent for 1968.[17] The same procedure gives an average tariff of 29.0 percent for the four CACM member countries in 1972. The comparable tariff averages adjusted for exemptions granted under fiscal incentives are 19.1 percent in 1968 and 10.6 percent in 1972.

It is a moot point whether the legal tariff rates or the rates after adjustment for exemptions should be used for the shadow price calculation. The latter are the actual tariffs paid, on the average. However, some importers must pay the full legal tariff because they do not have access to exemptions, which are available only under industrialization incentive schemes. As a result, it could be argued that the marginal cost price signal given by the tariff structure is the legal rate rather than the adjusted tariff. In practice, it seems reasonable to take the average of the two rates as the best estimate of the overall tariff level. On this basis, and using the Harberger approach, the shadow price for foreign exchange would have been 1.23 times the market rate for the Common Market of five countries in 1968, and 1.198 times the market rate for the Common Market of four in 1972.

In sum, the econometric model approach yields a foreign exchange shadow price premium of 60 percent, while the Harberger approach gives a premium of 23 percent for 1968 and 20 percent for 1972. The estimate from the econometric model appears to be too high. Because the shadow price of foreign exchange has a large weight in the overall estimates of integration benefits (see below), it is probably preferable to err in the conservative direction for this parameter, rather than to use a possibly overestimated value. Otherwise, the overall results might give an exaggerated estimate of the net economic benefits of integration. Accordingly, the central value used in this chapter is a shadow price premium of 25 percent for foreign exchange. This estimate is conservative, since it is much closer to the lower, tariff-based estimate than to the estimate from the econometric model. A heavier weight for the lower estimate is partly due to the fact that the 60 percent estimate appears excessive, and partly due to the fact that under the Bacha-Taylor method the shadow price premium would be still lower than that from the Harberger tariff-based method.[18]

Given the shadow price of foreign exchange, the welfare gain from integration due to foreign exchange scarcity may be estimated on the basis of the net impact of integration of each country's trade balance. Effects favoring the trade balance (increased exports to partners and import decreases through trade suppression) must be set against influences deteriorating that balance (trade creation and external trade augmentation). The net result is multiplied by the shadow price premium on foreign exchange to obtain the welfare gain from the saving of foreign exchange.

It is important to note that in this formulation, effects normally considered negative (trade diversion and trade suppression) and positive (trade creation, augmentation) have the reverse welfare effect. In fact, trade suppression will be beneficial on balance if the foreign exchange scarcity effect outweighs the traditional welfare loss from raising tariffs. Trade creation will be detrimental if the scarcity price on foreign exchange is sufficiently high that the welfare cost of losing foreign exchange exceeds the traditional welfare gains from duty free entry from partners. Moreover, because increased exports to partners due to integration derive from the partners' trade diversion, there will be a welfare gain to the customs union as a whole when trade diversion occurs, as long as the shadow price premium on foreign exchange exceeds the excess unit cost of importing from partners rather than from the rest of the world (the latter being the welfare cost per unit of trade diverted).

These paradoxical reversals of the traditional sources of gain and loss in the formation of a customs union represent the essence of the free trade dispute in developmental policy formulations: measures reducing imports will have beneficial effects if the scarcity of foreign exchange factor outweighs the "triangles of welfare" emphasized in the traditional theory of free trade.

Finally, it might be objected that the attribution of a welfare gain to integration's positive trade balance effect ignores an entirely different alternative: the member countries might have obtained similar welfare gains through stimulating their individual exports to the world market, rather than by improving their trade balance through the replacement of extraregional supply with regional products.

Here again the question is, what would the realistic "anti-monde" have been in the absence of integration? Those who argue that countries such as the Central American nations could have chosen a route of rapid general export expansion would appear to be unrealistic. Few observers suggest that rapid export growth would be possible relying solely on traditional raw materials exports such as coffee, sugar, bananas, and cotton. With price-inelastic demand and with quasi-oligopolistic supply conditions (for example, in coffee), rapid export expansion by the group of Central American countries would face serious limitations. Instead, dynamic export prospects are most often cited in the areas of nontraditional goods, especially light manufactures. The popularity of the notion of prospects for rapid export growth in such goods has been bolstered by the success of places such as Korea, Hong Kong, Taiwan, Brazil, and Colombia in recent years in such exports. However, it is often forgotten that the now buoyant exports of manufactured goods required a prior period of import-substitution industrialization in order to establish the necessary industrial base, especially in the latter two countries. Had the recommendation of free trade cum general export expansion toward the world market prevailed in the 1950s and 1960s, those industrial bases would very probably not have been established. The corresponding requisite phase in the case of Central America may reasonably be said to have been the formation of the Common Market and the expansion of industrial production for its supply. Before leaping to the establishment of export outlets for manufactured goods in industrial country markets, it is not surprising that Central American countries would have found it necessary first to gain experience through the development of export markets in their neighboring Common Market partner countries.

In short, a realistic assessment of the appropriate anti-monde must conclude that the foreign exchange savings provided by the Common Market represented real gains--because in the absence of integration the earning of foreign exchange through rapid expansion of nontraditional exports to world markets would have been an unlikely, unreliable alternative (as, indeed, the Central American policymakers appear to have judged at the time of the formation of the Common Market).

This assessment does not necessarily mean that export expansion today remains an impossibility; on the contrary, given the development of an industrial base there are likely to be more and more industrial goods in which the region has a comparative advantage. Even at present, however, the cloud of industrial country protectionism, as shown most strikingly by the rigid controls on textile imports under the multifiber arrangement of voluntary export quotas, looms over the prospects for exports of light manufactures.

7. Induced Intermediate Demand Effects

In the preceding analysis the effects captured stem from the direct changes in trade and output attributed to economic integration. It is important to consider the magnitude and direction of change in the results if indirect effects on intermediate inputs are considered as well. Thus, integration may increase the demand for output from a given sector as exports to partners rise (due to trade diversion and creation) or as total imports fall (due to trade suppression). However, there may be additional increases in output of the good to satisfy increased use of the sector's product as an intermediate input into other sectors also expanding due to integration. This "induced" expansion will confer additional "labor opportunity cost" and "economies of scale" welfare benefits not captured in the analysis above. At the same time, expansion of the sector may require the purchase of additional intermediate inputs from abroad. These induced imports will reduce the net foreign exchange savings, although a partial offsetting factor will be any increase in exports to partners due to their increased imports of intermediate inputs. Appendix C sets forth the measurement of these indirect effects and of their corresponding welfare effects.

8. Application to 1972

The methodology presented above is applied directly to data for all five Central American countries for 1968, the last year of unimpeded operation of the Central American Common Market. However, it is important to obtain in addition estimates for the most recent year for which data are available, 1972. For this later estimate the method must be adjusted to account for the fact that Honduras was no longer a member of the CACM in the economic sense; the country had restored the imposition of general tariffs on imports from the other CACM countries, which in turn had done the same for goods supplied by Honduras.[19]

The strategy chosen for treatment of 1972 in this chapter is to consider Guatemala, El Salvador, Nicaragua, and Costa Rica as a Common Market of four countries, and to consider Honduras as a member of the rest of the world. That is, for both the base year (1958) and terminal year (1972), all of the calculations which involve partners are made for the four countries alone, and all of the calculations involving the rest of the world (such as the change in propensity to import from outside the Common Market) are conducted by adding the data for Honduras to that for the rest of world. This approach essentially assumes that whatever structural changes the Common Market brought about linking Honduras and the other four countries by 1968, had been eliminated after four years of absence of the former from the union. Although this approach may understate the continuing links of the Honduran economy to the economies of the other four, it appears to be the only reasonable procedure for the analysis.

The results for 1972 give estimates only for the Common Market of four, not for Honduras. There is no direct computation of the loss or gain experienced by Honduras as the result of its withdrawal from the CACM. However, the method implies that as part of the rest of the world, gains or losses from the Common Market for Honduras were zero by 1972. Since positive net gains from integration are found for Honduras in 1968, the implication is that withdrawal led

to an economic cost of a magnitude at least as great as the sacrifice
of 1968 Honduran gains.

D.   Data

The data used in the estimates of the static welfare effects of
integration are from the following sources:

(i) The statistics division within SIECA provided data on
foreign trade;[20] special tabulations of trade data for individual
agricultural products; and computations of the ad valorem equivalent
common external tariff for 1968 at the most detailed tariff line
level (seven- or nine-digit NAUCA--Uniform Tariff Nomenclature for
Central America, equivalent to the SITC, Standard International Trade
Classification).

(ii) A special FAO study on agriculture in Central America provided data for agricultural production, agricultural wage rate, the wage
bill in agricultural product, and rural unemployment.[21]

(iii) The 1968 industrial census conducted in Guatemala, Honduras,
Nicaragua, and Costa Rica provided the plant level data on inputs and
output for calculating returns to scale, the industrial wage rate, unskilled wage bill as a share of gross output value, and the share of
value added in gross output.[22]

(iv) Individual country tariff books were the sources for tariff
rates in the base year, 1958.[23]

(v) A study by the International Monetary Fund on tariff exemptions in 1959 and 1967 was used to obtain estimates of tariffs adjusted
for exemptions in 1958 and 1968.[24]

(vi) Estimates of 1972 legal tariffs and tariffs net of exemptions
at the individual tariff line level were available from a special analysis prepared in the tariff division of SIECA.

(vii) An industrial census for Guatemala in 1971 provided the basis
for the input-output coefficients used in the analysis of intermediate
effects.[25]

Certain features of the data warrant special attention. The ratio
of Common Market price to world price, required for the calculation of
the cost of trade diversion, is based on sectoral indices of relative
unit values aggregated from ratios at the level of approximately 1,500
tariff line items. Each of these indices is constrained between (i)
unity, as a lower bound, and (ii) unity plus the tariff, as an upper
bound. That is, the Common Market price should be no lower than world
price if quality is identical, and no higher than world price plus
the tariff.

It may be asked whether the use of unit value import prices
accurately represents the relative price of CACM and world market
goods. When heterogeneous goods are included in a single category, import

value divided by quantity (kilograms) has little meaning. However, the estimates here employ unit import values at the most detailed tariff line level (seven or nine digits of NAUCA), so that the composition of goods should be relatively homogeneous for most categories. Nevertheless, the price information could definitely be improved if there were available detailed survey data comparing the import prices of individual goods from CACM partners against prices of comparable goods from the world market.

Tables C-3 and C-4 of appendix C present the estimates of the CACM price relative to the world market price for 1970 (used in the 1968 analysis) and 1972, respectively. The tables show three sets of these relative prices: unadjusted unit price ratios, relative prices constrained on the basis of legal tariffs, and relative prices constrained on the basis of adjusted tariffs (that is, net of exemptions). Separate estimates for 1972 are only available for the industrial sectors.

In all of the agricultural sectors and in more than half of the industrial sectors, for both 1958 and 1970, the unadjusted relative price indicates that the CACM unit value is lower than that for imports from the rest of the world. This fact suggests that goods traded intra-regionally are cheaper and of lower quality than are imports from outside the CACM. Moreover, this pattern also very probably reflects the particular bias resulting from the weight of specific tariffs in the CACM tariff structure. For many products the "specific" component of the tariff (dollars per kilogram) is quite onerous, resulting in a strong incentive to import from outside the CACM only varieties with very high quality and high price per kilogram, within a given tariff line product.

The relative prices for 1972 are similar, by sector, to those for 1970, suggesting that the relationships are reasonably stable. The "constrained" estimates (limiting the detailed relative prices to a minimum of unity and a maximum of one plus the tariff) show much less variation among sectors than does the unconstrained relative price. Several of the constrained relative prices are close to unity, especially when adjusted tariffs are the basis for constraining the estimates.

Critics of the Common Market may be surprised that CACM prices are not found to be higher relative to world prices in view of frequent complaints about high-priced regional production. Enthusiasts of the Market may on the contrary maintain that the analysis should not rule out CACM prices lower than world prices. In the absence of additional information on world and Common Market prices, it would seem there is no reason to expect the benefit cost calculations to be biased either optimistically or pessimistically by the relative price data used.

The next basic data variable is the base year tariff rate. The tariff for 1958 is computed at the most detailed NAUCA tariff line level, using legal tariff rates specified in the tariff books of each country. Since these rates include both ad valorem and specific tariffs for each category, it is necessary to convert the specific tariffs into ad valorem equivalents to arrive at the total ad valorem tariff. This conversion uses the 1958 data for each country's unit value of imports from the rest of the world within each tariff line item (that is, the specific duty per kilogram is divided by unit value per kilogram to obtain ad valorem equivalent). Limitation of the imports considered to the rest-of-world supply stems from the fact that the terminal common external tariff similarly applies specific tariff to unit value of imports, and in that instance the imports are solely from the rest of the world (since partner goods enter free). Thus, valid comparison of preintegration and post-integration tariffs will only be obtained by using import unit value from the rest of the world as the "price" in obtaining the ad valorem equivalent of specific levies.

Given the estimates of ad valorem tariff rates for each country at the seven-digit NAUCA (SITC) level (approximately 1,240 categories, the most detailed for which trade data are available for 1958), it is necessary to obtain an aggregate tariff rate for the three-digit ISIC level at which the benefit-cost analysis is conducted.

The more aggregative tariff estimate is a weighted average of the detailed tariff line item rates. The weights are based on values of imports from the rest of the world, again because it is undesirable to intermix measurement of tariff change from base year to terminal year with change in composition of trade as between CACM and the rest of the world.

Whenever an aggregate tariff estimate is involved, the question arises about whether weighting by import value is appropriate. The normal concern is that import value will be low in precisely those items for which the tariff is very high, so that such weighting will produce a downward bias in the estimate of overall protection. The remedy sometimes proposed is to use some "standard" set of import weights based on a "normal" composition of imports for various countries which are not subject to the tariff-biased composition of a single country. In the present case such an alternative appears to be of little use. There is no reason to believe that the bias introduced by the enforcement of such an exogenous weighting system would be less than the bias contained in using observed import value weights. Moreover, insofar as some of the benefit cost measures involve change from base to terminal tariff, the bias concerning tariff level becomes less important since the change would be accurately measured as long as the degree of bias is identical for the base and terminal estimates.

The 1968 terminal year tariff rate is calculated in the same way as the base year tariff, except that there is a single common external tariff for each good in the terminal year rather than five different country tariffs.[26] For 1972, individual tariff rates are used for each country; these are available from a special study by the tariff division of SIECA. Even for the four countries continuing the application of the common external tariff as of 1972, tariff rates may vary somewhat because of varying unit values, which give the specific component of the tariff different ad valorem tariff equivalents.

In addition to legal tariffs, an alternative set of estimates is made for tariffs net of exemptions. The widespread practice of exonerating duties on inputs imported under industrialization incentive schemes requires the consideration of tariffs adjusted for exemptions. The estimates of these adjusted tariffs are available for 1972, on the basis of actual tariff collections by tariff line category (from the SIECA tariff study).

For 1958 and 1968 the effect of exemptions on the tariff structure may be determined on the basis of a study conducted by the International Monetary Fund (IMF) for the years 1959 and 1967.[27] That study prepared estimates of tariffs and exemptions granted for a sample of 226 products, accounting for less than one-sixth of the total number of tariff line items but representing approximately three-fourths of the import value of the region.

For 1959 the total value of exemptions as a fraction of total value of imports, according to the IMF study, is computed as the "exemption proportion" for each tariff line item available. An aggregate exemption proportion at the three-digit CIIU level is obtained through weighting by import value the individual exemption proportions at the tariff line level for all available items included within the three-digit CIIU category. This aggregate proportion is then subtracted from the 1958 legal tariff to obtain the adjusted tariff. The same procedure is applied to the 1967 IMF data to obtain adjusted tariffs for 1968, except that only exemptions granted on imports from outside the region are considered, and weighting for aggregation involves only imports from outside the region (since intra-regional exports were free of tariffs). No estimates of exemptions were available for Nicaragua in 1959 or for Honduras in 1967. Therefore, it is assumed that for Honduras the proportion of legal duties exempted in 1967 was identical to the known portion in 1959; for Nicaragua, it is assumed that the proportion exempted in 1959 was the same as the proportion known to be exempted in 1967.

Estimates of tariffs adjusted for exemptions are made for the industrial sectors only, since the practice of granting exonerations for developmental incentives is limited to inputs imported for use in industrial activities. Furthermore, for the agricultural sectors, tariff estimates are made for 1958 and 1968 only, since the cost-benefit analysis is not conducted for these sectors for 1972 because of the lack of other data.

In order to obtain an idea of the general trend of tariff protection in Central America, the sectoral tariff estimates are aggregated into overall weighted average industrial tariffs. These averages are presented in table 4. Both legal and adjusted tariffs are shown, and two weighting schemes are used: sectoral shares in imports from the rest of the world, and sectoral shares in total apparent consumption.[28] The latter basis is included to take account of the fact that weighting by import value tends to understate the overall level of protection (because sectors with prohibitively high tariffs will have low import levels).

The following patterns are evident in table 4:

(i) Legal tariffs converged from their 1958 levels among the five countries to a uniform, intermediate level by 1968; the tariffs were reduced substantially in the process for Guatemala and Costa Rica.

(ii) By 1972, tariffs were somewhat more dispersed again. In Guatemala and Costa Rica, they still stood far below their original 1958 levels; in Nicaragua and Honduras, however, tariffs had crept up again.

(iii) If tariffs net of adjustment for exemptions are considered, there is a very strong pattern of reduction in protection both from 1958

Table 4. Weighted Average Industrial Tariffs, 1958, 1968, and 1972
(percent)

Tariffs	1958	1968	1972
Based on Import Value Weights			
Legal Tariffs			
Guatemala	53.8	28.1	27.9
El Salvador	25.2	28.9	26.2
Honduras	34.4	28.5	36.0
Nicaragua	30.7	25.5	34.5
Costa Rica	52.9	28.9	28.1
Adjusted Tariffs[a]			
Guatemala	48.8	19.5	10.4
El Salvador	13.3	23.4	12.6
Honduras	28.7	22.9	14.2
Nicaragua	15.4	14.9	12.0
Costa Rica	47.4	15.2	8.5
Based on Consumption Value Weights			
Legal Tariffs			
Guatemala	79.5	59.6	60.9
El Salvador	27.7	57.4	53.0
Honduras	56.7	60.4	59.3
Nicaragua	52.5	54.9	61.9
Costa Rica	69.5	54.8	58.1
Adjusted Tariffs[a]			
Guatemala	70.8	36.7	15.6
El Salvador	10.3	49.3	23.5
Honduras	45.2	49.1	27.7
Nicaragua	34.8	39.0	16.6
Costa Rica	59.4	40.7	19.8

[a]Adjusted tariff--adjusted for exemptions.

to 1968 and again from 1968 to 1972.[29] The reductions were the most extreme for Guatemala and Costa Rica. Only El Salvador had an increase in adjusted tariffs moving from 1958 to the integration tariffs of 1968, and by 1972, El Salvador's tariffs net of exemptions had again fallen to the relatively low level of 1958.

(iv) In terms of general level of protection, these tariffs appear quite modest--especially the rates adjusted for exemptions. In 1972 legal tariff rates on the order of 30 percent and adjusted rates on the order of 12 percent in the region represented very modest protection compared with that typical for most developing countries.

(v) As expected, the consumption-weighted averages are much higher than the import-weighted averages. The divergence is partly due to the high level of protection of basic consumption sectors (food products, 311; beverages, 313) and the lower levels of protection facing imports of raw materials and capital goods (industrial chemicals, 351; steel and iron, 371; metal and machinery products, 384). The weighting shifts from the latter to the former when consumption weights replace import weights.

(vi) For most of the countries the incidence of exemptions rose from limited impact in 1958 to very substantial impact by 1972, when actual tariff collections were between one-third and one-half of the legal duties hypothetically due in the absence of exemptions.

Tables C-5 through C-9 in appendix C present the detailed tariff estimates at the three-digit CIIU level. While these tables permit the evaluation of specific trends in protection by country and sector, detailed trends are not of direct interest to this chapter--although they of course enter into the cost benefit calculations, especially in the determination of whether observed negative trade creation and diversion are due to changing tariff policy or to exogenous factors.

Finally, for the intermediate demand effects, coefficients of intermediate input-output requirements are necessary. These have been estimated at the three-digit CIIU level on the basis of a 1971 industrial census in Guatemala.[30] Since similar data are not available for the other countries, the estimates of this chapter assume that the same input-output coefficients characterized production in the other countries as in Guatemala. Due to the lack of input-output coefficients for each country, and because of the uncertain reliability of the coefficients for Guatemala itself,[31] the results obtained for intermediate inputs must be considered somewhat tentative. However, as shown below, the results for intermediate effects constitute only a relatively minor adjustment to the results for direct effects, so that even sizable changes in the intermediate effect estimates would have only modest impact on the final overall effects estimated.

E.   Results

The basic results for the static welfare benefits and costs of Central American economic integration are presented in tables 5 through 10. These results include estimates for the raw materials sectors for 1968 (table 5); estimates of the direct effects of integration in the industrial sector for both 1968 and 1972 (tables 6 and 7); and the magnitude and distribution of the total effects of integration (tables 8 through 10). In addition, the induced industrial intermediate demand effects (tables C-10 and C-11) appear in appendix C.

The results for the raw materials sectors in 1968 are assumed to continue unchanged in the 1972 estimates, due to the lack of data on the raw materials sectors in 1972. This assumption is reasonable since a general growth in the scale of trade and integration effects between 1968 and 1972 should have been offset by a tendency toward interference with free trade in the primary sectors in this period. Different results for the "legal" and "adjusted" tariff cases are given for the industrial

Table 5. Integration Effects in Agriculture and Mining, 1968

Effects	Guatemala	El Salvador	Honduras	Nicaragua	Costa Rica	Total CACM
Basic effects						
Trade diversion	386	491	95	4	73	1,049
Trade creation	968	1,703	1,335	3,879	4,230	12,115
External trade augmentation	879	0	3,263	3,153	33	7,328
Trade suppression	0	1,587	167	0	0	1,754
DELTX	1,652	3,908	4,219	1,732	590	12,101
Foreign exchange savings	-195	3,792	-212	-5,300	-3,673	-5,588
Welfare benefits from						
Trade creation	431	178	694	2,160	902	4,365
External trade augmentation	213	0	416	201	6	836
Labor opportunity cost	57	105	158	28	1	349
Economies of scale	0	0	0	0	0	
Foreign exchange savings[a]	-45	948	53	-1,325	-918	-1,397
Total benefits	574	1,231	1,215	1,064	-9	4,075

Table 5 (continued)

Effects	Guatemala	El Salvador	Honduras	Nicaragua	Costa Rica	Total CACM
Welfare costs from						
Trade diversion	161	36	0	0	0	197
Trade suppression	0	160	17	0	0	177
Labor opportunity cost	0	0	10	11	94	115
Economies of scale	0	0	0	0	0	0
Total costs	161	196	27	11	94	489
Net welfare gains	413	1,035	1,188	1,053	-103	3,586

[a]Evaluated at foreign exchange shadow price premium of 25 percent.

Table 6. Direct Effects of Economic Integration in the Industrial Sectors
(Legal Tariff Basis), Central America, 1968 and 1972
(1,000 $CA)

Effects	1968						1972				
	Guate-mala	El Sal-vador	Hon-duras	Nica-ragua	Costa Rica	CACM-5	Guate-mala	El Sal-vador	Nica-ragua	Costa Rica	CACM-4
Total net benefits	37,582	20,938	4,169	6,334	11,486	80,509	46,680	32,039	18,687	18,374	115,780
Percentage shares	46.7	26.0	5.2	7.9	14.3	100.0	40.3	27.7	16.1	15.9	100.0
Basic effects											
Trade diversion	30,517	35,634	30,679	32,779	38,189		49,707	56,537	41,751	57,662	
Trade creation	5,823	9,090	6,214	5,576	3,694		11,807	8,160	5,951	5,114	
External trade augmentation	234	0	0	0	489		2,994	0	240	199	
Trade suppression	70,673	20,847	13,670	10,104	21,467		102,417	73,232	41,944	50,107	
DELTX	62,642	69,877	14,734	20,154	30,086		83,162	76,309	36,698	40,520	
Foreign exchange savings	127,258	81,635	22,189	24,682	47,369		170,778	141,380	72,452	85,315	
Welfare benefits											
Trade creation	1,374	522	1,130	1,043	1,503		1,502	537	1,147	1,571	
External trade augmentation	1	0	0	0	50		297	0	15	36	
Labor opportunity cost											
Economies of scale	8,432	5,724	1,346	1,327	1,556		12,360	9,436	3,416	2,616	
Foreign exchange savings	2,463	903	254	536	628		2,787	1,206	1,430	1,316	
(at f* = 1.25)	31,814	20,409	5,547	6,170	11,842		42,694	35,345	18,113	21,329	

Table 6 (Continued)

Effects	1968						1972				
	Guate-mala	El Sal-vador	Hon-duras	Nica-ragua	Costa Rica	CACM-5	Guate-mala	El Sal-vador	Nica-ragua	Costa Rica	CACM-4
Welfare costs											
Trade diversion	2,952	2,542	1,970	2,348	3,098		5,480	4,090	3,598	5,113	
Trade suppression	3,493	4,035	1,907	394	994		7,374	10,394	1,836	3,379	
Labor opportunity cost	58	41	230	0	0		106	0	0	0	
Economies of scale	0	1	0	0	0		1	0	0	0	

Table 7. Direct Effects of Economic Integration in the Industrial Sectors
(Adjusted Tariff Basis), Central America, 1968 and 1972
(1,000 $CA)

Effects	1968 Guate-mala	1968 El Sal-vador	1968 Hon-duras	1968 Nica-ragua	1968 Costa Rica	1968 CACM-5	1972 Guate-mala	1972 El Sal-vador	1972 Nica-ragua	1972 Costa Rica	1972 CACM-4
Total net benefits	35,871	19,878	4,524	5,261	9,068	74,602	44,913	37,670	17,048	13,680	113,311
Percentage shares	48.1	26.6	6.1	7.1	12.2	100.0	39.6	33.3	15.0	12.1	100.0
Basic effects											
Trade diversion	30,517	35,634	30,679	32,779	38,189		49,707	56,537	41,751	57,662	
Trade creation	5,823	9,090	6,214	5,576	3,694		11,807	8,160	5,951	5,114	
External trade augmentation	1,013	0	0	0	489		2,998	0	266	293	
Trade suppression	61,953	20,847	13,670	7,838	14,226		68,812	73,480	33,781	17,251	
DELTX	62,642	69,877	14,734	20,154	30,085		83,162	76,309	36,698	40,520	
Foreign exchange savings	117,759	81,635	22,189	22,416	40,129		137,169	141,628	64,263	52,364	
Welfare benefits											
Trade creation	1,134	0[a]	977	458	855		1,239	0[b]	655	491	
External trade augmentation	39	0	0	0	65		379	0	51	72	
Labor opportunity cost	7,577	5,724	1,346	1,276	1,406		9,470	8,975	3,062	1,882	
Economies of scale	2,312	903	254	628	2,787		1,169	1,250	542		
Foreign exchange savings			536								
(at f* = 1.25)	29,440	20,409	5,547	5,604	10,032		34,292	35,407	16,066	13,091	

Table 7 (Continued)

Effects	1968						1972				
	Guate-mala	El Sal-vador	Hon-duras	Nica-ragua	Costa Rica	CACM-5	Guate-mala	El Sal-vador	Nica-ragua	Costa Rica	CACM-4
Welfare costs											
Trade diversion	2,952	2,542	1,970	2,348	3,098		1,773	1,724	1,347	1,838	
Trade suppression	1,622	4,573	1,400	265	820		1,376	6,157	2,689	561	
Labor opportunity cost	58	41	1,400	265	820		1,376	6,157	2,689	561	
Economies of scale	0	1	0	0	0		1	0	0	0	

[a]Unadjusted figure: - 176. See text.
[b]Unadjusted figure: - 56. See text.

Table 8. Total Net Benefits from Integration (Legal Tariff Basis),
1968 and 1972
(1,000 $CA)

Effects	1968						1972				
	Guate-mala	El Sal-vador	Hon-duras	Nica-ragua	Costa Rica	CACM-5	Guate-mala	El Sal-vador	Nica-ragua	Costa Rica	CACM-4
I. Agriculture and mining	413	1,035	1,188	1,053	-103	3,586	413[a]	1,035[a]	1,053[a]	-103[a]	2,398
II. Industry: direct effects	37,582	20,938	4,169	6,334	11,486	80,509	46,680	32,039	18,687	18,374	115,780
III. Industry: intermediate effects	-2,775	-1,953	-1,222	-688	-2,270	-8,908	-3,654	-1,863	-2,484	-3,668	-11,669
IV. Total	35,220	20,020	4,135	6,699	9,113	75,187	43,439	31,211	17,256	14,603	106,509
Percent	46.8	26.6	5.5	8.9	12.1	100.0	40.8	29.3	16.2	13.7	100.0

NOTE: Evaluated at foreign exchange shadow price premium of 25 percent.

[a]Assumed equal to 1968 values. See text.

Table 9. Total Net Benefits from Integration (Adjusted Tariff Basis),
1968 and 1972
(1,000 $CA)

Effects	1968						1972				
	Guate-mala	El Sal-vador	Hon-duras	Nica-ragua	Costa Rica	CACM-5	Guate-mala	El Sal-vador	Nica-ragua	Costa Rica	CACM-4
I. Agriculture and mining	413	1,035	1,188	1,053	-103	3,586	413[a]	1,035[a]	1,053[a]	-103[a]	2,398
II. Industry: direct effects	35,871	19,878	4,524	5,261	9,068	74,602	44,913	37,670	17,048	13,680	113,311
III. Industry: intermediate effects	-2,494	-2,044	-1,230	-623	-1,894	-8,283	-2,214	-2,828	-2,399	-2,020	-9,461
IV. Total	33,790	18,869	4,482	5,691	7,071	69,905	43,112	35,877	15,702	11,557	106,248
Percent	48.3	27.0	6.4	8.1	10.1	100.0	40.6	33.8	14.8	10.9	100.0

[a]Assumed equal to 1968 values.

Table 10. Distribution of Integration Benefits Among Common Market Members, 1968 and 1972

Benefits	1968						1972				
	Guate-mala	El Sal-vador	Hon-duras	Nica-ragua	Costa Rica	CACM-5	Guate-mala	El Sal-vador	Nica-ragua	Costa Rica	CACM-4
I. % Share of net benefits[a]	47.6	26.8	6.0	8.5	11.1	100.0	40.7	31.5	15.5	12.3	100.0
II. % Share of											
Population	35.2	22.7	17.0	13.4	11.6	100.0	42.1	27.8	16.2	13.8	100.0
GDP	34.6	19.7	13.9	15.1	16.6	100.0	39.1	20.7	17.8	22.4	100.0
Industrial value added	32.0	23.0	10.6	15.5	18.9	100.0	33.5	22.9	20.0	23.6	100.0
Exports	24.0	22.3	18.5	17.1	18.0	100.0	28.9	24.4	22.0	24.7	100.0
III. Difference of % benefits from											
% Population	12.4	4.1	-11.0	-4.9	-0.5	32.9[b]	-1.4	3.7	-0.7	-1.5	7.3
% GDP	13.0	7.1	-7.9	-6.6	-5.5	40.1[b]	1.6	10.8	-2.3	-10.1	24.8
% Industrial value added	15.6	3.8	-4.6	-7.0	-7.8	38.8[b]	7.2	8.6	-4.5	-11.3	31.6
% Exports	23.6	4.5	-12.5	-8.6	-6.9	56.1[b]	11.8	7.1	-6.5	-12.4	37.8

Table 10 (Continued)

Benefits	1968						1972				
	Guatemala	El Salvador	Honduras	Nicaragua	Costa Rica	CACM-5	Guatemala	El Salvador	Nicaragua	Costa Rica	CACM-4
IV. Ratio, % net benefits to											
% Population	1.35	1.18	0.35	0.63	0.96	1.00	0.97	1.13	0.96	0.89	1.00
% GDP	1.38	1.36	0.43	0.56	0.67	1.00	1.04	1.52	0.87	0.55	1.00

[a]Simple average of % share in legal tariff and adjusted tariff variants.
[b]Sum of absolute values of differences.

sectors; for the primary sectors only the legal tariff case is examined since the practice of granting tariff exemptions on raw materials imports is generally nonexistent for economic activity in the primary sectors.

1. Total Welfare Gains

The central estimates for total static welfare gains from integration are $72.5 million annually by 1968 for the CACM of five, and $106 million annually by 1972 for the CACM of four (the average of results using legal and adjusted tariffs). These gains represented 1.62 percent of the GNP of the region in 1968 and 1.98 percent of the combined GNP of the four remaining member countries in 1972. These gains are large, especially considering the conventional findings of very small welfare gains from customs unions.[32] It is the nontraditional, developmental welfare effects in the analysis that are responsible for the relatively large results, as discussed below.

To place these gains into perspective it is helpful to consider their single once-for-all value as an estimate of the value obtained by the decision to integrate. This single value may be obtained by taking the present discounted value of a future annual flow of these integration benefits. Assuming that the figure for the CACM of four in 1972 were to grow annually at the same rate as total trade--say by 5 percent in real terms--and assuming a 10 percent social discount rate, the present discounted value of the future stream of annual benefits would be twenty times the annual rate, or $2.12 billion for the CACM of four.[33] In other words, counting only net static welfare benefits, the decision to integrate was worth a once-for-all gain on the order of $2 billion, or $160 for each inhabitant of the four CACM members (in 1972 prices).

An important aspect of the aggregate benefit is that it increased by approximately one-half between 1968 and 1972, even though Honduras had dropped out of the market in the latter year.[34] This result suggests that the basic gains of the integration were not seriously reduced by the withdrawal of Honduras.

Tables 8 and 9 permit a comparison of the results when legal and adjusted tariffs are used. The results on the two alternative bases are very close for 1968 and virtually identical for 1972. For 1968 the adjusted tariff basis does give slightly lower welfare gains, primarily because fewer instances of "trade suppression" are identified (since some cases with a rising legal tariff from 1958 to 1968 show a declining adjusted tariff).

The most important single variable in determining the magnitude of total gains is the shadow price for foreign exchange. The results presented in tables 5 through 10 are based on the central estimate used for this parameter, a 25 percent premium on the scarcity value of foreign exchange over the market rate. If instead a high premium of 60 percent is used (based on the econometric model of Siri), the estimate of total welfare gains rises dramatically--from $106 million annually in 1972 to $231 million. Similarly, the use of a much lower scarcity price premium of only 10 percent reduces the estimates of 1972 welfare gains to $53 million annually.[35] However, as discussed above, the scarcity premium of 25 percent seems much more reliable than either the lower-bound estimate (based on the Bacha-Taylor method) or the upper-bound estimate (based on the econometric model).

In sum, the total welfare gains are very substantial relative to GNP, especially compared to most estimates of integration effects (for the European Common Market, for example), and these estimates would be still much larger if a less conservative alternative were used for the most important parameter, the shadow price of foreign exchange.

2. Composition of Gains

Examination of tables 5 through 9 reveals the following main features concerning the composition of the effects by sector and by type of welfare effect:

(i) Gains from integration are much higher in industry than in agriculture (tables 8 and 9). This result stems from the fact that the great bulk of integration's effect on production and trade balance was concentrated on the industrial sectors, a phenomenon explored in greater detail in the discussion below of structural transformation.

(ii) In the industrial sectors, the traditional welfare gains from integration through trade creation are small relative to the nontraditional effects considered. Welfare gains from shadow pricing labor, from increased exploitation of economies of scale, and particularly from shadow pricing foreign exchange savings, far outweigh the traditional effects.

(iii) Similarly, the conventional approximate guide to a Common Market's welfare effect--trade creation compared with trade diversion--proves irrelevant. Trade diversion far exceeds trade creation (for example, in 1968 for industry, trade diversion amounted to $168 million while trade creation was only $30 million, on the legal tariff basis (table 6). Yet, the overall welfare effects of the Common Market are strongly positive.

(iv) In agriculture, on the contrary, it is the conventional effects which dominate. The principal welfare benefits derive from trade creation (and these are concentrated in three countries: Honduras, Nicaragua, and Costa Rica). The nonconventional effects are modest, and economies of scale benefits are forced to zero as the sector is assumed to have constant return to scale. The foreign exchange effect is actually negative for all countries except El Salvador. In essence, in agriculture integration resulted in a traditional improvement of efficiency through freeing internal trade in the CACM. Examination of the detailed computational results indicates that the principal effect was increased importation of rice and beans into Honduras, Nicaragua, and Costa Rica from El Salvador. Hence, El Salvador enjoyed foreign exchange gains while the other three countries enjoyed traditional gains from trade creation.

(v) Of the three nontraditional effects in the industrial sector, savings of foreign exchange is by far the most important, followed by the labor opportunity cost effect. Gains from economies of scale are relatively limited, although even this effect is more important than the traditional influences of trade creation and diversion in producing net benefits. The modest results for scale economies may reflect a downward

bias in the scale parameters used; for most sectors the empirically estimated returns to scale were zero, and yet it would seem that returns to
scale would be important in many of these sectors.

(vi) Trade suppression in the industrial sector is approximately
as important as trade diversion in magnitude and welfare impact. This
result indicates that negative trade creation is a prevalent feature,
suggesting a trend toward overall import-substitution industrialization
within the CACM. Despite the decline in the overall weighted average
tariff, the tariff for specific industrial sectors frequently rises,
yielding economically germane "trade suppression" when overall import
propensity declines.

(vii) The intermediate demand effects are negative on balance.
The results show that the welfare cost of increased import requirements
for intermediate inputs, attributable to integration, outweigh the gains
from increased use of labor with low opportunity cost and exploitation
of economies of scale in the domestic production of intermediate input
requirements. However, the intermediate demand effect merely dampens
the overall welfare gains to a limited extent, reducing them on the order
of 10 percent below what they would be otherwise (see tables 8 and 9).

(viii) These various patterns of composition of the welfare effects
are generally consistent for both 1968 and 1972, and for the legal versus
adjusted tariff basis. This stability of the nature of the results provides some reassurance about the reliability of the estimates.

3.   Distribution of Gains Among Countries

Tables 8 and 9 present the total annual welfare gains to each country,
on both the legal and adjusted tariff bases. These results indicate that
all five countries, including Honduras, had positive welfare gains from
integration in 1968, and that all four of the remaining participants had
even higher welfare gains by 1972. Even Honduras, the country with the
lowest absolute and relative net benefits, had gains in GDP of 0.67 percent,[36] a substantial amount for a customs union welfare gain. It is
noteworthy that although Honduran benefits in the agriculture and mining
sectors were more important relative to those in industry than in the
other countries, Honduran primary sector gains were still only one-fourth
the size of the industrial gains. This fact casts doubt on the common
viewpoint that Honduras became merely a raw materials supplier to the
other CACM countries but achieved no integration benefits in the industrial
sector.

The percentage participation of each country in total net welfare
gains is shown in table 10. These percentages are the averages of those
for the legal and adjusted tariff bases. For comparison the table also
shows the share of each country in the regional totals of population,
GDP, industrial value added, and exports.

It is evident from table 10 that the net benefits of integration were
not evenly distributed as of 1968. In terms of the equity of distribution
probably the best indicator is the ratio of share in benefits to share
in population. This ratio ranged from a high of 1.35 for Guatemala to a

low of 0.35 for Honduras. The country ranking of relative participation in net benefits for 1968 from most to least favored, was the following: Guatemala, El Salvador, Costa Rica, Nicaragua, and Honduras. This ranking is unchanged whether the benefit share is taken as a ratio of share in regional population or GDP.

It is particularly noteworthy that the ranking of countries by relative gains from integration in 1968 was precisely the same as their ranking by absolute size of industrial production as well as absolute size of GDP. By contrast, the ranking bore no relationship to country rank by per capita income.[37] This fact suggests that, at least in the initial stages, economic integration among developing countries confers the greater advantage on the countries with the larger economies and industrial sectors in absolute terms--not on the "most developed" countries in terms of per capita income.

Finally, the distribution of benefits in 1968 must be said to have been quite unequal, although all countries did gain from integration. Net benefits per capita were approximately four times as high in Guatemala as in Honduras. These results thus suggest that there was a reasonable economic basis for the complaint of Honduras that its share in the benefits of integration was unduly low.

The distribution of benefits by 1972 represents a very different situation. For the four remaining members, the benefits from the Common Market were distributed very closely relative to the share of each country in the total population. This fact may be seen in the figures in table 10 reporting the ratio of share in net benefits to share of population--all of which are close to unity.

The ranking of countries by relative share in benefits changed between 1968 and 1972: El Salvador became first and Guatemala second; Nicaragua moved to third and Costa Rica fell to fourth place, based on benefit share relative both to share in population and share in GDP. However, the ranking by 1972 meant much less than in 1968, because all four countries had very similar relative shares in 1972.[38]

Two crucial patterns may be seen in these results. First, the equality of distribution of benefits improved greatly between 1968 and 1972. In addition to the "relative share ratios," the figures for the absolute sum of percentage differences bear out this fact (section III of table 10). This sum measures the total absolute deviation of benefit shares from regional shares in other variables. For each of the four variables this measure showed more equal distribution in 1972 than in 1968, and the improvement was especially marked using the population share measure. Second, by 1972 the ranking of relative country shares in benefits no longer obeyed a strict relationship to the absolute size of industrial output and GDP.

These trends suggest two conclusions of the utmost importance. First, the Common Market of four probably had much more fundamental stability in 1972 than did the Common Market of five in 1968, because its pressure for internal redistribution should have decreased. Second, the advantage of a country with a larger GDP and industrial base, in common markets among developing countries, would appear to diminish over time, at least on the basis of the Central American experience. Both of these inferences suggest that Honduras might have enjoyed an increasing share in the integration benefits, as did the other countries with below average relative participation in 1968 (Nicaragua and Costa Rica), if it had remained inside the Common Market.

F. Dynamic Effects

An evaluation of the magnitude and distribution of welfare gains from the Central American Common Market cannot be based solely on the static effects considered above. Although much more difficult to measure and even to specify conceptually, the dynamic welfare gains must also be taken into account.

1. Structural Transformation

One of the prime objectives of economic integration in Central America was to establish a market large enough to permit the introduction and expansion of manufacturing activity to the point where the economies of the region would no longer remain so dependent on the export of traditional raw materials. There are two steps to evaluation of gains from this structural transformation. The first is to determine the extent to which integration increased the share of manufacturing industry in the economies relative to that of primary export production. The second is to establish the welfare gain, if any, associated with such a transformation.

a. Cross-Country Patterns

One method of measuring the impact of integration on the weight of industry in the economy is to apply cross-country norms which have been empirically estimated relating industrial share in GNP to important economic variables. By comparing the share of industry in GNP with that which would be expected on the basis of standard economic variables--both before and after integration--insight may be gained about the impact of integration on the structure of the economy.

Chenery and Syrqum[39] have conducted recent statistical tests for a large number of countries relating the share of manufacturing in GDP to per capita gross national product, population, foreign capital inflow, and trend over time. It is possible to apply the equations for these relationships to the relevant variables for Central American countries to estimate what the share of manufacturing would be expected to be on the basis of cross-country experience. Once the expected share of manufacturing is estimated, the actual share is compared with it. If integration caused a structural transformation favoring industry, then during the period of integration the Central American countries should have experienced an increasingly larger share of manufacturing in their GDP compared with that expected on the basis of the cross-country equations.

Garcia Marenco has carried out statistical tests along these lines to examine the structural effect of integration in Central America; the principal results are reported in table C-16 of appendix C. These results are mainly inconclusive, because most of the parameters are not statistically significant. Nevertheless they contain patterns suggesting a net increase in the share of manufacturing as the result of integration, as discussed in appendix C.

b. Direct Estimation

The basic cost-benefit methodology developed in this chapter provides a more direct basis for estimating structural transformation than the use of cross-country patterns. In obtaining the static welfare estimates reported above it was necessary to compute, by sector, the change in output attributable to integration, both direct and indirect. The gross increase or decrease in output due to direct effects are described in the discussion of methodology (above and in appendix C). The calculations for these effects provide a direct indication of the net impact of integration on the structure of production.

Tables C-13 and C-14 of appendix C present the estimates of change in output attributable to integration by three-digit CIIU sectors for industry and for the raw materials sectors. The estimates are for 1972 except for the case of Honduras, where data refer to 1968, the last year of that country's full participation in the Common Market. Although the specific industrial patterns of these effects are not of direct relevance to the issue of structural effects, and the net increase in output due to intermediate demand transformation, it is worth noting some of the detailed trends. The most important sectors in terms of output gain due to integration were: (i) basic metals and metal products (joint sector 371, 372, 381) in all countries except Honduras; (ii) chemicals (sectors 351 and 352) in all countries; (iii) textiles (321) and paper (341 in Guatemala, El Salvador, and Honduras; (iv) food products (311) in all countries except El Salvador; and (v) petroleum refining (353) in Nicaragua.

The fact that some of these most important industries are the same for most or all of the countries suggests that a substantial portion of the integration effect was derived from general import-substitution patterns common to all five countries (through "trade suppression") rather than from new production for trade specialization within the Common Market.[40]

To assess structural transformation the relevant figures concern output change for manufacturing industry as a whole compared with that for primary products. These figures are shown in table 11. It is evident from the table that the increase in industrial value added due to integration was much larger than that for agriculture and mining.

These changes in value added do not represent welfare gains; it would be inappropriate to compare them directly with GDP and conclude that the resulting ratio represented the proportion of GDP which would not exist in the absence of integration. In the absence of integration some or all of the investment which went into these activities would have gone into other activities so that GDP would not have been fully less than actual levels by the amount of "changes in value added attributable to integration." Nevertheless these changes do give a clear indication of the effect of integration on the sectoral structure of production.

The proportional distribution of activity with and without integration may be examined by subtracting the changes in output attributable to integration from the actual sectoral output data for 1972 (for Honduras, 1968).

98

Table 11. Change in Output Attributable to Integration, Primary and Secondary Sectors ($CA million)

Country	Year	Gross Output			Value Added		
		Industry	Agriculture & Mining Total	Cotton[a]	Industry	Agriculture & Mining Total	Cotton[a]
Guatemala	1972	219.2	7.0	1.5	95.6	6.3	1.1
El Salvador	1972	176.1	9.6	1.9	69.7	8.7	1.4
Honduras	1968	31.5	4.4	.3	7.6	4.1	.2
Nicaragua	1972	96.2	3.8	.2	37.0	3.2	.2
Costa Rica	1972	104.4	1.7	.4	33.4	1.5	.3

[a]Cotton shown separately as the only traditional raw material export good with measured output effects due to integration.

SOURCE: Tables C-13 and C-14, appendix C. Value added computed by applying to each three-digit CIIU sector the ratio of value added to gross output from the 1968 industrial census (with Guatemalan coefficients applied for El Salvador), as reported in SIECA, VI Compendio Estadístico Centroamericano, 1975 (Guatemala City: SIECA, 1975), pp. 163-69). Agricultural-mining value added/gross output ratios based on Grupo Asesor de la F.A.O. para la Integración Económica Centro-americana (GAFICA), "Plan Perspectivo Para el Desarrollo y la Integración de la Agricultura en Centroamerica," vol. II, part B, mimeographed (Guatemala City: GAFICA, 1972), table B10a. Ratio for cotton is based on part H, table H2.

The resulting hypothetical data indicate the extent to which the percent-age breakdown of value added between industry and primary production was changed due to integration. The results of this exercise are shown in table 12. The table presents the calculation first for the breakdown between industry and all primary products, and second, for that between industry and the raw materials export sectors.

It is clear from table 12 that integration had an important effect in shifting the composition of production away from the primary and toward the secondary sector. For Central America as a whole, the estimates indicate that integration raised the share of industry in the two sectors from 33 percent to 39 percent. Considering the export sectors of industry and raw materials alone, integration raised industry's share from 54 percent to 62 percent. Even for Honduras, the country most concerned that integration was insufficiently stimulating its transformation toward industry, the table indicates that the integration raised the share of industry in the combined primary and secondary sectors from 22.6 percent to 24.0 percent.

Moreover, the extent of these shifts is understated by the ap-proach used. If instead it were assumed that some of the "output due to integration" would have taken place in other activities without integra-tion, then the appropriate "hypothetical" base for comparison might in-volve substantially higher output levels in agriculture but only modestly higher levels in industry (that is, along the lines prior to integration), shifting the composition of the hypothetical base for comparison even further toward the primary sector and therefore yielding an even greater measure of the rise in industry's share in the two sectors because of integration.

c.   Welfare Gains

The preceding analysis establishes that integration played an important role in moving the Central American economies away from primary production toward manufacturing industry.

However, there is a second step remaining in the identification of the resulting dynamic benefits: a relationship must be established between structure of the economy and economic welfare. There is no generally accepted methodology relating the two. Even the advocates of import-substituting industrialization (such as Prebisch) have never specified the economic welfare gain associated with each percentage increase in the share of industry in GDP, and many recent studies question whether this type of industrialization in developing countries has in fact generally been beneficial or costly and inefficient.

Because of the importance attached to structural transformation by Central American policymakers (see for example the discussion in chapter 2), this chapter attempts to develop a measure of its welfare benefits. The model for this purpose is presented in appendix C. In essence the method captures the phenomenon of risk in producing traditional raw ma-terial exports which are noted for their wide fluctuations due to cycles in world prices as well as annual variations in domestic production. The model asks the following question, Given avoidance of risk, how much lower average output in a low-risk activity would be considered

Table 12. Change in Economic Structure Attributable to Integration, 1972
(value added, $CA million)[a]
(percentages in parentheses)

Change	Guatemala	El Salvador	Honduras	Nicaragua	Costa Rica	CACM-5
I. Industry versus primary products						
Actual						
Industry	344.3 (35.8)	220.1 (42.7)	82.7 (24.0)	186.2 (41.4)	227.5 (48.5)	1,060.8 (38.7)
Agriculture and mining	618.0 (64.2)	295.4 (57.3)	261.9 (76.0)	263.2 (58.6)	241.8 (51.5)	1,680.3 (61.3)
Total	962.3	515.5	344.6	449.4	469.3	2,841.1
Hypothetical[b]						
Industry	248.7 (28.9)	150.4 (34.4)	75.1 (22.6)	149.2 (36.9)	194.1 (44.7)	817.5 (33.0)
Agriculture and mining	611.7 (71.1)	286.7 (65.6)	257.8 (77.4)	260.0 (63.1)	240.3 (55.3)	1,656.5 (67.0)
Total	860.4	437.1	332.9	409.2	434.4	2,474.0

Table 12 (Continued)

Change	Guatemala	El Salvador	Honduras	Nicaragua	Costa Rica	CACM-5
II. Industry versus raw materials export sectors[c]						
Actual						
Industry	344.3 (68.4)	220.1 (60.5)	82.7 (45.4)	186.2 (66.3)	227.5 (58.1)	1,060.8 (61.6)
Raw materials exports	159.1 (31.6)	143.5 (39.5)	99.4 (54.6)	94.5 (33.7)	164.1 (41.9)	660.6 (38.4)
Total	503.4	363.6	182.1	280.7	391.6	1,721.4
Hypothetical[b]						
Industry	248.7 (61.2)	150.4 (51.4)	75.1 (43.1)	149.2 (61.3)	194.1 (50.0)	817.5 (54.3)
Raw materials exports	158.0 (38.8)	142.1 (48.6)	99.2 (56.9)	94.3 (38.7)	193.8 (50.0)	687.4 (45.7)
Total	406.7	292.5	174.3	243.5	387.9	1,504.9

[a] 1972 except for Honduras, for which data refer to 1968.
[b] Actual less change due to integration (table 3-14).
[c] Raw materials exports: bananas, coffee, cotton, sugar.

SOURCE: Actual data--SIECA, VI Compendio Estadístico Centroamericano, 1975 (Guatemala City: SIECA, 1975), pp. 278-82; 364-73.
Hypothetical--actual minus change in value added shown in table 11. For raw materials export case, only cotton subtracted to estimate hypothetical.

to generate the same level of welfare as a higher level of average output but with higher fluctuation in a high-risk activity? Under the assumption of a "utility function" frequently employed in welfare analysis (in which utility increases as the logarithm of income), this method permits quantification of the welfare gain associated with a given shift in the percentage distribution of output between low-risk and high-risk activities.

Table 13 shows the results of the estimation of welfare gain attributable to structural transformation for Central America on the basis of this methodology. These results apply the formulas developed in appendix C to the data in table 12 showing the change in percentage composition of industrial production relative to traditional raw material export activities. For the estimation it is assumed that the risk parameter is +0.2 for traditional raw materials exports and 0.0 for industrial.[41] As shown in table C-15 of appendix C, the percentage deviation around the time-trend line for export earnings in the four most important raw materials crops (bananas, sugar, coffee, and cotton) is on the order of 20 percent (excluding the extremely high fluctuation for Honduran cotton exports).

The results in table 13 must be considered to be primarily "indicative" rather than definitive, given the novelty of the methodological approach, the fact that risk avoidance may be only one aspect of gains from structural transformation (at least as perceived by policymakers), and the very simple assumptions involved. Nevertheless, the results do show an important pattern: they are all extremely small compared with the nontraditional static welfare gains estimated above. This result suggests that the general conclusions regarding magnitude and distribution of integration benefits based on those effects discussed above should remain valid even after the incorporation of dynamic welfare gains from industrial transformation--either on the specific basis proposed here or on a more refined approach following the same general lines of the analysis of risk avoidance.

2. Investment Effects

A second dynamic welfare effect of integration is its impact on investment. The expansion of national markets to a regional dimension should have stimulated the rate of investment in Central America, since the wider market offered better prospects of profit for both domestic and foreign firms deciding whether to invest in the region. Once again there are two steps required to reach conclusions about welfare gains; first, the increase in investment attributable to integration must be determined, and second, it is necessary to decide what are the net welfare gains associated with each unit of increased investment.

a. Change in Investment due to Integration

To examine the first of these steps, a sample survey of industrial firms was conducted in each of the five Central American countries.[42] The crucial content of the survey was a series of questions inquiring about the impact of the Common Market's formation on the investment decisions of the firm. The most senior financial officer of the firm available was interviewed for this purpose.

Table 13. Annual Welfare Gains Associated with Structural
Transformation, 1972

	Guatemala	El Salvador	Honduras (1968)	Nicaragua	Costa Rica
Weighted risk factor[a]					
Actual	.0632	.0790	.1092	.0674	.0838
Hypothetical without integration	.0776	.0972	.1138	.0774	.1000
Y_1/Y_2 [b]	1.0012	1.0008	1.0004	1.0008	1.0015
Welfare gain[c] ($CA thousands)	604	290	70	22	59

[a]Equals .2 times fraction of industry plus traditional raw material
exports comprised by the latter. See table 12.
[b]See equation (29), appendix C.
[c]Equals $[(Y_1/Y_2) - 1]$ times sum of industry, raw materials export value
added.

The sample design did not attempt to be sufficiently rigorous from
a statistical viewpoint to result in a reliably representative survey. Instead, in view of the limited resources for the survey, the sample was
designed (i) to allocate the number of interviews by country and industrial sector in proportion to the share of each sector in the industrial
value added of the region; and (ii) within each sector to include the most
important firms, in order to cover the maximum amount of investment with
a limited number of interviews. (Altogether, 142 firms were interviewed.)

The interviewers asked the firms to identify their total investment
during the periods 1960-68 and 1969-73, and then to state what portion
of this investment would probably have taken place even in the absence
of the Central American Common Market. By residual, the amount of investment attributable to integration was derived. The analysis necessarily
constituted an opinion survey with regard to the hypothetical question
of how much of the investment would have occurred without the CACM. However, the survey also included a question on the percentage of sales directed to exports to the Common Market, and the answer to this question
tended to confirm the subjective responses on the percentage of investment
attributable to the existence of the Market.

Table 14 reports the results of this survey. Two striking features emerge from the table. First, the proportion of investment attributed to economic integration by the firms was very high, except in the cases of El Salvador and Costa Rica. Second, the highest reported influences of integration on investment were in Honduras and Nicaragua, where over 60 percent of investment during the period 1960-73 was attributed to the existence of the Common Market. Yet these two countries were precisely the ones with the lowest relative share in integration benefits as of 1968 on the basis of the static welfare measures, and Honduras has been the country which has acted the most dramatically--by withdrawing from the Market--under the presumption that its gains from integration were inadequate relative to those of other members.

The table also indicates that approximately 45 percent of the investent attributable to integration came from foreign investments, reaching 69 percent in Costa Rica but only 23 percent in Honduras.[43]

In order to throw light on the reliability of these results, table 14 also includes an estimate of total industrial investment for the five countries from 1960 to 1968. The investment in that period by the sampled firms is also reported, and the ratio of sample to total investment is reported (in column G). One would expect the results to be more reliable in the countries where the sample constituted a higher proportion of total investment. Under this criterion, the three countries with the highest reported influence of integration--Honduras, Nicaragua, and Guatemala--were also those for which the results may be less reliable because the sampled firms represented smaller fractions of total investment than in the other two countries.

The direction of bias in the results for the effect of integration on investment is probably upward, especially for Honduras and Nicaragua. By including the largest firms first, the sample probably was biased toward those firms engaged in activity with regionwide dimensions. However, the large estimates for the impact of integration on industrial output discussed above and reported in tables 11 and 12 lend support to the large investment effects encountered in the investment survey, reducing the likelihood that the investment effects are seriously biased upward. Indeed, based on the estimates for the effect of integration on industrial structure, it would seem instead that for the two countries with relatively low "investment effects" as reported in table 14, El Salvador and Costa Rica, the investment effect estimates are downward biased rather than the reverse. Despite these qualifications the survey results suggest an extremely large effect of integration on industrial investment, especially in Honduras, Nicaragua, and Guatemala.

b. Welfare Effects

Some considerations on the welfare gains from the investment impact follow. First, if the investment is from outside the region, then the future stream of profits will accrue to foreigners, not nationals. In this case it is therefore only the wage bill resulting from additional economic activity that may confer a gain in the country. Even this gain would be nonexistent if workers were paid wages equal to their opportunity cost to the economy of the country. In the case of Central America, however, the industrial wage exceeds the opportunity cost of labor, so that

Table 14. Evidence on the Effect of Integration on Industrial Investment, Central America, 1960-73 (1,000 $CA) (survey results)

Country	A Number of Firms Interviewed	B Total Investment, 1960-73	C Investment Attributed to CACM	D Percent Attributed to CACM (C/B)	E Investment, 1960-68	F Total Industrial Investment, 1960-68	G Sample Investment, as % of Total (E/F)	H Foreign Capital as % of Column C
Guatemala	39	53,561	15,541	40.9	21,891	438,000	5.0	44.3
El Salvador	31	93,460	11,411	13.9	33,392	207,000	16.1	45.1[a]
Honduras	12	32,450	12,657	63.9	12,450	119,000	10.5	23.4
Nicaragua	27	64,600	24,358	60.5	31,100	364,000	8.5	43.2
Costa Rica	33	165,150	22,704	15.9	40,447	240,000	16.8	69.5

[a]Assumed equal to the average for the other four countries. Direct data not available.

SOURCE: Columns A through E; H: Horacio Bobadilla, "Encuesta Selectiva de las Inversiones de Centroamérica en el Subsector Manufacturero," SIECA/75/PES/IE/12, mimeographed (Guatemala City: SIECA, 1975). Column F: derived from Rosenthal, whose data for the eight-year period, 1962-63, are multiplied by 1.125 to obtain an estimate for the nine-year period, 1960-68. Gert Rosenthal, "The Role of Private Foreign Investment in the Development of the Central American Common Market," 1973.

a portion of the wage bill proportional to the excess of the wage over the shadow price of labor would be appropriate to count as a welfare gain from extra foreign investment. [44] In principle, another welfare gain would arise in tax payments by the firm, but in practice, Central American tax incentive systems have been so generous (and the underlying tax rates so low) that this gain is not important.

Second, if the extra investment is undertaken by domestic entrepreneurs, there is a "capital scarcity" welfare gain in addition to the gains due to the excess of the wage bill over the social opportunity cost of labor. This gain derives from the difference between the rate of return to domestic capital and the opportunity cost of the source of the extra capital.

If the funds are borrowed from abroad, there will be a welfare gain per unit of capital equal to the difference between the rate of return and the borrowing cost. If the funds come out of domestic savings, then essentially the impact is to reduce current consumption in return for investment. This tradeoff will generate a welfare gain if the rate of return on investment is higher than the time discount rate for consumption, and this condition will in fact generally hold true because imperfections in the capital market as well as risk maintain the average profit rate well above the interest rate for consumption (that is, the interest rate at which households would be prepared to give up more current consumption if firms wishes to borrow more funds).

Third, the welfare gains from the investment effect of integration should account for the extra investment which would have taken place in other activities in the absence of integration. That is, some portion of the investment funds going into activities attributable to integration would have gone into other activities in the absence of integration.

Fourth, the benefits from the investment effect must not be double counted with those identified under the static welfare effects. This possibility arises for the effect of the labor welfare gain associated with investment attributable to integration. That is, the static welfare analysis already identified the same type of "labor opportunity cost" welfare gain, and the estimate under the concept of investment effect may be an alternative but not an additive gain. The problem does not arise for the "capital scarcity welfare gain," which is a gain unique to the investment effect.

Although an exact formulation of the welfare gain from increased investment is by no means straightforward in theoretical terms, in light of the above discussion a reasonable specification of gain would be as follows:

(i) First, consider increased foreign investment. If this increase is known, then its resulting increase in output may be calculated by applying a capital-output ratio. (For example, if foreign investment increases by $50 million and the capital-output ratio is 2.0, annual production will rise by $10 million.) Then, a portion of this extra output will accrue to the national economy as welfare gain: that portion representing wage payments in excess of the social opportunity cost of labor hired.

(ii) Second, in the case of domestic investment attributable to integration, the welfare gain will include the same gain from labor earnings in excess of social cost, but in addition will include the welfare gain associated with the scarcity price of capital. The latter equals the difference between the rate of return and the opportunity cost of the funds, either from borrowing abroad or from the reduction of domestic consumption. It is not unreasonable to assume that both sources will have a similar opportunity cost, such as a 10 percent discount rate (for consumption) or interest rate (for borrowing abroad).

Appendix C sets forth the precise formulations for these calculations. The results of the estimations are shown in table 15. The calculations refer to cumulative investment over the period 1960-73 due to integration. The figure for extra investment due to integration in this period[45] is arrived at by first estimating total investment in the period and then applying to this total investment the percentages attributable to integration found in the survey, as reported in table 14. The breakdown between incremental foreign and domestic investment is based on the proportions of the survey, also reported in table 14. The computations employ an assumed incremental capital output ratio of 1.5, because estimated capital output ratios from the 1968 industrial census are too low (less than unity) to be accepted at face value.

The rate of return used is 20 percent, and the opportunity cost of funds used is 10 percent. The 20 percent rate of return is, if anything, understated, in view of the extremely high apparent profit rates encountered in the 1968 industrial census data.[46] Thus, $1.00 of investment is worth $2.00 of consumption. This fact may be seen by considering that $1.00 invested will yield an annual stream of 20 cents, which, discounted at the 10 percent consumption discount rate, is worth $2.00.

In this particular case the present discounted welfare value of extra investment due to integration is exactly equal to the face value of the extra investment. That is, using consumption price as the basic unit, the cost of the extra investment of, say, ΔI, is its face value; but its benefit is twice the face value, $2 \Delta I$, leaving a net welfare gain of the face value, ΔI. More generally the present value of the welfare gain from I extra investment will be $\Delta I \left(\frac{\rho}{i} - 1 \right)$ where "ρ" is the rate of return and "i" is the opportunity cost of the funds required.

Table 15 shows two variants to account for the possibility that, for the domestic investment effect, part of the investment attributed to integration comes at the expense of investment which would have occurred in alternative activities, rather than drawing on funds from abroad or from consumption. The "100 percent extra" case assumes that all the domestic investment effect is incremental, whereas the "50 percent" case assumes that only half of the welfare gain is realized because the other half of the extra investment attributed to integration came at the expense of investment which would have occurred even in the absence of integration.

For foreign investment it is assumed that 100 percent of the investment effect is incremental. One of the chief qualitative judgments on the CACM has been that it attracted foreign investment that otherwise would not have taken place. There is no reason to believe that the extra investment attributed by foreign firms in the survey to integration would

Table 15. Annual Welfare Gains from Increased Investment Attributable to Integration, 1973
(million CA pesos in average 1960-73 prices)

	Guatemala	El Salvador	Honduras	Nicaragua	Costa Rica	CACM-5
I. Basic effects						
Δ Foreign investment, 1960-73	137.3	22.1	29.5	150.8	51.5	391.2
Δ Domestic investment, 1960-73	172.7	26.9	96.6	198.2	22.6	517.0
II. Welfare effects						
Foreign investment labor opportunity cost	13.00	2.14	3.07	10.46	2.68	31.35
Domestic investment						
(1) 100% additional:						
Labor opportunity cost	16.35	2.60	10.05	13.75	1.18	43.93
Capital scarcity	17.27	2.69	9.66	19.82	2.26	51.70
(2) 50% additional:						
Labor opportunity cost	8.17	1.30	5.02	6.87	0.59	21.97
Capital scarcity	8.63	1.35	4.33	9.91	1.13	25.85
Total						
(1) 100% case	46.62	7.43	22.78	44.03	6.12	126.98
(2) 50% case	29.80	4.79	12.42	27.24	4.40	78.65

SOURCES: Calculated according to text equations based on following data:
Private investment: SIECA, VI Compendio Estadístico Centroamericano, 1975 (Guatemala City:
SIECA, 1975), p. 361.
Fraction due to integration, and fraction foreign: table 14.
Unskilled wage bill as share of value added and industrial wage: SIECA, VI Compendio Estadístico,
p. 163, 171.
Shadow price of labor: table 3.

have been available from alternative foreign enterprises investing in activities limited to individual countries, in the absence of integration.

The magnitudes of the investment welfare effects relative to those found under the concept of static gains and structural transformation are discussed below, as is the problem of possible double counting with regard to the labor opportunity cost welfare gain.

3. Competition

A final dynamic effect of integration is its influence on efficiency through an increase in competition. Appendix H to this volume is a study of industrial concentration in Central America. The study finds that when Central America is viewed as a whole free trade area, the degree of its industrial concentration is much lower than is the average concentration for each country viewed in isolation. While this result does not lead to a quantitative estimate of a welfare gain from integration, it is nevertheless highly suggestive that the freeing of trade within the CACM did provide a dynamic welfare gain through the resulting reduction in oligopolistic power from very high concentration levels in the individual country markets to much lower levels for the CACM as a whole.

4. Total Welfare Effects: Dynamic and Static

Because of the exploratory nature of the methodology and the basically illustrative nature of the data, estimates of dynamic welfare effects are much less reliable than those for the static welfare effects. Nevertheless, it is essential to obtain an overall estimate of the welfare gains from integration which includes both the dynamic and the static effects, given the importance of dynamic effects. On the basis of the average of the static gains shown in tables 8 and 9, the structural transformation gains of table 13, and the investment-effect gains of table 15, the totals of the dynamic and static effects are shown in table 16. These results represent ongoing annual welfare gains from integration.

Table 16 deducts from the sum of the three effects the overlapping welfare gain from labor wages in excess of opportunity cost in the static estimates on the one hand and the dynamic investment effects on the other. [47]

The results for Honduras in table 16 require special comment. The static welfare analysis based on trade propensities treats Honduras in 1972 as outside of the Common Market and therefore assumes zero gains from integration in that year. However, the dynamic analysis takes account of permanent changes in the structure of production and level of capital stock in the Honduran economy due to integration, and these ongoing dynamic effects are presumed to continue to generate annual welfare gains even after the withdrawal of the country from the Common Market. An overall assessment of Honduran gains relative to those of the other countries must consider both the static welfare gains and the structural and investment gains together. For this reason the table includes the

1968 static gains along with the 1972 dynamic gains for Honduras. As such the data are hybrid "actual" and "hypothetical" concepts; the dynamic gains are estimates of actual ongoing structural effects, while the 1968 static gains may be interpreted as a lower-bound estimate of the static gains which Honduras would be enjoying if the country were still inside the Common Market. Therefore the total is an overestimate of the actual Honduran gains from integration as of 1972, but an underestimate of the gains which Honduras could have expected for that year if the country had remained in the Common Market.

Two general conclusions emerge from table 16. First, the inclusion of dynamic welfare benefits approximately doubles the estimate of the gains of integration compared with the estimate based on static effects alone—raising the welfare benefits from integration to approximately 4 percent of Central America's GDP annually (3 percent in the 50 percent incremental domestic investment case). Second, the relative positions of Honduras and Nicaragua improve dramatically in the distribution of total benefits, mainly because these two countries are the ones for which a very high investment effect was found in the informal investment survey. At the same time, the relative position of El Salvador drops markedly, again because of the results found in the investment survey.

These "total" welfare estimates, and especially the distribution among members, must be viewed as less reliable than the static welfare estimates. Therefore, the main result of the incorporation of dynamic effects should be construed to be the following: (i) the dynamic benefits raise total benefits very substantially, perhaps doubling the overall estimate, and (ii) inclusion of dynamic effects makes the relative positions of Honduras and Nicaragua appear to be much more favorable than under the static analysis alone.

G.   Conclusions and Policy Implications

On the basis of the analysis of static and dynamic welfare gains from Central American integration the conclusions of this chapter are the following:

(i) The welfare gains from economic integration in Central America have been very substantial. Annual gains appear to be on the order of 3 to 4 percent of GDP for the whole region.

(ii) Two sources account for most of these gains. First, the static welfare gain derived from economizing on scarce foreign exchange by importing from partners goods that otherwise would have been imported from outside the region and by increasing exports to partners. Second, the dynamic welfare gain attributable to increasing total investment, both foreign and domestic, above what it would have been in the absence of integration.

(iii) The traditional measures of gains from customs unions—the welfare effects of trade creation and trade diversion—are negligible compared with these other effects. Three nontraditional effects are more important—increased use of labor with low opportunity cost, increased

Table 16. Total Annual Welfare Effects, Static and Dynamic, 1972
(1,000 $CA)[a]

Effects	Guatemala	El Salvador	Honduras	Nicaragua	Costa Rica	Total
I. Static	43,275	33,544	4,308[b]	16,479	13,080	110,686
II. Dynamic						
A. Structural transformation	604	290	70	22	59	1,045
B. Investment effect						
(1) 100% case	46,620	7,430	22,780	44,030	6,120	126,980
(2) 50% case	29,800	4,790	12,420	27,240	4,400	78,650
III. Less: labor opportunity cost double-counting						
(1) 100% case	-13,821	-4,742	-1,471	-4,101	-2,786	-26,921
(2) 50% case	-13,821	-3,440	-1,471	-4,101	-2,786	-25,619
IV. Total, net						
(1) 100% investment case	76,678	36,522	25,687	56,430	16,473	211,790
(2) 50% investment case	59,858	35,184	15,327	39,640	14,753	164,762
V. Percent share						
(1) 100% investment case	36.2	17.2	12.1	26.6	7.8	100.0
(2) 50% investment case	36.3	21.4	9.3	24.1	9.0	---
VI. Ratio, share in gains/share in population						
(1) 100% investment case	1.03	0.76	0.71	1.99	.67	---
(2) 50% investment case	1.03	0.94	0.55	1.80	.78	---

[a]Dynamic estimates for investment effect are for annual welfare effects of cumulative investment impact of Common Market, 1960-73.
[b]1968.

SOURCES: I: tables 8, 9 average; table 10. II: tables 13, 15.

exploitation of economies of scale, and improved welfare from the structural transformation of the economies toward industry--but these effects are also of limited importance relative to the foreign exchange savings and the investment effects.

(iv) The static welfare gains indicate that in the initial phase of integration there was an exact correlation between the rankings of the countries by relative share in integration gains and absolute size of the economy and industrial sector, but that later (by 1972) this correspondence had been broken--and in addition the distribution of gains was much more even. This result suggests that customs unions among developing countries favor the partners with the largest economies and industrial bases--not necessarily those with the highest per capita incomes--but that this advantage is only temporary, and that after longer periods of integration the gains will be more evenly dispersed.

(v) The dynamic welfare effects indicate that precisely the two countries with the lowest relative shares in static gains--Honduras and Nicaragua--had the most dramatic dynamic gains from increased investment attributable to integration. This result suggests that while the countries with the smallest industrial bases, in a customs union among developing countries, may have the smallest relative participation in industrial expansion based on changes in trade shares due to integration (and especially increased industrial exports to partners), they may nevertheless enjoy the largest relative impact of stimulus to investment on their economies. This phenomenon may represent the fact that investors are anticipating future growth through integration that does not make itself evident yet in data for trade among partners.

(vi) All five countries enjoyed positive gains from economic integration.

(vii) Only for the case of Honduras can an unambiguous case be made that the share in gains from integration were low. For all other countries the analysis shows either average or above average relative participation in the gains (Guatemala, El Salvador, and Costa Rica); or, for the case of Nicaragua, the relative gains reverse from a ranking of next to last for static effects alone to first place once dynamic effects are included.

The policy implications which flow from these conclusions seem relatively straightforward. First, the effort to integrate the Central American economies has been well justified since the gains have been very substantial, far above those more conventionally attributed to customs unions. Second, since Honduras was obtaining positive gains prior to withdrawal from the Common Market, it would appear to be in the interest of that country to reenter the integration scheme. By the same token, considering the fact that the other four members continued to enjoy sizable gains even without participation by Honduras, this country should be realistic about the amount of any special treatment that it can expect in return for reentry into the Common Market.

It is possible to carry further these implications to obtain an idea of the order of magnitude of special redistributive benefits which might be appropriate for Honduras in the process of reintegrating that country into the CACM. For background purposes it is useful to consider the mechanism which existed in the past for redistribution within the CACM: the Central American Bank for Economic Integration (CABEI). Table 17 shows the allocation of CABEI loans by country, since the inception of the institution. It is evident from the final column of the table that the share of Honduras in these loans has been higher than that country's share in regional GNP, so that there is already a precedent lending by CABEI that is more than proportionately concentrated on Honduras. (Nicaragua and Costa Rica also have loan shares in excess of GNP shares but by much smaller degrees than in the case of Honduras.)

The crucial questions about redistributive policy are: (i) What should be the size of any redistribution? (ii) Which countries should receive the redistribution? (iii) Which countries should pay for it? and (iv) Which channels should be used for redistribution? From the discussion above, the case for redistribution is clear only for Honduras. At the same time, the other four countries have relatively equal participation in benefits from integration, especially when the changes in ranking under static versus dynamic effects are considered. Therefore all four of the other countries would reasonably be expected to participate as sources of any redistribution, probably on the basis of the share of each in the total GNP of the four.

Table 17. Country Distribution of Lending by the Central American Bank for Economic Integration: Cumulative Total of Loans Approved through 31 December 1973

Country	A Value of Loans	B Percent	C Country's Share in Regional GNP: 1971-72 avg.	D = B/C
Guatemala	81,590	19.0	34.8	0.55
El Salvador	63,918	14.9	19.0	0.78
Honduras	94,338	22.0	11.8	1.86
Nicaragua	88,105	20.5	15.7	1.31
Costa Rica	101,431	23.6	18.7	1.26
Total	429,381	100.0	100.0	

SOURCE: Calculated from SIECA, VI Compendio Estadístico Centroamericano, 1975 (Guatemala City: SIECA, 1975), pp. 408, 358.

How large would an appropriate redistribution be? On the basis of equalizing the participation of Honduras in integration benefits with the average for the other four countries--probably an overly ambitious goal in light of the fact that the CACM of four is progressing even without Honduras--the general order of magnitude for redistribution may be calculated as follows. From table 16, the share of Honduras in total welfare gains relative to the Honduran share in population is 0.71. Therefore a 40 percent increase in Honduran gains would raise that country to a share in benefits approximately equal to its share in population (that is, 1.0/0.79 = 1.41). This calculation uses the case of 100 percent additional investment effect, and the share of Honduras under the 50 percent additional case is less favorable. However, while this fact may understate the amount appropriate for redistribution to Honduras, the fact that the overall estimate uses the 1968 static gains for Honduras understates that country's likely gains under full participation at the current time. These offsetting factors suggest that the 40 percent result is a reasonable, central estimate for an appropriate redistribution to Honduras.

Applying the 40 percent estimate to the total of annual Honduran gains for 1972 (table 16), the resulting estimate of the amount to be redistributed is $10.5 million. This amount would seem well within feasible ranges for redistribution to Honduras under alternative schemes--especially considering the fact that it would represent only 5.6 percent of the total annual integration gains for the other four countries (table 16).

Only the final question remains: Which channel would be ideal for redistribution? The most obvious channel would be the CABEI. Since this institution annually lends on the order of $50 million, if the bank could increase its lending to Honduras by the equivalent of $10 million in grants--or, loans with negligible interest rates and long-term repayment-- then the institution could carry out the redistribution, following past precedent but on a larger scale. Funding for such concessional lending, perhaps through a special loan window, might be available from development assistance entities outside the region.

A second possible channel would be contributions of tariff collections by the other four countries into a fund for redistribution. In 1973, tariff receipts of the four reached $150 million.[48] Therefore it would be sufficient for each of the four countries to contribute 6 percent of its tariff receipts to a fund for redistribution to Honduras in order to generate the $10 million amount in question; however, given the scarcity of budgetary receipts in all of the countries, in political terms this alternative might be less practical to implement than other options.

A third redistributive channel would be to permit Honduras to reenter the Common Market with free entry for its goods into the other countries, but with the maintenance of some tariff level facing goods from the other four partners. Honduran imports from the region were at their peak in 1968 at a level of $49 million.[49] Once trade relations were reestablished with El Salvador, one might expect a somewhat higher level of total imports at the present time, say $60 million. It would require only a 15 percent average tariff against Common Market goods for Honduras to receive in duties the $10 million target sum for redistribution. This rate would constitute somewhat more than a 50 percent exemption from legal tariffs facing the rest of the world (on the basis of table 4). In other words, it could be possible to generate the required redistribution merely through granting free entry to Honduran goods in the CACM but allowing Honduras to charge 50 percent of its external tariff rates for goods imported from the CACM.

These possibilities and especially these magnitudes should be considered indicative rather than definitive. Nevertheless, they do strongly suggest that the reintegration of Honduras into the Common Market on a basis of redistributive policy to raise the country's participation in the union's benefits could be achieved with reasonable amounts of redistribution using existing policy instruments, or new ones which it should be feasible to create.

116

Chapter 3

NOTES

1. These four products are the most important traditional exports of the region. From a base period 1949-51 to a terminal period 1959-61, the average prices of these exports changed by the following amounts: coffee, -16.1 percent; cotton, -37.6 percent; bananas, -10.1 percent; and sugar, -40.6 percent. By contrast, from the base 1959-61 to the terminal period 1967-69, the average price for each product, respectively, changed by: -2.2 percent, +8.3 percent, +9.7 percent, and -20.4 percent. Calculated from IBRD, Commodity Trade and Price Trends (1973 Edition), Report No. EC-166/73 (Washington, D.C.: 1973), pp. 48, 58, 82, 87.

2. SIECA, Acta del Quinto Periodo de Sesiones de la Tercera Reunión de Ministros de Economia de Centroamerica (Managua, Nicaragua: 17-20 November; San José, Costa Rica: 25 November - 2 December 1970). (Guatemala City: SIECA, n.d.), p. 63.

3. More completely, welfare benefits from trade creation equal the increase in consumer surplus (through lower prices) net of the reduction in producer surplus and in government revenue. See appendix C.

4. European Free Trade Association, The Trade Effects of EFTA and the EEC: 1959-1967 (Geneva: EFTA, 1972); and Mordechai E. Kreinin, "Effects of the EEC on Imports of Manufactures," The Economic Journal 82 (September 1972): 897-920.

5. Note that one important influence is the cyclical state of the economy. Nugent shows that Central American import growth rates are very sensitive to GNP growth rates. Imports can actually decline when GNP growth is very slow, yet they grow more rapidly than GNP when GNP growth is rapid. Jeffrey B. Nugent, Economic Integration in Central America: Empirical Investigations (Baltimore: Johns Hopkins University Press, 1974). Hence, if the base year is one of recession and the terminal year one of boom, the observed rise in import propensities will be biased upward. However, the base and terminal years used in this chapter (1958 and 1968) do not present difficulties in this regard. Central American GDP rose 17.5 percent in the three-year period 1955-58; it rose 17.8 percent in the period 1965-68, suggesting 1958 and 1968 were comparable in terms of cyclical status. Calculated from SIECA, VI Compendio Estadístico Centroamericana, 1975 (Guatemala City: SIECA, 1975).

6. W. Arthur Lewis, "Economic Development with Unlimited Supplies of Labor," The Manchester School 22 (May 1954): pp. 139-91.

7. Grupo Asesor de la F.A.O. para la Integración Económica Centroamericana (GAFICA), "Plan Perspectivo Para el Desarrollo y la Integración de la Agricultura en Centroamerica," Vol. 2, "Marco Cuantitativo," part J, "Empleo Agricola," mimeographed (Guatemala City: GAFICA, 1972).

8. GAFICA, "Plan Perspectivo."

117

9.   The positive trade balance effect of the Common Market is a well-
known phenomenon.   For example, Meade's classic work on trade and welfare
states: "If, therefore, a group of countries wish to form a preferential
area for the purpose of extending the protection of their own domestic industries, they are most likely to select for preferential tariff reductions those imports from each other of which important supplies are simultaneously imported from the outside world.   This is likely to protect
the industries of the area from the outside competition of these products . . . and by reducing the total expenditure on imports from the outside world to improve the balance of trade of the preferential area with
the outside world."   James E. Meade, Trade and Welfare (London: Oxford
University Press, 1966), p. 536.

10.   Hollis Chenery and Alan Strout, "Foreign Assistance and Economic
Development," American Economic Review 56(4) (September 1966):   679-733.

11.   See I. M. D. Little and J. A. Mirrlees, Manual of Industrial Project
Analysis in Developing Countries (Paris: OECD, 1969); and United Nations
Industrial Development Organization, Guidelines to Project Evaluation
(Vienna: UNIDO, 1970).

12.   Arnold C. Harberger, "Survey of Literature on Cost-Benefit Analysis for Industrial Project Evaluation." Paper presented at the United Nations Inter-Regional Symposium in Industrial Project Evaluation, Prague,
1965.

13.   The argument is as follows.   The existence of a tariff distorts
the incentive to produce for domestic sale rather than for export sale.
Suppose, for example, that there is a tariff of 25 percent and the market
rate of exchange is one peso per dollar.   Then the domestic price of a
good selling for $1.00 on the world market will be 1.25 pesos.   Therefore
producers will be prepared to devote domestic resources of up to 1.25
pesos to produce the good for home consumption, even though they would
only be willing to put one peso's worth of resources into production of
the good if it were sold abroad.   To eliminate this distortion and give
producers the incentive to devote equal resources per unit of production
to sale at home and abroad, the foreign exchange earned from exporting
$1.00 per unit of the good should be "shadow priced" so that it is given
the worth of 1.25 pesos rather than the market value of one peso.   The
shadow price premium therefore equals the tariff itself.

14.   Edmar Bacha and Lance Taylor, "Foreign Exchange Shadow Prices:
A Critical Review of Current Theories," Quarterly Journal of Economics
85(2) (May 1971).

15.   Note that there is also a problem of political-economy involved
in using the tariff-based approach to the shadow rate for foreign exchange.   The higher are tariffs, the higher will be the measured shadow
price for foreign exchange.   Yet if foreign exchange scarcity is then
used to justify import-substitution programs, and these in turn require
still higher tariffs, then there is a spiral process appearing to justify
higher and higher tariffs.

16.   Bacha and Taylor, "Foreign Exchange Shadow Prices."

17. Note that the "consumption-weighted" tariffs are irrelevant for the shadow price formulas, which are based on trade changes in response to trade price changes and therefore must operate on trade-based weights.

18. Exactly how much lower would depend on the import and export elasticities.

19. By 1972 there did exist some modest efforts toward bilateral tariff agreements among Honduras and Guatemala, Nicaragua, and Costa Rica. In broad terms, however, by that year Honduras was essentially outside of the free trade area.

20. At the three-digit CIIU (International Standard Industrial Classification, ISIC) level for 1958 and 1968, and at the tariff line level (for aggregation to three-digit CIIU) for 1972.

21. GAFICA, "Plan Perspective."

22. The data at the plant level were available for the analysis. For results of the census at a more aggregated level, see SIECA, VI Compendio Estadístico, pp. 159-211.

23. Republica de Guatemala, Arancel de Aduanas (NAUCA): República de Guatemala, 1959 (Guatemala: Unión Tipográfica, 1959); República de El Salvador, Diario Oficial 182 (15), 23 Enero 1959; República de Honduras, Arancel de Aduanas (Tegucigalpa: Ariston, 1958); República de Costa Rica, Ministerio de Economía y Hacienda, Arancel de Aduanas, Ley no. 1738 de 31 de Marzo de 1954 (San José: Imprenta Nacional, 1954); and unpublished SIECA study for Nicaragua.

24. International Monetary Fund, Western Hemisphere Division. Unpublished study on tariff structure in Central America for 1959 and 1967.

25. Guatemala, Ministerio de Economía, Dirección General de Estadística, Departamento de Estudios Especiales y Estadísticas Continuas, I Encuesta Industrial, 1971.

26. These common external tariff estimates are from a special SIECA study using legal tariffs and 1970 unit values. They exclude a 30 percent tariff increase under the San José Protocol, effective June 1968. Given the time lags characteristic of imports, it is unlikely that the impact of this surcharge would have appeared in the import magnitudes for 1968.

27. IMF, Western Hemisphere Division. Unpublished study on tariff structure in Central America for 1959 and 1967.

28. However, the consumption weights enter only at the level of three-digit CIIU categories. To obtain the average tariffs at the three-digit level, import share weights are applied to data at the tariff line level.

29. The reduction from 1968 to 1972 is especially remarkable considering that the tariffs for the latter year include the San Jose´ Protocol's

surcharge of 30 percent on all goods to which the Protocol applies (the large majority).

30. Guatemala, I Encuesta Industrial, 1971.

31. The study from which the data are taken was not designed primarily to measure input-output relationships. Furthermore, for several sectors some inputs from "unspecified sources" were reported. These had to be omitted from the input-output coefficients employed here, due to the unknown sector of origin. Finally, the "using" sectors for which input-output information is available include industrial sectors only, although the "supplying" sectors include agricultural and mining sectors as well.

32. For example, Balassa estimates that the static welfare gains of economic integration in the European Common Market amounted to 0.15 percent of GNP. Adding the dynamic welfare gains from increased investment and economies of scale raised the total estimate to 0.65 percent of GNP. Bela Balassa, "Trade Creation and Diversion in the European Common Market: An Appraisal of the Evidence," in Bela Balassa, ed., European Economic Integration (Amsterdam: North-Holland, 1975), pp. 113–115.

33. Since the magnitude of the benefit is assumed to grow at 5 percent yearly and the discount rate is 10 percent, the present value may be obtained by applying a "net" discount rate equal to the 10 percent gross rate less the 5 percent growth in base, for a net discount rate of 5 percent. An infinite stream discounted at 5 percent annually has a present discounted value twenty times its annual value.

34. Part of the increase was due to inflation. If the United States wholesale price index may be considered representative for the movement of prices of traded goods in this period, the real increase from 1968 to 1972 (after deflating to constant 1968 prices) was only 25.7 percent. U.S. wholesale price index calculated from International Financial Statistics 28 (4) (April 1975): 392.

35. The corresponding estimates for 1968 are: total welfare gains of $153 million with a shadow price premium of 60 percent, and $38 million with a 10 percent premium.

36. Calculated from SIECA, VI Compedio Estadístico, p. 369.

37. Per capita income in 1973, adjusted for different price levels among the countries (on the basis of the price study's results as reported in chapter 8 of this book) were the following: Costa Rica, $720; Guatemala, $451; Nicaragua, $442; El Salvador, $391; and Honduras, $304. See chapter 7, table 16.

38. El Salvador's high share relative to her share in GDP is a possible exception; however, the share relative to population is more meaningful for analysis of the degree of equality in distribution.

39. Hollis B. Chenery and Moises Syrquin, Patterns of Development, 1950-70 (London: Oxford University Press, 1974).

40. However, patterns of country specialization could exist at more detailed levels within the three-digit CIIU sectors without being evident at the more aggregate level.

41. See appendix C. The risk parameter, " δ ," is the percentage deviation from average output value expected for the activity in question. The model assumes simply that there is a 50 percent probability that actual output will be the average plus δ, and a 50 percent chance that it will be the average level minus δ.

42. Horacio Bobadilla, "Encuesta Selectiva de las Inversiones de Centroamerica en el Sector Manufacturero," Proyecto SIECA/Brookings, SIECA/75/PES/12, mimeographed (Guatemala City: SIECA, 1975).

43. Note that Rosenthal calculated that foreign investment provided close to 20 percent of total industrial investment in the period 1962-69 in Guatemala and El Salvador, 15 percent in Costa Rica, and 10 percent in Nicaragua and Honduras. These data, combined with those reported in table 14, imply that foreign concerns were relatively much more active in investment for projects oriented toward sales to the Common Market than in industrial investment for domestically oriented projects, especially in Costa Rica. Gert Rosenthal, "The Role of Private Foreign Investment in the Development of the Central American Common Market," 1973. See also the discussion in appendix A of this volume.

44. Another effect of foreign investment may be to raise the availability of capital sufficiently that the rate of return to capital in the country declines. In this case there is a welfare gain to the country, even if the opportunity cost of labor equals the wage rate. For example, if only domestic capital were available, the equilibrium rate of return would be ρ_0. If foreign capital is added, the equilibrium rate of return falls to ρ_1. Total production in the country equals the integral under the curve of marginal productivity of capital; however, the foreign investors only obtain a rate of return of ρ_1 on their investment. As may be seen by considering a graph of the marginal product of capital (vertical axis) against capital stock (horizontal axis), there will be a net gain for the country equal to one-half the difference between ρ_0 and ρ_1 multiplied by the amount of capital brought in by foreigners. As may be seen by considering a graph of the marginal product of capital (vertical axis) against capital stock (horizontal axis), there will be a net gain for the country equal (approximately) to one-half.

45. By obtaining the ratio of industrial investment in 1962-69 (reported by Rosenthal) to the national accounts totals for private investment in this period, and then applying this same ratio for the remaining years 1960-61 and 1970-73 to the national account private investment data.

Note that the data are not converted to constant prices because the Central American prices were remarkably stable through the entire period with the exception of the year 1973, when prices rose about 15 percent. Wholesale prices rose a total of only 11 percent between 1960 and 1972 in Guatemala, 12 percent in El Salvador, and 26 percent in Costa Rica. Consumer prices stood at the same level in 1972 as in 1960 for Honduras. SIECA, VI Compendio Estadístico, pp. 421-23; 417.

46. See chapter 4. Note that in the terminology of cost-benefit analysis, the existence of a 20 percent rate of return in the face of a 10 percent discount rate for consumption means that the "consumption price of investment" is 2.0 (see I. M. D. Little and J. A. Mirrlees, Manual of Industrial Project Analysis in Developing Countries, vol. I (Paris: OECD, 1969).

47. The procedure adopted is to accept the higher of the two alternative labor opportunity cost welfare gains--that is, from the static effects or from the investment effects. The labor effect may reasonably be assumed to be at least as high as the higher of the two alternative estimates, since neither one of them is necessarily completely comprehensive in capturing the welfare gain from extra employment due to integration.

48. SIECA, VI Compendio Estadístico, p. 386.

49. SIECA, VI Compendio Estadístico, p. 262.

Part II

THE EMPLOYMENT PROBLEM

CHAPTER 4

The Demand for Labor in Manufacturing
Industry in Central America

Charles R. Frank, Jr., Max A. Soto, and Carlos A. Sevilla

Widespread poverty and underemployment in Central America place the expansion of employment opportunities in a priority position among economic policy issues facing the region. This chapter presents a quantitative examination of the possibilities for increasing employment in manufacturing industry. The analysis focuses on whether changes in the relative prices of capital and labor would evoke substantial changes in the amount of employment provided by the sector. In addition, the analysis examines the impact of economic integration on employment in Central America. After a brief background discussion of the nature of the unemployment problem, the chapter sets forth the methodology for the analysis. It then presents the empirical results and the corresponding policy implications.

A. The Employment Problem: Brief Historical Background

Unemployment is not a new problem in Central America. It has been closely linked to poverty and to the development pattern of the region. Perhaps what is new is the recent interest in the problem within government, business, and labor circles.

There seems to be general agreement on the fact that the unemployment problem in developing countries will not be solved automatically by concentrating efforts on the rate of growth of the economy alone. It has also become socially and politically unacceptable that massive unemployment and underemployment be considered an inevitable feature of the economy of the region. Recognition of related serious political and economic implications has helped to change the policymakers' perception of unemployment

NOTE: Charles R. Frank, Jr., is responsible for the basic design of the methodology. Max A. Soto and Carlos A. Sevilla are responsible for the empirical implementation of the study as well as for selected methodological aspects.

The authors wish to thank Lic. Henry Lewin and Marilu Castellanos of SIECA for computational assistance, as well as the Bank of Guatemala and the Dirección General de Estadística of Guatemala for their cooperation.

as a temporary "social problem" peculiar to a particular group of the population. The structural characteristics of unemployment are now recognized and efforts made to reduce it are based on that recognition. Unfortunately, the appropriate policy measures for addressing the problem, and the institutional framework for the implementation of those measures, remain a subject of controversy.

The roots of the employment problem in Central America must be found in the particular pattern of development that has characterized the economic history of the region in the last century, the analysis of which is to be found elsewhere.[1] As brief historical background for this chapter, it will suffice here to outline some of the basic characteristics of the overall employment problem in the region.

One feature of the problem is its structural nature. Central America's insertion into the world market as a coffee producer during the last half of the nineteenth century was followed by significant changes in the the land tenure system, in social structure, and in the political system of the five countries.[2] One important result of these changes was the consolidation of what has been called the latifundio-minifundio system, embodied in the hacienda as the basic production unit. Under this system, the impoverished campesinos and semi-obreros agrícolas were forced--by necessity and in some instances by law--to work part of the time in the the larger haciendas. For their labor, they were paid partly in money and partly in kind. Such seasonal migratory labor has been an important source of agricultural labor supply, usually accompanied by low incomes and low productivity.

Later developments, such as the introduction of the banana "plantation" by the turn of the nineteenth century and of the modern cotton and sugar plantations afterward, have not changed substantially the very uneven distribution of land. However, they had an important impact on the labor market by introducing modern forms of organization and salaried work. The history of organized labor movements in Central America, in fact, starts with the plantation economy. It is in that sector that the first labor strikes took place.[3] Not until after World War II, however, did conditions become favorable for the consolidation and institutionalization of the labor movements. Since then, the major social reform laws have been enacted.[4] Labor regulations and social security benefits, nevertheless, have been restricted almost exclusively to urban areas--although to a lesser degree in Costa Rica--thus widening the income gap between the less privileged campesinos and the urban workers.

Thus, seasonal labor demand, an uneven land distribution, some forms of precapitalist labor relations, lack of organization among peasants in traditional agriculture, and frequent fluctuations in external demand for agricultural export products combine in such a way that conventional policy measures to fight unemployment and underemployment must be complemented with other measures specifically directed at modifying the above structural elements.

Another feature of the employment problem is that underemployment, and not open unemployment, is the prevalent situation. In the traditional agricultural sector, this is a natural result of the elements described above. Seasonal work, low incomes, and virtually nonexistent or ineffective labor legislation and social benefits force the creation of adaptive family mechanisms for the subsistence of a large percentage of the agricultural population. Agricultural underemployment estimates range from a low of 15 percent in Costa Rica to a high of 52 percent in Guatemala.[5] In the urban context, the underemployed concentrate in the services and handicraft sectors, and usually migrants from the rural areas are the ones who establish themselves in "marginal" areas of the cities. Generally these are people with a low average number of working hours, low average income, or both.

Frequently, underemployment is also found in the public sector, reflecting a government's efforts to reduce open unemployment rates in the face of slow labor absorption rates by the industrial and construction sectors. It is thus thought that urbanization in Central America has signified, to a certain extent, merely a transfer of underemployment from agriculture to the urban areas. Therefore, higher rates of industrial employment expansion have been looked upon as part of the solution to unemployment and underemployment. Industrial growth, however, is limited by several factors, one of them possibly being the weakness of internal demand caused by the uneven distribution of income. It has been estimated that only 13 percent of total income goes to 50 percent of the population, which represents an annual income per capita of about US$74 for half the total population.[6]

Finally, the employment problem has been aggravated by what has been referred to as labor-saving technological change in the main productive sectors of the economy, including agriculture. This kind of technical change makes it possible to replace labor with machinery, hence reducing labor demanded per unit of product.

Given that the above-mentioned limitations on employment opportunities--particularly among unskilled and rural workers--contribute to the existence of a large body of impoverished families in Central America, a development strategy which successfully expanded employment opportunities enough to reduce underemployment could certainly contribute to the reduction of overall inequality in the distribution of income. There can be little doubt, then, that policies are needed to stimulate the expansion of employment opportunities. The overall level of employment is determined by supply and demand in the labor market. The issue is therefore how to apply economic and social policy instruments to influence supply, demand, or both. On the demand side, if management reacts to changes in relative prices of labor and other inputs, then the fiscal, wage, and monetary policies influencing those relative prices should have a direct impact on the level of employment. These policies--as well as others explicitly directed at changing the distribution of income and wealth--could also indirectly affect the demand for labor through induced changes in the levels and composition of consumption and investment, considering the effect of these changes on levels of production in different economic sectors.

On the supply side, it may be possible to exert direct influence on the supply of labor through educational, migration, and population policies and, indirectly, to influence supply through policies affecting the distribution of wealth (such as agrarian and fiscal reform).

In the past, the supply side of the labor market has received the most attention. The predominant theories have identified "demographic explosion" as a major obstacle to development, and stressed the role of "unlimited supply" of the unskilled labor as the core element for profit and capital formation. Influenced by these ideas, employment policies in Central America traditionally have concentrated on the supply measures of reducing population growth and improving manpower qualifications and placement services. These approaches deserve vigorous pursuit, in view of the high population growth rate of the region and its low level of education and skills. Nevertheless, the existing high rates of underemployment in agriculture and services suggest that serious attention must also be given to possible lines of action on the demand side. A basic premise of this study is that there are possibilities for reducing the high levels of underemployment through policies that would substantially increase the demand for labor.

B. The Industrial Sector

The analysis in this chapter refers to employment in the manufacturing sector only. (Chapter 5 examines employment in the economy as a whole, using an alternative methodological approach.) Evaluation of manufacturing employment is important because of the strategic role of this sector in the program of Central American integration and because of the unresolved controversy about the prospects of addressing the employment problem through labor-intensive industrialization. Moreover, fairly abundant information from industrial censuses and surveys is available, making it possible to apply analytical techniques that require data at the firm level that are currently unavailable on a comprehensive basis in other sectors.

It is sometimes thought that the manufacturing industry holds little prospect of solving the employment problem because its share in total employment is so low that, even with very large proportional increases in employment, the sector could contribute little to goals for increasing overall employment. At first glance this thought would appear to have some relevance in Central America. As shown in table 1, manufacturing accounts for only 8 percent to 14 percent of the labor force in the countries of the region; however, these figures seriously understate the relative importance of industry in prospective employment generation. The reason is that the large part of the labor force is in agriculture, but one worker in the industrial sector represents more than one available worker in agriculture in terms of meaningful "job equivalents."

One way to establish this proposition is to consider degrees of underemployment. Urban underemployment typically occurs in the unorganized service sectors, whereas in manufacturing industry an employee is usually fully employed. As noted above, agricultural labor is markedly underemployed. Therefore, the share of industry in "full employment" terms would be higher than its nominal share of the labor force. The share of agricultural labor in full employment terms would be lower than its nominal share in the total labor force. As a result, increases in the growth rates of manufacturing employment would hold greater promise for making inroads into the overall employment problem than is typically thought to be the case.

Table 1.   Sectoral Composition of Labor Force in Central America

Country	Year	Agriculture, Forestry, Fishing	Manufacturing Industry	Construction	Commerce	Services	Other[a]
		Percentage of Labor Force Engaged In:					
Guatemala	1973	57.0	13.8	4.0	7.4	12.6	5.2
El Salvador	1971	46.7	8.2[b]	2.1	7.3	13.7	22.0
Honduras	1961	66.7	7.7	2.0	4.8	12.2	6.6
Nicaragua	1971	47.0	12.4	4.0	9.4	20.9	6.3
Costa Rica	1973	37.0	11.6	6.6	10.8	23.9	10.1

[a] Includes mining; electricity, gas, water, sanitation; transport, storage, communications; and unspecified activities.
[b] This figure probably underestimates the real one due to the inclusion of over 19 percent of the total labor force of El Salvador under the "nonspecified" category, which, in the rest of the countries, does not exceed 6 percent.

SOURCE: Calculated from SIECA, VI Compendio Estadístico Centroamericano, op. cit., p. 76.

C.   Outline of the Study

This chapter concentrates on three aspects of the demand for industrial labor. The first refers to the effect of relative factor prices on labor demand. To the extent that the economy of the region presents market imperfections which have led to the adoption of capital-intensive production techniques, it should be possible to influence the demand for labor and other factors by acting on their prices through fiscal and financial policies. Evaluation of these policies, in turn, requires analysis of the possibilities for substitution between capital and labor, and of the degree to which management responds to changes in relative factor prices. Analysis of the availability of economic policy instruments that could effectively alter factor prices in the desired direction is also required. An examination of the policy instruments best suited for raising national and regional employment levels must take into account the different effects that the harmonization of certain policies would have on the demand for labor in different countries.

The second aspect of this study of the demand for industrial labor refers to another central element in theories of economic development: technological change.   It is generally accepted that one of the characteristics of development is the increase in the productivity of labor over extended periods. It has also been maintained that technological

change in developing countries involves a bias against the use of manpower, giving rise to what has been called "technological unemployment."
This chapter distinguishes between the effects of technological change
on production itself, or the "intensity" of technological change (including the achievement of economies of scale), and the effect of technical
change on the factor proportions, or the "bias" of technological change.
The results should provide useful criteria for deciding among alternative
technological policies at the regional level consistent with the objective of raising employment levels substantially.

The last aspect of this study refers to the effect the Central American Common Market has in employment generation. The analysis of the employment effect of economic integration is very important because it throws
light on two controversial issues: the role of industrialization within
employment policies, and the limitations on achieving regional solutions
to the employment problem through policies related to the Common Market
itself, especially with the Common Market restricted primarily to the
industrial manufacturing sector.

Investigation of the problem of disappointingly low labor-absorption
rates through quantitative analysis of the demand for labor is by no means
new. However, certain features of the analysis here distinguish it from
most other studies of this nature.

(i) The analysis is made not for a single country or for a series
of unrelated countries but for a common market among developing countries
closely related by historical, geographical, and economic ties. In particular, the estimates include calculation of the impact of economic integration on the demand for industrial labor.

(ii) The estimates concerning technological change are the first available for Central America.

(iii) Estimates of the cost of capital are provided at highly detailed levels, permitting an unusually robust basis for policy implications directed at reasonably homogeneous groups of firms.

Finally, it is important to point out some of the limitations of the
chapter. The fact that the analysis refers only to the industrial sector
prevents the examination of factor substitutability and technical change
in the other sectors of the economy as well as the incorporation into
the model of dynamic or indirect employment effects of policies such as
changes in the distribution of income or in the sectoral composition of
investment. Furthermore, concentration on the demand for labor under
given labor supply conditions leaves aside the treatment of some important
factors which influence the supply of labor, such as the effect of trade
unionism and collective bargaining in establishing wages, the mobility
of workers, systems used for information on job opportunities, and the
influence of population on labor force growth. Another limiting factor
is that most of the analysis is based on data from the 1968 Central
American Industrial Survey, although, where possible, data from recent
industrial surveys have been incorporated in order to test the results.

D.   Elasticity of Substitution

The first question to be examined is whether industrial employment could be substantially increased by making the cost of labor cheaper relative to the cost of other inputs, especially machinery and equipment, through policies that change relative factor prices. The answer to this question hinges primarily on the extent to which the technical production characteristics allow for changes in the relative amounts of capital and labor used to produce given levels of output. It is frequently thought that industrial production is characterized by "fixed coefficients"--that one worker can be combined with one machine with no possible variation. If this were the case, then there could be no possibility of increasing employment through measures which change the relative prices of capital and labor. However, as discussed below, this chapter finds just the opposite: factor combinations (the amount of capital used with each worker) are reasonably sensitive to the relative prices of capital and labor, so policies affecting these prices deserve special attention.

The most satisfactory way to examine the responsiveness of factor combinations to relative factor prices is the estimation of "labor demand functions" or "production functions." The former state the response of labor demanded to relevant influences such as the wage rate and the cost of capital; the latter specify the level of output for given levels of inputs, and therefore the changes in output as factor combinations change. The fundamental assumption for these analyses is that entrepreneurs maximize their profits, a reasonable assumption in the Central American case where profit rather than tradition or ritual motivates industrial production.

In either labor demand or production functions, the key parameter for evaluating the responsiveness of factor combination to relative factor prices is the "elasticity of substitution." This elasticity tells the percentage change in the ratio of capital to labor used that will occur as entrepreneurs adjust to a 1 percent change in the ratio of the price of capital to the wage rate. (The elasticity is negative, but this chapter will refer to its absolute value so that a "higher elasticity of substitution" means greater responsiveness of factor combinations to factor prices.) If there are absolutely no alternatives to existing production techniques, this elasticity will be zero and the capital/labor ratio will not change despite changes in the prices of capital and labor. Under much more "responsive" production characteristics,[7] the elasticity of substitution is unity--so that the capital/labor ratio falls by 1 percent when the ratio of capital cost to wage rises by 1 percent. The extreme case is an elasticity of substitution of infinity; in this case a slight change in the factor price ratio causes a complete switch from the use of only one factor to the use of only the other.

There is widespread evidence that for industrial production the elasticity of substitution is somewhat less than unity but greater than zero. The form of a "production function" best suited to analysis in this situation is the "constant elasticity of substitution" (CES) function.[8] In this function (unlike the Cobb-Douglas function) the elasticity of substitution may be lower than unity (or higher), although the elasticity does have a single, constant value. The estimates presented in this study were obtained from a CES production function.

Before turning to the CES function and derivation of the statistical tests to be conducted, it is important to clarify the policy implications that follow from alternative results on the elasticity of substitution. Suppose that the elasticity is found to be close to zero. Then it will be of little help to employment generation to raise the price of capital or lower wages. Indeed, if policymakers were concerned about the labor force, in this circumstance they might raise minimum wages; the result would be to transfer income from profits to existing workers with no change in employment levels in the short run, although in the longer run new investment, and thus the creation of new jobs, might be discouraged by a reduced profit rate. By contrast, if the elasticity of substitution is unity or above, wage and capital cost policies will have a major impact on the level of industrial employment. Substantial increases in minimum wages should be avoided in that case because they will be counterproductive for labor as a group: wages lost by workers losing jobs due to replacement by capital will more than offset wage gains by those who remain employed. On the other hand, with a high substitution elasticity, policies raising the cost of capital will stimulate the hiring of more labor to replace the now more expensive capital. And, if profit rates are already extremely high (as is the case in Central America), an increase in the cost of capital will probably not cause major reductions in the pace of investment. In short, the case of high substitution elasticity is the optimistic case for employment policy because increases in the cost of capital will bring forth greater demand for labor in the industrial sector.

To assess the direction of response of the total wage bill to the unit wage, it is necessary to go one step beyond the elasticity of substitution to the "elasticity of demand for labor." The latter tells the percent change in employment for a 1 percent change in the wage rate. If the elasticity is above 1, a reduction in wages will raise employment by enough to raise the total wage bill even though the unit wage falls. Even if the elasticity is exactly 1, a reduction in the wage rate will have favorable income redistribution effects because it will shift income from existing industrial workers to newly incorporated workers (usually from the countryside) formerly earning much less, without changing the total wage bill.

There is a critical value of the substitution elasticity which represents the turning point between below unity and above unity for the elasticity of demand for labor. If the policy being considered is the reduction of industrial wages, then under reasonable assumptions, that critical value is merely the share of capital in value added. Although this conclusion is demonstrated mathematically[9] in appendix D, the logical basis for this result is the following. When wages fall, two effects occur: entrepreneurs replace capital with labor in their existing production, the "substitution effect"; and they expand the level of production to take advantage of greater profitability, the "output effect." If the capital share is very high, close to unity, then wage costs are trivial relative to value added, and a savings in wage costs generates little output effect--although the substitution effect still occurs. In this case the elasticity of labor demand is practically equal to the elasticity of substitution. At the opposite extreme, with capital share close to zero, wage costs form the bulk of value added, and a reduction in wage costs provides a large basis for increasing output; here, the elasticity of demand for labor is much larger than the elasticity of substitution because a large output effect supplements the substitution effect.

In Central America the share of capital in value added is on the order of 0.6 to 0.7.[10] Therefore, the elasticity of substitution need only be approximately 0.7 (absolute value) in order for the elasticity of labor demand with respect to wage to be at the turning point of unity. If the elasticity of substitution is higher (even if it is still less than unity), a reduction in wages will cause an increase in employment sufficient to raise rather than lower the total wage bill.

If the policy under consideration is raising capital cost rather than lowering wages, then the critical value of the elasticity of substitution is different. In this case there is no negative effect on the wage bill from lowering wages. At the same time, there is an output effect, which in this case is negative instead of positive. That is, with higher capital cost (instead of lower labor cost), producers will tend to reduce rather than raise output.

Because profit levels are already at exceedingly high levels in Central America,[11] it is highly likely that increases in the cost of capital would merely reduce "excess profits" but not cause producers to reduce output or investment. In this case, then the only effect on employment will be the substitution effect (the output effect will be zero); and as long as the elasticity of substitution is greater than zero, there will be an increase both in total employment and total wage bill when capital cost is increased.

In sum, the critical value for the elasticity of substitution need only be on the order of 0.7 or higher, in the Central American case, for reductions in wages to raise total wage bill as well as employment. Furthermore, it may be argued that the critical level may be much lower, even any value larger than zero, for an increase in capital costs (with wage constant) to cause an increase in employment and total wage bill.

A final qualification is necessary on the meaning of the elasticity of substitution for policy purposes. The estimates below are based on comparison of different firms facing different prices of capital and labor during a single year, 1968 (with variation due to regional differences in salaries, and differing interest levels, taxation rules, and tariff exemption practices). The estimates are not based on observed short-run adjustments made by individual firms in response to changing factor prices. Therefore, the results probably overstate the responsiveness of factor combination to factor price in the short run. They refer more appropriately to long-run flexibility of factor combinations in the installation of new plants. That is, even though before actual construction of a plant technical alternatives exist, once the machinery and equipment are installed it is much more difficult to change capital/labor ratios. (This difference between ex-ante flexibility and ex-post rigidity is known as the "putty-clay" phenomenon: malleable as putty before actual installation of plant, factor combinations are as fixed as fire-hardened clay afterward.) Thus, the responsiveness of employment to factor prices indicated by the substitution elasticities found here refers primarily to influences on factor choice in future investment. It is difficult to say what the responsiveness of employment in existing industries would

be, although this responsiveness would be lower than the long-run sensitivity of factor combinations indicated by the substitution elasticities
estimated.

Turning to the methodology for estimating the elasticity of substitution, we begin with the production function of the Constant Elasticity
of Substitution (CES) type. From this production function, it is possible
to derive the relationships which should exist between production, the
use of labor and capital, and the relative prices of labor and capital;
and, in the case of technological change, the influence of experience
over time. Once the algebraic forms for the relationships are determined,
then statistical tests employing these forms may be used to estimate the
major parameters (the elasticity of substitution, the degree of returns
to scale, and technical change).

The CES production function relates value added to the levels of labor
and capital applied. As is shown in appendix D, it is possible from
this relationship to derive a corresponding formulation relating value
added per worker to the real wage. In this latter formulation, the coefficient on the wage term is the elasticity of substitution. That is, when
the real wage changes by 1 percent, output per worker will change by a
percentage indicated by this coefficient. This form, thus, provides the
first basic estimating equation for statistical tests.

A second estimating form is obtained by placing the level of output on the right-hand side of the equation as an explanatory variable,
and calculating a labor demand function. In this case the level of labor
applied is the dependent variable. It is related to the wage rate and
the level of output as two separate variables. Here once again the coefficient on the wage rate represents the elasticity of substitution, but in
addition the output variable provides information on economies of scale.

A third estimating form may be derived from the same CES production
function but in a formulation allowing capital cost to vary. In this
version, the ratio of labor to capital is related to the ratio of capital
cost to labor cost. Here the elasticity of substitution is the coefficient
on the ratio of factor costs.

These three estimating equations provide the basis for the alternative estimates of the elasticity of substitution, presented below.

E.   Technological Change

The second aspect of our study of the demand for labor concerns the
characteristics of technological change in Central American manufacturing
industries. The importance of this topic stems from the emphasis that has
been placed on technological change as a source of economic growth. Relevant literature includes analyses of the contribution of different factors of production to growth of the product,[12] as well as attempts to
quantify "structural change" in partial equilibrium models.[13]

Empirical studies on the first of these two subjects have found
that "technological change" is as important as (or even more important
than) expansion of capital and labor in the growth of the product per

capita. Studies on the second subject have maintained that the bias
in technological change contributes to reinforcement of what has been
called the phenomenon of "technological dualism." The concept of "technological unemployment," whereby unemployment is due to scarcity of resources and to sectoral technology rather than to lack of effective demand, also attaches great significance to the issue of factor bias in
technical change.

Empirical examination of technological change requires a formulation
providing the basis for statistical tests and drawing upon the same basic
framework already applied to examine the elasticity of substitution. The
production function must be adjusted to incorporate technological change.
For this purpose the traditional neoclassical approach is followed here:
it is assumed that technological change grows at a constant, exogenously
determined rate.[14] The analysis must also differentiate between two effects of technological change: its impact on the level of production
while capital and labor remain constant (or the "intensity" of technological change), and its effect on the factor proportion used (or the bias
in technological change).[15]

The incorporation of technological change into the analysis begins
with the revision of the CES production function to express labor and
capital in terms of "effective" units that grow from technical change
with the passage of time, even without additional physical units of labor
or capital. This revision is accomplished by treating effective capital
(or labor) as equal to physical capital (labor) multiplied by an expansion factor that grows exponentially over time, at the rate of "capital-
augmenting" (or "labor-augmenting") technical change. In this formulation,
the "intensity" of technical change is defined as the rate of growth of
output that takes place spontaneously with physical inputs of labor and
capital held constant. The "bias" of technological change tells the extent to which technical progress causes a change in factor combinations.
For example, if the rate of labor-augmenting technical change is high
while the rate of capital-augmenting change is low, "effective" labor
units will grow relatively rapidly, and technical change will therefore
be biased against the absorption of physical units of labor. Moreover,
the extent of the bias depends on the degree of substitutability. If
the elasticity of substitution is low, then it is difficult to make use
of the extra effective units of labor caused by more rapid labor-augmenting change (in the example above) through compensatory substitution of
capital by labor, and the degree of bias against labor absorption will
be all the greater.

The CES production function allowing for technical change contains
parameters that state the degree of "intensity" and "bias" in technical
change, as shown in appendix D. Based on these parameters and the form
of the production function with technical change, it is possible to estimate the bias in technical change using an estimating form in which the
labor/capital ratio is related to the factor price ratio (cost of capital
divided by the wage rate) and time. In this statistical test, the coefficient on the variable "time" tells the bias of technical change. This
test, then, provides the basis for the results below on the bias of technological change. Estimation of the intensity of technical change, for
its part, requires reliable estimates of the individual parameters for
rates of capital-augmenting and labor-augmenting technical change, and

these prove to be impossible to obtain in the empirical application discussed below.

F. Economies of Scale

Another aspect of the technology of industrial production is the degree of returns to scale. This subject has been given much importance in integrationist circles. It is usually assumed that the broadening of the market size through the association of small countries in a common market facilitates the achievement of economies of scale. The exploitation of economies of scale in turn would allow for a greater degree of efficiency in the production systems, freeing funds for further increases in production capacity, stimulating the expansion of employment opportunities, and improving the balance of payments.

Stemming from this premise, the achievement of economies of scale has been established even as an objective itself within integration processes.[16]

Empirical evidence on the economies of scale of each country and sector of industrial activity should be valuable information for the direction of development policies and industrial programming within the framework of economic integration.

Economies of scale can be estimated either by using the results obtained in the equation for the derived demand for labor, or by estimating the production functions directly. The first approach uses the second of the three estimating forms discussed above in connection with the elasticity of substitution. In that equation, the demand for labor is related to the wage rate and the level of output. The coefficients estimated on the wage and output variables may be manipulated to show the degree of returns to scale (appendix D). In practice, however, this approach is subject to estimation biases which tend to exaggerate the degree of economies of scale, and to make it unstable when the coefficients on wage and output are of similar magnitudes.

For the alternative approach to estimating economies of scale, we apply a particular estimating technique for the CES production function, the Kmenta approximation. By contrast with the method using the labor demand function, estimation using the Kmenta approximation provides a direct estimate of the economies of scale parameter, for which tests of statistical significance can be conducted. The form produces highly reliable estimates of economies of scale.

Another estimating form used to test for economies of scale is the so-called "transcendental-logarithmic" production function. This form (a quadratic equation for the logarithms of inputs) permits different degrees of returns to scale for different sizes of firms.

In order to avoid confusing economies of scale at the plant level with economies of scale at the level of the entire market, data at the establishment level are used in this chapter. Estimates with aggregate data, in addition to economies of scale, would include the effects of external economies or diseconomies.

G.   Effect of Central American Integration on Employment

One of the most controversial aspects of the industrialization process in developing countries is its effect on employment-generating opportunities. One influential argument states that industrialization automatically leads to the absorption of "excess" agricultural labor. On the
other hand it has been repeatedly pointed out that the specific industrialization patterns followed--typified by labor-saving techniques as the
result of distorted incentives toward overutilization of capital--have
been a negative factor in the generation of employment. The problem takes
on other dimensions when industrialization efforts are conducted within
a process of economic integration, inasmuch as the growth of the industrial sector in each member country depends to a certain extent on its
participation in the increasing production resulting from the expansion
of the market under a common external tariff. It is interesting to note
that after fifteen years of integration in Central America, in spite of
the fact that the social implications of the employment effect of the
integration process is one of its most frequently and heatedly debated
aspects, there has been no analytical examination of this effect. The
data on employment used in the following chapter, combined with the estimates in chapter 3 of the effect of integration on the structure of production, make it possible to conduct this quantification for the periods
1958-68 and 1958-72. For each sector at the three-digit CIIU level, the
increase in employment is measured on the basis of the net increase of
the gross value of production attributed to integration between the time
spans mentioned above. Given the change in output attributed to integration, the corresponding increase in employment is calculated by three
alternative procedures.

First, on the basis of the labor demand function used to estimate
the elasticity of substitution (labor related to wage and output), it is
possible to express the percentage change in employment to be expected
from a percentage change in wage or in output. Given the incipient nature
of regional labor organizations and the absence of effective regional
compromises to harmonize labor and social security legislation, it is
highly unlikely that integration had any significant influence on the
prevalent wage rates. Changes in the wage rate probably respond to factors internal to each country. The first approach therefore reduces to
estimating the change in employment as a function of the change in output
attributable to integration--based on the estimated labor elasticity with
respect to output (percent change in employment resulting from a 1 percent
change in output).

Two alternative methods of estimation were utilized here. One makes
use of the actual empirical estimates of the elasticity of employment demand with respect to output at the three-digit industrial level, and the
other assumes constant returns to scale. The reason for this second assumption is that the estimated elasticity (the coefficient on output in
the labor demand function) is very likely to be biased, as discussed in
appendix D.

A third estimate was obtained by applying coefficients of labor per
unit of output (the inverse of labor productivity) to the output change
attributable to integration. Since this effect takes place throughout
time it is necessary to adjust average productivities to reflect this

fact. (In a strict sense, marginal and not average productivities ought
to be used. Estimates based on 1968 data indicate that the marginal productivity of labor exceed labor's average product, suggesting that this
third procedure probably overestimates the employment effect of integration.) For Costa Rica and Guatemala, the average of the initial and final
productivities of the two periods under consideration were used. For
Honduras and Nicaragua, 1968 productivity was assumed to represent the
average productivity for both periods. It was also assumed that Guatemala's labor inputs for 1968 applied to El Salvador.

Finally, the change in output attributed to integration used is that
discussed in chapter 3. It includes the increase in production necessary
to provide for (i) extra sales to partners in the Common Market and (ii)
the replacement of goods formerly bought from abroad (trade suppression),
net of reduction in output because of (iii) external trade augmentation
or (iv) trade creation. The estimates of change in output used in this
chapter do not include indirect integration effects, which are added
through the use of an input-output table as discussed below.

Chapter 5 of this volume presents an alternative approach to estimating the impact of integration on employment, constructed in such a way
that the calculation serves as a "worst case" or "lower bound" estimate.
That approach assumes that integration had no net effect on the aggregate
level of output, and asks what the change in the sectoral composition
of output resulting from integration implied for employment. Because the
central estimates of this volume conclude that there was a net positive
output effect of integration (see chapter 3), however, the employment
estimates presented below may be considered the central results of the
volume on this question.

H. Estimating Equations

As a summary review of the forms of the equations used for statistical tests (as discussed above), table 2 presents the forms for which
estimates are conducted. The left column of the table shows the dependent
variable being explained, and the remaining variables are those entering
the regression equations as explanatory or independent variables.[17]

I. Construction of the Variables

The data source for capital (K), labor (L), and the wage rate (w)
was the 1968 Industrial Census in Guatemala, Honduras, Nicaragua, and
Costa Rica. The capital variable is the unweighted sum of the value of
assets at the beginning of the year. Assets included buildings and other
construction; production machinery and equipment; vehicles and transportation equipment; and furniture, office equipment, and other physical
assets.[18]

The measure used for the labor variable is the number of production
workers, or the sum of those in the following categories: production
technicians, skilled workers, and unskilled workers.[19]

Table 2. Equations for Regression Estimates

Form	Equation	Text Equation, Appendix D
a	$\ln(V/L) = a_0 + b_1 \ln w + u_1$	(2)
b	$\ln w = a'_0 + b'_1 \ln(V/L) + u'_1$	
c	$\ln L = a'_3 + b_4 \ln w + c_2 \ln V + d_2 t + u_4$	(10)
d	$\ln L = a_3 + b_5 \ln w + c_1 \ln V + u_5$	(11)
e	$\ln(L/K) = a_1 + b_2 \ln(c/w) + u_2$	(5)
f	$\ln(L/K) = a_2 + b_3 \ln(c/w) + dt + u_3$	(9)
g	$\ln(V/L) = a_4 + h_1 \ln L + g_3 \ln(K/L)$ $+ g_4 [\ln(K/L)]^2 + u$	(13)
h	$\ln V = a_5 + h_2 \ln L + t_1 \ln K + k(\ln L)^2$ $+ m(\ln K)^2 + n_1 (\ln L \ln K) + u$	(14)

NOTE: V = value added, L = labor, w = wage, t = time, c = cost of capital, ln = natural logarithm.

Administrative personnel and unpaid workers are excluded from the labor estimate. The facts that in Central America administrative personnel represent a relatively stable proportion of total employment and that various methods of weighting labor categories yield similar results,[20] suggest that the estimates obtained would change little if the definition of the labor variable were modified to include one or both of these categories.[21]

As a measure of the cost of labor, the average annual salary of production workers was calculated. This salary included employer payments for social benefits.

The measure used in this study to represent the level of production is the value added, defined as gross output value less the value of intermediate inputs.[22] In a strict sense, value added is an appropriate measure of output for the production functions if it is assumed that: either (i) the elasticity of substitution between value added and intermediate input is infinite; or (ii) this elasticity is zero, in which case intermediate inputs represent a constant proportion of gross output value.[23]

If some element is erroneously omitted in the measurement of intermediate inputs (such as working capital or inventory), value added will overstate production. Nevertheless, because of its generally recognized superiority over gross output value for estimation purposes,[24] value added is the measure of output chosen in this study.

In order for the measure of the cost of capital (c_k) to be useful for deriving policy orientations, it should take into consideration a set of factors which have an influence on it such as interest rate policies, the price of capital goods, taxation rules, and tariff levels on imported capital equipment and machinery. (A formula for the cost of capital is derived in appendix D. In that formulation the cost of capital varies directly with the price of capital goods; it increases as the interest rate rises; and, paradoxically, it declines when the tax rate rises under the prevalent situation in which, because of accelerated depreciation, the depreciation rate exceeds the replacement rate.)

The variables for price of capital, replacement rate, and depreciation rate are indices weighted by the shares of structures (buildings and other construction) and of machinery, equipment, and vehicles within the fixed assets of each industry. It should be noted that the price of capital goods incorporates the ad valorem equivalent of the tariff and capital goods imports adjusted by authorized exemptions on those imports. The interest rate variable was calculated as the average interest rate for all loans from the banking system extended to firms in the industry in question, for the case of Guatemala. For all the other four countries, the sectoral interest rate was taken to be equal to the rate fixed by the national banking authorities for manufacturing loans.

The income tax rates were estimated for Guatemala by comparing the taxable income of each establishment in the industrial sector with the corresponding tax according to the income tax law and deriving a weighted overall rate for each industry. Exemptions granted by the laws of industrial development were taken into account. For the remaining four countries, the tax rate was assumed to be 6 percent, on the basis of tax information provided by the tax revenue offices of Guatemala and Costa Rica.

Estimates of the cost of capital for the five countries at the four-digit CIIU level are reported in table D-1 in appendix D.

Finally, it is important to note that all firm observations showing zero or negative values for one or more variables were eliminated from the data set.

J. Empirical Results

1. The Elasticity of Substitution

(a) Estimation at the establishment level

Table D-2 in appendix D presents the estimates of the elasticity of substitution for Central America for the functional forms "a," "b," and "d" (of table 2). These estimates are conducted at the firm level for groupings at the four-, three-, and two-digit levels of the CIIU industrial

classification.[25] Table 3 summarizes these results, including the comparable findings at the level of individual countries. The table shows the
percentage of cases in which the elasticity of substitution (σ) is not
significantly different from zero; falls between zero and unity; is not
significantly different from unity; or becomes greater than unity. These
frequencies are reported for the estimates conducted for individual countries and for the region as a whole using each of the three functional
forms and the alternative CIIU categories.

Table 3 indicates several important patterns in the results. First,
estimates of σ are very sensitive to the functional form applied. The
highest estimates are those from functional form 3 in the table, the regression of the logarithm of wage on that of value added per worker.
Functional form 1, the logarithm of value added per worker regressed on
that of wage, yields intermediate estimates of the substitution elasticity, and the lowest estimates are from functional form 2--the regression
of labor on wage and value added. Thus, for example, for Guatemala with
groupings at the four-digit CIIU level, the percent of cases in which σ
is zero increases from zero for functional form 3 to 41.6 percent for
functional form 1 and to 82.4 percent for functional form 2.

Second, abstracting from the functional form used, as the sample is
enlarged from groupings of four-digit industries to three- and two-digit
categories, there is a tendency for σ to rise from zero to the range of
greater than zero but less than unity. This change is primarily due to
the fact that, as the CIIU categories are broadened, each estimation
group includes a wider variety of products with distinct capital/labor
ratios. While this greater variation leads to a higher estimate of the
substitution elasticity, generally, it nevertheless means that the results
for broader industry groupings are less "pure" as indications of substitutability between capital and labor for individual industrial products.

Finally there are also significant differences in the substitution
elasticity among countries, as shown in the table. Honduras appears to
have the highest degree of factor substitutability; and Guatemala, the
lowest. These differences are discussed below.

The results demonstrate that both the functional form and the definition of groupings of firms play an important part in the specific estimates
obtained for σ. Therefore, it is necessary to confront the assumptions
underlying each of the estimation models with the prevailing economic
conditions in Central America, in order to choose the most appropriate
model and estimate from the available alternatives.

It is evident in table 3 that functional form 3 (logarithm of wage regressed on logarithm of value added per worker) consistently yields unacceptably high estimates of the elasticity of substitution. Therefore
the results from this form may be dismissed.[26]

The fundamental difference between the two remaining equations is
that the first (form 1) assumes constant returns to scale ($h = 1$), whereas
the second (form 2) eliminates this restriction. The final four columns
of table 3 report that the parameter associated with economies of scale,
the coefficient on value added in form 2, is significantly different
from unity in approximately 50 percent of the cases. It could be argued,

Table 3. Size of Elasticity of Substitution, b, for Three Functional Forms, with Observations at the Establishment Level Within ISIC Categories of 4, 3, and 2 Digits; and Economies of Scale Parameters, c (in percent)

Country	I. Size of b	$\text{Log } \frac{V}{L} = a + b \ln w$ Functional Form 1			$\text{Ln } L = o + b \ln w + c_1 \ln V$ Functional Form 2			$\text{Ln } w = a + b \ln \frac{V}{L}$ Functional Form 3	
		4 digits	3 digits	2 digits	4 digits	3 digits	2 digits	3 digits	2 digits
Costa Rica	b=0	38.5	54.5	28.5	47.1	69.2	42.8	0.0	0.0
	0<b<1	7.7	9.0	28.5	29.4	7.7	42.8	0.0	0.0
	b=1	53.8	36.4	42.8	23.5	23.1	14.3	0.0	14.3
	b>1	0.0	0.0	0.0	0.0	0.0	0.0	100.0	85.7
Nicaragua	b=0	16.7	16.7	14.2	60.0	64.2	57.1	0.0	0.0
	0<b<1	16.7	16.7	28.4	6.7	7.1	28.6	0.0	0.0
	b=1	66.7	66.7	56.8	33.3	28.6	14.3	11.8	0.0
	b>1	0.0	0.0	0.0	0.0	0.0	0.0	88.2	100.0
Honduras	b=0	6.7	0.0	0.0	18.2	33.3	14.3	0.0	0.0
	0<b<1	6.7	7.7	0.0	45.4	41.7	57.1	0.0	0.0
	b=1	86.7	92.3	100.0	36.3	25.0	28.5	13.3	0.0
	b>1	0.0	0.0	0.0	0.0	0.0	0.0	86.7	100.0
Guatemala	b=0	41.6	26.3	12.5	82.4	81.8	55.8	0.0	0.0
	0<b<1	29.2	42.1	50.0	8.8	13.6	44.2	0.0	0.0
	b=1	29.2	31.6	37.5	8.8	4.6	0.0	12.0	11.0
	b>1	0.0	0.0	0.0	0.0	0.0	0.0	88.0	89.0
Central America	b=0	12.0	8.0	0.0	53.3	43.0	11.1	0.0	0.0
	0<b<1	25.5	44.0	77.8	33.3	52.2	88.9	0.0	0.0
	b=1	61.7	48.0	22.2	13.3	4.3	0.0	12.9	7.1
	b>1	0.0	0.0	0.0	0.0	0.0	0.0	87.1	92.9

Table 3 (Continued)

Country	II. Size of c_1	Functional Form 2		
		4 digits	3 digits	2 digits
Costa Rica	$0<c_1<1$	56.5	76.5	87.5
	$c_1=1$	43.5	23.5	12.5
	$c_1>1$	0.0	0.0	0.0
	-	-	-	-
Nicaragua	$0<c_1<1$	53.8	66.7	100.0
	$c_1=1$	41.2	33.3	0.0
	$c_1>1$	0.0	0.0	0.0
	-	-	-	-
Honduras	$0<c_1<1$	50.0	64.3	100.0
	$c_1=1$	50.0	35.7	0.0
	$c_1>1$	0.0	0.0	0.0
	-	-	-	-
Guatemala	$0<c_1<1$	35.0	87.5	89.0
	$c_1=1$	65.0	12.5	11.0
	$c_1>1$	0.0	0.0	0.0
	-	-	-	-
Central America	$0<c_1<1$	91.8	83.5	100.0
	$c_1=1$	8.2	11.5	0.0
	$c_1>1$	0.0	0.0	0.0
	-	-	-	-

NOTE: The figures represent the percentage of cases in which the estimated value of b or c lies within the specified range.

SOURCE: Calculated from 1969 Central American Industrial Census.

therefore, that this form is preferable to form 1. However, it is necessary to examine certain considerations about the coefficient estimates for form 2 before reaching a conclusion on which of the two forms is preferable.

As discussed in appendix D, if the variable V is measured with error, the estimated coefficients on value added (c_1) and on the logarithm of wage (σ_5) will be biased downward, if the two variables are correlated. The data for Central America appear to indicate that value added does contain substantial errors of measurement.[27] Furthermore, the inclusion of ln V on the right-hand side of form 2 may cause biases of simultaneity in the event that this variable is not exogenous.[28]

These considerations suggest that both the estimate c_1--which is crucial for testing the validity of functional form 1--and the estimated elasticity of substitution will tend to be underestimated when form 2 is applied.

To obtain valid econometric estimates it is frequently preferable to impose a restriction, even if this restriction is not entirely correct, than to leave the estimating form unrestricted, particularly if there is a high degree of multicollinearity (that is, correlation among the various independent variables).[29] In the present case, the restriction which may be imposed is that of constant returns to scale. While this restriction may cause a bias in the estimates,[30] it is evident from the results obtained (table 3) that any such bias represents a much less serious problem than that caused by the instability of the parameters found for the unrestricted "form 2," which allows for economies of scale. Moreover, as discussed below, direct estimates of economies of scale using production functions indicate that the scale elasticity (h) is not statistically different from unity in the majority of cases. Also, form 2 presents multicollinearity, although not to a high degree (the coefficient of determination between ln V and ln w fluctuates between 0.1 and 0.6). Therefore, it is appropriate to impose the restriction of constant returns to scale, and for this reason the most reliable estimates of the elasticity of substitution are those obtained from functional form 1.

Table D-3 of appendix D reports the estimates for functional form 1 for four Central American countries individually. Table 4 of this chapter presents a comparative summary of the magnitudes of the elasticity of substitution for four-digit CIIU categories for the four countries, based on the estimates using the preferred functional form 1 (equation "a"). The table includes only these industrial categories for which at least two countries had six or more establishments in the census. Table 4 shows that the estimates of the elasticity of substitution fall within the range of 0.2 to 1.9, with the majority of the estimates centering around the value 0.8. The industrial branches which tend to produce the lowest estimates are CIIU categories 3211 (winding and beaming, weaving, and finishing of textiles), 3213 (knitted textiles), 3240 (shoes except those of rubber and plastic), and 3691 (clay products for construction).

In several instances the substitution elasticity for one country differs widely from the values encountered in the other countries for the same product.[31] It would be of great interest to determine the extent to

Table 4. Size of Elasticity of Substitution by Country and Industrial Category
(Four-digit CIIU), 1968

CIIU	Description[a]	Guatemala	Honduras	Nicaragua	Costa Rica	Average[b] Simple	Weighted[c]	Central America
3111	Slaughtering, preparation, and preservation of meat	0.8943	1.1219*	1.5574*	--	1.1914	1.0926	0.9734**
3112	Manufacture of dairy products	0.7417**	1.4165**	2.6793	--	1.6198	1.6569	0.8473*
3113	Canning, preservation of fruits, vegetables	0.7563	--	--	1.6955**	1.2275	1.0689	1.0031**
3116	Grain mill products	0.5483	1.9282*	0.4757_2*	0.6910**	0.9109	0.7395	0.5235_2**
3117	Manufacture of bakery products	0.6543_2**	0.9200**	0.0286_2	0.7036_1**	0.5768	0.6438	0.6534**
3118	Sugar factories, refineries	0	--	--	0.9426	0.4713	0.2164	0.6445**
3119	Manufacture of cocoa, chocolate, and sugar confections	0.5848_1**	--	--	1.5943*	1.0896	1.1357	0.7603**
3121	Manufacture of food products n.e.c.	0.5744*	0.9621*	0.5971	--	0.7112	0.5656	0.6501_1**
3131	Distilling, rectifying, blending spirits	--	0.3523	--	--	0.3523	0.1754	0.0990_2
3134	Soft drinks, carbonated water	2.0327	--	1.3713*	0.5801	1.3447	1.4644	1.5422**
3140	Tobacco manufactures	1.4829_1**	0.8090	--	--	1.1460	1.2956	0.9933**
3211	Spinning, weaving, finishing textiles	0.5443_1*	--	0.2320	0.4925	0.4731	0.4629	0.5962_1*

Table 4 (continued)

CIIU	Description[a]	Guatemala	Honduras	Nicaragua	Costa Rica	Average[b] Simple	Weighted[c]	Central America
3212	Manufacture of made-up textile goods, excluding clothing	1.3682	--	--	0	0.6841	0.8130	1.1692*
3213	Knitting mills	0.3028_2*	--	--	0.1669	0.2349	0.2608	0.2937_2*
3220	Manufacture of wearing apparel, excluding footwear	0.5303_1*	0.7027**	0.7574**	0.2553_2	0.5626	0.4745	0.6663_2*
3231	Tanneries, leather finishing	0.1263	--	1.1729**	0.0592_1	0.4528	0.6517	0.6273**
3233	Manufacture of leather products, excluding footwear	0	--	--	1.0875*	0.5438	0.7001	0.4276_1
3240	Manufacture of footwear, excluding rubber and plastic	0.2835_2	0.4933_2**	0.3091_2**	0.3453_1	0.3591	0.3196	0.3815_2**
3311	Sawmills, planing, other wood mills	0.2744	0.8931**	1.0224**	0.9951*	0.7963	0.8331	0.6924_2**
3319	Manufacture of wood, cork products n.e.c.	3.1443	0.6600	--	--	1.9022	1.3303	1.3971**
3320	Manufacture of furniture and fixtures, excluding metal	0.1276_2	0.7709**	0.8759**	0.9207***	0.6738	0.6503	0.5385_2*
3420	Printing, publishing and allied industries	0.4983_2*	1.1612**	0.6097	0.6322	0.7145	0.6400	0.8478_2**
3522	Manufacture of drugs and medicines	0.7674	1.0644*	1.1794	0.3746	0.8465	0.8378	0.6933**
3523	Manufacture of soap, perfumes, cosmetics	0.8305**	0	0.0706	0.4524	0.3509	0.5092	0.6803**

Table 4 (continued)

CIIU	Description[a]	Guatemala	Honduras	Nicaragua	Costa Rica	Average[b] Simple	Average[b] Weighted[c]	Central America
3560	Manufacture of plastic products n.e.c.	0.3681_1	0.7305	1.5411**	1.2028*	0.9606	0.9605	0.7496**
3691	Manufacture of structural clay products	0.1826_1	--	--	0.2535	0.1181	0.2443	0.4135_1
3699	Manufacture of nonmetallic mineral products n.e.c.	0.3083_2	0.5673**	0	--	0.4252	0.3876	0.5486_2**
3812	Manufacture of furniture, fixtures primarily of metal	0.2068_1	1.0439	--	0.9090	0.7199	0.6770	0.7545**
3813	Manufacture of structural metal products	0.4570_1	2.1128*	1.2212*	0.6459	1.1092	1.4738	0.9396**
3819	Manufacture of fabricated metal products n.e.c., excluding machinery, equipment	0.7162	--	--	0.0100_2	0.3631	0.4085	0.3155_1
3839	Manufacture of electrical apparatus n.e.c.	1.1435	--	--	0.0446	0.5966	0.7649	0.8560*
3909	Manufacturing industries n.e.c.	0.5286	1.3848	--	0.4064	0.7733	0.6284	0.7834**

[a]"n.e.c." = Not elsewhere classified.

[b]The negative regression coefficients were excluded from the calculation, except for those significantly different from unity, to which a value of zero was assigned.

[c]Weighting factor: share of each country in total value added for the countries included in estimates.

Symbols: * and **, significantly different from zero at 5 percent and 1 percent level, respectively.
Subscripts 1 and 2, significantly different from unity at 5 percent and 1 percent level, respectively.

SOURCE: Calculated from the Central American Industrial Census of 1969.

which these differing results reflect real differences among the countries with respect to productive structure, labor markets, and economic policies. In the absence of additional information, however, there is little basis for exploring these variations, and it may only be concluded that there do exist significant differences in the degree of substitutability between labor and capital among industrial sectors in each country, and among industries considering the region as a whole.

Table 5 presents the simple and weighted averages of the elasticity of substitution for industry overall and for industrial subgroups, for each country and for the region. The table shows that for the region as a whole both the simple and weighted averages indicate a value of approximately 0.8 for the elasticity for all manufacturing establishments. It is also evident in the table that the elasticity varies among countries. It is the highest in Honduras (close to unity), and successively lower for Nicaragua, Guatemala, and Costa Rica. The averages calculated for a more selective subset of results (excluding negative estimates and those not significantly different either from zero or unity) tend to be somewhat lower but basically do not alter the conclusions above on magnitude and country rank of the substitution elasticity.[32] Note that although data for El Salvador are unavailable, in view of the similarities between this country's labor and industrial structures and those in Guatemala, the elasticity of substitution in manufacturing industry in El Salvador probably would be close to that found for Guatemala in the estimates presented here.

An interesting feature of the results presented in table 5 is that except for Costa Rica, the average elasticity of substitution is slightly higher for "dynamic" industries (groups 3511-3909) than for "traditional" industries (groups 3111-3420).[33] This result contradicts the conventional thesis that the techniques of production in dynamic industries have lower factor substitutability than the techniques applied in traditional industries.[34] These results suggest that relative price policies would have a differential impact on employment absorption which would depend on the particular subsector to which those policies are directed.

Other insights may be obtained by reordering industries according to the magnitude of the elasticity of substitution. Tables D-4 to D-7 in appendix D, present the resulting arrangement for each country, at the three-digit level. Estimates of economies of scale, discussed below, and other technical information for each industry are also included to facilitate identification of patterns.

Interestingly, for Guatemala (table D-4), the industries with greater substitution elasticities also tend to present larger economies of scale, higher labor productivity, and higher capital-to-labor ratios. Furthermore, the industries with the largest shares in manufacturing employment generally have statistically significant factor substitution possibilities. Whereas industries with significant elasticities of substitution represent approximately 61 percent of manufacturing employment, the total share in employment of those with fixed coefficients only reaches 12 percent.

Even though the pattern found for Guatemala is not evident for the other countries, it may be said that, with the exception of Costa Rica, there are reasonable possibilities for substituting labor for capital in

Table 5. Simple and Weighted[a] Averages of the Elasticity of Substitution
for Manufacturing Sectors in Central America, 1968

Country/ Averages	I. All Industry[b]			II. Selected Industries[c]		
	Total	Groups 3111-3420	Groups 3511-3909	Total	Groups 3111-3420	Groups 3511-3909
Guatemala						
Simple	0.769	0.773	0.766	0.542	0.449	0.715
Weighted	0.682	0.664	0.724	0.339	0.518	0.732
Honduras						
Simple	1.004	0.985	0.913	1.151	1.088	1.036
Weighted	1.129	0.928	1.456	0.948	1.102	1.582
Nicaragua						
Simple	0.862	0.846	0.892	0.861	0.841	0.921
Weighted	0.962	0.936	1.039	0.626	0.906	1.119
Costa Rica						
Simple	0.607	0.698	0.473	0.736	0.760	0.606
Weighted	0.595	0.706	0.408	0.390	0.754	0.530
Central America						
Simple	0.858	0.830	0.878	0.831	0.766	0.911
Weighted	0.787	0.704	0.893	0.648	0.663	0.918

[a]The weighting factor used was the share of each industrial group (at four digits CIIU) in total value added of the groups included in the calculation.
[b]These averages, and those of the two following columns, are calculated excluding the groups that had negative elasticities, except those that were insignificant but were significantly different from -1 at the 5 percent level. In the latter case a value of zero was assigned.
[c]For the calculation of these averages we excluded all negative coefficients as well as those not significantly different from zero or from unity.

SOURCE: Appendix tables D-2 and D-3 (functional form 1) and data from the Central American Industrial Census of 1969.

the industries with largest employment shares. The Costa Rican case is partly explained by the fact that two of the more labor-absorbing industries—textiles and garments—show fixed coefficients. Nevertheless industry 311 (foodstuffs), which in 1968 employed about one-third of total manufacturing employment, shows an elasticity of substitution of approximately 0.65. The final section of this chapter elaborates further on the policy implications of these associations.

Up to this point, the results described are all based on 1968 data. It is important, however, to verify whether the elasticity of substitution has experienced any changes through time. Changes in the elasticity affect both the bias of technological change and the rate of growth of production which, in turn, have a direct bearing on the problem of low labor absorption in manufacturing.[35] Table D-8 in appendix D presents estimates of the elasticity of substitution for Guatemala, for the years 1964, 1968, and 1971. Firm data were used with three-digit CIIU groupings.

It is seen from table D-8 that the magnitude of σ shows a downward trend between 1964 and 1968, and increases again in 1971. However, these differences are not statistically significant and it cannot be concluded that the elasticity of substitution has changed between 1964 and 1971, for Guatemala. The estimate that appears in the next to the last column of the table is obtained by pooling the data of three years (equation 2a) and could be considered as an acceptable estimate of the substitution possibilities of each industry.[36]

On the other hand, the last column of table D-8 reports the estimates of the elasticity of substitution that result from incorporating the cost of capital (equation "f" of table 4-2). These estimates tend to be lower than those of equation (2a). The arithmetic averages for the two estimates are 0.683 and 0.908, respectively. Nevertheless, there is a positive association between both estimates, with a simple correlation coefficient of 0.67. The above results show that Central American entrepreneurs respond to changes in factor relative prices. Therefore, labor demand depends not only on the wage level but also on the cost of capital. The last section of this chapter discusses the relative price policies which could increase labor demand in manufacturing.

Finally, it should be noted that the models used require underlying assumptions that may not be valid for Central America. It is important to consider what types of biases would be introduced into the empirical estimates if this were the case. Probably the single assumption that raises the greatest doubt is that concerning perfect competition. That is, the maximization models presented here and in appendix D as the basis for the regression analysis generally assume that markets are perfectly competitive. Yet it is commonly believed in Central America that monopoly or oligopoly conditions prevail in the industrial structure; this belief tends to be supported by the indicators of industrial concentration presented in appendix H. Nevertheless, a more careful examination shows that perfect competition is not a condition as crucial for estimating the models as it may seem to be at first. Appendix D demonstrates that under a variety of conditions of imperfect competition, both in the product market and in the factor markets, the results obtained in this study hold valid. The assumption underlying the analysis is that entrepreneurs maximize profits, under different conditions in the product and in the factor markets, by equalizing marginal resource revenue to marginal resource cost, and marginal total revenue to marginal total cost. The problem of biases arises in most cases because observed market prices—in this case the wage rate—differ from those that are relevant for the profit-maximizing level of factor use (labor). These differences are due precisely to imperfections in either or both the product and factor markets. Consequently, use of observed market price leads to estimation biases which can be treated either as biases due to error of measurement in the variables or to omission of relevant variables.

It is shown in appendix D that estimation under certain assumptions, like competition, or the same degree of imperfect competition in the product market or in the labor market for all observations when those assumptions are not true, will bias the elasticity of substitution estimate toward unity. Other conditions, including simultaneous equation bias, will bias the estimate of σ downward.[37] However, unless the relative magnitudes of these biases are known, no conclusion can be made about whether the estimates obtained are biased in either direction.

(b) Estimation at the aggregate level

As an alternative to estimation using individual firm data for each observation, the equations examining factor substitutability may be calculated using, as each individual observation, the total of labor, capital, and output in a single industrial branch. Estimates of this type are reported in table D-9 of appendix D. These results are given for two alternative levels of aggregation: in the first, all firms in each four-digit CIIU category are collapsed into a single observation; in the second, all firms in each broader three-digit category are consolidated. Although four alternative estimation forms are applied, the results for the principal form (logarithm of value added per worker regressed on logarithm of the wage) suffice to establish the patterns found. These results are shown in table 6.

Table 6. Elasticity of Substitution with Aggregate
Observations at the Four- and Three-Digit
CIIU Levels, 1968

Country	4-Digit	3-Digit
Guatemala	1.672	1.337
Honduras	1.178	1.921
Nicaragua	n.a.	1.837
Costa Rica	1.258	1.262

SOURCE: Appendix D, table D-9.

The results using aggregated data for each observation (and estimating across all industries) yield a much higher elasticity of substitution than that typically computed using firm level data for a single industrial branch. The reason is that substitution between factors under the aggregate approach includes the influence of indirect substitution through changes in the product mix. Similarly, the effect of raising the level of aggregation at which the estimate is made is generally to raise the estimated elasticity of substitution. The simple average for the elasticity is 1.369 for the four-digit case and 1.579 for the three-digit case. Nevertheless, as may be seen in table D-9, these estimates tend not to differ significantly (in the statistical sense) from unity.

An interesting aspect of the results reported in table D-9 is that at the aggregate level, the estimates of the elasticity of substitution under functional forms 1 and 2 are quite similar. These results stem from the fact that the coefficient on value added (c_1) in functional form 2 approximates unity as the degree of aggregation rises. When this coefficient is unity, there is no difference between the two functional forms.

Because census data aggregated to the level of three-digit industries are available for earlier years, it is possible to obtain substitution elasticity estimates at the aggregate level for years prior to 1968. Appendix table D-10 presents these estimates. Even though the estimates do vary somewhat over time, in only two of the eleven cases does the elasticity differ significantly from unity. The implication is that at the aggregate level the elasticity of substitution is not only unitary but also stable over time.

(c) Summary

For econometric reasons, the most appropriate equation for estimation of the elasticity of substitution using firm level data is the basic form in which the logarithm of value added per worker is regressed on the logarithm of the wage rate. Using this form and plant level data, the average elasticity of substitution encountered for all industries and countries in the region is in the neighborhood of 0.8. The empirical evidence indicates that there exist differences in the magnitude of the elasticity of substitution, both among industries of a single country and among countries for the same industry. The results do not support the generally accepted notion that possibilities for the substitution of factors are greater in traditional industries than in dynamic industries. The results also suggest that substitutability generally is higher in some countries than in others, the highest being in Honduras and the lowest in Guatemala and Costa Rica.

There is no conclusive evidence that the elasticity of substitution has changed over time. Consideration of the possible biases in the estimates, particularly any biases posed by imperfect market structure, indicated that there was no basis for expecting the estimates obtained to be biased upward or downward.

Estimates based on aggregate data, on the other hand, show higher substitutability than those based on firm level data. The aggregate estimates generally do not differ significantly from unity and are stable over time. However, the two sets of estimates--firm level and industry level--actually measure different phenomena and are not comparable. The former refer to the possibilities of substitution between capital and labor for firms producing a single product, whereas the latter also include the possibility of substituting products. For this reason, it is the results obtained using the firm level data that are relevant for the examination of wage and capital cost policies which are designed to have their effect through the adjustment of entrepreneurs to changes in incentives for the use of capital and labor in their individual firms.[38] Therefore, the central estimate of this study of the relevant elasticity of substitution is the approximate value of 0.8, a result indicating considerable responsiveness of factor combinations to factor prices. The elasticity of labor demand with respect to the wage rate should then be unity or higher since the substitution elasticity exceeds the capital share. The policy implications of these results are explored further in the final sections of this chapter.

2. Economies of Scale

Two alternative equations are used to obtain estimates of economies of scale from the firm level data of the 1968 industrial census. In the first (form "d" of table 2), the logarithm of labor is regressed against the logarithm of wage (with coefficient b_5) and the logarithm of value added (with coefficient c_1). If returns to scale are constant, the coefficient on value added should be unity; the percentage rise in labor demand should be equal to the percentage rise in value added as firm size increases, abstracting from any change in wages.[39] In the second equation, the Kmenta approximation of the CES production function (form "f" of table 2), the parameter for returns to scale is estimated directly, as the coefficient on the logarithm of labor.[40] There are constant, increasing, or decreasing returns to scale when this coefficient is equal to, greater than, or less than unity, respectively.

Appendix table D-2 presents, for Central America as a whole, the results of estimation of the first of these two equations ("functional form 2," in the table).[41] Table D-2 indicates that in the great majority of cases the magnitude of the scale parameter "h" is greater than unity, implying a preponderance of increasing returns to scale. However, the scale estimates are of such large magnitudes that they cannot be taken seriously. The results frequently show values of "h" higher than 2, meaning returns to scale of 100 percent (that is, as inputs rise by 10 percent, output would rise by 20 percent). The discussion of appendix D sets forth the reasons why results from this estimating form might be expected to be biased upward, including the problem of errors in measurement of variables and the possibility that the production function is not homothetic. Results obtained below with the Kmenta approximation function suggest that the latter problem is not present; instead it seems to be that, in addition to the instability caused when b_5 is close to the value of c_1 in the calculation of h (or when b_5 approaches unity in absolute value), the principal problem is that of errors of measurement. These errors produce underestimates of b_5 and c_1 and, as a result, overestimates of the scale parameter h. In view of the severity of the problem as manifested by the frequency of unacceptably high estimates of economies of scale using this first equation, there is little alternative to simply abandoning it.

The second basic approach to estimating returns to scale applies the Kmenta approximation of the CES production function.[42] This estimating equation produces highly reliable estimates of the returns to scale parameter,[43] even though it is not very suitable for estimation of the elasticity of substitution. Moreover, by contrast with the parameters σ and δ, the parameter h does not depend on the units of measurement of capital and labor in this approach, so that the data on these variables may be used in their original form.

Table D-11 in appendix D presents the results of the Kmenta approximation for the region, using establishment level observations for CIIU three-digit groupings with data referring to 1968.[44] For an overview of the results table 7 shows the simple and weighted averages of economies of scale for the manufacturing sector of each country, and for the subgroupings of industries into traditional and dynamic categories.

The results indicate economies of scale for Guatemala, near to constant returns for Honduras and Nicaragua, and decreasing returns for Costa Rica. For the region as a whole, there are increasing returns on the order of 6 percent. In Guatemala, economies of scale are in the range of 12 percent to 17 percent; in Honduras, they are approximately 5 percent. The diseconomies of scale found for Costa Rica are approximately 12 percent. The results could be interpreted to mean that the exploitation of economies of scale attained from a widening of the market through economic integration would vary across the countries in the Common Market.

Although these differences among countries must be viewed with caution, given the lack of statistical significance of most of the individual estimates lying behind the summary in table 7,[45] it is particularly intriguing that the results find positive returns to scale only in the largest national market in the region, on the one hand, and in the smallest market, on the other. The finding that economies of scale for Honduras exceed those in Nicaragua and Costa Rica is consistent with the notion that for smaller markets the scale is so limited that firms exhibit very high returns to further scale expansion.[46] However, the finding that returns to scale then rise once again to higher levels for the largest market, that of Guatemala, requires additional explanation. This result is consistent with considerations of spatial economics, and in particular, considering the benefits of the "agglomeration" of activities. It is easily conceivable that the Guatemalan market represents a sufficiently larger size than the markets of Nicaragua and Costa Rica that it surpasses a "threshold" size beyond which higher internal returns to scale are feasible. These higher returns may be facilitated by the external economies of scale (including those in the supply of urban services) afforded by the agglomeration of activities in a polarization of of development.[47] Indeed, it can be expected that unless regional or multilateral action is taken to counterbalance these inherent polarizing forces, economic activity stemming from the integration effort will generally tend to concentrate in the countries with the largest markets.[48] In fact, chapters 2 and 3 of this volume show that, for Central America, benefits of integration have indeed been less than fully shared by Honduras, the region's smallest and least-developed economy. The alternative measures presented in chapter 3 generally show Guatemala as the highest or next to highest beneficiary country in the integration process, a pattern which is consistent with the "polarization" phenomenon and with the apparently higher degree of returns to scale in Guatemala than in the other countries of the region.

It is also interesting that except for Costa Rica, economies of scale estimates for "traditional" industries are higher than those of "dynamic" industries. Again, as in the case of the elasticity of substitution, this fact is in disagreement with conventional views and expectations. Nevertheless, the limitations of these overall averages must be

155

Table 7. Simple and Weighted[a] Averages of Economies
of Scale for Central American Manufacturing
Sectors, 1968

Country/Averages	Total[b]	Groups 311-342[b,c]	Groups 351-390	Regression Estimates[d]
Guatemala				
Simple	0.125	0.189	0.072	0.174*
Weighted	0.206	0.192	0.232	
Honduras				
Simple	0.045	0.066	-0.002	n.a.
Weighted	0.076	0.097	0.009	
Nicaragua				
Simple	-0.065	0.095	-0.248	-0.018
Weighted	-0.008	0.081	-0.274	
Costa Rica				
Simple	-0.131	-0.125	-0.139	-0.119*
Weighted	0.007	0.065	-0.154	
Central America				
Simple	0.043	0.108	-0.021	0.059*
Weighted	0.108	0.159	-0.003	

[a]The weighting factor is the share of each three-digit industrial group in the total value added for all the groups included in the average.
[b]These estimates are calculated using the coefficients of the three-digit groups.
[c]Excludes group 341 (fabrication of paper and paper products), which is included in the following column.
[d]These estimates are obtained from a single regression encompassing all of the establishments of the country. The asterisk indicates that the estimate is significant at the 1 percent level.

SOURCE: Table D-11 and SIECA/Brookings, Desempleo...., Tomo III, Cuadros 16-19, Apendice 5.

kept in mind and the individual industry estimates should be analyzed as well.

Table D-12, in appendix D, presents the results for each country and for the region at the industry level. Even though the general lack of statistical significance in the results means that they must be viewed with caution, certain interesting patterns may be seen. First, economies of scale vary widely among countries for a particular industry. For example, the foodstuffs sector (311) shows substantial economies of scale in Guatemala, much lower increasing returns in Honduras and Nicaragua, and diseconomies of scale in Costa Rica (although the last three cases do not differ statistically from constant returns). Second, the industry estimates are consistent with the country averages.[49] Third, except for Guatemala the impact of economic integration on production bears no close relationship to the existence of economies of scale at the industry level. However, for Guatemala in all but two of the ten industries in which integration had the greatest relative production effect, there are indications of increasing returns to scale.[50]

Finally, table D-9 of appendix D shows that, at the aggregate level, the patterns already described at the firm level for each country still hold. That is, estimates with aggregate observations at the four-digit level indicate positive returns to scale for Guatemala, close to constant returns for Honduras, fairly small decreasing returns for Nicaragua, and diseconomies of scale for Costa Rica. This result could be interpreted as an indication that external economies and diseconomies either have been negligible or have cancelled each other, since economies of scale at the firm and at the industry level could coincide only in the absence of external economies or diseconomies.

To recapitulate, the estimates obtained for economies of scale indicate--in a strict statistical sense--increasing returns to scale only for six three-digit industries in Guatemala and one in Costa Rica; decreasing returns are found for one industry in Nicaragua and for three in Guatemala; for the remaining industries, constant returns to scale cannot be rejected on the basis of the evidence presented.[51] Nevertheless, the signs and the magnitudes of the estimates suggest certain provocative patterns and raise some interesting questions. A geographical pattern from north to south is formed which starts with economies of scale in Guatemala and ends with diseconomies of scale in Costa Rica, suggesting the possibility of an uneven degree of exploitation of economies of scale through integration, among the five countries of the region.

Another interesting pattern found is that "traditional" industries, as a group, present higher economies of scale estimates than "dynamic" industries, contrary to conventional expectations.

Appendix D examines the question of whether economies of scale vary over different size ranges, using the transcendental-logarithmic production function. Although some evidence is found in support of variable returns to scale, the results vary by country and by the precise test applied (see appendix D).

Our central conclusion on economies of scale is that the hypothesis of constant returns cannot be rejected for most industries on the basis of the evidence presented. Nevertheless, divergent results are sufficiently suggestive to warrant further research on the question of scale economies in Central American manufacturing industry.

3.   Technological Change

Estimation of the different aspects of technological change require comparable data for more than one point in time. Since establishment level

157

data for years other than 1968 were available only for Guatemala, the following analysis refers to that country, although the results may well be
applicable to the other Central American countries.

Equation "f" of table 2 was fitted to three-digit industries using date
at the establishment level, for the years 1964, 1968, and 1971. From the
resulting parameter the bias in technical change was estimated according
to the methodology described above. The results are shown in table 8.

Table 8. Guatemala: Bias of Technical Change

Industry		Bias
311	Foodstuffs	1.4167
312	Foodstuffs	0.6298
314	Tobacco	0.5270
321	Textiles	0.2137
322	Clothing	0.5994
331	Wood products, excluding furniture	0.5224
332	Wood furniture	0.6995
341	Paper and paper products	0.7126
342	Printing equipment	0.6314
351	Chemicals for industry	0.5459
352	Chemical products	0.5808
355	Rubber products	1.9960
356	Plastic products	1.4454
362	Glass and glass products	1.0572
369	Nonmetallic minerals	0.5530
371	Iron and steel	0.5670
381	Metallic products, excluding machinery	0.5287
382	Machinery, excluding electrical	1.5616
383	Electrical machinery and appliances	0.1876
384	Transport machinery	2.0515
385	Scientific equipment	0.1621
390	Other industries	0.2846

With the exception of industry 321 (textiles), all of the estimates
turned out to have positive signs. This is a strong empirical indication that technical change in Central America's industry (at least in
Guatemala) has had an implicit bias against the use of labor. This fact
not only throws some light on the slow rates of labor absorption in industry but also helps to explain the exceedingly low participation of wages
in value added.[52] These and the policy implications of the labor bias
in technical change are discussed in the last section of this chapter.

Unfortunately, due to the unstable character of the formulas to calculate the rates of capital-augmenting and labor-augmenting technical
change, when the elasticity of substitution is close to unity, it was not
possible to obtain reasonable estimates for these parameters. And since

the effect of technical change on production, or intensity of technological change, is a function of the above rates, this effect could not be
estimated either.

4.   Employment Effect of Integration

The final subject for investigation in this chapter is the effect
of economic integration on employment in Central America. As noted in
section G of this chapter, the analysis of this effect is done for two
overlapping time spans. One refers to the years 1958 to 1968, which can
can be considered the "normal" period of the Common Market. The other
includes this period but goes four years beyond, to 1972. It is thus
possible to have an idea of the effect--if any--that the institutional
crisis of 1968 had on employment.

Of the three estimation methods described in the last section of
this chapter, only the third one was applied to all five countries. The
first two methods were applied only to Guatemala and Costa Rica, since
the required data were not available for the other countries.

The results for Guatemala and Costa Rica (table 9) show that method
1 gives the lowest estimate whereas method 3 gives the highest. For reasons mentioned earlier, it is reasonable to expect that the true employment
effect of integration lies within these two estimates. Thus, the total
number of direct jobs created by integration in Central America probably
was about 30,000 until 1968, and about 10,000 between 1968 and 1972. This
is equivalent to approximately 3,000 incremental jobs annually during
the first   ten years considered, and   2,500 new jobs per year after
1968. Although these are gross estimates, they suggest that there was
in fact a slowdown in the number of jobs created by integration after
the 1968 conflict between Honduras and El Salvador. Unfortunately, this
effect could not be singled out for these two countries.

The discussion that follows refers to the results of method 3 (application of labor coefficients to the increase in production attributed
to integration, as calculated in chapter 3).

One important pattern is the country distribution of new jobs created
by integration. Table 10 presents estimates of this distribution.

Bearing in mind the considerable limitations of the information relative to employment levels, it is interesting to note that Guatemala and
El Salvador benefited more than proportionally since their total share
in regional employment in 1958 was only 40 percent, but close to 70 percent of the new jobs created by integration in the region went to these
two countries. Partly as a consequence of the above phenomenon, Guatemala
and El Salvador increased their share in total regional employment to
53 percent in 1972. For these results and those discussed below, however,
it should be kept in mind that the estimates of job creation are derived
from the output changes identified under the static effects of integration
only. As discussed in chapter 3, the dynamic effects of increased investment are more pronounced for Nicaragua and Honduras, whereas the static
effects are concentrated in Guatemala and El Salvador. Therefore the

159

Table 9. Estimates of the Number of Direct
Jobs Created by Integration

| | 1958–68 | | | 1958–72 | | |
Country	Method 1	Method 2	Method 3	Method 1	Method 2	Method 3
Guatemala	6,130	11,098	17,152	7,118	13,186	21,287
El Salvador	...	...	12,898	...	...	21,075
Honduras	...	...	2,601	...	...	2,604
Nicaragua	...	...	2,966	...	...	5,732
Costa Rica	4,611	6,863	6,926	4,202	6,622	7,244
Central America	...	...	42,543	...	...	57,939

NOTE: Method 1: $dL = c(dQ/Q)L$;
        Method 2: $dL = (dQ/Q)L$;
        Method 3: $dL = dQ(L/Q)$.

See text.

Table 10. Country Shares in Jobs Created by Integration,
and Shares in Regional Manufacturing Labor Force
(in percent)

| | Share in direct regional employment generated by integration | | Share in regional manufacturing employment | | |
Country	1958–68	1958–72	1958	1968	1972
Guatemala	40	36	21	28	32
El Salvador	30	36	22	24	21
Honduras	6	6	17	14	13
Nicaragua	7	10	18	14	14
Costa Rica	16	12	22	20	20
Central America	100	100	100	100	100

SOURCES: Table 9 and estimates based on information of the country population censuses of the 1960s and 1970s, the industrial censuses of Guatemala and Costa Rica for 1958, the Industrial Census of El Salvador for 1956, the Central American Industrial Survey of 1969, and the Industrial Survey of Guatemala for 1972.

employment results discussed here may overstate the degree of concentration of new jobs in Guatemala and El Salvador and understate new jobs attributable to integration in Nicaragua and Honduras.

Table D-14 of appendix D shows the estimates of the employment effects of integration at the industry level, for each country and for the region. The same information is presented in percentage form in appendix table D-15. It may be seen in these tables that nine industries dominated the direct employment opportunities generated by integration in the region. Within each country, four or five industries can be identified which accounted for about two-thirds of the jobs attributed to integration.

For Guatemala, these industries were 321 (textiles), 381 (metallic products), 311 (food products), and 352 (other chemical products). In El Salvador, nearly 40 percent of integration-generated jobs concentrated in two industries: 321 and 381; also significant were the contributions of groups 352, 322 (apparel), and 383 (construction of electrical machinery).

In Honduras, industries 321, 322, 341 (paper), and 352 represented jointly a little over two-thirds of the increment in employment, while in Nicaragua and Costa Rica, two industries (321 and 381) accounted for over 40 percent of that increment.

Thus, the effect of integration on direct industrial employment was concentrated in a few industries, among which are metal products, textiles, nonelectrical machinery, "other" chemical products, foodstuffs, and construction of electrical machinery and accessories. About 40 percent of newly created jobs in the region were concentrated in the first two industries just mentioned.

So far, the effects considered refer only to the direct number of industrial jobs generated as a consequence of economic integration. There could be, however, important indirect effects which take place within the same industrial sector or outside of it, as a result of the increased demand for raw materials required to meet the increase in industrial production. Indirect effects also spread to the transport, service, construction, and commercial sectors of the economy.

Since economic integration in Central America has been mainly an urban phenomenon, the analysis that follows considers first the indirect effects of integration on urban employment and then makes an appraisal of the possible indirect effects on employment in agriculture and mining. It should be mentioned that the estimation of indirect effects on employment, and hence, on production require the use of an input-output matrix, unavailable at present for the Central American countries. As an approximation, we utilized a recent input-output table for Colombia, a country about the size of the five countries combined and with characteristics similar to those of Central America in several respects. Table 11 presents the results for the urban sector of each country.[53]

Although these estimates have to be taken as gross approximations, the results indicate an employment multiplier of about 0.82 for the urban sector. That is, for each job created in industry, 0.82 job is generated in the other activities of the urban economy. However, due to the input composition of industrial goods, the largest proportion of that effect

Table 11. Direct and Indirect Urban Employment
Induced by Integration (in thousands)

Country	1958-68			1958-72		
	Direct	Indirect[a]	Total	Direct	Indirect[a]	Total
Guatemala	17.1	13.2	30.3	21.3	15.9	37.2
El Salvador	12.9	12.9	25.8	21.1	18.2	39.3
Honduras	2.6	2.5	5.1	3.6	2.4	6.0
Nicaragua	2.9	3.2	6.1	5.7	6.6	12.3
Costa Rica	6.9	4.0	10.9	7.2	5.7	12.9
Central America	42.4	35.8	78.2	58.9	48.8	107.7

[a]Excludes agricultural and mining employment.

takes place within the industrial sector itself. Approximately 75 percent of the indirect urban employment effects are generated in the industrial sector, but only 13 percent and 12 percent of that effect takes place in the transport, and in the service and commercial sectors, respectively. These estimates already take into account that part of the raw materials required by industry are imported and the indirect employment effects are thus partly translated to the country supplying those imports.

With indirect urban employment effects considered, the number of jobs attributed to integration increases from 42,400 to 78,200 during 1958-68, and from approximately 59,000 to a little over 100,000 during the period from 1958 to 1972.

Table 12 relates the above estimates with the increases in each country's urban labor force between 1958 and 1972.

The table shows that, during the decade that followed the year 1958, the urban jobs generated by integration represented approximately 18 percent of the increase in the urban labor force in the region. The situation differed between countries, this proportion being higher in Guatemala and Nicaragua, and much lower in Honduras.

By comparing the two columns of table 12, it can be inferred that the employment effect of integration loses importance in relative terms after 1968. The contribution of the Common Market to the provision of jobs for the incoming urban labor force is reduced to about 10 percent by 1972. A final effect to be considered is the indirect employment generated in the primary sector. According to the Colombian input-output table, for each dollar of additional gross industrial production, 13.8 cents are required from agriculture and 1 cent from mining to meet incremental raw material demand. However, some exercises made for the Central American countries with Guatemalan data[54] suggest that agricultural inputs for industry are considerably lower—probably between 4 and 8 cents per

Table 12. Ratio of Total Urban Employment Increments
Attributed to Integration to the Change in the
Urban Labor Force Between 1958-68 and 1958-72
(in percent)

Country	1958-68	1958-72
Guatemala	25.3	13.2
El Salvador	15.3	9.3
Honduras	6.9	6.2
Nicaragua	23.5	12.2
Costa Rica	16.5	7.8
Central America	18.4	10.5

SOURCE: Table 10 and estimates based on data from the country's population censuses.

dollar—due to the weak linkages between the agricultural and the industrial sectors.

To give an idea of the possible orders of magnitude of the indirect effects of integration on primary production, table 13 presents three
alternative estimates. Considering the qualifications just mentioned, it
is probable that integration contributed between 22,000 to 46,000 indirect
jobs in agriculture and mining. The fact that average labor productivities
were used in deriving the above estimates actually overstates the indirect
employment in agriculture since these jobs are not "equivalent" to those
generated in manufacturing.[55] The difference between the first two estimates and the third one could be interpreted as the cost, in terms of
foregone employment opportunities, of the weak links between agriculture
and industry, having as reference the Colombian situation. Notwithstanding, indirect employment effects in the primary sector are substantial,
accounting for over 25 percent of total effects in the economy, even in
the most conservative case.

Table 14 shows the contribution of total employment effects (direct
and indirect) of integration to providing jobs for the new entrants to
the labor force during 1958-72. Except for Honduras, integration's share
in the provision of new jobs was substantial. For the region as a whole,
integration accounted for a minimum 10 percent of the new jobs required
to employ the increase in the labor force between 1958 and 1972.

The principal results of this section may be summarized as follows.
First it is shown that two of the five countries, Guatemala and El Salvador, benefited proportionately more than their other partners in terms of
direct employment opportunities generated by integration. Second, direct
employment effects of integration concentrated heavily in nine industries;
four to five industries within each country accounted for approximately
two-thirds of direct employment attributed to integration. Third, the

Table 13. Indirect Effects of Integration on Agricultural
and Mining Employment, 1958-72

Country	Minimum[a]	Intermediate	Maximum
Guatemala	7,334	15,326	23,317
El Salvador	8,316	16,467	24,618
Honduras	1,200	2,599	3,997
Nicaragua	3,697	7,693	11,688
Costa Rica	1,839	3,690	5,540
Central America	22,386	45,773	69,160

[a]The alternative estimates assume coefficients of 0.04, 0.089, and 0.138
for the value of agricultural inputs going into each dollar of manufacturing gross production.

SOURCE: Calculated from estimates of the direct increase in production
attributable to integration from chapter 3, and average labor
productivities in agriculture and mining from CEPAL, "Consideraciones sobre la situación del empleo en C.A." Op. cit.

Table 14. Ratio of Total Employment Effects of
Integration to Labor Force Increments, 1958-72
(in percent)

Country	Minimum	Intermediate	Maximum
Guatemala	12.2	14.3	16.6
El Salvador	8.1	9.5	10.9
Honduras	3.9	4.6	5.5
Nicaragua	13.4	13.6	18.8
Costa Rica	8.1	9.1	10.1
Central America	10.6	12.2	14.3

NOTE: The alternatives differ in the agricultural employment effect estimate considered, as presented in table 13.

SOURCE: Calculated from tables 11 and 12, and data from each country's
censuses of population.

estimates indicate that a significant number of indirect jobs were created
by integration in the secondary and tertiary sectors of the economies. In
general, for each ten direct jobs created in manufacturing, from twelve
to sixteen additional indirect jobs are generated in the economy; of these,

approximately eight take place in the urban sectors and from four to eight, in the primary sector. It is estimated that integration generated about 60,000 direct jobs and from 71,000 to 95,000 indirect jobs from 1958 to 1972. Of the latter, approximately 50,000 went to the urban sectors and the rest to agriculture and mining. The above estimates represent from 10 percent to 14 percent of the increment in the labor force during the reference period. Finally, the results indicate that the effect of integration on employment was stronger from 1958 to 1968 than from the latter year to 1972.

K.   Policy Implications

In view of the priority of the employment problem in Central America it is especially important to draw policy implications from the empirical findings of this chapter. Although the results are derived from partial analysis, in the sense that it deals only with the manufacturing sector and that it does not address direct or indirect employment effects of broad development strategies (such as emphasis on industry as opposed to agriculture, redistributive versus laissez faire policies, and so forth), the findings do provide the basis for some important policy conclusions.

1.   Relative Prices

The results of this chapter demonstrate that there do exist possibilities for substitution between capital and labor in industrial production. That is, prevailing technology in the Central American manufacturing sector is not characterized by "fixed coefficient" combinations of labor with capital. Instead, a range of possible techniques exists for each product. Moreover, the analysis demonstrates that entrepreneurs do respond to changes in relative prices of factors; the estimated elasticity of substitution is on the order of 0.8 in the region. Thus, a 1 percent change in the relative price of the factors produces a 0.8 percent adjustment in the factor ratio used, for a given level of production. More specifically, an increase of 10 percent in the real wage would probably lead to a reduction in employment of approximately 8 percent. Similarly, a rise of 10 percent in the cost of capital, holding real wages constant, would lead to an increase of 8 percent in manufacturing employment if the level of capital were held constant. To be sure, these responses represent the longer-run sensitivity of factor use to relative factor prices. In the very short run it is likely that existing plants would have lower flexibility for rearranging labor and capital combinations since their equipment is already installed. But over the longer run, as new equipment is purchased for expansion and as new equipment replaces existing capital, entrepreneurs would have the flexibility to revise their labor/capital combinations and respond to changes in wage and capital cost to the degree predicted by the empirical findings of substitution elasticities centering around 0.8.

Considering wage policy, the impact of wage changes would be even more significant if induced changes in output level (due to changing labor cost) were taken into account. Recalling that the elasticity of employment with respect to the wage rate is essentially equal to the substitution elasticity divided by capital share, the results of this chapter indicate that this employment elasticity is on the order of 1.14. Thus, an increase in wages would be more than offset by a larger proportional decline in employment (so that the total wage bill would decline as well as the number of hired workers).

The fact that the elasticity of substitution appears to vary by country points to the need to consider the special technological and institutional characteristics of each member country when formulating policies to harmonize wages and social benefits within the Common Market. For example, if the countries with low wage levels also have high elasticities of substitution, then a policy of equalizing wage levels across countries will have a negative impact on employment for the low wage countries.

At the same time, it must be recognized that it is _relative_ factor prices, not merely the wage rate, which determine the factor combination used. Therefore, a consistent policy of harmonization across Common Market countries must take into account capital costs as well as wages.

There are basically two alternative policies for stimulating employment through changes in relative factor prices. One is to reduce the cost of labor and the other is to increase the cost of capital. The first may be implemented by reducing wage levels or by subsidizing the cost of labor to the entrepreneur. Among the instruments commonly cited for this purpose are the elimination or reduction of minimum wages, the reduction of employer contributions to social benefits for workers, and the weakening of labor organizations. Instruments for subsidizing the use of labor include direct payments of wage subsidies (from the government to employers) to cover the difference between the market wage and the institutionally desired wage; or indirect subsidies in the form of tax deductions or credits based on the wage bill.

Although these measures should theoretically increase employment, they face practical problems in implementation. Salary reductions are politically undesirable. Furthermore, policymakers would have to be very confident indeed that the estimated sensitivity of employment to salary is accurate, for if in practice the responsiveness of employment to wages were lower, the net result of reductions in wages would merely be a regressive redistribution of income away from existing workers to entrepreneurs. On the other hand, fiscal limitations virtually rule out mechanisms that require direct subsidy payments from governments to firms for wage supplements.

Given the current low level of industrial taxation,[56] the alternative of subsidizing labor through employment-related tax deductions would have serious limitations. These tax deductions or credits would probably be too small to affect entrepreneurial decisions significantly. However, if the general level of taxation were increased so that deductions or credits had more impact, such a mechanism might hold promise for stimulating employment. More specifically, if it were desired to avoid an increase in the total level of taxation because of concern over adverse effects on the rate of new investment, then an increase in the tax level could be gauged such that, combined with new employment-related deductions, the total tax collections remained constant but their composition shifted heavily to favor firms using relatively more labor while imposing a heavier tax burden on those using relatively more capital.[57] As discussed

below, from the standpoint of the cost of capital, as long as the depreciation rate allowed is accelerated (that is, faster than actual replacement rates), raising taxes will have the paradoxical effect of reducing
the cost of capital. Therefore, if a policy along these lines were
adopted (raising taxes but granting deductions based on employment
levels), depreciation allowances would have to be reduced to actual replacement rates in order to avoid a counterproductive side effect on relative factor prices.

In short, the direct reduction of wages as well as direct government
wage subsidies appears to be an undesirable or unrealistic means of increasing employment, but an alternative policy worth further examination
is the extension of tax deductions related to employment, with an offsetting increase in the general tax level to avoid fiscal losses. That direct reduction in wages is inadvisable is all the more clear in view of
the very low share of wages in industrial value added in Central America,
on the order of 27 percent.[58] In the face of such low labor shares it
would be questionable to pursue policies further reducing, or restraining
the future growth of, real wage levels which, in any event, have been
in jeopardy during the recent period of heightened inflation.

With these policy limitations on stimulating employment on the wage
side, it is especially important to consider possibilities for action on
the side of capital cost. Measures in this area generally include the
elimination or reduction of subsidies to capital embedded in various
instruments of fiscal, monetary, and tariff policy. To examine the influences of these policies it is necessary to consider their effects on the
cost of capital. The following analysis indicates that the most powerful
instruments for changing capital cost in Central America are financial
and tariff policies.

The cost of capital used in this chapter depends on the price of capital goods, the rate of replacement for plant and equipment, the depreciation rate allowed for tax purposes, the interest rate, and the rate of
taxation of corporate income.[59] In order to evaluate the impact of each
of these factors on the cost of capital, it is necessary to consider the
rates which typically apply in Central America. Up to 1973 the following
rates could be considered as reasonable approximations: 7 percent for the
replacement rate, 8 percent for the interest rate, 20 percent for the depreciation rate, and 10 percent for the income tax rate. Using these
values, the resulting annual cost of capital is 13.55 percent of the
value of fixed capital assets.

On the basis of the equation for the cost of capital and the rates
just described, it is possible to determine the "elasticity" of capital
cost with respect to each component (that is, the percentage change in
capital cost for a 1 percent change in the rate in question).[60] This
analysis indicates the following elasticities of the cost of capital with
respect to the variables comprising it: price of capital, 1.0; interest
rate, 0.59; accelerated depreciation ratio v, −0.16; income tax rate,
−0.13. The most direct impact on capital cost comes from the price of
capital goods (a 1 percent rise in their price causes a 1 percent rise
in cost of capital). The principal policy which can affect the price of
capital goods is the rate of tariffs applied to imports of capital equipment, as discussed below. The other powerful influence is the interest

rate. The elasticity of 0.59 means that a 10 percent increase in the interest rate (for example, from 8 percent to 8.8 percent) will increase the effective cost of capital by 5.9 percent.

Accelerated depreciation and, under Central American conditions, taxation are negatively related to the cost of capital, although the small size of their respective elasticities limits their influence on capital's cost. A 10 percent rise in the accelerated depreciation ratio (depreciation rate divided by replacement rate) reduces the cost of capital by 1.6 percent. And, because of the tax savings conferred by depreciation allowances in excess of replacement costs, an increase in the tax rate by a proportion of 10 percent will reduce the effective cost of capital by 1.3 percent (by increasing the value of the tax shelter provided by capital through accelerated depreciation).

However, the elasticities themselves do not provide the basis for selecting the most appropriate policy instrument for affecting the cost of capital. The feasibility of introducing changes of the necessary magnitudes must also be considered.

Consider the price of capital goods; even though its elasticity for the cost of capital is the highest (unity), the principal policy instrument for altering the price of capital is the tariff rate on imports of capital equipment. Yet this tariff constitutes only a part of the total price of capital goods. Overall capital price is a weighted average of construction price and the price of machinery and equipment (as adjusted by tariff). Given the very low levels of nominal tariffs (as reduced by exemptions) for capital equipment imports--on the order of 6 percent-- the elasticity of the cost of capital with respect to changes in the tariff rate turns out to be merely 0.032.[61]

These considerations do not mean, however, that the tariff rate on capital goods should remain unaltered in a program of policies to raise the cost of capital. The low present level of these tariffs means that merely raising them to the average levels for other goods, and eliminating their exonerations, would lead to a large percentage increase in the tariff and thus a nontrivial increase in capital cost. For example, an increase in the tariff net of exemptions from 6 percent to 22 percent would lead to a 15 percent rise in the cost of capital as formulated above. Moreover, this type of policy would have the indirect effect of stimulating the domestic production of capital goods.

In the area of financial policy, traditional practice in Central America has been to maintain low interest rates. The typical rates of 8 percent probably represent only about one-half of the true scarcity price of capital in the region, so that financial institutions essentially subsidize entrepreneurs in an amount equal to approximately three-fifths of their capital costs. Clearly, financial policy plays a key role in the choice of technology; it represents a powerful instrument with room for change, considering the fact that interest ceilings are institutionally fixed. Yet under current practice, interest rates favor the use of capital-intensive techniques, discouraging the creation of employment opportunities. And this distortion becomes all the worse as inflation rates accelerate (primarily in response to international developments), turning the real rate of interest negative.

When considering the policy of raising interest rates to stimulate the replacement of capital by labor, it is of course necessary to determine whether there will be a negative impact on capital formation and thus on the creation of future jobs. As has been mentioned earlier, current profit rates in Central American industry are extremely high. Thus, it seems very likely that interest rates (and other capital costs) could rise substantially without significantly discouraging the rate of investment (although excess profit rates, primarily made possible by noncompetitive conditions, would fall).

A final qualification must be made with respect to the feasibility of rising interest rates to favor the use of labor-intensive techniques. Although interest rates are institutionally fixed in Central America, lack of control on external capital flows limits considerably the use of interest rates as a policy instrument for increasing employment. Under conditions of unrestricted capital flows, the effect of raising interest rates considerably above international rates may well be to increase substantially the internal public debt (interest on government bonds) while leaving unchanged the cost of capital to firms.[62] It is not surprising that in spite of the fact that interest rates in Central America are institutionally fixed, they are periodically adjusted to reflect changes in external interest rates. Therefore, unless control can be exercised on external capital flows, interest rate policies cannot be considered a suitable instrument to effect general policy measures with employment objectives.

In relation to tax policies, at present accelerated depreciation is common, as is the exemption of tax burden because of qualification under various criteria for industrial development tax incentives. Ironically, the second practice tends to nullify the first, from the standpoint of choice between capital and labor in production. The lower the tax rate, the lower the effect that accelerated depreciation has as a tax-saving mechanism. The rate of depreciation relative to the actual replacement rate is the pivotal influence; if the two rates were equal, an increase in the tax rate would be neutral to the choice of capital versus labor; and if depreciation were at a slower rate than actual replacement, an increase in the tax rate would raise the relative cost of capital and encourage more employment. In this last case capital would no longer endow the company with a tax shelter but instead would constitute a tax liability.[63]

This observation permits us to distinguish between two effects of tax policies on employment. One is the substitution effect which takes place when relative factor prices change as a consequence of modifications in the tax burden. The other affects employment through changes in the structure of production which are induced by profitability differences among industries. Several factors, such as unorganized capital markets, profit remittances abroad, and lack of internal demand prevent reinvestment of sizable profits in Central America. Thus, while not affecting employment significantly, tax policies may have resulted in high profit rates accompanied by unnecessary fiscal losses.

In fact, the most important consideration on taxation is probably the question of fiscal loss through exemptions, rather than the issue of taxation's influence on the capital-labor ratio. Even with higher tax rates it is unlikely that taxation of income per se could be used as an instrument favoring employment because it is unlikely that depreciation permitted would fall below the actual replacement rate even if the practice of accelerated depreciation were terminated. It would require the introduction of a new feature into taxation--deductions or credits related to employment--in order to turn the instrument into one capable of stimulating employment. Concerning revenue foregone, it would seem that widespread exemptions could be curtailed (thereby raising revenue) without serious threat to the pace of investment, considering once again the very high profit rates in the region. Harmonized steps in each of the Central American countries would be necessary to carry out such increases, because otherwise a fruitless competition to attract foreign investors away from partner countries would lead to continued or intensified exemption practices.[64] A side effect of a coordinated increase in corporate taxation would be that the instrument of deductions related to labor force would become more powerful as a means of stimulating employment.

On the basis of the above considerations on each of the policy instruments, the most promising policies for stimulating employment through altering relative factor prices are: raising tariffs on imported capital equipment; and, possibly, instituting tax deductions related to the firm's employment while adjusting depreciation rates and raising the general tax rate to avoid fiscal loss. Raising interest rates would require imposing restrictions on external capital flows to have the desired impact on relative prices. However, to the extent that interest ceilings exist which prevent rates from rising to the levels they otherwise would reach through market forces, a priority policy measure would be to eliminate these ceilings and allow rates to rise, since a corrective rise of this nature could take place without any control on access to foreign capital.

The empirical results of this chapter suggest further implications concerning such policies. For example, they could be applied in differing degrees across various economic sectors in light of the estimated degree of substitutability between labor and capital in each sector. Thus, relative price policies could be focused on sectors showing higher substitution elasticities--for example, dynamic industries rather than traditional industries.[65] As another example of sectoral selectivity, the case of Guatemala appears to show that the sectors having economies of scale also have relatively high degrees of factor substitutability. In these sectors, to the extent that industrial policy has been to grant incentives (especially financial) leading to artificially cheap capital, there has been a lost opportunity for achieving not only the gains from economies of scale but also employment expansion.

Relative prices in Central America demonstrate substantial disparity among countries in the cost of labor but great similarity across the countries in the cost of capital. Because the cost of capital appears to be well below its scarcity cost to the economies of the region, and in order to stimulate employment, policies raising the cost of capital should be pursued. These policies should probably be harmonized, raising capital cost similarly for all countries in the region. This harmonization is necessary not only to prevent the counter-productive competition for new investment (as experienced with fiscal incentives) but also because, within a common market, the price of a mobile factor such as capital should be expected to equalize. A coordinated rise in the cost of capital would still leave relative prices of factors free to vary among countries through variation in their relative labor costs, so that within the Common Market patterns of specialization would be free to reflect the relative endowments of labor (and natural resources) of each country.

2. Technological Change

The results of the models estimated indicate that technical change in Central American industry has been biased against labor. A useful insight into the implications of this fact may be gained if it is considered that labor absorption depends not only on the rate of growth of production but also on the degree of substitutability between capital and labor, on the rate of growth of relative factor prices, and on the bias of technical change. (See appendix D.)

Given that relative factor prices have not changed substantially--except perhaps for the last three years--due to the slow growth of both nominal wages and the cost of capital, employment growth has been limited by the bias in technology against labor. Furthermore, the results of estimating equation "f" of table 2 indicate a significant trend toward higher capital-labor ratios in Guatemalan industry. Again, if relative factor prices have not changed much and given that the elasticity of substitution is about 0.8, this trend toward more capital-intensive technology has to be attributed to biased technical change. Therefore, increasing capital-labor ratios and low absorption rates have resulted more from biased technical change than from relative factor price policies.

Another important implication to consider is that of technical change on the functional distribution of income. Given the assumptions of the models used in this chapter, the proportional rate of growth of labor's share can be expressed in terms of the elasticity of substitution, of the bias in technical change, and of the proportional rate of change in the capital-labor ratio. (See appendix D.)

The empirical results show that the bias is positive and that a capital-deepening process (increasing capital-labor ratios) has taken place in Central America. Moreover, the elasticity of substitution has been found to be about 0.8. These conditions imply a negative proportional rate of growth for labor's share. This means that the share of labor relative to that of capital is bound to decrease still more due to the bias in technical change. The above phenomenon may account for the very low observed relative shares of labor for developing countries in general, and for Central America in particular. It is thus shown that the present functional distribution of industrial incomes in Central America is affected by technological change and that this effect has been unfavorable to labor's income.

The results point out the necessity to formulate a policy to rationalize the selection, transfer, and adaptation of technology.[66] Since this is a long-term endeavor which involves scientific skills, substantial resources, and bargaining power, it is only natural that a joint effort be made by all five countries in this area. Emphasis should be given to measures that reduce the labor-saving bias in technical change (by reducing the difference between the proportional rates of growth of labor and capital), since it has not only signified low labor absorption rates but also hampered the increase in labor's relative income share.

A further implication is that relative factor price policies should play an important role in a strategy to raise unemployment levels. That biased technical change has been so important to the labor-absorption problem is partly due to the fact that relative factor prices have not been used with employment objectives. Therefore, these results strengthen the policy implications outlined before for relative prices.

3. The Common Market

The analysis of this chapter concerning employment creation through formation of the Common Market indicates that integration contributed to generate direct and indirect jobs by an amount equivalent to 10 to 14 percent of the total labor force increment from 1958 to 1972. It is not surprising that Guatemala and El Salvador benefited proportionately more than the other countries in terms of jobs created or induced by integration, since the two countries also had a larger share in the static gains from economic integration, as shown in chapter 3.[67] The implication of these results is that regional action is necessary to counteract the tendency of the output and employment effects of integration to concentrate in the relatively more industrialized countries.

Although the contribution of integration to employment generation is by no means negligible, the results suggest that integration effects per se should not be expected to yield very large inroads into the employment problem. In other words, though integration can help, it is not a substitute for the measures required at the national level to reduce unemployment and underemployment. Rather than approaching the employment problem indirectly through economic integration policies, it should be addressed directly at the national as well as the regional level. That is, explicit measures should be adopted with employment objectives. This chapter suggests that important employment and distributive gains may be achieved in the industrial sectors by raising the cost of capital and rationalizing the selection, transfer, and adoption of technology at the regional level. Still further gains could result from the incorporation of other important sectors, such as agriculture, into the mainstream of integration.[68]

Chapter 4

NOTES

1. For example, the study by SIECA, "El Desarrollo Integrado de Centroamérica en la Presente Decada," vol. 7, "Politica Social" SIECA/ID/ INTAL, 1973; C. M. Castillo, Growth and Integration in Central America (New York: Praeger, 1966); Torres Rivas, E; Interpretación del Desarrolla Social Centroamericano, 2d ed. (EDUCA, 1971); R. Quirós, "Agricultural Development and Economic Integration in Central America" (Ph.D. diss., University of Wisconsin, 1971); Tenencia de la Tierra y Desarrollo Rural en Centroamérica (CEPAL/FAO/OIT/IICA/SIECA/OCT/OEA) (EDUCA, 1973); and Monteforte Toledo, M., Centroamerica: Subdesarrollo o Dependencia, 2 vols. (Mexico, IIS, UNAM, 1972).

2. The character of these changes and the speed at which they took place in each country depended on different historical factors. The resolution of the conflict posed by the "liberal" influence in Central America was violent in Guatemala and El Salvador, peaceful in Costa Rica, and incomplete in Nicaragua and Honduras. See Torres, Interpretación del Desarrollo Social Centroamericano.

3. Nicaragua (1921, 1924, and 1926); Honduras (1925, 1930, 1932, and 1954); and Costa Rica (1934).

4. Among these are the drafting of modern labor codes, separate from the Civil Codes, the creation of Social Security Institutes, and the establishment of ministries of labor and social affairs.

5. These refer to "unemployment equivalent" rates which measure, in a grossly approximated way, the proportion of the rural labor force that theoretically could be withdrawn from agriculture without affecting agricultural production. See SIECA, "El Desarrollo Integrado de Centroamérica," vol. 7.

6. SIECA, "El Desarrollo Integrado de Centroamérica." There are, of course, differences between countries, the situation being relatively better in Costa Rica and Nicaragua.

7. In particular, those represented by the well-known "Cobb-Douglas" production function, which has the form $Q = AK^a L^b$, where Q is output, A is a constant, K is capital, and L is labor.

8. This well-known function was introduced in: K. Arrow et al., "Capital Labor Substitution and Economic Efficiency," Review of Economics and Statistics 43 p. (1961).

9. Where it is shown that, if constant returns to scale are assumed, the elasticity of demand for labor with respect to the wage rate equals the elasticity of substitution divided by the capital share.

10. Based on aggregates from the 1968 industrial census. Calculated from SIECA, VI Compendio Estadístico Centroamericano, 1975. (Guatemala

City: SIECA,   1975),   pp.   163,   170;   and from the original plant level data
from the census.

11.   On   the   basis of the   1968   industrial   survey,   estimated   rates of
return on investment of 30 percent and over are common in Central America.
These high   rates are   consistent   with the evidence of substantial oligopoly power because   of   industrial   concentration   in   the region, as reported
in appendix H, volume II.

12.   See   for   example,   M.   Abramowitz,   "Resources and Output Trends in
the United States since   1870,"   American Economic Review 46 (May 1956); R.
Solow,   "Technical Change and the Aggregate   Production Function,"   Review
of Economics and Statistics 39 (August 1957); or E. F. Dennison, The Sources
of Economic Growth in the United States, and the Alternatives Before Us (New
York: Committee for Economic Development, 1962).

13.   The principal   studies   in   this   stream of   analysis include: H.
Chenery,   "Patterns of   Industrial   Growth,"   American Economic Review 50
(September   1960);   K.   Arrow et   al.,   "Capital Labor   Substitution and Eco-
nomic Efficiency,"   Review of Economics and Statistics 43 (1961); R. Ec-
kaus,   "The Factor   Proportions   Problem in   Underdeveloped Areas,"   American
Economic Review 45 (September   1955); and H. Leibenstein, "Technical Pro-
gress, the Production Function   and Dualism,"   Banca Nacionale del Lavoro
Quarterly, no. 55 (December 1960).

14.   The alternative   approach of   incorporating technological change as
an endogenous   variable   remains   in   an   embryonic   state of   analysis.   See
E. Phelps,   "Models of Technical Progress and the Golden Rule of Research,"
Review of Economic Studies, no.   33 (April 1966); P. Samuelson, "Rejoiner:
Agreements,   Disagreements,   Doubts, and the Case of   Induced Harrod-Neutral
Technical Change,"   Review of Economics and Statistics   48 (November 1966);
J. Conrisk,   "A Neoclassical Growth Model   with   an   Endogenously Positioned
Technical Change Frontier,"   Economic Journal 78 (June 1968).

15.   This differentiation was used by A. Amano,   "Biased Technological
Progress and a Neoclassical Theory of Economic Growth,"   Quarterly Journal
of Economics   78   (1964),   and J.   Williamson,   "Capital Accumulation,   Labor
Saving, and Labor   Absorption Once More,"   Quarterly Journal of Economics
85 (1971).

16.   Thus,   for example,   during   the recent   proposal for restructuring
the Central American Common market,   twelve   years   after   the signature of
the General Treaty,   the   development   of   economies of scale is singled out
as one   of   the main   objectives   for   industrial development of the region.
SIECA, "El Desarrollo Integrado de Centroamerica."

17.   For the reader unfamiliar with regression analysis,   this statistical technique   essentially   chooses values of   "parameters" (or weights)
for each explanatory variable in the equation so that the predicted values
for the dependent   variable   being explained   are as   close as possible to
the reported   values actually observed.   The criterion for "closeness" is
the least sum of   squared residuals principle--weights on variables are
chosen so that, summing over all observations, the squares of the differences between the predicted and actual values are minimized.   The procedure has   certain   major   test   statistics   which   indicate   the   degree of

of success obtained in the estimation. The "R " or coefficient of determination, tells the percentage of total variation of actual observations which is explained by the equation estimated. The "t statistic" tells the ratio of an individual variable's parameter to the standard deviation (a measure of fluctuation) of that parameter, and the higher this ratio, the higher the "significance" of the estimate. (For example, a "t" ratio of 2 or higher generally will indicate that at the 5 percent level of significance the parameter estimated is significantly different from zero, meaning that 95 times out of 100 one would be correct in concluding that the relationship estimated in fact systematically does exist rather than being purely random.)

18. Beginning-of-period value for each of these categories was obtained by adding to the firm's initial book value (net of accumulated depreciation) the acquisition of new and used goods for all years prior to 1968 and subtracting the value of asset sales and depreciation during those years. (Note that, because of ambiguity in the census questionnaire, it is likely that some firms reported beginning-of-1968 assets as their "original book value".)

19. The questionnaire's criteria for distinguishing among these categories are vague. For this reason the data are probably unreliable for detailed analysis of differences in labor quality.

20. See, for example, Z. Griliches and V. Ringstad, Economies of Scale and the Form of the Production Function (Amsterdam: North-Holland, 1971) or P. Meller, "Estimación de Funciones de Producción para Establecimientos Industriales de Distinto Tamaño" (paper presented at the Seminar on Utilization of Econometric Models in Latin America, Mexico, November 1974).

21. Note, however, that other authors consider technical and professional workers as a distinct factor of production, making this distinction a central focus of analysis. In this case the estimated elasticity of substitution between "labor" (treated as a homogenous factor of production) and capital will not reflect the true elasticities of substitution between the two labor factors and capital. See C. Ullman, "The Professional in the Labor Force: An Econometric Study of the Growth of Professional and Technical Occupations in the U.S." (Ph.D. diss., Columbia University, 1972).

22. Gross output included value of sales of finished goods and products in process; change in stocks; and electricity sold. It excluded the value of services provided to outsiders, "other income," and sale of untransformed goods. The value of inputs included raw materials, packing materials, fuels and lubricants, and other materials, plus the change in inventory of each of these categories, plus the value of electricity purchased, insurance, advertising, contracted industrial services, and other expenses.

23. See Griliches and Ringstad, Economies of Scale. In the second case, if Q = gross output, and a = the constant ratio of value added to gross output, then if Q = f(K,L), M where M is intermediate inputs, Y = F(K,L) + aY, or Y(1 - a) = F(K,L). Thus, V = F(K,L).

24. Griliches and Ringstad, Economies of Scale.

25. International Standard Industrial Classification, revision 2.

26. The explanation of the unreasonably high estimates of from this form may be that errors in variables give a downward bias to the regression coefficient on the logarithm of V/L, and, as a result, an upward bias to the reciprocal of this coefficient, which is the substitution elasticity in this form. Furthermore, the relatively low R of either equations "a" or "b" implies a high value for the elasticity estimate through equation "b" due to the relation between both estimates, established above.

27. It is indicative of this problem that the coefficient of variation in $\ln V$ is 50 percent greater than the corresponding coefficient for $\ln w$, for the region as a whole. Besides, zero or negative values for V are frequent in some industries.

28. If the correct model is given by the two equations:

$$L = f(w, V) \, e,$$

where e is an error term, and

$$V = f(K, L),$$

then if the error term "e" increases, L increases, causing in turn an increase in V, such that V and the error term e are correlated—meaning that there will be biases in the estimates of the first of the two equations.

29. See H. Theil, Principles of Econometrics (New York: Wiley, 1971).

30. Suppose that the correct form is:

$$\ln L = a_5 + \sigma_5 \ln w + c_1 \ln V + u_5,$$

but that the estimating equation is:

$$\ln (V/L) = a_1 + \sigma_1 \ln w + u_1.$$

Then:

$$E(\hat{\sigma}_1) = \sigma_5 + p_1(1-c_1)$$

where p_1 is obtained from the auxiliary regression $\ln V = a + p_1 \ln w + e$ (where e is an error term). Given that $p_1 > 0$, then the estimate of σ_1 will be biased upward if $c_1 < 1$, and downward if $c_1 > 1$. The bias will diminish to the extent that the true value of c_1 approximates unity.

31. This is the case for Costa Rica in branches 3220 (clothing articles), 3522 (pharmaceutical products), 3819 (metal products), and 3839 (electrical appliances) for which the possibilities of substitution appear to be well below those in corresponding sectors in the rest of Central America. Similar cases of atypically low substitutability occur in

Guatemala's branches 3311, 3320, 3560, 3813, and in Nicaragua's category 3117. Unusually high elasticity estimates (compared with those for other countries in the same categories) occur for Guatemala (3523), Honduras (3420 and 3699), and Nicaragua (3231).

32. Except that the ranking of Guatemala and Costa Rica reverses.

33. The distinction between dynamic and traditional stems from growth rates for value added. Between 1963 and 1969 the former group had a growth rate of 16 percent annually while the latter group experienced annual growth of only 8.2 percent. Classifications based on other criteria, such as the modern or traditional characteristics of production techniques, tend to produce groupings similar to the grouping used here.

34. The same result contradicting the conventional view is found for Brazil in: E. Bacha and R. Modenesi, "Technologia, Custos e Absorcao de mao de cora na Industria Je Transformacao: a Evidencia das Series Temporais" (Rio de Janeiro: Fundacao Cetulio Vargas, 1972).

35. If the elasticity of substitution is less than one ($\sigma < 1$), and the productivity of labor grows more rapidly than that of capital, then reductions in the magnitude of σ can induce the adoption of more capital-intensive technologies. On the other hand, decreases in the elasticity of substitution can mean lower rates of growth of industrial production if there are significant differences between the rates of growth of capital and labor.

36. The estimating equation in this case assumes that the intercept and the elasticity of substitution did not change during the period under consideration, although changes in labor productivity are permitted. The resulting equation is

$$2a \qquad \ln \frac{V}{L} = a + b \ln w + dt,$$

where t represents time.

37. In the event that the wage is not exogenous to the decisions of the firm. Concerning this bias, see E.S. Maddala and J.B. Kadane, "Some Notes on the Estimation of the CES Production Function," Review of Economics and Statistics 48 (August 1966).

38. The broader impact of relative factor price changes on product mix cannot be examined merely through the use of substitution elasticity analysis. Changes in total product mix would have to take into account aggregate demand elasticities, foreign trade effects, and aggregate supply elasticities in order to arrive at meaningful conclusions about the substitution of labor for capital through product mix variations. For an examination of this question see H. Chenery and W. Raduchel, "Substitution in Planning Models," in H. Chenery, ed. Studies in Development Planning (Cambridge, Mass.: Harvard University Press, 1971).

39. More specifically, as noted in appendix D, volume II, the degree of returns to scale in this case is:

$$h = [1 + b_5]/[c_j + b_5],$$

where the sign of b is negative.

40. In the Kmenta estimation, the logarithm of value added per worker is regressed on the logarithm of labor, the logarithm of the capital-labor ratio, and the square of the logarithm of the capital-labor ratio.

41. Corresponding results for the individual countries are reported in Charles R. Frank, Jr., Max A. Soto, and Carlos A. Sevilla, Desempleo y Subempleo en Centroamérica, Study Project SIECA/Brookings, vol. 3 (Guatemala City: SIECA, 1977). Hereinafter referred to as SIECA/Brookings, Desempleo, vol. 3.

42. In addition to the two approaches used in this chapter, a third alternative applying production functions of the Cobb-Douglas type, which are particular cases of the CES function, is used in appendix I to obtain supplementary estimates of economies of scale. Note that the benefit-cost analysis of chapter 3 uses sectoral economies of scale parameters selected from both the results of this chapter and those obtained in appendix I.

43. See G.S. Maddala and J.B. Kadane, "Estimation of Returns to Scale and the Elasticity of Substitution," Econometrica 35 (July-October 1967).

44. Similar results for individual countries are reported in SIECA/Brookings, Desempleo, vol. 3.

45. Moreover, there are a priori reasons for doubting the results of decreasing returns to scale, even thogh statisticaly significant decreasing returns are found for three sectors in Costa Rica. It should be possible to obtain equal efficiency in larger plants merely by repeating in multiples the activities carried on in smaller plants. Furthermore, for the case of developing countries it is to be expected that returns to scale are increasing, due to the incorporation of more modern techniques in new, larger plants.

46. For this same reason, the gains from economic integration through the achievement of economies of scale in a wider market might be expected to be greater for member countries with smaller national markets than for those with larger markets. See M.E. Kreinin, International Economics: A Policy Approach, 2d ed. (New York: Harcourt, 1975), p. 266.

47. Concentration patterns also reflect structural imbalances related to spatial differentiation of resources, population, and markets. A considerable amount of literature has come out after the pioneering work by F. Perroux, "Note sur la Notion de Pole de Croissance," Economie Appliquée 7 (1955), aiming not only at explaining spatial concentration of economic activity but also at achieving polarization as a policy objective.

48. Kreinin, International Economics, p. 327.

49. For Guatemala, fifteen out of nineteen cases show increasing returns (although only five are statistically significant); in Honduras,

nine of the twelve estimates are positive (but none significant); in Nicaragua decreasing returns occur in half of the cases (with only one case significant); and for Costa Rica approximately two-thids of the industries show diseconomies of scale (with two cases being statistically significant).

50. The ten industries are: 311, 321, 322, 341, 352, 355, 381, 382, 383 and 390.

51. This conclusion--similar to that obtained in the supplementary analysis of economies of scale presented in appendix I, volume II--provides the empirical basis for the adoption of a constant returns to scale functional form for the estimation of the elasticity of substitution in the preceding section of this chapter.

52. This question is posed by H. Bruton in "Employment, Productivity and Import Substitution," Research Memorandum no. 44, Center for Development, Williams College, Massachusetts, March 1972.

53. Indirect employment was estimated by applying the increments in value added attributed to integration (derived from the results of chapter 3 and value added to gross production ratios from the regional industrial surveys of 1962 and 1969) to the input-output table of Colombia, taken from the study by E. Thorbecke and J. Sengupta, "A Consistency Framework for Employment, Output and Income Distribution," Developing Research Center, World Bank, 1972. Average sectoral productivities of labor taken from CEPAL, "Consideraciones sobre la Situación del Empleo en Centroamérica," April 1972, were also used.

54. W. Cline, "Additional Material for Cost-Benefits Study," mimeographed. SIECA/Brookings, June 1975. The input-output coefficients used in this exercise were taken from the Industrial Survey of Guatemala for 1972.

55. Adjustment by agricultural employment rates could bring these estimates down by approximately 40 percent.

56. Corporate income tax ranges from 4 percent in Guatemala to 10 percent in Costa Rica (tax deductions included), according to information supplied by the respective Tax Revenue Offices.

57. It should be noted that the general strategy of labor-related tax deductions is considered to be ineffective, in a recent World Bank study, H. Chenery et al., Redistribution with Growth (London: Oxford University Press, 1974). The study suggests that such mechanisms would have minimal impact on factor demand while possibly causing an unnecessary fiscal sacrifice. However, the study generally considers factor substitutability to be lower than that empirically estimated for Central America in the present study. Moreover, if the strategy suggested here were followed--raising general tax rates to offset new deductions--the problem of fiscal loss would be circumvented.

58. Calculations made on the basis of data from the Central American Manufacturing Survey of 1969.

59. Specifically,

$$c_k = \frac{1}{(1 - u)} \, [(1 - v) \, \delta + rq(1 - u)],$$

where c_k is the cost per unit of capital, q is the unit price of capital goods, r is the interest rate rate, δ is the replacement rate, u is the tax rate, and v is the ratio of the depreciation rate to the replacement rate (so that v greater than unity indicates accelerated depreciation).

60. The elasticity is derived, for each rate, by taking the partial derivative of capital cost (from the equation of footnote 59) and then dividing by the ratio of overall capital cost to the rate in question.

61. The price of capital, q, is defined as

$$q = ap_c + (1 - a)p_m \, (1 + T),$$

where a is the share of buildings and other constructions in the capital stock (excluding land), p_c and p_m are the prices of construction and machinery and equipment, respectively, and T is the ad valorem equivalent of the nominal tariff adjusted for exonerations. Then, the elasticity of the cost of capita with respect to T is:

$$e_T = \frac{\partial c_k}{\partial T} \, \frac{T}{c_k} = \frac{(1 - a)p_m}{1 - u} \, [(\delta - ud) + r(1 - u)],$$

where d is the depreciation rate and other variables are as before. Evaluated with the typical rates cited for Central America, this elasticity is 0.032.

62. A one-time capital inflow from abroad can take place in response to the interest rate differential created between Central America and other countries, but unless the use of those funds is considered, that inflow will not be relevant from the standpoint of employment policy. It is also true that the cost of investment capital to firms will rise to the extent that they finance their investments in machinery and equipment through the forward exchange market, since they will be charged for the difference between the local interest rate and that of the country from which the machinery is imported.

63. More formally, the partial derivative of cost of capital with respect to the degree of accelerated depreciation (ratio of depreciation rate to replacement rate) is:

$$\frac{\partial c_k}{\partial v} = - \frac{u \, \delta \, q}{(1 - u)} \, .$$

Similarly, the partial derivative of capital cost with respect to the tax rate is:

$$\frac{\partial c_k}{\partial u} = - \frac{q(\delta - d)}{(1 - u)^2}$$

The first equation shows that when the tax rate (u) is low or close to zero, accelerated depreciation has a negligible impact on the cost of capital. At higher tax rates, greater acceleration of depreciation (higher v) means lower cost of capital. The second equation shows that when the replacement rate is lower than the depreciation rate (δ < d), an increase in the tax rate reduces the cost of capital; when the replacement rate is higher than the depreciation rate (δ > d), increasing taxes will increase capital costs. When the two rates are equal, changes in the tax rate do not affect capital cost; profits, of course, are affected.

64. For example, a firm subject to a corporate tax of 6 percent in Guatemala and allowed to depreciate its investment at the rate of 20 percent annually, will face a similar cost of capital but higher profits than the same firm in Costa Rica, where the tax and depreciation rates are both 10 percent.

65. Although the fact that absolute employment levels in the latter exceed those in the former means that more employment might be forthcoming in the traditional industries in response to relative price changes, even though the proportional change would be less than in the dynamic sectors.

66. This need has been given much emphasis lately by different institutions and organizations. See, for example, SIECA, "El Desarrollo Integrado en Centroamérica," vol. 7, pp. 119-124; SIECA, "Documentos Seleccionados sobre Transferencia de Tecnología en Centroamérica, Grupo Andino, y oiros Paises en Desarrollo," SIECA/CAN-VI/D15, vols. 3-4 as well as "Serie de Estudios sobre el Desarrollo Científico y Tecnologico," Programa Regional de Desarrollo Cientifico y Tecnológico, Departamento de Asuntos Cientificos, OEA.

67. However, as discussed in the chapter, incorporation of dynamic gains substantially raises the relative share of Nicaragua and, to a lesser extent, Costa Rica and Honduras, in the benefits of integration. Note that the dynamic effects, most importantly those due to increased investment, are not included in the employment effects estimated in this chapter, due to the absence of reliable sectoral detail on the dynamic effects.

68. Analyses of employment generation in agriculture and in the construction sector of the Central American countries are currently being prepared by Carlos A. Sevilla and Max A. Soto, respectively.

Employment Problems of Export Economies in a Common Market: The Case of Central America

Clark W. Reynolds
with the collaboration of
Gustavo A. Leiva

A. Introduction

The Central American countries are characteristic "export economies," dependent upon foreign demand for raw materials and primary products.[1] With fixed exchange rates and large trade shares of gross domestic product (GDP), the levels and fluctuations of national income and product of these countries have long been influenced by world prices of their major exports and imports plus capital flows to and from the region. Moreover, internal fiscal and financial policies have been highly conservative, for the most part, avoiding anticyclical measures. During "boom" periods increases in export prices and sales have expanded domestic liquidity and fiscal revenues. Government expenditures have grown accordingly, joining with private demand to activate the economy. In periods of depressed export prices and sales the reverse process has taken place, perhaps even accentuated by disproportionate declines in private investment demand. Hence internal economic policy in pursuit of fiscal balance between taxes and real expenditures has served to accentuate trade cycles rather than to provide some modest alleviation of the dependence on foreign trade. Attempts to break this dependency pattern have led to inflation and balance of payments difficulties. Since fiscal revenues of these countries are derived primarily from foreign trade, and other indirect taxes and government expenditure depend on such revenues, the labor-absorptive capacity of these economies has been traditionally dependent upon external conditions of trade, technology, and finance. Even taste patterns which influence the structure of final demand and employment have been conditioned from abroad.[2]

Recognizing the limitations of their domestic markets as a basis for changes in the structure of production, the Central American republics have made a number of efforts to unify their economies in order to reduce their vulnerability to foreign economic conditions. Two approaches existed in the minds of regional policymakers. One was to establish planned integration industries on a regionwide basis to avoid excessive competition among the countries while attempting to balance the establishment of industrial capacity to serve the entire market by favoring those countries with fewer competitive advantages for industrialization. This was a Central American approach to the postwar trend toward import-substituting industrialization. There was considerable internal and external opposition to the implementation of the scheme (planning was anathema to many in those highly laissez faire systems), but the ideal of planned industrial integration was reflected in bilateral treaties and a multilateral accord signed in 1958. Nevertheless the results were minimal and had little effect on either employment or welfare of the working class.[3] The second approach was to form a common market with free trade among members and a common external tariff as its central features.

In the 1960s, long after most other Latin American countries had completed the first stages of import-substituting industrialization, Central America established a customs zone called the "Central American Common Market." A common external tariff was applied, with duty-free internal trade for most of the goods produced within the five countries and the adoption of a common external tariff, approximately equivalent to the arithmetic average of the five national tariffs. Exempted goods included those which were not expected to be produced regionally within the medium run, such as automobiles and fuels; some agricultural products such as sugar, coffee, and bananas, produced in common but primarily for export to the rest of the world; and other commodities which were subject to quotas (but essentially duty free) such as corn and beans (frijol).

The system was designed to facilitate both trade creation and trade diversion by shifting the structure of production toward industry and, implicitly, away from dependence on traditional export activities and the production of nontradables. The intended effect on the labor market was to make employment more responsive to internal economic conditions and more independent of export cycles and trends. There was little planning involved, as higher relative prices for manufactures were designed to attract both domestic and foreign capital toward the establishment of new industries. These industries were to reflect the comparative advantage of the respective countries, given the new levels of protection, fiscal incentives, and other inducements provided by regional and national policy. However, effective protection in many cases proved to be higher than expected, due to exemptions from import duties from primary and intermediate products and exemption from income and property taxes for such industries. Also in some cases the external tariff on competing final goods imports was raised.[4]

The SIECA/Brookings Project has attempted to analyze a number of factors associated with the Central American Common Market (CACM), to determine the net impact of integration policies on the level and structure of production (rural and urban), relative prices, employment, and the income of the working class. This chapter examines overall employment trends among the five countries during the period of the CACM in response to changing conditions of labor supply and demand. Special attention is given to the level and distribution of employment among activity sectors, wage levels, the degree of unionization, the process of labor mobility including migration, and skill composition of the work force. The findings are used to determine the impact of employment and labor productivity trends on labor income and the wage share of value added in all major sectors of the economies of the five countries.[5]

This chapter summarizes a wide variety of data from existing studies on production and employment in the CACM. The degree of aggregation of the present analysis is necessarily high in order to permit a comprehensive view of the problem. Throughout the chapter the reader is referred to the literature on detailed aspects of the employment problem for specific countries, regions, and activity sectors. Special mention should be given here to the indispensable work of ILO-PREALC on the employment problems of Central America and Panama, which has been one of our most important sources.[6]

1. Background

It is hypothetical for purposes of this study that significant changes in the level and distribution of income of most of the Central American population have resulted from the regional pattern of employment growth, and that employment has in turn been influenced by integration policies favoring industrialization and urbanization. We wish to determine to what extent the "productivity growth" associated with this experience has been shared by the working class in the form of higher real wages and better conditions of employment.[7] The study estimates the "employment gap" and analyzes its effect on the level and distribution of the wage bill among the various production sector and income groups. These findings are then used as a basis for recommendations of a regionwide approach to employment and social participation in the development process, with a number of specific policies suggested to achieve these goals.

2. Employment Problems of an Export Economy with Import-Substituting Industrialization

In an export economy the initial income-generating activity is determined by foreign demand as reflected in international prices for the domestic export products (translated into internal prices through the exchange rate). The response of producers to this demand causes a derived demand for labor, depending on the technology employed and its effect on output per worker (labor productivity). If productivity rises rapidly, the increase in demand for workers will be less than proportional to the increase in production and vice versa. Hence, the first and most important employment-generating activity in an export economy is production in the foreign sector. The income generated by exports in turn generates factor payments to labor, capital, land and other rent-earning resources (such as subsoil minerals, plus patents, licenses, entrepreneurship, and labor skills in naturally or artificially short supply). Some economic rent may derive from barriers to entry in markets or other obstacles to free competition reflecting monopoly or monopsony power. Government controls may also give rise to scarcity rents, such as tariffs and indirect controls on trade which protect domestic suppliers, and the government may participate in rents and other factor income through taxation. We shall see how the forces of demand and supply in the market provide a potential for a variety of distributions of factor income within the dimensions of "value added" that the export sector derives from foreign demand. It will also be shown how institutional conditions reflecting the social, political, and historical characteristics of specific markets will influence the specific functional distribution of factor income of such economies, as illustrated by the experience of the five Central American countries.[8]

The factor income stream in turn generates final demand within the economy depending upon the demand propensities of households, business, and government, and their respective income shares. It is quite likely that the composition of disposable income between upper-, middle-, and lower-income households will have a significant effect on both the structure of final demand and the labor intensity of goods and services in the national market basket. Internal demand will lead to a secondary derived demand for labor, depending on the kinds of goods and services desired, their factor intensities, and the prices of those factors (reflecting in turn their relative scarcity).

In Central America the export-led pattern of labor demand has characterized the region since Colonial times.[9] The kinds of raw materials and primary products that they were capable of producing, and the institutional, social, political, and psychological conditions that prevailed in the several countries all had a major influence on popular participation in the value of production, principally through payments to labor but also through land rents accruing to smallholders. Only in Costa Rica did historical conditions produce a relatively egalitarian land tenure system with broader participation in economic rent from the main export crop (coffee). In the other countries, to varying degrees, development policy favored the purchase of land by those who were dedicated to the cultivation of export crops (especially coffee). This led to a high concentration of land in the hands of a new class of commercial growers. Policies also favored the provision of adequate suppliers of labor for cultivation, especially during the harvest season. As land shifted toward commercial cultivation, peasants found it necessary to work for wages at least part of the year on large holdings producing export crops to supplement the declining income earned on their diminished subsistence plots. Labor supply in these economies has traditionally been tightly linked to the supply of land, and real wages are directly related to the laborer's access to remunerative employment on his own smallholding. A model which draws on this experience to illustrate how wages, employment, and the functional distribution of income are determined in an export economy appears in appendix E.

Since 1960 the CACM has offered incentives based on selective trade policies favoring the establishment of manufacturing industries in the region. The pattern of import-substituting industrialization is analyzed in detail elsewhere in this volume. Such incentives were provided in addition to fiscal measures adopted by individual countries in the 1950s in the form of industrial incentive laws. These laws favored import-substituting industrialization, but in an uneven way among the five countries. Subsequent efforts have been made to harmonize the legislation in the spirit of integration, but without major success. The resulting pattern of economic growth is therefore a product not only of the CACM policies but also of a variety of other measures imposed quite independently of the integration process.

For our purposes we are particularly concerned with the way in which the continued set of incentives has altered the conditions of labor demand as reflected in the level and distribution of employment, wages and nonwage benefits, and the wage share of national income and product. In principle one would suppose that the growth of industry in the region would offer an alternative form of employment, in competition with both export agriculture and subsistence farming. Given the supply of labor, this should have a favorable effect on wages and living levels of most of the population; however, the supply of wage labor has expanded rapidly as a result of high historical rates of demographic growth, increased participation of women in the work force, and inadequate access to land in smallholder agriculture. The high rent potential of export cultivation in large holdings has reduced the reserve of land for subsistence production. Moreover, the benefits of employment in manufacturing and related urban activities have been unevenly distributed, with extremely unequal earnings for workers in different occupational categories.[10] There is strong evidence that the labor market has been segmented so that the normal forces of supply and demand have failed to transmit productivity growth to workers at all levels.[11]

B. The Labor Market

1. Rent Partitioning--the Struggle for Shares[12]

The net value of production (value added) of any economy is comprised of the following elements:

(i)   Wages and salaries (normal return to labor).
(ii)   Interest and normal profits (normal return to capital).
(iii) Land rent (return to natural resources).
(iv)   Other economic rents (excess profits, excess wages and salaries, returns to other scarce factors such as entrepreneurship, patents, royalties, indirect taxes).

In an export economy which depends upon natural resources to produce raw materials and primary products, a significant share of the value of production may be represented by economic rents. Since such economies are well within the range of being marginal suppliers in the world market for a number of basic commodities, their rental share of value added is significant. Rent as used here represents the residual after subtracting from value added wage costs based upon the reservation price of labor plus the opportunity cost of capital and other factor inputs. As shown in appendix E, the price of labor is bounded at the lower limit by its productivity in the subsistence sector but may rise above this level to reflect alternative earning opportunities in other activities if the supply of labor is inelastic. As such an economy industrializes, this can have an impact on the level of wages in the export sector, to the extent that alternative employment opportunities arise. But industrialization behind protective barriers may also give rise to a new source of economic rents, in the form of excess profits of protected industry, especially where competition is restricted. In this case the composition of rents may shift from rural or urban activities, but their share in value added may remain high, especially where labor is abundant.[13]

Hence, the objective of each participating sector in an export economy is to maximize the level of rent subject to its share of the total (recognizing that the two main goals are often in conflict). This often involves a high level of political activity, with a variety of strategies on the part of participants. The first stage of rent partitioning occurs within the traditional export activities, particularly among labor, capital, and the public sector. The political process provides one means of strengthening or weakening the bargaining position (and even the legality of the institutional representatives) of the participants involved, depending on their respective power. Often the struggle for rent partitioning will occasion major political clashes and may even lead to the rise and fall of governments. In the past some governments were established and others removed as a result of the interests of local and foreign firms in the securing of rights to produce exports (such as coffee, bananas, or cotton), with the greatest possible quantity of rents accruing to the principals involved.[14] Where governments may threaten taxation of rents, the producers may be willing to use all their influence with public officials in order to preserve the maximum share of rents. Such behavior is more likely to occur as the level of rents rises, increasing the stakes for those capable of exercising monopsony power in factor markets and monopoly power in product markets.

How does rent partitioning affect the demand for labor and its share in the distribution of rents? This will depend upon conditions in the labor market which, as they are more competitive on the supply side, and monopsonistic on the demand side, will tend to push wages down to subsistence levels, leaving the maximum amount of rent to be divided among the owners of capital, natural resources, marketing firms, and the government. Central American countries have differed historically in the extent of monopsony power of export industries in the labor market, as they have also differed in the relative abundance of manpower available to be employed in the export sector. This is handled in considerable detail in the literature on the social history of the region, with Guatemala being characterized as an economy in which access to land was utilized as a means of forcing workers (especially Indians and mestizos) into the wage-labor market to permit increased production of labor-intensive exports such as coffee.[15] El Salvador was even more successful at this strategy, owing to its notable scarcity of cropland and given its large and burgeoning population. The recent mass expulsion of Salvadorians from Honduras has exacerbated this problem.

The more land-abundant economies of Honduras and Nicaragua have been less able to take advantage of low-wage labor based on policies which limit access to land. Costa Rica actually adopted policies from the earliest part of the nineteenth century in which a relatively broad distribution of land tenure permitted large segments of the rural population to participate in the rental income from coffee and other exports.[16] This different behavior among the five countries, with associated levels of wages and social participation in the rental "surplus" of the export sectors, indicates that there is no single solution to the problems of employment and income distribution in the region. Indeed, the pluralistic policies that have operated in Central America, dating back to the Colonial period in some cases, underscore the alternatives open for social participation in export development. The political consequences of these alternatives are also apparent, since Costa Rica combined its strategy with a long and virtually unbroken tradition of democratic administrations, while most of the other countries have ignored the problem, frequently relying on force to hinder a broader social distribution of the gains from growth.

What these divergent experiences suggest is that increasing the share of the mass of the population in the rental income of such economies need not necessarily have a detrimental effect on growth of the demand for labor. Even though redistribution of income may increase the supply price of labor, this may be offset by the economies of scale and lower capital requirements of wage goods production for consumption by the working class. Moreover higher labor incomes, associated with greater incentives for education and skill attainment, plus broader political participation of the work force, will have a favorable effect on further productivity growth. Hence the Costa Rican model illustrates the feasibility, over the long run, of combining growth with a more equitable social participation in export rents and a more balanced demand for the products of import-substituting industries, construction, and urban services. Despite the evidence from Costa Rica, most of the other countries of the region have, maybe unwillingly, tended to perpetuate the historical trends of extreme inequality in income distribution and social participation.

2. Unionization of Labor

The history of labor organization in Central America is long and turbulent.[17] It is impossible to do justice here to the fluctuating fortunes of those who have attempted to build unions in the region.[18] In many cases labor organization was used as a means of developing popular support for political parties favoring liberal reforms. In other cases, unions arose out of attempts to repartition rents in favor of workers, first in the more productive export enclaves and later in the urban industrial sector. Opposition to such efforts arose from many landowners and entrepreneurs who sought to preserve profit and rental incomes. The degree of unionization (measured not only in numbers of workers organized but in their effectiveness in collective bargaining) might be expected to vary as a reflection of differences in conditions of supply and demand for labor as well as in response to the degree of political support for the various income groups. Economies such as Costa Rica, which have the greatest relative scarcity of labor, with the longest history of access of workers to export rents and subsistence cultivation of their own land, would be expected to have the greatest degree of unionization. Similar conditions should also hold for Honduras, where land is relatively abundant permitting labor to reserve its supply, given the alternative of subsistence cultivation.[19]

Table 1 shows that about 60 percent of the union members of Central America in 1973 were in Costa Rica and Honduras, though these two countries had only 30 percent of the regional work force. And 60 percent

of the union workers in Honduras were in the agricultural sector (principally banana workers), reflecting the abundant land in Honduras and
its highly productive export enclaves. The comparable figure for relatively more urban Costa Rica was 20 percent, while the figure for all
Central America was 30 percent of union workers in the agricultural
sector, which in 1971 employed 56 percent of the regional labor force
(table 1).

Table 1. Number of Union Members in Central America, 1973

Country	Total	Agriculture	Manufacturing and Mining	Services, and Other
Guatemala	29,186	15,283	4,220	9,683
El Salvador	54,387	1,432	24,464	28,491
Honduras	67,958	39,251	7,573	21,132
Nicaragua	10,419	602	1,796	8,021
Costa Rica	58,263	11,353	3,976	42,934
Central America	220,213	67,921	42,029	110,261

SOURCE: Unpublished SIECA study by Lic. Thomas Barrientos, 1976.

One of the most striking factors reflected in table 1 is the low
degree of organization of rural workers in Nicaragua (less than 3 percent of the agricultural labor force), Guatemala, and El Salvador (16
percent and 3 percent, respectively). These three countries are traditionally characterized by "labor abundance," meaning that the land tenure systems force large numbers of landless workers and smallholders
into the rural proletariat. Moreover, in Nicaragua and Guatemala there
had been a trend to reduce the influence of labor organization, especially in the rural areas. On the other hand, El Salvador shows 12 percent of its manufacturing workers to be unionized, while Costa Rica shows
under 8 percent, indicating that despite the degree of labor abundance
in the rural sector, in El Salvador industrial workers are much better
organized even in comparison with the most developed of the five countries. In contrast, labor unions play a much more active political
role in Costa Rica than in El Salvador.

Table 2 shows that the degree of unionization in 1969 was highest
in Costa Rica, as might be expected in view of the relative scarcity of
labor available at wages anywhere approximating those elsewhere in the
region, plus the existence of a political system rather more favorable

to labor organization. The astonishing thing is that between 1969 and
1976 Honduras moved past Costa Rica in percentage of the labor force in
unions, while conditions in El Salvador and Nicaragua stagnated and Guatemala showed the lowest degree of unionization of the five countries.
The abundance of land in Honduras has undoubtedly had an influence on
the ability of workers to bargain collectively. Moreover, Honduras has
been characterized as one of the more "socially conscious" countries in
the area; and it should also be noted that the regional institute for
training of labor organizers is located in Honduras. The low degree of
unionization in Guatemala is particularly disturbing in view of the successful industrialization in that country which, on those terms, is one
of the leaders in Central American integration. There is clear evidence
that for Guatemala, unlike El Salvador, the lack of labor organization
predominating in the rural areas extends even into the most modern manufacturing industries. Notwithstanding this, recent efforts to strengthen
the formation and operation of agricultural cooperatives, especially in
the region of the altiplano, provide some indication that the government may be beginning to take a positive interest in such matters.

Table 2. Percentages of Active Population
in Labor Unions

Country	1969	1973	1976
Guatemala	1.7	1.9	n.a.
El Salvador	5.0	5.0	5.0
Honduras	4.3	8.7	14.6
Nicaragua	4.8	2.0	5.6
Costa Rica	9.7	10.7	11.6

SOURCE: Same as table 1.

The major conclusion one may draw from these figures is that labor
is relatively unable to defend its interests in an organized way in most
of Central America, with the exceptions of a minority of workers in
Costa Rica and Honduras, and the industrial labor elite of El Salvador.
Hence one may expect that if segmentation does occur, it will exist for
those export enclaves and modern urban activities in which employers see
it in their interest to pay higher wages despite the relative abundance
of unskilled labor. This may hold for cases in which there is on-the-
job training or the demand for special skills which are in short supply.
It should be stressed that the degree of paternalism in employer-employee
relations in these countries is significant, even where unionization does
exist, and since our figures do not differentiate between independent
and company unions they probably exaggerate the practical consequences
of unionization on wages and nonwage benefits.

The significant differentials in labor income that are observed within given countries in Central America are, for the most part, attributable not to union partitioning of labor markets for the benefit of their own workers at the expense of outsiders but rather to skill differentials and to segmentation along class lines, as well as to unequal access to the educational channels into higher paying jobs. Those who benefit by secondary and university education tend to be from the upper- or middle-income groups in the urban areas, and principally those from the capital cities of the region, with the exception of Costa Rica where education is more broadly diffused and where class and racial barriers are less evident. There is little question that if the demand for labor were to outstrip the growth of supply in the coming years, the objective conditions would exist for significant improvements in the degree of labor organization and in the capacity of workers to bargain for larger income shares. However, the success of such efforts would also depend upon political conditions being favorable to the working class. Thus far the lack of social integration in the region works against both of these factors. Sections C and D of this chapter deal with the growth of demand and supply of labor in the CACM between 1960 and 1975. The resulting "gap" between supply and demand (excess supply) may be said to have influenced trends in real wages, employment, and income of the working class both directly and through weakened opportunities for bargaining of labor for income shares through political and institutional channels.

C. Demand for Labor in the Central American Common Market

1. Methodology

We shall look primarily at demand factors as reflected in census data on the actual employed labor force, normalized for the years 1960 and 1971, and supply factors related to those age groups considered most likely to be participating in the labor force, applying participation rates from 1960 census data to subsequent demographic estimates. The sectoral pattern of demand will be studied in terms of its structure and evolution since 1960 in relation to output by the same production sectors. This permits employment to be related to the gross productivity of labor (output per man-year) by activity sector and country, as a basis for estimating the effect of supply and demand shifts on labor income. Labor income is represented in this chapter by average earnings per worker by major sector of economic activity for each of the five countries. This information is obtained from primary data consolidated for the SIECA/Brookings employment study from a variety of statistical sources. The results of this analysis have been compared with individual country studies for El Salvador, Costa Rica, Honduras, and Nicaragua prepared by the PREALC division of the ILO as a means of insuring consistency between the regionwide analysis and the work at the country level. The PREALC studies have been particularly helpful in understanding the problems of urban employment and underemployment, while those of GAFICA have been indispensable for work on the employment and underemployment conditions in the rural sector of all countries.[20]

Figure 1 illustrates the principal factors underlying shifts in supply and demand as they have been reflected in regional employment and

Change in Supply of Labor ————————

1. Δ Population (lagged)
2. Δ Desired participation rates
   a. Δ Income from other sources
   b. Δ Quality of working conditions
   c. Δ Nature of work performed
   d. Δ Customs and traditions
3. Δ Wages and salaries
   a. Δ Degree of competition in supply of labor
   b. Δ Other institutional factors such as labor laws, unionization, productivity of labor in alternative pursuits such as domestic employment and home employment in the "informal sector"

Change in Demand for Labor ————————

1. Δ Composition and level of production (based on changes in final demand)
   a. Δ Domestic demand
   b. Δ Foreign demand
   c. Δ Fiscal and financial policies affecting relative returns on capital, labor, and natural resources
2. Δ Labor productivity
   a. Δ Technology
   b. Δ Labor skills
      1) Education
      2) On-the-job training
   c. Δ Degree of competition in goods and factor markets
3. Δ Wages and salaries

Note: Δ Supply - Δ Demand = Δ Employment Gap.

Figure 1. Structure of Supply and Demand Conditions Affecting Employment and Labor Income

labor income during the period of the CACM. It should be noted that this chapter refers primarily to first differences in labor service flows (changes between benchmark periods) rather than to absolute levels of supply and demand for labor, since there is no consensus on base or terminal year factor gaps in the labor market. The concept of "unemployment" refers to the number of man-years of labor which would be available for employment at the going wage. This concept is primarily applicable to developed countries during periods of recession when there is excess industrial or agricultural capacity which could be used to absorb labor if aggregate demand were stimulated. This Keynesian concept, developed for use in England and applied to the United States and Western European industrial economies since the 1930s, is largely irrelevant to countries such as those in Central America; there the degree of underutilization of capital and natural resources, if it does occur, is associated less with failures of aggregate demand than with resource bottlenecks, imperfections in the degree of competition in goods and factor markets, sharp inequalities in income distribution, and small absolute size of the economies which limits domestic markets and prevents the realization of scale economies. In addition there is segmentation of the labor market which results in a skewed distribution of factor income with an excess demand for high-paying jobs and an associated excess supply of low-paying employment opportunities.

In section E of this chapter the employment gap is examined in terms of alternative measures of absolute levels of unemployment (from the censuses) and underemployment (from PREALC and GAFICA studies of the urban and rural sectors.) The main factor affecting adjustments between supply and demand in this chapter is the level of labor income (wages and salaries and nonwage benefits). A decline in the employment gap should be associated with a rise in labor income and vice versa. The pure theory of employment assumes frictionless labor markets in which supply and demand adjust through changes in factor prices (figure 1, item 3). Among submarkets, movement of labor from lower to higher wage activities (ceteris paribus) should further facilitate the clearing process and eliminate factor gaps; however, there is considerable evidence that labor market segmentation causes factor gaps to be sustained, leading to an excess supply of labor seeking higher wages and larger numbers of underemployed in the rural and urban informal sectors.

2. The Distinction between Physical and Value Productivity of Labor

There is a confusion in much of the employment literature due to the failure to define the concept "labor productivity" properly. This is especially evident when growth and structural change in an economy lead to changes in the value of output per worker among the various production sectors. The demand for labor is a function of the marginal value product of labor in a given occupation, given the product price and the offer price (wage) of labor. The marginal value product has within it two main elements, the physical product of labor (physical units of output produced per man-year, given the technology employed and the supply of other factors including capital, natural resources, and intermediate goods) and the unit value of that physical product. Unit value is a function of supply and demand conditions in the market. If labor is a major input, then a shift upward in the offer price of labor will influence the final price of the product, increasing the demand for labor (marginal value product) for every given level of physical productivity. For such cases there is an identification problem in attempting to separate supply and demand factors associated with a change in the level of wages and the value product of labor. Shifts in supply and demand are interdependent.

To give an example, take employment in the service sector (part of the "informal sector" which absorbs the majority of increases in labor supply in the region). The physical productivity of a service worker, such as a barber, is relatively fixed over time and the service provided is comparable among regions and countries despite the fact that it cannot be traded. The number of haircuts that a barber can give during a year will not vary greatly regardless of the economic conditions of the region. Similarly the amount of paperwork that a government bureaucrat can complete will not change remarkably over time, except with the introduction of highly capital-intensive data processing. Yet the wages of barbers in terms of real purchasing power vary by a factor of ten or more between developed and developing countries, and among the regions of Central America they may vary by a factor of two to four from rural to urban areas and from country to country, as well as from poor to rich barrios in a given city.

What accounts for this difference in marginal value product, if marginal physical productivity of the service worker is approximately the same? The difference results from the relative factor gaps that operate from region to region, so that where labor is in abundant supply the unit value of the service is much lower than where labor is in short supply, given physical productivity. How might such markets adjust to equalize the unit value of haircuts? Consumers could move to other cheaper regions to consume haircuts, lowering their price in the high wage area and raising their price in the labor surplus region. Or barbers could migrate, having the same effect on relative prices of haircuts. Where commodities and services are movable, international and interregional trade help to bridge factor price gaps. But for one-third to one-half of the employment in Central America this method of equalizing markets is impossible because labor is producing home goods and services that do not exchange effectively over long distances. This places the full burden for factor price equalization on the small segment of commodities and services produced which are tradable and which employ only a portion of the total work force. And, as we shall see, the portion of labor which is subject to factor price equalization is actually declining as a share of total employment in Central America.

For this reason the adjustment in the value product of labor will depend most importantly on internal supply and demand conditions, although some of this demand will be derived from the markets for exports and import-competing production. This is why employment gap analysis is so crucial. To the extent that the excess supply of labor gap narrows, through demand increases caused by union growth in the export and industrial and productivity sectors, there will be upward pressure on real wages. This will have a repercussion on the final price of labor-using goods and services, and particularly those produced in small-scale agriculture and the informal sector. This increase in relative prices may of course be partly offset by a shift in consumption away from such goods and services toward imports and more capital-intensive products. But the net effect should be a rise in the marginal value product of labor, increasing the incomes of the poorest workers. In this way gains in physical productivity and increases in world prices for the leading sectors will be passed on to workers in the rest of the economy.

It should be repeated and underscored that improvements in real income of the poor workers will be associated with a rise in relative prices of labor-intensive goods and services. This must be permitted to take place if a broadened distribution of productivity gains is to occur. Such gains will necessarily lower the real income (purchasing power) of middle- and upper-income households, a large portion of whose consumption is in labor-using goods and services (domestic help, residential construction, personal services, hotel and restaurant services, maintenance and repair of consumer durables). Hence for physical productivity growth in the capital-intensive sector to be translated into value product growth of labor in the tertiary sectors, there must be a redistribution of real income. This is certain to influence the pattern of final demand, as it has so obviously within the developed countries, shifting away from labor-intensive personal services toward manufacture. The technology of the service sector will also shift toward more capital-intensive methods of production (e.g., from restaurants to cafeterias toward drive-ins, from small grocery stores to supermarkets, from purchased services to do-it-yourself activities).

3. Confusing Changes in Relative Prices with Inflation

We have seen that the transmission of productivity gains through the labor market from the primary and secondary to the tertiary sectors requires changes in relative prices, and that these changes will alter the relative real incomes of the upper and lower income groups in favor of the latter. What then tends to happen is that the upper income groups, who usually dominate the political process, cry "inflation" as their real incomes begin to be eroded through the increased price of labor-intensive goods and services. Pressure is placed on the economic policymakers to permit increases in wages of skilled manufacturing and white collar workers to offset these cost increases, while entrepreneurs and rentiers call for increases in commodity prices to raise the real returns on capital and land. In short, the political process is used to contravene the redistributive tendencies operating through the labor market. Precisely this process occurred in the United States during World War II, as the labor scarcity placed pressure on the prices of labor-using goods and services. During this period the government instituted price controls for manufacturing and raw materials to prevent structural changes in employment from affecting commodity prices in capital and land-using sectors, but services were relatively free of controls and showed considerable relative price increases. It is not surprising that between the prewar and postwar periods hired domestic workers virtually disappeared in the United States, while postwar demand for consumer durables (to replace now-expensive wage labor) exceeded even the most optimistic projections.

One may expect a similar process to take place in some regions of Central America in the near future, particularly in countries such as

Costa Rica where the tertiary sector workers are on the threshold of
significant increases in real wages, provided that increases in excess
liquidity are not permitted which would cause offsetting increases in
the incomes of property owners and capitalists. In other words, pressures for relative price increases in labor-using sectors should not be
permitted to justify price increases in capital-intensive sectors or
increases in wages of middle and upper income employees in favored occupational categories. Otherwise the net effect will be a general rise
in the price level, continuing inflation, and a retarded process of
diffusion of productivity gains to the working class. Statistically it
is difficult to distinguish between changes in physical productivity
and changes in relative unit values among the sectors of the Central
American Common Market, except to note that the apparent "productivity
growth" of the tertiary sector is for the most part due to rising real
wages and associated increases in the relative prices of services. Needless to say such "productivity growth" will tend to lag behind the physical productivity growth of labor in the primary and secondary sectors.
It will also tend to be relatively smaller in labor-abundant economies
such as Guatemala and El Salvador than in Costa Rica.

4.   Changes in the Demand for Labor in the CACM, 1960-73

The demand for labor at the global level increased rapidly during
the initial period of the CACM, given traditional rates of labor absorption in developing countries. Since labor demand is derived from the
growth of output net of changes in labor productivity, one may trace
this performance to the impressive growth in output in the CACM as shown
in table 3.

Economic growth of the five Central American countries during the
decade and a half of integration (Honduras dropped out of the CACM in
September 1969) has been notable by any standards. However, table 3
shows that this rate has decelerated slightly in recent years, particularly in the primary sector. Industrial growth has also lost the momen-
tum of the first eight years of the program. These figures support the
current feeling that the early burst of growth resulting from both the
establishment of the CACM and recovery of agricultural export markets
in the 1960s is all but over. There is of course a dampening influence
on Common Market esprit from the embargo between El Salvador and Honduras plus the political difficulties of Nicaragua and the dispute between Guatemala and Belize. If these issues were to be resolved, one
might see a rebirth of "regionalism." But at present even those manag-
ers in the industrial sector who once provided the most enthusiastic
support for integration are hard pressed to see new opportunities for
major investments based on further extension of the CACM, though some
argue that expanded protection for intermediate and capital goods might
provide a next step. A main obstacle is that final goods producers are
currently benefiting by the transformation of low-duty intermediate
goods imports into finished manufactures behind the common tariff wall.
They resist any change that would diminish the profitability of such
operations which depend on tariffs that would have to rise if intermediate goods were also produced locally.

Table 3.   Growth of GDP, Central America, Based on
Constant 1960 CA Pesos[a]
(percent)

Sector	Compound Annual Growth Rates		
	1960-68	1968-71	1971-75
I. Primary Production (agriculture, mining)	4.8	4.7	3.6
II. Secondary Production (manufacturing, construction, energy, transportation)	7.8	5.7	6.3
III. Tertiary Production (commerce, banking, real estate, services, others)	5.5	4.7	4.7
Total = Gross Domestic Product	5.9	5.0	4.9
Exports (constant 1960 CA peso values)	9.5	3.4	7.7
Imports (constant 1960 CA peso values)	8.1	4.0	9.0

[a]Central America--Costa Rica, El Salvador, Guatemala, Honduras, and Nicaragua.   The Central American peso is valued at one U.S. dollar.

SOURCE: For 1960-71: SIECA, VI Compendio Estadístico Centroamericano, 1975 (Guatemala City: SIECA, 1975).
For 1971-75: SIECA, "Centroamérica: Estadísticas Macroeconómicas 1971-75," SIECA/76/PES/8, Guatemala, 11 June 1976.

Since the mid-1960s a number of incidents have occurred in the CACM in which Nicaragua and Costa Rica have restricted the import of sensitive goods such as shoes, cloth, and clothing.   These are symptoms of increasing competition from intraregional production which threaten to slow the gains from manufacturing trade.   Such problems dampen the enthusiasm of potential investors.   Also there are many industries which have partitioned regional markets to avoid what in Latin America is called competéncia desleal ("unfair competition").   For example, the Central American beer manufacturers have a gentlemen's agreement not to raid each other's markets.   As a result Central American beer companies have a monopolistic scheme of production and distribution within their own internal markets (under several brand names) and are protected from foreign competition in an industry with a large and growing market which includes all income groups.   Construction materials, such as cement, are also subject to import licenses. In the case of cement during Guatemala's earthquake reconstruction, while the demand for construction materials soared, licensing was used to restrict the quantity of imports, permitting the single cement producer to earn substantial profits despite protests of builders, merchants, and public officials involved in the reconstruction program. (Recently, after much pressure, a second cement company was allowed to begin production in Guatemala.)

These specific cases are illustrative of the general tendency in the region for import-substituting production to be controlled by one or a few dominating families. True integration, with free competition among suppliers, could serve to break this control of national markets, except in cases where scale economies permit one or a few manufacturers to drive out less efficient small producers, as perhaps in the shoe industry. A reduction in external tariff barriers or unlimited intraregional trade would serve to reduce the internal excess profits, even of national monopolies, by extending competition beyond their present closed markets. (Of course this would tend to favor those multinational firms which might enjoy even greater scale economies than regional suppliers.) Despite the present stresses and strains of integration, there is evidence of considerable success in the first stages of expansion of production from national to regional markets. But this process was not designed for the specific goal of employment generation. Instead the object was to increase the independence of the countries from the vicissitudes of foreign demand for traditional exports and to achieve productivity gains from a wide regional market without facing the competition of the world market. In this section we shall see to what extent the resulting increases in production influenced the level of employment and its distribution among major sectors of production.

The major components of increase in demand for labor focused on in this chapter are changes in output and changes in labor productivity. The change in demand for labor is composed of three parts: (i) the change in output, multiplied by the initial ratio of labor input to production; (ii) the change in labor productivity multiplied by the initial level of production; and (iii) an interaction term--the change in output multiplied by the change in labor productivity. The first element is positive and the second two are negative. That is, the first element shows the increase in employment that would have occurred from rising output if productivity had remained constant. The second two elements subtract from this extra employment amounts corresponding to the saving of labor through increased labor productivity with respect to both the initial level of output and the increase in output.[21]

It should be stressed that "labor productivity" as used here is a gross concept including all elements involved in the production process (capital, land and other inputs, plus technological change). "Labor" is not disaggregated to account for changes in skill composition of the work force from learning by doing, formal education, and other increments in "human capital." Hence labor productivity is a catch-all category comprehending a variety of changes in the conditions of production. In principle it can be ultimately broken down into these separate elements once the requisite data become available, but for the present we proceed with the information at hand, since even this degree of aggregation gives interesting results.

Table 4 provides data on the respective contributions of output and productivity growth to employment growth in the region, based on observed data for the years 1960 to 1971. Most notable about the results is the immense contribution of productivity growth to output, such that a 5.6 percent cumulative annual rate of production growth was accomplished with only a 2.7 percent rate of increase in equipment. More than half of the regional growth was due to new investment, technological change, improved skills, and other factors increasing the productivity of labor, while less than half was due to increased numbers of man-years employed.

Table 4. Central American Employment Growth in Relation to
Production and Productivity, 1960-71
(percent)

Sector	Growth of Real Output (Value Added in Constant 1960 Prices)	Growth of Employment (Man-Years)	Growth of Productivity (Value Added per Employed Worker)
I. Primary	4.8	1.9	2.9
II. Secondary	7.2	4.2	3.0
III. Tertiary	5.3	3.5	1.8
Total GDP, CACM	5.6	2.7	2.9

SOURCE: See table 3.

The primary activities, agriculture and mining, absorbed little labor relative to the growth in the estimated number of job seekers by 1971. Labor supply grew by an estimated 3.1 percent per year for the region as a whole, ranging from 4.0 percent for Nicaragua and Costa Rica to 2.3 percent for Guatemala (for the basis of these calculations see tables 10 and 11). As a result of the fact that productivity growth accounted for the highest share of output growth in the primary sector (60 percent), due to the introduction of new techniques of cultivation including mechanization, irrigation, application of pesticides and fertilizers, and the shift to export crops which responded well to such measures, labor was released in large numbers to find work in the secondary and tertiary sectors. This problem was exacerbated by the fact that most rural workers are only seasonally employed. In the immediate post-World War II period a larger share of these workers either owned or rented land which was used for subsistence cultivation and for production for internal markets. But with the boom of commercial export agriculture throughout the region from 1950 to the present, the opportunity cost of such land has sharply increased, as reflected in tripling or quadrupling of real rents charged to the peasants.[22] This is forcing ever-increasing numbers of workers to rely on the highly uncertain seasonal wage-labor market. Men, women, and children are faced with the option of either migrating to the cities or of taking their chances on rural employment as field hands. There is some evidence that in certain areas real wages (per day or per quantity of crop picked) may be rising for this type of work, but it is sporadic, and the income it provides is insufficient to support a family. Thus, despite possible rising real wages for field hands, annual real earnings of landless rural families seem to be declining, reflecting falling income from subsistence cultivation as land becomes increasingly scarce wherever export crops can be grown. This pattern is most pronounced in El Salvador and Guatemala. Only the increased employment of women and children permits family income to be maintained. The natural consequence is growing pressure on the cities, even in the relatively favored countries such as Costa Rica where slums are approaching San Jose for the first time, as export agriculture displaces rural households from the land, and as demographic growth exacerbates land hunger.

The slack in employment in the rural area has been somewhat absorbed by the secondary sector in Central America, with productivity growth accounting for 42 percent of changes in output due presumably to the very high rate of investment in manufacturing and transportation, which use relatively capital-intensive technology. Tertiary activities have absorbed a significant share of the increasing work force, with "productivity growth" only accounting for one-third of output growth in this sector. In fact, as table 4 shows, during the period 1960-71 the combined employment growth of the secondary and tertiary sector averaged almost 4 percent per annum, which was well ahead of the estimated rate of growth of labor supply (see sections D and E of this chapter). The problem then is not one of failure of growth sectors to absorb labor rapidly but of the failure of the agricultural sector to maintain its share of employment opportunities because of its higher relative rate of growth of output per worker. Hence the primary sector which employed 62 percent of the work force in 1960 fell to 57 percent in 1971, with the secondary sector rising from 17 percent to 20 percent and the tertiary sector from 21 percent to 23 percent. The share of output in the primary sector fell by less, or from 30 percent to 27 percent. While that of the secondary sector grew from 22 percent to 27 percent, the tertiary sector share fell from 48 percent to 46 percent.

The nature of rural production changed in response to rising world prices for cash crops, integration of previously isolated regions through road and communication grids, and resulting declines in transport costs (at least until the recent rise in petroleum prices), plus improved technology for irrigated farming, pesticides, fertilizers, and expanded marketing outlets. This amounted to a rural revolution in much of Central America. That revolution provoked rapidly increasing economic rents both absolutely and in some cases as a share of factor income (see section H). The dislocation of the labor force from land previously in subsistence farming and for domestic crop production swelled the rural proletariat, repressing wages in favor of rising rent shares and benefiting those with access to land. Some of the displaced labor provided a pool that was drawn upon for employment in the urban industrial and service sectors. The rest was relegated to land in more distant, less accessible regions; to sporadic employment as field hands; and to very low productivity occupations in the tertiary sector.

In short the Central American export economies, always rural-based, experienced increasing dependence on commodity exports in the 1960s, industrialization policies notwithstanding. And while low-cost labor was essential to the new cropping patterns that emerged, the consolidation of land and its mechanization led to a growing surplus of rural labor that is today well in excess of readily available employment opportunities, particularly in the most populous regions. Policies favoring migration among the five countries could alleviate this problem somewhat. Much seasonal migration does in fact take place from El Salvador to Guatemala, Guatemala to Mexico, and El Salvador to Nicaragua and Costa Rica (bypassing Honduras, which expelled scores of thousands of Salvadorians in 1969). Permanent migration also occurs, such as from southern Nicaragua to Costa Rica. But it is unlikely that formal policies permitting free labor mobility in the CACM will be forthcoming in the near future.

5. The Regional Pattern of Productivity Growth

Since it was productivity growth which prevented regional production growth from absorbing the increased labor force despite the fact that output grew in all major sectors and countries of the region, we shall trace the locus of productivity growth among the five countries. It should be stressed that the prospect of profit from such gains influenced investors to invest in land clearing, plant, equipment, education, and new methods of cultivation. This in turn led to growth in output per worker. Hence it is not suggested that productivity growth should be minimized in order to create jobs (in order to perpetuate the curse of Eden) but rather that the surplus from such gains be channeled into activities which by expanding employment opportunities raise the income and welfare of the working class. In fact, however, working class participation in factor income streams has declined in relative terms (and apparently in absolute terms for some landless families in the more populous regions) in all countries but Nicaragua. As a result, even though export-led rural growth and import-substituting industrial growth have permitted impressive productivity gains, these gains have not been shared by the population as a whole. This is not to suggest that such a result was the objective of the CACM development policies, although private enterprise is understandably interested in minimizing wage costs. It is argued rather that development led by the prevailing market structure, in conditions of abundant labor supply and involving a minimum of fiscal and financial transfers, tends to exacerbate income inequality. In at least four of the five countries analyzed below the results support this proposition.

In table 5 we have broken down regional productivity growth (4.2 percent per annum in current prices, or 2.9 percent in constant prices) into its national components in order to determine the relative contribution of each of the five countries. Productivity growth over the eleven-year period averaged $CA 485, which represents a nominal gain of 58 percent over the value of output per worker in 1960 and a real gain of 37 percent. Among the five countries, Nicaragua and Costa Rica alone

Table 5. Country Contributions to Regional Productivity Growth,
Central America, 1960-71

Country	(1) Growth in Output per Worker (CA pesos in current values)	(2) Share of Regional Employment	(3) Contribution to Output per Worker (1) x (2)	(4) Contribution Relative to Total (3) ÷ Σ (3)	(5) Contribution Relative to Share of Employment (4) ÷ (2)
Guatemala	423	.38	171	.33	.86
El Salvador	280	.23	64	.13	.57
Honduras	289	.17	49	.10	.59
Nicaragua	947	.11	104	.21	1.91
Costa Rica	1,077	.10	108	.22	2.20
Central America	485	1.00	485	1.00	1.00

SOURCE: For output growth, see table 3. Employment estimates are taken from numerous sources,
primarily based on census data for individual countries, as consolidated and adjusted
by Gustavo Leiva, SIECA Special Studies Unit, Guatemala, 1975-76.

accounted for 43 percent of total regional productivity growth, though their combined work forces represented only 21 percent of employed labor in the region (a share which did not change over the period). Lagging far behind were El Salvador and Honduras, with a joint contribution of 23 percent to the regional total relative to their combined 40 percent of the work force. Guatemala also lagged, but by a smaller amount. What these figures reveal is that over and above the given output per worker in 1960, and despite the rapid growth of employment during the period 1960 to 1971, there remained an additional $CA 485 per worker in productivity growth to be apportioned among the owners of labor, capital, natural resources, entrepreneurship, technology, and the government.

6. Actual Growth in Demand for Labor in Central America, 1960-71

The demand for labor in the region grew at 2.7 percent per annum between 1960 and 1971, or by 1.1 million workers over the period as we have seen. Because of the low productivity growth of Honduras, combined with its significant increase in output, labor demand increased by the highest rate in the region, or by 3.4 percent per year (table 6). Alternatively one might reason that the existence of abundant land in Honduras, plus access (until 1969) to the labor pool of El Salvador where wages were even lower, stimulated the growth of activities in the primary sector which involved little capital formation except in labor-intensive land clearing and planting. As other studies have shown, these developments did not depend essentially on the machinery of the CACM, though a number of processing industries were established around San Pedro Sula which did benefit from low-cost imports and other CACM incentives.

In general, however, the perception has been that in Honduras trade diversion raised the cost of imported final goods without providing commensurate benefits to local manufacturing.[23] This explains the lack of support for continued participation in the CACM, though it is difficult to explain the embargo on migrant labor from El Salvador on these grounds. One explanation for the eventual expulsion of the Salvadorians is said to have been the opposition of the local population to competition in the labor market and to land claims by their visitors from the west under the expanding agrarian reform program. The Honduran authorities appear to have responded reluctantly to these populist pressures for exclusion of Salvadorians, justifying their action in terms of preserving national resources for Honduran citizens. On broad economic grounds, both El Salvador and Honduras would doubtless have benefited from continued free migration and capital flows (the net flows were probably from El Salvador to Honduras in the 1960s, though they might have reversed later). But social pressures caused by migration were probably more detrimental to Honduras than to its neighbor before expulsion, while afterward the conditions were reversed.

After Honduras, El Salvador had the greatest increase in labor demand where employment rose by 2.9 percent per annum, followed by Costa Rica (2.6), Nicaragua (2.4) and Guatemala (2.2). The poor performance of Guatemala was due to its somewhat slower rate of output growth relative to that of the leading countries plus faster productivity growth compared with that of the lagging countries. Hence, from the point of view of employment, Guatemala had the worst of both worlds. This is partly because its growth depended more heavily on industry (manufacturing grew at 7.9 percent per annum) than on export agriculture. The growth of primary production (5.7 percent per annum) lagged behind that of all other countries except El Salvador (4.3 percent), which had the most rapid industrial growth. In view of the large share of the Guatemalan work force in agriculture, it contrasts unfavorably with that of other rapidly industrializing countries such as Costa Rica (which had annual growth rates of industrial and primary production of 11.0 and 7.4 percent, respectively) and Nicaragua (12.5 and 7.0 percent). El Salvador had a higher rate of industrialization than Guatemala (8.3 percent), permitting greater labor absorption into the urban sector.

Table 6. Actual Growth in Demand for Labor,
Central America, 1960-71

Country	Actual Employment			Employment	Output	Productivity
	1960	1971	(1960-71)			
	(thousands of man-years)			(cumulative annual growth rates)		
Guatemala	1,254	1,593	339	2.2	5.4	3.2
El Salvador	741	1,025	284	2.9	5.4	2.5
Honduras	567	826	259	3.4	4.5	1.1
Nicaragua	367	480	113	2.4	6.8	4.4
Costa Rica	338	452	114	2.6	6.3	3.7
Central America	3,268	4,376	1,108	2.7	5.6	2.9

SOURCE: See selected appendix tables. Figures for employment in 1971 are interpolated from the most recent census results, assuming constancy of participation rates and steady demographic growth rates for intercensal years.

Given the unequal land tenure conditions in Guatemala, its impoverished Indian peasantry, the slow rate of productivity growth, and low per capita income for the majority of the population, this country together with El Salvador poses the darkest spectre of labor redundancy. Later we shall see that it also has the lowest wage share of value added in Central America, with that share falling at the most rapid rate. This contrasts with the evidence of rising average real wages which are ahead of El Salvador and Honduras (though average and marginal earnings per worker need not be correlated, especially when all skill levels are considered). There seems to be the growth of a dualistic wage structure, as workers in the higher productivity urban and commercial agricultural occupations increase their share of the wage bill at the expense of the marginally employed. Since the February 1976 earthquake, wages appear to have been rising in real terms and construction jobs have drawn heavily on the number of wage laborers in agriculture. This is the direct result of the combination of dire necessity (with massive do-it-yourself reconstruction), and subsidized construction materials, machinery, and equipment provided through international disaster relief operations which have benefited a large share of the affected population.

There is evidence that the earthquake and widespread relief activities have had a profound impact on social consciousness at the grassroots level. What this will mean in practical terms remains to be seen. But even the poorest Indians from the smallest villages in the earthquake zone are now aware that despite many shortcomings of the relief programs, their welfare has been a matter not only of national but of international concern at least for a brief period. This is likely to give voice to a new force in politics that will become more strident as time goes by. Recent events have also galvanized strong pressures within the hitherto conservative Church hierarchy favoring social reform.

The rural earthquake relief program of Guatemala, and the urban reconstruction of Nicaragua after Managua was devastated by the December 1972 quake, illustrate that massive public expenditure programs can provide many additional jobs, although at the expense of severe (if temporary) inflation in the prices of basic consumables. While rising prices hurt those on fixed money incomes, the working class in both countries seem to have benefited from these disaster relief measures. These were the first real efforts in either country to mount major deficit spending programs. From a fiscal point of view the expenditures were financed externally rather than by the unsupported creation of liquidity. But they had the same functional impact as deficit spending programs, since output capacity was severely constrained by the disaster (especially in the Nicaraguan case). In Guatemala there was little excess capacity in wage goods production, so that in 1976 alone the increase in effective demand which did not leak into imports of basic consumables (as well as producers goods, construction materials, and other inputs for reconstruction) pushed up price levels by from 30 to 40 percent.

The forced experiment in earthquake relief was a shock treatment for the traditionally conservative fiscal policies of both countries. The consequences (taking account of the lack of precise time series data on employment) seem to have been favorable to the employment of unskilled labor, though there is still much underemployment due in large part to the seasonal nature of demand for agricultural workers. The lesson is that deficit spending (and attendant inflation), with foreign assistance for balance of payments support, and somewhat more flexible exchange rates (a divergence from existing policies) might allay the cyclical underemployment problem.[24] This would be especially true if public expenditures were directed toward labor-absorbing activities such as construction, the urban informal sector, small-scale agriculture (including land distribution programs and infrastructure), and processing industries in labor surplus regions. But barring continued natural disasters, the conservatism of most existing governments in northern Central America supported by less progressive members of the business, commercial, and landed elite stand in the way of such policies.

7. Alternative Labor Demand Patterns With and Without Productivity Growth

In order to assess the potential of regional growth for labor absorption in the absence of such rapid productivity growth as did occur, we have made an extreme assumption that labor requirements per unit of value added remained constant between 1960 and 1971. (Since there was very little inflation during the period, calculations made in current prices bias slightly upward the estimated demand for labor in 1971.) Under this assumption, table 7 shows that the observed growth of regional output during the eleven-year period would have required 3.6 million additional workers, compared with the observed increase in employment of only 1.1 million. In short, the "gap" under the extreme assumptions would have amounted to 58 percent of the economically active population in the region. Of course without the productivity growth and the rewards which it provided to investors, output growth almost certainly would have been much less; however, these calculations do show that under the unrealistic assumption that the same output growth would have been attempted at constant productivity levels, the demand for labor would have substantially exceeded supply by 1971 for all countries in the region. In short, productivity growth permitted the region to expand rapidly and still avoid a severe labor supply constraint. Indeed, it did the job all too well from the standpoint of the working class.

Those countries which would have been most affected by this hypothetical excess demand for labor, measured in terms of the gap as a percentage of 1971 employment, would have been: Nicaragua (101 percent), Costa Rica (90 percent), Guatemala (53 percent), Honduras (50 percent), and El Salvador (38 percent). Attempts to achieve observed output growth without investment in capital, natural resources, and technology would have almost certainly produced rapidly rising wage levels. The wage share of value added would likely have risen as well (given the evidence from chapter 5 that the elasticity of substitution between labor and capital in Central American manufacturing is less than unity). Without taking into consideration the effects of changes in income distribution on final demand, which might have permitted the realization of scale economies and provided additional investment incentives, the labor constraint eventually would have slowed output growth, reducing the excess demand for labor. But in fact the opening up of the regional market and the attractiveness of tariff protection for final manufactures, tariff exemption for intermediate inputs plus tax holidays for new investment, and the provision of rural and urban infrastructure permitted production to shift toward less labor-intensive activities. This was exacerbated by the availability of new labor-saving technology and methods of increasing land productivity in the region. These factors virtually eliminated the possibility of any labor constraint on Central American growth.

206

Table 7. Hypothetical Growth in Demand for Labor,
Central America, 1960-71
(thousands of man-years)

Country	Actual Growth in Employment	Hypothetical Growth in Demand for Labor	Difference
Guatemala	339	1,180	841
El Salvador	284	676	392
Honduras	259	670	411
Nicaragua	113	596	483
Costa Rica	114	523	402
Central America	1,109	3,645	2,536

SOURCES AND METHODS: Data on employment in 1960 and 1971, productivity in 1960, and output in 1971 are from selected appendix tables. The assumption is made that value added per worker remained constant between 1960 and 1971 in order to calculate hypothetical demand for 1971. This figure was then subtracted from that for actual employment in 1960 to obtain the hypothetical growth in labor demand.

In table 8, estimates are presented for the sectoral impact of productivity growth on employment demand, using similar assumptions about the demand for labor with and without productivity growth. These figures permit one to measure the sensitivity of employment to productivity growth in each of the three major production sectors. The ratio of labor demand without productivity growth to actual demand in the primary sector is 4.4. Up to four times as many workers would have been required in agriculture (and mining) to produce actual levels of 1971 output without the recent increases in investment, opening of new land to cultivation, shifts in cropping patterns, and technological progress (seed fertilization revolution). In the absence of such factors, food prices would almost certainly have risen relative to those of industrial goods, exports would have been reduced, and food imports would have risen. Paradoxically it would seem that the growth of secondary activities was heavily dependent upon a productivity revolution in the primary sector, despite policies providing incentives to manufacturing which tended to discourage agricultural growth during comparable periods of import-substituting industrialization elsewhere in Latin America. What seems to have happened is that overall incentives provided to the secondary sector were not accompanied by direct income transfers through fiscal or financial subsidies, such as occurred in Chile, Uruguay, Argentina, and other countries during the 1950s and 1960s. Instead the

Table 8. Growth in Demand for Labor by Major Production Sector with and
without Productivity Growth, Central America, 1960-71
(thousands of man-years)

	(1) Primary Sector (Agriculture, Mining)	(2) Secondary Sector (Industry, Construction, Energy, Transportation)	(3) Tertiary Sector (Commerce, Bank, Services, Other)	(4) Total
Change in Labor Demand without Change in Productivity but with Change in Output, 1960-71	1,998	880	767	3,645
Change in Labor Demand without Growth in Output but with Productivity Growth, 1960-71	-780	-212	-206	-1,198
Change in Labor Demand Due to Combined Productivity Growth and Change in Output	-763	-340	-234	-1,337
Actual Change in Labor Demand, 1960-71	455	328	327	1,110

NOTE: This table is calculated from the formula:

$$\Delta D_L = \Delta Q \left[\frac{Q}{L_0}\right] + \Delta \left[\frac{Q}{L}\right] Q_0 + \Delta \left[\frac{Q}{L}\right] \cdot \Delta \left[\frac{Q}{Q_0}\right]$$

where:

D_L is demand for labor,
Q is value added,
0 is base year, and
Δ is first difference between year 0 and year n.

fiscal and financial practices or measures of Central America during these years worked to minimize the degree of effective protection and artifical subsidization of the urban industrial sector, permitting agriculture to grow simultaneously with industry and services.

The labor-saving technologies in the rural sector further released labor for employment in secondary and tertiary activities. The parallel growth of agriculture and industry distinguishes the Central American model, accounting more than anything else for fifteen years of relatively rapid growth in both output and productivity. The secondary sector would have required 2.7 times as many additional workers without observed rates of productivity growth, while tertiary activities would have shown a factor of 2.1. The overall figure is 3.3 times as many new workers without productivity gains.

8.   Estimated Demand for Labor, 1971-75

The relationship between output and productivity growth in terms of the demand for labor was shown in table 4 for the period 1960 to 1971. These years were chosen because of their proximity to the dates of population censuses for the five Central American countries. This permits us to calculate the share of economically active population recorded as employed in those years. Data on production (gross domestic product) is available for the period 1971 to 1975 inclusive (appendix E, table 7) but precise employment figures are not available. Hence for the purpose of estimating labor demand growth from 1971 to 1975, changes in productivity must be hypothesized based on historical figures. The difference between observed output growth and estimated productivity growth is estimated employment growth. In table 9 some estimates are made under the assumption that 80 percent of the productivity growth for the period 1960-71 continued to hold for the period 1971-75. This assumption of less productivity growth in the 1970s is based on the fact that there was a deceleration in regional growth which almost certainly reduced the efficiency of capacity utilization. Also earlier rapid productivity gains were due to the assimilation of new technology and scale economies resulting from rapid growth of investment of the 1960s, while since then, new investment has decelerated sharply, especially for the private sector. In the case of the tertiary sectors, we have argued above that so-called "productivity gains" include increases in the relative prices of goods and services in this sector, which in turn reflect rising real wages in the lower skill levels. Thus it is implicitly assumed that the same trend continued into the 1970s, though at a decreasing rate commensurate with the slower rate of production and employment.

Because of the strong assumption about lower rates of productivity growth in the 1970s, employment is estimated to have grown by 2.6 percent annually during the 1970s compared to 2.7 percent in the 1960s, even though the rate of output growth declined by 13 percent (from 5.6 percent per annum to 4.9 percent from the 1960s to the 1970s). If in fact productivity growth did continue to maintain its earlier rate (2.9 percent per annum), which is very unlikely, then employment would have increased by only 2.0 percent annually. Of course the extreme sensitivity of these estimates to assumptions about productivity growth makes them highly suspect. In view of the absence of annual employment figures, all that

can be said with certainty is that it is unlikely that recent employment
growth has kept pace with the expansion of the potentially economically
active population, and that it is reasonable to expect that the employment
gap widened significantly between 1971 and 1975.

Table 9. Estimated Growth in Demand for Labor, 1971-75
(percent per annum)

	(1) Output Growth (Observed)	(2) Productivity Growth (Estimate)	(3) Employment Growth (Estimate) (1) - (2) = (3)
By Sector			
I. Primary Sectors	3.6	2.3	1.3
II. Secondary Sectors	6.3	2.4	3.9
III. Tertiary Sectors	4.7	1.4	3.3
Total CACM	4.9	2.3	2.6
By Country			
Guatemala	5.2	2.6	2.6
El Salvador	4.8	2.0	2.8
Honduras	2.5	0.9	1.6
Nicaragua	5.0	3.5	1.5
Costa Rica	5.6	3.0	2.6
Total CACM	4.9	2.3	2.6

SOURCE AND METHODS: Column (1) by sector is taken from table 3. Column
(1) by country is taken from SIECA, "Centroamérica:
Estadísticas Macroeconómicos 1971-75," SIECA/76/PES/
8, Guatemala, 11 June 1976. Column (2) by sector is
from table 4, assuming that 80 percent of annual productivity growth for 1960-71 was achieved in 1971-75.
Column (2) by country is from table 6, making the
same assumption of 80 percent of the productivity
growth of the 1960s continuing in the 1970s. Column
(3) is the residual of columns (1) and (2).

D.   Supply of Labor in the Central American Common Market

In order to relate the observed changes in employment to likely changes in the availability of labor, table 10 presents a rough estimate of labor supply increases in terms of additional man-years available (based on equal weighting for age and sex). These estimates rely upon the strong assumption that participation rates observed for the econom- ically active age groups (ages 10 to 64 in all countries except Costa Rica; 15 to 64 in Costa Rica) in 1960 were approximately equal to de- sired rates in 1975. This assumption ignores the effect of both posi- tive and negative influences on desired participation rates due to chang- ing income levels, urbanization, shifting age composition of the base population, increased educational demand, and other factors; however, the purpose of the measure is simply to provide rough orders of magni- tude for supply increases for the period under consideration.

Table 10.   Estimated Labor Supply Increases, 1960-75
(thousands of man-years)

| Country | Employment in 1960 | Estimated Labor Supply Increase | |
		1960-71	1971-75
Guatemala	1,254	362	151
El Salvador	741	318	151
Honduras	567	257	58
Nicaragua	367	131	59
Costa Rica	338	181	87
Central America	3,268	1,249	506

METHODS: See text. Employment in 1960 from table 6. Note that the growth rate is not based on the economically active population available for employment in 1960 but on the number of persons actually employed according to the respective census for that year. Hence the rate of growth is subject to a slight upward bias.

The assumed participation rates represent an outside limit of the number of workers potentially available for employment in 1971, given the demographic growth of the respective age groups considered repre- sentative of the economically active population. Note that as the level of education rises for most of the population, through improved oppor- tunities for schooling and higher returns to education, the lower thresh- old of the employable age groups will rise. For example, in the case

Table 11. Basis for Calculations of Estimated Labor Supply

Country	Population from Ages 10 to 64[a]			Participation Rates, 1960	Hypothesized Desired Participation Rates, 1971, 1975 (assumed equal to 1960)	Observed Participation Rates, 1971
	1960	1971	1975 est.			
Guatemala	2,527	3,232	3,534	.50	.50	.49
El Salvador	1,562	2,254	2,575	.47	.47	.45
Honduras	1,133	1,647	1,763	.50	.50	.50
Nicaragua	870	1,185	1,325	.42	.42	.41
Costa Rica[a]	583[a]	895[a]	1,045[a]	(.46) .58[a]	(.46) .58[a]	(.40) .51[a]
CACM[b]	6,823	9,462	10,543	.48[b]	.48[b]	.46[b]

[a]Ages 15 to 64 inclusive (Costa Rica only).
[b]Totals are for cohorts 10 to 64 for all countries (Costa Rica included). Figures in parentheses are participation rates for population 10 to 64 inclusive. Totals for Costa Rica are participation rates for population 10 to 64 inclusive.

SOURCE AND METHODS: See text. Population estimates interpolated from decennial census data. Participation rates from employed population figures in appendix E.

of Costa Rica we have used the age group 15 to 64 for purposes of calculation of participation rates in 1960 and as applied to the population
estimate for 1971 and 1975. In the other four countries we have used
the age group 10 to 64, reflecting the lower levels of educational participation of these populations. Table 11 provides the basis for the
calculation of labor supply in 1971 and 1975 as presented in table 10,
so that our estimates may be adjusted on the basis of alternative assumptions about participation rates and rates of demographic growth.

The growth rates of the relevant age cohorts likely to be seeking
employment, which of course reflect lagged demographic characteristics,
differ widely among the five countries. Costa Rica showed the highest
rate of growth of economically active population (ages 15 to 64) increasing at 3.9 percent annually. (The group 10 to 64 grew by even more,
or 4.1 percent annually in the same intercensal period, 1963-73.) For
the other four countries the growth of the 10 to 64 age cohorts for their
respective intercensal periods were: Honduras 3.4 percent (1961-73), El
Salvador 2.8 percent (1967-71), Nicaragua 2.8 percent (1963-71), and
Guatemala 2.2 percent (1964-73). Our calculations are of course solely
dependent upon demographic factors, due to the assumption of constant
desired participation rates. The plus factors of rising female participation and increased attractiveness of wage labor employment during
periods of rising wages, and the negative factors due to the effect of
rising family income which reduces the need for outside employment (this
could have been positive for some households in the rural sector where
there is evidence that family incomes for landless workers and smallholders actually fell in real terms) plus rising educational opportunities and investments of households, have offsetting effects on participation rates. As a result the net impact cannot be assessed with any precision in a study at this level of generality. For that reason we have
chosen the null hypothesis which assumes that the positive and negative
factors exactly offset each other in determining desired participation
rates, so that these rates remained constant for the relevant age cohorts
over the decade and a half.

The resulting figures for net increase in labor supply do not, of
course, include the number of "unemployed" or "underemployed" in the
base year. Despite the statistical and conceptual problems involved,
the unemployment figures should be added to those for the employed population in the base year plus the estimated growth in labor supply to
arrive at total labor supply in the terminal year.

E.   The "Employment Gap" in the Central American Common Market

1.   The Changing Employment Gap between 1960 and 1975

The concept of an "employment" gap is of less relevance to developing countries than to the United States or Western Europe in that invol-
untary unemployment (those willing to work at going wages but unable to
find jobs) is likely to be transformed into "underemployment" under circumstances in which wages, hours, and working conditions barely permit a
subsistence level of living. In such countries unemployment benefits are

minimal and there is little slack capacity which, if stimulated through increases in effective demand, might provide workers with more remunerative employment. Moreover, real wages tend to be more flexible downward (especially under conditions of price inflation), taking up some of the slack in employment at the expense of deteriorating living levels for the working class. Since wages are initially at low levels and accumulated savings are scarce, workers are forced to find gainful employment, migrate, rely on charity, or starve. This is particularly true for major sections of Central America in which per capita incomes are at the bare survival level.

Hence any attempt to match labor supply growth with changes in labor demand will produce "gaps" on paper that are only partly borne out in practice in the form of open unemployment. Nevertheless, such simulations are useful because they show the extent to which underlying supply and demand conditions combined to influence the ability of workers to bargain for higher real wages and improved shares of the benefits from growth. Here we examine the observed growth in employment in Central America from 1960 to 1971, based on population census data for the five countries. The increase in labor demand is then related to the estimated increase in labor supply based on calculations from section D of this chapter. The difference between supply and demand is termed the "employment gap." The gap indicates the extent to which hypothetical supply increases outstripped observed employment growth, thereby placing downward pressures on wages and forcing workers into less desirable occupations, emigration, withdrawal from the labor market, or open unemployment.

For the period 1971 to 1975 both demand and supply of labor have been estimated, the former based on observed output and assumed productivity growth as indicated in the footnotes to table 12. Labor supply growth is based on demographic projections and assumed labor participation rates as described in section D of this chapter. The results of these calculations are presented in table 12 in terms of changes in the employment gap ($\Delta D - \Delta S$). In this table an increase in the "excess supply" of labor appears as a negative item. The period 1960 to 1971 shows an increase in the employment gap of 140,000 workers, 48 percent of which was located in Costa Rica and 24 percent in El Salvador. In the case of Costa Rica, earlier rapid rates of demographic growth (which are now sharply decelerating) caused an expansion in the number of potential workers in the 1960s. In addition, more women entered the work force during this period. Enrollment in secondary schools and universities in this most educationally advanced country of the region helped to offset the growth of labor supply by reducing the participation of school age persons in the work force. But the net effect was to provide significant pressure for jobs in a country which until recently was noted for its capacity to absorb workers at rising real wages. In the 1970s the Costa Rican "gap" continued to grow, but its share of the regional total fell to 45 percent (table 12).

Migration toward Costa Rica continued, its employment gap notwithstanding, because of higher real wages and expectations of better jobs compared to conditions in neighboring countries. This exacerbated the employment problem caused by internal demographic pressures. Nicaragua for example also showed a large relative increase in its employment gap amounting to 3.8 percent of 1971 employment, although its share of the

Table 12. Estimated Increase in the Employment Gap, 1960-75
(thousands of man-years)

Country	(1) Change in Employment (Observed)	1960-71		(4) Change in Employment (Estimated)	1971-75	
		(2) Change in Labor Supply (Estimated)	(3) Change in Employment Gap (ΔD - ΔS)		(5) Change in Labor Supply (Estimated)	(6) Change in Employment Gap (ΔD - ΔS)
Guatemala	339	362	-23	167	151	16
El Salvador	284	318	-34	121	151	-30
Honduras	259	257	2	55	58	-3
Nicaragua	113	131	-18	30	59	-29
Costa Rica	114	181	-67	50	87	-37
CACM	1,109	1,249	-140	423	506	-82

SOURCES AND METHODS: Column (1) from table 7; columns (2) and (5) from table 10; column (14) was calculated from the output growth for 1971-75, SIECA, "Centroamérica: Estadísticas Macroeconómicas 1971-75," SIECA/76/PES/8, Guatemala, 11 June 1976.

regional "gap" was only 13 percent. The earthquake which devastated Managua in 1972 led to major reconstruction activities which increased the demand for manual labor, helping somewhat to relieve these pressures. Still, our figures for the period 1971 to 1975 show that Nicaragua's share of the employment gap of the 1970s grew to 35 percent (table 12).

One of the most severely overpopulated countries in the region, El Salvador, accounted for one-fourth of the increased employment gap in the 1960s (roughly proportional to its share of the regional work force), rising to one-third of the gap in the 1970s. This is a sobering situation with explosive potential for social and political stability in that country. Indeed, despite rapid industrialization and the second fastest rate of employment growth in the 1970s (table 6), El Salvador cannot keep pace with its burgeoning work force by pursuing current economic policies. This is especially true due to the consolidation of farm units into large-scale commercial agricultural operations which use increasingly capital-intensive techniques, thereby displacing workers from traditional rural occupations. El Salvador's employment gap is one of the most serious of the region, especially in view of the 10.5 percent rate of open unemployment in 1970 (table 13). This combined with the degree of underemployment in low-productivity occupations creates growing pressures for emigration and internal reform which cannot long be ignored.

Perhaps the most curious and interesting of the findings from table 12 is that Honduras showed no significant increase in its employment gap in either decade. Yet Honduras also had the lowest wage and labor productivity growth in the region. Table 6 shows productivity in that country rising at only 1.1 percent annually in the 1960s, compared with an average of 2.9 percent in the region. Indeed it was because of slow productivity growth that employment in Honduras rose by 3.4 percent annually, since output growth (4.5 percent) lagged behind that of all other countries (the regional average was 5.6 percent). Such a finding illustrates that the absence of an "employment gap" is not a sufficient condition for rising real incomes of the working class, since employment growth without attendant productivity increases is sterile. What must be accomplished are both employment and productivity growth.

In the case of Guatemala, another country with a hard-core poverty problem, the increased employment gap of the 1960s was 16 percent of the regional total (table 12), but there is evidence that in the 1970s the growth in demand for labor might well have exceeded that of supply. This is a most encouraging sign, since Guatemala was second in the region in output growth. In addition its productivity growth in the 1960s was well above the regional average and may be assumed to have remained so in the 1970s. Unlike Honduras, Guatemala appears to have the potential for employment demand growth which could eventually improve conditions in the labor market. The problem is that historically there has been active opposition to the organization and collective bargaining of workers in Guatemala, and in the rural sector the Indian population has been subjected to the most socially demeaning conditions leading to grinding poverty, disease, and malnutrition rivaling the most disadvantaged regions of the world.

Table 13 indicates that by the best available estimates, Guatemala faced 12 percent open unemployment as late as 1970. Compared with a

Table 13. Open Unemployment in Central America, 1970

Country	(1) Total Population	(2) Economically Active	(3) Employed	(4) Openly Unemployed	(5) Increase in Employment Gap (1960-71)	(6) Increase in Gap as % of Active Population (1970)	(7) Active Population Openly Unemployed
	(thousands of man-years)					(percent)	
Guatemala	5,179	1,623	1,428	195[a]	23	1.4	12.0
El Salvador	3,441	1,081	968	113[b]	34	3.1	10.5
Honduras	2,583	799	753	46[c]	-2	0	5.8
Nicaragua	2,222	659	600	59[d]	18	2.7	9.0
Costa Rica	1,798	535	508	27[e]	67	12.5	5.0
CACM	15,223	6,697	4,257	440	140	3.0	9.4

SOURCES AND METHODS: Column 6 from table 12; column 7 = column 6 divided by column 2.
a. Guatemala, Consejo Nacional de Planificación, "Caracterización Resumida de los Recursos Humanos en Guatemala," March 1972.
b. El Salvador, Censo de Población 1961, Ministerio de Trabajo; "El Desarrollo Social del Salvador y la Situación de la Familia," El Salvador, 30 March 1971, table 16.
c. Honduras, Dirección de Estadística, "Encuesta de Ingresos y Gastos Familiares," Tegucigalpa (1967-68), 1970.
d. Nicaragua, Censo de Población 1971, Cifras Preliminares.
e. Costa Rica, Encuesta de Hogares por Muestreo, 1967. Censos de Población 1950-63. See PREALC, "Situación y Perspectivos del Empleo en Costa Rica," March 1972.

regional average of 9.4 percent, this is a serious condition of labor
surplus which must be resolved if average productivity and incomes of
the poorest workers are to rise significantly. It should be noted, however, that the middle- and upper-income groups of Guatemala depend on
cheap labor for the provision of many domestic services and basic commodities. Were a positive employment program to be adopted, this would
hasten changes in the pattern of living against the interests of politically powerful groups. This makes the problem particularly difficult
to resolve; however, whatever policies are being applied, the reduction
of the employment gap in Guatemala must be accelerated simply to permit
the subsistence of those already in the work force, if social conditions
are not to deteriorate still further.

The relationships between changes in the "employment gap" as measured in table 12 and the absolute employment gap are shown in table 13.
Here the conditions of the several countries of the region are somewhat
reversed. Costa Rica shows the smallest rate of open unemployment as of
1970 (5.0 percent), though its increased gap is the highest share of 1970
employment (12.5 percent). Thus Costa Rica is moving from a condition
of relatively full employment to one of potentially serious underemployment. One may expect that this will work against rising real wages in
that country, or that in the case of wage increases, growing dualism in
the Costa Rican labor market will occur. (In a later section we deal
with the question of wage dualism and its effect on the profile of labor
earnings and income distribution in Central America.)

Clearly the hard-core unemployment problem in Central America is
focused in Guatemala and El Salvador, which together account for 70 percent of open unemployment in the region (table 13), though their share
of its labor force is only 40 percent. The growth of the regional economy in the 1960s apparently helped to prevent this problem from seriously
worsening, since the increase in the employment gap of Guatemala and El
Salvador as a share of the 1970 active population was only 1.4 and 3.1
percent, respectively. However, as we saw in table 6, employment growth
in Guatemala in the 1960s was slowest in the region, while that of El
Salvador was the second fastest (after Honduras). In the 1970s estimated employment growth in El Salvador moved into first place, growth in
Guatemala shared second place with Costa Rica, while that of Honduras
fell to last place. As in Nicaragua, natural disaster in the form of the
1976 earthquake brought an infusion of relief and reconstruction funds,
and this facilitated both output and employment growth in Guatemala,
though much of this was simply a replacement of destroyed homes and commercial buildings. It will take a long time for most of the impoverished
workers in Guatemala to be absorbed into higher productivity occupations
sufficiently to permit their incomes to rise significantly. Yet it appears that the location of labor-intensive activities in labor-abundant
regions such as Guatemala, El Salvador, and Honduras had much to do with
keeping their respective employment gaps from growing unduly.

2.   Relation of CACM Policies to the Employment Gap

The Central American Common Market is shown to have increased output in the region during the period 1960 to 1972 by from 3 to 4 percent of
GDP in the latter year.[25] This additional stream of income, expressed in

value terms, would presumably not have existed in the absence of import-substituting industrialization policies at the regional level which shifted the pattern of investment away from traditional raw material and primary product production toward manufacturing. Of course, part of the shift in relative shares of value added, as well as in total value of production, may reflect a bias in commodity prices arising from protection of finished manufactures, although average external protection did not rise during the course of integration (chapter 3, table 3). This bias raises the share of "value added" in manufacturing relative to primary and tertiary sector production, the output of which was less subject to import protection. Furthermore, these gains from integration may be overstated to the extent that in the absence of such policies, relative prices in the primary sector might have been higher, stimulating greater growth in agricultural production both for export and the home market. Needless to say the pattern of gains among the five countries would also have changed notably in the absence of CACM policies.[26]

However, it is not our purpose to extend significantly the counterfactual estimation of gains and losses from integration policy in this section, except insofar as it pertains to employment problems. Indeed such estimates must rely on strong ceteris paribus assumptions about factors such as expectations with and without the CACM. Much of the growth since 1960 was due to investments in all sectors, and not just in those directly associated with increased output for exports to partner countries or replacement of imports from outside the region. (In other words one must look beyond those sectors for which increased investment might be attributed directly to the CACM, such as in the investment survey discussed in chapter 3.) Overall investment behavior in the CACM reflected generally favorable expectations about the growth potential of the region. This psychology, which influenced both domestic and foreign investors, was associated with the goals of the Common Market. It is impossible to calculate the importance of Common Market rhetoric in generating the investment and entrepreneurship on which such growth depended. Quite likely the absence of a unified attempt at growth associated with CACM policies would have been accompanied by much greater pessimism among investors, so that even had savings been available from more traditional activities, these savings might have continued to flow abroad rather than being used to expand production along the different lines that counterfactual analysis assumes. In a case such as this where growth results from investments made on the basis of favorable expectations, the optimistic rhetoric of the private sector can be self-fulfilling, at least for a time.

The other side of the coin is, however, more sobering. That by the 1970s the outlook for the CACM seemed more pessimistic reflects the fact that production growth in the 1960s was not matched by a comparable expansion in the internal market for mass-produced goods and services. As we shall see, the income distribution arising from CACM growth which is closely related to conditions in the labor market did not facilitate a balanced expansion of demand. This had important consequences for profit expectations in manufacturing, the "leading sector" of the CACM strategy. For this reason investment decelerated, the real rate of growth of private investment falling from 6.7 percent per annum in the 1960s to 4.8 percent in the 1970s (1974 being the latest year for which regionwide data are available). Had the CACM introduced employment policies favoring rising real wages and a greater labor share of value added, demand growth would have been more balanced. Under such conditions the output growth of the 1960s might well have continued into the 1970s. This would ultimately have benefited both labor and capital. Unfortunately in the absence of adequate employment and income-distribution policies, the present gloomy prognosis of private investors about regional growth prospects may also be self-fulfilling.

Assuming that the effect of the CACM policies on output was as measured by Cline in chapter 3 of this volume, what consequences might this have had for growth in the "employment gap"? Is there evidence that the CACM policies might have directed growth in less labor-using directions, working against the goals of employment and improved income distribution? To examine this latter question we shall apply current levels of labor productivity by sector of production (primary, secondary, tertiary) to output estimates made under the alternative assumptions of the presence or absence of integration policies. These estimates are based on the study of costs and benefits of integration in chapter 3, with some modifications described below.

Table 14 shows the figures from chapter 3 for regional value added in 1972 in the primary and secondary sectors with and without integration. The remaining sectors ("other") are added to round out the total GDP for 1972 (Honduras figures are for 1968). The "actual" figures are for observed GDP for 1972. The "hypothetical" figures are those calculated by Cline under the assumption that CACM integration policies were not in effect. Note that Cline prepared these counterfactual estimates only for the primary and secondary sectors (agriculture and mining, and manufacturing, respectively). The handling of tertiary activities is difficult since it is not appropriate to assume that they would have grown in value added terms in the same manner with and without the CACM. For example, urban tertiary activities are far different from those in the rural sector and are more likely to be monetized and therefore to appear in GDP tables. Also, as shown above, if the pattern of growth makes labor relatively scarce, then real wages of tertiary workers are likely to rise more than those in primary and secondary activities, causing the share of value added in the tertiary sector to remain as a larger proportion of GDP (see for example the high share of "other production" in the Costa Rican GDP (62 percent) compared with the regional average (56 percent) or that of low-wage Honduras (47 percent).

What effect did integration policy have on the structure of value added? Taking the Cline estimates as a base for the region as a whole in 1972, integration policy is seen to have increased the value of industrial production and to have stimulated total agricultural and mining production as well. In table 14 the figures for the CACM show integration policy raising 1972 agricultural and mining production by $23 million and industrial production by $243 million, the total gain being $267 million or 4.3 percent of GDP in that year. (In table 12 of chapter 3, raw material export production is shown to have been $27 million lower for the CACM as a result of the reallocative effect of integration policy, but this was offset by a rise in nonexport crop and mining production resulting from the CACM sufficient to produce a net gain of $23 million in primary production.)

220

Table 14. Gross Domestic Product With and Without
Economic Integration, 1972
(value added $CA million)

Country	(1) Primary, Agriculture and Mining	(2) Secondary, Industry	(3) Tertiary, Other	(4) Gross Domestic Product
Guatemala				
Actual	618	344	1,202	2,164
Hypothetical	612	249		
El Salvador				
Actual	295	220	634	1,150
Hypothetical	287	150		
Honduras (1968)				
Actual	262	83	302	647
Hypothetical	258	75		
Nicaragua				
Actual	263	186	537	986
Hypothetical	260	149		
Costa Rica				
Actual	242	228	771	1,240
Hypothetical	240	194		
CACM				
Actual	1,680	1,061	3,446	6,187
Hypothetical	1,657	818		

SOURCE AND METHODS: Columns 1 and 2, chapter 3, table 12. Columns 3 and
4 from SIECA, VI Compendio Estadístico Centroameri-
cano, 1975 (Guatemala City: SIECA, 1975), pp. 362-73.

From the Cline figure of $267 million, the effect of integration
policy on employment might seem to have been positive, since both primary
and secondary production would have been higher than otherwise, assuming
of course that the integration policy had no influence on productivity
growth. If this were true, then only the reallocative shift from export
to domestic crop production might have had negative consequences for employment, but this is unlikely in view of the greater capital and land
intensity of much export cropping observed in the region. (Coffee and
banana production, which have relatively high labor-capital ratios, also
have high value added per worker and therefore complicate the situation

insofar as the relationship between factor intensity and employment are concerned.)

Based on 1970 productivity figures, the implied 4.3 percent growth in GDP which Cline attributes to integration policy (as calculated from table 12 in chapter 3) would have accounted for 178,000 jobs as of 1972, or 3.8 percent of the labor force in that year; however, such counter-factual estimates might well understate the alternative output and employment growth that would have taken place in the absence of integration policy.[27] For example, considering just the primary and secondary sectors by Cline's measure, integration policy increased industry's share of value added from 33.0 to 38.7 percent, with the agricultural and mining share correspondingly reduced from 67.0 to 61.3 percent. This represented an allocative shift by 5.7 percentage points between the two sectors. Let us suppose that in the absence of integration total output of the two sectors would have remained the same but the shares would have been 33 and 67 percent, respectively. This would have meant that of a total value of production of $2,741 million, agriculture and mining would have represented 67 percent or $1,837 million and manufacturing production would have been $904 million, rather than the observed totals of $1,680 million and $1,061 million, respectively. The employment consequences of this alternative allocation of resources based on 1970 labor productivity figures would have been considerable, as illustrated in table 15 of this chapter.

The counterfactual analysis of table 15 assumes no alteration in total regional GDP in 1972, but a shift in the composition of output from industry to agriculture corresponding to the implied sectoral shares in the absence of integration. Under such circumstances, employment would have grown enough by 1972 to totally absorb the increased "excess supply of labor" implied by our 1960-71 employment gap estimates. While the non-CACM growth path would have meant some 92,000 fewer industrial jobs, assuming the impressive labor-displacing productivity gains of the 1960s, the primary sector would have provided 245,000 more jobs than in fact existed in 1972. If to these estimates we add the reasonable assumption that CACM policies favored labor-saving and capital-intensive technologies in both the rural and urban sectors, then the counterfactual favorable impact on employment might have been greater than 153,000 jobs.

The strongest and most questionable assumption underlying the estimates is that without CACM policies growth in total output would have remained unchanged. Indeed, the relatively pessimistic employment results require that one dismiss in their entirety the integration benefits estimated in chapter 3. As such, the pessimistic alternative may be viewed as something of a "maximum damage" estimate corresponding to the most extreme statement of possible employment loss caused by integration, under the assumption that integration made no positive impact on total output but did reduce employment by shifting the composition of production from labor-intensive agriculture to capital-intensive industry. In fact, we are almost certain that total output growth would have been less without the CACM considering both the detailed analysis of integration benefits and the more general factor of the stimulative impact of the CACM rhetoric. Tertiary sector production (which is largely urban in character and derived from expenditure multipliers of industrial growth) would have lagged with that of the manufacturing sector, and urban demand for agricultural

Table 15. Employment Consequences of Integration, 1972
(negative impact assumption)

Sector	(1) Hypothetical Output Without Integration ($CA million)	(2) Percent	(3) Jobs per $CA million	(4) Total Jobs Without Integration (thousand man-years)
A. Without Integration				
Industry	904	33.0	582	526
Agriculture, Mining	1,837	67.0	1,563	2,871
Total	2,741	100.0		3,397

Sector	(1) Actual Output With Integration ($CA million)	(2) Percent	(3) Jobs per $CA million	(4) Total Jobs With Integration (thousand man-years)
B. With Integration				
Industry	1,061	38.7	582	618
Agriculture, Mining	1,680	61.3	1,563	2,626
Total	2,741	100.0		3,244

C. Difference in Employment Due to Integration

	(thousand man-years)
Industry	+ 92
Agriculture, Mining	- 245
Net Difference (1972)	- 153
Employment gap increase, 1960-71 (increase demand - increase supply)	- 140
Employment gap increase, 1960-75	- 222

SOURCES AND METHODS: See text. Labor productivity (1971) in column 2 from appendix E.
Increased employment gaps for 1960-71 and 1960-75 from table 12.

commodities would have slowed as well; however, the consequences of slower urbanization and secondary/tertiary sector growth on employment and welfare of the working class are less easy to estimate. Since we have seen that growth in value added in the tertiary sector depends somewhat upon the total balance between supply and demand for labor, it is not appropriate to take existing productivity estimates and apply them to alternative expansion paths as a basis for projections of either labor income or employment. Had the non-CACM growth path been more labor-using, then workers would have been less abundant in the urban sector and growth in labor income would have been more rapid. The labor share of GDP might also have risen. Moreover, the regional distribution of income among the five countries would almost certainly have been more equal.

To recapitulate, the above analysis considers the pessimistic end of the range of possible employment effects of integration in the region. This approach indicates that by favoring industry rather than agriculture, integration may have reduced potential employment by 153,000 jobs, or by 3.5 percent of actual employment. The alternative end of the range for employment effects is that which is based on the central interpretation of the SIECA/Brookings study. That more optimistic interpretation suggests that total output was higher as the result of integration and that new jobs in industry (and agriculture) did not come at the expense of jobs in traditional agriculture. The estimates in chapter 4 compute the employment effect under the optimistic interpretation, once again using the sectoral output effects of integration as identified in chapter 3. Those estimates conclude that the integration process created a total of 154,000 direct and indirect jobs in all sectors during the period 1958-72 (chapter 4, tables 11 and 13).[28]

F.   Labor Income in the Central American Common Market

The evolution of real wages in Central America may be presumed to reflect the direct influence of market forces and the indirect effect of changing demographic, political, and institutional conditions such as unionization and integration policies as discussed in the preceding sections. Labor income is derived from wage and nonwage benefits, the latter of which generally bear some proportion to wage levels. In this section we shall look at recent trends in wages and salaries in the five countries of the CACM in order to provide a basis for evaluation of the possible impact of the various forces causing changes in the labor market. While this section deals with trends in average wages, section G deals with the distribution of the wage bill as reflected in "wage profiles" by country and activity sector. This permits an assessment of the distributional impact of wage changes among the working class.

In table 16 the average levels of wages and salaries per worker are presented for the five countries in 1960 and 1971. The growth of nominal wages during the period averaged 3.9 percent annually for Central America, but price inflation prevented real wages from growing at more than 2.6 percent. In average terms, the leading countries in real wage growth were Nicaragua and Costa Rica, both relatively "labor-scarce" economies, followed in descending order by Guatemala, El Salvador, and Honduras. Since Guatemala and El Salvador are generally acknowledged to be "labor-abundant" economies, their lagging position is relatively understandable.

Table 16. Annual Average Wages and Salaries per Employed Worker

| Country | Average Annual Wages and Salaries Plus Fringe Benefits | | Compound Annual Rate of Growth 1960 to 1971 | | |
	1960	1971	Current Prices	Constant Prices	Productivity Growth
	($CA Current Prices)			(percent)	
Guatemala	339	470	3.0	2.5	3.2
El Salvador	328	431	2.5	2.2	2.5
Honduras	266	370	3.0	0.9	1.1
Nicaragua	481	991	6.6	4.5	4.4
Costa Rica	622	1,138	5.5	3.5	3.7
Central America	369	568	3.9	2.6	2.9

NOTE: Based on wage and salary (and fringe benefit) estimates by Gustavo Leiva, SIECA
Special Studies Unit, Guatemala, 1975. Appendix tables 3, 16, from SIECA and
governmental sources. The figures are average earnings and do not reflect trends
in distribution of the wage bill. In section G of this chapter the wage profile
is seen to have become more skewed over the period for all countries. Price level estimates are converted to constant prices using the implicit GDP deflators
for the respective countries from SIECA, VI Compendio Estadístico Centroamericano, 1975 (Guatemala City: SIECA, 1975). Productivity growth is from table 6.

However, the slowest growth in real wages, that of Honduras, is more difficult to explain, since it showed the smallest "gap" (excess supply of
labor) as of 1971 (table 12).

For these calculations we used the estimates of the wage share of
value added (including fringe benefits) and employment by sector and
country in order to calculate earnings per worker for 1960 and 1971. The
only comparable independent series of estimates on earnings per worker
are for the industrial sector as presented in the VI Compendio Estadistico
Centroamericano (SIECA, 1975). The advantage of our method is that it
permits a comprehensive measure of labor earnings for all economic sectors including manufacturing, and national averages on a comparable basis
for all countries. As for absolute wage levels by country, the rank
ordering indicates a high positive correlation with the growth in labor
productivity over the period 1960 to 1971, as shown in table 17.

Table 17. Rank Order of Wages, Productivity Growth, and the "Employment
Gap," Central America, 1960 and 1971

Country	Average Wage Levels		Growth in Output Per Worker (1960-71)	Employment Gap Increase (1960-71)
	1960	1971		
	(Current $CA)			(thousand man-years)
Costa Rica	622	1,138	1,077	67
Nicaragua	481	991	947	18
Guatemala	339	470	423	23
El Salvador	328	431	280	34
Honduras	266	370	289	-2
CACM	369	568	485	140

SOURCES AND METHODS: Columns 1 and 2 from table 16. Column 3 from table
5 and column 4 from tables 12 and 13.

With the exception of El Salvador and Honduras there is a perfect
positive rank correlation between productivity growth and average wage
levels in both years, suggesting that those countries with the highest
initial income per worker have experienced the most rapid productivity
growth. On the other hand, the correlation between wage increases and
the employment gap is by no means as clear. Costa Rica, with the highest
real wages and high productivity growth, also experienced the largest

increase in its employment "gap," which as shown earlier amounted to 12.5 percent of the active population in 1971. Admittedly the "gap" concept is artificial in that it does not imply open unemployment but rather an excess in predicted labor supply growth over observed demand. Part of the "gap" may reflect falling participation rates among the adult population. But there does seem to be evidence that the impressive growth in real wages in Costa Rica might well have been at the expense of significant underemployment of the work force and concentration of wage income among those workers more able to benefit from artificial or natural barriers to entry into the labor market.

Among the various sectors of the economies of Central America there is a wide diversion of labor earnings, as seen in table 18. In 1960 for the region as a whole the highest earnings (in commerce) averaged 4.7 times those in agriculture. This ratio was maintained through 1971, but the ratio of industrial sector wages to those in agriculture grew from 3.1 in 1960 to 3.4 in 1971. The compound annual rates of growth of wages in current Central American dollars were 3.3 percent in agriculture, 4.3 in industry, and 3.2 in commerce. The fact that industry was a leading sector during the first decade of the CACM had clear impact on the relative growth of wages there, while agriculture and commerce (more subject to the availability of surplus labor) showed a slower rate of growth.

The differences in the growth of labor earnings among the five countries are even more pronounced when one looks at individual sectors. For example, wage increases in industry varied enormously, from 12.6 percent per annum in Guatemala, which began the period at a low base with industrial wages little above those in agriculture, to only 1.2 percent annually in Honduras where industrial wages in 1960 were already 3.9 times those in agriculture. Because of this regional growth, industrial wages in Guatemala in 1971 reached 4.3 times those of agriculture compared to 1.5 to 1 in 1960, clearly establishing the evidence of wage dualism in that country. In El Salvador, where wage dualism was already pronounced in 1960 with industrial wages 2.9 times those in agriculture, industrial earnings grew at only 2.1 percent per annum during the 1960s.

In Costa Rica, wage dualism between industry and agriculture was the least evident at the beginning of the period with a ratio of 1.9 to 1 in 1960, but dualism rose to 3.0 by 1971 as industrial wages grew at 8.1 percent per annum, compared with a 4.1 percent annual rate of growth of agricultural earnings. Indeed, the country with the most serious underemployment problem, El Salvador, showed the slowest growth of agricultural earnings for the period, being only 0.7 percent per annum in current prices. This contrasts with growth rates for rural earnings of 6.2 percent in Nicaragua, 4.1 percent in Costa Rica, 2.6 percent in Guatemala, and 2.1 percent in Honduras.

Perhaps the most important findings of table 18 are the rapid movement in the absolute level of labor earnings in Guatemalan industry, from last place in 1960 to third place (behind Nicaragua and Costa Rica) in 1971, while El Salvador, which had notable growth in value added per worker in industry, moved from fourth to fifth place in industrial income per worker. Despite the caveats that must be raised about intercountry comparisons of undeflated figures, nothing illustrates more clearly the effect of El Salvador's labor surplus on the earnings of its workers. Moreover, capital-intensive agricultural development in the northern three countries, Guatemala, El Salvador, and Honduras, tended to swell the rural proletariat by displacing small farmers. The interdependence of rural labor markets in these countries, the border conflict between El Salvador and Honduras notwithstanding, tended to equalize labor earnings in the rural sector at low levels. In short, the regional employment gap was reflected most sharply in agriculture. As a result, money earnings rose slowly and real wages not at all between 1960 and 1971 in most of northern Central America's rural sector. On the other hand, in Costa Rica and Nicaragua, where rural employment conditions were more favorable, agricultural earnings grew slightly even though the gap between urban industrial and rural wages widened significantly during the 1960s.

Table 18. Average Earnings per Worker in Selected Sectors of the
Central American Economies, 1960 and 1971
(current $CA per year)

Country	Year	Agriculture	Industry	Commerce
Guatemala	1960	151	219	1,099
	1971	202	871	1,467
El Salvador	1960	171	498	707
	1971	185	629	940
Honduras	1960	146	565	706
	1971	184	645	865
Nicaragua	1960	364	771	669
	1971	718	1,962	1,229
Costa Rica	1960	322	622	1,065
	1971	504	1,520	1,644
CACM	1960	188	574	890
	1971	269	919	1,262

SOURCES AND METHODS: See note, table 16. Basic data on employment and labor shares of value added in appendix E.

Wage behavior since 1971 is difficult to determine with any precision because there are no reliable global figures on employment by sector since the population censuses at the beginning of the period. However, wage income has been influenced by two major factors during the post-1971 years, the slowdown in economic growth and the rapid increase in prices due to varying combinations of factors including world inflation, domestic deficit spending (mainly in Costa Rica), natural disasters (hurricane Fifi in Honduras and the earthquakes in Nicaragua and Guatemala), and the monetization of relief donations which swelled effective demand even as capacity was cut.

The sudden sharp inflationary impact of the 1972-75 period is reflected in the figures of table 19. Costa Rica showed the most severe inflation, 16 percent annually, followed by 14 percent in Guatemala, 12 percent in Nicaragua, 10 percent in El Salvador, and 7 percent in Honduras. Without clear indicators of post-1971 money wage trends, there is a consensus among most observers in the region that real wages probably declined for all countries during the period for those in the lowest skill levels, with lesser declines and even some increases for the higher skills, though at a much slower rate than in the 1960s.

Table 19. Price Level Increases in Central America, 1950-75
(consumer price index; first year of
each period = 100)

Country	1950-60	1960-70	1970-72	1972-75
Guatemala	111	107	97	150
El Salvador	101	104	104	137
Honduras	119	124	105	125
Nicaragua	161	124	103	143
Costa Rica	108	125	104	161

SOURCE: Consumer price index, SIECA, VI Compendio Estadístico Centroamericano, 1975 (Guatemala City: SIECA, 1975), tables 220-24, for years through 1972. For 1972 to 1975, the implicit deflators of GDP as prepared by the SIECA Special Studies Unit by country. Note the effect of the respective earthquakes in Nicaragua and Guatemala in 1972-75 price level changes. There is some tendency for temporary price rises to readjust downward in these countries. In Costa Rica the price inflation is rather a reflection of domestic monetary and fiscal policies and related wage adjustments in response to political pressures because of its relatively democratic system of government.

G. Wage Profiles in the Central American Common Market

Having examined average earnings per worker in the CACM in the preceding section, we now look at the relationship between labor income and productivity (value added per worker) as it evolved between 1960 and 1971 for the region as a whole. The evidence is based on the preparation of a set of "wage profiles" for the five countries, both in detail for the industrial and agricultural sectors and in summary for the main sectors of the economies. The summary tables for each of the countries for the years 1960 and 1971 are presented in appendix E. For the CACM as a whole, the summary tables are reproduced in figure 2 of this chapter. These "wage profiles" are based on a concept orginated by Richard Webb for application to the Peruvian situation.[29] They involve a presentation of labor income in graphical form by descending order of value added per worker, such that labor productivity becomes an envelope within which labor income is drawn. This formulation is particularly helpful in defining the limits within which labor income may be permitted to grow, since in no case may this exceed total value added per worker.

In a purely competitive market economy, if labor were perfectly mobile and skills homogeneous, then the wage profile as determined by aggregate supply and demand for labor would be relatively flat. In such an economy, as labor became more scarce relative to capital and other inputs, the wage profile would tend to shift upward. Wages as a share of value added would also tend to rise if the elasticity of substitution between labor and capital were less than unity (which is the case in Central America, as evidenced in other sections of this volume, at least for the industrial sector). Skewing of the wage profile, as observed in figure 2, will occur in a competitive economy whenever labor productivity differs among sectors due to varying skill content among the work force and skill requirements among sectors of production. In such cases, higher wages will reflect returns to a greater degree of labor skill, including investment in human capital.

Market imperfections on both the supply and demand side will also tend to skew the wage profile. Monopoly of labor supply, through unionization, collective bargaining, and the imposition of barriers to entry into the labor market for higher skills will permit workers to bid away a share of economic rent from the recipients of property income. Monopsony control over the demand for labor will tend to depress wages below competitive levels, skewing the wage profile in the other direction. Government policies may exacerbate both types of influences. For example, minimum wage policies work in favor of a higher offer price of labor than market conditions would permit, which could either complement monopoly forces or offset monopsony forces in less than fully competitive labor markets. In competitive markets a minimum wage policy would tend to reduce employment by skewing the wage bill above equilibrium levels.

The characteristics of the labor market as described in section B of this chapter determine the ability of labor to bargain for shares of value added within the productivity envelope. Clearly the more competitive the labor market and the greater the share of workers in low-productivity sectors, the lower the overall contours of the labor income curve. The more segmented the labor market, in terms of the ability of workers in higher productivity sectors to restrict entry into their jobs (through unionization, social solidarity, political preferences, and other measures), the more skewed will be the earnings profile. The skewing will, of course, tend to follow the contours of the overall productivity envelope. On the other hand, where the labor market has monopsonistic characteristics, such that employers can force down wages even below the

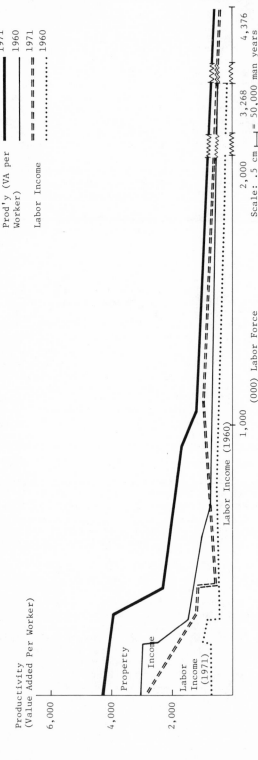

Productivity
(Value Added Per Worker)

6,000

4,000

2,000

Property
Income

Labor
Income
(1971)

Labor Income (1960)

Prod'y (VA per Worker)

Labor Income

1971
1960
1971
1960

1,000   2,000   3,268   4,376

(000) Labor Force

Scale: .5 cm ⊢——⊣ = 50,000 man years

Source: Appendix C (unpublished version of manuscript), tables 1 and 2. Based on "Webb curve" analysis of Richard Webb, Government Policy and the Distribution of Income in Peru, 1963–1973, Harvard University Press, Cambridge, Mass., 1977, chapter 5. Property income represents the sum of all non-labor income including profits, interest, and rent expressed on a per-worker basis as summed across main sectors of the economy. In descending order of per-capita productivity these sectors were, for both years, commerce, energy, transportation, mining, industry, construction, and agriculture. The profiles for the Industrial sector were also estimated for this project for the five countries in 1962 and 1968 for 20 two-digit subsectors, and for the agricultural sector for the five countries for 1960 and 1971 for the major export crops and all other sectors combined. For reasons of space, these diagrams have not been included in the published version but are available from the authors on request. Profiles for each of the five countries for the main sectors in 1960 and 1971, are included as Appendices in the unpublished manuscript.

Figure 2. Wage Profiles in Central America, 1960 and 1971
($CA per year)

marginal productivity of labor, or where product markets are monopsonistic so that product prices are forced down below competitive levels (thus reducing the marginal revenue product of labor), the wage profile will be depressed below the level that it might reach under purely competitive conditions.

In the Central American case both sets of pressures coexist, unionization and other forms of segmentation being present in the urban industrial and high-productivity agricultural export sectors, particularly in the southern countries. In other sectors (especially in agriculture), elements of monopsony obtain, particularly in the northern countries of the region where for generations the Indian population has been the victim of discriminatory employment practices. Some of the governments still employ police and military units to "discipline" labor markets, facilitating the maintenance of low wages. While this is generally done to forestall collective bargaining, strikes, and other means of reducing competition on the supply side, such measures are also used to support monopsony, forcing wages to below competitive equilibrium levels. However, growing opportunities for employment throughout the CACM have weakened the grip of employers on workers in the poorest regions by stimulating migration. Even though underemployment has grown, workers who relocate in urban areas are less susceptible to the traditional monopsonistic practices which predominate in much of rural Central America.

The wage profiles in figure 2 show some skewing of the wage bill for both 1960 and 1971, with visual evidence of increased inequality at the end of the period. Evidence is insufficient to trace out the market and nonmarket forces behind the level and trends in these wage profiles. It could be argued simplistically that growing skill requirements, due to integration policies and general development tendencies, outstripped growth in the supply of skilled labor. This would lead to a relative increase in earnings of skilled workers independent of imperfections in the labor market. Indeed we have suggested that relatively weak unionization and numerous legal and institutional barriers to collective bargaining in much of Central America tended to minimize upward skewing at the left-hand end of the wage profile. On the other hand, the stress on industrialization and capital-using agricultural growth required a rising proportion of skilled to unskilled labor in the work force. Lags in educational achievements in most countries (except Costa Rica) have tended to slow the supply response to growing demand for skilled workers.

The highest segment of the wage profile represents workers in commerce. The ratio of average earnings in commerce to those in agriculture remained 4.7 to 1 between 1960 and 1971 (table 18), showing that the "productivity gap" between the highest and lowest wage groups did not narrow during the first decade of the CACM. One may ask whether educational and other "skill requirements" in commerce justified this gap, or whether the force of urbanization and expansion of the market economy had a relatively favorable effect on the earnings of those employed in the commercial sector. To the extent that commerce has its own internal dualism, such that high-wage modern commercial enterprises and low-wage urban informal activities exist side by side, there may well have been a skewing of the wage profile in this sector as well.

At the right-hand end of the wage profile, which represents the majority of workers employed in the agricultural sector, there may have been some downward skewing due to nonmarket forces which restricted the ability of rural workers to bargain for increased shares of economic rent. Appendix E discusses this process in some detail and suggests that for high-rent export crops the wage profile has been shifted upward by such measures in several Central American countries. On the other hand, the withdrawal of land from subsistence cultivation will tend to swell the landless rural proletariat, depressing real wages at the far end of the distribution.

It should be stressed that "labor earnings" under the wage profile curve do not comprise the total income of working-class households. The remainder, property income, includes returns to capital, natural resources, technology, entrepreneurship, and other scarce factors. To the extent that such factors are in the possession of workers, this will increase their total income. From a policy point of view, there are alternative strategies for increasing incomes of workers. One method is to shift the ownership of land, capital, and technology toward the working class. This could be done gradually through increased labor participation in savings, investment in physical and human capital, management, and entrepreneurship. It could be done more abruptly by redistributing existing income or wealth in the direction of the workers, either through direct expropriation or through taxation and other measures (wealth is defined here in terms of claims on future income streams rather than ownership of assets per se). It is not clear whether in the Central American case the skewing of wage profiles has been accompanied by a proportional skewing of claims on property income, such that privileged workers have higher property incomes than poorer workers, but this seems likely.

What about the overall conditions of supply and demand in the labor market, and their effect on wage profiles in the region? The growth in the employment gap between 1960 and 1971 probably depressed the growth of labor earnings at the low end of the profile. In addition policies favoring investment in the urban and industrial sectors facilitated segmentation of the job market, raising labor incomes in these sectors, though a growing excess supply of labor probably diminished tendencies for upward skewing, especially in economies such as Costa Rica and Nicaragua. Hence, if current economic policies exacerbated inequality at the low end of the spectrum, their effect on inequality at the upper end is not clear. From table 18 we have seen that in those countries where the industrial sector already had high wages relative to other sectors in 1960, industrial wage growth was less. But where the industrial sector began with a lower wage level at the beginning of the period, incomes tended to soar between 1960 and 1971, increasing wage dualism relative to agriculture. This suggests that regional averages for wage profiles conceal quite different and even offsetting trends among both countries and sectors.

Some final points may be drawn from this section. In analyzing the Peruvian case, Webb stressed the importance of government policies in the growth of the productivity envelope within which wage profiles evolve. The favoring of capital-intensive activities will tend to skew the wage profile by skewing the productivity envelope to the extent that workers can bargain for a share of the increase in productivity. Taxation or expropriation of the rents of high-productivity sectors, for the benefit of workers in the same sectors, will skew the wage profile without necessarily altering the productivity envelope. Certain measures to increase wages such as minimum wage laws may skew wage profiles, while others, such as a reduction in wage-specific taxes (such as employer social security contributions), will tend to shift up the curve. The proportionality of the shift will depend on the extent of the tax incidence. Attention should focus not only on the employment and wage impact of development policies but on the distribution of employment and labor incomes among the working class. We shall argue in the following sections that in Central America the functional and size distributions of income are related and that functional income distribution reflects overall labor market conditions. Thus, future policies designed to combine growth in productivity with a broader and more equitable distribution of income must be directed toward the slope of the productivity envelope and to market and nonmarket forces which permit the wage profile to rise throughout its length and not in a skewed manner.

H. The Functional and Size Distribution of Income in the Central American Common Market

1. The Functional Distribution of Income

Here we examine the effect of Central American economic growth from 1960 to 1971 on the functional distribution of income in the region. The breakdown used for the factor income shares is as follows:

Labor income: wages, salaries, and fringe benefits

Cost of capital: a "normal return" to assets plus depreciation (as calculated by the Central Banks of Guatemala and Costa Rica; these average shares by sector applied to the remaining countries)

Economic rent: the residual of value added after deducting labor income and the cost of capital. (This includes profits in excess of a "normal return on capital," entrepreneurial income, returns to licenses and patents, other scarcity rents, and possible undercounting of labor and capital shares.)

Clearly the "economic rent" component of value added is the weakest of the three, being a residual sensitive to procedures for estimation of the labor and capital shares; however, it is important to separate out "economic rent" in view of the key role it plays in the distribution of income between labor and property owners. Yet "economic rent" should not be estimated as a simple "surplus" of value added after deducting labor income, since capital must receive at least a "normal return" (covering liquidity and risk bearing) for depreciation costs to be replaced and new investment to occur. In this respect the concept of "economic rent" used here is narrower than that of "surplus value" in the Marxian literature yet broader than Ricardian resource rents in the neoclassical literature.

An additional consideration is that a proper definition of economic rent should include that component of wages and salaries in excess of a "normal return" to labor. Since the "normal return" to assets is based on the concept that there is a shadow price of capital (the social opportunity cost of an increment of savings) plus a definable degree of compensation for risk and loss of liquidity, the cost of labor should also be based on the social opportunity cost of labor services per unit of time. Wages and salaries in excess of that amount would then be regarded as part of "economic rent." This more complete definition of rent would clarify the political-economic process of rent partitioning which occurs between labor and property owners (and the government) in every economy.[30] The earlier analysis has suggested that the tighter the labor market (less the relative supply of unemployed workers or those in marginal occupations) the greater the opportunity for labor to bargain for increasing shares of economic rent. Also the higher the productivity of labor the greater the potential for rent partitioning in favor of the working class. Needless to say, the greater the voice of labor in the political process, the more "political markets" will be used to increase the labor share of economic rents.

In the Central American case one can imagine that the highest productivity activities are characterized by a higher absolute level of true economic rent per worker and hence greater scope for labor to bargain for shares. Since our statistics reflect actual wages and salaries (plus fringe benefits) they almost certainly include some part of the true economic rent, especially for those sectors at the higher end of the productivity distribution. It is also likely that since productivity grew in a skewed manner between 1960 and 1971, labor in these favored activities was more successful in bargaining for rent shares, and that this also held for higher-productivity economies in the region. Hence, one would expect that there is an upward bias to the wage share in the high-productivity sectors and countries, and that this bias increased from 1960 to 1971 insofar as that share reflects a "normal return to labor." On the other hand there is a corresponding downward bias to the economic rent share for the same reasons.

A word about the data. Their numerous shortcomings notwithstanding, the factor share estimates for the five Central American countries are as reliable as most in Latin America and are suitable for broad comparisons; however, one should not attempt to use them for detailed analysis, and slight differences in trends should be minimized.

Those who quarrel with the arbitrary estimates of cost of capital might prefer to aggregate the respective capital and rent shares. Also as noted above, the rental share is almost certainly understated with respect to labor and may well be overstated with respect to capital. This is because of the difficulty of estimating a return to capital essential to elicit the full replacement of depreciating assets and historical levels of net investment. Finally the allocative function of economic rents should not be discounted by the concept employed here. If rents were channeled away from property owners to labor, those resources eliciting higher rents might not be drawn into production first, with obviously detrimental consequences for productivity. (On the other hand the monopoly profit component of rents may be associated with restricted output for purposes of profit maximization, so that a "tax" on potential rents might lead to fuller capacity utilization.)

Table 20 provides a rough breakdown of the functional distribution of income in the five Central American countries for 1960 and 1971.

Table 20. The Functional Distribution of Income, Central America, 1960 and 1971 (percent of value added)

Country	Year	National Averages			
		Wages and Salaries	Cost of Capital	Economic Rent	Total
Guatemala	1960	.407	.083	.510	1.00
	1971	.374	.094	.532	1.00
El Salvador	1960	.426	.086	.487	1.00
	1971	.412	.099	.489	1.00
Honduras	1960	.438	.084	.479	1.00
	1971	.413	.090	.497	1.00
Nicaragua	1960	.493	.077	.431	1.00
	1971	.515	.086	.399	1.00
Costa Rica	1960	.502	.036	.461	1.00
	1971	.492	.046	.462	1.00
Central America	1960	.441	.076	.483	1.00
	1971	.430	.085	.485	1.00

NOTE: Calculations prepared by Gustavo Leiva, SIECA Special Studies Unit, Guatemala, 1975-76, based on appendix E. See also footnote to table 23. The capital cost share estimated for Costa Rica is significantly below that of Guatemala (which provides the basis for the capital coefficients of the other three countries), suggesting that there is an upward bias to the rent share for Costa Rica for both years; however, the cost of capital coefficient rose by 28 percent between 1960 and 1971, clearly indicating a trend, notwithstanding the possible downward bias in absolute terms for both years.

The effect of the structure of the labor market on functional income shares can be indirectly inferred from table 20. First, it should be noted that the distributions listed are national averages reflecting not only changes within sectors but shifts in output among sectors, with associated changes in weighted averages. Also intrasectoral shifts in the composition of output will affect the functional distribution shares. Having made these caveats, there is evidence from the data that in all countries but Nicaragua the share of wages and salaries declined significantly between 1960 and 1971. And the country with the lowest wage share, Guatemala, also experienced the sharpest decline in wages as a proportion of gross domestic income, by 3.3 percentage points over the decade. Nicaragua, on the other hand, was the only country for which the wage share rose, by 2.2 percentage points, and it was second only to Costa Rica in the share of wages in GDP. Costa Rica, the highest productivity economy which also had the highest initial wage share, nevertheless experienced a slight decline in this share by 1.1 percentage points. By 1971 both Costa Rica and Nicaragua showed about 50 percent of income accruing to wages and salaries (plus fringe benefits).

We have already seen that in terms of "employment gap" analysis (table 13), Costa Rica as of 1971 had a large and growing underemployment problem. This might lead one to suspect that the falling wage share of value added reflected depressed bargaining power of labor for rental income shares; however, the declining wage share was offset by rising capital costs. These costs represent normal returns to plant, equipment, and other assets and do not include what might be called excess profits. The rent component of GDP did not rise significantly for Costa Rica during the period. This indicates that growing investments per worker led to rising normal costs of capital per worker. It is not possible to determine whether excess profits (which would appear under rental income in our estimates) rose disproportionately, offsetting other components of rent. One may simply affirm that the rent share as a whole did not grow and therefore the ability of workers to participate in economic rents was not significantly impaired, the employment gap notwithstanding.

The Costa Rican case is quite different from that of the poorer countries. For example in Guatemala the wage share fell by 3.3 percentage points, offset for the most part by increased rent shares (2.2 points) and only slightly by costs of capital (1.1 points). Abundant low-cost labor from the subsistence sector combined with conditions unfavorable to collective bargaining in Guatemala probably contributed to the fact that most productivity gains accrued to property owners. Since Guatemala was one of the countries most favored by CACM policies, these findings are sobering in terms of their distributional consequences. The situation was little better in Honduras, in which the wage share fell by 2.5 percentage points (table 20) offset by a 1.8 point rise in rent shares and a slight rise in the share of capital costs. Here again the struggle for shares of economic rent seems to have been won handily by the property owners. In the case of Honduras, however, the access of the lowest income groups to land (and hence the land-rent portion of total economic rent) is relatively greater than in Guatemala, so one may suppose that the consequences of these trends in factor shares for size distribution of income (distribution among households) would be less severe in Honduras than in Guatemala.

In El Salvador the functional share of wages and salaries in total value added fell by 1.4 percentage points, offset primarily by capital

costs which rose 1.3 points. Here, as in Costa Rica, the falling wage
share seems to have reflected growing capital intensity of production
leading to a larger share of "normal profits" in GDP. Finally Nicaragua, the only country to register an increase in the wage share, also
experienced a very slight rise in profit shares, both offset by a 3.2
percentage point decline in rental income shares. In terms of our hypothesis
that factor incomes in developing countries represent a struggle for shares
of economic rent, the strongest supporting evidence for this comes from
Guatemala on the negative side (rents rose relative to wages) and Nicaragua
on the positive side (wages rose relative to rents). Slight support is
provided on the negative side by Honduras, but for Costa Rica and El
Salvador, two of the most industrialized and urbanized countries, falling
wage shares are wholly offset by an increased normal return on capital.

Interestingly, both Guatemala and Nicaragua have strong export agricultural sectors, but the latter appears to have more potentially arable
land per rural worker. The effect on relative wage and rent shares
of value added in agriculture may be seen in table 21. As one would
expect, the rent share of value added was smaller in Nicaragua, the land-
abundant economy. Also the change in wage shares from 1960 to 1971 for
Nicaragua was positive, whereas in both Guatemala and Costa Rica it was
sharply negative.

Table 21. The Functional Distribution of Income in Agriculture
in Selected Countries

		National Averages			
Country	Year	Wages and Salaries	Cost of Capital	Economic Rent	Total
Guatemala	1960	.427	.110	.463	1.00
	1971	.349	.100	.551	1.00
Nicaragua	1960	.634	.110*	.256*	1.00
	1971	.758	.100*	.142*	1.00
Costa Rica	1960	.554	.110*	.336*	1.00
	1971	.455	.100*	.445*	1.00

*The Costa Rican and Nicaraguan cost of capital figures were adjusted
to equal that of Guatemala for both 1960 and 1971, thus altering the
residual for economic rent. Our independent estimates of capital cost
for Costa Rican agriculture give shares of .029 in both 1960 and 1971.
Figures are based on SIECA estimates as described in table 22.

The trend in the wage share of value added in manufacturing in Costa Rica and El Salvador was the reverse of that in the other three Central American countries, as indicated in table 22. Here again the performance of Guatemala stands out, since this was one of the most rapidly industrializing economies in the CACM. Nevertheless, its industrial wage share fell slightly, even as it did by a much larger amount in agriculture (table 21). The shift in Guatemala toward more capital-intensive activities appeared to have the most depressing effect on wage shares of any of the five countries (as shown in table 20).[31]

Table 22. The Wage Share of Value Added in Central American Industry
(wages ÷ value added)

Country	1960	1971
Guatemala	.579	.561
El Salvador	.580	.610
Honduras	.579	.452
Nicaragua	.637	.610
Costa Rica	.338	.395
CACM	.540	.535

SOURCE: Appendix E. Note that capital cost and rental shares are not given because there is a lack of comparability in estimating techniques for capital cost at the sectoral level. The low shares for Costa Rica, which is a high-wage country, suggest that the labor income estimates also have a comparability problem, so that trends may be more relevant than absolute levels for comparative purposes.

Bearing in mind the questions of comparability in data and trends in individual country shares, functional distributional averages for the region are presented for five major sectors of production in table 23. The wide range in labor shares among the sectors is evident, the highest share being in construction and the lowest in commerce. A rising trend in wage shares for construction, commerce, and industry (in El Salvador and Costa Rica) was offset by sharply declining shares in agriculture and transportation. The proportion of rural rents appears to have risen notably everywhere but in Nicaragua, as shown above, while rent shares in industry fell in every case but Honduras, where increased rents offset a sharp decline in wage shares. While these figures are far from the last word, they indicate the extent to which abundant labor may depress the wage share of value added and keep it low during a period of rapid economic growth.

Table 23. The Functional Distribution of Income in Key Sectors of the
Central American Economy, 1960 and 1971

Sector	Year	Wages and Salaries	Cost of Capital	Economic Rent	Total
		Sectoral Averages for Region as a Whole			
Agriculture	1960	.470	.100	.430	1.00
	1971	.426	.089	.485	1.00
Industry	1960	.540	.159	.301	1.00
	1971	.535	.217	.248	1.00
Construction	1960	.805	.067	.128	1.00
	1971	.829	.063	.108	1.00
Transportation	1960	.556	.098	.346	1.00
	1971	.509	.121	.370	1.00
Commerce	1960	.291	.074	.635	1.00
	1971	.319	.060	.621	1.00

SOURCE AND METHODS: Tables on factor incomes in appendix E, with wages
(salarios globales) calculated for each country and
sector, capital costs estimated for the six main
sectors of production (agriculture, industry, construction, energy, transport, and commerce) for Costa
Rica (Banco Central de Costa Rica and SIECA) and
Guatemala (Cuentas Nacionales, Banco de Guatemala,
Departamento de Estudios Económicos, 1968), with sectoral proportions for Guatemala for the years 1960
and 1971 applied to El Salvador, Honduras, and Nicaragua for the respective years. Economic rents in
each case are the residual.

In table 24 we show the trends in wage levels and shares in the
five countries from 1960 to 1971. These figures reflect the hard core
poverty problem in Guatemala and El Salvador associated with their "labor
surplus." Though each country had higher average wages than Honduras,
their wage share of value added was below that of Honduras in 1960 and
remained equal or below it in 1970. Guatemala had the lowest wage share
in both years, due primarily to the depressing effect of low-productivity
agricultural employment. In this respect we may note that despite the
abundance of cheap labor in El Salvador and Honduras, there is a double
migration outflow between both countries due to geographical proximity
and the different harvest times for the main crops. There is also seasonal migration from Guatemala into the poorest regions of southern Mexico to harvest coffee, sugar, and other cash crops. Dualism in the labor
markets of both Guatemala and El Salvador lies behind the wage share

figures, since higher wages in the more productive subsectors skew upward average wage levels, while the depressed condition of wages in most of agriculture, the urban informal sector, and a considerable part of industry permit rents to retain a higher share of value added than would otherwise obtain.   (This becomes more apparent when one examines the wage profiles within both industry and agriculture, though space limitations prevent the detailing of these findings here.)   Indeed our wage profile data indicate that wage dualism increased during the period 1960 to 1971, exacerbating income inequality and causing the wage share to decline for the three lowest-wage countries at the same time that average wages rose for each.

Table 24. Wage Levels and Shares of Value Added

Country	1960		1971	
	Wages per Worker	Wages Value Added	Wages per Worker	Wages Value Added
Costa Rica	622	.502	1,138	.492
Nicaragua	481	.493	991	.551
Guatemala	339	.407	470	.374
El Salvador	328	.426	431	.412
Honduras	266	.438	370	.413
CACM	369	.441	568	.430

SOURCES: Wage levels are expressed in current $CA from table 17; wage shares are from table 20.

For the "high-wage" countries, Costa Rica and Nicaragua, conditions were somewhat different. In the Nicaraguan case, despite its modest and growing employment gap, both wages and the wage share rose notably (table 24). On the other hand Costa Rica suffered the largest absolute and relative increases in its employment gap of any of the five countries between 1960 and 1971, and the effect was to increase dualism in the labor market perhaps more than in any other country. In this case average wages (in nominal terms) rose by 83 percent, while the wage share remained constant. If the elasticity of substitution were unity, one might expect this result independent of labor market dualism. If the elasticity of substitution were in fact .8 (less than unity) as evidence from other work in this chapter would suggest, then a rise in wages would be consistent with a rising wage share (just as has happened in all industrial countries during their development process). However, if dualism is intensifying in the Costa Rican case, such that a growing share of marginally employed workers is working at relatively low wages while queuing up for higher-productivity jobs, as is suggested by Costa Rica's new and growing urban slum problem, then a low elasticity of substitution in specific sectors of production (such as the urban industrial sector) would be consistent with rising average wages and yet a falling wage share of value added. We would argue that this is indeed the case, not only for Costa Rica but even more so for the rest of the region.

In the Costa Rican case one must qualify the implications of the pattern of functional distribution of income for the size distribution of income among individuals and households. Since land is more evenly distributed in that country, as is capital, the shares of profit, interest, and rent are more equitably divided among the population as well. Moreover the relatively high education of the Costa Rican work force causes the wage bill to be more evenly distributed among the population than in the other four countries of the region, even though as we have suggested the skewing of wages in Costa Rica may have worsened over the decade of the 1960s. Finally, earlier rapid rates of demographic growth had a lagged positive effect on the expansion of the labor force in Costa Rica during the 1960s, an effect which must continue at least through the 1980s, but this trend will fall sharply by the late 1980s to 1990s as the deceleration in fertility rates in the 1960s and 1970s begins its lagged dampening effect on growth of the work force. Such favorable inflections in the demographic transition have yet to be achieved for the other Central American countries, putting into the more distant future any alleviating influence this may have on the supply side of the labor market.

In summary, only Nicaragua experienced a significant rise in the wage share of value added between 1960 and 1971, while that of Costa Rica may have even declined (though the trend is barely significant). The other three "low-wage" countries showed significant declines in wage shares, indicating that the "surplus" in economic rents generated by the rapid growth of the 1960s was being distributed to owners of capital, land, and other scarce resources. Since there is no evidence that property ownership became more equal during the period, it is quite likely that the size distribution of income also became more skewed, particularly in those countries with a relative abundance of unskilled labor and greater inequality in wealth distribution. The next section presents comparative figures on the size distribution of income in the region.

2. The Size Distribution of Income

The quality of size distribution of income figures for Central America is so poor that it is impossible to draw any precise conclusions about relative income shares among individuals or households even at a single point in time since the formation of the CACM. In table 25 we have assembled a variety of estimates of size distribution as compiled by Shail Jain in a pioneering study for the World Bank and as prepared by SIECA primarily from surveys of INCAP, the Central American Nutrition Institute. In almost every case the results are flawed by the almost impossible task of reflating reported expenditures (and incomes) in the

underlying budget studies in order to derive a total figure for disposable income that would approximate that of the independently estimated
national income accounts. The ubiquitous problem of underreporting of
income in budget studies, associated with a disproportional undercounting of profit, income, and rental income, tends to seriously distort the
results. It is clear from table 25 that the range of estimates in even
the broadest cohorts is so large that it makes the figures almost mean-
ingless; however, one striking result does emerge, namely the evident
inequality in shares between the top 5 and next 15 percent of income recipients and the lower 80 percent.

For example, in no case does the top 5 percent show less than 15
percent of total personal income, and in the 15 percent case (Guatemala),
the upper end of the same range is 35 percent, indicating a wide margin
of error. In order to get a sense of the degree of income inequality in
the region, we have grouped the estimates in terms of the total range for
the upper 5 percent and lower 50 percent of income recipients in table 26.
For the lowest one-half of the population, Honduras shows the smallest
share, or 11 to 13 percent. After this Nicaragua, Guatemala, and El
Salvador compete for the next lowest positions depending upon which estimates are chosen. Costa Rica showed the largest income share for the
bottom 50 percent of households (since the high end of Guatemala's range
is suspect), but it is noteworthy that even in this "more egalitarian"
country, the lower half of the population only received about 20 percent
of total personal income. On the other hand the top 5 percent of households in Costa Rica enjoyed 23 to 33 percent of total income, a proportion comparable with that of the poorest countries of the region.

It would seem that the relatively high growth in output per worker
for Costa Rica has permitted income shares of the lower half of the population to reach higher levels than elsewhere in Central America but has
not significantly reduced the shares of the upper 20 percent. In the
Costa Rican case, trends in distributive shares for households between
1961 and 1971 may be seen from table 25. To the extent that the estimates are comparable, there is evidence that the middle-income groups
("next 30 percent") showed the most significant gains, rising from 24 to
29 percent of total income. Such trend data provide some support for
the alleged development of a "middle class" economy in Costa Rica. However when one looks at the same three deciles ("next 30 percent") in the
poorer countries, the shares for Guatemala and El Salvador are as high
as those in Costa Rica (one estimate in each case showing a share greater
than 30 percent). It would seem that "middle-class" income growth in
Central America may not be inconsistent with a small and even falling
share of income for the poorest workers. Hence the lowest 10 percent of
households in Costa Rica showed only 2 to 3 percent of total income,
comparable with the bottom deciles in Guatemala, El Salvador, and Honduras. The growing employment gap in Costa Rica during the 1960s would
help to account for the lag in shares of the poorest households.

As for the top 5 percent of households in Costa Rica and individuals
in El Salvador, the data show declining income shares over the 1960s,
falling by 10 percentage points in the former and 13 points in the latter.
Despite the weakness of upper-income range estimates in such studies,
this offers evidence that Central American growth involved some deconcen-
tration in income at the upper range in at least two of the relatively

Table 25. The Size Distribution of Income in Central America in the 1960s

Strata of Individuals (I) or Households (H)	Guatemala		El Salvador			Honduras		Nicaragua	Costa Rica			CACM
	H_{66}^a	I_{68}^b	I_{61}^a	I_{69}^a	I_{69}^b	$H_{67/68}^a$	I_{68}^b	$H_{no\ date}^b$	H_{61}^a	H_{71}^a	$I_{61/66}^b$	^{b}
(percentiles)												
(Lowest 10%)[a]	(3.8)		(2.4)	(1.1)		(1.4)			(2.6)	(2.1)		
Lowest 50%	29.7	13	16.1	18.6	16	10.7	13	15	17.8	20.8	18	13
Next 30%	31.3	24	23.1	30.6	24	21.6	24	25	23.6	28.8	26	26
Next 15%	24.2	28	26.8	30.2	33	31.7	30	32	25.6	27.4	27	30
Top 5%	14.8	35	34.0	20.6	27	36.0	33	28	33.0	23.0	29	31
Gini coefficient[a]	.30		.55	.47		.63			.52	.44		
Kuznets index[a]	.23		.43	.36		.51			.41	.34		

[a]Shail Jain, Size Distribution of Income (Washington, D.C.: IBRD, 1975). Details on sources and methods are presented in the publication.
[b]SIECA, "La Política de Desarrollo Social dentro de la Integración Económica Centroamericana," 28 PES/PS/ASI I, Guatemala City, Seminario sobre los Aspectos Sociales de la Integración, 11 July 1975. The original source of these data was GAFICA, "Plan Perspectivo," also repeated in Estudio de la Década, vol VII, Política Social, table II-3, p. 47. The primary sources for the respective countries are: Guatemala: Based on the distribution of wages and salaries of those registered in the Instituto Guatemalteco de Seguridad Social, assuming (incorrectly) that the distribution of wages as prepared by the IGSS reflects the overall distribution of income in Guatemala (GAFICA, "Perspectivas Para el Desarrollo y la Integración de la Agricultura en Centroamérica," vol II, "Marco Cuantitativo," May 1974, p. xiv); Nicaragua: used results of the sociocultural survey of INCAP (no date); El Salvador: two sources combined, the sociocultural survey data of INCAP (1965) and family income and expenditure survey data, Dir. General de Estadística (1969); Honduras: two sources, INCAP sociocultural survey data and family income and expenditure survey by Dir. General de Estadísta y Censos (1968). Since the respective Lorenz curves were similar, the INCAP survey data were used for consistency with other country results; Costa Rica: two sources, INCAP sociocultural survey (1966) and CEPAL estimates (1961). Because of comparability of the two sources, the INCAP data were used for consistency. The CACM aggregate measures are based on estimates of "gasto de consumo privado" (GCP) for the region in 1970, assuming savings out of disposable income to be insignificant. (This almost certainly biases downward the share of income of the upper-income groups.)

243

industrialized countries of the region. (No such comparisons are possible for the other three countries.) In both countries the functional
distribution changed adversely to wages and favorably to capital costs
and rents. Also in the size distribution of both, the lowest decile of
recipients indicated a decline in relative shares while the lowest 50
percent showed only a slight gain, so that the major beneficiaries of the
fall in upper-income shares seem to have been "middle-class" deciles six
through eight. The upper middle class ("next 15 percent") also registered significant gains in relative shares. It would seem that the size
distributional consequences of functional distributional shifts from the
wage shares toward capital costs and rents were passed on to those in
the middle- and upper-middle-income groups rather than to the wealthiest
5 percent and at the expense of the poorest 50 percent.

A final point is that comparisons of the CACM region with other Latin
American countries noted for their distributional inequality, Mexico and
Brazil, are far from favorable to Central America at both extremes in
the income distribution. Table 26 shows that except for Costa Rica the
Central American countries show at least as much inequality as do their
larger partners in the hemisphere. On the other hand Panama's figures
indicate considerably more equality between richest and poorest cohorts
than any Central American country but Costa Rica. Since both Panama and
Costa Rica have rather high levels of income and productivity, this suggests that income growth in the region might eventually even out the size
distribution if labor absorption were encouraged. As this chapter would
imply, one step in that process would be for labor markets to progressively tighten, such that wages profiles would flatten out at higher income levels for all cohorts. This could eventually lead to increased
wage shares of the functional distribution of income (at the expense of
economic rent), as has occurred in most developed countries. Perhaps
more importantly, agrarian reform and greater access by the working class
to the ownership of physical and financial assets and the acquisition of
human capital through a more equitable and efficient educational system
might help to improve the size distribution of income, even if the functional distribution remained skewed, since poorer households would be
able to increase their shares in total profits and rents. A democratiza-
tion of the net worth of households in Central America is long overdue
and should be regarded as an essential component of employment and incomes policy.

3.   Implications of Income Distributional Trends for Savings and
     Investment in Central America

It remains to be seen to what extent the observed sharp inequality
in the functional and size distribution of income in Central America might
have been associated with growth trends in the region since the 1960s,
not only as a consequence of the policies pursued but also as a source
of new savings and investment. This section examines the behavior of
gross savings and investment, public and private, during the periods 1960
to 1970 and 1970 to 1974. We shall seek to determine whether increased
rental and capital income shares, at the expense of wage income, might
have had a positive effect on economic growth by increasing the surplus
available for savings and investment and by providing incentive for further investment through higher adjusted rates of return on capital. Had

this been true, then Central American growth might be expected to continue into the 1980s despite worsening income shares for the lowest deciles of the population and perhaps even declining real income for the
poorest households; however, the facts are otherwise. The rapid expansion of profits and rents in the first phase of the CACM was followed by
a falling growth rate of private investment by the 1970s associated with
a dampening of Common Market *esprit*.

Table 26. Some Comparisons of Size Distribution of Income Estimates

Percent of Individuals or Households	Upper 5% of Income Shares	Lower 50% of Income Shares
Guatemala	15-35	13-30
El Salvador	21-34	16-19
Honduras	33-36	11-13
Nicaragua	28	15
Costa Rica	23-33	18-21
CACM	31	13
Mexico (68/69 avg.)	30-40	14
Brazil (70)	33	14
Panama (72)	22	22

SOURCE: For CACM countries, see table 25. For Mexico, Brazil, and Panama,
see Shail Jain, *Size Distribution of Income* (Washington, D.C.:
IBRD, 1975).

Table 27 shows the trend in savings and investment as a share of GDP
in the region for the 1960s and 1970s. Two facts clearly emerge. The
first is that the early expansion of the CACM depended significantly on
foreign sources of finance, the share of gross foreign saving in gross
investment being 13.5 percent during the 1960s. Gross domestic savings
accounted for only 13.4 percent of GDP during the period. Table 28 shows
that gross investment plus net inventory change grew at 7.6 percent per
annum in the 1960s while private investment grew at 6.7 percent, indicating the importance of public sector investment spending. The second

246

fact is that growth in the 1960s favored domestic savings. Regional savings grew by 8.8 percent annually while output grew at 5.7 percent, giving an elasticity of 1.5; however, private investment grew at only 6.7 percent, an elasticity of 1.2 with respect to income. In short, the increasing gains from income growth in the form of profits, rents, and middle-income wages led to rapid savings growth but to a less than proportional increase in private investment.

Table 27. Average Savings and Investment Rates in the CACM in
the 1960s and 1970s (based on data in millions
of 1960 CA pesos)

	Percentages of Gross Regional Product	
	1960-70	1970-74
Gross investment and net inventory change	15.5	16.3
(Private investment not including net inventory change)	(11.0)	(11.0)
Gross domestic savings	13.4	16.4
Gross foreign savings (imports of goods and services minus exports of goods and services)	2.1	-0.1

SOURCE: For the years 1960 to 1970; SIECA, VI Compendio Estadístico Centroamericano, 1975 (Guatemala City: SIECA, 1975), table 193. For the years 1971 to 1974; SIECA, "Centroamérica: Estadísticas Macroeconómicas 1971-75," SIECA/76/PES/8, Guatemala, 11 June 1976, table 7. For an independent assessment of post-1973 trends in the balance of payments, with increasing evidence of the role of gross foreign savings inflows in recent years, see Clark Joel, "Economic Assessment of the CACM Region as of Mid 1976," ROCAP, Guatemala, 21 July 1976.

By the 1970s the annual rate of growth of private investment in plant and equipment had slowed to 4.8 percent, as seen in table 28, though faster growth of public investment and net inventory accumulation between 1970 and 1974 led to an increase in gross investment of 8.0 percent annually (compared with 7.6 percent in the 1960s). Indeed the income elasticity of private investment was .9 while gross savings grew by 9.2 percent annually. The income elasticity of gross savings was 1.7 while that of gross investment was 1.5. Also though the gross domestic savings share of GDP rose from an average of 13.4 percent in the 1960s to 16.4

percent in the 1970s, this was accompanied by a regional shift from net
importer to net exporter of capital, as gross foreign savings fell as a
share of GDP from 2.1 to -0.1 percent (table 27). This was partly due
to the repayment of earlier borrowing. But we also suggest that a major
contributing factor was that the increased capacity to save from earlier
CACM expansion was not matched by a proportional growth in the perception
of new investment opportunities. In short, the CACM expansion of the
1960s, rapid as it was, did not bring with it sustained growth in private
investment demand. We would argue that this is intimately associated
with the kind of income distribution that occurred during the 1960s, a
distribution which derived directly from crowded labor market conditions,
lagging real incomes for the poorer households, and growing skewedness in
the wage bill.

In order to understand this point it is important to note a number
of factors responsible for the astounding resistance in much of the region
to policies and programs which would have served to widen social participation in gains from the Common Market. These include slow growth in
unionization and education of the working class in most countries, opposition to more equitable land distribution, and inadequate access to
financial capital, health, nutrition, and technical assistance programs.
An observer unfamiliar with Central American history might wonder why the
"integration" of markets for manufactures did so little to reduce the
"disintegration" of the work force in much of the region. If Central
America were indeed resource poor (as does hold for many heavily populated parts of the Guatemalan highlands and rural areas in the subtropic
zones which have serious health and climatic problems), the use of political and sometimes military measures to preserve privileges for a few
might be better understood. But there are broad areas of underutilized
land and mineral resources throughout Central America, even in the most
"overcrowded" countries, which might be brought into the national economy
through further construction of roads, communication networks, and other
works of infrastructure. Such programs could make use of part of the
abundant rental income "surplus" which past growth has generated. Moreover the impoverished populations of highland Guatemala, coastal El
Salvador, and other subsistence regions could benefit greatly from the
abundant arable land remaining to be opened in eastern Guatemala, Honduras, Nicaragua, and much of the Costa Rican highlands, if greater re-
location of the population through migration were encouraged. Of course
this would call for "integration" on a social as well as economic scale
unheard of to date.

In conclusion, CACM growth by favoring import-substituting industrialization and export agriculture failed to broaden regional demand by
drawing large numbers of workers into the national market for basic manufactures, consumer durables, high income elasticity food crops, and services. A large potential regional market remains to be tapped. We suggest
that an alternative option has not yet been tried throughout Central
America, namely programs implemented country by country which would lead
to what one might call the true regional integration of Central America.
This would involve policies which would have as their goal the incorporation of the mass of rural and urban workers into the economies of their
respective countries. This would involve programs to stimulate employment, increase real wages, and facilitate wealth accumulation by the

poorer households. It would presuppose fuller social and political integration at the national level as well. Such an approach would require as
much or more private sector esprit, domestic political support, and foreign
cooperation as the initial phase of the CACM. There is little question
that a redirection toward true integration of the economy and society of
individual countries is a sine qua non for successful future integration
at the regional level.

Table 28. Savings and Investment Behavior in the CACM, 1960-74
(millions of 1960 CA pesos)

Year	Gross Investment & Net Inventory Change	Private Investment[a]	Gross Domestic Savings	Gross Foreign Savings	Gross Domestic Product
1960	373	275	288	85	2,701
1961	355	252	320	35	2,816
1962	406	291	368	38	3,009
1963	487	344	430	57	3,242
1964	551	391	433	118	3,463
1965	631	426	496	135	3,691
1966	624	437	517	107	3,908
1967	697	497	600	97	4,113
1968	673	496	621	52	4,315
1969	688	507	686	2	4,549
1970	801	538	692	109	4,775
1960/70 Compounded annual rate of growth	7.6	6.7	8.8	---	5.7
1971	819	552	782	37	4,971
1972	704	535	873	-168	5,285
1973	914	608	926	- 13	5,611
1974	1,104	653	998	107	5,918
1970/74 Compounded annual rate of growth	8.0	4.8	9.2	---	5.4

[a]Does not include net inventory change.

SOURCE: See table 27; especially SIECA, VI Compendio Estadístico Centroamericano, 1975 (Guatemala City: SIECA, 1975), table 193, pp.
362f. Note that growth rates are between end-years of periods.

I. Summary and Conclusions

1. Employment and Income Distribution in the Period, 1960-75

The central theme of the analysis in this chapter, as presented in section A, is that income distribution in export economies, such as those of Central America, is closely related to the nature of labor markets and their effect on the wage bill. The degree of competitiveness in labor markets influences the extent to which objective conditions of demography, technology, and final demand affect the amount and distribution of the wage bill. That is because such economies tend to be well within the margin as suppliers of high unit value exports in the world market, such that export value added includes a significant component of economic rent (return over and above the opportunity cost of labor and capital). The distribution of the rent share among competing income groups depends upon the ability of each to organize economically, socially, and politically to benefit from the rents generated. While rents normally accrue to property owners, it is common in such economies for labor groups in certain sectors to participate in the rent share through a variety of measures which push up wage and nonwage benefits. This is especially true for workers directly involved in the production of high-rent exports, whether in agriculture or the extractive industries such as mining and petroleum.

The ability of labor to partition rents in its favor depends on historical factors including the legal and institutional ability to organize and bargain collectively, the capacity and willingness of the government to tax and redistribute scarcity rents, the lagged demographic and migratory effects on the supply of labor, and the education and skill formation of the work force (which influences its own ability to attract scarcity rents as well as to appropriate those rents accruing to other inputs). Rents of export economies are augmented by those accruing to import-substituting industry based on their ability to earn profits over and above the opportunity cost of capital plus risk owing to high rates of effective protection. These rents are also subject to partitioning, in cases where the work force is well organized. In addition firms may also elect to pay wages which include some rent component (payments above the reservation price of labor) in order to "internalize the externalities" of on-the-job training and learning-by-doing. Finally industries which can capitalize on research and development to market innovative new products in less than fully competitive markets will tend to earn scarcity rents in the form of excess profits. Here too some rent partitioning is possible for workers, though this is less relevant for developing countries since rents for innovation tend to be concentrated in the more industrialized countries where most research and development are located and where intellectual property rights are legally protected.

We have proceeded to examine conditions in the five Central American countries to determine the extent to which considerations of rent generation and partitioning affect the level and distribution of the wage bill and its share of total income. The first step in section B was to examine the degree of unionization, as a measure of labor's ability to organize and bargain collectively. As of 1973, 60 percent of union members in Central America were concentrated in Costa Rica and Honduras, which had only 30 percent of the regional work force. And in Honduras 60 percent of unionized workers were in the agricultural sector, primarily in banana exporting, supporting our argument that high-rent export "enclaves" tend to facilitate labor organization and collective bargaining, especially since such enclaves are prone to legislation favoring domestic labor over foreign capital. In Costa Rica, on the other hand, a long history of liberal social legislation, not unrelated to favorable land/labor ratios and relatively productive peasant agriculture, has favored the formation of labor unions. Also scarcity rents generated in the rural sector have accrued to a broader segment of the population because of a more equal land tenure system. Among the five countries, Guatemala appears to be the most retarded in the extent of unionization and the ability of the working class to increase its participation in the rental share of income.

In addition to the legal and institutional factors working for or against the ability of workers to bargain for income shares, growth in output, technology, and changing structure of production have affected the wage bill through the derived demand for labor. Rapid production growth was accompanied by impressive productivity gains, so that while output in the Common Market countries expanded at 5.6 percent annually between 1960 and 1971, employment grew at only half that rate, or 2.7 percent. The fastest rate of employment growth was in manufacturing (secondary sector) and the slowest in agriculture. The highest rate of productivity growth was in agriculture, since primary production grew at 4.8 percent annually while employment only grew by 1.9 percent. This was the essential cause of Central America's "employment problem"--workers displaced from agriculture, which shifted increasingly from subsistence to commercial production during the period 1960-1971, could not be sufficiently absorbed in urban activities, despite the rapid growth of employment in manufacturing (4.2 percent per annum) and tertiary activities (3.5 percent).

Productivity growth by country favored Nicaragua and Costa Rica, which together accounted for 43 percent of the regional total, yet having only 21 percent of the CACM work force. Guatemala followed, with El Salvador and Honduras lagging far behind. In Honduras, the effect of slow productivity growth on labor demand was positive, however, in that this country showed the highest growth in employment (3.4 percent annually), the lowest rates being in Guatemala (2.2 percent) and Nicaragua (2.4 percent). Guatemala showed the greatest gap between output and employment growth, since its shift toward import-substituting manufacturing and commercial agriculture led to a relatively high rate of output and productivity growth (5.4 and 3.2 percent, respectively) but the slowest rate of employment growth. This is reflected in the large amount of seasonal migration of Guatemalan highland cultivators to Mexico, El Salvador, and Honduras. El Salvador is the other center of greatest labor redundancy and here again rapid development was based on the expansion of commercial agriculture and manufacturing so that productivity growth was 2.5 percent and employment growth was only 2.9 percent. Meanwhile Salvadorian workers continued to migrate to Honduras (until the 1969 border war), Nicaragua, and Costa Rica.

To illustrate the unbalancing effect of productivity growth on regional employment, we calculated some counterfactual historical estimates of employment, given observed rates of production growth and the assumption of constant 1960 productivity levels. It was found that the number of new jobs created from 1960 to 1971 under this assumption would have more than doubled, from 1.1 to 2.5 million worker-years. Of course the largest gainers would have been productivity growth leaders Nicaragua and Costa Rica, but for Guatemala constant productivity would have meant a 53 percent increase in worker-years required relative to 1971 employment levels. This is not to suggest that productivity gains were inadvisable from an employment viewpoint but just that the capital- and land-intensive production techniques employed during CACM growth failed to reflect the social costs (negative externalities) of increasingly redundant labor and associated deterioration in the income position of the poorest members of society. The sectoral impact of productivity growth based on such counterfactual measures shows up most importantly in agriculture (up to four times as many additional rural workers would have been required had growth occurred without productivity gains). There was clearly a productivity revolution in agriculture which exceeded that of any other sector, giving rise to growing rental incomes and strengthening our argument that land tenure and labor market conditions were crucial to the level and distribution of working class income in the CACM. As for the development of import-substituting industrialization in Central America, unlike so many Latin American cases, it grew apace with the expansion of export agriculture. The prevailing fiscal mechanism and commercial policy within the region did not distort exchange rates or the internal terms of trade in favor of industry sufficiently to prevent commercial agriculture from responding to favorable market conditions abroad.

Labor demand estimates for the 1960s and 1970s prepared in section C are related to supply growth estimates in section D. These estimates apply adjusted 1960 labor force participation rates to active population cohorts in 1971 and 1975, based on census data and demographic growth projections. The estimated "labor supply" growth is then matched with observed employment levels for the two periods to determine the changes in "employment gaps" for each country. Of the total increased regional employment gap of 140,000 worker-years between 1960 and 1971, 48 percent applied to Costa Rica and 24 percent to El Salvador. In the Costa Rican case this was largely due to earlier rates of demographic growth which are now much reduced but are likely to continue to push labor supply beyond demand for another two decades. In the case of El Salvador a shift toward export agriculture together with productivity growth in manufacturing plus rapid historical rates of demographic growth have produced a much more serious spectre of labor surplus. This country has fewer resources per worker than most of its neighbors and lower average income levels from which savings may be drawn to invest in increased productivity and job opportunities for the work force. Moreover in El Salvador, as in Guatemala and Nicaragua, rents are mostly concentrated in the hands of a small number of property owners, so that political opposition to income redistribution has been intense.

An attempt was made to assess the effect of CACM policies on the employment gap from 1960 to 1972 by drawing on independent estimates of the effect of the CACM on production. By our measures the net employment effect of Common Market policies through increased growth was as much as 178,000 new jobs by 1972 (3.8 percent of employment in that year). However, there was a negative structural effect on employment caused by the shift from more labor-intensive agriculture to manufacturing. This led to a net loss (gain in manufacturing minus loss in agricultural jobs) of 153,000 worker-years. Hence the difference between a gain of 178,000 jobs through increased growth and a loss of 153,000 jobs caused by shifts in the composition of output toward more capital- and land-intensive techniques left a net benefit of 25,000 jobs. Technological choice within both industry and agriculture did not favor labor-intensive methods of production. Instead incentive schemes of the five countries favored the direct application of foreign production techniques and product mixes (extreme examples including the proliferation of capital-intensive fast food operations such as Chicken Delight, Colonel Sanders, and MacDonald's in upper-income suburbs). Our quantitative analysis does not take into account the negative effects on employment of such policies.

It is impossible to differentiate between the effects of the CACM on technology choice and the structure of production, and the effects of the independent policies of the five countries especially with regard to import-substituting industrialization and the development of export agriculture. All that can be said is that the net results from the stimulus of urban manufacturing and related service employment did not sufficiently absorb the displacement of workers from the rural sector. The General Treaty of Integration only proposed to provide a general framework of free trade within the region. It is the new Project for Central American Economic and Social Community, yet unapproved by the respective governments, which proposes to deal with the underlying social and institutional problems of the region in the context of integration.

Real wage growth in the region is estimated in section F. The average increase of 2.6 percent annually (1960 to 1971) lagged behind productivity growth (2.9 percent). Country by country there is a perfect positive rank correlation between productivity and wage growth, the rates being respectively: Nicaragua (4.4/4.5), Costa Rica (3.7/3.5), Guatemala (3.2/2.5), El Salvador (2.5/2.2), and Honduras (1.1/0.9). The correlation between wage growth and increase in the "employment gap" is less clear. The country with the highest gap, Costa Rica, had the second highest wage growth, while the lowest gap country, Honduras, had the slowest growth in wages. This supports the hypothesis of labor market segmentation, in which high-productivity growth may be passed on to privileged members of the work force despite depressed conditions at the lower end of the labor market. Hence the problem of underemployment and low marginal productivity of labor is more closely associated with the skewing of the profile of wages than with average earnings.

This chapter looks briefly at the distribution of wages within the region. The "wage profile" is not only sharply skewed in 1960 but becomes more uneven by 1971. While the ratio of incomes of the highest-wage workers (commerce) to those in the lowest-wage group (agriculture) remained at 4.7 to 1 over the period, those in other high-productivity urban activities (including manufacturing) showed an upward drift relative to agricultural earnings. We found that regional averages were poor measures of segmentation, since factors leading to the partition of labor markets vary widely among countries, sectors, and skill levels. One important finding is that countries which began the period with relatively low industrial earnings showed much greater wage growth in that sector than did the higher-wage countries. The evidence of increased labor market dualism is greatest where manufacturing has shown relatively rapid growth and where the agricultural sector is characterized by expanding high-rent enclaves such as coffee and bananas.

The final section deals with the level and trends in the functional distribution of income among wages, normal costs of capital, and economic rents. It also compares the size distribution of income in the five countries. For the region as a whole the rent share appears to rise slightly, together with that of capital costs, while wages and salaries show a decline. Two of the lowest wage economies, Guatemala and Honduras, showed impressive increases in rental income shares and declines in wage shares, while in another labor-abundant economy (El Salvador), the rent share rose slightly while that of wages fell sharply. For all countries the share of income reflecting normal costs of capital went up significantly, due to the increasing investment intensity of CACM growth. At the sectoral level rural rent shares rose in all countries but Nicaragua, while industrial rent shares fell for all but Honduras.

The size distribution of income in the five countries shows some relation to the functional distribution in that countries which have higher absolute wage levels and wage shares (such as Costa Rica and Nicaragua) also have more equal income distribution among individuals and households. In the case of Costa Rica, the more equal distribution of land and other assets augments this effect by smoothing the size distribution of property income. Still the general pattern of size distribution of income in the region is very unfavorable to most of the population, rivaling some of the worst examples in the hemisphere. Moreover those countries with remarkably lower wage shares of value added (namely Guatemala, El Salvador, and Honduras) show very skewed size distributions of income as well. The final part of section H indicates that the Central American process, growth favoring profits and rental income, has given rise to rapid growth in regional savings but lagging investment rates. We suggest that failure to integrate fully the working class into the markets of the respective countries has held back demand growth, discouraging further investment. It is also suggested that resulting instability in social and political conditions have dampened investment incentives in several countries. A new approach is called for which combines integration of the working class into the economy and policy at the national level, through improved wages, employment conditions, and political representation, with longer-term goals of political-economic integration of Central America. Some suggestions along these lines follow.

2.   Toward True Regional Integration: A Strategy for Central
      American Employment and Incomes Policy

Given the present size of the effective regional market, the opportunities for import substitution under the present set of incentives are limited. One obstacle to further progress is the state of uncertainty about the integration process due in particular to the post-1969 crisis between Honduras and El Salvador. Given the eventual resolution of this problem and the reentry of Honduras into the CACM, the outlook might well improve. For further investments two new directions are possible. One is to alter external protection, favoring capital and intermediate goods production over the protection of current consumption goods. The other is to shift toward a program of export promotion. The latter would seem preferable in terms of employment goals, but it would probably require additional incentives such as direct subsidies or devaluation of local currencies, since the hope for further fiscal incentives is limited after more than a decade of such policies. Drawback arrangements would also favor the export promotion of value added manufacturing in which raw materials and intermediate goods are assembled with local labor, following the models of Hong Kong, Taiwan, Korea, and Brazil. This would mean the integration of local assembly plants with transnational production and marketing operations. However there is little likelihood that this strategy alone would significantly alter predominant conditions of labor surplus and attendant lack of social and economic integration in most of the region.

A third approach, perhaps in combination with that of export promotion, would be to follow the Costa Rican model and to attempt to improve the distribution of income through employment-generating programs in construction, labor-intensive manufacturing of wage goods for sale to the working class, state-sponsored distribution systems for wage goods, the stimulation of agricultural production for domestic consumption, and land distribution schemes to provide the rural work force with a higher floor on incomes based in part on subsistence production and in part on broader access to rental income from the sale of cash crops. This approach would require sharp increases in public expenditures in all countries, following the fiscal policy objectives of Costa Rica, which, despite difficulties, has made the most effort to achieve progress along distributive lines through intervention by the public sector. Economic rents would be taxed at a higher rate than is now the case to permit such programs to proceed without resorting to inflationary fiscal deficits, an approach which is technically feasible since the tax shares of most of the countries are among the world's lowest. Exchange rate policies also may have to become more flexible to permit balance of payments equilibrium.

An additional source of finance for employment-generating programs could be increased rates of financial savings by middle- and upper-income households. A great portion of the large and growing rental income stream accruing to the elite is being spent on importation of Mercedes Benz automobiles, foreign tourism, luxury housing, land acquisition, and domestic retainers. Financial savings which do occur tend to flow abroad. One explanation for this is the desire to shelter wealth accumulation from taxation. Another is the present underdeveloped state of financial intermediation in the region. Growth of financial institutions has been constrained by a complicated set of governmental regulations that inhibit the formation and operation of banks and other financial institutions in the five countries of the region. This has resulted in the concentration of banking in the hands of privileged groups, such that the financial savings captured by these institutions are channeled primarily to the same groups, namely those with significant economic and political power. In addition there are portfolio requirements and ceilings on deposit rates which tend to discourage financial saving, causing local funds to be diverted into the acquisition of foreign financial assets, unproductive self-financed investments, or consumption. Moreover the financial system is scarcely integrated among the five countries, so that

funds tend to flow more readily between the region and the rest of the
world than among surplus and deficit sectors within Central America.
Here fiscal and financial reforms could go hand in hand, serving the goal
of savings, investment, and employment-generation in both the private
and public sectors. But neither approach would in and of itself improve
social participation in the development process without the requisite
political will.

In spite of the general conditions stated above, it may not be necessary to sacrifice growth for distribution in Central America if attention
is directed toward development policies which make employment and labor
income explicit goals. In order to facilitiate the formulation of such
employment and incomes policies to bring about true regional integration,
some suggestions follow:[32]

(i) Some form of land tenure transformation is essential in
most of Central America to permit greater access to fertile land and the
rents accruing to it. The precise nature of land reform must be worked
out country by country, but this is a key area for labor absorption consistent with rising income and productivity of the rural poor.

(ii) Regionwide migration should be encouraged to permit more
effective access to land-abundant areas and centers of industrial growth
for workers from the poorest regions. There is already considerable
voluntary migration. The gathering and dissemination of information about
job opportunities elsewhere and of land availability in areas for new
settlement could be a CACM undertaking. Efforts should also be made to
resolve the Honduran-Salvadorian dispute, to permit freer movement of
labor and goods between the two countries.

(iii) Capital market reforms should be made to facilitate the
accumulation of voluntary financial savings. Banking laws should be
changed to permit more competition for the attraction of savings and
investment lending to all sectors of society. This would involve raising ceilings on deposit rates of existing institutions to competitive
levels for those countries which maintain artificially low interest rates
on deposits. It also would entail programs to facilitate the holding
of bearer instruments such as bonds perhaps denominated in dollars or
"Central American peso" units, to attract capital which might otherwise
seek shelters abroad. At the national level recent experiments in the
issue of dollar-denominated coffee bonds have met with significant success in Costa Rica. The Central American Bank of Economic Integration
(CABEI) should be employed at the regional level to facilitate the local
sale of financial assets lending to support labor-intensive private and
mixed-enterprise investment and infrastructure formation. Special incentives should be provided for new financial institutions and especially those which would serve lower-income groups, including those in the
rural areas. The experience of financial cooperatives in Central America
and elsewhere should be explored to determine their effectiveness in
stimulating savings and wealth creation for the working class. Fuller
financial integration of the CACM should be pursued, in terms of facilitating net borrowing and lending flows among the five countries, since
employment-generating innovation and investment depend upon increased
sources of financial capital.

(iv) Minimum wage policies should be designed to protect workers against cost-of-living increases without encouraging cost-push inflationary pressures or the discouragement of employment of low-income
workers. Heretofore minimum wage policy has tended to pursue the criterion that wages should be uniform throughout the region. But this would
have a negative impact on those areas in which labor has relatively low
productivity. Moreover it fails to take into consideration the existence
of different elasticities of substitution between labor and other inputs
sector by sector. A policy of uniform wages would tend to displace labor
in low-productivity occupations and regions while having little impact on
wages in high-productivity areas. Productivity guidelines for minimum
wages would help to avoid this danger, as would regional differentials
in minimum wages, reflecting differences in the opportunity cost of
labor.

(v) Social contributions for the work force, such as social
security, might be financed from general revenues or through direct taxation rather than indirect taxes linked to employment. This would lower
the cost of labor to the firm while at the same time preserving the fiscal base of public welfare benefits for workers. The pricing of capital
goods should reflect their social opportunity cost, minimizing subsidies
and preferential tariffs for imports of machinery and equipment. Those
incentives which are provided should be justified by evidence that the
resulting investments would be complementary rather than competitive to
the goals of net employment growth.

(vi) Labor organization and collective bargaining should be
supported by enabling legislation and enforcement machinery throughout
the region, so that those countries which now inhibit the development
of labor organization would be less able to bid away new investment at
the expense of their more socially conscious neighbors. This would also
lessen the burden on the latter from immigration of those seeking dif-
ferentially better wages, hours, and working conditions because of re-
pressive measures at home. However, the use of labor organizations to
permit the segmentation of labor markets and skewing of the wage bill in
favor of a "labor elite" should be discouraged. The rents of high-
productivity sectors should, instead, be channeled through taxation and
voluntary financial savings into investment which would benefit the
lowest-income workers by expanding overall labor demand and increasing
education and skill levels.

(vii) Expansion in the level and distribution of the wage
bill, and of net worth of the working class, will lead to a broadening
of regional markets by increasing the regional demand for wage goods and
basic commodities. This would stimulate investment through increased
profit potential. Investments in wage-good manufacturing, the cultivation of cash crops for domestic markets, and the provision of services
for the working class could be further incentive for providing credit,
markets, and managerial training. Commercial activities should also be
encouraged along these lines, including government-sponsored enterprises
for the low-cost mass distribution of wage-goods. The experience of
CONASUPO in Mexico and IDEMA in Colombia deserve study for possible application to Central America.

(viii) A broadened social base from which to generate both innovation and entrepreneurship is required. Central America has not begun
to tap the creative potential of its human resources. Improved national
educational programs for applied science, technology, marketing, management, and finance would be useful in mobilizing the latent pool of talent
in the region. Regionwide training programs in science and engineering
could be supported by funds raised at the regional level (perhaps through
the issue of Central American Integration Bonds by CABEI in cooperation
with local financial institutions). These programs could be linked into
regional industrial and commercial development by making funds available
for small business and by providing legal safeguards for the accumulation
of intellectual property. Patent laws, licensing arrangements, and other
measures, with safeguards against sustained monopoly power, are needed to
provide incentive to local innovators and entrepreneurs and especially
to those emerging from among the poorer segments of society.

(ix) Since economic policy does not develop in a political
vacuum, programs favoring employment, income, and social participation
of the working class require for their formulation and implementation
effective representation of the lower-income groups, both rural and urban.
The precise form for such "political openings" is a matter for each country to determine independently. But for much of Central America the
present political situation is not conducive to the achievement of the
above social objectives. We would argue that much scope remains for
incorporation of the working class into the political system in each of
the five countries. The first step for most would be to permit the
organization of political parties reflecting the interests of workers.
An additional goal would be to provide legal and institutional safeguards
for free elections, where necessary.

The planning and design of employment and incomes policies presented
in these nine points would best be accomplished by the broadest possible
representation of all political and interest groups in an atmosphere of
free discussion and debate with full safeguards for human rights.

Chapter 5

NOTES

1. The term "export economy" employed in this chapter refers to the strictly economic relationship of the economy to the foreign market for its exports. Export economies, which depend importantly upon fluctuations in world prices, and which are influenced by foreign capital flows, are often characterized by close ties with external political and economic decisionmaking which affect the internal structure of production and distribution. In extreme cases the political conditions of countries with export economies, heavily dependent upon trade, are influenced by foreign governments and business. The literature on this subject, associated with several versions of "dependency theories," should be distinguished from the analysis presented here, which is rather more economic than political-economic.

2. The relationship between exports and political-economic development is central to most writings on development problems in Central America by local scholars. See, for example, Edelberto Torres Rivas, et al., Centroamérica hoy (Siglo Veintiuno Editores, S.A.), selected readings. Guillermo Molina Chocano, Integración Centroamericana y Dominación Internacional (Editorial Universitaria Centroamericana, 1974). Mario Monteforte Toledo, Centroamérica Subdesarrollo y Dependencia, 2 vols. (Instituto de Investigaciones Sociales, Universidad Nacional Autónoma de México, 1972).

While to the foreign observer the preoccupation of these works with "dependency" of the political and economic behavior of Third World countries may seem obsessive, it becomes understandable as one studies the social history and contemporary economic structure of the region. A striking feature of econometric models of income determination in the region is the evidence of the continuing dominating effect of terms of trade and other export-related fluctuations on the level of domestic income and product. This is so, despite almost two decades of integration policy designed to diversify these economies to reduce their vulnerability to foreign trade cycles.

In this chapter the focus is on the effect of the integration process on employment, wage levels, and the share of labor income in domestic income products. Despite the fact that the Central American economies remained heavily dependent upon foreign trade, the pattern of production and employment (especially of rural and urban employment), both within the five countries and between them altered radically during recent years. While the analytical framework developed for this study deals primarily with the economic dimensions of production, employment, and income distribution, the social and political implications of our findings may well be of greater importance. Indeed Central America may prove to be one of the regions in which contemporary changes in trade and production patterns have the most evident impact on social and political institutions, especially the impact on income levels and shares.

3. A more detailed statement of postwar efforts at integration in Central America is presented by E. Delgado in chapter 2 of this volume.

In the eventual CACM the two ideas of "planned integration" and free trade area coexisted as goals, but the General Treaty of Integration of December 1960 dealt exclusively with the latter. As a result Costa Rica withdrew from the integration scheme until the idea of planned integration was incorporated into the treaty.

The work of Eduardo Lizano, "El Proceso de Integración Económica," in Torres Rivas et al., Centroamérica hoy, is a brilliant synthesis of the process of economic integration dealing as it does with factors underlying the failure of the more politically oriented Organization of Central American States (ODECA) formed in 1962. He maintains that ODECA "is and has been of almost no significance from the viewpoint of economic integration," due in part to the difficulty of bringing about meetings of its steering group, composed of the foreign ministers of the five countries, and perhaps more importantly to the "globalist" and somewhat "messianic" character of its goals. ODECA was built on a nineteenth century patria grande model of regional statecraft. Since the five countries are so different in terms of their social, political, and economic institutions, it is not surprising that the more pragmatic economic integration program has achieved far greater results. However it is increasingly evident that the very economic changes which the CACM has brought about intensify the need for new pragmatic approaches to political and social evolution, if the economic process itself is to continue to develop.

4. For more detail on the elements distorting effective protection, see chapters 3 and 7 of this volume.

5. No work on Central American integration can ignore the basic SIECA research projects summarized in a series of volumes entitled "The Study of the Decade." SIECA, "El Desarrollo Integrado en la Presente Década: Bases y Propuestas para el Perfeccionamiento y la Reestructuración del Mercado Común Centroamericano," (Buenos Aires, INTAL, 1973). _____. "La Evolución de la Economía Centroamericana durante el Periodo 1960-1970 y sus Perspectivas para la Próxima Década," (Buenos Aires, INTAL, 1973). _____. "El Desarrollo Integrado de Centroamérica en la Presente Decada: La Política Social y el Desarrollo Integrado," (Buenos Aires, INTAL, 1973). Volume 6 on social policy and integrated development deals most directly with issues addressed in this chapter.

6. Important macroeconomic analyses of Central American employment problems and a statement of the central issues in the PREALC research program as of the mid-1970s are contained in ILO/PREALC. The present chapter uses much of this material as a point of departure for its analysis at the regional level. International Labor Organization (ILO/PREALC), "Diagnóstico de la Situación Actual de las Estadísticas de Empleo y de las Instituciones Relacionadas en Centroamérica y Panamá: Conclusiones y Recomendaciones," Santiago, Chile, September 1975. _____. "Situación y Perspectivas del Empleo en Costa Rica," Santiago, Chile, October 1973a. _____. "Situación y Perspectivas del Empleo en Nicaragua," Santiago, Chile, October 1973b. _____. "Situación y Perspectivas del Empleo en El Salvador," Santiago, Chile, October 1973c.

International Labor Organization (ILO), "Situación y Perspectivas del Empleo en Panamá," Geneva, 1974.

7. The underlying model linking value added per worker to the wage level and quality of employment is developed in appendix E. The source for the concept of wage profile is Richard C. Webb, Government Policy and the Distribution of Income in Peru, 1963-1973, Harvard Economic Studies, vol. 147 (Cambridge, Mass.: Harvard University Press, 1977). However, the expansion of this approach whereby wages are shown to reflect participation in the rent share of value added ("partition rents") originates in this study, which also presents the first expanded estimation of wage profiles (Webb curves).

8. An illuminating summary of the socioeconomic history of political power in Central America from the viewpoint of "dependency theory" appears in the paper by Edelberto Torres Rivas, "Síntesis Histórica del Proceso Político," in Torres Rivas et al., Centroamérica hoy.

9. Some of the most fundamental relationships among land tenure, social structure, and economic behavior during the Colonial period are treated in depth in Severo Martínez Peláez, Algo sobre Repartimientos (Instituto de Investicaciones Económicas y Sociales, Serie Investigaciones para la Docencia No. 2, Universidad de San Carlos de Guatemala, 1977). _____, La Patria del Criollo (Editorial Universitaria Centroamericana, 1975). _____, La Política Agraria Colonial y los Origenes del Latifundismo en Guatemala, Instituto de Investigaciones Económicas y Sociales, Serie Investigaciones Para la Docencia No. 3, Universidad de San Carlos de Guatemala, 1977.

10. See Asfura for information on wage and nonwage benefits in Central America. Victoria Asfura, "Consideraciones sobre la Situación Laboral en Centroamérica" (Thesis Licenciado en Economía, Universidad Autonoma de Honduras, 1965).

11. The additional effect of import-substituting industrialization on employment and income distribution in an export economy is analyzed in the second part of appendix E.

12. Parts of this section first appeared in the author's monograph, "Fissures in the Volcano? Central American Economic Prospects," Stanford, Food Research Institute, Fall 1976. The concept "normal profits" or "normal return on capital" reflects the social opportunity cost of installed plant, equipment, and goods in process. This opportunity cost equals the shadow price of capital (shadow interest rate) plus a discount for risk, times the value of assets, plus an allowance for depreciation and obsolescence. (Assets may be valued at original cost or replacement cost to allow for inflation.) Net of "normal profits" and a "normal return to labor" (the opportunity cost of eliciting labor services), the residual in value added represents economic rent to be divided among the owners of natural resources, capital, and government, as well as entrepreneurs, skilled workers, and others who can command a scarcity value for their services.

13. Two basic works on income distribution are Orellana (1967) and Orellana et al. (1972). Both their methodological framework and statistics are extremely useful for studies that go well beyond the case of Guatemala, with which they specifically deal. Rene Arturo Orellana, Encuesta sobre Ingresos y Gastos de la Familia del Campesino Asalariado de Guatemala, 1966 (Guatemala, IIES, 1967). Rene Arturo Orellana and Adolfo Enrique de Leon L., Ingresos y Gastos de Familias Urbanas de Guatemala (Guatemala, IIES, 1972).

14. The political-economics of rent generation and partitioning in Central American export sectors has been primarily the domain of authors in the dependency school, e.g., Bodenheimer and Torres Rivas. The problem deserves far more comprehensive attention than it has received by economists of all persuasions, not only in the Central American cases but on a much broader basis throughout the developing world. Susan Bodenheimer et al., La Inversión Extranjera en Centroamérica (Editorial Universitaria Centroamericana, 1974). Torres Rivas, Centroamérica hoy.

15. On the different historical tenure, employment, and income patterns in the coffee sectors of Central American countries, see Martínez Peláez, La Patria del Criollo, and Monteforte Toledo, Centroamérica Subdesarrollo y Dependencia.

16. Torres Rivas, Centroamérica hoy.

17. Gonzalez contains analyses of two major labor uprisings, the Salvadorian insurrection in 1932, and the Honduran strike of 1954. Vinicio Gonzalez, "Movimientos Laborales en Centroamérica. I." ("La Insurrección Agraria Salvadorena de 1932"; "La Gran Huelga Hondureña de 1954"), Segundo Seminario sobre Estructura Social Rural Centroamericana, Guatemala, 2-6 July 1973.

18. Organización de los Estados Americanos, "El Movimiento Cooperativista como Instrumento para el Desarrollo Integral," Washington, D.C., OAS, January 1975. Max Diamant, "Sindicatos, Cooperativas, y Dictadura," in Léctura y Desarrollo, no. 1, San José, Costa Rica, January 1969.

19. Monteforte Toledo, Centroamérica Subdesarrollo y Dependencia.

20. Consejo Superior Universitario Centroamericano (CSUCA) Población, Desarrollo Rural y Migraciones Internas en Centroamérica (II Seminario Técnico Regional) San José, Costa Rica, 2-5 August 1974. Researchers in the Central American universities have done much to systematize the diverse sources of information on Central American employment, this work being a basic source of detailed information for our study.

21. Specifically:

$$\Delta D_L = \Delta Q \cdot \frac{L}{Q_0} + \Delta \frac{L}{Q} \cdot Q_0 + \Delta \frac{L}{Q} \cdot \Delta Q$$

| Change in Labor Demand | = | Change in Output Effect | + | Change in Productivity Effect | + | Combined Output and Productivity Effects |

where: D_L ≡ Number of man-years.

Q_0 ≡ Value added (constant prices) in year 0.

$\dfrac{L}{Q}$ ≡ Reciprocal of gross productivity of labor (average product of labor) without deleting the productivity of land, capital, and other inputs in value added.

Δ ≡ First difference of a specific variable (annual or between specific benchmark years) from year 0 to year t.

22.   This was confirmed by the authors in numerous interviews with smallholders and rural wage laborers throughout the region (August 1976) and supported by documentation of GAFICA and related studies.

23.   It should be noted that this Honduran opinion is controverted by evidence from the SIECA Comparative Price Study at the Level of Final Demand, which indicated that prices in Tegucigalpa in 1973 were slightly higher than those in the other countries of the region, with the exception of Nicaragua.

24.   Central bankers in the region resist full flexibility of exchange rates, arguing with reason that due to the heavy trade orientation of the economies and their vulnerability to export price fluctuations, freeing exchange rates would lead to violent changes in the purchasing power of local currency, discouraging incentives for domestic investment.

25.   This and related calculations on the impact of the CACM on regional growth are taken from chapter 3 of this volume.

26.   Editor's note: However, insofar as the analysis of chapter 3 accurately identifies excess costs of trade diversion, by comparing regional price to world price excluding tariff, the analysis will not overstate net income gain for that component of increased industrial activity related to trade diversion; and the increased activity associated with the other integration effects cannot meaningfully be said to be "overvalued," despite the presence of tariffs, without an assessment of the marginal cost of obtaining increased industrial goods indirectly through expanded traditional exports, as opposed to directly through protected regional production.

27.   Cline himself declares that "the extent of these shifts is understated by the approach used. If instead it were assumed that some of the 'output due to integration' would have taken place in other activities without integration, then the appropriate 'hypothetical base' for comparison might involve substantially higher output levels in agriculture but only modestly higher levels in industry (that is along the lines prior to integration), shifting the composition of the hypothetical base for comparison even further toward the primary sector and therefore yielding an even greater measure of the rise in industry's share of the two sectors because of integration" (chapter 3).

28.   Editor's note: Under the central interpretation of this book, integration raised total output and, as a result, increased total employment as well, by approximately 3 percent of total employment in all

sectors (4.4 million workers in 1971). By contrast, under the pessimistic alternative explored in the present chapter, integration might have re-duced employment by about 3 percent below the level it otherwise might have reached. Although the pessimistic alternative has limited signifi-cance, because of the contrary conclusions reached in the detailed analy-sis of integration's economic effects (chapter 3), it does serve the function of setting an outer limit on the extent of any possible negative impact of integration on employment. Viewed in this way, even the pessi-mistic alternative suggests that critics of the region's employment ex-perience should look elsewhere than in the realm of economic integration policy to identify the basic causes of employment problems. That is, even under an extreme negative interpretation, integration could have had only a very small detrimental effect on the expansion of total employment. On balance, of course, it is our assessment that the increased output ef-fect of integration created, rather than reduced, employment opportuni-ties in the region (as spelled out in chapters 3 and 4).

29. Webb, Government Policy and the Distribution of Income in Peru, chapter 5.

30. Galbraith saw this as related to the "countervailing power" of participants in the struggle for shares.

31. The fact that Guatemala showed the largest corresponding rise in the rental share of income is to some extent explained by the common cap-ital cost coefficients applied to all countries but Costa Rica, which caused the residual rental component to move in a direction opposite to that of wages and salaries.

32. Many of the suggestions are amplified in works detailing the problems of underemployment and low labor income and productivity in spe-cific Central American countries. These include earlier studies of SIECA, and studies by the Regional Employment Program for Latin America and the Caribbean, PREALC, specifically for El Salvador: "Situación y Perspecti-vas del Empleo en El Salvador," vols. I-II, working document, PREALC/80, April 1975; Nicaragua: "Situación y Perspectivas del Empleo en Nicaragua," vols. I-II, working document, PREALC/63, October 1973: Costa Rica: ILO, Situación y Perspectivas del Empleo en Costa Rica (Geneva, 1974); and Panama: ILO, Situación y Perspectivas del Empleo en Panamá (Geneva, 1974). For Guatemala: "Los Recursos Humanos en Guatemala," prepared by the Sec-retaría General del Consejo Nacional de Planificación Económica, Sección Programación de Recursos Humanos, Guatemala, July 1972. Also helpful was PREALC's study by Peter Gregory, "Estudio sobre Políticas de Salarios y Redistribución de Ingreso en Costa Rica," prepared for the Ministry of Labor, OFIPLAN, Central Bank, and the Presidency, July 1976 (draft). It should be stressed that the opinions reflected are those of the writers and do not reflect the official policies of SIECA or the Brookings Institution.

Part III

SECTORAL POLICIES AND COMPARATIVE ADVANTAGE

CHAPTER 6

Industrial Comparative Advantage in the Central American Common Market

William R. Cline and Alan I. Rapoport

A. Introduction

The purpose of this chapter is to provide empirical analysis which will aid in identification of Central American manufacturing sectors that have present or potential "comparative advantage" and should thus have a high priority in future industrial expansion in the region. The chapter examines two dimensions of this question: (i) comparative advantage of the region as a whole vis-à-vis the rest of the world; and (ii) comparative advantage of each of the five Central American countries vis-à-vis the other four.

The policy implications of the chapter bear directly on two major instruments currently used in the region for industrial incentives: tariff policy (including practices of granting tariff exonerations for intermediate inputs and capital goods) and corporate tax policy (in particular, the granting of tax exemptions). The chapter holds implications for other policy areas as well, including broad developmental strategies such as whether import substitution should be extended into additional industries; specific measures such as the sectoral focus of official loans through entities such as the Central American Bank for Economic Integration or through the international lending agencies; and the elaboration of country development plans. One vital area of policy application is in the designing of measures for improving the degree of balance among member countries in the Central American Common Market (CACM). To the extent that the CACM introduces measures to improve the position of the relatively backward members (especially Honduras, given this country's relatively low share in past benefits of the CACM),[1] knowledge about comparative advantage of each member country should make possible the efficient pursuit of an "allocational" policy wherein industries are established in countries with indicated comparative advantage within the region.[2]

The chapter examines only the manufacturing industry. All of the analysis is at the level of detail of four-digit industry classifications within the International Standard Industrial Classification,[3] or approximately seventy-five sectors in Central America. The analysis excludes the agricultural and mining sectors. For a comprehensive view of comparative advantage it is obviously necessary to address those sectors as well, in order to encompass all tradable goods. Nevertheless many policy questions involve choice among products within the manufacturing sector itself, and for these issues the present chapter, limited to this sector by constraints of data availability and project scope, should be relevant.

The analysis of comparative advantage is a subject on which there exists no well-defined method of economic analysis. This chapter is by necessity exploratory. Although some of the individual "indicators" of comparative advantage considered are familiar in the general literature on international trade, their precise formulations as well as their combination with other measures new with this chapter, constitute essentially a new methodology. The reader should be forewarned that the results are therefore not as "unequivocal" as might be the result of more standardized economic methods, such as traditional cost-benefit analysis of projects. In principle, direct cost-benefit analysis of projects by sector and country might provide an alternative approach to examining the issues of comparative advantage and sectoral allocation of resources. In practice, however, a comprehensive analysis such as the one provided here would face insurmountable difficulties of the unavailability of detailed project data required for cost-benefit analysis. Precisely because the analysis here is comprehensive for the manufacturing sector, it cannot achieve the degree of detail that would be necessary to reach firm conclusions about specific investment programs. Instead, the results should be considered as initial identifications of promising or unpromising sectors, to be followed by more specific project analysis before actual investment programs are undertaken.

The structure of this chapter is as follows. Section B sets forth the methodological framework for the study. Section C examines the present comparative advantage of Central America as a whole, as well as the probable future evolution of its comparative advantage. In addition, the section examines the structure of industrial incentives existing in the region. The empirical results permit the identification of the individual manufacturing sectors which show the greatest promise from the standpoint of comparative advantage (both present and future). The results also provide information on industrial sectors in which the current relative levels of incentives appear to be excessive or inadequate, on the basis of a comparison between comparative advantage rankings, and rankings of levels of industrial incentives. This section also examines the relationship between import substitution and comparative advantage. In the areas of tariff structure and fiscal incentives, our results would appear to be sufficiently robust to contain policy implications even without additional information (such as cost-benefit analyses). In these areas, different incentives by sector already exist, and the extreme cases of excessive or low incentive identified here should be prime candidates for changes in tariff or fiscal policies unless there is compelling evidence to the contrary in each case.

Section D addresses the issue of comparative advantage of individual member countries vis-à-vis the CACM as a whole. The empirical results of the section provide an enumeration of the industries most suited for each of the five countries of the region as well as a harmonization of these "allocational" results with the findings concerning the most suitable industries for the region as a whole.

B.   Methodological Framework

1.   Background

There exists no unique, commonly accepted methodology for evaluating present or future comparative advantage. The general approach of this chapter is to apply a number of "indicators" to obtain rankings of industrial sectors by comparative advantage. Similar approaches have been used in previous studies, although they do not necessarily use the same quantitative indicators or ranking methods.[4]

The use of relative sectoral rankings for examining comparative advantage provides advantages over the direct examination of cost and competitiveness in the world market. By incorporating fundamental phenomena such as relative factor abundance, a rankings approach can transcend the vagaries of temporary changes in domestic production costs relative to those abroad. At the empirical level, direct comparative cost analysis would require price observations on thousands of highly specified products. At the conceptual level, any prices thus observed might fail to tell anything about comparative advantage in any event, because in the absence of barriers all world prices would equalize in the presence of trade even though ex ante prices in a nontrading world would vary widely.

Although there are precedents for identifying areas of present comparative advantage using rankings of indicators such as those discussed below, there is practically no precedent for quantitative analysis of the evolution of comparative advantage toward its future structure.[5] Ideally analysis of future comparative advantage would probably involve a large-scale world model for optimization over time, given projected trends in technologies and factor availabilities in major trading areas. A comprehensive approach of this sort is beyond the scope of this chapter, which relies instead on a number of partial indicators of probable future changes in comparative advantage (as discussed below).

2.   Theory and Measurement of Present Comparative Advantage

Three broad theoretical approaches exist for the evaluation of "present" or "static" comparative advantage: (i) Ricardian, or "classical" analysis; (ii) Heckscher-Ohlin, or "factor proportions" analysis; and (iii) the approach of "revealed comparative advantage."

Classical trade theory, especially as stated by Ricardo, maintains simply that it is advantageous for a country to specialize in exporting the good in which it is relatively efficient, importing the good in which it is relatively inefficient--regardless of absolute levels of efficiency in the two goods. The classical measure of efficiency is output per worker. The principle of comparative advantage holds that if England, for example, produces three yards of cloth per worker and two bottles of wine, while Portugal produces one yard of cloth per worker and one bottle of wine, then it would be to England's advantage to export cloth in exchange for imported wine even though England is more efficient than Portugal in both products in absolute terms. That is, through foreign trade England could obtain one bottle of wine for one yard of cloth,[6] whereas domestically it would require one and one-half yards of cloth sacrificed to obtain one bottle of wine (half of a worker's output in both products).

The classical or Ricardian analysis takes as given differing efficiencies among countries without particular concern about the source of these differences (by contrast to the Heckscher-Ohlin approach as discussed below). The traditional measure of efficiency, output per unit of labor, was understandable within the context of classical theory, which held that all economic value was created by labor. A modern formulation of the Ricardian approach, however, requires that at least two other separate factor inputs be considered in the measurement of efficiency: capital and skilled labor (as distinguished from raw, unskilled labor). The corresponding measure of efficiency is "total factor productivity," the ratio of output (value added) to total factor inputs of capital, skilled labor, and unskilled labor evaluated at appropriate prices. Once total factor productivity is measured for one country, its ratio to the corresponding measure of total factor productivity in its trading partners will provide a neo-Ricardian indicator of comparative advantage. Such a measure is used in this chapter, in sections C and D.

A second broad theoretical approach is that of factor proportions. The original "Heckscher-Ohlin" theorem holds that trade will follow patterns consistent with "relative factor abundance." For example, countries with much labor and little capital will specialize in exporting "labor-intensive" goods (products using much labor and little capital). A central premise of this approach is that underlying production functions are identical everywhere; there are no basic differences in overall efficiency among countries, merely differences in the cost and combination of factors they tend to apply in producing any given product.

There are various problems associated with the factor proportions approach. One problem is that once more than two unique factors of production are admitted to exist, it becomes ambiguous what the relatively "abundant" factor of a given country is (although in principle this question may be answered by examining the ratio of the available stock of the factor in question to the sum of the stocks of all other factors multiplied by their respective reference prices, where a standard set of reference factor prices would be applied to all of the countries being compared). In addition, there is the problem that the factor proportions theory has been cast into doubt by the famous "Leontief paradox," in which Leontief's input-output analysis for the United States indicated that the country seemed to be exporting goods which used relatively much labor and importing goods using relatively much capital, the opposite of the pattern predicted for the labor-scarce and capital-abundant U.S. case. More recent research has tended to conclude that the Leontief paradox disappears when the quality of labor (skills) is taken into account along with other factors (especially natural resources),[7] so that the basic factor proportions theory of comparative advantage appears to retain its validity.

Another aspect of the factor proportions theory subject to question concerns its assumption that a "labor-intensive" sector will maintain its relative intensity in all countries. The contrary possibility that a sector might be characterized by relatively labor-intensive techniques in one country but capital-intensive techniques in another raises the possible problem of "factor reversibility." Namely, if the relative factor intensity of two sectors reverses itself between countries, then no conclusion about comparative advantage of the two countries may be drawn from information on the relative abundance of the various factors in the two countries. Citing evidence that some sectors have lower "substitutability" between factors than others, Minhas[8] has argued that the phenomenon of factor reversal may exist. That is, a sector with no possibility of substitution will have the same capital-labor ratio in all countries; a sector with a high degree of substitutability will have a high capital-labor ratio in a capital-abundant country and a low capital-labor ratio in a labor-abundant country; so that there may be a reversal of the relative factor intensity of the two industries between the two countries. Here again, however, subsequent literature suggests that this critique of the factor proportions theory is not a damning one and that there is insufficient evidence, by far, in support of the hypothesis of factor reversibility to warrant rejection of the factor proportions approach.[9]

Two other aspects of comparative advantage analysis represent variants on the factor proportions approach: the "technology factor" and the "product cycle" phenomenon.[10] These considerations attribute great importance, respectively, to the degree of technological sophistication and the life cycle stage of a product. Technologically sophisticated goods will be more efficiently produced by countries with an extensive infrastructure for research and development. Similarly, technologically advanced countries will have an advantage in "new" products, whereas other countries, the "followers," will have an advantage in producing goods for which production methods have long been known. In practice, relative requirements for skilled labor are often used to measure the degree of technological sophistication required by a product,[11] so that the "technology factor" tends to coincide with a factor proportions approach which treats skilled labor separately from unskilled labor.

In sum, the Heckscher-Ohlin factor proportions theory of trade represents a second central vehicle for analyzing comparative advantage. Under this approach, once the relatively abundant factors of a country are identified, then if the factor requirements by the industrial sector are known, it is possible to identify the relative rankings of sectors in terms of comparative advantage for the country in question. In this process, however, it is especially important to take account of two essentially different factors of production--skilled labor versus unskilled labor--in addition to the capital factor; and in addition to consider the technology intensity of the product.

A third basic approach to comparative advantage is inductive rather than deductive: "revealed comparative advantage." This approach directly examines indicators of trade specialization in order to identify sectors that in fact manifest apparent comparative advantage (high exports relative to imports) or disadvantage (low exports relative to imports). Within the same approach other measures of "revealed performance" are also logical candidates for assisting in the identification of comparative advantage--measures such as product price compared with international price, and sectoral rate of return to capital.

The analysis of this chapter uses all three of these broad approaches in assessing comparative advantage. The particular variables chosen for measurement within these approaches are discussed below. Of the various theories of causes of international trade, two others deserve attention. The "product differentiation" approach of Linder[12] attributes much of international trade to the existence of distinct product types (and brands) among countries for a given good. For example, some U.S. consumers may purchase European automobiles, even though automobiles are available domestically, because of major style and performance differences between domestic and foreign cars. In this approach it is consumer taste differences and differences among national product styles that matter. These influences do not lend themselves to the analysis of comparative advantage, so that the approach helps explain why there might be deviations from normal patterns of specialization, but it does not help in the assessment of the basic patterns themselves.

Finally, "interindustry trade" represents another theme which attempts to explain the existence of trade but is of little help in identifying comparative advantage. This approach[13] emphasizes the fact that even with very finely divided categories of products most countries conduct two-way trade--they both export and import. One explanation of this fact may be that countries tend to produce more than needed domestically in some items in order to achieve economies of scale (or "longer production runs") in those items, while importing other similar items within the same general industrial category.[14] In any event, the approach serves as a reminder that specialization by sector is by no means complete, although it sheds no light on the development of a methodology for identifying areas of comparative advantage.

3. Dynamic Comparative Advantage

Despite the extreme importance of analyzing "dynamic" comparative advantage--or the evolution of static comparative advantage over time--there is practically no existing methodology for conducting such analysis. The traditional theoretical basis for differences between dynamic and static comparative advantage is the "infant industry" argument: an industry may develop comparative advantage in the future if it is established now, even though it would appear not to have immediate "static" comparative advantage.

The literature which comes closest to addressing the issue of dynamic comparative advantage is that which examines patterns of industrial composition by sector in relation to levels of economic development, especially the studies in this field by S. Kuznets and H. Chenery.[15] This literature documents the fact that economic development is associated with a rising share of manufacturing industry and a falling share of agriculture in the economy (with the services sector tending to maintain a steady share). Higher per capita income raises the fraction of expenditure going to manufactured goods and lowers the share spent on food (according to Engle's Law); capital--as a rule more intensively used in manufacturing than in agriculture--becomes relatively more abundant and labor relatively scarcer in the course of development; and necessary economic size conditions for economies of scale are progressively met as

the economy matures. These and other influences lead to a central tendency for the share of manufacturing industry in economic activity to rise
as development proceeds.

The literature on patterns of industrial growth strongly implies
that comparative advantage in international trade evolves over time as
well. The implication is that currently less-developed countries specializing in raw materials exports may be expected to evolve toward having
a greater emphasis on manufactured exports (and indeed the vigorous growth
of manufactured exports from developing countries is already an important
feature of world trade). The one drawback in applying the findings of
these studies in this way is that the studies of industrial growth typically compare countries at different per capita income levels and derive conclusions about the evolution of the poor countries based on patterns observed in the richer countries. Yet in the future both the
poorer and richer countries will evolve still further, and since comparative advantage depends on relative status rather than absolute levels,
there is reason to expect that projected change based on cross-country
comparisons may overstate the degree of likely emerging change in reality.
For example, if the United States made no further accumulation of capital and technology while Mexico grew rapidly, then comparison between
industrial patterns for Mexico and the United States today might tell
much about the future patterns to be expected for Mexico. But since the
United States will continue economic growth as well, the information
about Mexico's future contained in a comparison between the two countries
at present is obscured.[16] Despite their limitations, cross-country patterns of industrial growth do provide one of the few analytical bases
for examining the prospective evolution of comparative advantage, and
the approach is adopted in the analysis of this chapter.

A second approach to the problem is the dynamic counterpart to the
analysis of "revealed" static comparative advantage. In this approach,
also used in this chapter, growth rates of exports are assumed to provide a practical indicator of the direction of change in comparative advantage. This analysis considers those sectors with the highest export
growth rates to be the industries exhibiting the most rapid increase in
comparative advantage over time.

4. Comparative Advantage and the Structure of Incentives

Empirical analysis of static and dynamic comparative advantage sheds
light on the economic rationality of existing or alternative incentives
across industries. Specifically, those sectors receiving relatively high
incentives may be scrutinized to determine whether in fact they are
suited for the country in terms of either static or dynamic comparative
advantage; if not, the sectors are candidates for reduced levels of incentives. Similarly, sectors showing strong signs of potential comparative advantage but which are discriminated against under current incentives policies represent candidates for increased levels of incentives.

One school of thought, of course, is that there should be no differentiation among sectors of the economy in terms of economic incentives

provided by government policy. If import tariffs exist at all, according to this school, they should be equal for all sectors. Similarly, in
this viewpoint taxes applied to firms should be equal for all sectors.

The issue of intervention to differentiate incentives among sectors
is one of continuing debate. From Viner's early advocacy of free market
determination of trade and industry patterns in developing countries[17]--
to the Prebisch doctrine supporting import-substitution industrialization
to overcome stagnant raw materials export markets;[18] to the theoretical
work on failures of the market to send proper price signals in the context of changing comparative advantage and the particular conditions of
developing countries;[19] and, finally, to an apparent recrudescence of
emphasis on the merits of free market price signals even for developing
countries[20]--the literature on the subject represents a protracted and
unfinished debate.

This chapter accepts as a fact of political reality the existence
of incentives to stimulate industry. The focus of the chapter is therefore on the rationality of the structure of incentives. Given the existence of incentives, it is important to determine whether some sectors
receive excessively high incentives without justification on grounds of
comparative advantage, while others may be discriminated against by receiving very low levels of incentives even though these sectors are promising on the basis of comparative advantage.

In the comparison of comparative advantage with incentive levels, it
is necessary to incorporate the analysis of both "static" and "dynamic"
comparative advantage. It might be argued that incentives are warranted
only in sectors which do not now have comparative advantage but are likely to develop it in the future--in other words, incentives would be judged
solely on the basis of "dynamic" comparative advantage; however, analysis
of static comparative advantage contains many elements that represent
"potential" rather than "realized" advantage; only the elements of "revealed" comparative advantage strictly represent already existing patterns of demonstrated competitiveness. For this reason there are elements in the measure of static comparative advantage which point to
sectors warranting incentives in order to realize their potential static
comparative advantage, even before consideration of future evolution.
Furthermore, comparative advantage tends to be persistent and to change
only slowly over time. Therefore measurements of potential "static" comparative advantage are fully as germane for policy purposes over a period
of several years as are indicators of the future change in comparative
advantage.

The analysis below does not address two important aspects of incentive structure: the particular type of incentives that ought to be used,
and the optimal absolute levels of incentives. It is well known that
economic analysis shows government subsidies to be far preferable to
import tariffs as a form of industrial incentive. It is equally well
known that governments facing fiscal constraints find it more feasible
to erect tariffs than to disburse subsidies. In Central America, tariff
protection--the exoneration of tariffs on inputs and capital goods--and
the exemption of corporate taxes constitute the main system of industrial incentives. The analysis of this chapter examines the structure
of these incentives and attempts to indicate areas of relative excess or

shortfall in the light of information on comparative advantage; the chapter does not address the issue of whether the incentive instruments used should be replaced by others such as direct subsidies, although implications for relative stimulus by sector should hold regardless of the instrument used.

Neither does this chapter assess the optimal average level of incentives. Instead, it examines the relative levels of incentives among industrial sectors. Evaluation of the optimal absolute average level of incentives for the industrial sector as a whole raises even more fundamental methodological difficulties than those discussed above in connection with identifying comparative advantage; and, in any event, the optimal average level of incentives cannot be determined by the examination of only one broad economic sector--manufacturing industry--to which this chapter is limited.

5. Regional and Intraregional Analysis

The analytical framework described above applies to a single country. It may also be applied to an entire region in relation to the rest of the world, as in this study of the Central American region. In a regional study, however, there are two dimensions of comparative advantage to examine: that of the region relative to the outside world, and that of each member country relative to the rest of the region. The intraregional comparisons are especially relevant when the region is a common market with free trade.

At the level of individual Central American countries in relation to the CACM, this chapter repeats several of the analytical approaches used for the region as a whole to determine comparative advantage. There are two main differences between the regional and intraregional analysis, however. First, in the absence of any basis for predicting significant differential changes in factor endowments or other relevant economic features, as among the five CACM countries, this chapter focuses only on the structure of realized and potential static comparative advantage among the five countries, without attempting to assess future evolution in that structure. (By contrast, the analysis for the region as a whole examines prospective future change in comparative advantage as well.) Second, the intraregional analysis of static comparative advantage is richer than that for the region as a whole because certain measurements are possible that are not available for the region relative to the rest of the world. The most important of the additional measures are a linear programming model used for identifying the optimal pattern of intraregional industrial specializaton, and comparisons of "producer prices" based on recent surveys.

6. Value-added Activities

Finally, the methodology applied in this chapter considers manufacturing activities at the level of value added rather than vertically integrated activities including backward linkages to intermediate inputs. There are theoretical as well as practical grounds for adopting a value-added approach. At the theoretical level, a processing industry is a separable activity from the production of its required inputs, and should be analyzed separately. Purchased inputs need not come from the country in question but can be obtained from the world market. One important area of theoretical literature, that on the effective rate of protection, deals with industries defined at the value-added stage, and several empirical studies analyze comparative advantage at this stage.[21] At the practical level, the case of Japan is an excellent example of relevance of analyzing comparative advantage at the level of value-added activities. Under an approach examining vertically integrated industries requiring domestically produced inputs, Japan would be judged as having little basis for comparative advantage in any products requiring substantial inputs of raw materials, given the country's poor resource base. But judged on criteria focusing on the value added of transformation industries, Japan manifests a comparative advantage in products such as steel because modern techniques outweigh the disadvantage of having to purchase inputs abroad.

Nevertheless, in the analysis below it must be kept in mind that inclusion of intermediate inputs might change the sectoral rankings of comparative advantage. Generally, those sectors that use inputs produced regionally (especially agricultural products) would be likely to show improved rankings relative to those sectors using inputs from abroad. To some extent, however, the relationship of value added to factor costs will already reflect advantages of locally available raw materials because with lower input costs, value added will tend to be higher. Another mitigating factor is that in the analysis of comparative advantage among the five Central American countries, the exclusion of raw materials will not alter conclusions insofar as transport costs are low enough to make raw material costs similar among the five countries.

C. Empirical Measures of Comparative Advantage for Central America As a Region

1. Static Comparative Advantage

Our first three measures of regional comparative advantage are indicators of the factor intensity of each sector's production, for three factors: unskilled labor, capital, and skilled labor. The three indicators represent the "factor proportions" approach to comparative advantage as discussed above. Table F-2 of appendix F shows the ratio of each of these factors to value added by industrial sector (in 1968). These ratios represent "factor intensity"; for example, a sector with a high ratio of capital to value added (relative to other sectors) is a "capital-intensive" sector.

The use of value added as the base for measuring factor intensity circumvents the problem of ambiguity in assessing relative factor intensity when there are more than two factors. Value added equals the sum of all factor inputs times their respective unit factor payments. On the average these unit factor payments will equal prevailing "factor prices" in the region. Thus, the ratio of one factor to value added represents assessment of the intensity of use of that factor relative to the price-weighted measure of the use of all factors.

277

Given these factor intensity ratios, it is possible to rank all
seventy-five four-digit ISIC industrial categories in the region by their
presumptive static comparative advantage vis-à-vis the rest of the world.
As a developing region, Central America may be considered to be abun-
dantly endowed with unskilled labor but scarce in skilled labor and capital relative to world trading partners. Therefore one may rank industries
from lowest comparative advantage (rank = 1) to highest comparative advantage (rank = 75) according to progression from (i) lowest ratio of
unskilled labor/value added to highest ratio, (ii) highest ratio of
capital/value added to lowest; or (iii) highest ratio of skilled labor/
value added to lowest.   Rankings R1 through R3 reported in table F-1
of appendix F indicate the relative positions of the seventy-five sectors
on the bases of these three factor intensity measures.

The next two indicators represent "revealed" comparative advantage,
or actual "performance."   One is the rate of return to capital for each
sector (annual profits divided by capital stock); the other is the trade
ratio, (exports - imports)/(exports + imports).   The rate of return
variable represents the assumption that sectors with demonstrated comparative advantage will also be sectors with high rates of return to capital.
The trade measure represents an even more direct indicator of revealed
comparative advantage because it explicity records the degree of export
or import specialization. It varies from -1 (for sectors with no exports)
to +1 (to sectors with no imports).[22]   The underlying values for these
two variables are shown in table F-3, appendix F.   Their corresponding
sectoral rankings appear as R4 and R5, respectively, in appendix table
F-1.

The final indicator of static comparative advantage for Central
America represents the Ricardian, or classical, theme of relative factor
productivity (regardless of factor proportions and endowments). The measure used is the ratio of "total factor productivity" in Central America
to that in the United States, for each individual sector.   The United
States is assumed to be a relevant base for comparison because of its high
weight in Central America's industrial trade with the rest of the world.
Total factor productivity for Central America is measured as the ratio
of value added to the sum of: capital stock evaluated at a 15 percent
opportunity cost, plus wages paid to skilled labor, plus the number of
unskilled workers multiplied by the "shadow price" or opportunity cost
of unskilled labor.[23]   The data source is the 1968 industrial census,
from which detailed plant level data are available.[24]   For the United
States, total factor productivity is measured as the ratio of value added
to the sum of capital evaluated at an 8 percent annual opportunity cost,
plus the wage bill for skilled and unskilled labor.[25]

Table F-4 of appendix F presents the estimates of Central American
and U.S. total factor productivity, and the ratio between them, for each
industrial sector. Appendix table F-1 reports the corresponding rankings
of sectors by implied Central American comparative advantage, as ranking
variable R6.   (The higher the ratio of Central American total factor
productivity to that for the United States, the higher is a sector's
ranking under R6 in the table.)

These six indicators complete our measurements for regionwide static
comparative advantage of Central America.   Appendix table F-1 presents

two composite rankings based on all six individual rankings; the first (C1) is based on an unweighted average of the six. The second composite rank (C2) is more meaningful because it assigns weights broadly representative of the importance of each individual ranking variable. In the weighted composite rank, the following procedure is used: (i) the broad influence of "factor proportions" receives a weight of one-third (hence, a weight of one-ninth on each of its three components, R1, R2, and R3); the influence of "revealed comparative advantage" receives one-third weight (with greater consideration given to the more direct trade performance indicator—2/9 in overall weight—and lesser consideration to rate of return—1/9 overall weight); and the Ricardian approach using total factor productivity (R6) receives one-third of total weight. An examination of the two alternative composite rankings shows them to be quite closely correlated.

The weightings used to obtain composite rankings are necessarily arbitrary to some degree. To the extent that the rankings under individual variables tend to parallel each other, however, the composite rankings will be little affected by the particular weights chosen. Table F-5 in appendix F shows the Spearman rank correlation coefficient between each pair of individual rankings. Overall the rankings adhere to each other relatively well. The Kendall "coefficient of correspondence" is 0.238, significant at the 1 percent level. Therefore, considered as a group the six variables show a statistically significant correlation in their rankings. The one exception to the pattern is the first variable, unskilled labor/value added. The variable's rankings are negatively correlated with those of the other variables. When this variable is omitted, the Kendall correspondence coefficient rises to 0.439, significant at the 1 percent level.

The reason for the negative correlation between the ratio of unskilled labor to value added (R1) and the other variables is probably the fact that shifts in total sector productivity across sectors make value added fluctuate considerably, and value added appears in the denominator of R1 but in the numerators of R2, R3, and (indirectly) R4 and R6. Despite the negative correlations found for R1, however, we do not discard the measure. It has been found to perform well in explaining manufactured exports of developing countries.[26] It contains the only direct information about relative intensity of the most clearly abundant factor, unskilled labor. Therefore we retain the variable, while noting that it is the only one that is out of step with the others. Because the variable's weight in the composite ranking is only one-ninth, the composite variable primarily reflects the much closer adherence of the other five variables taken together, however.[27]

Specific composite rankings for individual sectors are shown in table F-1; however, it is more meaningful to discuss overall sectoral comparative advantage only after taking into account "dynamic" evolution of comparative advantage as well.

2. Dynamic Comparative Advantage

To assess "future" comparative advantage it is necessary to examine the probable relative <u>changes</u> of comparative advantage in the future from current or static levels. Our first indicator of this prospective change is one of "revealed degree of change," the rate of growth of exports. The higher a sector's export growth rate, the higher is its future ranking in comparative advantage likely to be relative to its current ranking.

"Exports" refers to the sum over the five countries of total exports, including those to CACM partners. Inclusion of intraregional exports is important to capture information on the dramatic evidence of the region's changing comparative advantage, shown by the rapid growth in intraregional industrial trade in the 1960s, with much of that trade representing regionwide import substitution vis-à-vis the rest of the world. Appendix table F-6 presents the sectoral rankings by export growth. The underlying data on growth rates refer to the period 1963-65 to 1970-72, and are reported in table F-7.

The two remaining indicators of prospective change in comparative advantage represent the approach of "cross-country" patterns of industrial development. The first uses statistical estimates of individual growth patterns across small developing and developed countries to rank sectors by "growth elasticities." These elasticities represent the percentage rise in a given sector's output per capita associated with each percentage increase in per capita income. The elasticities encompass the effects of income elasticities of demand as well as changing factors on the supply side. The higher the growth elasticity for a sector, the greater is the increase of that sector's share in the economy and, therefore, the greater is the prospective increase in comparative advantage in the future relative to the sector's present comparative advantage. As shown in appendix table F-8, the growth elasticities tend to be lowest for "traditional" products such as textiles and food, and highest for nontraditional products such as paper, metal products, and rubber. The twelve broad industrial category rankings are translated into corresponding rankings for the seventy-five more disaggregated categories, as shown in column F2 of appendix table F-6.

The second cross-country evolutionary indicator is simpler. It considers three "control countries" reasonably characterized as having economic structures similar to that which Central America could be expected to obtain in the future. We have chosen Chile, Colombia, and Peru as the control countries. Colombia and Peru both have per capita incomes ($340 and $450 in 1970 dollars, respectively) and populations (21.6 million and 13.6 million in 1970) similar to what might be expected for Central America in the next few years (with a 1970 regional per capita income of $367 and population of 15 million).[28] Chile has a higher per capita income ($720 in 1970) but lower population (9.8 million),[29] so that its economic size is somewhat larger and its economic structure more "developed" than that of Central America. In addition the three countries are geographically close to Central America, facilitating meaningful comparisons.[30]

Table F9 of appendix F shows the percentage shares of each sector in total value added of manufacturing industry for Central America and for the three "control countries," along with an unweighted average of these shares for the three control countries. For comparability the shares are based on industry totals excluding sector 372, nonferrous metals. The extremely high share of copper production in Chile (and, to a lesser extent, in Peru) requires the elimination of this sector in order that meaningful comparisons may be made with Central America (because of the highly natural resource-specific basis for the copper industry in Chile and Peru). For the remaining sectors, the ratio of the average sector share among the three control countries to the corresponding share in Central America is shown in table F-9. This ratio provides the second indicator of cross-country evidence on prospective change in comparative advantage. The higher the ratio, the greater is the probable future growth rate of a sector in Central America, and thus the higher the prospective increase in comparative advantage in the future. Sectoral rankings based on this ratio are shown in appendix table F-6 (column F3). (These more disaggregated sector rankings are derived from the ranks of the broader industrial classes on which table F-8 is based.)

It may be asked whether Chile, Colombia, and Peru have had policy distortions that make their industrial structures unfortunate ones for comparison. To be sure, all three countries have followed policies of import-substituting industrialization, making some errors of excess in the process.[31] Nevertheless, their experiences contain information about the industrialization patterns that are feasible for countries comparable with Central America as a regime, and that information should not be completely discarded even though it may contain some misleading evidence along with its more relevant trends. Moreover, to the extent that policy error has been a general overemphasis of manufacturing industry rather than agriculture, the experience of the control countries will not be misleading for our purposes because we are examining changes in relative weights among manufacturing industries, not between industry and agriculture. Finally, despite the common criticisms of import-substitution policies in the control countries, the emergence of successful exports in the cases of some manufactured products provides evidence that not all of the import-substitution efforts were necessarily bad over the longer run.[32]

Given the three ranking variables for prospective increase in comparative advantage, a composite rank is obtained using a weight of one-half for the export growth variable (F1) and one-quarter for each of the two cross-country variables (F2 and F3). These weights reflect the following considerations: (i) The "revealed" changing comparative advantage approach (R1) is given equal weight with the cross-country hypothetical evolution approach. (ii) Within the cross-country approach, the statistical elasticities (Chenery-Taylor) are more comprehensively based, but the control-country ratios provide more sectoral detail, so each of the two alternatives receives equal weight. As shown in appendix table F-5, the rankings for the three variables adhere closely to each other. The Kendall coefficient of correspondence for the three indicators is 0.597, significant at the 1 percent level. Therefore the composite rank should not be sensitive to the weights chosen.

3.   Combined Static and Dynamic Comparative Advantage: Detailed Sectoral Results

As the best single basis for evaluating overall comparative advantage we have chosen a combination of the sectoral rankings on the composite static basis (table F-1, "C2") and the composite dynamic basis (table F-6, "FC"). A weight of two-thirds is assigned to the static composite ranking and one-third to the composite dynamic ranking.

For the reasons discussed above, both static and dynamic rankings must be included in an overall evaluation of comparative advantage. The particular weights chosen represent two facts. First, the prospective level of (as opposed to change in) comparative advantage is based on current level plus indications of change, and for a relevant intermediate time horizon (say five to ten years) the static or current comparative advantage should be more dominant in determining the level of comparative advantage than the ranking by dynamic change. (An analogy may be made to the path of average versus marginal rates over time; in the near-term future, average rates dominate, while in the longer-run future, marginal rates dominate.) Second, the various indicators of static comparative advantage are somewhat better grounded in theory than are the indicators of prospective future change in comparative advantage.

As shown in appendix table F-5, the composite static ranking (C2) is negatively correlated with the ranking by prospective future change in comparative advantage (FC). This result is not surprising; it states that some sectors not currently enjoying a comparative advantage will experience the largest increases in comparative advantage. Dynamic sectors may be expected to supplement or replace traditional sectors. The divergence between the two rankings does mean that different weights would alter the overall comparative advantage rankings. Nevertheless, experimentation with the weights shows that the overall ranking is relatively stable. In particular, the static ranking is already fairly close to the overall ranking, so that raising the weight on the static ranks would cause little change.[33] The "dynamic change" rankings differ more from the overall rank, and raising the weight of the dynamic rankings would introduce more changes in overall ranks.[34] Nevertheless, the maximum weight acceptable for the dynamic change ranks would be one-half.[35] Yet, when weights of one-half each are applied to the static and dynamic change ranks, the resulting overall rankings are relatively similar to those under the weights actually used in the analysis (two-thirds and one-third, respectively).[36]

The combined comparative advantage ranking is shown for all sectors in table 2 of this chapter, which also reports rankings by degree of incentive received. However, before turning to the question of incentives in relation to comparative advantage, it is useful to consider the individual sectors found to have the highest overall comparative advantage. These sectors, reported in table 1, should represent the most likely candidates for efficient expansion of activity in Central America.

Inspection of table 1 reveals that several industries for which a high regional comparative advantage is to be expected are traditional industries such as tobacco, sugar refining, meat, the canning of fish and fruits, wood products, and grain mill products; however, the list of industries with strong actual or potential comparative advantage also includes several industries more typically considered "dynamic" and not necessarily suited for specialization by a developing region, products such as: electrical apparatus and machinery, radio equipment, fertilizers, paints, metal-working machinery, pulp and paper, and rubber products.[37]

Table 1. Twenty-Five Industrial Sectors Ranked Highest for Overall
Comparative Advantage, Central America

Sector	Description	Combined Rank, Static and Dynamic Comparative Advantage[a]
3839	Electrical apparatus not elsewhere specified	75
3140	Tobacco manufacturers	74
3131	Distilling spirits	73
3832	Radio, television, communication equipment	72
3111	Meat: slaughter, preparation	71
3512	Fertilizers, pesticides	70
3843	Motor vehicles	69
3312	Wooden containers	68
3114	Canning, preserving fish	67
3559	Rubber products not elsewhere specified	66
3113	Canning, preserving fruits and vegetables	65
3813	Structural metal products	64
3521	Paints, varnishes	63
3311	Sawmills, planing mills	62
3823	Metal- and wood-working machinery	61
3213	Spinning, weaving, finishing textiles	60
3831	Electrical industrial machinery	59
3116	Grain mill products	58
3411	Pulp, paper, paperboard	57
3132	Wine industries	56
3118	Sugar factories and refineries	55
3412	Paper, paperboard containers and boxes	54
3134	Soft drinks	53
3710	Iron and steel basic industries	52
3551	Rubber tires and tubes	51

[a]See table 2 of this chapter, column 5.

Although these specific sectoral results should be viewed with caution,
they do at least suggest that these sectors deserve particular attention
for possible attractive projects in future development planning for the
area.

4. The Structure of Industrial Incentives

Two instruments are the primary source of industrial incentives in Central America: exemptions of corporate income taxes and the structure of tariffs on imports. Tariff policy affects industrial incentives in two ways: final products receive protection and therefore higher prices than in the absence of tariffs, and tariffs on imported intermediate inputs and capital goods are typically exonerated for industries enjoying incentives.

In order to compare the structure of incentives with the structure of comparative advantage, it is first necessary to obtain an estimate of the overall degree of incentive given to each industrial sector. Appendix table F-10 presents estimates of (i) the effective rate of protection, and (ii) the fraction of income taxes exempted, by industrial sector, for Central America as a whole. The underlying estimates for effective protection rates are presented in appendix K. For the purposes of the present chapter, the effective protection rate refers to "actual" protection net of all exonerations of import duties. An aggregate rate for Central America is obtained by weighting the effective protection rates of each individual country by the share of each in total regional value added in the sector in question.

The effective rate of protection--that is, the stimulus provided by protection expressed as a fraction of value added--represents an incentive to production. Nominal rates of protection are less directly indicative of the existing incentive because they are not specified in terms of the production activity (value added) but in terms of the gross product value (including inputs).[38] As shown in table F-10, effective protection rates in the region are not extremely high. Only nineteen of the seventy-five sectors show rates in excess of 50 percent; another twenty show quite low rates (under 10 percent). The highest rates of effective protection tend to be concentrated in the "traditional" industries, which appear early in the numerical order of industrial classifications.

Tax exemptions, the other instrument for incentives, are clearly widespread in the region. Table F-10 indicates that a large majority of sectors have from 70 percent up to 100 percent of their income taxes exempted.

To obtain a total measure of incentives granted it is necessary to specify the tax and tariff incentives in comparative units. For this purpose we have constructed a measure of the "proportional contribution of incentives to after-tax profits." Conceptually, if a firm has trivial profits then its tax exemption will provide little incentive. It is the contribution to after-tax profits through tax savings that constitutes the incentive impact of exemption. Similarly, higher effective protection means higher domestic value added and thus higher profits.

The specific measure of contribution of tax exemptions to after-tax profits equals the fraction of taxes exempted, multiplied by taxes due. For their part, taxes due equal the average corporate income tax rate for the sector, multiplied by profits before taxes.[39]

Because graduated income taxes exist in the region, it is necessary to compute for each sector in each country the average tax rate (based on estimation of taxes due for each firm using firm level profits data from the 1968 industrial census).[40] Before-tax profits are similarly obtained from the census. Estimates of the fraction of taxes exempted are based on the classification of firms reported in the census by industrial incentives category.[41]

The measure of the contribution of effective protection to after-tax profits equals the effective rate of protection multiplied by value added as adjusted by terms to account for leakage to taxes.[42] The rationale behind this measure is that higher prices permitted by higher effective protection raise profits by the amount of the effective protection rate multiplied by the base of value that it protects--value added. These higher profits translate into higher after-tax profits only after netting out the leakage to taxes, but including an adjustment for tax exemptions (the final expression in brackets in equation(2) of note 42).

The measure of total incentives combines these two measures and expresses them as a proportion of after-tax profits.[43] The final three columns of appendix table F-10 report the incentive measures for tax incentives, effective protection, and the combined effect of the two footnote equations (1) through (3), respectively. The third measure is the estimate of total incentive by sector which is used for the following analysis of incentive structure.

Table F-11 of appendix F, presents rankings of industrial sectors by degree of incentives received, for Central America as a whole.[44] The table reports tax and tariff incentives separately as well as the combined incentive. Given the sectoral rankings of incentive levels, it is possible to analyze the structure of incentives in comparison with the structure of comparative advantage. Table 2 presents a comparison between incentive and comparative advantage rank.

For each sector the difference between incentives rank and comparative advantage rank provides an indication of the rationality of relative incentive level. If incentive rank (or "score") is high and comparative advantage rank low, then the large positive difference indicates that excessive relative incentive is going to the sector. In the reverse case, the implication is that the sector receives relatively too little incentive. Columns 6 through 9 report these differences between incentive and comparative advantage rank. Column 6 uses static comparative advantage for the comparison, column 7, dynamic, and column 8, our combined measure of comparative advantage (based on two-thirds weight for static and one-third weight for dynamic rankings). Columns 9 and 10 classify these differences into categories AA--for strong evidence of insufficient incentive--through DD--for strong indication of excessive incentive, with intermediate cases as noted in the table.[45]

Table 3 shows the sectors for which incentives strongly appear to be relatively inadequate or excessive, reporting for each sector the level of effective protection and the percentage of income taxes exempted. The criterion for classification is that based on the combined comparative advantage indicator; the alternative basis implicitly gives equal weight

Table 2. Ranking by Incentive Minus Ranking by Comparative Advantage, Industrial Sectors, Central America

(1)	(2)	(3)	(4)	(5)	(6)	(7)	(8)	(9)	(10)
		Comparative Advantage Rank			Incentive Rank Minus:			Class[b]	
Sector	Incentive Rank	Current (C2)	Future (FC)	Combined[a] (R*)	(C2)	(FC)	(R*)	Case I	Case II
3111	20	73	27	71	-53	-7	-51	AA	AA
3112	41	36	32	33	5	9	8	D	D
3113	57	71	23	65	-14	34	-8	B	A
3114	61	75	17	67	-14	44	-6	B	A
3115	4	20	11	5	-16	-7	-1	A	A
3116	69	62	26	58	7	43	9	DD	D
3117	73	35	24	27	38	49	46	DD	DD
3118	25	60	20	55	-35	5	-30	B	AA
3119	66	55	7	41	11	59	25	DD	DD
3121	42	57	10	47	-15	32	-5	B	A
3122	15	32	14	17	-17	1	-2	B	A
3131	72	68	50	73	4	28	-1	D	A
3132	59	69	6	56	10	53	3	DD	D
3133	16	63	3	49	-47	13	-33	B	AA
3134	56	66	2	53	-10	54	3	B	D
3140	71	74	46	74	-3	25	3	B	D
3211	40	29	37	28	11	3	12	B	D
3212	58	45	22	35	13	36	13	D	D
3213	67	58	44	60	9	23	7	DD	D
3214	75	4	33	2	71	42	73	DD	DD
3215	23	40	5	22	-17	18	1	B	D
3219	74	31	52	39	43	18	35	DD	DD

Table 2 (continued)

(1)	(2)	(3)	(4)	(5)	(6)	(7)	(8)	(9)	(10)
		Comparative Advantage Rank			Incentive Rank Minus:			Class[b]	
Sector	Incentive Rank	Current (C2)	Future (FC)	Combined[a] (R*)	(C2)	(FC)	(R*)	Case I	Case II
3220	63	50	13	36	13	50	27	DD	DD
3231	31	48	21	42	-17	10	-11	B	A
3232	3	18	4	1	-15	-1	2	A	D
3233	62	47	8	32	15	54	30	DD	DD
3240	70	44	34	46	26	36	24	DD	DD
3311	50	72	18	62	-22	32	-12	B	A
3312	48	67	35	68	-19	13	-20	B	AA
3319	38	13	39	10	25	-1	28	B	DD
3320	64	53	15	44	11	49	20	C	DD
3411	29	41	65	57	-12	-36	-28	DD	AA
3412	32	43	49	54	-11	-17	-22	AA	AA
3419	35	17	62	30	18	-27	-5	A	A
3420	13	8	51	11	5	-38	2	C	D
3511	9	3	53	7	6	-44	2	C	D
3512	21	64	45	70	-43	-24	-49	AA	AA
3521	51	49	64	63	2	-13	-12	C	A
3522	26	21	57	31	5	-31	-5	C	A
3523	65	23	47	26	42	18	39	DD	DD
3529	33	22	36	18	11	-3	15	C	D
3530	5	12	31	6	-7	-26	-1	A	A
3540	6	1	66	12	5	-60	-6	C	A
3551	47	38	56	51	9	-9	-4	C	A
3559	36	54	58	66	-18	-22	-30	AA	AA
3560	53	30	28	23	23	25	30	DD	DD

Table 2 (continued)

(1)	(2)	(3)	(4)	(5)	(6)	(7)	(8)	(9)	(10)
		Comparative Advantage Rank			Incentive Rank Minus:			Class[b]	
Sector	Incentive Rank	Current (C2)	Future (FC)	Combined[a] (R*)	(C2)	(FC)	(R*)	Case I	Case II
3610	54	42	30	38	12	24	16	D	D
3620	52	26	63	40	26	-11	12	C	D
3691	28	10	55	14	18	-27	14	C	D
3692	30	34	9	16	-4	21	14	B	D
3699	12	39	40	43	-27	-28	-31	AA	AA
3710	27	37	60	52	-10	-33	-25	AA	AA
3720	19	33	19	21	-14	0	-2	B	A
3811	44	5	59	13	39	-15	31	C	DD
3812	43	51	29	50	-8	14	-7	B	A
3813	22	61	42	64	-39	-20	-42	AA	AA
3819	49	15	54	20	34	-5	29	C	DD
3821	11	28	72	48	-17	-61	-37	AA	AA
3822	17	9	43	9	8	-26	8	C	D
3823	8	46	69	61	-38	-61	-53	AA	AA
3824	2	11	73	29	-9	-71	-27	AA	AA
3825	45	19	70	34	26	-25	11	C	D
3829	18	24	74	45	-6	-56	-27	AA	AA
3831	14	65	25	59	-51	-11	-45	AA	AA
3832	39	59	61	72	-20	-22	-33	AA	AA
3833	68	7	68	19	61	0	49	DD	DD
3839	46	70	71	75	-24	-25	-29	AA	AA
3841	10	27	38	25	-17	-28	-15	AA	A
3843	37	52	67	69	-15	-30	-32	AA	AA
3844	55	25	41	24	30	14	31	DD	DD

Table 2 (continued)

(1)	(2)	(3)	(4)	(5)	(6)	(7)	(8)	(9)	(10)
		Comparative Advantage Rank			Incentive Rank Minus:			Class[b]	
Sector	Incentive Rank	Current (C2)	Future (FC)	Combined[a] (R*)	(C2)	(FC)	(R*)	Case I	Case II
3845	1	6	48	8	-5	-47	-7	AA	A
3851	24	1	75	15	23	-51	9	C	D
3852	34	16	16	3	18	18	31	D	DD
3901	7	56	1	37	-49	6	-30	B	AA
3909	60	19	12	4	41	48	56	DD	DD

NOTE: Incentive rank is from 1 for lowest incentive to 75 for highest. Comparative advantage rankings are from 1 for lowest comparative advantage to 75 for highest.

[a]Based on the following weights: C2, two-thirds; FC, one-third.
[b]Case I: Based on columns 6, 7.

AA = Strong case for increased incentive. Average shortfall of incentive rank relative to comparative advantage rank is 20 or more.

A = Weak case for increased incentive. Columns 6 and 7 both negative but by less than 20, average.

B = Ambiguous; column 6 negative, column 7 positive.

C = Ambiguous; column 6 positive, column 7 negative.

D = Weak case for reducing incentive; columns 6 and 7 both positive but by less than 20, average.

DD = Strong case for reducing incentive. Average excess of incentive rank over comparative advantage rank is 20 or more.

Case II: Based on column 8.

AA = Strong case for increased incentive; column 8 < -20.

A = Weak case for increased incentive; -20 ≤ column 8 < 0.

D = Weak case for decreased incentive; 0 ≤ column 8 < 20.

DD = Strong case for decreased incentive; column 8 > 20.

Table 3. Industrial Sectors with Evidence of Relatively Excessive or
Insufficient Incentives in Light of Comparative
Advantage, Central America

Sector	Incentive Rank - Comparative Advantage Rank[a]	Effective Rate of Protection (percent)	Percent of Income Taxes Exempted (percent)
I. Insufficient Incentive			
3111	-51	4.5	89.7
3118	-30	17.4	47.7
3133	-33	23.6	2.8
3312	-20	14.8	98.0
3411	-28	3.1	99.9
3412	-22	17.1	84.1
3512	-49	5.1	98.1
3559	-30	16.8	92.8
3699	-31	10.0	37.3
3710	-25	4.1	100.0
3813	-42	6.0	95.8
3821	-37	12.5	0.0
3823	-38	1.0	100.0
3824	-27	1.2	3.1
3829	-27	11.0	91.4
3831	-45	1.8	99.5
3832	-33	19.6	100.0
3839	-29	30.6	97.7
3843	-32	21.6	93.5
3901	-30	10.4	5.3
II. Excessive Incentive			
3117	46	1,239.5	63.1
3119	25	125.5	93.9
3214	73	162.4	100.0
3219	35	50.7	100.0
3220	27	78.9	79.0
3233	30	56.7	89.4
3240	24	90.0	81.6
3319	28	34.0	7.8
3320	20	73.9	29.3
3523	39	117.0	96.9
3560	30	36.1	86.6
3811	31	27.3	100.0
3819	29	33.2	93.2
3833	49	105.9	96.8
3844	31	41.2	99.5
3852	31	39.1	5.1
3909	56	58.8	68.9

[a]Combined static and dynamic comparative advantage ranking basis.

SOURCE: Table 2, column 10; appendix table F-10.

to the static and dynamic comparative advantage indicators, whereas a heavier weight to the static measure is preferable (as discussed above).

The following features emerge in table 3:

(i) There is no strict division of the so-called "traditional industries" versus "dynamic industries" by category of excessive or inadequate incentive. Sectors 3111-3901 are frequently considered "traditional" and the remaining sectors 3551-3909, "dynamic."[46] There are sectors from both groups in each of the two classes of the table--insufficient and excessive incentives.

(ii) Nevertheless, there is some tendency for the "dynamic" sectors to predominate in the class of insufficient incentives.

(iii) The broad industrial group most dominant among sectors apparently receiving relatively "inadequate" incentives is the 3800 series, machinery and metal products. Nine of the twenty sectors of part I in the table (insufficient incentive) are in this series.

(iv) It is the effective rate of protection rather than the income tax exemption which dominates the overall incentive level and industry classification by incentive adequacy. Almost all sectors with inadequate incentives have quite low effective protection and almost all sectors classed under excessive incentive have high or extremely high effective protection. By contrast, a fairly wide dispersion of income tax exemption rates exists in each of the classes.

A principal pattern of industrial policy evident in these results appears to be that the overall structure of incentives tends to favor traditional sectors and discriminate against machinery and metal products, basically capital goods. This pattern reflects the fact that, in general, effective protection is substantially higher for traditional than for nontraditional industries (see appendix K), combined with the fact that it is effective tariff protection rather than income tax exemptions that dominates the overall impact of incentives. That is, even though tax exemption policies tend to favor "new industries," these policies are inadequate to offset the even greater favoritism to traditional sectors provided by the structure of tariff protection. That structure, in turn, is the heritage of the typical import-substitution process in which high protection goes to the simpler goods being replaced by domestic production, while capital goods imports enter under little protection because of their use in investment in other sectors.

Despite this broad pattern, the results of table 3 indicate that it is dangerous to generalize. Instead, there are some sectors in both traditional and nontraditional groups with insufficient incentives and some in both groups with excessive incentives.

Finally, in order to evaluate the overall structure of incentives it is possible to conduct a statistical rank correlation relating the sectoral rankings by incentive to sectoral rankings by comparative advantage. This test gives the following results:

Incentive Rank Correlated with:	Spearman Rank Correlation Coefficient	T-Statistic
Static comparative advantage rank	0.318	2.86
Dynamic change comparative advantage rank	-0.11	-0.97
Combined comparative advantage rank	0.476	4.62

As shown in these results, the overall structure of incentives does appear to have a rational consistency with the structure of comparative advantage. There is an approximately 50 percent correlation coefficient between incentive rank and overall comparative advantage rank, and the relationship is strongly significant in the statistical sense (high T-statistic). The implication of this finding is that the political-economic process which has generated the current incentive structure appears to have made a reasonably successful effort--consciously or not--toward building incentives that reinforce rather than frustrate rational development along lines of regional comparative advantage.

An intriguing aspect of the rank correlation results is that neither individual comparative advantage ranking, static or dynamic, shows as strong a correlation with incentives as does the combined comparative advantage rank. Indeed, only the static ranking by itself shows a significant positive correlation with incentives. The fact that addition of the dynamic ranking into the combined ranking improves the overall correlation between comparative advantage and incentive rank suggests that policymakers in the region have to some extent taken into account those adjustments to a static-based incentive system which are called for when considering future evolution of comparative advantage as well.

Together, the results of table 3 and those of the rank correlation analysis imply that (i) although there is ample room for improvement in the rationality of incentives structure, especially by reducing some extremely high sectoral levels of effective protection while moderately raising several very low levels (especially for capital goods), (ii) the broad central patterns of incentive structure do appear to conform rationally with the structure of current and prospective comparative advantage.

5. Import-Substitution Policy

An important area of development policy in Central America may be examined in the light of our analysis of comparative advantage, import-substitution industrialization. A major question now facing policymakers in the region is whether to extend import substitution still further into remaining sectors in which imports from outside the region still dominate supply, or whether instead to follow an industrial strategy more oriented toward production in other sectors for domestic consumption or export.

A recent SIECA study on tariff policy contains estimates on imports, exports, and output by industrial sector that are convenient for analysis of import substitution.[47] These data may be combined with our estimates of sectoral comparative advantage in order to test a central policy issue: Would further extension of import substitution push Central America into production in industrial sectors in which the region has a substantial comparative "disadvantage"?

Table 4 presents evidence on this question. Part I of the table reports data on the twelve industrial sectors in which imports from outside the region are very substantial. In most of these sectors extraregional imports constitute a high percentage of supply of apparent consumption (column B). Thus these sectors are probably the most significant in terms of categories in which major scope remains for further import substitution.

Columns C and D in the table report the static and combined (static-dynamic) comparative advantage rankings estimated in the present chapter for these sectors. The results are striking: out of the twelve sectors, only three have favorable comparative advantage rankings--in order of preference: rubber, electrical machinery, and paper (the last on grounds of the "combined" ranking only). All of the other sectors in part I of the table show poor rankings by comparative advantage, including those on the combined basis taking into account dynamic comparative advantage. Out of a possible high score of 75, practically all of these nine sectors show rankings well below an average rank of 38. The policy implication of this finding is dramatic: <u>future efforts to industrialize by the mere replacement of industrial imports would be ill advised</u> in most major sectors with important remaining scope for import substitution. Further generalized import substitution is likely to lead to the expansion of sectors with comparative <u>disadvantage</u>, on the basis of part I of table 4.[48]

Part II of the table presents our rankings of comparative advantage for industrial sectors with large extraregional export values. It is evident that in the three export sectors with a high share of exports in output (the first three listed) the comparative advantage ranking is high (ranging from 46.7 to 71). For the other three sectors the comparative advantage rank is low--a finding that is consistent with the quite low fractions of output going to extraregional exports in these sectors (despite their sizable absolute levels of exports).

For all of industry disaggregated into thirty-three sectors, we have compiled estimates of imports as a fraction of apparent consumption and of exports as a fraction of gross output, for the region as a whole. After calculating the corresponding sectoral rankings by comparative advantage based on the present study (with averaging of four-digit ISIC ranks into broader categories where necessary), it is possible to conduct statistical regressions to examine two hypotheses about import substitution and export activity. The first hypothesis is that the existing degree of import substitution is positively related to comparative advantage. If this hypothesis is verified, then there is evidence over the entire structure of industry that still further import substitution will force Central America into sectors with lower and lower comparative advantage. The second hypothesis is that "export performance" (measured by extraregional exports relative to output) is positively related to measures of comparative advantage.

Table 4. Import Substitution and Export Activity in Relation to Comparative Advantage, Central America

Sector Old ISIC	Sector New ISIC	Description	A Imports from Rest of World 1972 ($1,000)	B A as % of Apparent Consumption	C Static Comparative Advantage Rank	D Combined Comparative Advantage Rank
		I. Sectors with major scope for import substitution				
360	3821,3822, 3823,3824	Machinery, excluding electrical	160,689	88.6	23.5	36.8
38	3841,3843, 3844,3845	Transport material	141,989	81.5	27.5	31.5
311	3511,3512	Industrial chemicals	105,276	66.5	33.5	38.5
319	3512,3533, 3523,3529	Diverse chemicals	84,562	44.2	32.5	36.3
27	3411,3412, 3419	Paper, paper products	68,801	50.2	33.7	47
370	3831,3832, 3833	Electrical machinery	67,717	63.5	43.7	50
34	3710,3720	Basic metals	62,916	71.1	35	36.5
231	3211,3214	Thread, textiles	54,401	23.4	16.5	15
350	3811,3813, 3819	Metal products	47,560	32.2	27	32.3
32	3530,3540	Petroleum refining products	26,141	21.0	6.5	9
33	3610,3620, 3691,3692, 3699	Nonmetallic mineral products	16,798	17.5	30.2	30.2
300	3551,3559	Rubber	16,681	36.2	46	58.5

Table 4 (continued)

Sector			A	B	C	D
Old ISIC	New ISIC	Description	Exports to Rest of World 1972 ($1,000)	A as % of Gross Output	Static Comparative Advantage Rank	Combined Comparative Advantage Rank

II. Sectors with major extraregional exports

201	3111	Beef, preparation and conservation	103,785	34.7	73	71
207	3118	Sugar refineries	67,364	50.1	60	55
25	3311,3312, 3319	Wood, cork products excluding furniture	36,140	44.0	50.7	46.7
312	3115	Animal, vegetable fats	10,502	14.1	20	5
319	3512,3522, 3523,3529	Diverse chemicals	9,185	7.9	32	36.3
231	3211,3214	Thread, textiles	6,732	3.7	16.5	15

NOTE: Ranks are from 1 for lowest comparative advantage to 75 for highest. For multiple sector entries, columns C, D refer to simple averages of individual sector ranks.

SOURCES: Columns A, B: SIECA (Study in Tariff Protection in Central America); Tomo I: Informe General Sobre Alcances, Contenido y Procedimientos, Anexo 3, Estadísticas. Column C: Table 2, column 3. Column D: table 2, column 5.

The specific regression results for these two tests are as follows: First, imports/apparent consumption as the dependent variable is regressed on the ranking by comparative advantage as the independent variable. The regression is conducted once using the static ranking, and a second time using the combined static-dynamic ranking. (Existing import substitution could be more closely related to static comparative advantage than to the combined rank which also takes into account future evolution.)

The first regression shows a statistically significant relationship in the predicted direction, confirming our hypothesis that the sectors with ample room for future import substitution are also those sectors with low static comparative advantage.[49] The second regression, however, shows the correct sign, but the relationship between import substitution and combined static-dynamic comparative advantage is not significant in statistical terms (the T-statistic is quite low).

The remaining tests regress exports/output on the static and combined rankings of comparative advantage. These tests also find results with the predicted direction--higher comparative advantage associated with higher exports/output performance--but the results are not statistically significant.[50]

Overall these regression results represent (i) strong evidence that existing import substitution is more advanced in sectors with higher current or static comparative advantage, (ii) weaker evidence that import substitution is more advanced in sectors with greater comparative advantage after taking into account prospects for dynamic evolution, and (iii) weak evidence that export performance is positively related to both static and static-dynamic measures of comparative advantage.

In summary, the comparative advantage estimates of this chapter shed light on the important policy issue of import substitution. The data strongly suggest that further industrialization through import substitution should be on a very selective basis because generalized import substitution will lead systematically to inefficient expansion of sectors that have comparative disadvantage for Central America relative to the outside world.

D. Intraregional Comparative Advantage Among Central American Countries

1. Introduction

In a common market among developing countries it is important to know patterns of comparative advantage among members as well as those between the region and the rest of the world. Measures for improving the degree of balance among member countries may require the "allocation" of industries to selected countries (or priority access to development loans for these countries). Knowledge of intraregional comparative advantage should increase the efficiency of the necessary allocational decisions. Overall development planning in a common market should similarly consider country comparative advantage in relating national to regional development plans.

The analysis of this section examines intraregional comparative advantage in Central America by industrial sector. On the basis of a number of indicators, each of the five countries is ranked for a given sector from 1 (lowest comparative advantage) to 5 (highest). Several of the indicators are the individual country versions of regionwide indicators used in the previous section. Other indicators are included as well, and a more comprehensive analysis of comparative advantage is therefore possible at the intraregional level than for the region as a whole.

All of the measures are basically of static comparative advantage. There is little basis for predicting differential evolution among the five countries in terms of factor endowments or other aspects underlying intraregional comparative advantage. Nevertheless, the final portion of the analysis reintroduces dynamic considerations indirectly. The sectors indicated in the regional analysis as most promising (on the basis of both static and dynamic rankings) are considered in relation to the findings on intraregional comparative advantage. An indicative listing is thus obtained for each country of sectors warranting special attention for prospective expansion on the joint basis for regional and intraregional comparative advantage.

2. Comparative Advantage Indicators and Country Rankings

The first area of analysis is that of industrial factor proportions in relation to factor endowments by country. As in the previous section, we consider three factors, unskilled labor, capital, and skilled labor. A first step is to determine, for each sector, whether production in the region is "intensive" in each factor (requires relatively much of the factor). The procedure chosen is to make a simple dichotomy for each factor: on the basis of the ratio of value added to the factor input, half of the sectors are classified as "intensive" in use of the factor (low ratio of value added/factor) and the other half are by default nonintensive in use of the factor. For a given sector, a single value added/factor ratio is enforced for the whole region. The use of data on variations of the value added/factor ratio among the five countries would rule out factor intensity analysis, which requires an unambiguous classification of each sector as either intensive in use of the factor or else not.

Table F-12, appendix F, presents the classifications of sectors by factor intensity, with a "Y" indicating that the sector is intensive in use of the factor in question and an "N" indicating that the sector is nonintensive for the factor.[51]

Given the classification of sectors as either intensive or nonintensive in the use of each factor, it is necessary to evaluate the relative factor abundance of each country in order to compare the two sets of information in an analysis of comparative advantage. Table 5 presents basic information on the relative abundance of each factor among the five countries in the region. Our indicator of unskilled labor abundance is the ratio of the shadow price of labor to the average industrial wage. The more "surplus labor" that exists in the "traditional sector" of a "dual economy," the lower the labor's "shadow price" or "opportunity cost" relative to the going wage for industrial labor. On this criterion the rankings, from most to least abundant in unskilled labor, are: Honduras, Guatemala, Nicaragua, and Costa Rica. For El Salvador we do not have direct estimates of the relevant wage rate (in the absence of industrial census results for 1968), but there is far more eloquent data on the question: the massive flow of migration from El Salvador to Honduras (a phenomenon largely responsible for the war between the two countries). From the evidence of migration it is unequivocal that unskilled labor is more abundant in El Salvador than in Honduras and, therefore, than in any other country in the region.

The evidence on capital abundance is more indirect.[52] Here we resort to first principles: among similarly situated countries (with respect to geography, natural resources, and access to technology) per capita income will be primarily determined by capital stock per capita. Therefore real per capita income should be a good index to relative abundance of capital. Table 5 shows real per capita income (adjusted for price differences among the five countries) and the corresponding rankings from the least to most capital-abundant country (Honduras, El Salvador, Guatemala, Nicaragua, Costa Rica).

We have ranked Nicaragua higher than Guatemala in terms of real per capita income, despite the fact that the precise estimates obtained in appendix A show a slightly higher real per capital income for Guatemala. The reason for this exception is that official national accounts show per capita income in Nicaragua to be approximately 20 percent higher than that in Guatemala, and a factorial analysis of several socioeconomic indicators also shows a higher level for Nicaragua (chapter 2). Nicaraguan prices observed in the price survey described in appendix A were probably temporarily high because of the earthquake in Managua. Therefore, if there exists any significant difference between real per capita income in Guatemala and Nicaragua, the higher level is probably found in Nicaragua (although by considerably less than is implied by national accounts unadjusted for relative prices).

The measure for skilled labor abundance is the ratio of high school and university enrollment to total population. Among country populations with similar age profiles this measure should be a reliable guide to the relative abundance of supply of skilled manpower. The resulting rankings show Costa Rica as most abundant in skilled labor and Guatemala as the least. Despite its low per capita income El Salvador is next to highest in skilled manpower abundance; next is Nicaragua, followed by Honduras—which has more abundant skilled manpower than Guatemala. The lowest ranking of Guatemala suggests the extent to which the country's relatively large industrial, urban sector is cut off from an even larger indigenous, uneducated rural populace.

Given (i) country rankings by factor endowment, and (ii) the "on" or "off" classification of a sector by intensive use of a factor, it is possible to rank the five countries on the basis of the factor-proportions concept of comparative advantage. If a sector is intensive in a particular factor then the ranking of the countries by abundance of that factor applies. If the sector is not intensive in the use of the factor, then precisely the opposite country ranking is assigned. Tables F-13 and F-14, appendix F, report the resulting country rankings on the basis of factor

Table 5. Indicators of Relative Factor Endowments among the Five
Central American Countries

	Guatemala	El Salvador	Honduras	Nicaragua	Costa Rica
I. Unskilled labor abundance					
1. Average industrial wage unskilled labor ($CA)	760.6	n.a.	1,028.1	907.1	751.4
2. Shadow wage rate ($CA)	107	93	93	202	340
3. Ratio, b/a	.141	n.a.	.091	.223	.452
4. Ranking	3	5[a]	4	2	1
II. Capital abundance					
1. GDP per capita, 1973, adjusted to comparable prices ($CA)	451	391	304	451	720
2. Ranking	3[b]	2	1	4[b]	5
III. Skilled labor abundance					
1. Secondary and university enrollment (1972) (1,000)	97.5	130.8	50.2	73.6	105.7
2. Population (1,000)	5,590	3,685	2,767	2,152	1,836
3. Percent, a/b	1.71	3.55	1.82	3.42	5.76
4. Ranking	1	4	2	3	5

NOTE: Rankings are from 1 for relatively least abundant to 5 for relatively most abundant.

[a]See text.
[b]Nicaragua ranked above Guatemala for reasons stated in text.

SOURCES: I.1, 1968 industrial census; I.2, III.1, III.2, SIECA, VI Compendio
Estadistico Centroamericano, 1975 (Guatemala City: SIECA, 1975).

intensity.   As an example, sector 3211 is classed as intensive in the
use of unskilled labor (table F-12).   Accordingly, on the basis of the
unskilled labor criterion countries are ranked (in ascending order) from
least labor abundant (Costa Rica) to most labor abundant (El Salvador).
By contrast, sector 3115 (for example) is nonintensive in unskilled labor.
Therefore the country rankings are precisely reversed, with El Salvador
ranked least favorably and Costa Rica ranked highest (table F-13).

In sum, regionwide factor intensity requirements by sector compared
with country rankings by factor abundance provide the basis for the first
three indicators of intraregional comparative advantage--based on the intensity of unskilled labor, capital, and skilled labor.

A fourth indicator is that of economies of scale.   On the basis of
the estimates in appendix I, a parameter on economies of scale is available
for each sector.   In table F-12 an affirmative "Y" appears if the sector
is, or is a member of, a category for which increasing returns to scale
in Central America were estimated.   A negative "N" appears otherwise.
The index to relative advantage from the standpoint of economies of scale
is merely the magnitude of gross domestic product (for 1973, smallest
for Honduras, and larger, in ascending order, for Nicaragua, El Salvador,
Costa Rica, and Guatemala).[53]   That is, we assume that a larger domestic
market facilitates the achievement of scale economies for industries in
the country in question. Accordingly, in those sectors with economies
of scale, table F-14 reports country comparative advantage rankings most
favorable for Guatemala, least favorable for Honduras, and so forth.
By contrast, in the absence of economies of scale all five countries
should have equal prospects of efficient production. Therefore, a single
"intermediate ranking"--"3"--applies to all five countries in sectors
without economies of scale.

The fifth indicator of comparative advantage is an intraregional
trade performance measure: the ratio of exports minus imports to exports plus imports, with data restricted to trade among the five Central American countries.   This measure is a strong, direct indication
of "revealed" intraregional comparative advantage.   The country rankings
under this criterion for each sector are presented in appendix F, table
F-15. (Underlying data on intraregional trade performance are available
on request.)

Our sixth indicator of intraregional comparative advantage is the
most powerful and theoretically appealing.   For this indicator we have
estimated a linear programming model of optimal intraregional specialization in the industrial sector.   Using data from the 1968 industrial
census, the model selects the level of value added which should be produced in each country and industrial sector in order to maximize total
regional value added in industry.   The model imposes the following constraints: (i) the technical coefficients (value added/factor ratios)
for each production activity in each country are the same as reported
in the 1968 industrial census; (ii) regionwide value added in a single
sector must be at least 90 percent as high as the actual 1968 level; and
(iii) the maximum level of value added allowed in any sector for the
region as a whole is 200 percent of the 1968 regionwide total.

In algebraic terms the model is the following:

(4) $\text{Max } V^* = \sum_i \sum_j V_{ij}$,

subject to:

$$\sum_j \alpha^u_{ij} V_{ij} \leq N^u_i,$$

$$\sum_j \alpha^s_{ij} V_{ij} \leq N^s_i,$$

$$\sum_j \beta_{ij} V_{ij} \leq K_i,$$

$$\sum_i V_{ij} \leq 2.0 \, V^0_{jr},$$

$$\sum_i V_{ij} \geq .9 \, V^0_{jr},$$

where subscripts i and j refer to country i and sector j,

V_{ij} = level of value added,

α^u_{ij} = unskilled labor per unity of value added,

α^s_{ij} = skilled labor per unit of value added,

β_{ij} = capital per unit of value added, and

V^0_{jr} = regionwide value added in sector j in base year, actual.

The model falls short of a comprehensive optimization model for planning purposes. It omits intermediate input-output relationships, implicitly assuming that changes in intermediate requirements from the reference base will be feasible through foreign trade or from domestic production (although of course only value added, not gross output, is included in the maximand). The model sets crude upper and lower bounds to sectoral levels of value added rather than applying more refined sector shares based on the composition of demand (following income and price elasticities) or assumptions about export prospects. (The bounds are necessary in order to prevent extreme solutions in which all output occurs in only a handful of sectors.)

Despite these simplifications the model should be a powerful tool for investigating intraregional comparative advantage. Essentially it determines the answer to the question posed by comparative advantage inquiry: What products (and in what amounts) should be produced by each member country in the region, in the light of factor productivities and the available resources in each country?

The results of this linear programming exercise (which are available on request) indicate that, in all but a few sectors, there is complete specialization of sectoral production in a single country for the provision of total regional supply. This pattern of results provides a clear-cut basis for identifying the country most suited for specialization in each sector within the region. Appendix table F-16 reports the country rankings by intraregional comparative advantage based on the linear programming results. Unlike the other indicators, this ranking is binary (for most sectors): it is "on" for the country selected to specialize in the product and "off" for the others. The question therefore arises as to how the indicator's ranks, or "scores," should be computed for comparability with the other rankings. The ranking procedure is complicated further by the fact that El Salvador is omitted from the linear programming computations (for lack of 1968 industrial census data), so that special provision must be made for El Salvador's ranking.

The highest rank possible for a country on other indicators is "5" (that is, there are five countries in the region). In principle, then, it is reasonable to rank the single country selected for specialization in each sector (by the linear programming model) at the level "5," while assigning zeros to the other countries. However, in a probability sense the chances are one out of five that, in any sector, El Salvador would have been chosen for specialization had it been included in the calculations. Therefore we reduce the "score" for the specializing country from five to four, and assign in every sector a score of 1 to El Salvador. The resulting country rankings on the linear programming basis appear in table F-16.[54]

The seventh and eighth indicators are similar to measures used in the regionwide analysis of section 3: total factor productivity and rate of return to capital. The underlying measures of these two variables for each country are available upon request. The variables are measured in the same way as in the regionwide case above.[55] Their corresponding country rankings appear in appendix table F-17. Once again special treatment is necessary for El Salvador, for lack of industrial census data. For these two indicators it is assumed that El Salvador has production characteristics identical to those of Guatemala given the similarities of the industrial sectors in the two countries. As a result in each sector there is a "tie score" between the two countries.[56]

The final indicator of intraregional comparative advantage is a variable not available for the regionwide analysis of section C: an index of "producer prices" for each sector. Producer, or factory, prices constitute a very direct indication of comparative advantage insofar as they represent production cost differences for identical products rather than differences in product quality or in level of excess profits because of differing market concentration. The producer price indices are based on a large sample survey of industrial firms, conducted in 1976 by country teams in collaboration with SIECA. Although the full results of the survey are not yet available, a selected list of commodities price comparisons at the factory level have been computed by J. Salazar and J. Borstcheff.[57] The commodities in question are highly specified according to the same product description applied in the study of consumer prices in the region, described in appendix A.

Appendix table F-18 presents the country rankings corresponding to the producer price indices, with countries ranked from 1 for the highest price to 5 for the lowest (and therefore most competitive, within the region). Table F-19 of the appendix reports the basic producer price indices for each sector having data available. Note that the weights used to obtain the indices from multiple products within an industrial sector are the "expenditure" weights estimated for each product in the earlier consumer price study. As may be seen in table F-19, the price indices are available for only twenty-two out of the seventy-five industrial sectors in the region at the four-digit ISIC level.

To recapitulate, nine indicators are measured in this section for the determination of the comparative advantage of each country within Central America, for each sector. On the basis of these underlying indicator measurements, there is a ranking of the five countries on each criterion. It is thus necessary to obtain a consolidated, weighted ranking based on all nine indicators in order to obtain a single central assessment of the comparative advantage of each country in each sector. In assigning indicator weights, the following considerations are relevant: (i) The single most important indicator is that based on the linear programming exercise, because it incorporates a formal (if simplified) maximization analysis of intraregional comparative advantage. (ii) Three indicators represent the "factor-proportions" approach to comparative advantage--the three factor intensity criteria. (iii) Three indicators represent a "revealed comparative advantage" approach: the trade performance measure, the rate of return, and the producer price index. (iv) One indicator, total factor productivity, represents the Ricardian concept of relative efficiency.

Taking these considerations into account, we have assigned a weight of unity to each of the following criteria: unskilled labor intensity, capital intensity, skilled labor intensity, economies of scale, intraregional trade performance, rate of return, and producer price index. To the linear programming criteria we assign a weight of 3--giving it equal importance with the entire "factor proportions" and "revealed comparative advantage" indicator clusters, each. To the important Ricardian indicator (total factor productivity), a weight of 2 is assigned.

Table 6 presents the composite score for intraregional comparative advantage, for each sector--that is, the sum of separate indicator ranking weighted as just described.[58] The table also shows in brackets the corresponding country ranks from 1 for the lowest comparative advantage to 5 for the highest.

Table 6 shows that Guatemala achieves the greatest incidence of highest ranking, with a rank of "5" in twenty-three out of seventy-five sectors. It is followed by Costa Rica, with twenty-two sectors; Nicaragua (sixteen sectors); Honduras (nine sectors); and El Salvador (four sectors). The results suggest a more concentrated pattern of comparative advantage for Honduras and El Salvador, and a fairly dispersed pattern for Guatemala, Costa Rica, and Nicaragua. The small number of highest rankings for El Salvador very probably represents the country's exclusion in the linear programming criterion (as discussed above). Note that, instead, El Salvador has an extremely high number of sectors (forty-four)

Table 6. Composite Rankings[a] of Intraregional Comparative Advantage, by Industrial Sector, Central America

Sector	Guatemala	El Salvador	Honduras	Nicaragua	Costa Rica
3111	49.5 (5)[b]	33.5 (4)[b]	25.0 (3)[b]	23.0 (2)[b]	19.0 (1)[b]
3112	20.5 (1)	25.5 (3)	25.0 (2)	44.0 (5)	35.0 (4)
3113	45.5 (5)	28.5 (4)	21.0 (2)	22.0 (3)	18.0 (1)
3114	33.5 (3.5)	33.5 (3.5)	21.0 (1)	37.0 (5)	25.0 (2)
3115	31.5 (4)	30.5 (3)	17.0 (1)	49.0 (5)	22.0 (2)
3116	32.5 (4)	25.5 (2)	39.0 (5)	31.0 (3)	22.0 (1)
3117	28.5 (2)	32.5 (4)	16.0 (1)	44.0 (5)	29.0 (3)
3118	44.5 (5)	28.0 (2.5)	16.0 (1)	33.5 (4)	28.0 (2.5)
3119	34.5 (4)	27.5 (3)	13.0 (1)	20.0 (2)	40.0 (5)
3121	31.5 (3.5)	31.5 (3.5)	19.0 (1)	25.0 (2)	43.0 (5)
3122	21.5 (2)	16.5 (1)	23.0 (3)	44.0 (5)	30.0 (4)
3131	24.5 (2)	25.5 (3)	19.0 (1)	27.0 (4)	39.0 (5)
3132	46.5 (5)	30.5 (4)	21.0 (2.5)	16.0 (1)	21.0 (2.5)
3133	30.5 (4)	24.5 (3)	40.0 (5)	32.0 (2)	18.0 (1)
3134	45.0 (5)	29.5 (3)	22.0 (2)	32.0 (4)	21.5 (1)
3140	33.5 (4)	30.5 (3)	25.0 (2)	19.0 (1)	42.0 (5)
3211	42.5 (5)	35.5 (4)	29.0 (3)	26.0 (2)	17.0 (1)
3212	41.5 (5)	33.5 (4)	24.0 (3)	19.0 (2)	17.0 (1)
3213	28.5 (3)	32.5 (4)	33.0 (5)	27.0 (2)	14.0 (1)
3214	36.5 (5)	32.5 (4)	18.5 (1.5)	18.5 (1.5)	29.0 (3)
3215	23.5 (2)	29.5 (4)	26.0 (3)	17.0 (1)	39.0 (5)
3219	17.5 (1)	29.5 (4)	20.5 (2)	24.5 (3)	43.0 (5)
3220	29.5 (3)	40.5 (5)	25.0 (2)	18.0 (1)	37.0 (4)
3231	18.5 (1)	25.5 (3)	19.0 (1)	43.0 (5)	29.0 (4)
3232	19.0 (1)	25.0 (3)	27.5 (4)	22.5 (2)	41.0 (5)
3233	36.5 (4.5)	36.5 (4.5)	20.0 (1)	22.0 (2.5)	22.0 (2.5)
3240	24.5 (2)	35.5 (4)	33.0 (3)	40.0 (5)	17.0 (1)
3311	28.5 (4)	26.5 (2)	40.0 (5)	27.0 (3)	13.0 (1)
3312	27.5 (3)	33.5 (4)	23.0 (2)	16.0 (1)	35.0 (5)
3319	25.5 (3)	32.5 (4)	18.0 (1)	20.0 (2)	39.0 (5)
3320	25.5 (3)	38.5 (4)	21.0 (1.5)	44.0 (5)	21.0 (1.5)
3411	42.5 (5)	28.5 (4)	19.5 (1)	20.5 (2)	24.0 (3)
3412	29.5 (3.5)	29.5 (3.5)	22.0 (1)	23.0 (2)	31.0 (5)
3419	18.5 (2)	28.5 (3)	17.0 (1)	41.0 (5)	30.0 (4)
3420	41.5 (5)	35.5 (4)	28.0 (2)	27.0 (1)	30.0 (3)
3511	26.5 (3)	24.5 (2)	31.0 (4)	24.0 (1)	33.0 (5)
3512	25.5 (3)	27.5 (4)	20.0 (1)	21.0 (2)	41.0 (5)
3521	26.5 (3)	30.5 (4)	36.0 (5)	20.0 (1)	22.0 (2)
3522	42.5 (5)	29.5 (4)	20.0 (1)	22.0 (3)	21.0 (2)
3523	33.5 (4)	32.5 (3)	28.0 (2)	34.0 (5)	22.0 (1)
3529	30.5 (3)	35.0 (4)	36.5 (5)	28.0 (2)	20.0 (1)
3530	25.5 (3)	26.5 (4)	41.0 (5)	23.5 (2)	18.5 (1)
3542	36.5 (5)	32.5 (4)	22.0 (2)	20.0 (1)	24.0 (3)
3551	43.5 (5)	22.5 (2)	25.0 (3.5)	19.0 (1)	25.0 (3.5)
3559	34.5 (4)	32.5 (3)	19.0 (1)	35.0 (5)	26.0 (2)
3560	26.5 (3)	29.5 (4)	31.0 (5)	22.0 (1)	26.0 (2)

Table 6 (continued)

Sector	Guatemala	El Salvador	Honduras	Nicaragua	Costa Rica
3610	28.5 (4)	19.5 (2)	15.0 (1)	28.0 (3)	44.0 (5)
3620	46.5 (5)	28.5 (4)	13.5 (1)	20.5 (2)	26.0 (3)
3691	27.5 (4)	24.5 (2)	14.0 (1)	42.0 (5)	27.0 (3)
3692	45.5 (5)	27.5 (4)	19.0 (1)	23.0 (3)	20.0 (2)
3699	45.5 (5)	32.5 (4)	23.0 (3)	19.0 (2)	15.0 (1)
3710	30.5 (4)	24.5 (3)	13.5 (1)	19.5 (2)	47.0 (5)
3720	28.5 (3)	31.5 (4)	16.5 (1)	19.5 (2)	39.0 (5)
3811	25.5 (3)	28.5 (4)	10.0 (1)	23.0 (2)	48.0 (5)
3812	26.5 (2)	32.5 (4)	30.0 (3)	20.0 (1)	41.0 (5)
3813	28.5 (4)	26.5 (3)	40.0 (5)	21.0 (2)	19.0 (1)
3819	28.5 (3)	32.5 (4)	14.0 (1)	19.0 (2)	41.0 (5)
3821	26.5 (4)	32.5 (5)	21.0 (2)	20.0 (1)	23.0 (3)
3822	24.5 (2)	30.5 (4)	17.0 (1)	27.0 (3)	36.0 (5)
3823	22.5 (2)	26.5 (3)	29.5 (4)	19.5 (1)	37.0 (5)
3824	37.5 (5)	32.5 (4)	24.0 (2.5)	17.0 (1)	24.0 (2.5)
3825	32.5 (5)	27.5 (3)	26.5 (2)	20.5 (1)	28.0 (4)
3829	20.5 (2)	33.5 (4)	23.0 (3)	41.0 (5)	17.0 (1)
3831	22.5 (2.5)	30.5 (4)	22.5 (2.5)	18.5 (1)	41.0 (5)
3832	27.5 (3)	29.5 (4)	20.0 (1)	36.0 (5)	22.0 (2)
3833	38.5 (5)	34.5 (4)	17.5 (1)	19.5 (2)	25.0 (3)
3839	43.5 (5)	33.0 (4)	28.0 (2.5)	28.0 (2.5)	17.5 (1)
3841	36.5 (5)	32.5 (4)	21.0 (1.5)	21.0 (1.5)	24.0 (3)
3843	30.5 (4)	33.5 (5)	26.5 (2)	17.5 (1)	27.0 (3)
3844	23.5 (3)	31.5 (4)	21.5 (2)	18.5 (1)	40.0 (5)
3845	38.5 (5)	34.5 (4)	24.5 (3)	18.5 (1)	19.0 (2)
3851	24.5 (3)	31.5 (4)	19.5 (1)	37.0 (5)	22.5 (2)
3852	36.5 (5)	31.5 (4)	21.0 (2)	20.5 (1)	22.5 (3)
3901	23.5 (2)	36.5 (4)	29.0 (3)	43.0 (5)	18.0 (1)
3909	29.5 (3)	39.5 (5)	23.0 (2)	20.0 (1)	38.0 (4)

[a]Sum of weighted individual rankings, with the following weights: 1.0 each for rankings based on unskilled labor, capital, skilled labor, scale, trade performance, rate of return, and producer prices; 2.0 for total factor productivity; and 3.0 for linear programming basis.
[b]Figure in parentheses is ordinal ranking corresponding to composite sum rank, with 1 for lowest comparative advantage and 5 for highest.

in which it is ranked next to the highest comparative advantage (rank of 4).

The results in table 6 show a dispersal of comparative advantage across the whole schedule of industrial categories of each country. Thus despite what one might expect a priori, the analysis does not indicate that the relatively less-developed countries (for example, Honduras) should specialize in simple traditional goods (the early categories in the schedule) nor that the countries with relatively ample capital and skilled labor (Costa Rica) or large industrial park (Guatemala) should specialize in more sophisticated, nontraditional goods (toward the end of the category schedule).

3. Integration of Regional and Intraregional Analyses

Finally, it is possible to integrate the analysis of intraregional comparative advantage with that of comparative advantage for the region as a whole. We may consider, say, the highest ranked one-half of all industrial sectors from the standpoint of the entire region's comparative advantage relative to the rest of the world (based on the combined static-dynamic measure; table 2, column 5). Then, these sectors may be "distributed" across the five Central American countries by specifying that the country ranking highest on the basis of intraregional comparative advantage (table 6) is the indicated CACM member country for priority expansion in the sector in question. Table 7 presents the result of this exercise, combining the findings of the regional and intraregional analyses of comparative advantage.

As shown in table 7, except for El Salvador there is a reasonably even distribution of industrial sectors across all five countries as the result of "allocating" each of the "top" half of all industries in the region (from the standpoint of comparative advantage) to the individual country showing the highest intraregional comparative advantage for the industry in question.[59] This finding suggests that it should not be difficult to harmonize the two objectives of "balanced growth" and efficiency. In particular, policies favoring expansion in Honduras to compensate for the country's relatively low share in past integration benefits[60] could focus efforts on some of the six industrial sectors listed on Honduras in table 7 without fear of encouraging inefficient industrial allocation from the viewpoint of intraregional comparative advantage.

The sectoral specialization by country shown in table 7 appears plausible, with the possible exception of the allocation of pulp and paper to Guatemala and paperboard containers to Costa Rica despite the more abundant availability of forestry resources in Honduras (the location of an actual major pulp and paper prospect). Here the absence of special treatment to vertical integration of intermediate inputs with transformation activity becomes evident. Similarly, the meat preparation industry is allocated to Guatemala, even though Nicaragua has the foremost cattle raising sector in the region (in both absolute and relative terms). Nevertheless, it is possible that even after taking into account the backward linkage to intermediate inputs in cases such as these, the optimal allocation of the processing activity would still be unchanged, because advantages caused by other factors outweighed the disadvantages of higher transportation costs for raw materials.

Going one step beyond the initial allocation of industries, it is possible to make "second-best reallocations" of sectors in order to increase the numbers of sectors identified as desirable for each country to approximately one-fifth of the total--or a minimum of seven sectors

Table 7. Preferred Country Allocation (by Intraregional Comparative
          Advantage) of Thirty-Eight Industrial Sectors (One-Half)
          Ranked Highest on the Basis of Comparative
          Advantage, Central America

	Country, ISIC Category				
	Guatemala	El Salvador	Honduras	Nicaragua	Costa Rica
I. Unadjusted	3,111	3,821	3,116	3,114	3,119
	3,113	3,843	3,133	3,231	3,121
	3,118		3,213	3,240	3,131
	3,132		3,311	3,320	3,140
	3,134		3,521	3,559	3,219
	3,411		3,813	3,829	3,312[a]
	3,551			3,832	3,412
	3,620				3,512
	3,699[a]				3,610
	3,839[a]				3,710
					3,812[a]
					3,823[b]
					3,831[a]
II. Transfers	...	(3,312)	(3,511)	...	...
		(3,812)			
		(3,831)			
		(3,839)			
		(3,699)			

[a]Transferred to El Salvador under balanced, "second-best" allocation.
[b]Transferred to Honduras under balanced, "second-best" allocation.

each.[61] This reallocation will be most efficient if industries so transferred are ones in which the "receiving" country shows intraregional
comparative advantage very close to that of the highest ranked country.
By consulting the raw "scores" for intraregional comparative advantage
reported in table 6, it is possible to choose the sectors for transfers
with the minimum sacrifice in relative efficiency. These sectors are
listed in part II of table 7, in order of efficiency of the transfer.
(For example, the first transfer is sector 3312, from Costa Rica with
a composite score of 35.0 in table 6 to El Salvador with a composite
score of 33.5.) Note that after the transfers suggested in part II
of table 7, there are nine sectors allocated to Costa Rica, eight to
Guatemala, and seven each to El Salvador, Honduras, and Nicaragua.

E. Conclusion and Policy Implication

In this chapter, on the basis of extremely detailed data, we have
constructed six variables for ranking Central America's static comparative advantage by industrial sector and three variables for ranking the
region's prospective dynamic change in comparative advantage. Similarly,
the chapter estimates nine variables for ranking the five Central American
countries by intraregional comparative advantage within each industrial
sector. On the basis of broad theoretical considerations the individual
rankings are weighted into one composite set of industry comparative
advantage rankings for the region as a whole and another set of composite country rankings of intraregional comparative advantage within
each sector.

In addition, this chapter presents measures of the degree of incentives received by each sector through the effective protection provided by tariffs net of exonerations (including those on intermediate
inputs) and through income tax exemptions.

On the basis of the comparative advantage and incentive measures,
the chapter reaches the following conclusions:

(i) We identify a listing of industrial sectors which appear to
have the greatest promise for the region in terms of static and dynamic
comparative advantage (table 1). These sectors include categories from
both the conventionally named "traditional" and "dynamic" groups.

(ii) The chapter identifies specific sectors which appear to receive too much incentive in view of their limited comparative advantage,
and other sectors which may receive relatively too little incentive considering their favorable comparative advantage (table 3).

(iii) We find that it is the effective rate of protection that
dominates the total incentive impact. Income tax exemptions are relatively less important.

(iv) The analysis of incentive suggests that there is some tendency to provide excessive incentive to traditional sectors and insufficient incentive to capital goods sectors because effective protection is
high for the former and low for the latter.

(v) Nevertheless, a statistically significant positive correlation exists between sectoral rankings by incentive and by overall comparative advantage, so that the central pattern of incentives does appear to be consistent with efficiency considerations (although the average level of incentives may or may not be appropriate).

(vi) Comparison of comparative advantage rankings with the degree of import substitution strongly indicates that for the most part, Central America has already exhausted import substitution possibilities which are favorably matched to the region's comparative advantage. Thus, great caution should be exercised in future extension of import substitution in order to avoid emphasis on sectors in which the region has comparative disadvantage.

(vii) A quite thorough analysis of intraregional comparative advantage yields the result that each of the five Central American countries has a strong comparative advantage intraregionally in a number of sectors widely dispersed across the range of traditional and nontraditional industries.[62]

(viii) An integration of results on comparative advantage for the region relative to the rest of the world with those on intraregional comparative advantage provides an indicative "allocation" of the region's most favorable industrial sector across the five member countries. This allocation shows that each of four of the five countries--including the critical case of Honduras--excels in a relatively proportionate number of the sectors indicated as advantageous for the whole region. Thus, "allocation policy" need not sacrifice efficiency. Furthermore, the analysis notes those sectors which would be "transferred" to El Salvador in order to obtain a greater balance in the "allocation" with minimum loss of efficiency.

The overall policy implications of these results are, first, that reforms in the structure of import tariffs, duty exonerations policy, and income tax exemptions may usefully take into account the specific sectoral results of this chapter. For example, high priority sectors for the reduction of tariff rates would be those sectors shown to have excessive incentives relative to comparative advantage (table 2).[63]

A second main area of policy application is that of industry allocation. Development loans through CABEI or any other program designed to improve the degree of balance in development among the countries of the region may take into account the chapter's specific sectoral results concerning intraregional comparative advantage. Finally, individual country development plans may consider the results on priority sectors identified for each country on the joint bases of regional and intraregional comparative advantage (table 7).

Chapter 6

NOTES

1. See W. R. Cline, "Benefits and Costs of Economic Integration in Central America," in W. R. Cline and E. Delgado, eds., "Industrial Employment, Consumer Prices, and the Benefits of Economic Integration in Central America," mimeographed (Washington, D.C.: Brookings Institution, 1976), hereinafter referred to as SIECA-I Study.

2. Note that the original scheme of "integration industries" within the CACM would have involved specific allocations of industries among the members. Although this instrument has been virtually unused, if applied, the mechanism would benefit greatly from information on the areas of comparative advantage of each member.

3. See United Nations, International Standard Industrial Classification of All Economic Activities, Statistical Papers, Series M, No. 4, Rev. 2 (New York: United Nations, 1968).

4. See for example D. Keesing, "The Impact of Research and Development on United States Trade," Journal of Political Economy (February 1967), pp. 38-48; W. R. Cline and L. Hayes, "Competitiveness Rankings and Disaggregated Industrial Trade Liberalization Effects," mimeographed; and G. C. Hufbauer, "The Impact of National Characteristics and Technology on the Commodity Composition of Trade in Manufactured Goods," in R. Vernon, ed., The Technology Factor in International Trade (New York: National Bureau of Economic Research, 1970), pp. 145-231.

5. An exception is that offered in M. Bruno, "Development Policy and Dynamic Comparative Advantage," in R. Vernon, ed., The Technology Factor, pp. 27-64. Bruno's approach is similar in some aspects to that used in this chapter. Nevertheless, Bruno's analysis, which uses a formal maximization model, is focused on somewhat tangential issues such as the impact of foreign aid on comparative advantage, and would not appear to represent the most promising approach for the purposes of the present chapter even if all the data it required were available for Central America.

6. The example assumes that the Portuguese price ratio between the two products would prevail. More generally, the price ratio would settle somewhere in between that in England (3 cloth to 2 wine) and that in Portugal (1 cloth to 1 wine).

7. For a summary of these studies, see R. Stern, "Testing Trade Theories," in P. B. Kennen, ed., International Trade and Finance: Frontiers for Research (Cambridge: Cambridge University Press, 1975), pp. 3-49.

8. B. S. Minhas, An International Comparison of Factor Costs and Factor Use (Amsterdam: North-Holland, 1963).

9. See for example H. B. Lary, Imports of Manufactures from Less Developed Countries (New York: National Bureau of Economic Research, 1968).

10. See R. Vernon, ed., The Technology Factor.

11. See for example, Keesing, "The Impact of Research and Development."

12. S. Linder, An Essay on Trade and Transformation (New York: Wiley, 1961).

13. For a discussion of the approach see H. Grubel, "Intra-Industry Specialization and the Patterns of Trade," Canadian Journal of Economics and Political Science 33 (August 1967): pp. 324-88.

14. This theme represents a microeconomic "vent-for-surplus" concept, an old idea in theory about the causes of international trade.

15. See for example S. Kuznets, Modern Economic Growth (New Haven: Yale University Press, 1966); and H. Chenery and M. Syrquin, Patterns of Development, 1950-1970 (London: Oxford University Press, 1975).

16. This problem is partially circumvented in those studies which examine patterns of industrial composition using time series data as well as cross-section data when comparing countries.

17. J. Viner, "The Economics of Development," in A. Agarwala and S. Singh, The Economics of Underdevelopment (New York: Oxford University Press, 1963), pp. 9-31.

18. R. Prebisch, "Commercial Policy in the Underdeveloped Countries," American Economic Review (May 1959).

19. T. Scitovsky, "Two Concepts of External Economies," Journal of Political Economy (April 1954); and H. Chenery, "The Interdependence in Investment Decisions," in M. Abramovitz, The Allocation of Economic Resources (Stanford: Stanford University Press, 1959).

20. I. Little, T. Scitovsky, and M. Scott, Industry and Trade in Some Developing Countries: A Comparative Study (Paris; OECD, 1970).

21. D. Keesing, "The Impact of Research and Development on United States Trade"; G. C. Hufbauer, "The Impact of National Characteristics and Technology on the Commodity Composition of Trade in Manufactured Goods"; H. B. Lary, Imports of Manufacturers; Bela Balassa, "A 'Stage Approach' to Comparative Advantage" (Paper presented to International Economic Association, Tokyo, 29 August - 3 September 1977).

22. Note that exports and imports in this measure are for trade with the rest of the world. Intraregional trade is omitted. Note that the numerator of the measure would omit intraregional trade even if it were considered, since the exports of one country in the region would be the imports of others, and these flows would cancel out in the term "exports - imports."

23. Estimated as follows (annual shadow wage): Guatemala, $107; El Salvador, $93; Honduras, $93; Nicaragua, $202; Costa Rica, $340. See W. R. Cline, "Benefits and Costs," SIECA-I Study.

24. Note, however, that El Salvador was excluded from the census, so that the measurements for "Central America" refer to only the other four countries of the CACM.

25. Note that comparison between Central America and the United States requires the determination of corresponding industrial categories between the U.S. classification ("Standard Industrial Classification"), (SIC) and the International Standard Industrial Classification (ISIC). We have conducted an estimate of this correspondence on the basis of category descriptions in addition to the use of existing correspondences between the SITC (Standard Industrial Trade Classification) and the SIC, on the one hand, and the ISIC on the other.

26. See for example H. B. Lary, Imports of Manufactures.

27. A further aspect of the rankings concerns their ability to "predict" export performance (R5). Studies of comparative advantage often use this predictive ability as a test of the adequacy of the ranking variables. The results here indicate that only one variable, value added/ skilled labor (R3), correlates well with the variable for export performance, R5 (see table F-5); however, the value of individual indicators cannot be judged by their prediction of export performance alone. If export performance were the sole criterion, all other indicators would be superfluous, and one would be left with the empty result that comparative advantage is precisely what it is revealed to be by current trade patterns.

28. World Bank Atlas, IBRD, 1972.

29. Ibid.

30. Mexico is inappropriate as a control country because it is much larger than Central America; Ecuador is inappropriate because it is poorer and smaller.

31. Carlos F. Diaz-Alejandro, Foreign Trade Regimes and Economic Development (New York: Columbia University Press, 1976).

32. See Diaz-Alejandro, Foreign Trade Regimes, pp. 45-47, for a discussion of manufactured exports from Colombia.

33. With two rankings of seventy-five elements, the maximum sum of absolute values of differences between the two sets is 2,736. The corresponding sum of divergences between C2 (static) and R* (overall) is only 666, or 24 percent of the possible maximum.

34. The sum of absolute divergences between FC (dynamic change) and R* is 1,765, or 65 percent of the maximum.

35. With the reliability of FC inferior to that of C2, the weight for FC would be one-half at most, and preferably lower. Note that in the case of equal weighting of FC and C2, the overall ranks would be merely based on the sum of the separate static and dynamic change rankings. In turn, this sum could be interpreted as the "terminal comparative advantage" ranking, that is, "current" ranking plus rankings of "future changes."

36. The sum of absolute differences between R* and an alternative overall ranking using weights of one-half on C2 and FC, respectively, is 610, or 22 percent of maximum possible divergence.

37. In addition the list includes motor vehicles and iron and steel. Neither sector seems a likely candidate for comparative advantage in the region on a priori grounds; however, the inclusion of iron and steel may be reasonable, given iron deposits within the region.

38. Note however that there is a close correlation between nominal and effective protection rates (see appendix K).

39. That is,

(1) $C_{tx} = \delta \bar{t} \Pi_o$,

where:

C_{tx} is the contribution of tax exemptions to after-tax profits,

δ is the fraction of taxes exempted,

$\bar{t}$ is the average corporate income tax for the sector, and

Π_0 is before-tax profits.

40. Legal tax rates for these estimates are from SIECA, "El Desarrollo Integrado de Centroamérica: Década de 1970," Study 10 "Armonización Tributaria," Washington, D.C., Inter-American Development Bank, 1975, pp. 28-29.

41. Because these classifications generally had either complete income tax exemption for three, five, or ten years, or else no exemption at all, a weighted average exemption rate was computed for each sector based on either a complete or zero exemption for each firm (depending on class code reported) applied to the firm's profits.

42. Specifically,

(2) $C_p = E_D \, VA \left[1 - \bar{t} + \delta \bar{t} \right]$,

where:

C_p is the contribution of protection to after-tax profits,

E_D is the effective rate of protection expressed at domestic prices,

VA is value added, and

$\bar{t}$, δ are as before.

Note that E_D is related to the more usual effective rate of protection at world prices, E_w, in the following way:

$$E_D = \frac{E_w}{1 + E_w}$$

43. Specifically,

$$(3) \quad Z = \frac{\delta \bar{t} \, \Pi_o + E_D \, VA \, (1-\bar{t} + \delta \bar{t})}{\Pi_o \, (1-\bar{t} + \delta \bar{t})},$$

where Z is the total incentive as a fraction of after-tax profits, and other variables are as before.

44. Note that the rankings and the estimates in appendix tables F-10 and F-11 are based on only four countries; El Salvador is omitted because it is not included in the 1968 industrial census, the source of information on profits and tax exemptions.

45. Column 9 examines the rank differences using static and dynamic comparative advantage separately and registers a strong insufficient (or excessive) incentive case when (i) both comparative advantages bases show agreeing signs, (ii) their average shows an average difference of at least 20 between incentive rank and the two comparative advantage ranks. Column 10 considers differences between incentive rank and combined comparative advantage rank, again showing a strong case for insufficient (or excessive) incentive when incentive rank is less than (or greater than) overall comparative advantage rank by 20 or more.

46. See chapter 4.

47. SIECA Tariff Study, SIECA/75/FIA/24, June 1975.

48. Note that these findings are not biased by any circularity of the comparative advantage rankings in relationship to the import-substitution variable. Nine separate indicators go into the composite measure of comparative advantage. Only one of those measures is related to import substitution, and even that measure--the trade performance variable (exports - imports)/(exports + imports)--is specified quite differently from the import-substitution measure (imports/apparent consumption).

49. The regression equations are:

(a) $\quad M/C = .517 \;-\; .00697 \, R_1; \quad \overline{R}^2 = .194,$
$\qquad\qquad (4.8) \qquad (-3.0)$

(b) $\quad M/C = .321 \;-\; .00243 \, R_2; \quad \overline{R}^2 = -.005,$
$\qquad\qquad (2.7) \qquad (-.92)$

where M/C is imports divided by apparent consumption, R_1 is ranking by static comparative advantage, and R_2 is ranking by combined static-dynamic comparative advantage. T-statistics in parentheses. Note that the negative coefficient means a positive correlation between the degree of existing import substitution and comparative advantage, because the dependent variable falls as import substitution rises.

50. The regression equations are:

(a) $X/Q = -.018 + .00211\ R_1;\ \overline{R}^2 = .06,$
   $(-.32)\quad\ (1.75)$

(b) $X/Q = .0014 + .00172\ R_2;\ \overline{R}^2 = .03,$

where X = exports (extraregional), Q = output, and R_1 and R_2 are as before.

51. Note that in several sectors there are Ys for all three factors or else Ns for all three. These cases register a sector as "intensive" in all factors or "nonintensive" in all, respectively. However, factor intensity by definition refers to levels relative to other factors, so that each sector should be intensive in at least one factor and nonintensive in the other(s). The problem here is that value added per factor represents the combination of two influences: total efficiency and factor combination. If a sector is very efficient overall relative to other sectors, it will have a high ratio of value added to each factor and will be classified as "nonintensive" in the use of all factors.

52. Note that one attempt at measuring capital abundance directly produced results which were rejected out of hand. Total capital stock from the industrial census was divided by total skilled workers multiplied by regional average skilled worker wage plus total number of unskilled workers multiplied by regional average shadow wage. The results indicated Honduras as the most capital-abundant country in the region and Costa Rica as the least--the opposite on a priori assessment. It appears that two influences rule out the approach of measuring ratios of total existing factors. First, actual factor use may reflect inappropriate policies, so that a capital-scarce country might nevertheless show the highest overall ratio of existing capital to other factors. Second, the ratio is theoretically ambiguous. Despite free trade in imported equipment, the unity price of a capital good is likely to be higher in the intrinsically more capital-scarce country. If the elasticity of factor substitution is below unity, then the implication is that higher capital price could mean higher stock value of capital relative to other factors in the capital-scarce country, even though "physical" capital units (for example, lathes per worker) might show the opposite.

53. SIECA, VI Compendio Estadístico Centroamericano, 1975, national accounts section.

54. Two further details require explanation. First, in sectors where more than one country specializes in production, the possible score of 4 is divided among the optimal producers in proportion to their respective proportional increases of optimal over actual production levels. Second, in ranking under this indicator there is the question of whether the criterion receives influence comparable with that of another indicator with a full set of rankings, 1 through 5. In particular, with a criterion having full rankings the total of country rank scores is 15 for each sector (one plus two, etc., through five). But for the linear programming indicator the sum is 5 for the sector. At first glance it would therefore appear that insufficient influence will be given to the indicator compared with the others. However, the unit weight of an indicator depends not on

its total level but on its variance around the country average. (If there is no variance--say, all countries ranked at "3"--then a combined ranking based on several indicators will be unaffected by the inclusion of the indicator.) The maximum variance on most indicators is essentially from -2 to +2 (that is, from 1 to 5 around the mean of 3). In fact, therefore, this indicator is equally influential as the others. Taking an average of "1" (total across all countries of 5, divided by five countries) the indicator ranges from +3 for the specializing country to -1 for the nonspecializing countries--a range with the same total as that applicable to the other indicators.

55. Except that for total factor productivity a different shadow price of labor is used for each country in the analysis of this section (see table 5).

56. Note that this approach for treating El Salvador is not an option for the linear programming indicator because of the binary, "on-off" nature of that indicator, in which a single country is usually chosen to specialize in a given sector.

57. Internal SIECA calculations.

58. Note that for those sectors with no data on producer prices, the last indicator is merely omitted. Comparisons are among countries, not across sectors, so that for any given sector it is possible to choose a different set of ranking criteria, and thus, it is possible to obtain a composite ranking while excluding the producer price criterion.

59. Although Guatemala and Costa Rica tend to have somewhat disproportionately high numbers of the sector allocated in this way. Note that the high share of the two countries are contrary to what one might expect a priori. Costa Rica has the greatest relative abundance of capital and skilled labor and thus tends to have the highest intraregional comparative advantage in sectors intensive in these factors. Yet precisely those sectors would be expected to have comparative disadvantage for the region relative to the rest of the world. The results of table 7 therefore suggest that many of the other measures of intraregional comparative advantage provide different patterns of evaluation than those based on factor proportions alone.

60. See W. R. Cline, "Benefits and Costs," SIECA-I Study.

61. Note however that the number of industries allocated to each country is of limited meaning because the industrial classifications are such that some represent large sectors and others very small sectors.

62. Although the specific data base leads to an understatement of the number of sectors in which El Salvador has the highest intraregional comparative advantage.

63. Although tariff policy directly affects nominal tariffs, given the very close correlation found between nominal and effective rates of protection (see appendix K), the sectors shown to have excessive effective protection very probably have extremely high nominal protection as well.

CHAPTER 7

A Model of Agricultural Production and Trade in Central America

Carlo Cappi, Lehman Fletcher, Roger Norton
Carlos Pomareda, and Molly Wainer

A. Introduction

Research reported earlier in this book supports the hypothesis that economic integration was an important factor in the substantial increase in growth rates that occurred in the Central American Common Market (CACM) countries compared with their growth rates prior to integration. Integration is estimated to have raised gross domestic product for the region by 3 to 4 percent above levels that would have been achieved in the absence of the Common Market. The gains from integration came from two major sources. First, production grew from the stimulus of importing from regional partners goods that otherwise would have been imported from outside the region. Second, a larger market encouraged increased investment that further stimulated growth via the multiplier effect. The gains from integration, however, were found to be much higher in industry than in agriculture. In agriculture, the gains stemmed essentially from improvements in efficiency through freeing trade internally in the CACM. The principal effect was the increased importation of rice and beans into Honduras, Nicaragua, and Costa Rica from El Salvador. This produced gains from trade-creation for the region as well as direct foreign exchange gains for El Salvador.

In the case of industry, the intercountry distribution of gains from integration has been definitely skewed. In particular, the results of other chapters show that the country with the smallest industrial base, Honduras, has had relatively slight gains from integration. These conclusions reinforce questions about the overall role of the agricultural

NOTE: This chapter is based on the results of a collaborative research effort involving the Secretaria de Integración Económica de Centroamérica (SIECA), the Brookings Institution, the Development Research Center of the World Bank, and FAO. Other contributors to this research were Ivan García, Carlos Selva, Arnaldo Gomez, and Willy Flores--all of SIECA--and Richard Inman, Vihn Le-Si, and Scott Sirles of the World Bank. Opinions expressed here are those of the authors alone and do not reflect the official views of the sponsoring institutions.

sector in influencing the distribution of benefits from further integration in Central America.

It may well be the case that allowing intraregional agricultural trade to conform more closely to patterns of comparative advantage would give greater benefits to the poorer countries. But this hypothesis has yet to be tested; if it proves to be the case, there are corollary questions concerning the costs of integration and who would pay them.

In order to address these questions, we have constructed a linked five-country agricultural model (MOCA) which describes conditions of production, demand, trade, and price and income formation, in each of the countries. It encompasses twenty-three agricultural products, processed and unprocessed, and production possibilities are specified for three farm-size groups in each country.

The model was designed for approximate simulation of the actual behavior of markets subject to certain kinds of government policy interventions. Its structure is based on the assumptions that (i) prices differ within and between countries but are responsive to changes in aggregate supply and demand; (ii) farmers and marketing firms individually are price takers; (iii) the farmers with the smallest plots tend to give priority to home retentions of their maize production; and (iv) when farmers market their produce, they attempt to maximize profits.[1] Transportation and processing activities, and their costs, are included in MOCA, as are subsidies, tariffs, and import quotas.

In its mathematical structure, MOCA is an optimization model in the style of the Mexican model CHAC;[2] maximization in the model is a device to insure that the solution represents the specified kind of market equilibrium. Policy goals are not maximized directly, but rather the model may be solved repeatedly under different values of policy instruments.

In attempting to represent both supply and demand conditions in some detail, MOCA is designed to capture the main determinants of comparative advantage in the five countries. Solutions are conducted under alternative assumptions about the level of institutional barriers to trade; and the responses to changes in those barriers demonstrate the basic patterns of comparative advantage.

But more than tracing out comparative advantage--which is an efficiency consideration--MOCA has been used to explore the multiple consequences of steps toward greater economic integration. Increased trade in agricultural products will make some groups of consumers better off and others worse off. The same holds for producers, in the aggregate, by country, and by farm-size class. It is these price and income consequences--the incidence of trade impacts--that MOCA is designed to analyze.

While the model results presented here are provocative, and on the whole plausible, we would like to issue a precautionary warning that they should not be taken too literally. The present version of MOCA was designed explicitly as a demonstration model; the work program of SIECA calls for carrying out considerable refinement of this version before utilizing MOCA as a policy model. The main limitation of the demonstration version is that product supply possibilities are treated in rather aggregate fashion within each country (compared to, say, the supply specification in CHAC). The current set of supply activities will be replaced with a more detailed one, while retaining the existing overall framework (and matrix generating computer program) for MOCA.

Given these considerations, we would consider the present results from MOCA to be only indicative. In the aggregate, the qualitative results probably are reliable, particularly as they address the possibilities of small changes from the observed values. But we would not like to impute an unwarranted degree of exactitude to the results.

The remainder of this chapter is organized as follows: section B provides some of the relevant historical background; section C describes the structure of the model; section D further discusses the model and the processes of validating it; and section E gives the principal numerical results. Full details of model structure are given in the appendix.

B.   Recent History in Numbers

1.   Agricultural Production in Central America

During 1960 to 1974, total agricultural production in Central America (including Panama) increased at an average annual rate of 3.9 percent (table 1). El Salvador experienced the lowest growth rate of 3 percent per year. All other countries achieved growth rates of 4 percent or better per year over this fifteen-year period. But output growth was much less impressive in per capita terms. Due to population growth rates averaging around 3 percent per year, per capita agricultural production increased only about 1 percent per year for all of Central America.

The dispersion of agricultural output growth rates by country has been larger since 1970 than it was in the 1960s. The average annual changes in agricultural sector output for 1970-74, measured at factor cost, are given in table 2. Honduras experienced the lowest growth in this recent period, while both Guatemala and Nicaragua increased production more rapidly than other countries and more rapidly than in the 1960s.

Table 2 also compares agricultural output growth to overall growth in gross domestic product (GDP) for the Central American countries in 1970-74. While the dispersion of overall growth in the countries has been less than for agriculture, the overall growth rate is clearly associated with growth in agricultural output. This tendency reflects both the absolute importance of the agricultural sector and the export-oriented growth pattern of the Central American countries. Traditional agricultural products still account for the bulk of exports.

Some selected statistics on the structure of the Central American economies are shown in table 3. Agricultural output accounted for slightly less than a third of total output for the CACM countries in 1974. And, with the exception of Costa Rica, well over half of the population is considered rural. This means that output per person is much less in agriculture than in the other sectors. Output per person in agriculture in 1974, as a percentage of output per person in the nonagricultural economy,

Table 1. Indices of Total Agricultural Production by Country, Central America, 1960-74[a]
(1961-65 = 100)

Country	1960	1961	1962	1963	1964	1965	1966	1967	1968	1969	1970	1971	1972	1973	1974	Growth Rates 1960-74
Costa Rica	102	101	103	98	93	103	114	120	124	136	141	143	153	165	155	4.1
El Salvador	81	92	98	105	110	96	100	106	104	114	115	131	119	130	142	3.0
Guatemala	77	83	96	104	103	114	102	114	118	115	122	142	149	163	165	4.8
Honduras	85	96	97	98	99	109	115	124	129	125	125	141	136	141	139	4.4
Nicaragua	62	76	89	101	121	113	118	116	115	110	118	135	130	153	137	4.3
Panama	81	92	91	95	104	116	118	124	141	152	144	153	155	145	140	4.3
Central America	80	89	96	101	106	108	109	116	119	121	125	139	139	150	148	3.9

[a] Latin American regional producer price weights.

SOURCE: Agriculture in the Americas: Statistical Data, FOCD working paper, Economic Research Service, U.S. Department of Agriculture, April 1976.

320

Table 2. Growth in Gross Domestic Product
and Agricultural Sector Product,[a]
Central America, 1970-74

Country	Gross Domestic Product	Agricultural Sector Product
	(annual percentage change)	
Costa Rica	5.9	4.1
El Salvador	5.4	3.9
Guatemala	6.3	7.1
Honduras	3.0	1.6
Nicaragua	4.9	6.0

[a]At factor cost.

SOURCE: CEPAL, on the basis of official country statistics.

ranged from a low of 25.6 percent in Honduras to 41.8 percent in Costa Rica. Moreover, the countries with the largest share of population in agriculture have the smallest relative per capita output in that sector.

Agricultural production for export continues to represent a large proportion of output in that sector in Central America. In 1974, the percentage of production for export relative to total agricultural output was:

Country	Percent
El Salvador	50.5
Costa Rica	48.6
Guatemala	46.5
Nicaragua	41.7
Honduras	29.6

2.   Evolution of Trade During the 1963-65 to 1970-72 Period

The basic conditions of trade are specified in the General Treaty of Economic Integration of Central America (1960), which established the Central American Common Market. The agreement posited free trade for products originating in the region, with some important limitations (see Anexo A of the Tratado de Integración Económica de Centroamérica).

A number of products were excepted from coverage under the 1960 Treaty for a transitory period of five years. In particular, imports and

Table 3. Agricultural Output, Agricultural Population,
and Output per Person, Central America, 1974

Country	Agricultural Output as Percent of Total GDP	Agricultural Population as Percent of Total Population	Agricultural Output/ Person as Percent of Nonagricultural Output/Person[a]
Costa Rica	23.4	42.2	41.8
El Salvador	28.9	55.0	33.2
Guatemala	31.0	61.1	28.7
Honduras	32.6	65.4	25.6
Nicaragua	27.3	53.7	32.5
Central America	28.8	57.3	30.2

[a]More precisely, agricultural output per person in rural areas, divided by nonagricultural output per person in nonrural areas.

SOURCE: CEPAL/FAO.

exports of basic grains were controlled in all countries under this clause. Later, in 1965, the five countries signed the Convenio de Limon to codify the regulation of trade in basic grains (defined to be maize, rice, sorghum, and beans). Export to countries outside the region was to be authorized only in the event that no buyers within the region could be found. There have been subsequent periodic revisions of the trade agreements, but in practice quota arrangements have prevailed, often formally justified by plant sanitation requirements.

In spite of the patchwork character of trade-liberalization steps, trade in agricultural products has grown faster than incomes in the region. During the 1963-72 decade, agricultural exports expanded at a rate of 6.7 percent per annum,[3] and total exports grew by 8.3 percent annually. Growth rates varied substantially by country, as shown in table 4. Agricultural exports represented approximately 80 percent of total exports in the CACM in the period 1963-65, but because of their slower growth compared with that of total exports, their share within the total declined over the following decade in every country (table 4). Agricultural imports, as a share of total imports, also declined for every country during the period under consideration. Table 5 gives the value of agricultural exports for the periods 1963-65 and 1970-72. In spite of agriculture's declining share within total trade, it must be pointed out that the export markets are the most dynamic source of demand for the region's agricultural products.

Table 4. Structure and Growth of Trade, Central America, 1963-65 to 1970-72[a]

Country	Rates of Growth, 1963-65 to 1970-72				Percentage Share of Agriculture to Total			
	Total Exports	Agricultural Exports	Total Imports	Agricultural Imports	Exports 1963-65	Exports 1970-72	Imports 1963-65	Imports 1970-72
Guatemala	8.7[a]	6.2	...	2.0	80.6	68.1	19.2	14.5
El Salvador	5.0	2.7	...	-0.3	77.6	66.5	23.9	17.2
Honduras	9.0	8.4	...	8.5	76.0	73.5	15.5	14.4
Nicaragua	7.1	5.6	...	2.2	79.8	72.2	19.3	14.6
Costa Rica	12.6	11.7	...	12.5	82.9	78.4	16.3	15.8
CACM	8.3	6.7	7.9	...	79.4	71.5	19.2	15.3

[a]Exports and imports measured as three-year averages of values in current U.S. dollars.

SOURCE: SIECA.

Table 5. Traditional and Nontraditional Agricultural
Exports, As a Percentage of Total Agricultural
Exports, Central America

Country	Years	Traditional Agricultural Exports		Nontraditional Agricultural Exports	
		Current US$1,000	% of Total Agricultural Exports	Current US$1,000	% of Total Agricultural Exports
Guatemala	1963-65	126,990	94.3	7,676	5.7
	1970-72	175,778	85.9	28,854	14.1
El Salvador	1963-65	127,057	94.3	7,665	5.7
	1970-72	145,670	89.7	16,923	10.4
Honduras	1963-65	65,332	86.1	10,556	13.9
	1970-72	123,309	92.3	10,350	7.7
Nicaragua	1963-65	89,278	88.1	12,097	11.9
	1970-72	123,525	83.4	24,632	16.6
Costa Rica	1963-65	176,429	94.2	5,144	5.8
	1970-72	176,429	91.6	16,173	8.4
CACM	1963-65	492,174	91.9	43,138	8.1
	1970-72	745,211	88.5	96,431	11.5

SOURCE: SIECA.

3. Traditional Versus Nontraditional Exports

Considering Central America as a whole, traditional exports--coffee,
cotton, sugar, bananas, and beef--constituted 73 percent of total exports
and 92 percent of agricultural exports during 1963-65. This picture
changed little between 1963-65 and 1970-72; at the end of this period,
exports of traditional agricultural commodities represented 89 percent
of agricultural exports and 63 percent of total exports. (See tables
6 and 7.)

Exports of coffee and cotton alone accounted for 70 to 90 percent
of agricultural exports in Guatemala, El Salvador, and Nicaragua in 1963-
65, while coffee and bananas accounted for 70 to 80 percent of agricultural exports in Honduras and Costa Rica in the same period. The situation remained essentially the same at the end of the period, with a
slight tendency for the shares of coffee and cotton exports to decrease
and the shares of sugar and beef exports to increase. Exports of beef

Table 6.   Traditional and Nontraditional Agricultural
Exports, As a Percentage of Total Exports,
Central America

Country	Years	Traditional Agricultural Exports	Nontraditional Agricultural Exports
		(percent of total exports)	
Guatemala	1963-65	75.9	4.6
	1970-72	58.5	9.6
El Salvador	1963-65	73.2	4.4
	1970-72	59.5	6.9
Honduras	1963-65	65.4	10.6
	1970-72	67.8	5.7
Nicaragua	1963-65	70.3	9.5
	1970-72	60.2	12.0
Costa Rica	1963-65	78.1	4.8
	1970-72	71.8	6.6
CACM	1963-65	73.0	6.4
	1970-72	63.3	8.2

SOURCE: SIECA.

became fairly important for Nicaragua, where they accounted for 21 percent of agricultural exports in 1970-72.   Banana exports also showed an
increase in most countries during the period of the study, particularly
in Honduras and Costa Rica (table 7).

In conclusion, it is evident that traditional agricultural exports
still constitute the bulk of total exports in the CACM.   The slight trend
of a declining contribution of traditional products to total exports has
not been strong enough to change the basic structure of trade in these
countries.   When the data are put in terms of growth rates, however, it can
be seen that the nontraditional exports are now much more dynamic than the
traditional ones, with the exception, as noted, of Honduras (table 8).

4.   Self-Sufficiency in Basic Grains

Domestic production of basic grains--maize, beans, rice, sorghum--
did not grow very rapidly during the decade covered.   In a few countries,
production of grains diminished over the period.   This happened in Honduras with production of beans and sorghum; and in Costa Rica with

Table 7. Traditional Agricultural Exports, As a Share of Each
Country's Total Agricultural Exports,
Central America

Product	Guatemala	El Salvador	Honduras	Nicaragua	Costa Rica
		Average, 1963-65			
Coffee	59.37	65.07	23.39	21.34	52.87
Banana	4.83	0.02	53.30	1.42	29.73
Sugar	4.65	1.72	0.13	5.66	5.59
Beef	3.14	0.04	3.78	7.44	5.38
Cotton	22.31	27.46	5.49	52.20	0.63
Total	94.30	94.31	86.09	88.06	94.20
		Average, 1970-72			
Coffee	49.35	63.21	18.87	21.25	36.39
Banana	7.67	-	62.09	0.82	37.30
Sugar	5.81	7.04	1.21	8.25	6.26
Beef	7.75	1.02	9.51	21.04	11.56
Cotton	15.33	18.62	0.58	32.01	0.09
Total	85.91	89.89	92.26	83.43	91.60

SOURCE: SIECA

production of maize, beans, and rice (table 9). Regarding the degree of
self-sufficiency in grains, the following conclusions can be drawn:

(i) Overall, CACM is effectively self-sufficient in the production of food grains (with some year-to-year fluctuations).

(ii) El Salvador shows an increasing degree of self-sufficiency
over time; except for beans, El Salvador is now a net supplier of basic
grains.

(iii) Guatemala was self-sufficient in rice and sorghum at the
beginning of the period, but it turned into a deficit country by the end
of the period.

(iv) Honduras shows a trend of diminishing surplus in basic grains,
but it is still self-sufficient in maize and beans. Honduras and Nicaragua
are the main suppliers of beans in the area.

(v) Nicaragua has shown a slight improvement in all self-sufficiency indexes, particularly in beans and rice where it has generated
surpluses in recent years.

Table 8. Average Annual Growth Rate of Traditional
and Nontraditional Exports, Central America,
1963-65 to 1970-72

Country	Traditional Agriculture	Nontraditional Agriculture
	(percent per year)	
Guatemala	4.75	20.82
El Salvador	1.97	11.98
Honduras	9.50	-0.28
Nicaragua	4.75	10.69
Costa Rica	11.28	17.78
CACM	6.11	12.18

SOURCE: SIECA.

(vi) Costa Rica is the only country which is experiencing a real
deterioration in domestic production of basic grains. Costa Rica was in
a deficit position in all grains at the end of the period.

(vii) Given that growth in grains production is slight, it is questionable whether the rapid increases in grains exports can be sustained
for very long (table 10). So far, grains exports represent a miniscule
portion of grains availability, but that portion is growing.

5. Trade in Agricultural Inputs

Agricultural inputs still figure importantly in agricultural and
total imports of the region. They accounted for 43 percent of agricultural
imports of the whole area in the initial period, and 37 percent of agricultural imports at the end of the period. With respect to total
imports, agricultural inputs accounted for 8 percent in 1963-65 and for 5
percent in 1970-72, for the region as a whole. These imports experienced
slower growth than imports of agricultural products, but they still remain a major import category. Within agricultural inputs, fertilizers
and other chemical products account for around 80 percent of total imports of agricultural inputs.

6. Relative Prices

In spite of a decade and a half of expansion of intraregional trade,
the potential for further trade remains substantial. Perhaps the most
direct measure of this potential is the dispersion of agricultural prices
among the five countries: significant price differentials are signals
that there could be overall gains if the products were to be shipped from

Table 9. Volume of Production and Rate of Growth
of Production of Basic Grains, Central America,
1963-65 to 1970-72

Production	Guatemala	El Salvador	Honduras	Nicaragua	Costa Rica	5 CACM
			(production in metric tons)			
Maize						
1963-65	625,900	200,500	316,900	157,300	72,100	1,372,700
1970-72	778,400	325,700	309,900	199,700	35,800	1,649,500
Rate of growth (%)	3.17	7.18	-0.32	3.47	-9.53	2.66
Beans						
1963-65	55,200	18,100	50,100	44,800	16,300	184,500
1970-72	62,900	30,600	47,200	44,300	7,600	188,100
Rate of growth (%)	1.88	7.80	-2.26	-0.16	-10.34	0.27
Rice						
1963-65	17,000	29,500	10,300	51,100	72,100	180,100
1970-72	32,700	35,000	10,500	89,100	65,300	237,000
Rate of growth (%)	11.85	2.47	0.28	8.28	-1.41	4.00
Sorghum						
1963-65	33,160	94,900	52,700	44,900	10,300	234,400
1970-72	35,500	149,800	74,600	41,600	11,400	285,900
Rate of growth (%)	1.68	6.75	-1.44	-1.09	1.46	2.88

SOURCE: SIECA, Series Estadisticas Seleccionadas de Centroamerica y Panama, December 1975.

Table 10. Value of Nontraditional Exports: Grains
and Other Products, Central America,
1963-65 and 1970-72

Country	Years	Grains	Other Nontraditional Products	Total
		(thousand U.S. $)		*
Guatemala	1963-65	277	7,399	7,676
	1970-72	1,514	27,340	28,854
El Salvador	1963-65	693	6,972	7,665
	1970-72	2,912	14,011	16,923
Honduras	1963-65	6,823	3,733	10,556
	1970-72	2,869	7,481	10,350
Nicaragua	1963-65	956	11,141	12,097
	1970-72	5,740	18,892	24,632
Costa Rica	1963-65	126	5,018	5,144
	1970-72	77	16,096	16,173
Central America	1963-65	8,877	34,261	43,138
	1970-72	13,112	83,319	96,431

SOURCE: SIECA

the low-price country to the high-price country. Tables 11 to 15 show the 1970 or 1973 relative prices for five principal products of the Central American countries.

Transportation costs no doubt account for some of the observed differentials, but those costs should account for no more than 5 to 10 percent of product value, so there obviously remain unexploited trading opportunities. The tables show that, although the patterns vary by crop, Guatemala and Honduras are low-cost producers rather consistently while Costa Rica is, on the whole, the highest-cost producer. These differences foreshadow to some extent the possibilities of trade expansion which are traced out with MOCA in section E below.

7. Labor Force and Employment

In a sense, there is more pressure for labor migration than there is for movement of agricultural products among Central American countries. But, in actuality, while there is substantial seasonal and permanent migration within each country, very little international migration has been permitted.

Table 11. Relative Consumer Prices, Maize, 1973

	Guatemala	El Salvador	Honduras	Nicaragua	Costa Rica
Guatemala	1.000	0.791	0.722	1.053	1.148
El Salvador	1.264	1.000	0.912	1.330	1.451
Honduras	1.386	1.096	1.000	1.458	1.590
Nicaragua	0.950	0.752	0.686	1.000	1.091
Costa Rica	0.871	0.689	0.629	0.917	1.000

NOTE: Relative prices are computed as the column country's price
divided by the row country's price.

SOURCE: SIECA/Brookings Consumer Price Survey, 1973.

Table 12. Relative Consumer Prices, Rice, 1973

	Guatemala	El Salvador	Honduras	Nicaragua	Costa Rica
Guatemala	1.000	0.963	0.773	0.898	1.027
El Salvador	1.039	1.000	0.803	0.933	1.067
Honduras	1.294	1.246	1.000	1.162	1.329
Nicaragua	1.113	1.072	0.861	1.000	1.143
Costa Rica	0.974	0.937	0.752	0.875	1.000

NOTE: Price relatives are computed as the column country's price
divided by the row country's price.

SOURCE: See table 11.

Table 13. Relative Consumer Prices, Beans, 1973

	Guatemala	El Salvador	Honduras	Nicaragua	Costa Rica
Guatemala	1.000	1.222	0.788	1.044	1.128
El Salvador	0.818	1.000	0.645	0.854	0.923
Honduras	1.269	1.551	1.000	1.325	1.432
Nicaragua	0.958	1.171	0.755	1.000	1.081
Costa Rica	0.887	1.084	0.698	0.925	1.000

NOTE: Relative prices are computed as the column country's price
divided by the row country's price.

SOURCE: See table 11.

Table 14. Relative Prices at the Farm Gate Level, Sugar Cane, 1970

	Guatemala	El Salvador	Honduras	Nicaragua	Costa Rica
Guatemala	1.000	1.025	0.790	0.667	1.123
El Salvador	0.976	1.000	0.771	0.651	1.096
Honduras	1.266	1.297	1.000	0.844	1.422
Nicaragua	1.500	1.537	1.185	1.000	1.685
Costa Rica	0.890	0.912	0.703	0.593	1.000

NOTE: Price relatives are computed as the column country's price
divided by the row country's price.

SOURCE: GAFICA, "Plan Perspectivo para el Desarrollo y la Integracion
de la Agricultura Centroamericana," vol 2, (Guatemala City:
GAFICA, May 1974), tables H.1.1-H.1.31.

Table 15. Relative Prices at the Farm Gate Level, Coffee, 1970

	Guatemala	El Salvador	Honduras	Nicaragua	Costa Rica
Guatemala	1.000	1.420	0.899	0.992	1.203
El Salvador	0.704	1.000	0.633	0.698	0.847
Honduras	1.113	1.581	1.000	1.103	1.339
Nicaragua	1.008	1.432	0.906	1.000	1.213
Costa Rica	0.831	1.181	0.747	0.824	1.000

NOTE: Price relatives are computed as the column country's price
divided by the row country's price.

SOURCE: See table 14.

Table 16 shows the rural population density in each country; the
figures speak eloquently of the demographic tensions which contributed to
the recent war between Honduras and El Salvador.

International political circumstances are such that it is not possible to contemplate significant movements of agricultural labor between
countries in Central America. The MOCA model does allow for intracountry
labor movements, but to conform to reality it does not allow for movements across international boundaries.   It does of course allow for international movement of products and, given contemporary realities, the
more pertinent question is, To what extent will movement of products
compensate for lack of factor mobility?

Table 16.   Rural Population per Hundred Acres
of Land in Farms, Central America,
1965 and 1970

Country	1965	1970	% Annual Rate of Change
Guatemala	93	98	1.1
El Salvador	122	130	1.3
Honduras	68	76	2.2
Nicaragua	29	31	1.3
Costa Rica	38	43	2.5
Central America	64	69	1.5

C.   MOCA: A Spatial Equilibrium Model

1.   Introduction to the Model

In broad terms, the principal objective in building MOCA was to construct an analytic instrument that could be used to simulate the consequences of changes in Central American agricultural trade policies. "Policies" chiefly means quotas (formal or informal), tariffs, and export
subsidies, and "consequences" refers to changes in trade patterns, production levels and prices by commodity and country, incomes by farm group
and country, and levels of employment and the use of other factors.

More narrowly, the initial uses of MOCA have concerned an assessment
of the incidence of benefits and costs of more liberalized agricultural
trade among the CACM countries.   The model solutions reported later in
this chapter contain measures of the magnitude of gains and losses by
country and by groups within each country. While the overall gains from
expanded trade are positive, it is clear that not everyone benefits.   Indeed, exactly this perception has hindered the full implementation of the
freer trade regime which is codified in the CACM agreements.

Although fears of unequal incidence of economic costs have been
widespread, there has been no frank attempt to set out what those costs,
and the corresponding gains, might be, and who will incur the costs and
reap the gains. MOCA was constructed to help fill this void. A clearer
appreciation of the incidence of benefits and costs perhaps can contribute to the design of compensatory programs, thereby promoting expanded
trade.

A byproduct of this study is a quantification of patterns of comparative advantage, over products and countries in the region.   MOCA is
a modified market equilibrium model, and as such it operates on the basis
of comparative advantage at the margin.   This last qualification is important: we consider that MOCA's validity is restricted to cases of marginal change away from the observed situation.

MOCA is based on cross-sectional data within each country. Supply
elastics are not estimated independently and then put into the model, but
rather are derived from the model's solutions.[4]   The representation of
agricultural supply behavior is derived from an activity-analysis specification of supply possibilities, plus the assumptions of home retentions
of basic foods on the part of small-scale farms, and profit maximization
with regard to the marketed portion of output. This latter assumption
is enforced by the objective function.

MOCA is an optimization model in terms of mathematical solution procedures, but it is a simulation model in the economic sense. The objective function in particular, and other equations as well, is designed so
that the model gives a solution which corresponds to the market-clearing
equilibrium in prices and quantities, for each product. The supply functions underlying that equilibrium are defined by the description above,
the demand functions by a set of previously estimated price and income
elasticities.[5]

The equilibrium described by MOCA is a conditional one, conditional upon values of the policy instruments. Thus the mode of using MOCA is to alter the instrument values and then, via model solution, to see whether the new equilibrium is significantly different from the previous one, and in what ways. MOCA is a static model for the base period, so its solutions consist of explorations of hypothetical policy-induced variations around observed base-year behavior, in the spirit of comparative statics.

As it is a static model, the policies addressed are current policies such as pricing and trade policies. Investment in agriculture is not included in this version, but it could be included in future versions.

The structure of MOCA is based on national agricultural models. MOCA comprises five linked national models, the linkages being the activities for international trade. The market-clearing objective function is defined over all products and all countries of the region. If there were no barriers to trade, the model would equalize prices (subject to transport costs) across countries for the same product. However, the degree of production reallocation required to achieve price equalization could be very substantial, and the model's technology coefficients probably would no longer be valid under such changes. Therefore, as mentioned, we restrict the analyses to marginal changes.[6]

Within each national model, three farm-size groups are specified on the supply side. This degree of disaggregation could differ from country to country, and will in future versions, but the data base used was uniform with respect to farm-size groups. There are a total of twelve primary products and eleven processed products in MOCA, of which thirteen may be traded internationally. Of the traded products, nine have markets both inside and outside the region, one has a market only outside, and three have markets only inside. Ten products are not traded at all outside the country of their origin; five of those products are processed into other forms before being sold at all, and five are final products which have strictly domestic markets (table 17).

Each national model also contains consumer demand functions for agricultural products and transportation and processing activities. Another major limitation of MOCA is its partial equilibrium character with respect to income formation. It captures the first-round process of agricultural income formation, but it excludes the multiplier effects on nonagricultural incomes and the consequent further round of changes in agricultural incomes. To put it another way, the price-elastic demand functions for agricultural products have a fixed position in price-quantity space, and they do not shift with income changes. Also, it regards foreign exchange rates as fixed within Central America. Again, as long as we restrict ourselves to studying marginal changes, these limitations probably are acceptable. In later versions, building in a link between incomes and demand functions probably would be desirable.

2. The Structure of MOCA

The model is assembled in a diagonal block arrangement of five independent country models, linked together through interregional trade of products and factors, and through an objective function for the Central

Table 17. MOCA, Flow of Products Into
Processing and Final Sales

Primary Product	Processed Product	International Trade Within Region	Outside Region
Maize	--	Yes	Yes
Wheat	Wheat flour	Yes	Yes
	Wheat bran[a]	No	No
Rice	Polished rice	Yes	Yes
	Rice bran[a]	No	No
Sorghum	Sorghum meal	Yes	Yes
Beans	--	Yes	Yes
Export bananas	--	No	Yes
Banano[b]	--	Yes	No
Guineo[b]	--	Yes	No
Plantain[b]	--	Yes	No
Sugar cane	Lump molasses	No	No
	Feed molasses	No	No
	Refined sugar	Yes	Yes
Coffee	--	Yes	Yes
Raw cotton	Cottonseed oil	Yes	Yes
	Cotton fiber	Yes	Yes
	Cottonseed cake	Yes	No

[a]Wheat and rice bran are regarded as the same product for sales
purposes.
[b]Banano, guineo, and plantain are three varieties of bananas.

American agricultural sector as a whole. Each of the country models follows the same general structure of CHAC-style agricultural sector models.
The international trade activities included in the model make its structure particularly interesting.   The complete set of MOCA equations is
given in the appendix.

A general overview of MOCA is given in figure 1.   There are three
major groups of column variables (activities): country model activities,
intraregional trade activities, and activities for trade with the rest

Figure 1 presents a schematic linear‑programming tableau. Column groups are: **Country Models** (P1–D3), **Intraregional Trade** (T12–T32), and **Extraregional Trade** (E1–M3), with a right‑hand‑side (RHS) column.

	Country Models												Intraregional Trade						Extraregional Trade						RHS
	P1	S1	F1	D1	P2	S2	F2	D2	P3	S3	F3	D3	T12	T13	T21	T23	T31	T32	E1	E2	E3	M1	M2	M3	
OBJ		−	−	+		−	−	+		−	−	+	−	−	−	−	−	−	+	+	+	−	−	−	Max
FB1		+		−											+		+					+			≥ 0
PB1	+	−											−	−					−						≥ 0
IB1	−		+																						≥ 0
R1			+																						$\leq RA1$
C1				+																					≤ 1
FB2						+		−					+					+					+		≥ 0
PB2					+	−									−	−				−					> 0
IB2					−		+																		≥ 0
R2							+																		$\leq RA2$
C2								+																	≤ 1
FB3										+		−		+		+								+	≥ 0
PB3									+	−							−	−			−				≥ 0
IB3									−		+														≥ 0
R3											+														$\leq RA3$
C3												+													≤ 1

See text for explanation of symbols.

Figure 1. Schematic Tableau for MOCA

of the world.   Only three countries (indexed 1, 2, 3) are shown in order
to save space.

The subgroups of activities within each country are as follows:

P = primary production activities,
S = transportation and processing activities,
F = factor supply activities, and
D = domestic demand activities.

The symbol Tij signifies trade flows from country i to country j in
the region, and E and M stand for exports to and imports from the rest of
the world, respectively.

In the body of the matrix, the plus and minus symbols indicate the
sign of the coefficient entries.   The row designations are as follows:

OBJ = objective function,
 FB = final sales balances,
 PB = processing balances,
 IB = input balances,
  R = resource availability restrictions, and
  C = the convex combination constraints for the segmented de-
      mand functions.[7]

Figure 1 effectively represents the steps in the process of transforming raw materials into purchased agricultural products.   First, the
basic inputs enter the production process, as governed by equations IB
and the resource availability restrictions, RA.   The harvested products
either are sold directly (shown by the + in the intersection of column P
and row FB) or they are sold to processing industries (according to equations PB).   Then the goods for sale, both directly from the farm and from
processing factories, are allocated to three markets: domestic, foreign
but within CACM, foreign but outside CACM.   The process is completed by
adding imports to the supply possibilities.

The objective function is defined to be the maximization of producer
and consumer surplus across all markets.[8]   This serves to replicate the
actual market equilibria for all products.   To implement this kind of
objective function, factor costs enter the OBJ row with a negative sign
and the areas under consumer demand functions enter with positive signs.
Following Takayama and Judge,[9] for international sales only the costs of
trade activities enter the objective function.

3.   The Structure of a Country Model

Each country model in MOCA has its own block-diagonal structure.
Primary production possibilities are subdivided according to whether they
occur on small farms (<4 hectares), medium-sized farms (4 to 35 hectares),
or large farms (>35 hectares).   The first group includes farmers who produce mainly for subsistence, and market only their surplus; they have
little access to advanced technologies; yields are low and these farmers
are in a disadvantageous position to market their product.   These farmers
depend only on family labor and, after having fulfilled their minimum food

requirements, they can work for wages on medium-sized and large farms. A significant proportion of their family time is devoted to various activities besides farming itself, such as wood cutting and carrying products to rather remote markets.

Medium-sized farms are market-oriented although they typically retain a part of their production, especially grains, for family consumption or for animal feed. They have access to more advanced technologies, which implies the use of oxen power, fertilizer and chemical inputs. Tractor services usually are rented. These producers depend on their own family labor and they hire landless workers but only after having utilized their own available family labor. Their access to the market is generally better than that of small farmers.

Owners of the large farms usually do not work their lands directly but rather they depend on hired labor supplied by landless laborers and, on a part-time basis, smallholding farmers. The large farms tend to specialize more in the traditional export crops and they have access to a wider range of production technologies.

These different characteristics were reflected in the FAO (GAFICA) [10] coefficients and they have been incorporated in MOCA in varying ways (which are not shown in the aggregate schema of figure 1). The main distinctions are found on the side of labor markets. MOCA specifies that smallholding farmers may work their own farms and also offer themselves for employment on the largest farms. At the other extreme, on large farms there are no activities allowing for field labor on the part of the owner, but rather all labor requirements are met through hiring either smallholders or landless labor. Owners of medium-scale farms exclusively work their own holdings, but they also may hire labor.

The technology vectors in MOCA are defined in accordance with these differences in factor endowments. The least-mechanized tilling procedures are specified for the smallest farms and the most-mechanized for the largest. Hence, the present version of MOCA does not allow for direct capital-labor substitution at the field level. Indirect substitution may occur, however, via changes in the crop mix in the aggregate and across farm-size groups. This treatment of micro-level factor requirements was dictated by the nature of the GAFICA set. Additional production technologies for each size class will be included in future versions.

This is the principal area for which improvements are planned in the more detailed version of MOCA to be implemented by SIECA. It would be desirable to allow choice of technique at the farm level and also to specify labor requirements on a monthly basis rather than on an annual basis, in order to better capture peak and off-peak season effects. Both land and labor inputs to crop cultivation are expressed in aggregate annual terms at present. In some cases, nevertheless, the land availability in MOCA is not exhausted in all categories because of the frequently poor economic returns obtained from further production. This result is in accord with observed experience.

Figure 2 is a mini-tableau for the labor market portion of MOCA, for a single country. Table 18 shows five representative production vectors in MOCA, for Nicaragua.

		Labor Demands in Cropping Activities			Sources of Labor Supply			
		Small Farms	Medium Farms	Large Farms	Small Farms 1 2 3	Medium Farms	Landless Laborers 1 2	RHS
Labor use Balances	Small	+			−			≤ 0
	Medium		+		−	−	−	≤ 0
	Large			+	−		−	≤ 0
Labor Constraints	Small				+ + +			≤ LS
	Medium					+		≤ LM
	Landless						+ +	≤ LL

Figure 2.   MOCA Mini-Tableau for Rural Labor Markets,
Within a Country

It can be seen that technologies vary significantly by farm group. The aggregate figure for purchased inputs conceals some composition effects; for example, for maize, large farms use a lower proportion of total purchased inputs than do medium farms, but large farms are more intensive in the use of fertilizers (hence their higher yields). Yields also vary, but the relative yields do not necessarily indicate comparative advantage. For example, the largest farms do not necessarily have a comparative advantage in coffee production, although their yields are higher. (It is likely that the yield differences are caused in part by land-quality differences.)

In the case of grains, the larger farms take advantage of the mechanization possibilities, and thus there is a certain amount of capital-labor substitution across farm-size groups. However, a crop like coffee is not as susceptible to mechanization. The labor input per hectare for coffee increases with farm size, in response to these factors: medium-scale farms purchase few inputs for coffee cultivation but nevertheless they tend the crops more carefully during the growing season; and large farms combine intensive cultivation practices with purchase and application of agrochemicals.

Table 18. Sample Production Vectors in MOCA, for Nicaragua
(all inputs given per hectare)

Input	Unit	Maize			Rice			Coffee		
		Small Farms	Medium Farms	Large Farms	Small Farms	Medium Farms	Large Farms	Small Farms	Medium Farms	Large Farms
Labor	Man-days	57.3	67.0	62.4	81.5	86.3	62.3	93.5	128.1	161.8
Purchased inputs	$	1.2	12.3	9.3	8.6	66.9	59.6	--	--	12.9
Yield	Kg	640	870	1,000	1,740	2,340	3,200	300	340	380

NOTE: Purchased inputs include the total value of expenditures on machinery, animal traction, fertilizer, other agrochemicals, and seeds. These figures are adapted from GAFICA data. GAFICA, "Perspectivas para el Desarrollo y la Integracion de la Agricultura Centroamericana," (Guatemala City: GAFICA, May 1974).

Another significant detail which is not revealed in the aggregate tableau of figure 1 concerns the retentions of production for home consumption. As a minimally restrictive assumption, it was required that a subsistence quantity of maize production be retained on the smallest farms only. It is implicit that they can either retain more or supplement their retentions with purchases from the market. (Throughout the construction of MOCA, the spirit has been to introduce as few assumptions as possible, so that the model retains as many degrees of freedom as possible.)

Four of the crops in MOCA are perennials: coffee and the three kinds of bananas. For the present version of the model, since it addresses only marginal changes away from the actual situation, only the (average) recurring annual production costs and returns to these crops have been included. In later versions, the investment cost also will be incorporated, in a full present-value formulation. Hence the present MOCA has a bias toward overstating the profitability of coffee and the bananas. In general, the subject of perennials in the context of sector programming models is one that is being studied intensively, and there is the possibility that new methods will evolve soon in this area.

Agroprocessing industries are represented in MOCA in a simple, abstract manner. When products are processed, their yield coefficients are entered into the processing balances instead of the national final sales balances. Then they are discounted for the wastage portion which occurs in handling and processing, and total unit processing costs are subtracted from the objective function. The labor and other specific inputs to processing are not included, as the processing sector is not part of agriculture proper. This is a simple but effective treatment of agroindustries, and in this respect MOCA constitutes an improvement over the CHAC model of Mexico.

4.   The MOCA Demand Structure

Household demands for agricultural products are assumed to behave according to a set of price elasticities. The method used for incorporating such demand functions in a linear programming model is that of Duloy and Norton.[11] The unique aspect of demand in MOCA, as a planning model, is the procedure for deriving the price elasticities. Given that only income elasticity estimates were available, Frisch's scheme was utilized to obtain corresponding price elasticities.[12]

Frisch's approach allows price elasticities to be computed from the expenditure distribution and the Engel elasticities. The main advantage of this approach is that the data required to estimate expenditure (or income) elasticities are more easily available than the time series data required for estimation of direct price elasticities. The expenditure distribution, that is, the per capita consumption for each one of the different categories of consumption, is also available in most countries.

Frisch bases his analysis on certain basic assumptions:

(i) The market behavior may be described by the behavior of a "representative individual."

(ii) There is "want independence" among groups of commodities (discussed below).

The last assumption may not be realistic if elasticities are estimated at a very disaggregated level of commodities. Nevertheless, the problem is minimized as the level of aggregation increases.

The general formulation of the Frisch approach can be summarized as follows: If X_1, X_2, ..., X_n are the quantities of commodities consumed by the representative consumer, and p_1, p_2, ..., p_n are the respective prices, then,

$$p_1 X + p_2 X_2 + \ldots + p_n X_n = Y$$

is the consumer total expenditure. The traditional condition for the equilibrium of the consumer is, in terms of his utility, U:

(1) $$\frac{U_1}{P_1} = \frac{U_2}{P_2} = \cdots = \frac{U_n}{P_n} = w,$$

where:

$$U_k = \frac{\partial U\,(X_1,\ X_2,\ \ldots,\ X_n)}{\partial X_k}, \quad (k = 1,\ 2,\ \ldots,\ n).$$

The common ratio w in (1) may be regarded as the marginal utility of money:

$$w = \frac{\partial U}{\partial Y},\ \text{all prices constant.}$$

Frisch then defined a concept which describes how w varies as total expenditure Y increases. He called it the "money flexibility" coefficient or:

$$\tilde{w} = \frac{\partial w}{\partial Y}\ \frac{Y}{w},\ P_i\ \text{constant.}$$

He then derived the relations between this coefficient and the usual demand elasticities:

(2) $$e_{ii} = -E_i\left(\alpha_i - \frac{1 - \alpha_i E_i}{\tilde{w}}\right),$$

(3) $$e_{ik} = -E_i \alpha_k \left(1 + \frac{E_k}{\tilde{w}}\right),$$

where the additional symbols are as follows:

e_{ii} = own-price elasticity, good i,

e_{ik} = cross-price elasticity, good i with respect to the price of good k,

E_i = Engel elasticity, and

α_i = budget share.

Given values of $\tilde{w}$ and E_i, (2) and (3) can be used to compute all the e_{ii} and e_{ik} directly. The assumption implicit in this scheme is that all pairs of goods i and k have the following property: the marginal utility derived from consuming more of good i is independent of the quantity of good k consumed.[13] Frisch called this property "want-independence."

Want-independence may not be a plausible assumption in many cases,[14] but the scheme does offer an attractive short-cut for obtaining price elasticities. However, a problem is how to obtain information about reasonable values for the money flexibility coefficient $\tilde{w}$. Frisch himself suggested that the value of $\tilde{w}$ would decrease as income increases. Johansen was one of the first to use the Frisch scheme; he turned it around and computed values of $\tilde{w}$ from price and income elasticity information.[15] For quite different products, he found values of w which were similar and around 2.0.

De Janvry, Bieri, and Nuñez[16] used the same approach, relying on existing demand parameters for different countries to get values of $\tilde{w}$. They then regressed those values against levels of real per capita income and obtained the following relationship:

(4) $\log_e (- \tilde{w}) = 1.5910 - 0.5205 \log_e \frac{Y^*}{P}$,

where Y^* is per capita real income and P is the overall price index. The negative sign on the second parameter in equation (4) confirms Frisch's conjecture about the inverse relationship between values of w and real per capita income.

More recently, in an unpublished work, Lluch and Williams[17] took up Frisch's suggestion for building a series of estimates of the money flexibility coefficients. The authors used time series data on income and expenditures data for fourteen countries of income levels ranging from $129 per capita (Thailand) to $3,348 per capita (United States), and four levels of commodity aggregation. The following regression equation was obtained for values of $\tilde{w}$:

(5) $\log_{10} (-\tilde{w}) = 1.434 - 0.331 \log_{10} Y,$

where Y is GNP per capita in 1969 dollars. On the basis of this result, the following interpretation was made: An economy with a GNP per capita of $1,000 has a money flexibility coefficient of about -2.7. This number declines in absolute value by about one-third of 1 percent for each GNP increase of 1 percent.

The money flexibility coefficient can also be obtained directly from estimation of the parameters of cardinal utility functions and from the estimation of systems of demand equations where the assumption of additivity is made. De Janvry, Bieri, and Nuñez[18] also surveyed the literature on values of w which were estimated using this approach and they calculated the following additional regression equation of w and income:

(6) $\log_e (-w) = 1.7595 - 0.5127 \log_e y/P.$

Finally, it should be mentioned that another group of authors[19] recently obtained results which appear to contradict the Frisch conjecture. Their estimates of w ranged from -0.9445 to -1.0497 for a cross-country sample.

In conclusion, while there remains some confusion about Frisch's conjecture, his scheme appears to be a powerful tool and there is some econometric evidence in favor of the conjecture. We have employed all three cross-country equations (4), (5), and (6) to see how their results differ when applied to income strata in Central American countries. Table 19 defines the income strata and associated per capita income levels, and table 20 gives the results of equations (4) to (6) in terms of values of w.

It can be seen that the results do not differ notably, and so for deriving the MOCA demand parameters the average money flexibility coefficients (column 5 of table 20) were used. The consequent values of the direct price elasticities are given in table 21 (including some products which do not appear in the first version of the model). For this initial version, cross-price effects are omitted. However, some recent work[20] has suggested efficient ways of including cross-price effects in linear programming models, so they probably will be added to later generations of MOCAs.

Table 19. Per Capita Income by Strata (in Central
American Pesos of 1970)

Country	Low (50% of Population)	Medium (30% of Population)	High (15% of Population)	Very High (5% of Population)	Average
Guatemala	79	247	589	2,194	311
El Salvador	82	227	605	1,538	278
Honduras	59	187	458	1,540	231
Nicaragua	105	286	723	1,895	340
Costa Rica	193	466	954	3,153	537

NOTE: The original figures on per capita income were expressed in Central American pesos of 1960. Consumer price index for each country was used to express those figures in Central American pesos of 1970.

SOURCE: GAFICA, "Perspectivas para el Desarrollo y la Integracion de la Agricultura Centroamericana," vol. 2 (Guatemala City: GAFICA, May 1974), p. 33.

Table 20. Computed Money Flexibility Coefficient Values, by Income Strata

Income Stratum	Country	(1) Per Capita Income (1970 CA$)	(2) w^1	(3) w^2	(4) w^3	(5) Average w
Low Income	Guatemala	79	-5.5494	-6.5558	-6.3957	-6.1670
	El Salvador	82	-5.4428	-6.4317	-6.3172	-6.1639
	Honduras	59	-6.4600	-7.6142	-7.0445	-7.0396
	Nicaragua	105	-4.7856	-5.6660	-5.8208	-5.4241
	Costa Rica	193	-3.4960	-4.1470	-4.7586	-4.1306
Middle Income	Guatemala	247	-3.0659	-3.6543	-4.3855	-3.7019
	El Salvador	227	-3.2037	-3.8160	-4.5098	-3.8432
	Honduras	187	-3.5438	-4.2147	-4.8086	-4.1890
	Nicaragua	286	-3.8407	-3.3897	-4.1778	-3.4694
	Costa Rica	466	-2.3033	-2.6391	-3.5544	-2.7989
High Income	Guatemala	589	-1.9504	-2.3405	-3.2892	-2.5267
	El Salvador	605	-1.9234	-2.3085	-3.2602	-2.4973
	Honduras	458	-2.2232	-2.6627	-3.5748	-2.8202
	Nicaragua	723	-1.7530	-2.1070	-3.0734	-2.3111
	Costa Rica	954	-1.5174	-1.8278	-2.8039	-2.0497
Very High Income	Guatemala	2,194	-0.98367	-1.1926	-2.1284	-1.4349
	El Salvador	1,538	-1.1835	-1.4308	-2.3940	-1.6694
	Honduras	1,540	-1.1827	-1.4299	-2.3929	-1.6685
	Nicaragua	1,895	-1.0616	-1.2856	-2.2341	-1.5271
	Costa Rica	3,153	-0.81447	-0.99025	-1.8877	-1.2308
Total	Guatemala	311	-2.7194	-3.2472	-4.0635	-3.3434
	El Salvador	278	-2.8830	-3.4394	-4.2172	-3.5132
	Honduras	231	-3.1747	-3.7820	-4.4838	-3.8135
	Nicaragua	340	-2.5961	-3.1021	-3.9453	-3.2145
	Costa Rica	537	-2.0465	-2.4540	-3.3914	-2.6306

SOURCES: Column (1): Table 19.
Columns (2)-(4): Obtained through equations (4), (5), and (6), respectively, using figures from column (1).

Table 21. Direct Price Elasticities for Food, Central America[a]

Product	Guatemala	El Salvador	Honduras	Nicaragua	Costa Rica
Wheat (flour)	0.19	0.21	0.20	0.23	0.16
Sorghum (meal)	0.06	0.06	0.05	0.06	0.08
Rice	0.18	0.17	0.16	0.13	0.12
Maize	0.03	0.03	0.03	0.03	0.04
Root crops	0.15	0.14	0.13	0.16	0.08
Plantain	0.09	0.06	0.05	0.06	0.08
Guineos	0.09	0.06	0.05	0.06	0.08
Sugar	0.15	0.15	0.17	0.13	0.04
Lump molasses	0.06	0.06	0.05	0.06	0.08
Beans	0.12	0.12	0.11	0.07	0.12
Fresh vegetables	0.16	0.19	0.18	0.27	0.24
Fruit	0.21	0.30	0.20	0.18	0.18
Bananas	0.09	0.09	0.08	0.06	0.08
Beef	0.28	0.25	0.23	0.25	0.31
Pork meat	0.15	0.15	0.14	0.16	0.19
Poultry	0.30	0.29	0.27	0.31	0.38
Eggs	0.25	0.24	0.27	0.26	0.27
Seafood	0.30	0.17	0.21	0.19	0.23
Milk and derivatives	0.26	0.22	0.22	0.15	0.21
Vegetable oils	0.25	0.21	0.22	0.19	0.23
Animal fats	0.12	0.14	0.11	0.16	0.19
Coffee	0.15	0.24	0.19	0.16	0.19
Alcoholic beverages	0.28	0.33	0.26	0.30	0.33

[a]Estimated according to the average income levels and average values of the Frisch money coefficient in table 20 and the income elasticities in table 22.

Table 22 gives the expenditure elasticities that went into the computations of price elasticities. There were some additional problems in obtaining base-year values of product prices and per capita income levels, but these were resolved eventually.

D.   Validation of MOCA

The model has been designed to simulate actual (1970) behavior of the sector; therefore before using it for policy analysis, its predictive capacity must be tested. There are no formal tests of validation for mathematical programming models, but measures of goodness of fit can be used to check how closely the model predicts the levels of areas planted, production, prices, and levels of input use.

Table 22. Income Elasticities for Central America[a]

Product	Guatemala	El Salvador	Honduras	Nicaragua	Costa Rica
Wheat (flour)	0.60	0.70	0.70	0.70	0.40
Sorghum (meal)	0.20[b]	0.20	0.20[b]	0.20[b]	--
Rice	0.60	0.60	0.60	0.40	0.30
Maize	0.10	0.10	0.10	0.10	0.10
Root crops	0.50	0.50	0.50	0.50	0.20
Plantain	0.30	0.20	0.20	0.20	0.20
Guineos	0.30	0.20	0.20	0.20	0.20
Sugar	0.50	0.50	0.60	0.40	0.10
Lump molasses	0.20	0.20	0.20	0.20	0.20
Beans	0.40	0.40	0.40	0.20	0.30
Fresh vegetables	0.50	0.60	0.60	0.80	0.60
Fruits	0.60	0.70	0.60	0.40	0.40
Bananas	0.30	0.30	0.30[c]	0.20	0.20[d]
Beef	0.80	0.80	0.80	0.70	0.70
Pork meat	0.50	0.50	0.50	0.50	0.50
Poultry	1.00	1.00	1.00	1.00	1.00
Eggs	0.80	0.80	1.00	0.80	0.70
Seafood	1.00	0.60	0.80	0.60	0.60
Milk and deriva- tives	0.80	0.70	0.70	0.40	0.50
Vegetable oils	0.80	0.70	0.80	0.60	0.60
Animal fats	0.40	0.50	0.40	0.50	0.50
Coffee	0.50	0.80	0.70	0.50	0.50
Alcoholic beverages	0.80	1.00	0.70	0.80	0.80
Total, nonfood[e]	0.81	0.81	0.81	0.81	0.81

[a]Elasticities estimated for 1965.
[b]The elasticity for this product was assumed to be equal to the corresponding elasticity for El Salvador.
[c]Elasticity taken from Guatemala.
[d]Elasticity taken from Nicaragua.
[e]Elasticity for nonfood expenditures estimated by Musgrove for Colombia.

SOURCES: GAFICA, "Perspectivas para el Desarrollo y la Integración de la Agricultura Centroamericana," vol. 2, (Guatemala City: GAFICA, May 1974), pp. 57-61. Philip Musgrove, "Income and Spending of Urban Families in Latin America: The ECIEL Consumption Study," preliminary draft (Washington, D.C.: ECIEL, October 1975).

The model, as it has been mentioned before, is a demonstration version at this stage, and it contains a limited number of restrictions as well as behavioral specifications. Because of these limitations, the model is not expected to provide an adequate representation of the rural sector at the level of the "representative producer." However, because demand functions are specified on a national basis, and because foreign trade is restricted, the model can be expected to provide reasonable results in the aggregate and for each country as a whole.

To recapitulate, the basic conditions under which the model is solved for the base period are as follows:

(i) each producer group has a maximum amount of land available for cultivation equal to the total area planted in the base year;

(ii) each producer group can use up to a maximum amount of family labor, equal to the level available in the base year;

(iii) the availability of landless workers is equal to the total actual use (hired by medium and large farmers) in the base period;

(iv) there is only one technology for production of each crop, by each group of producers;

(v) no crop is restricted in its area planted;

(vi) purchased inputs are available in infinitely elastic supply; and

(vii) commodity demand functions are specified at the national level and producer and consumer prices are determined endogenously.

Table 23 gives the actual values used for the 1970 land and labor restrictions. In addition to the conditions listed above, the following treatment of trade was adopted to reflect trade policy and external market conditions:

(viii) there are upper bounds on the total imports that each country may purchase from within the region and also from outside the region, but imports by product and by CACM country are endogenous to the model; and

(ix) each product shipped out of the region faces an export upper bound by country, reflecting demand conditions and quotas in importing countries; these bounds are varied in the policy experiments.

MOCA was solved under these initial conditions and its predictive ability was tested in terms of areas planted, production levels, prices, and trade patterns. To measure goodness of fit, the percentage absolute deviation (PAD) between observed and predicted values was used.[21]

Table 24 gives the observed and predicted levels of production (in 1970) by crop and country. The percentage absolute deviation is less than 10 percent for all countries. Generally, the model overestimates production, except in Nicaragua where more crops are underestimated than overestimated.

Table 23.   Endowments of Labor and Cultivable Land in MOCA, 1970

	Guatemala	El Salvador	Honduras	Nicaragua	Costa Rica
	(thousand man-years)				
Family labor in:					
Group 1 farms	69.6	24.1	32.7	16.0	10.0
Group 2 farms	123.7	40.7	96.2	165.5	46.3
Landless labor	228.8	121.5	85.1	126.1	117.0
	(thousand hectares)				
Land held by:					
Group 1 farms	306.7	113.0	129.8	70.9	31.5
Group 2 farms	594.2	228.2	308.6	232.3	148.2
Group 3 farms	422.0	220.8	133.0	263.8	201.2

SOURCE: GAFICA, "Perspectivas para el Desarrollo y la Integración de la Argicultura Centroamericana," vol. 2 (Guatemala City: GAFICA, May 1974), tables J.4a-J.4d, pp. 265-69, and tables H.1.1-H.1.31.

The tendency toward overproduction in MOCA appears to be a consequence of underestimated costs of production, and possibly overestimated yields, and hence underestimated prices (tables G-1 through G-5, appendix G). Due to the relative inelasticity of the demand curves, the price errors are greater than the quantity errors in percentage terms. Management skills and miscellaneous cost items are omitted from the MOCA production structure, as is risk. There are known methods of incorporating producers' risk in this kind of model,[22] and future versions of MOCA will include it. In any event, it should be recognized that the present MOCA has a downward bias with respect to prices and an upward bias with respect to production.

Each reader can draw his own conclusions from these tables, but to the authors, the production fit of the model turned out to be somewhat better than expected. It is comparable to CHAC's degree of approximation to reality,[23] even though the latter model had many more activities to describe the production process.

On the trade side, not surprisingly, the fit is weaker, although MOCA captures the major tendencies within the region. Table 25 shows intraregional trade patterns, in MOCA and in actuality, for maize and beans. Similar comparisons for other commodities are given in appendix G.

In the case of trade in maize, MOCA's pattern of exports from Honduras to the other countries very much resembles the actual situation, with a significant underestimation only in the case of the exports to Costa Rica. Also for maize a (vertical) comparison of imports in Guatemala shows that the model represents very closely the trade pattern observed in the base period. A very accurate representation of imports is

Table 24. A Comparison of the MOCA and Actual Levels of Production, 1970
(thousand metric tons)

Costa Rica

Commodity	Observed	MOCA	Deviation
Maize	73,400	73,926	- 526
Rice	97,400	101,646	-4,246
Sorghum	11,500	14,792	-3,292
Beans	15,100	14,899	201
Banano (export)	717,300	829,130	-111,830
Banano (domestic)	117,000	113,991	3,009
Guineo	90,000	91,543	-1,543
Plantain	57,500	65,474	-7,974
Sugar cane	1,644,200	1,710,743	-66,543
Coffee	74,800	77,892	-3,092
Cotton	4,000	6,000	-2,000

Average absolute deviation 18,569
Percentage absolute deviation 7.038

El Salvador

Commodity	Observed	MOCA	Deviation
Maize	279,000	281,874	-2,874
Rice	37,600	34,841	2,759
Sorghum	218,100	126,980	1,120
Beans	26,300	27,516	-1,126
Banano (export)	43,000	43,889	- 889
Plantain	17,600	30,074	-12,474
Sugar cane	1,367,500	1,602,606	-235,106
Coffee	116,300	116,484	- 184
Cotton	127,900	128,778	- 878

Average absolute deviation 28,611
Percentage absolute deviation 12.014

Table 24 (Continued)

Guatemala

Commodity	Observed	MOCA	Deviation
Maize	709,200	713,613	-4,413
Rice	26,500	26,684	- 184
Sorghum	54,100	59,707	-5,607
Wheat	32,600	43,441	-10,841
Beans	55,500	54,521	979
Banano (export)	157,300	156,437	863
Banano (domestic)	35,500	35,500	0,000
Guineo	284,500	298,116	-13,616
Plantain	35,600	15,882	19,718
Sugar cane	2,658,600	2,411,512	247,088
Coffee	119,000	119,332	- 332
Cotton	151,500	152,884	-1,384

Average absolute deviation 25,419
Percentage absolute deviation 7.061

Honduras

Commodity	Observed	MOCA	Deviation
Maize	339,200	354,445	-15,245
Rice	6,500	26,057	-19,557
Sorghum	47,900	48,402	- 502
Wheat	1,000	3,864	-2,864
Beans	54,700	75,259	-20,559
Banano (export)	1,037,900	986,606	51,294
Guineo	67,900	68,246	- 346
Plantain	78,200	78,608	- 408
Sugar cane	1,240,200	1,083,066	157,134
Coffee	32,700	29,862	2,838
Cotton	9,200	10,413	-1,213

Average absolute deviation 27,724
Percentage absolute deviation 9.328

Table 24 (Continued)

Nicaragua

Commodity	Observed	MOCA	Deviation
Maize	231,300	228,693	2,607
Rice	123,600	106,649	16,951
Sorghum	76,900	74,307	2,593
Beans	55,700	49,410	6,290
Banano (export)	63,000	63,149	- 149
Guineo	148,800	173,783	-24,983
Plantain	60,100	68,792	-8,692
Sugar cane	1,371,700	1,502,222	-130,522
Coffee	37,100	26,471	10,629
Cotton	199,900	197,935	1,965
Average absolute deviation			20,538
Percentage absolute deviation			8.673

Table 25. Predicted and Actual Intraregional Trade in Maize and Beans, 1970
(thousand metric tons)

	To Costa Rica		El Salvador		Guatemala		Honduras		Nicaragua	
Product From	Actual	Model	Actual	Model	Actual	Model	Actual	Model	Actual	Model
Maize										
Costa Rica	-	-	-	-	-	-	-	-	-	-
El Salvador	-	1.9	-	-	13.51	10.1	-	-	-	.3
Guatemala	-	-	-	-	-	-	-	-	-	-
Honduras	16.7	5.0	-	-	2.85	5.3	-	-	3.9	3.0
Nicaragua	-	9.8	-	-	-	.2	-	-	-	-
Beans										
Costa Rica	-	-	-	-	-	-	-	-	-	-
El Salvador	-	1.0	-	-	-	2.1	-	-	-	-
Guatemala	-	-	-	-	-	-	-	-	-	-
Honduras	16.2	4.4	6.3	-	2.6	2.6	-	-	1.8	1.8
Nicaragua	-	5.0	-	1.6	-	.1	-	-	-	-

also achieved for El Salvador, Honduras, and Nicaragua. In the case of beans, import patterns for Guatemala, Honduras, and Nicaragua are represented with very high precision. In the case of Costa Rica and El Salvador, however, the upper bounds in imports are not reached and the import patterns are more diversified than in the base periods.

The final test of MOCA's validity concerns the wage rate charged for family field labor. Like CHAC, MOCA uses an exogenous wage rate for hired labor, corresponding to prevailing practices. The question is: What percentage of that market wage is approximately charged for the use of family labor to represent the opportunity cost of their time? This percentage is called the "reservation wage ratio."

This is the only parameter in the model which is estimated by "simulation" (to use that much-abused word). The method, if it can be dignified with that term, is to solve the model under different values of the reservation wage ratio in order to see which one gives the closest fit to reality. In the papers on CHAC, there is considerable discussion of this issue and the empirical conclusion.[24] Without repeating that here, it is worth noting that the CHAC reservation wage ratio turned out to be about 50 percent for irrigated zones and about 30 percent to 40 percent for rainfed zones. Values near 0 or 1.0 gave very poor fits.

Basically, the reservation wage ratio reflects the imperfect mobility of the farmer in the short run. To leave the farm for the city, say, after he has planted his crop would imply significant financial losses. This is even more true in irrigated areas, so it is reasonable to expect the reservation wage ratio to be higher there.

Table 26 gives the results of the reservation wage tests. Building on the CHAC experience, it was decided to explore more carefully the range of 0.3 to 0.5. It can be seen that there is not much to choose in this range; 0.4 is chosen by the barest of margins. On the other hand, values of 0 and 1.0 definitely distort the results.

The fact that the model is relatively insensitive to variations within the 0.3 to 0.5 range is reassuring, on the one hand, because this is a parameter whose value we cannot expect to know with much precision. On the other hand, it is slightly disturbing because it indicates that the model's aggregate annual treatment of labor inputs has made it relatively unresponsive to changes in the cost of production. Again, the more disaggregated SIECA version should give a different picture here.

E. Preliminary Policy Results

As it now stands, the preliminary MOCA model appears to constitute a reasonably good static representation of Central American agriculture. We reiterate, however, that it should be regarded as a demonstration version, and that a better version is in the process of development.

"Policy results" are presented in this section, not so much to provide concrete recommendations as to as suggest issues and broad qualitative results, and to demonstrate some of the uses to which this kind of programming model can be put.

Table 26. MOCA Results Under Variations in the
Reservation Wage Ratio

	Value of the Reservation Wage Ratio												
	0		0.30		0.35		0.40		0.45		0.50		1.00	
Country	A	B	A	B	A	B	A	B	A	B	A	B	A	B
Costa Rica	–	–	13.4	7.0	13.4	7.0	13.4	7.0	13.4	7.0	13.4	7.0	–	–
El Salvador	–	–	23.9	12.0	23.9	12.2	23.9	12.2	23.9	12.2	23.9	11.9	–	–
Guatemala	–	–	19.5	7.1	19.5	7.1	19.5	7.1	19.5	7.1	19.5	7.1	–	–
Honduras	–	–	27.0	9.3	26.4	9.2	26.3	9.2	27.1	9.2	27.3	9.4	–	–
Nicaragua	–	–	17.2	8.7	17.2	8.7	17.2	8.7	17.2	8.7	17.2	8.7	–	–

NOTE: Column A: Percentage absolute deviation of consumer prices.
Column B: Percentage absolute deviation of quantities produced.

Two sets of results are given: country-level results, for the case of Costa Rica as an example, and full regional results. To set up the Costa Rican model for stand-alone solutions, the simple expedient of fixing international trade variables at their MOCA base-solution values was used. The Costa Rican model then was addressed to two issues: measuring the supply response to price changes, and finding the price level which is necessary to attain national self-sufficiency in basic grains. The two are clearly related.

1. Country-Level Results for Costa Rica

One of the most appropriate uses of a linear programming model is the "estimation of supply response." The model is built using cross-section microeconomic information and behavioral assumptions that effectively define the conditions for supply response to economic policies and investment; it is a simple matter to trace out the supply response functions which are implicit in the model.

Given the static formulation of the model, these are equilibrium short-run supply response functions; equilibrium in the sense of allowing all adjustment processes to work themselves out but short run in the sense of excluding investment. They are called supply _response_ functions, instead of supply functions, because when one product's price is varied, the price and quantities of other products are allowed to vary also. In MOCA, most of the responsiveness arises from substitution of land area among crops.

The procedure for tracing out the functions consists of rotating the product demand functions rightward, one at a time, by varying the right-hand side value of the convex combination constraint,[25] as shown in figure 3. In this rotation, the intercept on the price axis is held constant. The original demand function is D_0, and the rotated functions are denoted D_1 to D_4. Arc elasticities of supply response are then calculated ex post from the price-quantity solutions (A, B, C, D, E in figure 3). The procedure was carried out for maize, rice, and beans. The rotations of the demand curve were by the following percentage amounts:

D_1 : 20 percent down from D_0,
D_2 : 20 percent up from D_0,
D_3 : 40 percent up from D_0, and
D_4 : 60 percent up from D_0.

Table 27 gives all the relevant quantity responses for changes in the rice demand curve, along with the corresponding changes in the rice price, defined as the price of polished rice. The quantities refer to the raw product at the farm gate. Figure 4 is a graphic presentation of the information in table 27.

Qualitatively, the following points are evident from these results: (i) the "elasticity" of supply response is not at all constant; indeed, why should it be except to facilitate econometric curve-fitting? (ii) at low prices of rice, one set of substitute crops tends to respond more (maize, beans) and at high prices another does (sorghum). This is the

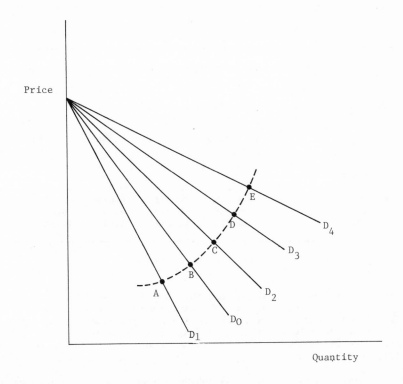

Figure 3. Tracing out an Implicit Supply Response Function

kind of multivariate information that can be extremely helpful in the course of setting price support policies.

Table 28 gives some computed arc elasticities, for the widest range of points explored in each case. Both direct and cross-price elasticities are shown, and three product demand functions were rotated in turn. The own-price elasticities of around +0.5 generally accord with other econometric estimates of short-run supply elasticities for grains.[26] The cross-elasticities show that some crops are more likely to drop in production than others are when prices of competing crops are raised. Beans, for example, happen to be more responsive in a negative direction than other crops, and sorghum is the least sensitive when the rice price is changed.

Finally, tables 29 and 30 apply this kind of analysis to the fairly typical concern of internal self-sufficiency, allowing trade variables to respond in this instance. It can be seen that for Costa Rica, a high-cost producer of grains, self-sufficiency in maize would come very dearly indeed. To analyze the consequences of attempting to achieve maize self-sufficiency, it was assumed that prices to consumers would not be changed,

Table 27. Supply Response Functions for Costa Rica, Under Variations
in the Rice Price

	Point on the Supply Response Function				
	A	B	C	D	E
Price of Rice (CA$/kg)	.1782	.1843	.1968	.2930	.4158
Quantities (000 metric tons)					
Rice	88.240	110.299	131.343	144.180	147.166
Maize	83.926	72.593	64.673	62.839	62.839
Beans	10.690	8.750	8.217	6.885	6.884
Sorghum	14.499	14.499	14.499	14.343	14.186

SOURCE: MOCA Solutions for Costa Rica (see text).

and hence a subsidy would be implied. It can be seen that the required
subsidy becomes enormous as self-sufficiency is approached, so in all
likelihood consumer price rises could not be prevented. But from table
30, it can be calculated that, at total self-sufficiency, even doubling
the price to consumers would not quite eliminate the net government out-
lays on this program.

These are, of course, illustrative figures, and they do not take into
account possibilities for expanding the amount of arable land or increasing yields. Nevertheless, it probably is true that maize self-sufficiency
is not a practical economic goal for Costa Rica.

2. Policy Results for All Five Countries

The actual recent patterns of CACM agricultural trade were discussed
in section B of this chapter. It will be recalled that there is a network of trade agreements which restricts intraregional trade, particularly
in basic grains. The basic solution of the model was designed with constraints reflecting these realities.

Further steps toward economic integration in Central America are
likely to depend on an adequate answer to the following question: What
will be the consequences of removing some of these trade restrictions,
by country and by socioeconomic groups within each country? To assist in
answering this question, we have designed two regionwide "policy experiments" with MOCA. The first consists of a solution under a 100 percent
increase in the limit on each country's grains imports from other Central
American countries. The second consists of an analysis of the incremental
gains from exports to the rest of the world. A large percentage increase

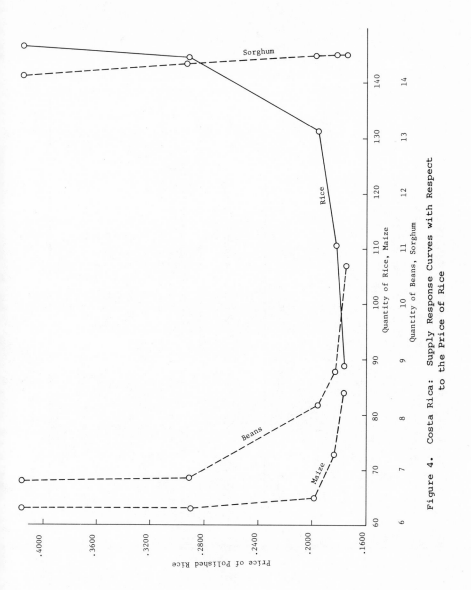

Figure 4. Costa Rica: Supply Response Curves with Respect to the Price of Rice

Table 28. Direct and Cross-Price Supply Response
Elasticities Generated by the Model, Costa Rica

	Quantity Response of:			
	Rice	Maize	Beans	Sorghum
Price change for:				
Rice	0.501	-0.188	-0.266	-0.017
Maize	-0.205	0.565	-0.490	-0.021
Beans	-0.048	-0.045	0.489	-0.009

Table 29. Production, Trade, and Degree of Self-Sufficiency at
Alternative Producer Prices of Maize, Costa Rica

Producer Price (CA$/kg)	Gross Production	Net Production	Imports (-) Exports (+)	Domestic Consumption	Coefficient of Self-Sufficiency
		(thousand metric tons)			
.080	62.69	59.55	-41.65	101.2	58.8
.093	75.12	72.03	-29.17	101.2	71.2
.133	95.83	91.04	-10.16	101.2	90.0
.258	115.79	110.00	+8.8	101.2	108.7

SOURCE: MOCA solutions.

Table 30. Other Consequences of Self-Sufficiency
in Maize, Costa Rica

(0) Producer Price	(1) Gross Income, Producers	(2) Gross Income, Intermediaries	(3) Maize Import Cost	(4) Total Cost of Maize Supply	(5) Average Cost of Supply	(6) Consumer Expenditure on Maize	(7) Maize Export Revenue	(8) Subsidy (-) or Tax (+) to Consumers	(9) Subsidy (-) on Exports	(10) Government Revenue (+), Expenditure (-) for this Policy	(11) Maize Import Tax (+)	(12) Balance of Payments
.080	5.02	6.49	3.33	14.84	0.147	16.19	-	+1.35	-	1.35	1.35	-3.35
.093	7.00	6.53	2.33	15.86	0.157	16.19	-	+0.33	-	0.33	0.33	2.33
.133	12.79	6.59	0.81	20.19	0.199	16.19	-	4.00	-	-4.00	0.18	0.51
.258	29.91	7.20	-	37.11	0.337	16.19	0.71	-17.95	-2.26	-20.21	-	+0.71

NOTES: Price and cost in CA$/kg and all other items in millions of
CA$.

(1) = (total production) x (producers' price).
(2) = (total production + imports) x (transformation cost
       coefficient).
(3) = (imports) x (import price).
(4) = (1) + (2) + (3).
(5) = (4) - [(net production) + (imports)].
(6) = (total consumption) x (consumers' price).
(7) = (exports) x (export price).
(8) = (total consumption) x (cost of supply - consumer
       price), or (8) = (4) - (6) - (7) - (9).
(9) = (exports) x (cost of supply - export price), or (9) =
       (4) - (6) - (7) - (8).
(10) = (8) + (9).
(11) = (imports) x (import tax).
(12) = (exports x export price) - (imports x import price).

SOURCE: MOCA solutions.

was hypothesized for intraregional trade in grains because the base is so small.

The projected consequences of these possible policies are discussed extensively. In particular, the distribution of income between countries and within countries is seen to be affected significantly.

Let us start with table 31 concerning the experiment on liberalization of intraregional trade. Liberalization leads to a significantly different allocation of production and trade although, by and large, the present tendencies toward importation and exportation are accentuated. Guatemala and Costa Rica become even greater importers than they were in the base periods, and Honduras, El Salvador, and Nicaragua increase their exports. Some exceptions: El Salvador increases its imports of beans and Nicaragua increases its imports of maize; also, Nicaragua switches from being a net importer to a net exporter of beans.

Looking back at tables 11 through 13, the changes in trade tend to follow from the observed price differentials, although transportation cost differentials also affect the results. For example, Nicaragua, not

Table 31.   MOCA Simulation of Intraregional Trade Liberalization in Basic Grains: Production and Trade Variables (thousand metric tons)

Country	Maize		Rice		Sorghum		Beans	
	A	B	A	B	A	B	A	B
Part I. Production								
Costa Rica	73.9	41.4	101.6	93.8	14.8	14.9	14.9	–
El Salvador	281.9	301.7	34.8	34.8	127.0	127.0	27.5	21.0
Guatemala	713.6	696.8	26.7	20.3	59.7	59.7	54.5	51.8
Honduras	354.4	390.0	26.1	–	48.2	75.3	75.3	82.8
Nicaragua	228.7	226.4	150.5	106.6	74.3	74.3	49.4	67.5
Central America	1,652.5	1,656.3	297.6	297.4	324.0	324.0	221.6	223.1
Part II. Imports (+) and Exports (–)								
Rest of the world	–15.10	–15.1	+ 4.8	+ 4.8	–	–	–	–
Costa Rica	+31.80	+63.6	+ 5.3	+ 5.3	–	–	+16.2	+32.4
El Salvador	–13.15	–32.0	– .2	– .2	–	–	+ 6.3	+12.6
Guatemala	+16.00	+32.0	+ 4.1	+ 8.2	–	–	+ 2.6	+ 5.2
Honduras	–23.45	–56.2	–	+15.1	–	–	–26.9	–34.7
Nicaragua	+ 3.90	+ 7.7	–14.0	–38.5	–	–	+ 1.8	–15.5

NOTES: Column A: basic MOCA solution values.
              Column B: MOCA solutions under trade liberalization.

El Salvador, increases its beans exports to Costa Rica, even though El Salvador is the lower-cost producer in this case. Geographical proximity makes the difference. Honduras is an even-lower-cost producer, so its beans exports to neighboring El Salvador are increased.

So far there is not too much that is surprising in the model; in the main it helps by attaching magnitudes to directions of changes which could be guessed by knowledgeable persons. In terms of prices (table 32), there are countervailing effects. Costa Rica's increased import bill is compensated for, in a sense, by lower prices to its consumers. The reverse holds for Honduras, and for the other countries this volume of additional trade is not sufficient to affect prices.

From the foregoing, it is clear that Costa Rican consumers would benefit from trade liberalization. Whether farmers would gain or lose depends on whether price effects are offset by quantity effects. The consequences for the rural income distribution are shown in table 33, and there it is evident that the lower prices to Honduran producers are more than offset by increases in production for export. Costa Rican producers suffer in net terms, and the net positions of producers in other countries are relatively unchanged (last column of table 33, part I).

Within countries, the picture varies. In Costa Rica, liberalization improves the rural income distribution. The large-scale farmers, and to some extent the medium-scale ones, are the sellers of grains--which are more susceptible to mechanization and hence to larger-scale cultivation

Table 32. MOCA Simulation of Intraregional Trade Liberalization
in Basic Grains: Consumer Prices
(CA$ per kilogram)

Country	Maize		Rice		Sorghum		Beans	
	A	B	A	B	A	B	A	B
Costa Rica	.126	.106	.189	.162	.071	.060	.369	.209
El Salvador	.069	.069	.150	.150	.063	.063	.255	.255
Guatemala	.095	.095	.214	.214	.060	.060	.196	.196
Honduras	.057	.070	.113	.119	.062	.073	.150	.171
Nicaragua	.130	.130	.101	.101	.058	.058	.185	.185

NOTES: Column A: basic MOCA solution values.
Column B: MOCA solution under trade liberalization.

Table 33. MOCA Simulation of Intraregional Trade Liberalization in Basic Grains: Income Distribution (million $CA)

Country	Landless Laborers		Small Farms		Medium Farms		Large Farms		Total	
	A	B	A	B	A	B	A	B	A	B
I. Total Group Incomes										
Costa Rica	35.29	30.01	5.73	5.01	19.96	16.35	5.49	1.01	66.47	52.40
El Salvador	28.95	29.19	5.57	5.57	12.62	12.62	4.41	4.42	51.54	51.79
Guatemala	27.67	26.88	14.74	14.74	27.70	27.71	10.42	10.42	80.54	79.75
Honduras	16.70	16.46	8.06	9.95	9.85	14.75	5.85	9.17	40.46	50.33
Nicaragua	30.73	30.98	4.45	4.45	8.09	8.82	9.14	9.13	52.40	53.38
Central America	139.32	133.52	38.55	39.72	78.22	80.25	35.31	34.15	291.40	287.64
II. Income Shares										
Costa Rica	53.1	57.3	8.6	9.6	30.0	31.2	8.3	1.9	100.0	100.0
El Salvador	56.2	56.4	10.8	10.8	24.5	24.3	8.5	8.5	100.0	100.0
Guatemala	34.4	33.7	18.3	18.5	34.4	34.7	12.9	13.5	100.0	100.0
Honduras	41.3	32.7	19.9	19.8	24.3	29.3	14.5	18.2	100.0	100.0
Nicaragua	58.6	58.0	8.5	8.4	15.5	16.5	17.4	17.1	100.0	100.0
Central America	47.8	46.4	13.3	13.8	26.8	27.9	12.1	11.9	100.0	100.0

NOTES: Column A: basic MOCA solution values.
Column B: MOCA solution under trade liberalization.

than are other crops. The reduction of production on larger farms adversely affects the employment and incomes of the poorest, the hired laborers, but on the whole the rural Costa Rican income distribution is made
more equal. In Honduras, it is made less equal, but all farmer groups
benefit in absolute terms.

Although large farms, the principal employers of hired labor, expand
their output considerably in Honduras, the incomes of landless laborers
drop somewhat under liberalization. This consequence arises from product
substitution effects: the increased Honduran exports are maize and beans
which are considerably less labor intensive than the rice which they
displace. Landless workers also suffer somewhat in Guatemala, but there
it is because total production drops.

By now it is fair to say that the model is telling us some things
which we could scarcely have known otherwise, but nonetheless the results
appear plausible. It seems evident that there are strong grounds for
some compensatory schemes to accompany trade liberalization.

To summarize at a more aggregate level, the costs and benefits of
expanded intraregional trade are summarized in table 34. The groups
which gain are (i) producers in Honduras, (ii) by a smaller margin, producers in Nicaragua, and (iii) consumers in Costa Rica. The losers are
(i) consumers in Honduras, (ii) producers in Costa Rica, and (iii) landless laborers in Costa Rica. Among countries, trade liberalization can
be said to be redistributional: the poorest countries gain at the expense
of the richest. But nevertheless, the poorest group in Costa Rica is one
of the losers. They gain partial but not full compensation through lower
consumer prices.

For the final piece of analysis, the dual solution of the model was
analyzed with respect to the constraints on exports to the rest of the
world. The shadow price on an export upper bound signifies the gain to
the objective function of one additional unit of exports of that product.
MOCA's objective function is the sum of Marshallian surpluses (consumer
and producer surplus), so it leads to a solution which maximizes "social
welfare" in the sense of competitive equilibrium. Hence the shadow prices
tell us the gains in "welfare," under this definition, from an additional
ton of exports.

Since tons of different products are not directly comparable, we
have chosen to express the shadow prices as ratios to the export prices
(table 35). For example, a shadow price/export price ratio of 40 percent implies that the social cost of producing another unit for export
is only 60 percent of the export price. These computations take into
account the fact that additional exports may mean fewer sales--and hence
higher prices--on the domestic market.

In table 35, the crops are grouped into four sets, and within each
set they are listed in rank order, according to the value of the shadow
price/export price ratio. It is apparent from the table that there are
not many easy generalizations as far as the crops are concerned; by and
large the results depend on location as well as crop. However, the
following rough patterns emerge:

Table 34. Aggregate Impacts of Trade Liberalization
Within Central America

Country	Total Producers' Income			Landless Laborers' Income			Consumer Price Index
	A	B	Index	A	B	Index	B
Costa Rica	31.18	22.37	71.7	35.29	30.01	85.0	74.2
El Salvador	22.60	22.61	100.0	28.95	29.19	100.8	100.0
Guatemala	52.86	52.87	100.0	27.67	26.88	97.1	100.0
Honduras	23.76	33.87	142.6	16.70	16.46	98.6	108.5
Nicaragua	21.68	22.40	103.3	30.73	30.98	100.8	100.0
Central America	152.08	156.12	101.3	139.32	133.52	94.4	-

NOTES: Column A represents the base solution values from MOCA.
Column B represents the MOCA solution under intraregional trade
liberalization.
The consumer price index is defined to be 100.0 for each country
in the base solution.
Incomes are stated in million CA$.
The income index is column B divided by column A.

(i) Export bananas and rice exports are highly profitable regardless of location (with one exception).

(ii) Cotton fiber is almost as universally profitable for export.

(iii) Plantain bananas are the less profitable item; in fact, in
Guatemala the ratio is slightly negative, implying that they are exported
only with a slight subsidy.[27]

(iv) The returns to extraregional sugar exports are highly variable according to country of origin, and coffee returns are variable also.

(v) No country has a comparative advantage with respect to its
Central American neighbors in traditional exports in general. However,
by crop there are significant differences across countries.

Comparing table 35 with table 7 of section B, it can be seen that
the comparative advantage rankings correspond roughly, but only roughly,
to historical changes in export shares by crop. Of the group I crops in
table 35, six out of nine increased their export share over the 1963-65
to 1970-72 period (including rice, which is not shown in table 7). Except for cotton, six of six increased their shares. In groups II and III,
shares of most crops decreased over time. It would appear that MOCA's
production coefficients are unduly high, or the yields are too low, as
in the case of cotton.

Table 35. Ranking of Crops by Comparative Advantage
in Extraregional Exports

Crop	Country

Group I. Social Returns Greater than 70 Percent of Export Price

Rice	Nicaragua
Cotton fiber	Honduras
Export bananas	Honduras
Sugar	Guatemala
Export bananas	Guatemala
Export bananas	Costa Rica
Cotton fiber	Nicaragua
Rice	El Salvador
Cotton fiber	El Salvador

Group II. Social Returns 40 Percent to 70 Percent of Export Price

Coffee	Honduras
Sugar	Costa Rica
Cotton fiber	Guatemala
Coffee	Costa Rica
Coffee	El Salvador
Sugar	El Salvador
Cotton fiber	Costa Rica

Group III. Social Returns 20 Percent to 40 Percent of Export Price

Coffee	Nicaragua
Plantain	Costa Rica
Coffee	Guatemala

Group IV. Social Returns Less than 20 Percent of Export Price

Sugar	Nicaragua
Sugar	Honduras
Export bananas	Nicaragua
Plantain	Honduras
Plantain	Guatemala

It is natural to ask whether there is any simple explanation of the
cross-country differences in table 35. Recall that we are dealing with
comparative advantage at the margin, and not on the average. And that
depends principally on the opportunity cost of land, the price on the
domestic market, and the way in which technologies differ across farm-
size groups. As an attempt to cut through this complex network of inter-
actions, we have compiled the ratios of labor inputs per unit of output
for the traditional crops listed in table 35. These ratios are entered
in table 36, along with the country comparative advantage rankings (by
crop) from table 35.

Table 36. Labor Input per Kilogram of Yield, Traditional Exports
(man-days per kilogram per hectare)

Country	Rice	Cotton	Export Bananas*	Sugar	Coffee	Plantain
Guatemala	.060	.073 (4)	.011 (2)	.0024 (1)	.320 (5)	.027 (3)
El Salvador	.027 (2)	.057 (3)	n.a.	.0047 (3)	.172 (3)	.016
Honduras	.080	.052 (1)	.013 (1)	.0057 (5)	.328 (1)	.015 (2)
Nicaragua	.037 (1)	.081 (2)	.019 (4)	.0057 (4)	.377 (4)	.013
Costa Rica	.067	.076*(5)	.011 (3)	.0036 (2)	.915 (2)	.016 (1)

NOTES: The fractional numbers represent labor inputs per unit of output on medium-scale farms, except where asterisked to indicate large-scale farms.

The numbers in parentheses represent country rank, for that crop, in table 35 (that is, an index of comparative advantage).

For rice and sugar, relative labor costs (or rather, their inverse) explain the comparative advantage rankings quite well. On the other hand, they do not explain the rankings for the other crops.

It may be suggested that total unit costs would constitute a better simple index than labor input. But that route leads to difficulties: How are land and family labor valued? Their value is their opportunity cost in alternative uses, that is, in the cultivation of other crops. This effect is captured by the programming model and figures importantly in the model's comparative advantage rankings. It therefore appears that this is an area where a full-sector model provides information that cannot be obtained by simple calculation of costs of production.

Chapter 7

NOTES

1. At a later stage, when more adequate data are available, risk aversion will be added to the list of behavioral characteristics.

2. For descriptions of CHAC and its uses, see L. M. Bassoco and R. D. Norton, "A Quantitative Approach to Agricultural Policy Planning," Annals of Economic and Social Measurement 4 (October-November 1975): pp. 571-94; and J. H. Duloy and R. D. Norton, "CHAC: A Programming Model of Mexican Agriculture," in L. Goreux and A. Manne, eds. Multi-Level Planning: Case Studies in Mexico, (Amsterdam: North-Holland, 1973), chapter IV-1. The equations for MOCA are given in the appendix.

3. All rates of growth in this section were calculated for the 1963-72 period, taking the 1963-65 average and the 1970-72 average as the beginning and the end of the period, respectively. Exports and imports are measured by changes in current U.S. dollar values.

4. With so many products, the number of potentially non-zero supply cross-elasticities is very large, and hence the available time series data would not offer sufficient degrees of freedom to be able to estimate the supply functions econometrically.

5. This is the central methodological aspect of MOCA. In this respect, it follows the Mexican model, CHAC. For a more complete discussion of methodological issues, see Duloy and Norton, "CHAC: A Programming Model"; and "Prices and Incomes in Linear Programming Models," American Journal of Agricultural Economics 57 (November 1975): pp. 591-600.

6. When the economic cost of trade barriers is included in a broader definition of price, then it is possible to say that the MOCA solution always equalizes prices.

7. See Duloy and Norton, "Prices and Incomes."

8. Ibid.

9. T. Takayama and G. Judge, Spatial and Temporal Price and Allocation Models, (Amsterdam: North-Holland, 1971).

10. GAFICA, "Perspectivas para el Desarrollo y la Integración de la Agricultura Centroamericana," (Guatemala City: GAFICA, May 1974).

11. Duloy and Norton, "Prices and Incomes."

12. R. Frisch, "A Complete Scheme for Computing All Direct and Cross Demand Elasticities in a Model with Many Sectors," Econometrica 27 (1959).

13. In some circumstances, a slightly weaker assumption can be inserted for some of the pairs of goods.

14. An evident exception is the case of clear complements, such as coffee and cream.

15. This work is cited in Frisch, "A Complete Scheme."

16. A. de Janvry, J. Bieri, and A. Nuñez, "Estimation of Demand Parameters under Consumer Budgeting: An Application to Argentina," American Journal of Agricultural Economics 54 (August 1972): pp. 422-30.

17. C. Lluch and R. Williams, "Cross-Country Patterns in Frisch's Money Flexibility Coefficient," unpublished draft (Washington, D.C.: Development Research Center, World Bank, September 1973).

18. De Janvry et al., "Estimation of Demand Parameters."

19. P. Pinstrup-Anderson, N. Ruiz de Londoño, and E. Hoover, "The Impact of Increasing Food Supply on Human Nutrition: Implications for Commodity Priorities in Agricultural Research and Policy," American Journal of Agricultural Economics 58 (May 1976): pp. 131-42.

20. W. Candler and D. Norton, "Linear Transformations in Mathematical Programming," Discussion paper no. 21 (Washington, D.C.: Development Research Center, World Bank, January 1977).

21. That is:

$$PAD = \frac{\sum\limits_{i=i}^{n} \left| x_i^o - x_i^p \right|}{\sum\limits_{i=i}^{n} x_i^o},$$

where:

x_i^o = observed value of the variable, product i, and

x_i^p = predicted value of the variable, product i.

22. P. B. R. Hazell and P. L. Scandizzo, "Competitive Demand Structures under Risk in Agricultural Linear Programming Models," American Journal of Agricultural Economics 56(2) (May 1974).

23. L. M. Bassoco and R. D. Norton, "Una Metodología Quantitativa de la Programación Agrícola," Demografía y Economía 9 (1975): pp. 432-81.

24. See, for example, L. M. Bassoco, R. D. Norton, and J. S. Silos, Appraisal of Irrigation Projects and Related Policies and Investments," Water Resources Research 19 (December 1974): p. 1073.

25. Duloy and Norton, "Prices and Incomes."

26. See, for example, J. R. Behrman, Supply Response in Underdeveloped Agriculture (Amsterdam: North-Holland, 1968).

27. This result may well reflect an error in model data, but in qualitative terms it seems safe to say that plantain bananas are less profitable in export than the other crops.

The Comparison of Prices, Purchasing Power, and Real Products in Central America

Jorge Salazar-Carrillo
and Jorge Bortscheff

This chapter presents empirical estimates of the price levels in the member countries of the Central American Common Market and, correspondingly, of their respective purchasing power parity exchange rates. Appendix A sets forth the methodology underlying these estimates, as well as details about the data used.

On the basis of the results concerning comparative prices, the gross domestic products (GDP) of the five Central American countries are compared in real terms. The aggregate and sectoral results are analyzed for implications concerning the integration experience and possible policy changes suggested by the empirical evidence.

All of the results refer to the period of November 1973. In addition, the research was repeated at the end of 1974 and at the beginning of 1975 in Guatemala and El Salvador, respectively.[1] However, the analysis of this chapter refers only to the November 1973 survey because of the objective of comparing all five Central American countries. The information concerning prices and production or expenditure covers the following areas of GDP: private consumption, public consumption, and gross domestic investment. In addition to these sectoral levels the results are presented at the aggregate level of GDP. Furthermore, individual categories within the three broad areas are examined separately, if they represent an important part of total product. For example, within private consumption separate results are examined for the categories of food, clothing, and textiles.[2]

The various price indices discussed in appendix A have been computed using the price data collected in the five countries. For purposes of

NOTE: The authors thank Ricardo Lira and Molly Wainer at The Brookings Institution for important supporting research. Special thanks go to George P. Montalván, of the Organization of American States, for preparation of the results for the machinery and equipment sectors. This study was made possible through the cooperation of the statistical and census offices of the Central American countries, and the Central Banks of Honduras and Nicaragua. Finally, the assistance of the Department of Statistics and Computation of SIECA is gratefully acknowledged.

analysis in this chapter, the Walsh index is the basic alternative used. This index is the most satisfactory for simultaneous comparisons among a number of countries (rather than for comparisons between only two countries, for which the Paasche, Laspeyres, or Fisher indices may be used). The version of the Walsh index used here is that with geometric weights.

A matrix of these Central American price indices, with each one of the Central American countries used alternatively as the base, appears in table 1. Given the circularity of the Walsh indices, the comparisons are transitive and thus identical no matter what base country is used. Nevertheless, in order to facilitate analysis of the indices, this chapter will concentrate on the column of the matrix in which Guatemala is used as the base country.

Table 1 indicates that El Salvador has the lowest level of prices for private consumption in Central America, and Nicaragua, the highest. Honduras has a level of prices slightly lower than that of Nicaragua, but more than 6 percent higher than that of Guatemala, the base country. Costa Rica has prices somewhat lower than Guatemala.

It must be clear that in order to make these comparisons, the prices of all the countries have to be expressed in terms of a common currency during the process of constructing the index. In this case all currencies were converted into Guatemalan quetzales, using for that conversion the official exchange rates prevailing in Central America in November 1973. In the case of Costa Rica, the rate of exchange is a weighted average of the two rates which were in force in this period, supplied by the Central Bank of that country. On the basis of these rates the economic sectors of each one of the countries involved make their decisions

Table 1. Matrix of Price Indices in Private Consumption,
Central America, November 1973[a]

	Base Country				
	Costa Rica	El Salvador	Guatemala	Honduras	Nicaragua
Other country					
Costa Rica	1.00000	1.10208	0.97555	0.92349	0.82081
El Salvador	0.90737	1.00000	0.88518	0.83795	0.74478
Guatemala	1.02506	1.12971	1.00000	0.94664	0.84138
Honduras	1.08285	1.19339	1.05637	1.00000	0.88881
Nicaragua	1.21831	1.34268	1.18852	1.12510	1.00000

[a]Each column of the matrix offers equivalent results, but with the country which appears at the head of each respective column as base. The rows show the index of the country which heads the row, with respect to all the possible bases.

concerning what they are going to export and import, and these rates are also those that the authorities must use in the construction of international price indices, especially concerning integration plans.

In order to carry out a more detailed analysis of the price levels for the total of goods and services in private consumption, it is necessary to consider their structure. This implies the construction and examination of Central American price indices for the principal categories of goods and services in private consumption.

Taking Guatemala as a base, considering that it has an intermediate price level within the Central American area, one observes that, in general, food products have lower prices in El Salvador and are more expensive in Nicaragua. (See table 2.) The dispersion of prices is relatively small, with a coefficient of variation of 0.122. Both Honduras and Costa Rica have price levels much lower than Guatemala in this category.

Table 2. Matrix of Price Indices for Food Products, Central America, November 1973

	Base Country				
	Costa Rica	El Salvador	Guatemala	Honduras	Nicaragua
Other country					
Costa Rica	1.00000	1.15990	0.95684	1.04367	0.83443
El Salvador	0.86214	1.00000	0.82493	0.89980	0.71940
Guatemala	1.04511	1.21222	1.00000	1.09075	0.87207
Honduras	0.95816	1.11136	0.91680	1.00000	0.79951
Nicaragua	1.9842	1.39005	1.14669	1.25076	1.00000

In table 3 the same type of price matrix appears, this time referring to beverages. Although consumer behavior differs concerning beverages and food, the ordering of the countries for beverages is quite similar to that of the previous category. The similarity is probably attributable to the fact that the agricultural sector provides the main inputs for both product groups, although their industrial processes differ. The results for the category of tobacco repeat the same general pattern of relative price levels across countries, as shown in table 4.

Considering the category for clothing and textiles, it is notable that Guatemala's relative position is substantially different from that found in the previous categories. (See table 5.) In clothing and textiles, El Salvador has the lowest prices, although these are almost equal to those of Guatemala. By comparison, the prices of Honduras and Nicaragua are relatively high. The dispersion in this category, although it could be considered low if we compare it with that found in similar studies in the Latin American Free Trade Association (LAFTA), is well above that of the two previous categories.[3]

Table 3. Matrix of Price Indices for Beverages,
Central America, November 1973

| | Base Country | | | | |
	Costa Rica	El Salvador	Guatemala	Honduras	Nicaragua
Other country					
Costa Rica	1.00000	1.07839	0.88453	1.17522	0.83874
El Salvador	0.92731	1.00000	0.82023	1.08979	0.77777
Guatemala	1.13055	1.21917	1.00000	1.32865	0.94824
Honduras	0.85090	0.91760	0.75264	1.00000	0.71369
Nicaragua	1.19225	1.28572	1.05458	1.40117	1.00000

Table 4. Matrix of Price Indices for Tobacco,
Central America, November 1973

| | Base Country | | | | |
	Costa Rica	El Salvador	Guatemala	Honduras	Nicaragua
Other country					
Costa Rica	1.00000	1.00870	0.83320	1.01022	0.76433
El Salvador	0.99137	1.00000	0.82601	1.00151	0.75774
Guatemala	1.20019	1.21064	1.00000	1.21246	0.91734
Honduras	0.98988	0.99849	0.82477	1.00000	0.75660
Nicaragua	1.30833	1.31972	1.09010	1.32171	1.00000

Table 5. Matrix of Price Indices for Clothing and Textiles,
Central America, November 1973

| | Base Country | | | | |
	Costa Rica	El Salvador	Guatemala	Honduras	Nicaragua
Other country					
Costa Rica	1.00000	1.13637	1.09938	0.80091	0.72784
El Salvador	0.87999	1.00000	0.96745	0.70480	0.64050
Guatemala	0.90960	1.03364	1.00000	0.72851	0.66204
Honduras	1.24857	1.41884	1.37266	1.00000	0.90876
Nicaragua	1.37392	1.56128	1.51047	1.10039	1.00000

In the category containing fuels, electricity, and water, the relative price indices (with Guatemala as a base) are quite different from
those before, as can be seen in table 6. Not only does the ordering of
the countries change substantially but also the dispersion or variation
of index numbers from country to country is much greater.

Table 6. Matrix of Price Indices for Utilities and Fuel,
Central America, November 1973

	Base Country				
	Costa Rica	El Salvador	Guatemala	Honduras	Nicaragua
Other country					
Costa Rica	1.00000	0.60418	0.68729	0.43518	0.55868
El Salvador	1.65514	1.00000	1.13757	0.72028	0.92469
Guatemala	1.45498	0.87907	1.00000	0.64417	0.81287
Honduras	2.29792	1.38835	1.57934	1.00000	1.28379
Nicaragua	1.78994	1.08144	1.23021	0.77894	1.00000

This surely is due in great part to the fact that, in contrast to the
previous categories, trade in this type of goods and services generally
does not go beyond national borders. In table 6, note especially the very
low level of prices in Costa Rica, which suggest the possible existence
of subsidies for these products which are usually of a public nature in
that country. We should note that the prices in Honduras are very high
in this category, surpassing even these prices in Nicaragua.

As explained in appendix A, the comparison of prices concerning housing
services is based upon a survey of the middle third of the distribution
of families according to income, in each one of the capital cities of the
Central American countries. The survey had as its objective the acquisition of information on rents and on a series of important characteristics
about the residences. The imputed rents for those houses inhabited by
the actual owners were not investigated, given the difficulty of obtaining this type of data and the growing conviction of the investigators in
this field that the movement of these prices, whether it be across time
or countries, is parallel to that of the rented residences.

A detailed examination of the values of the characteristics of the
houses in each of the Central American countries shows that their main
patterns are very similar. It was verified that the major differences
occur in the variables of constructed area and total area (including patio
and garden) in square meters.

On the basis of all this information hedonic regressions are estimated which permit the comparisons of the same services provided by
housing in each Central American country. The price indices which appear

in table 7 are based upon the results of these comparisons using the regression method. It is interesting to verify that El Salvador presents the lowest prices, followed by Guatemala.

In regard to the rest of the countries, the rents in Costa Rica were the highest, being almost 15 percent higher than those in Guatemala. On the other hand, the rents in Honduras and Nicaragua have levels almost equal to those of Guatemala. The dispersion in rents across the region is not very great if one considers that this is one of the goods not traded between countries. (The coefficient of variation is 0.159.) This result suggests that in an area which has been experiencing a process of integration, the mechanisms of price equalization affect not only the tradable goods.[4]

Table 7. Matrix of Price Indices of Services Provided by
Housing Units, Central America, November 1973

	Base Country				
	Costa Rica	El Salvador	Guatemala	Honduras	Nicaragua
Other country					
Costa Rica	1.00000	1.58553	1.14497	1.13018	1.13164
El Salvador	0.63070	1.00000	0.72214	0.71281	0.71373
Guatemala	0.87339	1.38478	1.00000	0.98709	0.98836
Honduras	0.88481	1.40290	1.01308	1.00000	1.00129
Nicaragua	0.88367	1.40109	1.01177	0.99871	1.00000

A group of very important products is that of durable consumer goods, given the possibilities of growing industrial specialization in the production of these goods by some of the countries in the area, with a consequent substitution for imports from their countries. Clearly, Guatemala seems to have the lowest prices in this category (see table 8), perhaps in part due to its large market which assures Guatemala definite economies of scale (when these goods are produced in the region) as well as advantageous import facilities (for the portion of supply imported from outside the region).

By contrast, it is also notable that there are very high prices in this category in Honduras. In general, the dispersion or variation of prices across the countries is greater in this group of goods, which suggests that intrazonal trade of these goods is relatively limited.

Contrasted with the behavior of prices described earlier, the variation in price index for the group on nondurable goods is quite small (table 9). In this type of product, which appears to have substantial regional trade, Costa Rica seems to have a certain price advantage. Surprisingly, the prices in El Salvador are higher than those of Honduras.

Table 8. Matrix of Price Indices for Durable Consumer Goods,
Central America, November 1973

| | Base Country | | | | |
	Costa Rica	El Salvador	Guatemala	Honduras	Nicaragua
Other country					
Costa Rica	1.00000	1.14713	1.52260	0.93264	1.03573
El Salvador	0.87173	1.00000	1.32731	0.81301	0.90289
Guatemala	0.65677	0.75340	1.00000	0.61253	0.68024
Honduras	1.07222	1.22999	1.63257	1.00000	1.11054
Nicaragua	0.96549	1.10755	1.47006	0.90046	1.00000

Table 9. Matrix of Price Indices for Nondurable Consumer Goods,
Central America, November 1973

| | Base Country | | | | |
	Costa Rica	El Salvador	Guatemala	Honduras	Nicaragua
Other country					
Costa Rica	1.00000	0.67151	0.94272	0.71410	0.81470
El Salvador	1.48917	1.00000	1.40388	1.06342	1.21323
Guatemala	1.06075	0.71231	1.00000	0.75748	0.86420
Honduras	1.40035	0.94036	1.32016	1.00000	1.14087
Nicaragua	1.22744	0.82424	1.15714	0.87652	1.00000

After Costa Rica, Guatemala has the lowest prices of consumer nondurables suggesting possible production advantages in these as well as in durable goods.

Table 10 shows the Central American price index for private consumption services. These range from transportation to domestic services and in general are nontradable. They are susceptible, nevertheless, to the competition produced by the mobility of factors of production across countries. Taking this fact into consideration, the finding that there is one of the lowest dispersions of prices in this category is of particular significance. (The coefficient of variation is 0.165.) This result seems to indicate that the degree of movement of workers and capital across Central American borders is much greater than one might assume.

Table 10. Matrix of Price Indices for Services,
Central America, November 1973

	Base Country				
	Costa Rica	El Salvador	Guatemala	Honduras	Nicaragua
Other country					
Costa Rica	1.00000	1.09340	0.85231	0.85657	0.71378
El Salvador	0.91457	1.00000	0.77950	0.78339	0.65280
Guatemala	1.17328	1.28287	1.00000	1.00499	0.83746
Honduras	1.16745	1.27649	0.99503	1.00000	0.83330
Nicaragua	1.40100	1.53186	1.19409	1.20005	1.00000

As would be expected, El Salvador has the lowest prices in services. This surely is determined fundamentally by the relatively low levels of wages and salaries that prevail in El Salvador as a consequence of population pressure and high density. On the other hand, the prices of these services are very high in Nicaragua, coinciding with the relative price levels in this country in private consumption as a whole. It is also notable that Costa Rica possesses one of the lowest price levels in services, suggesting that Costa Rican salaries are not markedly higher than those in the rest of the region.

Returning to overall price levels for private consumption of goods and services, the results for Nicaragua are particularly noteworthy (table 1). The prices in this country are close to 20 percent higher than those in the other Central American countries, with the exception of Honduras. This divergence tends to make it more difficult for Nicaragua to sell to the other countries in the region and makes it easier for these countries to offer their goods on the Nicaraguan market. It also means that in real terms, considering the purchasing power of the cordoba, Nicaragua's level of relative development is lower than implied by per capita income figures converted at the official exchange rate. Similar observations apply to Honduras, although to a much lesser degree.

A. Price Levels in the Public Consumption Sector

Comparisons of the prices of public consumption follow the same procedures as those for private consumption, utilizing the same formula of Walsh's index in order to calculate Central American price indices. Governmental services pose the special problem that market prices do not exist for the great majority of those services supplied by the governmental agencies. Therefore, the comparisons are based on the costs of providing a similar amount of these services. According to the classification followed in the national accounts, these costs are of two basic types: the wages and salaries paid to the public administration, and the goods and services bought by the government. Thus, wages and salaries paid to public functionaries in each of the Central American countries will be compared within the same categories of jobs and duties. Also comparisons are made for the prices of goods and services, defined in an equivalent form for categories of expenditure typically comprising the basket of goods and services bought by the various Central American governments.

It is assumed that the sum of these costs is equivalent to the price at which the public services would be sold by each one of the governments, given that they do not seek a profit.[5] And, as the components of cost are defined in identical form, the composite product also will be equal.

Although the special characteristics of this sector require different solutions, one must not lose sight of the fact that the importance of the sector within total expenditure in the GDP is relatively small. In general, public consumption expense is slightly above 10 percent in the Central American national accounts. Of this amount, the majority of the costs correspond to wages and salaries paid to public officials. Specifically in the case of Central America, nearly 85 percent of public consumption expense goes to the payment of wages and salaries to public employees, leaving approximately 15 percent for public purchases of goods and services.

In table 11 the comparisons of public consumption costs are presented. These are shown in aggregated form given that the importance of the public consumption sector, in contrast to the private consumption sector, does not merit a more detailed classification.

Using Guatemala as a base, it is confirmed that the costs of the public services in that country are the highest in the Central American area, while those of El Salvador are the lowest. Honduras has public services costs which are only higher than those in El Salvador. Finally, Costa Rica and Nicaragua have cost levels lower only than those of Guatemala.

Table 11. Matrix of Price Indices in the Public Consumption Sector, Central America, November 1973

| | Base Country | | | | |
	Costa Rica	El Salvador	Guatemala	Honduras	Nicaragua
Other country					
Costa Rica	1.0000	1.2879	0.8736	1.1395	0.9506
El Salvador	0.7764	1.0000	0.6783	0.8848	0.7070
Guatemala	1.1447	1.4743	1.0000	1.3044	1.0424
Honduras	0.8776	1.1303	0.7666	1.0000	0.7991
Nicaragua	1.0982	1.4544	0.9594	1.2514	1.0000

The results for Nicaragua in table 11 are somewhat surprising. This country has intermediate government costs, which are primarily a reflection of public wages and salaries, even though its prices of consumption of private services are approximately 20 percent above the region's average (table 10). By contrast, the low wage structure of El Salvador gives it the lowest prices in government services as well as in private services.

The dispersion of the costs of the labor factor in the governments of the different Central American countries (of which table 11 is a good indication) is much less than one might expect, given the existing obstacles to labor mobility, especially in regard to labor in the government sector. Again the implication is that a surprisingly high degree of integration exists in Central America.

In reality there are three countries--Costa Rica, Guatemala, and Nicaragua--whose salary levels are apparently similar. El Salvador and Honduras are on levels similar to each other but much lower than those of the rest of Central America. It is notable that the differences between these two groups of countries seem large, and that the government salaries in Guatemala are much greater than those of El Salvador.[6]

The dispersion of the price index values of the government services is much less in the Central American case than has been found in similar studies done by the ECIEL Program in collaboration with its member institutes.[7] One assumes that the indices of the total cost of the public services are reflected in the prices that would be charged by the different governments, if these services were sold. El Salvador presents the lowest prices in public services (table 11), with Honduras having the next lowest prices, although the difference of levels between these countries is more than 10 percent. On the other hand, the prices of the public services in Guatemala, Nicaragua, and Costa Rica seem to be more than 30 percent higher than those of El Salvador and Honduras. Thus, although these prices in Central America show variation that is much smaller than in the Latin American Free Trade Association (LAFTA), they nevertheless do show appreciable differences.

B. Price Levels for Machinery and Equipment

In Central America, machinery and equipment are almost totally imported from foreign countries. For the purpose of this study,[8] machinery and equipment were divided into two principal groups, the first of which corresponds to equipment for transport and communication and the second to other types of machinery and equipment. This division follows the lines of national accounts.

With respect to the indices in table 12, Nicaragua presents the highest price levels (using Guatemala as the base country). Guatemala, in turn, appears to have the lowest prices for machinery and equipment. El Salvador has price levels closest to those of Guatemala in this category, while Honduras and Costa Rica present price levels for machinery and equipment approximately 10 percent higher than those of Guatemala, and only slightly lower than those of Nicaragua.

Table 12. Matrix of Price Indices for Machinery and Equipment,
Central America, November 1973

	Base Country				
	Costa Rica	El Salvador	Guatemala	Honduras	Nicaragua
Other country					
Costa Rica	1.00000	1.04388	1.10519	1.00758	0.99503
El Salvador	0.95797	1.00000	1.05874	0.96523	0.95320
Guatemala	0.90482	0.94452	1.00000	0.91168	0.90032
Honduras	0.99248	1.03602	1.09688	1.00000	0.98754
Nicaragua	1.00500	1.04909	1.11071	1.01261	1.00000

Compared with the price variation between countries found in the previous study done by ECIEL in LAFTA, and with what has been found in the other sectors, the price dispersion of these goods in Central America appears to be reduced even further. This undoubtedly is due to the fact that almost all of these goods are imported.

Another important factor to be considered is that the import tariff system is the same for the whole region. Moreover, the tariffs generally have a very small impact on the c.i.f. price because of the frequent existence of tariff exoneration for capital goods.

The differences in prices between the Central American countries can be explained in terms of transport costs, internal taxes, trade margins, market size, and so on. It is evident that the economies which are the largest and closest geographically to the United States (Guatemala and El Salvador) have the lowest prices. This pattern also suggests that there exists some competition or at least a potential for competition among the Central American countries in the supply of these goods, based upon reexporting the same goods. The potential for reexport also tends to maintain the price differences within certain levels.[9]

C.   Prices at the Level of GDP

The results of the relative price indices at the level of GDP include all of the previous sectors. These sectors correspond to the components of the GDP concerning expenditures, excluding expenditures in construction.[10] Nevertheless, given that expenditures in construction represent less than 10 percent of total GDP, their inclusion would very probably not alter the results of the total index presented in table 13.

Table 13 shows that El Salvador and Costa Rica have the lowest overall price levels in the region, while Honduras and Nicaragua have the highest. Prices stand at an intermediate level in Guatemala.

Table 13. Matrix of Price Indices for the GDP,
Central America, November 1973

	Base Country				
	Costa Rica	El Salvador	Guatemala	Honduras	Nicaragua
Other country					
Costa Rica	1.0000	1.0893	0.9727	0.9432	0.8230
El Salvador	0.9181	1.0000	0.8930	0.8660	0.7556
Guatemala	1.0281	1.1199	1.0000	0.9698	0.8462
Honduras	1.0602	1.1548	1.0312	1.0000	0.8726
Nicaragua	1.2150	1.3234	1.1818	1.1460	1.0000

It is interesting to note that, at the level of GDP, the dispersion of prices is relatively low, with a coefficient of variation around 0.094. If one compares the dispersion at the level of the total product with that of the sectors previously examined, we can verify that although some discrepancies exist, they are not pronounced. The private consumption sector, which represents the fundamental part of total expenditure, has a coefficient of variation which is slightly higher (0.110). Expenditures in public consumption have the highest coefficient of variation (0.186), equivalent to twice the registered dispersion of prices for total product.[11]

This result is undoubtedly due in part to the low mobility of the public goods and services between the different Central American countries, which in turn does not allow competition to reduce variation of prices within the region. This is in accord with the basic nature of these products which are produced nationally, and usually nontradable. In addition, the government sector is somewhat immune to market forces, so that a political decision favoring high public wages in one country may give rise to differing public prices from those in another country having similar private sector prices and factor costs. In comparison to the other sectors, the prices of machinery and equipment show the least interregional variation for the reasons cited in the previous section.

The regional dispersion found in all of these prices offers no surprise. Except in the case of machinery and equipment, the higher the level of aggregation the lower the variation, as one would expect. As we have seen, in the case of machinery and equipment, the small variation is explained by the fact that most of these goods are imported.

On the other hand, the price variation in Central America is much less than in LAFTA. The difference reflects the higher level of trade and integration among the Central American countries, as well as a greater homogeneity in their economic characteristics, including the incidence of economic policies affecting prices and even geographical proximity.

For the aggregate level of GDP, we observe that the prices of Nicaraguan goods are 15 percent higher than those of Guatemala, the base country, and whose prices reflect an approximation of the Central American average. It would be interesting to examine the extent to which this price disequilibrium is a consequence of the earthquake which devastated Nicaragua at the end of 1972 and which may have produced a lasting effect on the price structure, especially of those products included in private consumption and investment (machinery and equipment). Prices in El Salvador on the other hand are almost 15 percent lower than those in Guatemala, and for that reason, 15 percent lower than the Central American average. An important feature of El Salvador's lower prices is their consistency across the principal sectors. This result appears to reflect lower costs in El Salvador, especially in the labor market.

D. Purchasing Power Parity

The exchange rates usually considered in the examination of economic activity are those which refer to the exchange of one currency for another, with the aim of carrying out international transactions. These exchange rates are determined by: the exports and imports of goods and services, interchange of productive factors (essentially capital), and by payments and remittances for services rendered.

As indicated in appendix A, purchasing power parity rates constitute an alternative for conversion purposes. These are determined by the prices of all the goods and services consumed in the different countries including, more or less directly, the services of the productive factors. These exchange rates are more complete, including not only the actual international transactions but also the potential ones. Similarly, some products are considered even if they are not potentially tradable goods because they may influence the prices of those goods, services, or factors which are traded or which could be traded in the future.

It is generally accepted that rates of this type, and not those of international trade, must be utilized in the conversion of general monetary values (as the GDP, the total consumption, and so on) from one country to another. What is most often debated is whether or not these purchasing power parity rates reflect with a certain amount of precision the equilibrium exchange rates in international trade.[12]

Although it has been recognized that this is not the case in a strict sense, and especially when countries with very diverse levels of development are compared, doubt also remains concerning the usefulness of employing parity exchange rates in order to estimate the exchange rates within the systems of integration of countries with similar levels of development.[13] This seems to be in the process of becoming accepted in regard to the relative version of the parity exchange rates, which would imply that once the absolute values of the equilibrium exchange rates within a determined period are defined, the movement of purchasing power parities across time could be utilized in order to adjust the equilibrium exchange rates.[14] Nevertheless, from an analytical standpoint, it seems logical to assume that there must exist a relation between the price levels and the exchange rates for a given moment for those countries which form part of an integration system. In effect, it is not very different

384

to accept the fact that the exchange rates must generally follow the
price movements across time than to consider--following the absolute version of the theory of purchasing power parity--that the same exchange
rates must also respond a great deal to the differences in existing levels
of prices at a given moment. This is especially true when the countries
maintain a high level of trade and a certain degree of mobility of factors across their borders as well as a certain coincidence in economic
policies (monetary, fiscal, and so on), all elements which characterize
integration groups.[15]

The parity exchange rates are based on all prices of the economies,
while the exchange rates which determine international transactions are
based upon the prices of tradable goods, the monetary flows determined
by movements of capital and other productive factors, and grants. These
last two factors do not affect the balance of payment of the countries
of the Central American Common Market in a very different manner and, as
such, the international exchange rates. On the other hand, it would seem
that in order to determine the equilibrium exchange rates, not only are
the prices of the trade goods relevant but also of those goods which
potentially can be traded, including prices of those nontradable goods
which influence the prices of tradable goods. Those countries which
have lower price levels and more favorable price structures enjoy undeni-
able advantages in the exportation of their products and in the defense
of new internal markets against imports from other countries.

Tables 14 and 15 report the purchasing power parity rates (based on
the price comparisons of this chapter) and the official exchange rates,
respectively, for the Central American countries in 1973.

In order to analyze the results of the calculations of the parity
rates, Guatemala is once again taken as the base country. Apart from
the reasons previously cited for taking this country as a base, it must
be added that the quetzal possesses great stability and furthermore it
is equivalent to the dollar. In table 14, in the Guatemala column, the

Table 14. Matrix of Purchasing Power Parity Rates Among the
Central American Currencies, November 1973

| | Base Country | | | | |
Other country	Costa Rica	El Salvador	Guatemala	Honduras	Nicaragua
Costa Rica	1.00	3.29	7.35	3.57	0.89
El Salvador	0.30	1.00	2.23	1.08	0.27
Guatemala	0.13	0.45	1.00	0.48	0.12
Honduras	0.27	0.93	2.06	1.00	0.25
Nicaragua	1.13	3.71	8.27	4.01	1.00

385

Table 15. Official Exchange Rates, Central America,
November 1973

Exchange Rate of:	For 1 Guatemalan Quetzal
Costa Rica[a]	7.56
El Salvador	2.50
Honduras	2.00
Nicaragua	7.00

[a]Weighted average of the various exchange rates which were found in Costa Rica at this date, as taken from the Central Bank of Costa Rica.

parity exchange rates for each one of the Central American countries appear with respect to one quetzal. As examples we can cite that 2.04 lempiras are equivalent to one quetzal and that 8.02 cordobas also are equivalent to one quetzal. Interpreting these rates from the point of view of what signifies the exchange rate, the corresponding column in table 14 indicates the specified quantities of other Central American currencies which should be given up in order to obtain one quetzal.[16]

Comparing tables 14 and 15 and using the quetzal as a base, one can state that there are countries whose national currencies possess a greater internal than external purchasing power and vice versa. The internal purchasing power of Nicaraguan and Honduran currencies is lower than their external purchasing power. The opposite occurs in the currencies of El Salvador and Costa Rica.

To the extent that the parity rates are considered as an estimate of the equilibrium exchange rate, certain normative conclusions could be derived from these comparisons. In the case of equilibrium, the internal and external purchasing power must coincide within certain ranges.[17] When this does not occur, the implication is that official exchange rates should be altered. When internal purchasing power is less than external purchasing power (or when parity is greater than the official rate), this could indicate that the official exchange rate is overvalued and that a devaluation is necessary. In the opposite case, when a parity rate is less than the official exchange rate (internal purchasing power is greater), it would seem that the official exchange rate would be undervalued and that a revaluation would be necessary.

Taking the Central American case in order to illustrate the application of these principles, it could be said that during the time in which the study was carried out, a disequilibrium between the internal and the external purchasing power existed in both Nicaragua and Honduras. The magnitude of this disequilibrium is indicated by the ratio PR/OER, which is slightly higher than unity in Honduras but appreciably greater in the case of Nicaragua.[18]

This would be an indication that both the Honduran lempira and the Nicaraguan cordoba could be overvalued with respect to the quetzal, but it is only in the latter case that the difference is sufficiently large to provide a meaningful empirical basis for the recommendation of a foreign exchange policy, which in this case would be devaluation.

The cases of Costa Rica and El Salvador are opposite. In these countries, the parity rate is less than the official rate, which therefore is evidence of a greater internal than external buying power. This situation would indicate that a revaluation is needed. Now, given that the parity rate is merely an estimate of the equilibrium exchange rate and that the difference between internal and external purchasing powers is only slightly significant, a revaluation of the Costa Rican currency is not justified, although it could be considered in the case of El Salvador where the PR/OER ratio is significantly lower than unity.[19]

Finally, it is necessary to point out that besides changing the external exchange rate, other measures can be implemented to restore the balance between the internal and external purchasing power of a currency. The most evident method is a change in the tariff levels, but also one can manipulate such things as taxes, subsidies, quotas, and exchange controls.

E.   Gross Products in Real Terms

The results of the survey of prices at a final demand level, and the parity exchange rates for 1973, permit the calculation of GDP in real terms for 1973. In this calculation, GDPs at current values for the five Central American countries are divided by the Central American price indices corresponding to this aggregate. All of these figures appear in table 16, with Guatemala as the base country. The estimates of the GDPs in real terms are also expressed in per capita terms in the table.

Comparing columns (c) and (e) of table 16, corresponding respectively to per capita GDP at current levels of 1973 and to the same values expressed in real terms, Costa Rica per capita income changes from 700 to 720, and El Salvador's rises even more in relative terms. On the other hand, per capita GDP in Nicaragua--which shows a GDP per capita of approximately $CA522 according to the latest revisions--upon adjustment to real terms undergoes a considerable decrease to $CA442, bringing it slightly below the level for Guatemala. Lastly, the position of Honduras worsens slightly upon expressing its product in real terms.

As one can verify by comparison, the rank ordering of the countries by per capita income is not altered substantially by converting their GDPs per capita into real terms, although Nicaragua changes places with Guatemala.[20]   In fact, the divergence between the top- and bottom-ranked countries widens when nominal GDP figures are adjusted by the purchasing parity price indices. The income of Honduras, the poorest country, decreases, and that of the richest country, Costa Rica, increases. On the other hand, the increase of the GDP per capita in El Salvador and the decrease in the GDP per capita of Nicaragua are striking when they are adjusted by the price levels.

Table 16. GDP per Capita in Real Terms, Central America, 1973

Country	(a) GDP[a] (million CA$)	(b) Population[b] (000 inhabitants)	(c) GDP per Capita (CA$)	(d) Index of Relative Prices	(e) GDP per Capita in Real Terms (CA$)	(f) GDP in Real Terms (CA$)
Costa Rica	1,321.3	1,887	700	0.9727	720	1,358.4
El Salvador	1,329.7	3,814	349	0.8930	391	1,489.0
Guatemala	2,591.0	5,751	451	1.0000	451	2,591.0
Honduras	899.0	2,864	314	1.0312	304	871.8
Nicaragua	1,160.9	2,222	522	1.1818	442	982.3

[a]Estimated values at current market prices. SIECA "Central America: Macroeconomic Statistics 1971-74," Statistical Annex II, SIECA, RMECA XIII/D.T.2 II, February 1975; CELADE, Demographic Bulletin, IV Year, No. 8, June 1971, Interpolations effected in the SIECA.

[b]It has been observed that the data on population of Costa Rica differ from the figures from other sources. Nevertheless, the information on population utilized seems to be the most reliable available.

In real terms, the GDP per capita of Guatemala, Nicaragua, and El Salvador differ little although that of the last country is somewhat lower. Honduras and Costa Rica are the extreme cases in Central America in real production per capita, with levels considerably below and above the other three countries, respectively. Concerning total GDP in real terms, it is evident that Guatemala and El Salvador are the largest economies of the area, while the economies of Honduras and Nicaragua are relatively small. (See table 16, column (f).) The economy of Costa Rica has an intermediate size within the Central American region due to the fact that its high real product per capita is offset by its lower population.

F.   Conclusions

The coordinated price surveys in the five Central American countries afford a rare opportunity for a reliable evaluation of comparative price behavior in an area of economic integration. A general conclusion is that prices are quite similar in the five countries at the aggregate level as well as for major expenditure components.   This similarity confirms our expectations for tradable goods in view of the free trade within the region, but it also applies to nontraded housing and private services consumption, suggesting a price equalizing factor of integration beyond the sphere of trade alone. (One additional explanation of the similarity is that the main reason for divergence of nontraded prices would be major differences in standards of living, and correspondingly, of the costs of labor-intensive services; and in Central America the national discrepancies in standard of living are relatively small.) The finding of a relatively wide divergence of government consumption prices (despite similarity of private service prices) suggests differing degrees of political departure from market-related wage policies in the government sector.

The sectoral price differences indicate that (i) capital goods show very similar prices, mainly because they are dominated by imports at the world price; (ii) sectors dominated by wage costs show El Salvador to be particularly lower in price, reflecting that country's relatively abundant labor and low wages; (iii) Guatemala's lower prices or durable consumer goods imply its favored position for comparative advantage in these goods, many of which are natural candidates for economies of scale (although conclusions on comparative advantage must be only tentative when based on consumer prices, which may be distorted by varying tax policies and commercial margins).

Two results stand out as the most important at the aggregate level. First, correction of nominal per capita income figures by the purchasing power parity indices leaves the ranking of countries in the region essentially unaltered, and even widens the measured discrepancy between the richest (Costa Rica) and poorest (Honduras) countries.   This result is especially important as a confirmation of the fact that any special measures adopted favoring Honduras within the Central American Common Market would be appropriately directed toward the region's poorest country.

Perhaps the second major conclusion is a quite specific implication for the case of Nicaragua: that the country might give full consideration to devaluation in view of the fact that it is the only country whose prices are unambiguously well above the general level of the other countries. The fact that Nicaragua has faced consistent trade deficits with the region and overall (see table 2, chapter 3) is consistent with this possible diagnosis. However, a fuller evaluation of the question is obviously necessary before adoption of the specific policy of devaluation. In this evaluation, factors such as the following would have to be taken into account: (i) the extent to which November 1973 was an atypical period because of the then recent earthquake in Nicaragua; (ii) the evolution of regional and Nicaraguan prices since then; (iii) the overall status of the country's balance of payments and financing prospects at the current time.

Finally, the favorable experience of this study in marshalling cooperative efforts for comparable surveys in each of the countries of the region suggests the strong desirability of periodic repetitions of the effort in order to construct comparable price indices over time for the countries within the region.

Chapter 8

NOTES

1. The annual rate of increase for consumer prices was found to be 27 percent in El Salvador. Similar results were encountered in Guatemala.

2. These comparisons of the levels of prices refer to a period when rapid world inflation had begun but had not reached its peak. New surveys of prices are being planned in order to update the comparisons.

3. See Jorge Salazar-Carrillo, The Structure of Prices, Purchasing Powers and Real Products in ALALC (Washington, D.C.: Brookings Institution) and "The Prices of Private Consumption Goods," Summary of the 19th ECIEL Seminar, São Paulo, Brazil, 1972.

4. The structure and the process of price determination of nontradable goods influence the prices of the products which enter or could potentially enter into international trade.

5. State industries are not included within the public sector in the national accounts, given that they sell goods and services which are produced or traded. For this reason the expenditures on these products are considered under the category of private consumption or capital formation.

6. The comparative level of wages generally in Central America is a subject requiring further study. The 1968 industrial census showed the following average wages for manufacturing production workers (in Central American pesos): Guatemala, $750; Honduras, $769; Nicaragua, $818; Costa Rica, $545. Calculated from SIECA VI Compendio Estadístico Centroamericano (Guatemala City: SIECA, 1975), pp. 159, 170.

This pattern ironically shows Costa Rica, the country with the highest per capita income, as having the lowest actual industrial wages. By contrast, Costa Rica has the highest level of minimum wages. The approximate daily levels in 1970 for industrial labor were: Guatemala, $1.60; El Salvador, $1.28; Honduras—no minimum wage; Nicaragua, $1.71; and Costa Rica, $2.55. SIECA, "El Desarrollo Integrado de Centroamerica en la Presente Decada," study no. 6 (Guatemala City: SIECA, 1972), table 43. Similarly, Costa Rica had the highest agricultural wages in 1970; and Honduras, the lowest. (See table 2 of chapter 3 in this volume.)

The general implication of these differences is that the barriers existing between sectors are greater in Honduras (with a large gap between industrial and agricultural wages) and lowest in Costa Rica (with a much smaller gap). Concerning government costs, the implication is that the public salaries are perhaps artificially high in Guatemala, since that country has the highest government wages but intermediate levels of industrial and agricultural wages.

7. See Jorge Salazar-Carrillo, "A Comparison of Prices of Public Consumption Goods in Latin America," mimeographed (Washington, D.C.: Brookings Institution, 1973).

8. The underlying analysis for this sector was prepared by George P. Montalván of the Organization of American States. See George P. Montalván, "Tipos de Cambio de Paridad para Bienes de Capital en Centroamérica: Metodología y Resultados Preliminares," mimeographed (Washington, D.C.: March 1975).

9. It is interesting to observe that in the case of LAFTA, domestic production of these goods on the part of some countries causes an increase in the price dispersion in this category. See Jorge Salazar-Carrillo, "Investment Goods Prices in Latin America," Summary of the 14th ECIEL Seminar, Quito, Ecuador, 1973.

10. Severe difficulties in the specification of comparable activities or products in construction required delays in the field work and analysis of this sector, for which results remain incomplete.

11. Note that the price dispersion for total product is essentially a weighted average of the dispersion measures for each of its components.

12. See, for example, Joseph Grunwald and Jorge Salazar-Carrillo, "Integration, Rates of Exchange and Value Comparisons in Latin America," in Don Daly, ed., International Comparison of Prices and Output (New York: National Bureau of Economic Research, 1971).

13. Jorge Salazar-Carrillo, "Price Purchasing Power and Real Product Comparisons in Latin America," Review of Income and Wealth (March 1973).

14. Edmar Bacha and Lance Taylor, "Foreign Exchange Shadow Prices: A Critical Review of Current Theories," Quarterly Journal of Economics (May 1971).

15. This is even more probable when there are no large differences in the levels of income between the member countries of the integration group, as in the Central American case where the difference in the GDP per capita between the poorest and the richest country is approximately $400 per year in absolute terms, and as a ratio, a little greater than 2 in relative terms.

16. The equivalent of these parity rates is real in terms of purchasing power. That is to say, these are the rates which are equal to the purchasing power (or the inverse of the same, which are the prices) of the currencies under consideration. More formally, if these parity rates are utilized instead of these official exchange rates in the calculation of the matrix of Central American price indices, this would be a unitary matrix.

17. It is necessary to recognize that, although the hypothesis has been established that the parity rates represent approximated estimates of the equilibrium exchange rates in certain integration schemes, this does not necessarily mean that a slight variation in the former should bring consequent variations in the official exchange rates. It is only when the differences between the official exchange rate and that of parity surpass a certain limit that devaluations and revaluations should be considered.

18. PR - Parity rate.

OER - Official exchange rate.

19. Note that if one had compared the PR with the OER of Costa Rica before the effective devaluation of its currency, which had already occurred by November 1973, the relationship would then have been opposite, indicating the possibility of the utility of a devaluation. The results therefore tend to confirm the appropriateness of the devaluation of the Costa Rican colon which became formalized early in 1974.

20. It should be noted that preliminary data for revised national accounts of Nicaragua show a GDP at current values about 5 percent below those used here, based on previous official estimates. With revised figures, the real GDP of Nicaragua would be below that of Guatemala, changing the ranking.

CHAPTER 9

Conclusion

William R. Cline
Enrique Delgado

A. Major Findings

In chapter 2 of this volume, Enrique Delgado traces the institutional experience of economic integration in Central America. Focusing on the tension between overall economic success and intercountry imbalances within the Central American Common Market (CACM), the chapter begins by remarking that the ideal grouping for economic integration would include countries at comparable levels of development but with disparate, complementary resource bases. Such countries would have a maximum to gain from integration and little to worry about in terms of possible distortion in the distribution of benefits in favor of rich member countries at the expense of poorer members. Within common markets containing countries at different stages of development, however, the issues of balanced growth and equitable distribution of the benefits of integration take on primary importance. Thus, these policy issues have greater salience in the CACM, the Latin American Free Trade Association (LAFTA), the Andean Pact, and integration efforts in Africa and Asia than in the European Common Market and the European Free Trade Association. Turning to the Central American experience, the chapter highlights the policymakers' original motive of reducing the region's dependence on exports of traditional raw materials and their mercurial fortunes. The early phase of integration involved efforts led by the Economic Commission for Latin America (ECLA), in the 1950s, in the direction of establishing jointly programmed plans of regional industrialization. At odds with this approach was the other basic theme of the then nascent integration movement, free trade. The countries with larger industrial sectors, Guatemala and El Salvador, advocated regional free trade, while the other three countries leaned toward industrial programming. The scheme of "Integration Industries" was to be the principal vehicle for planned allocation of industries among the five member countries.

    The Northern Tripartite agreement in 1960, providing for free trade among Guatemala, El Salvador, and Honduras, precipitated a concrete choice between the two basic options. Left with little alternative, Nicaragua, and subsequently Costa Rica, joined with the other three countries in the free trade regime of the General Treaty on Economic Integration in 1960, subscribing as well to the companion institution, the Central American Bank for Economic Integration (CABEI).

Based on meteoric increases in intraregional trade, euphoria dominated the CACM in the early 1960s. Industrial projects related to
regional trade multiplied; the region undertook impressive joint projects in highway construction and communications. The guiding principle
of integration was one of the unfettered expansion of economic activity.
Far from restricting specified industries to selected countries through
joint decisionmaking, the member countries outdid each other in competitive tax and tariff incentives in the race to attract foreign investment.

Within the atmosphere of free-for-all competition the latent relative weaknesses of some member countries soon rose to the surface. By the
mid-1960s Honduras and Nicaragua were registering complaints about the
absence of measures to insure balanced development among the member countries. They cited the failure of the integration industries scheme,
under which only two projects were actually realized. The scheme had
been turned into a dead letter by the adoption of free industrial trade
and by the "Special System for Promotion of Productive Activities," a
program that allowed new tariffs for industrial promotion but without
requiring the planned allocation of new industries among countries. Honduras delayed for several years the ratification of the Agreement on Common Treatment of Fiscal Incentives, hoping to negotiate meaningful special advantages relative to the other countries. The eventual special
provisions specified for Honduras in 1967, although too meager to supply
much developmental impact, encouraged Nicaragua to press for special
treatment as well. More dramatically, on grounds of balance of payments
difficulties Nicaragua unilaterally imposed tariffs on goods from the
other countries in early 1969, only to back down within the space of a
few months when faced with the threat of retaliation from the others.

By early 1969, then, serious strains existed within the CACM because
of the absence of special measures to benefit the lesser-developed member countries. But open rupture of the CACM came that year when war broke
out between El Salvador and Honduras, the two countries with perhaps the
closest historical ties. Migration from densely populated El Salvador to
land-rich but backward Honduras had reached a point of political crisis.
Large numbers of migrants were expelled by Honduran authorities. Actual
or at least alleged excesses in the treatment of their expelled compatri-
ots led the Salvadorians to attack.

Although short, the war left a legacy of unsettled boundaries, trade embargo between the two countries, and lack of road access through Honduras
for goods from El Salvador bound for markets in Nicaragua and Costa Rica.
The war set the stage for the complete withdrawal of Honduras from the
Common Market. After the failure of an attempt to establish a modus operandi with new, special provisions for Honduran participation in the CACM,
in late 1970 Honduras imposed the common external tariff on imports from
Central America, thereby opting out of the Common Market. Bilateral trade
agreements with Nicaragua, Guatemala, and Costa Rica, negotiated in 1972
and 1973, constituted only limited reintegration of Honduras into the
CACM, and in large part the Common Market has been a customs union among
only the four remaining members since 1969.

Chapter 2 concludes with an examination of the relative levels of
development of the five countries. Applying factorial analysis of several indicators of development, the chapter concludes that Costa Rica is

clearly much more developed than the others, and that Guatemala--although the largest industrial center--is relatively close to Honduras and El Salvador at the underdeveloped end of the range within the region. The result for Guatemala reflects the backward conditions of the rural and indigenous population; for the capital city, Guatemalan development levels are among the highest in Central America. This social dichotomy within Guatemala highlights the fact that policy measures for redistribution of the economic benefits from integration must take account of income distribution within member countries as well as among them.

Chapter 3 turns to quantitative investigation of two central policy questions: How large were the net economic benefits of integration in Central America? What was the distribution of benefits and costs of integration among the five member countries? Previous economic analyses of these issues have tended to examine highly aggregated data without relating them in a rigorous way to the impact of integration. Several studies have remarked on the increase in growth rates during the integration period, in comparison with preintegration years, but have not demonstrated the causal role of economic integration as opposed to other factors. Similarly, earlier studies have treated intercountry trade balances, within the CACM, as indicators of country gains or losses from integration, and this approach is unsatisfactory for examining the distribution of benefits among countries.

The methodology developed in chapter 3 takes as its point of departure the two traditional components in economic analysis of customs unions: trade creation and trade diversion. It then uses these estimates as building blocks for the calculation of several other economic effects not conventionally treated in analysis of economic integration but of fundamental importance in the case of developing countries. These effects include, at the level of static effects: (i) gains from increased economies of scale; (ii) benefits from increased employment of unskilled labor with low cost to the economy; and (iii) savings of foreign exchange, as partner supply replaces imports from outside and country exports rise by virtue of increased sales to partners. At the dynamic level, the same building blocks, trade creation and diversion, are used to identify structural changes in the economies, away from raw materials exports and toward manufacturing industry. Finally, an additional dynamic effect is estimated: the impact of economic integration on the pace of investment.

The cost-benefit study applies detailed sectoral data to estimate these various effects, using 1958 as the base and computing effects of integration for two terminal years, 1968 (the last year of full operation of the CACM including Honduras) and 1972. The principal results encountered are the following:

(i) Total net economic benefits of integration were large, amounting to 3 or 4 percent of regional product by 1972. Expressed as a single present discounted value for all future years, the decision to integrate was worth an estimated $3 billion.

(ii) The most important economic benefits arose from foreign exchange savings and from the Common Market's stimulus to investment. Economies of scale and employment effects were also important but less so. Economic benefits from structural transformation were minimal, even though the shift in sectoral composition from agriculture to industry was considerable (although here the methodology for calculating welfare benefits is embryonic). Finally, the traditional effects of a common market, trade creation and trade diversion, had extremely small benefits and costs. This finding highlights the fact that an assessment of customs unions among developing countries will fail to capture the principal economic effects if it does not go well beyond the conventional approach focusing on trade creation and diversion. However, the absence of high costs of trade diversion does throw light on one controversial aspect of integration. This finding rejects the common critique that the CACM established highly inefficient industries behind high tariffs. Indeed, the data developed in the analysis show that CACM product costs were reasonable compared to world prices, and that, if anything, average tariffs fell instead of rising as member countries moved to the common external tariff.

(iii)   The distribution of net benefits of integration across countries was relatively equitable. By 1972 the percentage shares of member countries in net benefits resembled their shares in regional population. The only clear case of low relative benefits was that of Honduras. Even for Honduras net benefits were positive, however, indicating that by dropping out of the Common Market Honduras has lost economic opportunities rather than improving her position. The special policy implications for the case of Honduras are discussed below.

The benefits did show a pattern of evening-out over time. As of 1968 there was a high concentration of net benefits in Guatemala and El Salvador, but by 1972 the distribution was much more uniform among the member countries. This evolution makes sense in that one would expect the countries with the largest industrial sectors to dominate regional trade at the beginning of a free trade movement. Thereafter, as new investments occurred in the countries with smaller industrial bases, stimulated by their now regionwide sales horizons, one would expect a rise in the shares of these smaller economies in regional industrial output and exports. Indeed, the investment survey found that it was precisely in the two economies with the smallest industrial bases, Honduras and Nicaragua, that the greatest proportional stimulus to investment occurred as a result of the CACM.

Part II of this volume turns from the general integration experience to a specific area of economic policy, the employment problem. Chapter 4 examines the problem in terms of quantitative analysis of production conditions in the industrial sector. The central question in this assessment is: To what extent does substitutability between labor and capital exist in manufacturing? The answer to this question determines whether it is feasible to accelerate the growth of employment by favoring policies that make capital more expensive relative to labor, thereby encouraging the use of labor and the economizing of capital. Three other questions are also examined: (i) Has technical change in Central American industry been biased against the use of labor? (ii) Are there economies of scale in industry in the region? (iii) What was the impact of economic integration on employment?

On the basis of detailed statistical analysis carried out in several different forms, chapter 4 concludes that there does exist considerable substitutability between capital and labor in the industrial sector. On the average, the elasticity of substitution is 0.8, so that a 10 percent rise in the cost of capital relative to that of labor will induce an 8 percent rise in the amount of labor combined with each unit of capital. This degree of flexibility is relatively high compared with that found in past studies for developing countries. The finding is therefore an optimistic one in that it points to the possibility of expanding industrial employment through use of policies that make capital expensive or labor cheap.

At the level of industrial product sectors, the chapter finds that the elasticity of substitution is as high in the "dynamic" sectors as in the "traditional" industrial sectors. This result rejects the common perception that there is almost no flexibility of factor combinations in the dynamic industries even though there might be flexibility in the traditional sectors.

Based on the elasticity of substitution and on the shares of capital and labor, the chapter identifies an elasticity of demand for labor. This elasticity incorporates both substitution between labor and capital, and an "output effect" in response to a change in wages. The labor demand elasticity is 1.14, indicating that a rise in real salaries will reduce total employment sufficiently to reduce the total wage bill of all employees despite the rise in wages for those who remain employed.

With respect to technical change, chapter 4 finds that for Guatemala (the only country for which data are available over a period of several years), most industrial sectors show a clear bias in technical change against the use of labor. The presence of this bias is relevant to an understanding of the slow growth of industrial employment as well as the low share of labor in industrial value added in the region. The results of the chapter concerning economies of scale generally indicate the presence of moderate or low returns to scale for the region on the average. Results by country suggest interesting divergences, with higher returns to scale in Honduras and Guatemala but diseconomies of scale in Nicaragua and Costa Rica. However, the statistical properties of these more detailed country results qualify them as tentative.

The impact of the Common Market on employment is estimated in chapter 4, using the sectoral estimates of change in output induced by integration as measured in chapter 3. Counting both direct and indirect jobs, in industry, agriculture, and the services sectors, economic integration appears to have created approximately 150,000 jobs. This employment effect represents about 3 percent of total employment in the region, and about 14 percent of the increase in the total labor force from 1958 to 1972. Thus, while integration provided no massive solution to the employment problem, it did generate significant employment. The amount of employment generation appears to have been roughly comparable to the contribution of integration to gross national product, as measured in the cost-benefit study in chapter 3.

Chapter 5 approaches the employment problem from a global and political-economic standpoint. As an initial indication of the relatively weak position of labor in the region the chapter first notes the low incidence of labor unionization. Within this low average level there are variations. There is a relatively higher incidence of unionization in Costa

Rica, where labor is the most scarce; a relatively high fraction of industrial workers are unionized in El Salvador, despite a low degree of unionization overall; and there has been an impressive expansion of rural labor unions in Honduras in recent years.

The study then turns to an examination of the gap between labor supply and demand. On the basis of population data and labor force participation rates, it is estimated that from 1961 to 1975 the potential supply of labor rose by more than the increase in actual jobs, widening the "employment gap" for the region as a whole by 150,000 workers, or approximately 3 percent of the labor force. The analysis then calculates the expansion in employment that would have occurred if output had grown as observed but productivity per worker had remained unchanged. This resulting increase in demand for labor would have been far greater than the increased supply of labor. Thus, the forces that stimulated rising productivity, including in all probability low costs of capital, bias in technical change against labor use, and rapid technical change in the production of traditional export crops, frustrated what otherwise might have been a rapid expansion of employment consistent with the rapid rates of output growth. Of course, at least some rise in labor productivity through natural "learning by doing" would have occurred even in the absence of policies stimulating the use of capital-intensive techniques.

In an innovative discussion of employment and income distribution in the export economy, the chapter points out the nature of competition among factors for rents generated by the economy. A crucial determinant of the outcome is the scarcity of labor and, correspondingly, the cost of labor-intensive service sector activities. Greater scarcity of labor would raise the price of labor, raising the cost of services and shifting rents in the economy from landlords and industrialists toward labor. The real income of the upper classes would decline doubly, given their heavy consumption of labor-intensive services. Linking this general approach to the estimates on the employment gap, the chapter points out that if policies favoring employment rather than capital intensity had dominated in the past fifteen years, the employment gap very probably would have narrowed instead of widening. The resulting upward pressure on wages would have had favorable income distribution effects, operating through the process of shifting rents and raising service sector costs.

The critical role of the political atmosphere in determining the outcome of changes in employment and income distribution is highlighted by a comparison of Costa Rica with other countries in the region. The greater equality of income and more favorable employment situation in Costa Rica, stemming in part from a more equal land distribution since Colonial times, serves as evidence that there is nothing inevitable about the income distribution resulting from the nature of the developing, raw materials export economy. Indeed, past episodes of nascent social change, including changes in regimes and subsequent counterchanges, highlight the role of political control in the determination of the distribution of rents in the system. Furthermore, recent experiences with increased labor demand during reconstruction after earthquakes in Nicaragua and Guatemala show the powerful stimulus to employment, wages, and the rent-shifting process that can come from public programs. The nature of political control, however, sets the limits within which such programs are likely to be pursued in more normal times.

The chapter then turns to a consideration of the employment effects of the integration movement. While reiterating the basic estimates of employment gains prepared in chapter 4, the discussion does call attention to a caveat about the employment effects of the Common Market. Because the CACM raised the sectoral participation of capital-intensive industry relative to more-labor-intensive agriculture, it is conceivable that integration may even have reduced employment. A "worst case" calculation assuming that total gross national product would have been just as high without integration, but that it would have been composed of more agricultural and less industrial production, concludes that integration might have reduced employment by about 3 percent of the labor force. The calculation serves not as the central estimate of this book but rather as a cautionary note. At the same time, it also serves as an estimate of the maximum possible damage to employment that integration conceivably could have caused. Because of the low estimate, the result suggests that even a highly pessimistic interpretation would not support the case of critics who contend that the integration process provoked serious new employment problems instead of helping reduce existing underemployment.

Finally, chapter 5 explores the nature of the distribution of rent between labor and capital in the Central American economies. On the basis of capital costs as applied to information on capital inputs, the chapter calculates the amount of economic rent going to owners of capital as the excess of returns to capital over capital cost. These estimates suggest that there exists a large component of rent to owners of capital, rent that could be redistributed to labor if the relationship of labor demand and supply were to tilt toward greater labor scarcity and if labor's relative bargaining strength were improved generally.

Sectoral development strategy and the issue of comparative advantage are next addressed. The studies concern industrial comparative advantage and agricultural policy and comparative advantage as assessed through a programming model.

Chapter 6 examines the structure of comparative advantage within manufacturing industry for the region as a whole compared to the rest of the world and for individual member countries relative to the CACM. The analysis has implications for concrete policies in at least three areas: tariff structure, industrial incentives, and the allocation of industries among member countries within any scheme of integrated regional planning. That is, although past tariff structures have reflected primarily the vagaries of pressure groups and tax revenue requirements, the future tariff structure should be geared more to development strategy. If a sector has extremely high tariff protection but shows no evidence of comparative advantage, present or future, then it is a prime candidate for reduced protection. A promising sector for at least future comparative advantage that currently is discriminated against by receiving no protection or protection far below the average would represent a candidate for increased tariff incentives. Similarly with industrial incentives through tax exemptions. For industrial allocation policy, knowledge of comparative advantage of each member country relative to the others will permit efficient planning of the allocation of industries across countries.

The analysis of chapter 6 applies a series of indicators to obtain rankings of seventy-five industrial sectors (at the four-digit levels of the International Standard Industrial Classification), from the sector with highest comparative advantage to the sector with the lowest. First the analysis considers the region as a whole. Under the Ricardian approach it calculates relative efficiency by sectors, computing "total factor productivity" in Central America and relating it to the same measure for each sector in the United States. Then three indicators of the factor-proportions concept of comparative advantage are applied: capital intensity, unskilled labor industry, and skilled labor intensity. As a region with relatively scarce capital and skilled labor but abundant unskilled labor, Central America is judged to have comparative advantage in unskilled-labor-intensive sectors but not in capital-intensive or skilled-labor-intensive sectors. A third approach is that of "revealed comparative advantage," or sectoral performance regardless of cause. Here the trade performance of each sector is measured (exports minus imports, divided by exports plus imports) to obtain comparative advantage rankings. A second indicator of revealed comparative advantage is the rate of return to capital in each sector.

A weighted average of rankings under all of these indicators provides a composite ranking of static comparative advantage. But it is also essential to examine the probable dynamic changes in comparative advantage--a task for which practically no precedent exists in the economics literature. The analysis of future evolution of comparative advantage adopts three indicators. The first uses "patterns of growth" identified by Chenery and others to rank industrial sectors by their prospective relative growth rates--based on past intercountry experience. A second indicator examines the same concept of ranking by prospective growth rate but uses comparison with a group of "control" countries in Latin America to obtain the estimates. The third indicator is the dynamic counterpart of the static measure for revealed comparative advantage: the growth rate of exports.

A final composite indicator incorporates both the static and "dynamic change" rankings. The top industries in this composite ranking are then identified as industrial sectors warranting special attention in development plans because of their overall comparative advantage for the region. In addition, sectoral rankings by incentives currently received through effective rates of protection or tax exemptions (the latter much less important, given low tax rates to begin with) are compared with the rankings by comparative advantage. Cases of strong excesses in either direction--high incentive for low comparative advantage or low incentive for high comparative advantage--are identified by sector. These results should provide information for revisions currently in progress in the tariff and tax incentive systems.

An overall correlation of comparative advantage ranking with incentive ranking is statistically significant, suggesting that as a whole the current system of incentives is rational even though cases of excessive or unduly low incentives exist. Comparison of major exporting sectors with comparative advantage ranking shows that except for a few sectors the largest remaining import sectors do not show comparative advantage, so that it would be an inefficient strategy to pursue import substitution per se without a careful analysis of comparative advantage for particular sectors.

Finally the chapter examines comparative advantage among the five member countries. Several of the same concepts used for the regional analysis are used once again to differentiate among the five member countries (total factor productivity; factor proportions--after identifying each member country as relatively abundant or scarce in a particular factor, in a regional context; and revealed sector trade performance). In addition, the intrazonal analysis incorporates economies of scale (the largest national markets have advantage for sectors with economies of scale); observed producer prices (the lowest cost producers, based on firm surveys, have comparative advantage); and a special linear programming model that assigns industrial sectors across the five countries to maximize regional value added subject to factor availability and demand constraints.

The result of the intrazonal analysis of comparative advantage is a ranking of countries from 1 to 5 for each sector. When combined with the sublist of sectors found to have comparative advantage for the region as a whole, the result is an indicative listing of appropriate industries for expansion in each country.

The results of these analyses show that industries with comparative advantage are drawn from the whole gamut of industrial sectors, not just from traditional sectors such as textiles. The intraregional results show that each country has comparative advantage in a sizable list of sectors--there is no overwhelming concentration of indicated sectors in a single country such as Guatemala.

The detailed results must be taken with caution when actual policies are formulated. An important qualification is that special attention must be given to national resource availability in the relevant sectors. Thus, Guatemala is indicated as the country with comparative advantage in pulp and paper, but if natural resource availability had been included in the analysis Honduras probably would have been the indicated country for specialization in this sector, given Honduran forestry reserves.

In sum, chapter 6 provides new methodology as well as detailed estimates for the assessment of present and future comparative advantage by industrial sector. The effort represents a first step that ideally should be followed by the incorporation of the nonindustrial sectors (omitted because of the absence of comparable data under each of the concepts used in measuring comparative advantage).

Chapter 7 reports on early results of a model of the agricultural sector in Central America. The model was designed as a planning instrument, and further elaboration of the model is anticipated, with more complete detail for country submodels and with improved data bases with respect to matters such as the alternative technologies available and seasonality of labor requirements.

In its present form the model provides the basis for conducting a number of important analyses. One area explored in the chapter is the price responsiveness of product supply. The model is an optimizing, programming model that solves for the best levels and locations of production of various agricultural products when given a set of product prices, and other relevant information such as patterns of demand and limits on trade. By solving the model for a whole set of alternative prices for a given product, it is possible to trace out the response of production supply to alternative prices. The resulting output levels for the product in question identify the "price elasticity of supply." In addition the experiments tell the indirect effects on other products that are cut back as land and labor are switched into the production of the good for which the price is being raised. This scheme for identifying output response to price is particularly suited to the analysis of government minimum price policies.

Another policy area examined in chapter 7 is that of agricultural trade, especially trade in basic grains within Central America. Since the beginning of the CACM, trade in agriculture products, unlike industrial trade, has been subject to numerous restrictions. Individual countries have pursued self-sufficiency in grains, ignoring the cheaper sources of supply available through importing from partner countries. Therefore, a second broad policy analysis in chapter 7 examines the possible economic gains that could be achieved through liberalization of trade in basic grains within the region. This analysis concludes that even a partial liberalization of this trade would provide considerable welfare benefits in the form of cheaper grains. The analysis presents details on the changes in trade flows that would occur with intrazonal trade liberalization in these sectors. In addition the results presented include information on the distribution of economic effects among classes of producers (large landowners, medium and small farmers, and landless workers) and consumers, by country.

In broad terms the liberalization of trade in basic grains would increase production and exports in Honduras and Nicaragua and increase imports in Costa Rica, causing little change in trade for Guatemala and El Salvador. There would be corresponding benefits for producers in Honduras and consumers in Costa Rica, with erosion in the incomes of producers, particularly of large farmers, in Costa Rica and substantially increased incomes of farm owners in Honduras.

The final set of analyses described in chapter 7 concerns comparative advantage with respect to the rest of the world. On the basis of the values of "shadow prices" of the constraints on the level of exports to the rest of the world, for each crop, it is possible to examine the rankings of the countries by comparative advantage in each crop. The results here show a diversity of specialization possibilities among the five countries. No single country or subgroup of countries shows a monopoly of comparative advantage in all export crops. Rather, each country shows favorable specialization prospects in specific alternative products.

The longer-term objective of the agricultural sector research described in chapter 7 is to establish a policy planning model that can be used to simulate the economic impacts of a wide variety of policies. The results reported here may be considered as initial and as illustrative of the type of policy questions that may be analyzed in greater depth and on a continuous basis through the further development of the sector model.

Before turning to the final chapter of this book, it is appropriate to consider possible qualifications on the results of the two sectoral chapters in light of the fact that the sector analyses are conducted separately rather than jointly. More specifically, What are the likely biases in analysis of comparative advantage by product, when the analysis is conducted first for industry and then, separately for agriculture? Ideally, comparative advantage analysis would treat all sectors jointly in a unified analysis.

One type of bias arising from separate analysis has been mentioned above: the absence of natural resource inputs in assessment of industrial comparative advantage. Self-evident in cases such as forestry or mineral products, this type of bias could also arise in assessing comparative advantage of, say, food processing industries. Thus, for example, labor abundance in El Salvador might indicate that country for specialization in a labor-intensive food processing sector, but once the scarcity of land and agricultural production were taken into account, the optimal country for specialization in the sector could be one with more abundant agricultural resources despite the greater scarcity of labor in the alternative country. The extent of bias of this nature will be limited, however, if intermediate inputs can be purchased from partner countries at prices not much higher than those charged to user industries within the country supplying the input. Given the small area of Central America, it would appear that this condition could be close to being met, especially if there were no agricultural trade restrictions within the CACM.

It may be argued that by and large the comparative advantage results of optimization by separate sectors, industrial and agricultural, will yield results similar to a comprehensive optimization. Consider agriculture. The land factor is specific to the sector. Patterns of relative yields by crop are unlikely to change if analysis is expanded to incorporate industry simultaneously. Only the labor factor might change under joint analysis. That is, conceivably the labor-abundant country could become the labor-scarce country in the agricultural sector if there were such a great specialization in industry that little labor were left over for agriculture. But a reversal of this sort is unlikely. The labor-abundant country in terms of industrial analysis is very likely to be abundant in agricultural labor as well. So even for the factor not specific to the sector, joint treatment of industry and agriculture would be unlikely to shift the relative factor abundance among countries, and therefore unlikely to alter conclusions about comparative advantage by product, reached through separate sector analyses.

These considerations do highlight the room for further analysis of comparative advantage through methodologies considering all economic sectors at once. There is of course ample need as well for improved methodologies for the examination of the future evolution of comparative advantage.

Chapter 8 presents the final main study of the SIECA/Brookings research on comparative prices in the CACM. This chapter follows the approach previously used for price comparisons among several countries within the ECIEL program of coordinated economic research in Latin America.

Information on comparative prices has several policy uses. It permits an examination of relative levels of real income per capita as opposed to nominal income per capita based on the actual exchange rate. For countries within an integration movement information on relative prices affords insight on the extent to which integration equalizes prices through the freer movement of goods and, sometimes, of labor. Price data contain

information relative to assessing the effect of specific government policies, such as direct taxes or subsidies. Product prices also may help
identify comparative advantage, although here prices at the producer level
are more relevant than those at the level of final demand. Furthermore,
when repeated in subsequent years, price surveys provide the basis for the
assessment of the pace of inflation on an accurate basis, and one that is
comparable among the countries examined. This last objective has taken on
heightened importance within Central America in recent years as worldwide
inflation has heightened the inflationary problem inside this region despite its traditional price stability.

The study presented in chapter 8 compares prices at the level of final
demand in the five Central American countries. The prices refer to capital
cities and to the time period of November 1973 when specially prepared
uniform consumer price surveys were carried out in the five countries.

Comparisons of prices are presented in three broad categories: private consumption, public consumption, and capital formation. Within each
category highly detailed products are specified to permit the calculation
of indices comparing the five countries. The indices are then weighted
(under alternative procedures) to obtain overall category price indices
at broader levels. These broader levels include subcategories (for example, within private consumption: food, beverages, and tobacco; clothing,
textiles, and shoes; and so forth). For one important spending item,
housing services, a special analysis is conducted, using statistical regression analysis to insure that the different classes of housing units
are in fact uniform and comparable across countries. Expenditures shares
within existing family budget surveys provide the basis for weighting
various spending terms. For public spending, public salaries for comparable personnel represent the principal information on relative prices.
In the area of capital formation, prices of imported machinery and equipment are considered; in addition, prices from a special survey on construction costs are included. In order to arrive at final global price comparisons, the shares of the various expenditure categories within the gross
national product are used as the basis for weighting.

The results of the price study show that in late 1973, compared with
Guatemala as the base, average prices in Costa Rica were almost the same;
prices in El Salvador were the lowest (10 percent below those of Guatemala); and those in Nicaragua, the highest (20 percent above those of
Guatemala). Honduran prices were 7 percent above the Guatemalan base.
This range of variation is narrow compared with the degree of dispersion
in prices found among the countries in LAFTA, for example. The relatively
limited dispersion of price levels suggests that integration in the CACM
has contributed to price equalization, both through free trade for tradable
goods and through migration's harmonizing impact on wages, which affect
nontradables sectors.

The high price level found for Nicaragua suggests that the cordoba was
overvalued at the time of the survey. This interpretation is consistent
with the presence of persistent Nicaraguan trade balance deficits within
the CACM, and overall. However, it is also true that the results for
Nicaragua reflect temporarily high prices as a result of the earthquake
that occurred in Managua approximately one year earlier. This effect is
most obvious in the high costs of construction.

For El Salvador, the low price level would not appear to represent an undervalued exchange rate. The lowest prices occur in nontradables sectors, and El Salvador had been experiencing trade balance deficits in the period 1971-73. For the case of Costa Rica, which had just devalued the colon for most imports in the months prior to the survey, the finding of an intermediate price level represents a form of confirmation that devaluation had been an appropriate measure.

Finally, the results may be applied to determine real levels of gross national product per capita. This analysis concludes that the real gap is even wider than the nominal gap between Costa Rica and Honduras, the two extreme cases in the region. Otherwise, the use of per capita income figures corrected for price differences makes little difference in the rankings of the five countries. The exception is the case of Nicaragua, where the price level is sufficiently high that the country is found to have a real per capita income lower than that of Guatemala, even though Nicaragua's nominal per capita income is higher.

B. Policy Implications

Several of the major findings of the empirical studies of this book have implications that bear directly on policy issues currently facing Central America. The study of benefits and costs of integration indicates a fundamentally important policy conclusion: the net economic benefits of integration have been large. Therefore the formation of the Common Market made an important contribution to the economic development of the region, and the continuation and strengthening of the integration effort should continue to play a key role in future economic development of the region.

A second policy implication of the cost-benefit study is that special measures for assuring balance in the distribution of the benefits of integration are necessary in the case of Honduras. Indeed, in the light of our results Honduras has good reason to ask for special measures as a condition for reentry into the CACM. However, in view of the evening-out of the distribution of benefits between 1968 and 1972, even the special measures for Honduras could be established on the basis that they would eventually be phased out after a specified period.

Chapter 3 examines various alternatives for special treatment of Honduras and concludes that the most feasible measure would be for the CACM to allow Honduras to reenter the market with free access to the markets of other member countries but with the maintenance of some level of Honduran tariffs against imports from the other member countries. In fact the bilateral treaties between Honduras and Nicaragua, Guatemala, and Costa Rica already contain precedents for this type of preferential treatment. On the basis of the specific estimates of benefits and costs, and considering likely levels of trade, the maintenance of Honduran tariffs on partner goods at a level of approximately one-half the common external tariff would generate tariff revenues of an amount sufficient to equalize Honduran per capita benefits from integration with the overall average for the CACM countries.

A third realm of policy implications of the study on the benefits and costs of integration is at the international level. The main implication on this plane is that economic integration among developing countries warrants renewed attention as an instrument for economic development. Given the considerable economic impact of integration in the CACM, it is reasonable to expect that sizable economic gains could also be achieved by other groupings of developing countries if they were prepared to adopt a thoroughgoing free trade regime like that of the CACM. The option of free trade areas among developing countries merits all the more attention at a time when industrial countries appear to have exhausted their political scope for the opening of their own markets to developing countries through tariff preferences and, on the contrary, are resorting to more protective measures (especially voluntary export quotas) in sensitive product areas important to developing countries, such as textiles and shoes.

A final policy implication of chapter 3, again with significance for developing countries generally and not just Central America, is that the nontraditional integration benefits arising from savings of foreign exchange and from integration's stimulus to investment are the dominant forces in the process of integration among developing countries. Similarly, in integration movements among developing countries, special measures are likely to be necessary in favor of the poorest member countries, although the need for these measures may diminish over time as the natural forces of maturation work in the direction of equalization in the country distribution of the benefits of integration.

The appendices to this book contain several implications for employment policies. First, with respect to industrial employment, serious consideration should be given to raising capital costs. The most direct means of doing so is to raise the interest rate--by raising legal ceilings on interest rates for business loans in the region--and to raise the tariffs (net of exemptions) on imports of capital goods, at least to the point where they stand at the average level of tariffs. Tax policies for stimulating industrial employment could include a tax on deductions on credits geared to the number of employees of the firms. In order to offset any fiscal loss, credits or deductions of this type could be balanced by an increase in the general corporate income tax rate (which is currently extremely low due to the system of fiscal incentives). To avoid a counterproductive side effect of higher tax rates, accelerated depreciation could be reduced so that depreciation equaled actual replacement rates. (Otherwise higher tax rates would favor the use of capital, which provides a tax shelter when depreciation exceeds replacement rates.) Increased capital cost would be unlikely to discourage new investment, at least within some range of increase, because the very high profit rates at present (made possible in part by a concentrated market structure) leave room for continued investment incentive even after squeezing out some excess profits. Moreover, to the extent that interest rates are raised, the response could be greater availability of savings and therefore increased rather than decreased total investment.[1]

Second, both chapters 4 and 5 suggest that economic integration as such had only a limited impact on the generation of new jobs--yielding new positions for perhaps 3 percent of the labor force in the region (chapter 4) or possibly even less in view of the sectoral shift toward capital-intensive industry and away from agriculture (chapter 5). The limited employment impact suggests the possibility that economic integration's effect on the distribution of personal income in each country was at best neutral and perhaps regressive. This study does not evaluate this question, which warrants analysis. Nevertheless, it is almost certain that the far more important determinants of personal income distribution are basic national phenomena such as the structure of landownership, education, and personal income tax policies, rather than policies directly related to economic integration.

Third, although considerable research remains to be done before a precise policy formulation is possible, the analyses in part II of this study suggest that economywide programs favoring employment, including labor-intensive public works and construction programs (especially in the light of experience with earthquake reconstruction programs), could reverse the trend of a widening gap between available labor supply and demand for labor. The resulting upward pressure on wages would improve the distribution of income, currently dominated by the effects of an extremely low labor share in industry and a high share of agricultural rents. However, the likelihood and the success of employment and distributional programs probably will continue to depend critically on the structure of political control in each country.

Chapters 6 through 8 of this volume contain policy implications for sectoral strategy. Chapter 6 identifies specific product sectors in individual member countries where comparative advantage appears to exist and, therefore, where developmental efforts may be focused usefully. The chapter also pinpoints sectors with either excessive tariff and tax incentives or, perhaps, relatively inadequate incentives, on the basis of measured sectoral incentives as compared with sectoral comparative advantage. The chapter casts serious doubt on the efficiency of continued import substitution as a general policy for industrialization. Instead, further import substitution appears efficient in only a limited number of remaining major import items. Outside of these products, expansion for export in areas with comparative advantage would appear to be the appropriate strategy for further industrial development.

Chapter 7 reports results indicating the economic gains available through further extension of integration into the agricultural sector. Freer trade in basic grains would provide consumer benefits, particularly in Costa Rica. The analysis also points out the corresponding redistribution of income among producer groups that would be involved. But rather than any single set of policy recommendations, the primary contribution of the agricultural sector model is that it provides an instrument for ongoing policy analysis. Estimation of supply elasticities and of country comparative advantage by agricultural product (discussed in chapter 9) represent two additional examples of the policy issues that may be analyzed through simulations with the model. Other policy areas, including questions about agrarian structure, agricultural employment, and subregional income disparities should also lend themselves to analysis once greater detail is built into subsequent revisions of the model.

Finally, the chief policy implication of the study of prices (chapter 8) is that a serious examination of Nicaragua's exchange rate was in order as of November 1973. Higher prices in Nicaragua than in the rest of the region would suggest the need for devaluation, a possibility that is consistent with the negative balance of trade which Nicaragua has experienced vis-à-vis the region (see table 2, chapter 3). A second implication is that, because relative price data confirm Honduras as the country with lowest real per capita income in the region, special measures in favor of Honduras within the integration program are relevant not only for the purpose of assuring a sufficient distribution of integration's benefits among countries to encourage continued participation by all but also for the purpose of improving equity within the region. A final policy implication is that periodic price surveys similar to that carried out for this study would be a desirable practice for the Central American countries. A first repetition of the consumer price survey was carried out in the spring of 1977. That survey and potentially others like it in the future should provide the basis not only for ongoing price indices but also for indices drawn from comparable baskets of goods and using comparable methodologies across the five countries.

C. Future of the Common Market

In the light of the results of the studies presented in this book, there are grounds for considerable optimism about the future of the Central American Common Market. The net economic benefits of integration appear to warrant the political costs of achieving the various commitments and compromises of national autonomy that are required. Full participation of all countries should be feasible upon the implementation of relatively modest special measures in favor of Honduras. The fuller extension of integration into the agricultural sector should provide the region with more efficient sources of food supply. Improvements in the common external tariff and in the system of fiscal incentives should make it possible to achieve a more rational set of incentives for development along lines of comparative advantage, and in directions encouraging use of the region's unskilled labor while economizing on the use of capital. All of these improvements should be eminently possible in the next few years of the integration movement.

The recent draft treaty, or Tratado Marco, designed to cover the next twenty-five years of integration, contains several of these policy approaches. It also contains other features that represent more ambitious integration goals. These include the introduction of joint industrial programming for large industrial projects, development planning on a regional scale, and considerable authority for the intergovernmental Common Market agency.

Although political prediction is even more difficult than economic forecasting, it appears likely that at best the structural changes in the CACM will be of a consolidating nature in the next few years, rather than a dramatic movement to fundamentally more intense forms of economic union. In the last few years the international economic shocks of higher oil prices, world inflation, and world business cycle contraction have left little time for policy efforts in the direction of the maturation of a more highly developed integration movement. Within the region, these shocks did have at least the beneficial side effect of stimulating joint efforts at confronting international economic problems (as in the case of joint positions on requests for financial support to cope with higher oil prices, as well as in the case of new efforts at agricultural cooperation in response to the radical increases in food import prices during 1972 to 1974).

Nongermane political tensions also confront the region and limit the energies left over for new integration efforts. If the state of war between El Salvador and Honduras is well in the past, the increasing possibility of independence for Belize has heated up old possibilities for armed conflict between Guatemala, potentially with support from other countries in the region, and England. At the same time new political initiatives by the Carter administration in the area of human rights represent new political preoccupations for some of the countries in the region.

If extraneous political issues divert attention from the political efforts necessary for the further economic integration of Central America, the Common Market also faces resistance in the form of direct criticisms of the model of economic integration itself. These criticisms include the charges that (i) integration has benefited primarily the foreign multinational firms; (ii) integration has benefited industrialists but at the expense of regional consumers who must now pay higher prices for inefficient local production; (iii) integration has prevented improvements in income distributions, or has actually made the distribution of income more unequal and worsened social conditions.

Although such criticisms are common and operate against the development of more complete integration, there is little basis in fact for these charges. The idea that only foreign firms benefited from integration is rejected by the analysis of benefits and costs of integration in chapter 3 of this study. The economic benefits found there are large; yet they exclude any benefits to foreign firms. For example, in the measurement of the welfare benefits of integration's impact on investment, that analysis explicitly excludes the profit share of foreign firms. While there would appear to be room for higher taxation of foreign investment once fiscal incentive schemes are coordinated instead of set up in competition among the countries, there is no basis for the notion that integration represented benefits to foreign firms with little gain or even losses for Central Americans.

Again, the charge that regional businessmen were the only local beneficiaries, and that they gain only at the expense of local consumers, is belied by the data. The Common Market did not set up a series of hothouse industries and then force consumers to buy local goods at exorbitant prices. Instead, the level of tariffs facing the outside world declined over time. Therefore prices to consumers should have fallen, not risen, as the result of integration, for two reasons: (i) newly free entry for goods from partner countries, and (ii) declining tariff charges even for supply from outside the area.

Nor is the charge that the Common Market thwarted goals of social justice credible. The basic determinants of income distribution are internal structural factors such as the distribution of landownership. It would be naive in the extreme to suppose that alternative integration policies could have changed these basic structural factors substantially. If the region had not integrated and had relied more on traditional raw materials exports, the rental share of large landowners would have been even higher. Or, in the absence of integration if each country had pursued independent industrial import substitution, then the sectoral shares in income would have been relatively similar to those experienced under integration, but there would have been less total income to go around.

It would appear that the realistic way to look at social and income distributional problems in relation to integration is to consider these basic structural issues soluble only through strong measures within each national polity, not through conceivable changes in integration policies. What economic integration <u>can</u> do is to provide a larger total gross national product, supplying <u>more</u> resources that may be used for the sometimes costly and painful restructurings required for significant income redistribution.[2]

Economic integration in Central America faces real opportunities for economic gains through feasible but significant policy changes. These include special measures for the reentry of Honduras, the extension of freer trade to basic grains, and rationalization of the tariff and tax incentive systems. It will require strong leadership in the member countries to pursue these opportunities, despite disruptions of a political nature and critiques of economic development strategy. In the latter area, the scientific, intellectual, business, and official communities in the region would appear to bear a special obligation to develop responsible positions based insofar as possible on careful analysis and empirical evidence. One purpose of this book is to contribute to the base for responsible policy analysis within the communities of informed opinion in Central America. Another objective of this book is to advance understanding of the question of economic integration among developing countries more generally, using for this purpose the experience of one of the most dynamic integration efforts so far observed among developing countries, the Central American Common Market.

Chapter 9

NOTES

1. The phenomenon emphasized by Ronald I. McKinnon, Money and Capital in Economic Development (Washington, D.C.: Brookings Institution, 1973).

2. For example, with larger gross national product made possible by integration, a country may be in a position to carry out a land purchase scheme for improving land access to small farmers. With lower gross national product and government revenue, the country might be forced to choose between no action whatsoever and land expropriation without compensation to owners, in the area of agrarian policy.

Comparing Prices, Purchasing Power, and Real Products in Central America

Jorge Salazar-Carrillo and Jorge Bortscheff

A. Methodology

Comparative studies have fascinated economists since Adam Smith. Such studies are especially useful among countries engaged in international trade, and their importance is still greater when they involve countries which are integrating their economies.

In particular, there are some variables whose comparative study is crucial for an understanding of the requirements and possibilities of integration. Prices, incomes, and expenditures are variables of this type. Thus, the comparison of their structures and levels is usually one of the first studies to be undertaken when a region is undergoing an integration process.

Although such comparative research has lately been given a boost by the needs of integration movements in Europe and Latin America, the origin of the research can be traced to the comparison of living costs and conditions among European countries (with the United States sometimes included) at the beginning of this century. To understand the nature of this chapter better, the studies that have preceded it are reviewed briefly.

1. Review of Previous Studies

The United Kingdom Board of Trade carried out the first comparative studies of wages and costs of living known to have been published.[1] The studies consisted of comparisons of wages and prices for food and rent in Germany, France, Belgium, the United States, and the United Kingdom for the period 1908 to 1911. These were limited studies covering only part of the living costs of the wage earners and obviously undertaken to study the basis of actual and future trade among these countries.

Almost since its inception, the International Labour Office (ILO) has been involved in research on wages and living costs. For many years this organization has collected materials on wages, consumption patterns of working-class families, and prices paid for the principal categories of goods in several countries. Part of these data are regularly published in the ILO Yearbook of Labor Statistics. The ILO has also undertaken special comparative studies. In one case the institution sought to determine the wages paid to employees of the Ford Motor Company in a study comparing the levels of living of employees in each of fourteen European countries with that of the same class of workers in Detroit.[2] More recently an ILO study on the textile industry (cotton and wool) attempted to measure the real purchasing power (in terms of food) of the wages paid in this industry in various countries.[3]

The most outstanding empirical study in the field prior to World War II was the pioneering work carried out by Colin Clark.[4] Clark was the first to attempt a comparison, not just of wage income but of total income expressed in real terms. This was done by estimating the purchasing power of the currencies involved in order to convert total monetary income into real income.[5] Clark made use of available data on prices, income and expenditure, and production patterns, but had to collect a considerable amount of information on his own. Not only was Clark's coverage on the concepts of income much broader but the price data used were more comprehensive as well.

In the early 1950s, interest in the type of comparisons pioneered by Clark reemerged. This prompted efforts by the OECD, under the direction of Milton Gilbert and Irving Kravis, which went much further in attaining comparability and inclusiveness.[6] In these efforts, gross national product (GNP), or the total income originated in generating it, was taken as the basis of comparison. A study was made of the composition of GNP in some OECD countries in order to collect comparable price information at an appropriate level of disaggregation. From the latter, the purchasing power of the currencies involved could be calculated with greater precision than before, making possible a detailed conversion of the GNP, or the total income originated, into real terms. As may be surmised, these studies broke new methodological ground and gathered much larger sets of data on expenditure and prices.

With the beginning of economic integration in Western Europe, studies comparing incomes, expenditures, and prices became more important. Both the High Authority of the European Coal and Steel Community and the Office Statistique of the European Economic Community carried out real wage comparisons among their member countries.[7] The latter organizations and a group of statisticians from Denmark, Finland, Norway, and Sweden compared price levels and determined purchasing power parities on the basis of very detailed collections of prices in their respective groups of countries.[8] However, these research bodies did not generally attempt to compare overall incomes in the tradition of Clark, Gilbert, and Kravis.

The integrationist spirit of the Economic Commission for Latin America (ECLA) led to a study, covering the years 1960-62, in which an attempt was made to measure and compare price levels and calculate purchasing power parities in Latin American countries. The study also compared the price levels in those countries with levels in two U.S. cities (Houston and Los Angeles).[9] The ECLA study was the first to focus explicitly on developing countries. In 1968 Stanley Braithwaite used the detailed purchasing power parities estimated in that study to calculate Latin American gross domestic products (GDP), or total income originated, in real terms.[10]

At the end of 1966 the ECIEL Program[11] decided to undertake another Latin American study comparable with that of the ECLA. As a result Latin American comparisons of prices, purchasing power, and real product were obtained for 1968. The ECIEL study was more ambitious than the ECLA study in terms of goods coverage, amplitude of the price surveys, expenditure breakdowns, and methods used, but it only covered the eleven Latin American Free Trade Association (LAFTA) countries rather than the nineteen Latin American countries included by ECLA.[12] Results and other details of this research effort, which can be considered a stepping stone to the present study, have been reported in the literature.[13]

More recently an effort has been mounted by the University of Pennsylvania, the World Bank, and the United Nations to estimate purchasing power parities (p.p.p.) and GDP in real terms for a small set of developed and developing countries, covering, however, most of the regions and socio-political systems in the world. The countries involved are the United States, France, Germany, Japan, India, Kenya, Colombia, Italy, the United Kingdom, and Hungary. The study is done in the tradition of Gilbert and Kravis, being directed by the latter, with a comprehensive coverage of the data required for the estimation of the purchasing power adjustment factors needed for converting total income (GDP) into real income. This project of international comparisons is being extended to cover a larger set of countries.[14]

2. Purpose and Nature of the Study

The process of economic integration in Latin America gained strength about fifteen years ago with the formation of the Central American Common Market (CACM). Immediately afterward, LAFTA was created, which came to include all the Spanish- and Portuguese-speaking countries of South America plus Mexico. Within LAFTA, the five western South American countries plus Venezuela later formed the Andean Common Market.

These efforts toward economic integration have been hindered by lack of comparative information about the economic conditions of the member countries. Furthermore, for integration to be a tool in the economic development of Central America, it is necessary to understand better the problems and the potentialities of these countries, for which similar data are required. If such information is gathered under a common methodology, it would help the analysis of regional development and integration.

Obviously, a careful comparison of the level and structure of prices, real incomes, and product for the Central American nations is an important step toward the achievement of these research goals. It will permit, through the application of the p.p.p exchange rates, all sorts of value comparisons among these countries.[15] It will also throw light upon trade prospects within Central America, and on its export competitiveness. Finally, it will illuminate the recent price trends in Central American countries and the role of tariffs, taxes, and price controls in the determination, through the price system, of the expenditure and production patterns in the area.

In order to accomplish the objectives of the study, the research had to be more complex and complete than that briefly reviewed above. Both greater comparability and inclusiveness were required. Price,

income, and expenditure comparisons have usually involved advanced countries, so an extra effort had to be mustered to achieve these comparisons
for developing countries.

In terms of the price and income comparisons, the present study
blends the approaches of ECLA and the Office Statistique with that of
Kravis and his collaborators in the International Comparisons Project.
This is the case because in this study price comparisons and purchasing
power estimation within the content of integration schemes are combined
with the comparison of real incomes and expenditures. The countries are
compared in pairs and multilaterally.

The national accounts breakdown, on the expenditure side, served
as a basis for the estimates and comparisons presented in this study.
Gross domestic expenditure had to be more disaggregated than that published by the national accounts offices in each country. For this reason
it was necessary to use unpublished data available in the worksheets of
these offices or obtained from other unpublished sources or special surveys. Thus, not only are real income and expenditure comparisons presented but their disaggregations are also compared among the Central
American countries at a quite detailed level. In order to insure uniformity in the various aggregates compared across all Central America,
a common methodology was used in the data gathering and survey stages,
and homogeneous definitions were used throughout.[16]

From all the goods and services included in the expenditure breakdown, certain items were selected, using various criteria, for the collection of the information required for the comparison of prices and
the estimation of p.p.p. rates. Market prices, at the final demand level,
were gathered in the countries involved. Price surveys were organized
for this purpose and a data file of more than 400 items, with several
observations per item, was compiled for each country.

The type of survey and number of items and observations varied for
the different expenditure categories. However, a common methodology was
followed for every country in the price surveys, and common market
baskets were chosen. These common Central American market baskets, selected using national price and expenditure information, were verified
as representative. Only in the case of investment in machinery and
equipment and consumer durables was flexibility allowed in the items
priced in the various countries. Generally, the goods were identically
specified in the various price surveys.

The prices, simultaneously collected in November 1973 in all countries, were submitted to a series of tests for cleaning purposes. After
corrections and adjustments, they were averaged and weighted using corresponding detailed expenditure information, and aggregated to correspond
with the expenditure breakdown referred to above.

On the basis of this information the p.p.p. rates were calculated
as the implicit rates among the weighted prices of the various countries. A more straightforward price comparison is presented after expressing the prices in a common currency by the use of the official
exchange rates. This allows the construction of Central American price
indices at various levels of aggregation. Finally, when the expenditure

categories are adjusted by the level and structure of prices in each country, real expenditure and product comparisons result.

This study is also singular because the results and information contained in it may be used to clarify other aspects relevant for research in economic integration and development. The several price indices computed can provide some rough indications of both absolute and comparative advantage.[17] These are not precise because they are based on final market prices which may be affected by taxes, subsidies, imports, and so on. However, given that both the level and structure of prices are available for the set of countries examined, the wealth of information makes up for its limitations. In particular, the number of observations per product and the number of products involved make the prices resulting from the study much more amenable to trade analysis than have been results of previous research. The fact that the countries being compared are experiencing an integration process also favors the use of the price data for this purpose.

Furthermore, some of the price limitations can at least be partly compensated. The examination of the price levels and structures in the determination of trade advantages can be made much more realistic by considering which prices correspond to imported goods and which to locally produced items. This information can be derived from the price survey and can sharpen the determination of possible exports and imports for each country.[18]

In addition, information was especially gathered on taxes, tariffs, and on other imports as well as price controls, in order to estimate how they might affect prices in the various countries.[19]

3. Scope and Plan of the Study

The comprehensive price surveys on which the price comparisons and the estimation of the p.p.p. rates are based were undertaken only in the capital cities of the Central American countries. A large number of price observations were amassed for the study, most of which were simultaneously gathered during a brief period, and all referred to the month of November 1973. This coordination was possible only through the regional auspices of the Permanent Secretariat of the General Treaty of Central American Economic Integration (SIECA), which secured the collaboration of institutions in each of the Central American countries.

The use of a computer helped in the experimentation with regression techniques involving one of the most difficult problems in studies of this type: the assurance that the goods encompassed were of comparable quality insofar as was possible. For certain classes of goods, comparability is difficult to obtain directly and hedonic adjustment techniques must be used.[20] This study is also one of the first to use hedonic regression techniques. However, it should be noted that even though this new approach was helpful in deriving homogeneous cross-country specifications, the difficulties encountered limited its applicability to a fraction of what was contemplated originally.

The national account estimates of the various countries were the starting point for the comparison of production and expenditures in real terms. In particular, the gross domestic product as estimated from the expenditure side was used as the standard of comparison.

It should be recognized that in some instances the definitions and procedures used by the Central American countries in their product and expenditure estimation do differ. Some of the incomparabilities have been removed, but others remain, clouding the comparisons. On the other hand, it is believed that the remaining discrepancies are not important enough to affect the results significantly. It is reassuring in this context that the surveys undertaken in the various countries to complement and supplement the national accounts used the same methodology and are strictly comparable.[21]

B. Alternative Methods

In general terms, there are two approaches to the international comparisons of prices and income. The first is to use a few goods and services as indicators (usually physical) of the country's economic activity, and the second is to use each country's own estimate of income and the prices from a selected but large sample of all these goods and services. The first approach, "short-cut methods," bases the comparisons on a few "indicators of stocks or flows of goods and services or structural characteristics of economies."[22]

For the second approach, the national accounts of each of these countries are used. To compare the national accounts, it is necessary to convert the figures from national currencies to a common unit of measure. For the purpose of income or real product comparisons, the p.p.p. rates calculated from the overall price sample are used. In order to obtain the price comparisons, the p.p.p. rates are divided by the official exchange rates, thus providing an indication of relative price levels. Before turning to the method employed in this study, it is useful to consider the nature of the short-cut methods and to demonstrate that they are no better than the comprehensive national accounts methods used here.

1. Short-Cut Methods

Many studies have been made using this approach. A representative study, and one of the best, is Beckerman's comparison of consumption in fifty-seven countries.[23] He correlates per capita private consumption with indicators such as the consumption of steel, and cement production. The advantage of these methods is that they are simple enough to use figures available for a wide variety of countries.

In principle a single indicator considered to be highly correlated with real income could provide the basis for real income comparisons. Alternatively, a series of indicators could be aggregated into one index for comparing income across countries. It would be difficult to evaluate the reliability of either type of comparison. A more reasonable approach would be to correlate statistically the chosen indicators with real income.

Suppose we have a series of indicators X_{ij}, i = 1, ..., n, for countries j, j = 1, ..., m, correlated with real income, y. We can form the equation

(1) $$y_j = \beta_0 + \sum_{i=1}^{n} \beta \ i \ X_{ij} + u_j.$$

Estimating the β 's by regression methods, we can compute a real income y_j^C:

(2) $$y_j^C = \hat{\beta}_0 + \sum_{i=1}^{n} \hat{\beta} \ i \ X_{ij}.$$

For countries lacking reliable data on real income but having easily available figures on the indicators, it may be desirable to compare predicted income, y_j^C, rather than measured income, y_j. Suppose we wish to estimate income of country m + 1 and we have data on X, m + 1, i = 1, ..., n.

Then:

(3) $$y_{m+1}^C = \beta_0 + \sum_{i=1}^{n} \beta \ i \ X_{i,m+1}.$$

We have assumed here that the figures for the first m countries accurately represent real income.

In conclusion, the short-cut methods may be useful as extensions of income comparisons to countries for which it is very expensive to get data good enough to estimate real income; when we have countries with reliable estimates for an existing set of countries; and when to those of the group lacking reliable estimates, that the parameters estimated from the first group of countries may reasonably be applied.

Richard and Nancy Ruggles developed a short-cut method applicable to price or p.p.p. comparisons,[24] based on principles similar to those outlined above. Given that prices for the products included in the expenditure side of the GDP are intercorrelated, the levels and movements of some of them may replicate rather well those of more comprehensive lists. This is determined statistically, category by category, by determining which goods and services better explain their overall variation, up to certain explanatory levels. It has been found that a limited number of products are capable of explaining practically all of the price variation in the private consumption categories, rents excluded. No experiments were conducted for public consumption or capital formation, but even so, this short-cut method seems to be more reliable than others commonly used for income comparisons across countries. However, the method still requires careful testing, especially in relation to the reliability of the price or p.p.p. comparisons at the category level, which may require larger samples than those suggested by the Ruggles.[25] However, as short-cut estimators of overall price differences, or p.p.p. rates among a group of countries, this method appears promising.

2. National Accounts Approach

With the generalized use of a relatively well-defined system of national accounts, it is now possible to begin with each country's own measure of income and with composites of prices fully reflecting each country's structure of goods and services. The national accounts income or product estimates are probably the best available, and their methodology is quite standardized. Of course, the national accounts contain many deficiencies, but when the method of their calculation is similar among countries, comparisons are nevertheless meaningful. This is the case when we compare income or production among Central American countries. It is more difficult to compare countries with very different systems of national accounts and different conventions.[26] Although the methodology is not as well established, the same could be said about the price comparisons, especially since wide surveys of prices can be undertaken more easily.

Because national accounts data are stated in each country's currency, it is necessary to convert them to a common unit of measure. The most generalized practice has been to convert the different currencies by the official exchange rate. A more refined rate of conversion is needed than the official exchange rate.[27] This turns out to be the p.p.p. rate, which is derived from a comparison of prices in national currencies.

The national accounts can be compared either from the production side, that is, the sum of the value added of each of the sectors of production, or the expenditure side, that is, the sum of the various classes of expenditures, such as consumption, investment, and so on. Either alternative provides more information than the simple comparison. The components of either the production or the expenditure side of the gross product can be compared among countries, if proper care is taken with the level of disaggregation, depending principally upon the objectives of the study. Such disaggregation probably has the beneficial effect of bringing greater accuracy to the comparison because it makes the total comparisons dependent on comparisons of the parts, and of also insures adequate attention to each of them. Moreover, instead using an overall p.p.p. exchange rate to normalize the influence of prices in the value figures, we can use as alternatives individual indices referring to separate components of the GNP.

Finally, the concept of GDP was chosen for this study over that of GNP because the latter is less amenable to international comparisons in that the "net factor incomes received from or paid abroad" varies substantially from country to country, and because the GDP estimates are in wider use in Latin America.

It has already been established that given the favorable state of statistics in the SIECA countries, comparisons based on direct rather than short-cut methods are preferable. Now we have to decide which side of the national accounts to use: production or expenditure.

Depending on the side of the national accounts selected, we will need different prices to estimate the p.p.p. rates. If we take the production side we need two sets of prices at the level of producers—the sales prices and the cost of inputs—which makes this method more difficult. The expenditure side requires only one set of prices at the level of consumers and investors, and it is a simpler task to obtain this single set of prices.

We have organized the discussion up to now attaching a very large importance to the comparisons of income and product. This is not to deny the importance of price comparisons from which, as indicated in the beginning, many further applications derive. Thus, at this point it is important to decide which sets of prices are more useful for different purposes. We can make the income comparisons using either the prices at the level of the final purchasers (consumers and investors) or the prices at the level of the producers.

To study costs of production and comparative advantage the prices at the level of the producers would be preferable because they are better estimates of the relevant variables. To study costs of spending, prices at the level of the final purchasers are preferable. We could cite many examples of these comparisons, some favoring the use of producers' prices; others favoring the final purchasers' prices and the expenditure side of the national accounts for two reasons: (i) it is much easier and substantially less expensive to collect data on purchasers' prices and (ii) the availability and reliability of the price and income data are greater at this level in Latin America, where there are no producer and input prices and no reliable value added data.[28] In sum, the producers' prices approach would have required efforts and resources beyond the scope of this initial study.

Taking then the expenditure side of the national accounts, goods and services are to be classified in three broad categories: private consumption, public consumption, and gross capital formation. These categories are further divided into a large number of subcategories. In each subcategory a representative sample of goods and services is selected. The subcategories are so defined that they minimize the number of commodities required to explain their price and real product variations across countries.[29]

3.   The Purchasing Power Parity Rate

With the generalization of a relatively well-defined system of national accounts, numerous comparisons of income and product among countries appeared, generally made by the simple device of converting each country's currency to a common currency using the official exchange rates. Long ago economists pointed out the inaccuracy of such comparisons because official exchange rates many times reflect the distortion in the international trade and refer only to tradable commodities.[30]

When we see that a country suddenly devalues or revalues its official exchange rate, we probably do not want to say that its real income or product decreased or increased when compared with those of other countries. Or when we observe that internal prices in one country experience a big surge but the country's official rate of exchange is kept unchanged, we do not want to say that its income, when compared with that of other countries, has increased. But using an exchange rate reflecting actual trade conditions, a sort of shadow or equilibrium rate, is not the solution because the rate could vary for the same country depending on the assumptions made regarding capital flows, and so on. Even if we could somehow define and compute the same type of shadow or equilibrium rate for all countries, we would be limited to the flows crossing national boundaries, or international flows. But could we apply the rate to convert not only the international but the strictly national flows on a comparable basis?

Given that the gross product estimates mostly reflect national flows, the idea of applying an official, shadow, or equilibrium exchange rate can be discarded. It would seem that a rate taking into account both the international and the national flows would be the one to use in comparing national accounts across countries. The p.p.p. is this type of rate, as it is determined by a comparison of the prices of a set of mostly national but also international goods and services entering the gross product calculations.[31]

Here is the connection between the product or income comparisons and the price comparisons. To obtain good comparisons of national product a relatively large sample of goods and services must be selected, following the particular national accounts classification in question.[32] The prices of these commodities must be compared when expressed in national currencies. Such price comparisons, when weighted by the corresponding gross product values and aggregated, constitute the p.p.p. rates.

In comparing the prices of a large number of commodities, the cost of the given basket of goods is determined in the various countries. The purchasing power parities of the currencies from the countries involved are easily derived from such relative costs.[33] The commodities may refer to either (i) a collection of items each of which is considered to satisfy "wants" or "needs" in the same or an equivalent way in the various situations, known as the "market basket" approach, or (ii) a collection of items which in total provide the same or an equivalent amount of satisfaction in each of the situations involved, even though individually the items may provide different amounts of satisfaction, known as the "cost of living" approach.[34]

Various kinds of price comparisons can be constructed from this information. By converting the total cost of the common basket of goods in each of the countries involved into a common unit by means of some sort of exchange rate, their overall price levels can be compared.[35] Such comparisons can be carried down into lower levels of disaggregation, with reliability being the only constraint. Thus, the price levels of groups of commodities could also be compared across countries. In the simpler "market basket" approach, the prices for an identical basket of items is collected for every country, and using index number formulas, price levels are compared across countries, and their p.p.p. rates are calculated.

4.   Cost-of-Living versus Market Basket Approach

The first approach, "cost-of-living," has been proposed by many researchers on the grounds that it avoids the difficulties attributable to the interdependence of prices and quantities. Also its proponents claim that this approach would circumvent problems due to differing availabilities of different goods among countries, and to factors such as climate

which, although influencing costs and prices, have in themselves no monetary value capable of adequate measurement in these comparisons.

However, this approach has a number of disadvantages. For instance,
it is difficult to demonstrate that a given collection of goods and services actually provides a specific amount of well-being, or that the satisfaction of wants or the levels of well-being are precisely equated in the
various situations. The use of indifference maps and income elasticities
of demand to indicate equivalence has been advocated, but at the present
stage of statistical development, this "cost-of-living" approach is not
likely to provide practical results except under very restrictive
conditions.

The second is the "market basket" approach. As its name indicates,
it consists of selecting a basket of goods and services, each of which
is assumed to provide equivalent satisfaction in two or more situations.
This implies that if individual commodities provide equivalent amounts
of satisfaction, the aggregate of the items will also provide an equivalent in total satisfaction in the countries being compared. A second
assumption implied in this approach is that the cost of the basket in
the various situations will indicate the comparative level of prices,
the comparative purchasing power, and the p.p.p. rate.

There are a number of limitations and disadvantages to the market
basket approach. It demands precise identification of each item in each
situation; it assumes that the same item meets and performs the same
function, no matter which country is concerned; it assumes homogeneity,
both of income and of expenditure (as well as of prices), within a country, which usually is not true; it demands a mass of precisely calculated
statistical material relating to prices, quantities, values, incomes, and
so on, which is not readily available; and its results may be restricted
in application by the limited coverage of the study and methodology
employed.

In spite of all this, the market basket approach has the overriding
advantage that it is mathematically precise, free from ambiguities in
interpretation, and that it does not rest on the subjective judgment of
the researcher using it. In addition, its application can be extended
through all sectors of expenditure, whereas the cost-of-living approach
has so far been applied experimentally to only a restricted part of consumer expenditure, and to particular levels of income. Accordingly it
was decided to adopt the market basket approach in this study. The market basket is defined in section B below.

5.   The Index Number Formulas

In this section we present the main price index formulas used in
estimating the p.p.p. rate and the cross-country price relations. Suppose we calculate an index PI_{12}, indicating the prices of country 1 relative to the prices of country 2. The notation in the formulas is the
following:

P_{ij} = prices,

q_{ij} = quantities,

i = 1, ..., n:goods, and

j = 1, ..., m:countries.

Let us now consider the index number formulas one by one.

    a. Laspayres Index

    The Laspeyres index is the most frequently used in intertemporal price comparisons. In interspatial comparisons it can be expressed as follows:

$$L_{12} = \frac{\sum\limits_{1=1}^{n} p_{i1}\, q_{i2}}{\sum\limits_{i=1}^{n} p_{i2}\, q_{i2}} \; .$$

In this case we answer the question of how much would a basket of goods representative of country 2 cost, when purchased in country 1. It will cost L_{12} times as much as in country 2. The purchasing power of the currency of country 1 relative to the currency of country 2 will be $1/L_{12}$.

    This formula is often transformed to use price relatives combined with expenditure weights,

$$L_{12} = \sum\limits_{i=1}^{n} \frac{p_{i1}}{p_{i2}}\; v_{i2},$$

where:

$$V_{i2} = \frac{p_{i2}\, q_{i2}}{\sum\limits_{i=1}^{n} p_{12}\, q_{i2}} \; .$$

    b. Paasche Index

    The interspatial correspondent of the intertemporal Paasche price index uses the quantities purchased in country 1 as the weights:

$$P_{12} = \frac{1}{\sum\limits_{i=1}^{n} \frac{p_{i2}}{p_{i1}} \cdot v_{i1}} \; ,$$

$$V_i = \frac{p_{iI} \; q_{iI}}{\sum\limits_{i=1}^{n} p_{i1} \; q_{i1}} \qquad .$$

c. Fisher Ideal Index

We know that because of the inverse relation between prices and quantities, the Laspeyres index will overestimate the aggregate price relative and the Paasche index will underestimate it. A practical solution is a compromise between the two of the forms, called the Fisher Ideal price index:

$$F_{12} = \sqrt{L_{12} \cdot P_{12}} \qquad .$$

These three indices are the most widely used for binary comparisons. They do well with most of the tests usually applied to the prices indices. In particular they meet what Dreschsler has called the "characteristicity" test, which is incompatible with the "circularity" (or "transitivity") test. The requirement is that the weights used in the index be characteristic of the two countries being compared. In the first index we use the weights of the base country; in the second, the weights of the other country; and in the third, a combination of the two. But when we want to compare more than two countries, we would like an index satisfying the circularity test. For example, in three countries, A, B, and C, we would like an index such that the index for A/C is equal to the product of the indices A/B and B/C.

It is very easy to verify mathematically that none of the three indices mentioned satisfies circularity. The more characteristic the weights are to any particular couple of countries, the less appropriate the index will be when applied in comparisons with other countries. To compare a group of countries we have to sacrifice characteristicity for the sake of circularity.

d. The Walsh Index

There are many indices that satisfy the circularity requirements. One of them is the Walsh price index.[36]

$$W_{12} = \prod_{i=1}^{n} \left(\frac{p_{i1}}{p_{12}} \right) V_{ix}$$

where

$$V_{ix} = \frac{\left(\prod\limits_{i=1}^{m} \cdot V_{ij} \right)^{1/m}}{\sum\limits_{i=1}^{n} \left[\left(\prod\limits_{j=1}^{m} \right) V_{ij} \right]^{1/m}} \qquad .$$

This index is a geometric weighted average of the price relative. The weights are the geometric means of value shares of the countries considered. Alternatively the same formula could have been applied
using arithmetic weights.

6.   Other Formulas

Many other price index formulas could be used in the intercountry
comparisons. A comprehensive list of these is discussed in the seminal
contribution of Irving Fisher, The Making of Index Numbers. More recent
surveys of the literature have been undertaken by Ruggles and Kravis,
Kenessey, Heston, Summers et al., focusing especially on the interspatial comparisons.[37]

Of the formulas appearing in these sources which were not discussed
above, a few offered interesting possibilities. These are the simultaneous equation method of estimating p.p.p. rates and cross-country price
indexes developed by Geary and later on by Khamis; the Van Izeren method
used by the Office Statistique of the European Economic Community, which
from a set of binary rates among all the countries involved derives a
transitive index, and the Theil index, similar to the previous one but
using regression in logs to derive transitivity. The Geary-Khamis method,
which crosses the weights of the countries involved, rather than the
binary index themselves, appears to have the best properties among these,
being the circular index used in the international Price Comparison Project
of the United Nations.[38]   However, it has two main defects; it uses
quantity rather than expenditure weights and does not give the same weight
to each of the countries included, consequently introducing a bias dependent on the per capita income differences of the countries compared. The
Van Izeren and Theil solutions have the disadvantage of requiring the
calculation of the full set of binary comparisons, which becomes somewhat
problematical when more than ten countries are compared.[39]

In the results of this study, we present the computations of the
four indices. The first three are useful for binary comparisons, and
the fourth for the circular comparisons of all the countries. The discussion of the results is based on the circular Walsh index.

7.   Special Problems of Cross-Country Comparisons

The accuracy of a method such as that employed in this study depends upon the identification of specific commodities for each point of
comparison, and while this is generally a minor problem for intertemporal indexes (since a commodity identified in one time period can as
a rule be identified again in succeeding or preceding time periods),
this is not the case for comparisons across space. Very often items
described by the same name may be of quite different quality in different countries, or they may be marketed under completely different conditions. It should be noted, however, that when intertemporal comparisons
are made for a given product over even a relatively short period of
time, the effect of technological changes can create the same problem
of identification that is faced in interspatial comparisons. In fact,
for long periods of time it may be impossible to find the same item in

intertemporal comparisons (for example, television sets), while this is seldom the case in comparisons across space.

A second problem is that of selecting a set of commodities for which information about the relative importance of each is either available or could be collected. This is further complicated by the wide variety of expenditure patterns existing across countries. For a price index over time, for instance, the difference in the relative importance of commodities in successive time periods is not sufficient to cast doubt on the validity of the index, unless the time periods are extended over five years, or unless some fundamental change has occurred in the meantime (for example, the outbreak of war). Among countries, and even among different cities in the same country, the difference in consumption patterns, however, is usually appreciable. If income levels, climatic and geographic conditions, tastes and customs, tax structures, transport costs, and the relative cost of producing the items differ to any extent, the expenditure patterns can be so divergent that the adoption of the common weighting system, needed for circularity, becomes problematical.

A final difference between intertemporal and interspatial comparisons concerns the scope and nature of the research. Usually intertemporal comparisons have dealt with certain types of prices and particular classes of purchasers. For final expenditure categories they have generally covered consumer prices for baskets of goods purchased by wage earners and employees. By contrast, interspatial comparisons have normally covered all types of prices and have given results that are representative of all classes within the communities considered; otherwise they could not be considered fully representative of the country.

Given the above difficulties one might tend to doubt the validity of interspatial comparisons. But there are other considerations that lead one to think they are valid, and which make their undertaking easier than they seem.

It is possible to regard the basic needs and desires of man as quite similar in different places. In this view, what changes from place to place is not so much what men would like to have but what the economy affords them. What differs is first the extent to which the economy is capable of satisfying their needs, and second, the means by which they are satisfied, that is, the physical identity of the goods. Differences in technology and differences in relative factor prices have been mainly responsible for variations in the physical forms of goods produced by the economy to satisfy basic wants that remain constant in different places.

There are reasons to believe that it is this latter view that in the main is the more valid approach to the international differences that are observed in the goods that satisfy particular wants. Any traveler around the world cannot help but notice the similarity of goods found in the shops of the major cities. Plumbing facilities in houses and the possession of automobiles and other durable goods, once regarded to a considerable extent as idiosyncrasies of the people in the United States, are becoming common in other parts of the world as economic levels rise. The emergent middle classes of Central America typically pursue the same patterns of consumption as their counterparts in the United States and Western Europe. It is reasonable to say that the consumption patterns of the peasants in less-developed economies are different from those of the urban middle classes in the same countries, not because of differences in taste. The measurement of relative income levels between the rural and urban sectors of the less-developed countries, and among less-developed countries as well (whose income levels differ substantially) is in principle a valid exercise. The problem then becomes one of finding criteria of equivalence between the different physical forms of goods that are used to satisfy practically the same wants. This may be difficult but not objectionable in principle.

The basic criterion is that of the physical identity of the goods being compared. This means that a product satisfying a particular want is very carefully specified in terms of its characteristics, and then an effort is made to find products fitting such description in the various countries. Actually, it will be practically impossible to find identical goods and services in different nations, but given that productive technology is similar around the world, and that the same companies are involved in the production of many items, it is possible to come quite close.[40]

When it becomes difficult to use, the physical identity criterion can be supplemented by the criterion of identity in the want being satisfied, or in the function performed. This criterion implies that products satisfying the condition of fulfilling the same need will be selected in certain countries, even though their physical characteristics differ.[41]

C.   Procedural Details

The following section reports on detailed aspects of the study. This section and the next (on the hedonic technique) constitute supplementary materials. The principal analysis and empirical findings of this appendix are contained in the preceding section and in chapter 8.

1.   The Private Consumption Sector

The object of this survey is to compile the market prices for a representative selection or basket of goods and services[42] in the different countries. In an investigation of this type, it is not possible to cover all of the items of the consumption sector, and as such, a representative list of 244 goods and services has been chosen. In this selection, the following aspects are taken into account; the composition of the expenditures, the importance of each group of articles, the availability of prices, and the definition of the item. This is done in order to make the identification of each one of these articles easy and precise.

a.   Design of the Questionnaire

The questionnaire included the following:

Name of the product,
Detailed specification of the product to be surveyed,
Date of the survey,

Name of the establishment,
Price per unit,
Price control: yes or no,
If imported, country of origin,
Sales tax, and
Comments of the surveyor.

In order to maintain the highest degree of comparability in statistical information between the five Central American countries, special care was taken to conduct the interviews in the following manner:

(i) The article should correspond to the specification. The products should be described in such a way that they can be identified adequately and thus assure product comparability between countries.

(ii) The article should be merchandise in good condition. Goods or articles in poor condition should not be selected, or in general, goods that for one reason or another are not desirable should not be priced.

(iii) The quality should reflect the most common kind in Central America, taking Guatemala as base for quality uniformity. When a difficulty arises in choosing among two or more brands of similar quality, the price of the brand which is most frequently used should be used for the survey.

(iv) Some of the goods specified in the list of prices are seasonal. In reference to this type of good, the lowest price which appeared immediately before the survey should be used.

b. Data Collection

The prices in stores, and so on, were compiled by the institutions preparing the price indices in each of the five countries.

For each good or service five to seven prices from different establishments were taken. The retail prices were obtained including taxes on the final sale price.

Table A-1 shows the coverage of the price survey corresponding to the private consumption sector in each of the Central American countries.

c. Weights

After reviewing the final selection of articles comprising the representative list for the preparation of the relative price index, as well as the parity rates, the corresponding weights were derived, on one of the following alternative bases.

(i) Certain weights were attributed to the goods and services on the basis of the results of the "Studies of Expenditures and Incomes" done in each of the five countries of Central America by the following institutions: Costa Rica--General Bureau of Statistics and Census; El Salvador--General Bureau of Statistics and Census; Guatemala--Institute

Table A-1. Private Consumption Sector, Coverage of the
Price Survey, Central America

Private Consumption Sector	Number of Observations				
	Costa Rica	El Salvador	Guatemala	Honduras	Nicaragua
Food, beverages, tobacco	405	405	558	405	400
1. Meat	35	35	49	35	35
2. Fish	25	25	35	25	25
3. Dairy products and eggs	45	45	63	45	45
4. Cereals and derivatives	55	55	77	55	50
5. Fruits	40	40	56	40	40
6. Vegetables	70	70	98	70	70
7. Fats and oils	20	20	28	20	20
8. Beverages (hot and cold)	25	25	35	25	25
9. Tobacco	10	10	12	10	10
10. Other foods	20	20	28	20	20
11. Foods (outside the home)	20	20	28	20	20
12. Beverages (nonalcoholic)	10	10	12	10	10
13. Beverages (alcoholic)	15	15	17	15	15
14. Beverages (bought outside home)	15	15	20	15	15
Clothing, textiles, and shoes	180	185	218	185	150
Fuels, electricity, and water	30	27	32	18	22
Durable consumption goods	125	108	142	122	97
Nondurable consumption goods	140	140	157	140	135
Services	140	143	164	121	141
Total	1,020	1,008	1,271	991	945

of Economic and Social Research of the University of San Carlos; Honduras--Central Bank of Honduras; Nicaragua--Central Bank of Nicaragua.

(ii) Others were estimated on the basis of the apparent consumption of the product. In this way the weights of the goods and services that were studied but do not appear in the "Study of Domestic Expenditures and Incomes" were completed.

(iii) A minimum weight ("nominal weight") was assigned to the goods and services that appear to be insignificant, whether due to infrequent use or because of difficulty of obtaining the data for corresponding consumption.

(iv) Some weights were based on the experience obtained in other Central American countries having a similar consumption structure, in order to fill gaps in the data.

The derived weights were added together, usually indicating a total weighted coefficient greater than 1.00. The weights were then normalized to adjust the sum to unity.

    d.   Correspondences

Correspondences among categories were required to allocate the weights identified on the above alternative bases to the appropriate corresponding items in the basket. Redistribution of the weights among the goods and services of the basket was done in the following ways:

(i) The weight was attributed exclusively to one good in the basket;

(ii) The weight was divided in equal parts among various goods in the basket; and

(iii) The weight was divided into unequal parts between two or more goods in the basket.

The products included in the survey were arranged under the subcategories listed in table A-2.

    2.   Rents

In order to make a relative price index compatible at a country level for this subcategory, which is part of the private consumption sector but is considered separately, a survey was made in each one of the five Central American countries.

    a.   Design of the Questionnaire

The questionnaire on rents asked for the following information: (i) address; (ii) year of construction; (iii) number of years of residence; (iv) house or apartment and what floor; (v) total number of rooms (detailed as to number of bedrooms, servants' rooms, kitchen, living room, dining room, living-dining room, other rooms); (vi) number of bathrooms; (vii) total area of the dwelling in square meters; (viii) elevator (yes or no); (ix) garden or patio area as a fraction of the dwelling; (x) heating (yes or no); (xi) air conditioning (yes or no); (xii) physical state--good, average, poor; (xiii) monthly rent; (xiv) rent controlled (yes or no); and (xv) taxes--ad valorem and specific. Conforming with the questions asked, a list was prepared which served as a basis for uniform criteria of comparability within the Central American region.

    b. Selection of Sample

    The survey covers only the capitals of each one of the Central American countries. In order to make the data collected compatible in terms of being representative, it was necessary to choose a minimum of 150 units in each country as a basic requirement.[43]

    The survey of rents in 1973 was based upon a random sample of rented units taken from neighborhoods or zones whose occupants belonged to that sector of the population defined as the middle third, in an ordering of families according to total annual income.

Table A-2. Private Consumption Subcategories

---

 1. Meat
 2. Fish
 3. Milk products and eggs
 4. Cereals and derivatives
 5. Fruits
 6. Vegetables
 7. Oil and fats
 8. Other foods
 9. Food outside of the home
10. Beverages (hot and cold)
11. Tobacco
12. Clothing for men and boys
13. Clothing for women and girls
14. Materials and articles for the home
15. Footwear
16. Rents
17. Combustibles
18. Furniture and utensils for the home
19. Automobile accessories
20. Electrical or similar equipment for the home
21. Nondurable articles for the home
22. Pharmaceutical products for personal care and hygiene
23. Educational and recreational materials
24. Transportation and communication
25. Health services
26. Personal and other services

---

c. Methodology Used for the Estimates

The main problem in price studies of the housing sector is that of comparability. What is usually done is to compare measured rents for "comparable" rented units. The main difficulty arises in defining "comparable" units. Housing units differ from country to country, and even within a country or region. Because of this, the "hedonic technique" was used to obtain estimates of rents for the five Central American countries.[44]

The hedonic technique is based on the idea that the price of each good depends on certain characteristics, whose implicit prices can be estimated by the use of regression analysis. The basic idea is that the consumers, when buying a good, or, in this case, when renting a house, are expressing their preferences for a specific set of characteristics. By using the regression method, implicit prices of these characteristics can be determined and the quality of the houses compared can be made relatively homogeneous.

The general regression equation would be:

$$R = \beta_0 + \beta_1 x_1 + \beta_2 x_2 + \ldots \beta_m x_m + u,$$

where R is a vector of product prices, in this case of monthly rents; each set of x_1, x_2, $\ldots$ x_m is a vector of values of the characteristics; and u is a vector of random disturbances.

In order to determine a few "typical" housing units, a frequency distribution was determined for almost all variables. Some statistics were calculated for the same variables: mean, standard deviation, median, and so on. With these elements, a few "typical" or more frequently occurring housing units could be specified. Nevertheless, it must be acknowledged that when deciding on the "typical" unit, value judgments were introduced in making final decisions.

In using the hedonic method, a decision had to be made on the kind of technique to be used when running the regressions. There were three possibilities: (i) running the regressions for each country separately; (ii) pooling all the information from the five countries, while including intercept dummy variables for each; and (iii) pooling cross-country data and using slope as well as intercept dummy variables.

In this study, alternatives one and two were used. Alternative three was discarded to avoid the creation of too many dummy variables which, given the number of observations, could complicate the analysis. The technique used in both alternatives was a stepwise regression in all the variables, and afterward, a regular multiple regression was run on the most significant variables only.

After running regressions for separate countries, and for all countries together, the most significant variables in all cases turned out to be the number of rooms and the number of baths. At this point the frequency distributions and statistics had helped to determine the following "typical" houses (considering these two variables):

(i) five rooms and two baths,

(ii) four rooms and one bath, and

(iii) three rooms and one bath.

Prices for these three units were estimated, using a semilog form for the regressions equations.[45] In order to get one final price a weighted average of the three prices obtained was calculated. Weights for this purpose were estimated using again the frequency distributions.

d. Public Consumption

In the system of national accounts, contrary to the expenditure sectors whose goods and services are sold in the market and have a price, the goods produced by the state--the public sector--are not sold on the market.

Thus it was first necessary to define the method of collecting the prices for this sector in a different way from that of the private sector, separating the goods produced by the state in terms of the wages and salaries paid and the goods and services purchased for such production.

It was also considered desirable to distribute the wages and salaries, as well as the purchases of goods and services, among the branches of government which follow: Ministries of Interior, Foreign Relations, Finance, Agriculture, Economics, Public Works, Education, Health, Labor, Defense, the Judicial Branch, and the rest of the central government.

3. Wages and Salaries

a. Design of the Questionnaire

On the basis of the experience obtained by various international institutions, and earlier price surveys by ECIEL in LAFTA countries, a design for a questionnaire was worked out to be used in the survey of wages and salaries. This was applied then to a sample of the principal categories of public employees, divided into technical and administrative, with respective definitions of their positions.

The questionnaire on government wages distinguished between starting salaries and those after three years of service and after five years. It identified basic annual salary as well as family allowances and rent in kind; hours of work per year; and number of years of education or experience required for the job.

b. Weights

The central banks in the Central American countries do not have the detailed classifications for government expenditure as part of the estimates of the GDP. In order to fill this gap for estimating the weights of different categories of public employees, it was necessary to turn to information contained in the registers of the technical offices

of the state budget of each Central American country; there information
was collected on the wages and salaries paid by the central governments
at the different ministerial branch levels, disaggregated into technical and administrative personnel.

4. Government Purchase of Current Goods and Services

Government purchases of current goods and services are of relatively
little importance in Central America, and an extensive survey of these
prices was not justified. An indirect investigation was made of the
principal goods consumed by the state, utilizing the prices of the private consumption sector as well as a survey of the prices of intermediate
goods. Once the prices of the principal goods and services bought by the
state were determined, a relative weight was assigned to each in accordance with the structure of total goods and services bought by the central
government. The goods purchased by the government were classified into
the seven subcategories shown in table A-3.

Average prices were calculated for each subcategory geometric mean
of the prices of the goods included in it. The prices of each product
correspond to those paid by the private consumption sector. However, in
category 6 the results of the survey on the prices of intermediate goods
were added.

5. Investment

The purpose of this survey was to collect the final market prices
for a selected number of capital goods, in this case machinery and equipment, as representative of patterns of investment in the five Central
American countries.[46]

Based on the statistics on industrial production and on external
trade, a basket of goods was formulated including the principal items
which made up gross domestic investment in machinery and equipment in
Central America. The questionnaire provided for the following information to be collected: (i) year and model (the models recommended were
those manufactured in 1973, or else the most recent available); (ii)
country of origin; (iii) unit price (for each model suggested, the list
or nominal market price, as well as the price of the cash transaction,
were both obtained in national currency); and (iv) the principal characteristics (a verbal description of the technical characteristics of
the products that influenced price).

After selecting the articles on the representative list of the ideal
direct comparisons, the next step was to assign weights to the components
of investment in machinery and equipment. These were based on the values
of imports of capital goods, since imported supply represents almost all
of the investment in machinery and equipment in the area. These data
existed for 172 subgroups under the Central American Uniform Customs
Nomenclature (NAUCA).

Table A-3. Subcategories and Grouping in Public
Consumption and Investment

Public Consumption[a]

Wages and Salaries

1. Primary teacher
2. Director of primary school
3. Secondary school teacher
4. Doctor
5. Nurse with a degree
6. Nurse without a degree
7. Police
8. Economist
9. Lawyer
10. Agricultural engineer
11. Office help
12. Secretary
13. Messenger
14. Accountant
15. Mailman
16. Assessor
17. Fireman
18. Electrician
19. Accounting help
20. Administrator

Purchase of goods and services

1. Foods, beverages, and tobacco
2. Clothing and textiles
3. Rents
4. Fuels and utilities
5. Transportation
6. Intermediate and other goods
7. Other services

Investment[b]

1. Automotive vehicles
2. Nonautomotive vehicles and communications equipment
3. Tractors and accessories
4. Construction and mining machines
5. Internal combustion engines
6. Electrical machinery and equipment
7. Machines and tools
8. Reproduction and printing machines
9. Other machinery and equipment
10. Office equipment

---

[a] Government categories are also aggregated into the following agencies: Education, Health, Interior, Other.
[b] These subcategories are aggregated into "Transport and communications equipment" and "Other."

A total of 156 goods were included in the price survey on machinery and equipment. The survey was carried out through interviews with the principal suppliers of machinery and equipment in each country.

D. Estimation of Housing Rents Using the Hedonic Technique

This section explains the methodology used to determine rents for comparable units in the five Central American countries. What is normally done in price studies, with respect to the housing sector, is a comparison among measured rents for "comparable" units that are in fact rented. The main difficulty arises when "comparable" units need to be defined: housing units differ from country to country. What is a typical house in one country may not even exist in another country. Furthermore, it is also very difficult to define what a typical house is within a country or a region.

The methodology chosen in this study to estimate "prices" or rents for comparable housing units is known as the hedonic technique and will be briefly described here. Next, the regression equations employed in this study will be shown, and finally, the estimation of a final weighted average price of typical housing units in each one of the five Central American countries will be explained.

1. The Hedonic Technique

This technique has been used in many studies to measure price changes through time and space with respect to adjustment of quality differences. The first contributions in this area were made by Court, Stone, and Griliches. Recently, the technique has been used in a series of studies on consumer and producer durables such as automobiles, tractors, and houses. A most recent application is one by Robert Gillingham from the Bureau of Labor Statistics, who uses the hedonic technique to make comparisons of rent levels among ten major U.S. cities.[47]

The conceptual framework of the hedonic technique is based on the Lancasterian approach to consumer demand or consumer behavior. This approach relies on the assumption that the price of each good is related to a certain number of characteristics, and that their implicit prices can be estimated by using regressions. The consumers or investors, in acquiring these goods, are expressing their preferences for specific sets of characteristics. They are free to decide if they want more or less of a particular characteristic of a specific product, and are aware that the price will vary accordingly.

In determining the implicit prices, regressions are applied to samples of goods with different characteristics for the periods or regions in question. The general equation can be expressed as

NOTE: This section was prepared by Molly Wainer. She wishes to thank Joseph Tu of the Brookings Social Science Computation Center for his invaluable assistance.

438

$$R = \beta_0 + \beta_1 x_1 + \beta_2 x_2 + \cdots \beta_m x_m + u,$$

where R is a vector of product prices--in this case of monthly rents; each set of x_1, x_2, ... x_m is a vector of values of the characteristics; the β's are the vector of the coefficients of those characteristics which correspond to their implicit prices; and u is a vector of random disturbances.

There are different ways to implement the hedonic technique to estimate price differentials among countries: (i) one alternative consists of running the regression separately for each region or period of time; (ii) the second alternative consists of pooling all the data from different regions, including intercept dummy variables to measure price differences introduced by the region effect. This technique assumes that implicit prices of the characteristics do not vary across regions, and the only differences in prices are attributed to "region or country effects"; (iii) the third alternative, known as the "flexible pooling" approach, consists of pooling all the data but including slope dummy variables to measure implicit price differentials among countries. The results in this case are equivalent to the results obtained through the first alternative.

If the three alternatives are compared, the first and the third appear to be superior to the second one which assumes that implicit prices would not vary significantly across time or countries. The second alternative would ignore an important element in price variation and, thus, would constitute a biased estimate of the price differentials. Furthermore, alternatives one and three should give equivalent results if the same data are used.

2. The Approach Followed in This Study

Alternative one was chosen in this study because of a priori superiority over alternative two[48] and for its simplicity compared with that of alternative three. Three types of regressions were estimated: arithmetic, semilog, and double log. The selection of the final functional form of the equation was done on the basis of a priori conceptions and explanatory power. One would expect that rents would change proportionally with the change in values of the characteristics of the housing unit, suggesting a semilog form of the equation. This criterion did help in the final choice of a semilog form for the regression equation. However, this was not the only criterion used to make the final decision. All three forms of the equations were tested, and a statistical procedure which allowed for a direct comparison of the residual sums of squares of the two equations constituted the ultimate basis for choosing the final functional form. By standardizing[49] the dependent variable in such a way that its variance does not change with different units of measurement, both equations were expressed in terms of these new variables, and the residual sums of squares in the two equations could then be compared directly. The functional form having the lowest residual sum of squares was the one chosen for the rent estimates.

With respect to the criteria followed for excluding or retaining the coefficients of the independent variables, the main considerations were: (i) only coefficients with expected signs were used; and (ii) only those of a size twice their standard errors were accepted. When comparing equations of the same functional form, the one with the highest R^2 was chosen.

A stepwise multiple regression program was first used on all the variables. This method was very useful in the analysis of the significance of the coefficients and in the determination of the impact of each independent variable on the others.

After running the regressions, a high intercorrelation among the independent variables was frequently encountered. When this occurred, one or more variables were eliminated. The equation chosen was one whose independent variable explained the highest share of the total price variation.

Regressions were initially run on selected variables: year built, year rented, number of rooms, number of baths, garden or yard as a percentage of total area, and area built.[50] The results of the regressions, either in arithmetic or semilog form, for separate countries or pooling all data together, were consistently very similar with respect to the most significant variables. Some of the results appear in tables A-4 and A-5. The number of rooms and number of baths were always the most significant variables. In some cases, such as in Guatemala and Honduras, the number of years rented was a significant variable, but in all cases, the coefficient of this variable or "implicit price" of this characteristic was almost negligible.

After determining the most significant variables--number of rooms and number of baths, and in some cases, number of years rented--the "best" functional form of the equation had to be chosen.

After standardizing the different functional forms of the equations on the most significant variables, the semilog form turned out to be the best; comparing the sums of squares of the residuals of the standardized equations, the one corresponding to the semilog form was the lowest.

3. Determining a Typical Housing Unit

Once the hedonic regressions were estimated, a decision had to be made on the "best" or "most appropriate" characteristics of the housing units. If "prices" or rents were going to be estimated using the semilog form of the rent equation on number of rooms and number of baths, the next question to be answered was how many rooms and how many baths were representative of a typical house in each one of the five Central American countries included in the survey. The methodology employed to determine a "typical" house consisted of determining frequency distributions of those two characteristics previously surveyed for each of the countries involved. The process involved the use of a program[51] to determine maximum and minimum values of the variables; absolute, percentage, and cumulative frequencies; and the calculation of statistics such as the mean, the standard deviation, and the median.

It was estimated that the most "frequent" housing units consisted of three rooms and one bath, four rooms and one bath, and five rooms and

Table A-4. Hedonic Coefficients of Rent Equations
(Independent Variables: Number of Rooms, Number of Baths;
Dependent Variable: Rent)

Arithmetic Form, Separate Equations for Each Country

	Costa Rica		El Salvador		Guatemala		Honduras		Nicaragua	
	Coeff.	T-Stat.	Coeff.	T-Stat.	Coeff.	T-Stat.	Coeff.	T-Stat.	Coeff.	T-Stat.
Constant	-38.5760	----	-10.147	----	-6.3309	----	-12.907	----	-12.089	----
Number of rooms	7.0670	6.1244	2.4830	3.1854	6.6033	11.736	7.6647	8.1619	9.2609	8.171
Number of baths	43.4230	11.715	24.250	9.0757	15.1430	5.6904	18.201	5.1173	21.334	5.529
R^2	0.69		0.52		0.54		0.46		0.48	

Table A-5. Hedonic Coefficients of Rent Equations
(Independent Variables: Number of Rooms, Number of Baths,
Number of Years Rented; Dependent Variable: Log Rent)

Semilog Form, Separate Equations for Each Country

	Costa Rica		El Salvador		Guatemala		Honduras		Nicaragua	
	Coeff.	T-Stat.	Coeff.	T-Stat.	Coeff.	T-Stat.	Coeff.	T-Stat.	Coeff.	T-Stat.
Constant	2.0036	----	2.2973	----	2.4131	----	2.3492	----	2.2722	----
Number of rooms	0.17912	6.3651	0.0817	2.7880	0.1976	11.974	0.2074	8.7434	0.2480	8.3705
Number of baths	0.7226	6.6186	0.5230	4.2081	0.2847	3.1687	0.3673	4.2651	0.3991	3.3377
Number of years rented	-0.104	-1.6433	-0.0093	-1.3850	-0.0105	-2.0990	-0.0202	-3.4884	-0.0104	-0.0223
R^2	0.56		0.40		0.45		0.50		0.41	

two baths. The percentage distribution for each country of these three types of housing units varied, as can be seen in table A-6. Smaller houses occur more frequently in Nicaragua and Honduras, and larger ones in Costa Rica, Guatemala, and El Salvador.

In order to use the information on percentage distribution of "types" of housing units to construct weights for the final calculation of prices of a "typical" and comparable house for the five Central American countries, the figures of table A-6 were normalized and table A-7 was obtained.

Next, prices or rents for the three types of houses were estimated using the regression equation. The rents obtained appear in table A-8.

Using the normalized distribution of housing units which appears in table A-7 as weights, and the prices estimated by the hedonic method, a unique "price" or rent was calculated for each Central American country. The three rents estimated for the three typical houses were weighted then by the percentual distributions. The final rents appear in table A-9.

4. Conclusion

The hedonic technique seems to be a very useful tool for price estimates in international comparative studies. Specifically, in this case of rent comparisons, it allowed for the calculation of implicit prices of the characteristics of housing units in the five Central American countries.

It is true that it can still be argued that there are some arbitrary decisions concerning the more relevant characteristics, the best functional form of the regression equation, and so on. After these decisions are made, the decision on how to define a typical house in each country also involves some arbitrariness, better than that, some "value judgments." In this study, the problem was solved by estimating three different "prices" for each country by using three different sets of characteristics of houses through the hedonic regression equation. Finally, a weighted average of these three prices determined an estimation of one "price" or rent which can be called the rent paid for the most frequently occurring and comparable housing units in the five Central American countries.

In spite of the problems mentioned, the objective of the study--international price comparisons--minimizes the impact of the level of arbitrariness on the final results of the study. This is due to the importance of relative prices for comparable units rather than the final price estimates in each country separately.

443

Table A-6. Percentage Distribution of "Types" of
Housing Units in the Five Central American Countries

Characteristics	Costa Rica	El Salvador	Guatemala	Honduras	Nicaragua
4 rooms, 1 bath	0.3750	0.3968	0.2102	0.2881	0.1379
5 rooms, 2 baths	0.2647	0.1825	0.2727	0.2599	0.1034
3 rooms, 1 bath	0.1912	0.1111	0.2045	0.3220	0.3908
	0.8309	0.6904	0.6874	0.8700	0.6321

NOTE: This table does not include the whole sample. It shows only the more frequently
occurring houses. For this reason, the figures in each column do not add up to
1.00.

Table A-7. Percentage Distribution of Housing Units
in the Five Central American Countries
(Normalized Figures)

Characteristics	Costa Rica	El Salvador	Guatemala	Honduras	Nicaragua
4 rooms, 1 bath	0.451318	0.574739	0.305790	0.331149	0.218162
5 rooms, 2 baths	0.230112	0.160922	0.297498	0.370115	0.618256
3 rooms, 1 bath	0.318570	0.264339	0.396712	0.298740	0.163582
	1.000000	1.000000	1.000000	1.000000	1.000000

SOURCE: table A-6.

445

Table A-8. Rents Estimated Through the Hedonic Equation
(in U.S.$)

Characteristics	Costa Rica	El Salvador	Guatemala	Honduras	Nicaragua
4 rooms, 1 bath	30.63	22.85	32.05	33.30	38.18
5 rooms, 2 baths	75.47	41.83	51.91	59.16	72.91
3 rooms, 1 bath	25.61	21.06	26.30	27.06	29.79

SOURCE: table A-5.

Table A-9. Rents Estimated for a "Typical" House
in Each Central American Country
(in U.S.$)[a]

	(1) Costa Rica	(5) El Salvador	(4) Guatemala	(2) Honduras	(3) Nicaragua
Rent	43.76	27.58	38.22	38.72	38.67

[a]The exchange rates used to make conversions from national currency prices to dollars correspond to the rates employed in the whole Price Study. They are: Costa Rica, 7.56; El Salvador, 2.50; Guatemala, 1.00; Honduras, 2.00; and Nicaragua, 7.00.

BIBLIOGRAPHY

Bailey, M. J., Muth, R. F., and Nourse, H. O. "A Regression Method for Real Estate Price Index Construction." Journal of the American Statistical Association 58 (1963).

Cagan, Phillip. "Measuring Quality Changes and the Purchasing Power of Money: An Explanatory Study of Automobiles." National Banking Review 3 (1965).

Fetting, Lyle P. "Adjusting Farm Tractor Prices for Quality Changes, 1950-1962." Journal of Farm Economics 45 (1962).

Lancaster, K. J. "A New Approach to Consumer Theory." Journal of Political Economy (April 1966).

___. "Change and Innovation in the Technology of Consumption." American Economic Review (May 1966).

___. Consumer Demand (New York: Columbia University Press, 1971).

Musgrove, J. C. "The Measurement of Price Changes in Construction." Journal of the American Statistical Association 64 (1969).

Triplett, Jack E. "Automobiles and Hedonic Quality Measurement." Journal of Political Economy 77 (1969).

448

Appendix A

NOTES

1. United Kingdom Board of Trade, Official British Publications, vol. 3864 (1908), vol. 4032 (1908), vol. 4512 (1909), vol. 5065 (1910), and vol. 5609 (1911).

2. International Labour Office, A Contribution to the Study of International Comparisons of Costs of Living, Studies and Reports, Series no. 17 (Geneva: ILO, 1932).

3. International Labour Office, Textile Wages: an International Study, Studies and Reports, New Series no. 31 (Geneva: ILO, 1952).

4. Colin Clark, Conditions of Economic Progress, rev. ed. (London: Macmillan & Co., 1960).

5. The purchasing power of a particular currency is a measure of its buying power in terms of actual goods and services. It is inversely related to the price level.

6. Milton Gilbert and Irving B. Kravis, An International Comparison of National Products and the Purchasing Power of Currencies (Paris: OEEC, 1954); and Milton Gilbert, et al., Comparative National Products and Price Levels (Paris; OECD, 1958).

7. See High Authority, European Coal and Steel Community, Informations Statistiques 2 (5) (August-September 1965), and Office Statistique des Communautes Europeennes, Couts de la Main d'Oeuvre - 1966, Statistiques Sociales (1969), and Structure et Repartition des Salaires - 1966, Serie Speciale. Again, similar publications followed later on. Some of these studies were the first of a series undertaken by these institutions.

8. Purchasing power parities are those exchange rates which equalize the prices of the countries in question. On the European studies, see Nordisk Statistik Sksiftserie no. 1, Leunadskostnader och reallöner i de nordiska Luvidstardena (Stockholm, 1954), and Office Statistique des Communautés Européennes, Prix, Taux d'Equivalence de Pouvoir d'Achat à la Consommation et Revenue Réels dans les Pays de la C.E.C.A., 1954-1958 (1960).

9. United Nations, Economic Commission for Latin America, A Measurement of Price Levels and the Purchasing Power of Currencies in Latin America, 1960-1962 (Argentina, 31 March 1963).

10. Stanley N. Braithwaite, "Real Income Levels in Latin America," Review of Income and Wealth (June 1968).

11. ECIEL is the Spanish acronym for Joint Studies on Latin American Economic Integration.

12. The LAFTA countries are Argentina, Bolivia, Brazil, Chile, Colombia, Ecuador, Mexico, Paraguay, Peru, Uruguay, and Venezuela. These

449

countries cover over 90 percent of Latin American income, production, and population.

13. See, in particular, Joseph Grunwald and Jorge Salazar-Carrillo, "Economic Integration, Rates of Exchange and Value Comparisons in Latin America," in Don Daly, ed., International Comparisons of Prices and Output (New York: National Bureau of Economic Research, 1972); Jorge Salazar-Carrillo, "Price, Purchasing Power and Real Product Comparisons in Latin America," Review of Income and Wealth (November 1973), and "Una Comparacion de los Precios de los Bienes de Inversion en la Zona de la ALALC," Revista de la Integracion 19/20 (May-September 1975). For a fuller treatment consult Jorge Salazar-Carrillo, Prices and Purchasing Power Parities in Latin America, 1960-1972 (Brookings Institution, forthcoming).

14. See Irving Kravis, Zoltan Kenessey, Alan Heston, Robert Summers, et al., A System of International Comparisons of Gross Product and Purchasing Power (Baltimore: Johns Hopkins University Press, 1975). Only studies involving comparisons of wages, income, and prices among more than two countries are covered in this brief survey. There have been very interesting studies of a strictly binary type, usually comparing other developed countries with the United States.

Other relevant studies not reviewed here include those by the U.S. State Department, the United Nations, and the German Statistical Office. Even though published by various nations, the studies are mainly applicable to international civil servants or diplomatic staff, and are partly reported by such personnel. Finally, lack of information has precluded any reference to comparisons undertaken in Eastern Europe. For a more comprehensive though somewhat dated survey see Wilfred Beckerman, International Comparisons of Real Incomes (OECD, Paris: 1966), chapters 2-3.

15. For an explanation of this point see Grunwald and Salazar-Carrillo, "Economic Integration."

16. Data were collected on private consumption expenditures at the family level, apparent consumption of machinery and equipment, values of different types of construction, and government expenditures.

17. The results of this study are only partly used to illuminate these aspects both in chapter 8 and in chapter 6, which deals with future comparative advantage.

18. This study forms part of a more comprehensive effort including other Latin American countries, the United States, and Western Europe. The inclusion of other countries in the comparisons also helps in the study of potential trade within the area, as it suggests the extent to which trade with third parties might be affected.

19. Of course, the validity of the comparisons of the level and structure of prices for trade advantages within the area is also dependent on the assumption that the relationship of prices to marginal and average costs, as well as distribution margins, do not vary significantly across the regions.

20. For a treatment of the hedonic approach, see Zvi Griliches, ed., Price Indexes and Quality Change (Cambridge, Mass.: Harvard University Press, 1971).

21. Of course, perfect comparability is illusory. Advanced countries implementing the new Standardized National Accounts, for example, have altered the system in different ways. In certain cases the differences can be substantial, as in those existing between the French, U.S., and Japanese estimates. The situation is worse when different kinds of developing and developed countries are compared.

22. Alan Heston, "A Comparison of Some Short-Cut Methods of Estimating Real Product Per Capita," Review of Income and Wealth (March 1973): p. 82.

23. See Beckerman, International Comparisons, which also contains an account of other studies using these methods.

24. Richard and Nancy Ruggles, "Price Measurement for International Comparisons," mimeographed, presented to the ECIEL Seminar, Mexico City, December 1966; also appearing in the Review of Income and Wealth.

25. The Ruggles suggested that just over sixty products would be sufficient to estimate price and purchasing power comparisons across countries for overall private consumption, not including rent. However, they admit that for other reasons (like reliability at lower levels of disaggregation, inclusion of easy-to-price products, and so on), such a list should be expanded.

26. See Kravis, Kenessey, Heston, Summers et al., A System of International Comparisons.

27. See Joseph Grunwald and Jorge Salazar-Carrillo, "Economic Integration, Rates of Exchange and Value Comparisons in Latin America," in Don Daly, ed., International Comparisons of Prices and Output (New York: National Bureau of Economic Research, 1972).

28. In fact, for these reasons there have been only one or two studies comparing income and prices that have used the production side approach, and then only involving two countries at a time.

29. For criteria to classify the commodities, and for an empirical study showing that after the few most representative commodities are included in the sample, the rest are redundant in the explanation of price differences in a subcategory, see Ruggles, "Price Measurement."

30. For a recent statement see Grunwald and Salazar-Carrillo, "Economic Integration."

31. For a fuller elaboration of the previous points, see Grunwald and Salazar-Carrillo, "Economic Integration."

32. In our case, the GDP from the expenditure side.

33. The term purchasing-power-parity exchange rate was coined by Gustav Cassel in "Abnormal Deviations in International Exchange," Economic Journal (September 1918), and has continued to be used, respecting tradition. Other terms could fit with equal or perhaps greater effectiveness, as purchasing power parities is rather long and confusing.

34. These terms are taken from the field of intertemporal price measurement, which is based on consumer theory.

35. Various kinds of exchange rates could be used depending on the purpose. If research on actual or potential trade flows on the basis of existing conditions is pursued, then the prevailing or official exchange rates, which are those on which traders base their decisions, should be used. However, the optimal allocation of resources for the countries considered demands the use of shadow or equilibrium exchange rates. Of course, if values are compared, then p.p.p. rates should be used. Obviously the latter would imply that prices at or below the category level are being compared, using the p.p.p. rates for higher levels of aggregation, or those defined by the total basket of goods and services considered.

36. For a recent study examining the Walsh index, see Richard Ruggles, "Price Indexes and International Price Comparisons," in Ten Economic Studies in the Tradition of Irving Fisher, Wiley, 1968.

37. See Ruggles, "Price Indexes"; Kravis, Kenessey, Heston, Summers et al., A System of International Comparisons; and Lazlo Dreschsler, "Weighting of Index Number in Multilateral International Comparisons," Review of Income and Wealth (March 1973).

38. See Kravis, Kenessey, Heston, Summers et al., A System of International Comparisons.

39. The whole set of binary comparisons requires n(n - 1) calculations.

40. Multinationals are sometimes involved directly, and other times indirectly, when they sell their patents or technical know-how.

41. Of course, if they fulfill the same need, the physical characteristics of the goods in all probability will be similar.

42. The basket of goods and services is that prepared by the ECIEL Program, as modified by the SIECA/Brookings unit in July 1973.

43. The number of units included in the survey were: Guatemala, 250; El Salvador, 150; Honduras, 201; Nicaragua, 202; Costa Rica, 151.

44. This method has been utilized in a series of studies on consumer and producer durables. The pioneering contribution was made by A. T. Court, The Dynamics of Automobile Demand (New York: General Motors Corporation, 1939); Richard Stone, Quantity and Price Indexes in National Accounts (Paris: OEEC; 1956); and Zvi Griliches, "Hedonic Price Indexes for Automobiles: An Econometric Analysis of Quality Change," in The

<u>Price Statistics of the Federal Government</u> (New York: National Bureau of Economic Research, General Series no. 73, 1961). A recent application to rent comparisons was done by Robert Gillingham in "Place to Place Rent Comparisons," <u>Annals of Economic and Social Measurement</u> (April 1975).

45. Arithmetic, semilog, and doublelog equations were tried, but semilog forms gave the "best" results from a statistical point of view.

46. For a full description of the data sources and methodology used for this sector, see George P. Montalván, "Tipos de Cambio de Paridad para Bienes de Capital en Centroamérica: Metodología y Resultados Preliminares," March 1975, mimeographed.

47. See Court, "Hedonic Price Indexes with Automotive Examples," in <u>The Dynamics of Automobile Demand</u>; Stone, <u>Quantity and Price Indexes</u>; Griliches, "Hedonic Price Indexes for Automobiles"; and Gillingham, "Place to Place Rent Comparisons."

48. Alternative two was tried, but the results were not considered for the study.

49. The dependent variables were standardized by dividing them by their geometric mean. For a better explanation, see Potluri Rao and R. L. Miller, <u>Applied Econometrics</u>, (Belmont, Calif.: Wadsworth, 1971).

50. The other variables surveyed were not included, since they were relatively constant for most units. This occurred in the cases of heating, air conditioning, and elevators.

51. The program utilized is the UNIVAN Program, written by Marcia Mason of The Brookings Institution for use in the ECIEL (Joint Studies on Latin American Economic Integration) Consumption Study.

A Survey of Literature on Economic Development in the Central American Common Market

William R. Cline
and
Alan I. Rapoport

A.   Introduction

There is an ample body of literature on the political economy of integration in Central America. This appendix attempts to summarize and evaluate the more important studies in that literature, with the objective of providing perspective for the SIECA/Brookings research reported in this volume. Some of the studies examined below bear directly on issues analyzed here (such as the magnitude and distribution of benefits arising from the Common Market); others contain work important to an overall understanding of the Central American Common Market but focusing on issues only tangentially treated in the SIECA/Brookings analyses (for example: role of foreign investment; tax incentives policy; tariff policy). The review does not include studies of individual economies in the region, and certain sectoral areas are omitted as well (including the important recent FAO study on agriculture in Central America). Instead, the survey concentrates on research most directly concerned with economic integration in the region.

B.   Institutional Evolution

An important study tracing the development of the Central American Common Market (CACM) is that by Castillo (1966). The study seeks to justify the use of the integration instrument as a means of bringing about economic change in Central America. It begins by showing, through historical analysis, the inadequacies of the export economy. It then presents a program of regional integration as a means of overcoming these inadequacies.

The historical analysis closely follows the "ECLA" view of the primary export economy. There are two tenets of the analysis. One deals with the nature of the world market: the secular decline in the terms of trade and the inherent instability of primary products markets. The second tenet deals with the internal social structure resultant from reliance on export agriculture: the landed oligarchs with their externally oriented consumption patterns, the landless laborers, and a dampening of the growth of a middle class. When both of these tenets are

combined with a rapidly increasing population and a desire by the population to emulate the oligarchy's consumption patterns, great internal
pressures for change arise.   On the one hand the export economy cannot
provide a stable solution for these pressures and, on the other hand,
maintaining a classic export economy maintains obstacles for an internal solution in import substitution.

Although import substitution is seen as a method of deepening internal demand structures by providing employment to local labor and investment opportunities to local entrepreneurs, the Central American
economies are individually so small that the width of the market prevents
efficient plant scale and inhibits the possibility of effective competition.   The institution of the Common Market, then, is seen by Castillo
as making the strategy of import-substitution industrialization a viable
solution to the pressures for change outlined above.

In addition to supporting regional integration as a general strategy
and outlining the agreements of the CACM, the second section deals with
particular goals which the regional program should encompass.   These
goals include: balanced growth and equitable distribution of the benefits of integration, vertical integration and diversification of industry, and local participation in the management and ownership of foreign-
controlled enterprises.

Castillo departs from earlier ECLA doctrine in not suggesting integration (or import substitution for that matter) as a solution to export
dependence.   Quite to the contrary, he says that due to increased imports of capital goods and intermediate products the Central American
economies can expect, if anything, an increased dependence on export
agriculture (p. 97), since nothing inherent in integration will diversify exports to the rest of the world in the short run.   He does not
see integration, then, as providing a buffer from the nature of the world
market in primary products.   He does see the Common Market as a tool to
stimulate social and structural change toward a modern capitalistic environment in Central America.

Hansen (1967) provided another early comprehensive study on the evolution and effects of the CACM.   After presenting a history and description of the Central American economies, the study discusses the background
and organization of the CACM, stressing the role of the ECLA in its
formation.   The author examines the ECLA integration doctrine, referring
in particular to controversies regarding the future path of Latin American development: demand deficiency versus supply deficiency of traditional exports; import substitution versus export promotion; static
versus dynamic aspects of integration.

The author then traces the principal achievements of the CACM, which
he considers to include: (i) improved allocation and use of existing
Central American resources through trade creation; (ii) structural
change--expansion and diversification of industry; (iii) attraction of
increased international assistance, especially infrastructural.

The author then evaluates important unresolved issues for the CACM:

(i) <u>Import substitution and protection</u>--Hansen fears that high protection (especially effective protection) will lead to high-cost industries utilizing imported inputs and thereby contributing to balance of payments problems as well as impeding export growth.

(ii) <u>Industrial duplication</u>--Here the main problem is seen as an overemphasis on production for the regional market with no plans for the world market, thus neglecting export diversification.

(iii) <u>Foreign investment</u>--In this area the author feels the main question to be raised is "For whose benefit is Central America integration?"

(iv) <u>Balanced regional growth</u>--The author considers this to be the crucial issue which will determine the future of the CACM.

(v) <u>Agriculture</u>--The author also emphasizes that the agricultural sector cannot continue to be ignored as it has been in the past. He maintains that the main tasks of governments are to provide a physical infrastructure as well as a political environment conducive to economic development.

Ramsett (1969) reported on the integration industries scheme in the CACM. He found that the scheme had not fulfilled its main purpose of promoting regionally balanced industrialization. The scheme has suffered from many problems. An industry desiring the full advantage of the program must undergo a long and cumbersome application process. The ratification process which involves the consent of all five participating countries presents another stumbling block to implementation of the program. National priorities dominate over regional orientation, causing many conflicts. Furthermore the threats of nonratification and delay are used for bargaining leverage on other matters. These various obstacles continued to block the creation of integration industries even after a liberalization of integration in 1964 by the Treaty, which encouraged a surge of new applications for integration industry status.[1]

According to the author, another major problem has been the U.S. attitude toward the integration industries scheme. In the past, the U.S. Government has opposed this program, believing that it would prompt monopoly enterprises. (Note that Cohen Orantes also cites U.S. opposition as a cause of failure of the integration industries scheme.) The United States allowed none of its development assistance funds going into the Central American Development Bank to be used for integration industries, according to the author.

Ramsett then examines four alternative approaches that the CACM considered adopting.

(i) <u>Convention of fiscal incentives</u>--This was an attempt to prevent costly competition among the countries in trying to attract investment funds. Limits would be imposed on tax and tariff concessions that countries could offer to attract investments. This program was ratified only after long delay, and it has yet to be implemented.

(ii) <u>Special industries receive quite high tariff protection</u>--In order for an industry to be selected under this program, it must be new, and the high tariffs do not become effective until it has sufficient productive capacity to satisfy 50 percent of the region's demand.

(iii) <u>Assembling industries</u> and (iv) <u>Textile industry</u>--These two programs were in an embryonic stage at the time Ramsett undertook his study.

Finally, Ramsett assesses the interrelationships between the various schemes. He finds the fiscal incentives and integration industries schemes quite complementary but feels the integration industries and the special system could come into conflict. Since there are no limitations to the number of firms in a given industry under the latter scheme, there exists a possibility of duplication of investment which could create excess capacity. The special system may also lead to oligopolistic competition, since there is no provision for regulation. In contrast, under the integration industries scheme a legal monopoly could exist, but it would be subject to substantial regulation and probably also relatively limited protection. The special system could also lead to more unbalanced industrial development if firms tend to concentrate in areas where there is already a great deal of industrialization. The major advantage of the special system is that it is much easier to implement than the integration industries scheme.

As policy measures to improve the existing integration industries scheme Ramsett advocated streamlining the ratification procedure for integration industries, establishing a specialized industrial commission, and empowering the regulatory commission to demand information on profits for use in setting prices through tariff or price policy.

A more recent work describing institutional evolution in the CACM is that by Holbik and Swan (1972). After reviewing the background of the CACM as well as the fundamentals of trade diversion and creation theory, the study concentrates on the instruments for the goals of trade and industrial expansion. Problems in balance of payments, budgetary balance, and delays in CACM negotiations are cited as the chief obstacles to integration. Tariffs, special incentives, and integration industries are identified as the main instruments for integration, although no quantitative evolution of their impact is presented.

C. Political Dynamics

A second separable set of studies on the CACM contains a limited number of analytical investigations by political scientists. These studies focus on the dynamics of political cohesion and conflict in the integration effort. A relatively early study by Nye (1967) stresses the role of the ministers of economy in separating economic from political considerations in their drive toward implementation of the Common Market. Nye maintains that this technical independence coupled with support first from ECLA and later from the United States helped achieve the reality of the CACM. He supports this claim by contrasting the achievements of the economic ministers, who constituted themselves as the Autonomous Committee for Economic Cooperation of the Central American

Isthmus (CCE) with ECLA as their secretariat, with the experience of the foreign ministers, who established the organization of Central American States (ODECA). CCE was able to meet, while ODECA, subject to political conflict, stagnated. He then points out that U.S. support through direct contribution to the Central American Development Bank (CABEI) helped speed up the integration process by luring hesitant countries into the scheme so they could have access to the funds in CABEI, which were only available to countries that had ratified the general treaty.

A subsequent study by Fagan (1970) deals principally with the problem of balanced development. The author is quite pessimistic regarding the future of the integration process in Central America. He states:

> In fact, however, the war did not interrupt an integration process which had been characterized by significant spillovers in tasks, by a growth in the mutual responsiveness of national elites, or by the delegation of increasing authority to regional institutions. Even before the July war, the CACM was on the verge of collapse, primarily because of its inability to deal satisfactorily with the problem of unbalanced development. The war reinforced prevailing political and economic trends in Central America rather than interrupting them.

Fagan maintains that the lack of coordinated planning coupled with the reliance on the free operation of market forces led to an unequal distribution of benefits among Common Market partners, and that this unequal distribution is the greatest threat to the integration process. Citing tariff policy, the author notes that free trade within the CACM as well as fixed common external tariffs deprived the governments of their traditional instrument for dealing with imbalances--tariff protection. At the same time, the unwillingness to regulate assembly industry activities created large import requirements.

Fagan also blames the absence of regulation for fiscal shortages which governments confronted by the mid-1960s. Although partly a consequence of an import-substitution policy which reduced tariffs on some capital and intermediate goods, these shortages were also attributable to the failure to implement a common fiscal incentives agreement, and the subsequent attempts of each country to offer greater tax and tariff concessions than the others.

It should be noted that the tariff and fiscal situations in question were not in reality cases of unregulated markets. The common external tariffs represented regulative intervention, as did the tax and tariff concessions. Therefore, the relevant questions are: Which types of regulation or interference with the market would be beneficial to the growth of the Central American countries? and How can the countries better coordinate their policies instead of competing with each other in a nonconstructive manner?

In another study of political dynamics of the CACM, Isaac Cohen Orantes (1972) maintains the thesis that the CACM would not have been established in the absence of outside influence. Cohen notes that the development of the CACM was fostered initially by ECLA's collaboration with the newly emerging tecnicos in Central America. ECLA shielded these technicians from political repercussions so that they could resolve as many aspects of the integration process as possible. The author argues that when the movement began to stall, government began to provide a major thrust for the integration process, but in doing so it changed some of the original objectives and attempted to replace ECLA as the dominant mentor.

The study examines the many regional agencies that sprang up along with the integration movement, and demonstrates the high degree of dependence of almost all of these agencies on external sources of financing. This dependence provides evidence for Cohen's view that the CACM would not have developed (and would not survive) if its support had been limited to internal interests.

Another political analysis is provided by Tobis (1970). His study focuses on the effects of the CACM with regard to relations between the United States and Central America. The author argues that the CACM promoted by the U.S. Government since 1960 (i) will permit the United States to increase its economic penetration of Central America and Central America's dependence on the United States; (ii) will rationalize capitalism in Central America; (iii) will preserve U.S. hegemony in the area.

Tobis notes that while it is true that the volume of intraregional trade has increased substantially due to the CACM, the composition of that trade has changed quite markedly, with a shift from trade in unprocessed agricultural goods to trade in nondurable consumer goods, processed foods, and chemicals. He infers that this change has been quite advantageous to U.S. business interests because these interests control a great deal of the production of these newly traded goods. Moreover, the transformation involves a growing dependence on the United States for raw materials and intermediate inputs.

Tobis maintains that prior to the CACM the United States was losing its dominant trade position in Central America to Japan and Western Europe, and hence that it was to the advantage of the United States to push for the formation of the CACM in order to close these markets through the imposition of the common external tariff. After this closure, U.S. firms were able to move into these markets via the route of direct investment, due to their greater advantage over European and Japanese firms in investment as opposed to trade in Central America. (This alleged advantage remains undocumented.) The author states that most of the foreign investment going into Central America comes from the United States, and that the market increased opportunities to invest and made investments much more lucrative by offering a myriad of fiscal incentives as the five countries competed with each other for foreign capital.

Tobis then argues that capitalism in the area will be rationalized by a series of occurrences. Economies of scale and efficiency will become more important because of the regional market and, according to Tobis, will lead local producers to sell out to foreign interests because the producers will not have enough know-how to be efficient. The high protective tariff structure will stabilize the market by keeping out external competition. Tobis argues that the common external tariff has increased both nominal and effective protection by substantial amounts (although the data presented in chapter 3 of this book indicate no such increase). The author predicts that there will be both loss of foreign exchange and loss of revenues to the CACM countries, making them more dependent on foreign sources of funds. He also states that Central American capital will now participate more actively in the region, which will lead to the creation of a tiny bourgeoisie dependent on U.S. interests (although he fails to deal with the inconsistency between this fear and the belief that increasing numbers of local capitalists will sell out to foreign firms).

Tobis postulates that U.S. hegemony in the region is being brought about by (i) the creation of a middle class in Central America which is dependent for its survival on U.S. interests, and (ii) by the creation of regional identifications and decisionmaking entities, which leads to a breakdown of nationalism.

Although most of these opinions are either unverified by relevant data or impossible to test, the study does state a viewpoint antithetical to the CACM because of its alleged domination by the United States. This viewpoint appears to enjoy a certain degree of support in the region and hence merits future empirical examination, with special attention to the question of whether the region's populace would have been better off if the presence of U.S. firms (and hence investment and jobs) had been more limited.

D. Quantitative Estimates of Integration Effects

Another genre of literature on the CACM concerns quantitative estimates of the benefits of integration. Such estimates are of course important in evaluating political analyses which assert (or imply) that some members have gained relatively more than others. One study containing such estimates is that by McClelland (1972), who also provides one of the best general descriptions of the CACM.

In analyzing the Common Market's contribution to economic growth, McClelland argues that the CACM principally worked on the manufacturing sector, which then induced indirect effects on the transportation, commerce, and infrastructure sectors.

The author uses the following methodology to measure the growth attributed to the CACM. He first estimates minimum normal growth, defined as the growth not attributable to leading sectors but due instead to constant factors such as population growth, usual rate of adoption of new techniques, and normal investment. To calculate this minimum normal growth McClelland uses trends over different periods: 1951-58, 1958-61, 1961-66. He also estimates growth caused by "normal" export expansion, assuming an export multiplier of one. The residual growth he then attributes to the CACM. The author is conscious that the method is basically unsatisfactory, noting that the estimates are no more than a first approximation. The author sees the limitations of both his data and his assumptions and states "It is possible that modernizing forces might have led to accelerated growth rates even without the Common Market."

In descriptive terms he feels the main effect has been the widening of the market and the concomitant effect of stimulating industrial production.

The major part of the study, however, deals with the author's perceptions of the CACM's impact rather than with specific measurements. Considering structural change, the author notes the increase not only in regional trade but also in imports from outside the region. He sees the latter as due either to high income elasticity of demand—or to increased demand for imported inputs. Examining composition of imports, he finds very little change (1962-66) among three broad categories—manufactured consumer goods, industrial inputs, and agricultural inputs. He investigates the structure of the prices of import substitutes and finds they have not risen as much as generally believed, although he does not take into account quality differences (which would tend to be rather important, especially in the case of Central America where there is a high preponderance of specific rather than ad valorem tariff rates).

Assessing the growth impact of import protection (both nominal and effective), McClelland concludes that tariffs have had little effect on industrial production. Instead, he holds that the wider market due to the CACM has increased competition and has had the greatest effect on industrial production. Concerning fiscal incentives the author contends that these have led to excessive competition among countries to attract investment and have influenced the location but not the regional total of the investment. The level of incentives has been determined mainly by chance, leading to both inadequate and excessive incentives. Furthermore, "Tariff exemptions tended to benefit most those industries that were highly dependent on imported materials . . . ," giving the strongest incentives in sectors where the contribution to growth has been least—those with little domestic value added. He also emphasizes the concept of alternatives, suggesting that certain incentives have negative contributions to development since alternative uses of the revenue might have contributed more.

Addressing the problem of balanced growth, the author postulates that:

> The minimum requirement in economic terms is that all members benefit. This is not necessarily—perhaps unfortunately-the minimum political requirement. For one thing, the benefits need to be visible and recognized, and even the assessment of benefits already realized has major elements of uncertainty. The projection of long-run economic benefits is even less certain. Political leaders are concerned with more than just economic considerations, and it is understandable that the leaders of the countries that appear to be benefitting the least will bargain strenuously, and perhaps take some risks, to get changes or preferential treatment that they hope will increase their share.

A more traditional and narrowly focused analysis of the economic benefits of the CACM is that by Wilford (1970). This study seeks to identify static welfare gains from net trade creation in the Common Market. The study employs the method of Balassa (1967), in which the effect of the market in increasing imports is determined by measuring the pre- and post-union income elasticities of importation. The change, attributed to the common market, is translated into an absolute value amount of increase in imports, then multiplied by an "import efficiency conversion factor" of 0.3 (apparently taken from the Balassa article which in turn drew the coefficient from historical U.S. data) to determine the welfare gain to national accounts from the customs union.

Examining the change in import elasticities would seem to have methodological drawbacks. The static welfare gains from integration constitutes a once-for-all outward shift for the economy beyond its production possibility frontier in isolation to a level of welfare attainable by free trading with partners (permitting greater efficiency of specialization, although not as great as that from complete free trade, according to traditional theory). This one-time shift is more appropriately captured by a shift in import propensities (share of consumption provided by imports), since elasticities concern growth rates rather than absolute levels.[2] Even more dubious is the resort to a mysterious import efficiency conversion factor. Finally, as Nugent (1973) has noted, Wilford's base and terminal periods are such that there is an upward bias in the estimate of change in import elasticities. These facts qualify Wilford's conclusion that the CACM was beneficial because the measured income elasticity of demand for imports rose over preintegration years.

Another quantitative study is that by Dagum (1972). The study estimates an econometric model of each country separately as well as for the Common Market as a whole. To examine the impact of integration on growth, Dagum calculates trend rates of growth for the two subperiods 1950-61 (preintegration) and 1961-68 (postintegration). He then conducts statistical tests showing that the trend of growth during the integration period is significantly higher than that prior to integration, for both the Common Market and for each individual member except Costa Rica. The author concludes that integration was responsible for higher rates of growth during the 1961-68 period in four of the five countries, and permitted Costa Rica to maintain its high rate of growth throughout the 1961-68 period.

The study then examines the hypothetical paths of consumption, income, and investment if (i) integration had not taken place, (ii) the war in 1969 had not taken place, (iii) integration continues in the 1970s, and (iv) integration does not continue in the 1970s. These calculations employ trend growth rates considered relevant for each hypothesis (for example, the 1950-61 trend for the nonintegration case for the 1970s).

Unfortunately the exercises in the study amount to little more than the outright assertion that observed changes in growth rates were due solely to economic integration (although the author does attempt to remove the influence of spectacular traditional sector export growth in Honduras in the integration period). At a very minimum such a global approach ought to examine only the excess of accelerated growth over that experienced by comparable countries outside the Common Market. (When such a comparison is made with Panama, the seeming conclusion is that integration contributed nothing, since Panama's growth accelerated even more than that of the CACM in the periods in question.)

Brewster (1972) has conducted another quantitative estimate of the Common Market's benefits. The author defines the gain from integration as G = (TC + KTC - TD)/Y, where G is the gain as a percent of GNP, TC is trade creation, K is a Keynesian multiplier, TD is trade diversion, and Y is GNP. Unfortunately, this measure is subject to serious shortcomings. While trade creation generates a benefit of economic integration and trade diversion, a cost, the corresponding welfare benefits and costs can only be calculated after appropriate incorporation of information on tariff levels and discrepancy between partner price and world price. The absolute differences between the values of trade creation and trade diversion tell nothing about the gains from integration.

The multiplier "K" is defined as K = 1/(s' + m'), where s' is the marginal propensity to save and m' the marginal propensity to import. The multiplier is then applied quite asymmetrically to trade creation but not to trade diversion. In addition to the inappropriateness of applying Keynesian multiplier analysis to the supply-constrained developing economy there are other conceptual difficulties with the analysis which need not be described in detail. Brewster then examines the "fiscal component" in the cost of trade diversion. This concept refers to the fact that if partner A sells goods to partner B which require intermediate inputs imported from the rest of the world, and the producer (A) collects duties on these inputs, there exists in effect a "fiscal transfer" to country A of tariff collections which would have accrued to partner B in the absence of integration. Brewster usefully notes that this transfer (and hence a case for compensation) exists only in the instance of trade diversion, not in the case of normal country specialization within the region. Using his estimates of trade diversion (which appear to be quite unreliable), the author concludes that the actual "fiscal transfer cost" is relatively unimportant.

Nugent (1973) has prepared perhaps the most comprehensive and sophisticated effort to date to measure the effects of the CACM on the region's economies. Nugent first applies the Balassa method (change in import elasticities) to measure trade creation, using the early 1950s as a base (rather than the late 1950s used by Wilford) to provide a base with GNP growth (and hence import growth) more comparable with that of the 1960s. Nugent uses the same import efficiency conversion factor (.3) as Wilford and finds that the CACM accelerated the growth rate for Central America by 0.31 percent per annum.

The weaknesses of this method are discussed above, and Nugent himself gives little weight to the result. Next the study conducts cross-country regressions relating export growth of developing countries to variables such as exchange rate, domestic prices, export commodity prices, gross domestic product, export taxes, and so on, and a specific dummy variable for participation in common markets. Applying the dummy variable coefficient found for the CACM, Nugent estimates that the Common Market accelerated the export growth rates of Central American countries by 1.4 percent annually above the rate which could have been expected on the basis of other factors. This estimate appears open to question, since the data observations are single averages of country growth rates over the entire period 1947-67, prohibiting analysis of the CACM countries before as opposed to after integration. Nugent then applies an export "efficiency conversion factor" to obtain the welfare effect of the increased export growth rate. This procedure (which again appears highly questionable)[3] yields an increase in annual growth rate of 0.38 percent due to integration.[4]

After brief examination of benefits from tariff homogenization (based on assumed parameters) and of industrialization (using Chenery's cross-country regressions), Nugent conducts his principal estimate of the Common Market's effect. The method is to estimate aggregate production functions for Central America and for each of the five member countries, in which the author regresses the logarithm of GNP per worker against (i) the logarithm of capital per worker, (ii) the logarithm of an index of international terms of trade, (iii) a dummy variable for completion of major transport links, (iv) two dummy variables for Common Market (one, a once-for-all shift, and the other, a cumulative growth effect), and (v) time. Although the transport and time variables turn out to be insignificant, Nugent concludes that on a basis of the Common Market dummy variables, the market contributed 0.6 percent to annual growth in the region. (Note that the data referred to 1950-66.)

It is surprising that Nugent does not discuss the probable bias introduced by the coincidence of the period of integration with higher export and GNP growth, in large part sparked by recovery of commodity prices in the early 1960s. Given the fact that the capital data are presumably very weak, what the regression results essentially pick up is that growth was on the average higher in the 1960s than in the 1950s, but that the effect was essentially a shelf shift rather than a secular acceleration (in which case the secularly increasing time variable would have swamped the common market variable). Thus, it seems quite doubtful that the production function approach succeeds in escaping the drawbacks of a simplistic assessment that because growth was higher in the integration period, the cause was integration.

Nugent's alternative estimates of the growth effects of the CACM all represent interesting but unconvincing measurement attempts. They all involve rather circuitous means, and they all appear to confuse ongoing growth rate effects (estimated) with what should be once-for-all shifts in the economic welfare base. It is interesting to note, however, the quite narrow range of all of the estimates: each estimate falls between 0.31 percent and 0.6 percent contribution of annual growth. (Note that Nugent points out that these measures are not additive but essentially substitute calculations of the same thing.)

The final and most important empirical analysis of the Nugent study consists of a set of econometric models estimated for the Central American economies. Once estimated, these models are used to simulate the welfare gains from "policy harmonization." As the econometric models are less directly related to calculation of past integration costs and benefits than the analyses discussed above, they are not reviewed in detail here. However, certain fundamental observations on the models are in order. The models are Keynesian in nature, building on the national income accounting framework commonly found in econometric models for advanced countries. This structure leads to strange results in that it is essentially demand-constrained and the models accordingly attribute real growth to influences that in the developing country context would frequently be counterproductive. For example, since imports enter negatively in the national accounting identity, raising tariffs and thus lowering imports permits more rapid growth; yet in a meaningful analysis this relation would represent an erroneous policy prescription (as Nugent points out himself). Similarly, government spending is attributed a real "multiplier," such that one dollar of extra government spending generates (through the normal Keynesian mechanism) two dollars, for example, of total extra GNP. Yet the developing country context is not one of Keynesian underemployment of both capital and labor, and it is generally considered erroneous to attribute real income multiplier analysis to the LDC case. Instead, increased government spending unaccompanied by increased taxation is generally considered to generate only inflation in the LDC contest. The essential ingredient that is missing in the models is a capital or foreign exchange constraint, to turn the models into supply-constrained systems. In this type of alternative approach, GNP would be the minimum of either the demand-determined level (in the Keynesian manner) or the supply-constrained level attainable. It would also be necessary to integrate into such an approach savings and feasible capital inflow equations, so that the available capital stock and foreign exchange at a given time would be determinate.

The other principal observation which may be made on the models concerns the way in which they simulate "policy harmonization." Nugent sets up a linear programming maximization problem in which GNP of the region is maximized by obtaining the optimal levels of policy variables in each country. He then demonstrates that this joint maximization yields higher total GNP than does individual maximization for each country's model in isolation. A fundamental question about this procedure is whether it represents in any sense a practical type of "policy harmonization" prescription. Usually harmonization is conceived as a series of "similar" policies: money supply grows at similar rates, similar exchange rate depreciation policies are followed, similar tax rates are employed, and so on. However, in Nugent's approach just the opposite happens: if regional income will be maximized by one country's inflating rapidly while another deflates, one country's appreciating while the other depreciates, so be it: that is the optimal solution. While there is nothing wrong with this approach in principle, in practice it would require the unquestioning commitment of all policymakers in the region to the economist's black box. Since no simple rules of thumb could be followed (everyone increases money supply at 6 percent, for example), only the econometric model with its particular parameters could provide the oracular truth on the optimal combination of policies.

Despite the caveats discussed above, the Nugent study provides a useful contribution toward further analysis of the effects of the CACM and represents careful empirical application of several imaginative methodologies.

E.   General Economic Development and Balanced Growth

Studies with more generalized evaluations of economic development in the CACM include two documents by ECLA (1966 and 1971). The first traces the development of the postwar Central American economies, emphasizing their export orientation. Turning to the political economy of integration, the study emphasizes that the prevention of conflict is much more important than the identification of solutions after problems

already occur. Regarding sectoral development, the importance of agriculture is stressed. ECLA cautions that agriculture must not be allowed
to stagnate because of excessive attention given to the industrial sector.
Import-substituting industrialization is viewed as an indispensable aid
to growth, but there is also an awareness of its limits. The study notes
the importance to Central American industry of becoming more efficient
over time through taking advantage of economies of scale, diversifying
exports, and developing the necessary infrastructure. The study concludes
with a description of the roles of existing regional institutions, and
examines their sources of funding.

The later ECLA study (1971) analyzes three major problem areas: balance of payments, public finance, and regional disequilibrium. The balance of payments is found to have become more negative over time, and
the import component to have become more inflexible due to a shift in
the structure of imports from finished products to capital goods and
intermediate inputs used in the import-substitution production process.
The net balance has also deteriorated for services such as freight, insurance, and other transport activities. The expansion of external debt
in the 1960s has led to an increase in interest and amortization payments,
adversely affecting the balance of payments.

Although the strengthening of the public sector has facilitated development, the public sector has grown little in absolute terms despite
reorganization and shifting of priorities. The main problem in terms
of public finance has not been so much the increasing expenditures of
the state as its inability to increase financial resources. Expenditures
on current account seem to be quite inflexible; yet if the governments
were not to increase their capital account expenditures this could lead
to future economic and social conflicts.

The ECLA study takes the position that the balance of payments and
fiscal problems were structural disequilibrium that would have occurred
with or without the existence of the CACM. In fact the study argues that
structural defects would have been worse and income growth would have
been slower without the CACM. An evaluation of this view is difficult
since the study presents no supporting analytical estimations.

The other major problem associated with the CACM concerns development of regional disequilibrium and the ensuing tensions and conflicts,
as well as a falling off of trade. Disputing the impression that the main
cause of decelerating trade has been exhaustion of import-substitution
activities, ECLA asserts that a wide range of industrial goods, in particular consumer durables and intermediate goods, remain to be introduced or expanded in the region (although the study acknowledges that
many of the easier opportunities had already been exploited).

While noting that the 1969 war had disastrous effects on the integration process, including the exit of Honduras from the Common Market
and declines in trade, the study points to the many problems already
present which might have led to a breakdown even without the catalyst
of the war. From the perspective of 1971, ECLA expressed the hope that the
war might have some long-range positive effects. It illustrated vividly
the limitations of the Central American transport mechanism, with roads
as the only major connecting source for transport of goods. It may also

have led to a firmer commitment to finding mechanisms for reducing imbalances among the members. The document reports the efforts of the countries to formulate a _modus operandi_ which would reestablish integration between Honduras and the rest of the CACM.

The package would have provided for a fund for agricultural and industrial development to be administered by CABEI-partly externally financed, partly financed by the members--with those countries considered as least developed paying a smaller percentage and being awarded a larger percentage of financing. Other provisions included the establishment of regional policies on industry, agriculture, and tariffs; revision of tariffs, flexibility in the application of the common external tariff; criteria for origin of goods; safeguard clauses; application of measures for economic stabilization; and fiscal incentives. Unfortunately this effort at reconstructing integration foundered on persistent opposing interests (especially between El Salvador and Honduras).

A study examining the issue of unbalanced growth is that by Garbacz (1972). The author concentrates on the problem of polarization--the "tendency for an economic union of countries with widely divergent levels of development to result, barring policies to the contrary, in further extreme concentration of economic activity at a few industrial poles, or centers." The study considers this problem in the context of a Latin America Common Market and various subregional markets, including the CACM.

The basic tenet argued by Garbacz is that if market forces were allowed free play, polarization would result, and the ensuing pressures would lead to the disintegration of any economic integration unit. The main focus of the study is on the steps taken in the CACM and LAFTA to grant concessions to the least-developed countries.

The CACM used three basic instruments to counteract polarization: (i) integration industries--where each member is assured one industry with monopoly status before the other member countries are regarded eligible for a second monopoly industry; (ii) CABEI--the regional development bank which tries to favor the less-developed countries in its lending policies; and (iii) special fiscal incentives--favoring less-developed member countries. The author discusses the above policies and concludes that they have been much less effective than originally envisioned.

The study by Garbacz includes a discussion of LAFTA's main approaches to the polarization problem. These included preferential tariff treatment for goods from the least-developed countries (LDCs); complementation agreements under which LDCs and MDCs (more-developed countries) would agree to the assignment of some stage of production in the LDC, coordinated with industries in the MDCs; financial and/or technical assistance to LDCs; and subregional integration among more homogeneous countries, reducing the possibilities of polarization. Once again in the LAFTA case, the author demonstrates that these instruments have only been slightly effective.

Overall the author concludes that more coordinated financial and investment allocation planning and more attempts at subregional integration are the two most promising avenues of achieving broad economic integration and economic development over time. Regarding the latter, he notes that "In a group of relatively poorer countries it may be possible to build much of the industry from scratch taking account of comparative advantage, dynamically construed, and emphasizing complementarity without having to retrench because of the disruptive forces of vested interests." Yet the subregional integration option, while valuable for Latin America as a whole, would not appear to be an option for the already small CACM, so that other measures countering polarization are necessary. (Indeed, others have noted that the very success of the CACM owed much to the type of "absence of vested interests" described by Garbacz, which in turn stemmed from a traditional policy of relatively free trade in comparison with other Latin American countries.)

Brewster (1972) has also considered the balanced growth problem. He begins with the thesis that there will be some tradeoff between different distributions of the benefits of the Common Market and the total benefits to the market, that is, between distribution and efficiency. He further assumes that the market solution will lead to the optimal solution in terms of the efficiency criteria through the process of comparative advantage. (This assumption raises the question of appropriate identification of dynamic as opposed to static comparative advantage.) In Brewster's view, the main task of any attempted regional allocation of industries is to maximize the benefits or to minimize the costs to the CACM of a given distribution of the net benefits. There are of course many difficulties in accomplishing the latter task--the major ones being the decision as to what is a suitable distribution of the net benefits and the appropriate calculation of benefits and costs (and associated data and shadow pricing problems).

Noting that industry allocation generally should be confined to those industries needing a minimum market size to produce efficiently, Brewster points out that the determination of which industries are subject to economies of scale constitutes one problem, and selection of the industries themselves may be an even greater problem. The inclusion of too few industries in an allocation plan may make it physically impossible to divide industries among all the participants in an equitable manner; inclusion of too many may lead to interminable wrangling among the participants over their distribution. Brewster also notes the possibility of partial integration: a subset of countries may find there are greater benefits available through combining among themselves than through integration.

The crucial problem of determining an acceptable distribution amounts to a value judgment. The basic principle according to Brewster must be that the least-developed countries should obtain relatively greater benefits than the more-developed countries. However, there may not be agreement as to which countries are least developed, nor agreement as to criteria for measuring development. Brewster lists possible criteria for distributional policy: distribution

  (i) of equal per capita benefits,
 (ii) of equal absolute benefits,
(iii) positively related to per capita income,
 (iv) inversely related to per capita income,
  (v) positively related to absolute income, and
 (vi) inversely related to absolute income.

Another criterion mentioned is the existing degree of industrialization in the countries.

Brewster later offers a possible categorization scheme of industries into regional, subregional, and national, which he feels might help to strike a balance between regional and national considerations. Regional industries would be those subject to programming at the regional level. They would be selected via discussion among the national governments utilizing such criteria as economies of scale, growth potential, and contribution to balanced development. Subregional industries, which would consist of those industries whose production exceeds 50 percent of regional demand and which are not included in the regional category, would have their location chosen by the individual countries with some sort of regional consultation. National industries would be the remaining industries--those based on the national market or up to 50 percent of the regional market. They would not be subject to intervention at the regional level. The most important category in this type of scheme would be the subregional industries, and the type of consultation scheme would also be of critical importance. Brewster correctly points out that some sort of enforcement potential is necessary for this scheme to work. Thus some kinds of sanctions would have to be applied to those countries which infringe on the carrying out of this regional scheme.

Rosenthal (1973) has carried out an important study on the role of foreign investment in the development of the CACM. He estimates that the book value of foreign direct investment in the region was $750 million in 1969, of which four-fifths was from the United States. Noting the major shift away from the traditional sectors of raw material export enclaves and related public utilities toward a focus in industry (with the fraction of outstanding foreign direct investment in industry rising from 15 percent in 1959 to 31 percent in 1969), the author maintains that:

> Both the high rate of foreign investment in the region during the decade of the 1960s as well as the rapidly increasing importance of those investments in the manufacturing sector can be explained by the creation of the Central American Common Market and the regional industrialization policies that formed part of the integration movement. (p. 436)

In terms of aggregate capital supply, foreign savings provided 23 percent of gross investment in the region (1962-70), and of this inflow one-third was in the form of direct foreign investment. Moreover, the reinvestment of domestic profits added capital accumulation equal to 40 percent of the foreign capital inflows registered in the balance of payments. Rosenthal estimates that in the manufacturing sector, at least 15 percent of investment in the period came from direct foreign investment, and another 10 percent came from other forms of foreign financing. The corresponding creation of jobs was important; the author estimates that foreign plants account for one-third of total wages paid in the manufacturing sector of Guatemala. Regarding the current importance of foreign firms, Rosenthal estimates that 30 percent of all industrial output in the region in 1968 was from foreign firms, which possessed one-third of the fixed assets in manufacturing (with the share somewhat higher in Honduras and Nicaragua and lower in El Salvador and Costa Rica).

Foreign firms have become dominant primarily in the newer industrial sectors (especially chemicals, metals, plastics, petroleum, tobacco, rubber, glass), while domestic firms remain dominant in the more traditional manufacturing sectors (clothing, wood, leather, food, beverages, textiles, nonmetallic minerals). Another critical feature of foreign investment is its intensive activity in intraregional trade. Rosenthal estimates that foreign manufacturing firms in Guatemala export 45 percent of their total sales to the other CACM countries. He calculates that fully 40 percent of the trade within the CACM comes from foreign firms. In contrast, the activities of these firms in exporting outside of the region have been only "marginal," dependent on intracompany marketing arrangements. These trade patterns provide strong indirect evidence that the formation of the Common Market was instrumental in attracting increased foreign investment.

Foreign investment has been extremely free of controls in the region. There has been no CACM policy of channeling the investment, and one result has been a concentration of foreign investment during the 1960s in the more-developed member countries. Indeed, it is quite interesting to note that the country ranking of foreign participation in total industrial investment exactly parallels the ranking of participation in net static benefits of integration as calculated in chapter 3 of the present study.[5] Citing this aggravation of the balanced growth problem, Rosenthal concludes that "this fact alone justifies the adoption of some type of regional policy towards overseas capital." However, some of the more aggressive popular criticisms of foreign capital are countered by the author. He notes that the royalties of foreign interests for technology transfer do not appear to be excessive. Also, based on his interviews, the local firms which sold existing plants to foreign interests did so not because of forced sale under external pressure but because they were unable to adopt to the dynamism and competition introduced by the freeing of trade within the CACM.[6]

Finally, an important study from the standpoint of policymakers' perceptions of balanced growth is that prepared at the Central Bank of Honduras by Bueso (1970). The study first notes that the CACM was founded on the rationale of ECLA that the potential of raw materials exportation had been exhausted, that import-substituting industrialization was essential for growth, and that a regional market was necessary to permit the economies of scale required for this industrialization. The failure of the CACM to achieve this objective for Honduras is depicted in the following overview:

> . . . in our opinion the level of protection in the Common External Tariff has been excessive, with the consequent result of proliferation of inefficient industry to the detriment of the consumers, and, on the other hand, the absence of regional industrial planning has led to unnecessary duplication of plants and excessive fiscal incentives granted by the governments. . . . This lack of planning at the regional level has contributed to the unequal growth of the manufacturing

sector among the countries of the region, and consequently has led to the concentration of the benefits
of integration in two or three countries, imposing
economic sacrifices on the others and forcing them, to
a still greater degree than in the preintegration period, to remain dependent on exports to the rest of the
world as a source of dynamism for their growth. (p. 12;
our translation)

The analysis of the Bueso study relies on the following tenets:

(i) The benefits from integration are equivalent to its influence
in increasing industrialization.

(ii) Increased exportation of industrial products within the region
is the proof of this stimulus to industry for other partners; in contrast,
Honduras has exported raw materials to the partner countries, which it
did even before integration, showing that the Common Market has stimulated
neither Honduran industrialization nor exports.

(iii) Moreover, Honduras has paid the price of the partners' industrialization by sacrificing foreign exchange earned by exporting to the
rest of the world to purchase a reduced volume of high-cost manufactured
items from CACM partners (since its own exports to the region have shifted
from a surplus to a shortfall from its imports from the region). (The
study cites CACM supplier prices higher than world prices for five items,
which are reported as representative.)

It is clear that this line of analysis too simplistically identifies
industrialization with integration benefits, and confuses the observed
balance of payments with the structural shift in exports attributable
to integration (for the analysis of which see chapter 3 of the present
book). Even the study's authors appear to find the assessment too harsh,
since the study contains a separate estimate of integration benefits (following McClelland's methodology) and finds that these have been positive
for Honduras, equaling a 0.7 percent rise in the percentage growth rate
from 1962 to 1968 (p. 24), only modestly below the 1 percent estimated by
McClelland for the CACM as a whole.

The study concludes with policy recommendations focusing on (i) the
regional assignment of industries (although it is unclear what incentives
will induce private investors to locate where it would not be profitable
to do so otherwise); (ii) the outright transfer of income from partners
benefiting relatively more from integration to those benefiting relatively
less; and (iii) a reduction in the CACM's tariff protection, especially
for items with a low value added component derived from within the region.
The study is most important for what it reveals about the perception of
gains from the CACM; these clearly focus on the market's apparent impact
on industrialization and exports.

F.   Tariff Policy

Various studies have been carried out which examine the use of specific policy instruments within the CACM. A major review of tariff policy
by SIECA (1972) is one such effort.

Noting that the idea of a common external tariff (CXT) originated
in the 1950s and was finally put into operation under the Common Market
in the early 1960s, the study points out various problems associated
with the CXT, the most important being that in reality there does not
exist a common external tariff. Not all products were originally included
under the CXT and, though more have been added over the past decade, the
procedure has been rather slow, subject to lengthy negotiations and unusually long delays in ratification. Even among the included products
there exist problems. The nomenclature associated with international
commerce in Central America is imprecise and does not meet some of the
objectives of the CACM, especially those relating to industrial development. Another problem concerns enforcement of the CXT. There appears
to be substantial misevaluation of products with tacit approval of customs
authorities. There are also many unilateral exemptions of duties for
certain importers of certain goods, primarily in relation to schemes
of industrial incentives of individual countries.

The second major component of the CACM was the creation of free
trade among the member countries. Although the free trade involves a
large proportion of trade there still are many goods not yet included
in the agreement. The process of inclusion of goods has been slow, subject to the same types of negotiation and ratification problems as the
extension of the CXT. Instead of a system set up in advance providing
for successive widening of free trade to additional goods, there has been
a series of bilateral and multilateral negotiations between the participating countries. Regional trade has increased dramatically since the
inception of the CACM, and the volume of intraregional trade has also
expanded. Yet there have been problems contributing to decline in trade
over the past few years, especially since the conflict between Honduras
and El Salvador in 1969. One major problem has been the absence of
procedures for solving conflicts. Countries experiencing problems related
to trade tend to take unilateral action. Sometimes after arduous negotiation a regional solution may be found, but the lack of a mechanism for
solving problems in advance has been very costly to the integration movement, according to the SIECA study.

Another matter relating to trade and tariffs deals with the origin
of goods. There is no clear definition of what constitutes a Central
American product. Thus, any disagreements have to be solved by costly
negotiation procedures which are usually bilateral in nature rather than
regionally applied. Without some definite customs rules for the determination of origin, there will continual conflicts over whether a good
should or should not be included in free trade among the countries of
the CACM.

The SIECA volume makes several proposals for future tariff policy.
SIECA proposes a change in nomenclature from the existing NAUCA (SITC)
method to the Brussels Tariff Nomenclature. The study considers the latter superior because it utilizes a progressive ordering system of stages

of production, facilitating study of the effects of industrial policy--and the analysis of effective rates of protection. The study also proposes that the tariff system be changed from a mixed system including specific rates to one completely based on ad valorem duties, both because it would be easier to administer and because it would prevent discrimination against particular products or countries. The study advocates the streamlining of procedures for revising tariffs and the adoption of a comprehensive commercial policy to replace the ad hoc system presently in effect in the region. Tariffs have been used in the past to solve balance-of-payments and fiscal problems rather than to promote regional production. The study recommends that the former objectives should be controlled by means other than by commercial policy and that the proper functions of the tariff are protection and external commercial policy. The study recognizes the possible conflicts which can develop from a protectionist system: inefficiency in production, discrimination against exports, high prices to consumers. The authors propose these problems be handled by measures such as a scaling tariff system, export subsidies, drawbacks, and case-by-case analysis. SIECA also believes more use should be made of internal taxes (excise), especially to prevent the production of luxury goods. It is also felt that the common external tariff can be a negotiating instrument of the region with the rest of the world. The study also emphasizes the importance of a more detailed analysis of each individual case that arises, looking at such criteria as employment, balance of payment, and savings. It is also mentioned that 20 percent to 35 percent effective protection would be reasonable rates; however, an approximate final product tariff schedule is offered which seems to contradict the 20 percent to 35 percent range (p. 72).

To improve the free trade area, the SIECA study contends that the tendency of member countries to take unilateral action in trying to solve balance-of-payments and fiscal problems must be arrested. Free trade should also be extended to products not currently eligible.[7] The study goes on to propose additional improvements on several trade issues (including country of origin, imperfect competition, conciliation of free trade with internal consumption taxes, fiscal incentives, dumping, border procedures, and safeguard clauses).

Brewster (1972) has studied tariff policy in the Central American Common Market. This author also reports that although in theory the five countries have a common external tariff (CXT), in reality their tariffs differ substantially. This fact is principally due to the presence of a multitude of tariff exemptions which not only differ among products but also among countries for the same products. Other factors that have prevented the realization of the CXT are the haphazard application of the San José Protocol (30 percent import surcharge) of 1968, the specific components so prevalent in the CACM tariffs scheme, and a rather important list of excluded goods. All these factors, of course, affect both nominal and effective protection. Brewster points out that even if there were a functional CXT, effective rates of protection would still differ among countries because domestic value added ratios seem to vary quite widely.

The author ranks industrial goods in terms of national protection: nondurable consumer goods (122 percent), durable consumer goods (42 percent), intermediate goods (35 percent), and capital goods (11 percent). The data sources and the tariffs measured remain obscure (for tariff estimates in the present book, see chapter 3). The author then criticizes the system's absence of flexibility, noting that very few changes have been made in the CXT since the beginning of the Common Market. Yet he maintains that many Central American prices are lower than rest-of-world c.i.f. prices[8] and that many Central American products have declined in prices since the establishment of the CACM. He assumes that there must be ample "water" in the tariff system. He also criticizes the structure of protection for the way in which it concedes very high effective protection to goods with a small component of domestic value added.

Brewster then turns to the design of tariff policy. The author argues that the purpose of protection is not to shelter the inefficiency in production but to correct for divergences between private and social costs (for example, for labor, capital, foreign exchange, land). Furthermore, according to Brewster, the society may desire to industrialize in order to reduce external dependence, to affect the distribution of income, to modernize the society. The author recognizes that there is a limit to adequate protection, and that beyond that limit an economy can become quite distorted. He also recognizes that a tariff is a second-best way to promote industrialization (the first-best method being a production subsidy), and that tariffs often discriminate against the agricultural and export sectors in favor of import-substituting industry. Another possible use of protection is to correct structural deficiencies in the economy. When there are multiple objectives which are sought through a single policy, there tend to be conflicts between the objectives.

Arguing that fiscal and balance-of-payments problems should be dealt with through other policy instruments, Brewster formulates the following principles for protection policy:

(i) The "overall" rate of protection should be equal to the proportional difference between marginal private cost and marginal social cost measured in terms of exports.

(ii) The structure of nominal tariffs should be in conformity with the desired structure of consumption.

(iii) The structure of effective protection should give priority to the commodities which make the greatest contributions to the objectives of industrial policy. Finally he proposes that "the efficient rate of change for overall effective protection may be estimated as the change in the average Central American commodity terms of trade index."

This last proposal appears to stray far from any theoretical foundation. (The traditional relationship of "optimal protection" to terms of trade applies only to very large countries who by their monopsony power can affect international prices.) Regarding the other principles, while it is true that average tariff protection could reasonably be a function of the shadow price of foreign exchange, in practice there can be a vicious circle of policy reasoning in which a tariff is justified by a scarcity of foreign exchange, and then in turn the scarcity price of foreign exchange is measured by height of the tariff (as in Bacha and Taylor [1971]). Moreover, the "desired" consumption and industrial characteristics require complicated analysis, but unfortunately are likely to be chosen by ad hoc presentiments. Rather than Brewster's propositions, probably the principal basis for protective policy should be the assessment of divergence between present and future comparative advantage--a difficult task.

Bell (1974) has conducted another study on Central American protection. This study is considered by Bell to be only a first attempt at estimating nominal and effective protection in the region.

The study employs a sample of 400 items (encompassing 70 percent of import value) found to be "representative" on prior studies for other countries. For each item the procedure is to first estimate the components of nominal protection (specific duty, ad valorem tariff, San José Protocol surcharge, exonerations, ·export tax or subsidy, and "water"--excess of protection over amount required to raise import price to that of local production). To assess the "water" in the tariff, the author confines the analysis to goods in which there is intraregional trade and national production but which have little importation from the rest of the world, and compares unit values for local and rest-of-world imports. This last method can be quite misleading when there exist quality differences, as is likely with specific tariffs. Bell is well aware of this problem but has no alternative data base. Finally, the author employs coefficients from the 1963 input-output table for the United States to measure effective protection, recognizing that the procedure is less than ideal.

In view of the various short-cuts required for the analyses, the tariff study by Bell is primarily useful as a first effort at effective tariff estimation as groundwork for more comprehensive efforts.

G. Tax Incentives

Another economic policy instrument within the CACM is the system of incentives for industrial development. Joel (1971) has provided a useful assessment of this instrument. Exemptions have been granted by the CACM countries for (i) corporate income taxes, and (ii) import duties on capital intermediate goods. The liberality of such exemptions has varied with the country (with Guatemala and El Salvador more restrictive than the other countries) and the classification of applicants as "new" (more liberally treated) or "existing" industries.

Policymakers realized early that tax exemptions to attract foreign investment could merely lead to competitive underbidding by the individual countries and a consequent loss in revenue for them all. Accordingly, an Agreement on Fiscal Incentives for Industrial Development was drafted in 1962, but only adopted after finally being ratified by Honduras in 1969. Joel notes that even the common policy continues to confer a high degree of exemption for new industries, although containing somewhat tighter provisions for existing industries than applicable before in some member countries.[9] Moreover, the common policy perpetuated one of the most costly tax incentives practices: a producer of a good in one member country could apply for and receive exemption similar to that granted to a producer of the same good in any other member country (even if the industry were "new" in the latter but already existing in the former).

Joel considers the income tax exemption to have had very little effect in stimulating foreign investment in the region (although he warns that the impact on investment out of domestic capital is much more uncertain). This conclusion stems from a consideration of necessary conditions for a stimulative impact as well as from surveys of entrepreneurs by other analysts. Requisite conditions for impact include: (i) expected realization of profit during the exemption period (frequently not the case for investors primarily seeking to establish a base rather than expecting early profits); (ii) relatively high tax rates (the rates are only 10 percent to 25 percent in Central America). The attitudinal surveys cited found that U.S. firms generally regarded other factors (for example, tariff protection, freedom of profits repatriation, political stability, market size) to be much more important than tax exemption in their investment decisions--(although the surveys in question were not for Central America).

In contrast to income tax exemption, tariff exemptions for capital goods and intermediate imports seem to have been important to investment decisions, according to Joel. The reason is that legal tariffs on these items have been so high that exemptions have been essential to warrant investment. Nevertheless, one attitudinal survey of foreign investors found even tariff exemption played a limited role in investment decisions.

Turning to costs of incentives, Joel reports that import duty exemptions equaled from 19 percent to 46 percent of tariff revenue actually collected in the five countries in 1967, and from 6 percent to 15 percent of total government revenues, correspondingly. The author cites data for Costa Rica indicating a growth of tariff exemptions from only 2.5 percent of total tax revenue in 1962 to 13.8 percent in 1967. He then notes the probable contribution of the exemption schemes to the observed deterioration in government revenues and budget balances during the 1960s. Joel concludes by recommending drastic curtailing of new tax exemptions, combined with a reduction in tariffs in intermediate goods (to make elimination of exemptions on them feasible).

In a study of the Guatemalan tax structure, Hinrichs (1974) provides support to the thesis that tax incentives in the CACM have been excessive in terms of their revenue loss compared to their impact in stimulating investment. Citing data for import tariff exonerations and probable income tax exemptions for Guatemala in 1970, Hinrichs notes that the total exemptions equaled or exceeded the total value of increased investment in that year, suggesting prima facie evidence that the "costs" of the incentives were greater than their benefits.[10] Hinrichs also points out that Guatemala had applied tax incentives for a long period (especially 1959-70), so that the 1967-70 investment boom could not be attributed to them. Instead, investment was much more heavily influenced by export booms, development of the CACM, and the political climate.

H. Industrial Policy

SIECA (1972) has reviewed policy in the industrial sector. Besides the stimulus to industry during the 1960s from the formation of the CACM, the study identifies the formation of the Central American Bank for Economic Integration as an important stimulus to development of the industrial sector. In addition there were liberal fiscal incentives to industrial growth. The general belief in the period was that industrialization was essential for development and should be stimulated as fully as possible. Intraregional trade in industrial products grew most in the categories of textiles, chemicals, machinery, and electrical apparatus. The countries were affected differently: El Salvador and Guatemala tended to be net sellers; the others, net buyers. Exports to the rest of the world remained basically traditional, with small increases in manufacturing exports.

Detailed investment data are quite difficult to obtain, which necessitates the use of proxy measures to estimate both the amount and effects of financing. It is believed that industrial investment increased quite substantially over the decade, especially from foreign capital. The World Bank estimates that between 1962 and 1967 about 72 percent of industrial investment came from Central American sources and the other 28 percent from foreign sources, according to the SIECA study.

Central American inputs into the industrial process have been slowly increasing over time. Prices of industrial goods produced in Central America seem to be quite competitive with international prices. The effects on industrial employment seem to be quite uncertain in view of the conflicting data. In any case, there seems to have been no well-defined employment policy.

The SIECA study catalogs the various programs stimulating industry, including the Special Systems of Promotion and the national fiscal incentives (discussed above). The study notes that practically no policy considerations (exports, employment) have entered into the fiscal incentives scheme.

Looking toward the 1970s the SIECA study foresees possible problems of excess capacity. Increases in technology could also have a negative effect in that the sizes of efficient or optimal plants could grow faster than the Central American market, making it almost impossible to produce some products efficiently in the region. The study holds that industrialization can best be furthered through increasing internal demand by economic expansion, improvement of the distribution of income, and development of increased external demand for Central American products (or potential products). But in order to increase growth of the industrial sector, specific policies will be needed because this growth is not likely to occur spontaneously.

Assessing the future role of the industrial sector, the SIECA study reiterates the view that industry is more dynamic than agriculture; notes the objectives of improving income distribution and distribution of industrial benefits among member countries; recognizes the need to stimulate competition; and advocates development of manufactured exports outside the region. Instruments for these purposes include a protectionist but not indiscriminate tariff structure with protection diminishing over time to stimulate efficiency, and "industrial programming" (especially in basic industries and industries facing excess capacity).

I.   Conclusion

A number of salient themes emerge from the various studies surveyed here. Politically the formation of the CACM owed much to outside impetus, first from ECLA, then from the United States. From the outset the objective was to permit industrialization in a region where the markets of individual countries were inadequate to achieve economies of scale—although the instrument of regional industrial monopoly to achieve this goal gave way to free trade in industrial goods as U.S. influence replaced that of ECLA.

Against the unifying objective of industrialization was the disintegrating influence of differences perceived in the distribution of the markets' benefits. Honduras especially felt the objective of industrialization had been met by other partners at Honduran expense. The 1969 war merely brought into the open elements of conflict already inherent due to this perception. Another influence weakening support of the CACM has been the perception by some groups that the market's benefits have gone to foreign firms and increased U.S. hegemony in the region (a possibility not inconsistent with the impressive evidence of foreign participation in the industry and trade of the region, but a viewpoint which, nevertheless, fails to consider whether the alternative of lower foreign activity combined with slower growth would have been preferable).

Despite the charges of "polarization" and foreign influence, all quantitative estimates of the CACM's benefits yield positive estimates for all partners. The past estimates cluster in a range of 0.3 percent to 1 percent incremental per annum growth rate as the impact of the Common Market. The estimates presented in the present volume (chapter 3) are based on very different methodology. Prior estimates tend to confuse ongoing growth effects with once-for-all efficiency shifts, and to attribute to the CACM the observed changes in growth rates which happen to coincide with the institution of the Common Market. The estimates of this study are based on a detailed examination of the changes in trade and production patterns caused by integration. When both dynamic and static effects are considered, integration is found to have raised the absolute level of GNP in the region by 3 to 4 percent above what it otherwise would have been (as of 1972). This estimate represents a large economic benefit from integration. On the other hand, it is difficult to compare with earlier estimates, because those estimates are in terms of an increased growth rate (not level) of GNP; and in the absence of any specified period over which the increased rate would be expected to continue, those estimates cannot be compared with one stated (more appropriately) in terms of level instead of growth rate. (Clearly, any study purporting that integration raised the growth rate permanently by 1 percent per annum would imply far larger gains than those identified in chapter 3 of this study.)

Regarding policy measures required for improvement of the CACM, the studies considered here agree about the need for measures to insure equitable participation of all members in the Common Market, but they also indicate (i) the ambiguity in determining which countries are "least developed" as well as how much and what type of redistribution should occur; (ii) the political difficulty of implementing any redistributive scheme (as shown by the fate of the proposals for a modus operandi).

The studies on tax incentives concur that these have been excessive; those on tariff policy generally point to the need for a developmental (rather than fiscally oriented or accidental) tariff policy as well as the need to reduce high effective protection for products with little value added from within the region. Industrial studies point the need for revitalization of the integration industries scheme and for regional planning and country allocation of industries, but they remain vague on the incentive system that will lead to these results in the face of private investment signals pulling investment toward the more industrialized poles.

The research results of the SIECA/Brookings program tend to confirm several of the themes of the previous literature while providing, in many cases, a more complete quantitative assessment of these themes. The measurements of benefits and costs of integration confirm positive gains from integration (and show them to be larger than commonly thought, at least if the "growth rate" effects of earlier studies are interpreted to be for relatively short, transitional periods). The results here also confirm the problems of equity in distribution of benefits with respect to Honduras, while the new results provide a more precise basis for gauging the size of the imbalance and, therefore, the extent of redistribution policies required. The studies here on employment provide quantitative evidence on the scope for substituting labor for capital, on the employment effects of integration, and on the trends in income distribution and their relationship to wages and to the forces determining the division of rents between labor and capital. The study on comparative advantage provides sectoral measurements that should contribute to an assessment of tariff and fiscal incentives policies. The study on the agricultural sector measures the extent of economic gains available through a more complete extension of integration to the sector, and the study on comparative prices provides a rigorous basis for examining comparative levels of real income (as well as indicative information for areas such as exchange rate policy). In broad terms these studies tend to confirm that part of the previous literature that has recognized the positive achievements of the CACM while at the same time calling attention to the need for improvements in policy areas such as those of balanced growth among partners, employment and income distribution, tariffs and fiscal incentives, and agricultural integration.

BIBLIOGRAPHY

Bacha, E., and Taylor, L. "Foreign Exchange Shadow Prices: A Critical Review of Current Theories." Quarterly Journal of Economics 85(2) (May 1971): pp. 197-224.

Balassa, B. "Trade Creation and Trade Diversion in the European Market." Economic Journal 77 (305) (March 1967): pp. 1-21.

Bell, H. "El Uso de Una Muestra Representativa del Universo Arancelario como Instrumento de Trabajo para el Estudio del Sistema Arancelario del Mercado Comun Centroamericano," mimeographed (Guatemala City, 1974).

Brewster, H. "The Choice between Efficiency and Industrial Balance: Protection and Employment in the Central American Common Market," mimeographed (Guatemala City: SIECA, 1972).

Bueso, G. La Integración Centroamericana y el Desarrollo Económico de Honduras (Tegucigalpa: Banco Central de Honduras, Departamento de Estudios Económicos, 1970).

Castillo, C. Growth and Integration in Central America (New York: Praeger, 1966).

Cohen Orantes, I. Regional Integration in Central America (Lexington, Mass.: Lexington Books, 1972).

Dagum, C. "La Evolución de la Economía Centroamericana Durante el Período 1960-70 y sus Perspectivas para la Próxima Década" (Guatemala City: SIECA/72-VII-6136, October 1972).

Fagan, S. Central American Economic Integration: The Politics of Unequal Benefits (Berkeley: Institute of International Studies, 1970).

Garbacz, C. Industrial Polarization under Economic Integration in Latin America (Austin: Bureau of Business Research, University of Texas, 1972).

Hansen, R. Central America: Regional Integration and Economic Development (Washington, D.C.: National Planning Association, 1967).

Hinrichs, H. "Tax Reform Constrained by Fiscal Harmonization within Common Markets: Growth without Development in Guatemala," in D. Geithman, ed., Fiscal Policy for Industrialization and Development in Latin America (Gainesville: University of Florida Press, 1974).

Holbik, K., and Swan, P. Trade and Industrialization in the Central American Common Market: The First Decade (Austin: Bureau of Business Research, University of Texas, 1972).

Joel, C. "Tax Incentives in Central American Development." Economic Development and Cultural Change 19(2) (January 1971): pp. 229-52.

McClelland, D. The Central American Common Market: Economic Policies, Economic Growth and Choices for the Future (New York: Praeger, 1972).

Nugent, J. "Empirical Investigations in Central American Economic Integration," mimeographed (Los Angeles: University of Southern California, 1973).

Nye, J. Central American Regional Integration (New York: Carnegie Endowment for International Peace, 1967).

Ramsett, D. Regional Industrial Development in Central America: A Case Study of the Integration Industries Scheme (New York: Praeger, 1964).

Rosenthal, G. "The Role of Private Foreign Investment in the Development of the Central American Common Market," mimeographed, 1973.

SIECA. "El Desarrollo Integrado de Centroamérica en la Presente Década," study no. 2, "El Perfeccionamiento del Mercado Común Centroamericano: Regimen de Libre Comercio, Unión Aduanera y Arancel Común" (Guatemala City: SIECA/72-VII-6/36, October 1972).

SIECA. "El Desarrollo Integrado de Centroamerica en la Presente Decada," study no. 3, "Programa de Desarrollo Industrial Integrado" (Guatemala City: SIECA/72-VII-6/36, October 1972).

Tobis, D. "The Central American Common Market: The Integration of Underdevelopment" NACIA Newsletter 3(9) (January 1970) North American Congress on Latin America, New York: pp. 1-8.

United Nations, Economic Commission for Latin America. Evaluación de la Integración Económica en Centroamérica (Santiago: ECLA, E/CN.12/751 Rev. 1; E/CN.12/762, 1966).

United Nations, Economic Commission for Latin America. The Central American Common Market and Its Recent Problems (Santiago: ECLA, E/CN.12/ 885; E/CN.12/CCE/363/Rev. 1, 1971).

Wilford, W. "Trade Creation in the Central American Common Market" Western Economic Journal 8 (1) (March 1970): pp. 61-69.

Appendix B

NOTES

1. The Treaty provided that "The contracting states shall not desig-nate a second plant in the same country until each of the five Central American countries has been assigned a plant...." The original interpre-tation was that no country could have a second plant set up in any indus-try until every other country had at least one industrial plant. The new interpretation was that no country could have a second plant in a given industry unless a plant in that industry had been assigned to each of the other countries.

2. Suppose integration raises the import share in consumption from m_0 to m_1, but after the absolute shift the growth rate of imports is the same as before ($g_1 = g_0$) although operating in a larger base. Attributing trade creation to changes in elasticities would yield a zero estimate of trade creation, although creation had in fact occurred (in the amount $\left[m_1 - m_0\right] C_1$), where C_1 is terminal consumption).

3. The conversion factor is based on the coefficient for exports in the regression: $\ln (1 + g_r) = 2.9 + .276 \ln (1 + g_E) + .122 \ln (1 + g_I)$, where $\ln$ = natural logarithm, g = growth rate, and Y, E, I are GNP, ex-ports, and investment, respectively. This procedure does not take account of the simultaneity problem caused by the fact that exports are a compo-nent in GNP. Indeed, the coefficient on exports appears suspiciously close to the trade share in GNP, indicating that nothing other than this accounting definitional relationship has been captured.

4. It is worth reiterating that estimates attributing ongoing in-creases in growth rates to the static effects of integration are inconsis-tent with the theoretical basis of these effects, which indicate a once-for-all gain but not an acceleration of growth rate into the indefinite future.

5. Rosenthal estimates the following foreign shares of total indus-trial investment, 1962-69: El Salvador, 20.8 percent; Guatemala, 18.8 percent; Costa Rica, 15.0 percent; Nicaragua, 10.2 percent; Honduras, 9.8 percent. However, the point of concentration in more-developed countries is somewhat at odds with Rosenthal's report that the share of foreign in-dustrial investment in the total amount outstanding is higher in Nicaragua and Honduras than in the other three countries (p. 448). Combined, these two sets of information suggest high foreign presence in industry in the less-developed partners prior to the CACM (due presumably to a weak do-mestic entrepreneurial class), but a shift of foreign efforts to the more natural poles for industrialization once the CACM eliminated intraregional tariffs.

6. Rosenthal does cite the importance of the transfer of existing fiscal incentives benefits from one owner to the next in the decision of foreign firms to buy out local plants, and he suggests the termination of such transfers.

7. Of which the more important include coffee, sugar, cotton, meat, tobacco, pastas, breads, alcohol, cigarettes, petroleum derivatives, fabrics, packing materials, and matches.

8. Although the comparison appears to rest on unit values of imported goods, which are subject to problems of noncomparability (especially when the categories examined are broad).

9. For example, for new industry in favored "Group A" (raw materials and capital goods fields, as well as other goods deriving at least half of their material imports from the CACM), the agreement grants 100 percent exemption on import duties for machinery, raw materials, semifinished products, and fuels, for periods of five to ten years, as well as 100 percent exemption of income tax and tax on assets for eight to ten years.

10. It should be noted, however, that an incentive structure that truly increased total investment over time could be unfairly judged by such a comparison. The very estimate of foregone revenues may be premised on output value which includes a portion that would not have existed in the absence of incentives. Furthermore, a "transfer" (that is, between government and the private sector) would not appear legitimately identifiable as a cost when the "benefit" involves a net increase to the economy's welfare rather than a mere redistribution among sectors.

Benefits and Costs of Economic Integration: Methodology and Statistics

William R. Cline

A. Introduction

Chapter 3 examines the benefits and costs of economic integration in Central America. The chapter sets forth the methodology in intuitive terms. This appendix reports the equations of the analysis and elaborates on their derivation. In addition, further details on data are reported, and supplementary statistical tables are presented.

B. Trade Creation and Diversion

The analysis begins with the traditional concepts of trade creation and trade diversion. In order to approach the measurement of these effects, it is useful to review their conventional graphical treatment.

Consider a country with original tariff rate, t_0, importing from the world market as shown in figure 1. The country pays price P_w for the good, although consumers must pay the price including tariff: $P_w (1 + t_0)$. Total consumption of the good is Oc, of which Ob is produced at home and bc is imported.

The country joins a Common Market, freeing imports from partners who supply the good at price P_c. Importation expands to Q_1^M as more is demanded at this lower price and less is produced at home in view of the lower domestic price. The increase in total imports, $Q_1^M - Q_0^M$, represents trade creation. Its welfare benefits are the two triangles, A + B. The first represents the savings from releasing domestic resources originally producing the good. (The opportunity cost of producing a unit of the good is given by the supply curve, so that whereas domestic resources worth "aefb" went to produce ab of the good, this quantity may now be imported for aegb, a savings of A.) The second triangle, B, represents the gain in consumers' surplus[1] net of the loss of producers' surplus[2] and original government tariff collections. (Movement down the demand curve from h to j has transferred to consumers the total area lkhj in new consumers' surplus at the expense of a loss of lkfe for producers' surplus and of gfhi in foregone government tariff revenue, leaving net social gain of A + B, of which we have already counted A.) Note that the transfer away from producers and government toward consumers contains

484

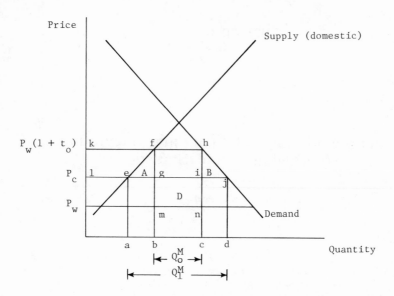

Figure C-1

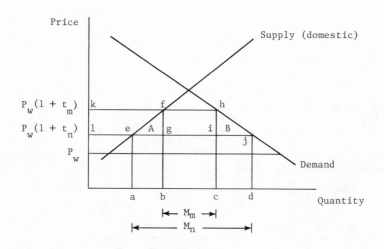

Figure C-2

political implications: the "trade creating" effects of Common Market formation may not be popular to the politically organized groups--producers and bureaucracy--although they are beneficial to the consumers.

It should be noted that the customs union literature narrowly defines "trade creation" as only the domestic output reduction, "ab." The expansion in consumption, by "cd," is referred to as the "consumption effect." Our measures below will combine the two and refer to the "trade creation and consumption effect" (TCCE).

While total trade creation and consumption effect was $Q_1^M - Q_0^M$, the integration also involved a switching of import supply from the rest of the world to a partner. That is, in the diagram, partner supplied nothing before and everything, Q_1^M, after integration; the world market supplied Q_0^M before integration and nothing after. There was therefore "trade diversion" away from the supply of the rest of the world (ROW) to the supply of partner in the amount Q_0^M. There is a welfare cost of this diversion, represented by rectangle D. That is, the country previously imported Q_0^M at price P_w; it has now switched this portion of imports to partner supply at the higher price, P_c. The loss is therefore $(P_c - P_w)$ (Q_0^M), or the area D. Note that this loss is also equivalent to the gross loss of tariff revenue (originally mfhn) minus that portion of tariff revenue transferred to consumer surplus (gfhi).

It is illuminating to consider who gains and who loses from trade diversion. The government loses, and the loss comes wholly out of tariff revenue; however, the producers of exports in partner countries gain because they will now sell goods previously purchased from the world market. Traditional analysis omits those "partner exporter" gains, under the assumption that such exports carry full opportunity costs, but the analysis below will measure welfare gains associated with those increased partner exports--meaning that our own analysis can attribute welfare gains to trade diversion as well as to trade creation.

Turning from graphical to algebraic analysis, the anti-monde assumed is that in the absence of integration, import propensities would have remained unchanged from their preintegration patterns. Therefore trade diversion may be measured as:

(1) $TD = (n_0^R - n_1^R) \, C_1$,

where:

n^R is the average propensity to import the good from the rest of the world, measured as M^R/C where M^R is value of imports from ROW;

C is apparent consumption of the good, measured as domestic production plus total imports minus total exports of the good; and

Subscripts 0, 1 refer to base and terminal year, respectively.

Equation (1) measures trade diversion as the shortfall of importation from ROW, from that magnitude which would have been expected if the preintegration import propensity had still applied to the post-integration import propensity level of consumption.

The "trade creation and consumption effect" is measured as:

(2) $TCCE = (\eta^T_1 - \eta^T_0) \, C_1,$

where variables are as before, with superscript T referring to total importation.

In terms of figure 1, total imports (and hence the total import propensity) will have increased due to integration by the amount $Q^M_1 - Q^M_0$. The increment is represented by the total increase of imports above what would have been expected if the preintegration import propensity had continued, i.e., the measure in equation (2).

Given the sectoral estimates of trade diversion and trade creation-consumption effect for each country, the corresponding welfare estimates are:

(3) $CTD = (\lambda - 1) \, TD,$

where:

CTD = welfare cost of trade diversion,

$\lambda = P_c / P_w,$ and

P_c, P_w are partner supply price and world supply price, respectively.

Equation (3) states that of the total value of imports switched from world to partner supply in the amount TD, the fraction $\dfrac{P_c - P_w}{P_w}$ or $(\lambda - 1)$, will constitute welfare loss to the importing country due to purchase of partner goods at a higher price than that available on the world market.

In terms of figure 1, the result in equation (3) may be seen as follows: trade diversion cost is rectangle D, or

(3a) $D = (P_c - P_w) \, Q^M_0.$

The measure TD is the value equivalent of the quantity "switched" (Q^M_0). This foregone importation from ROW would have been purchased at price P_w (in the absence of integration), so that TD is the equivalent of $P_w Q^M_0$ in figure 1. Thus, since (3a) may be written:

(3b) $D = \dfrac{(P_c - 1)}{P_w} \, P_w \, Q^M_0),$

the equation may also be written

(3c) $D = [(\lambda - 1) \, TD],$

yielding the original equation (3) for welfare cost of trade diversion.

The welfare gain from trade creation and consumption expansion is:

(4) $\text{BTCCE} = (1/2)(\text{TCCE}) \left[\dfrac{1 + t_0 - \lambda}{(1 - \phi_1^R)\,\lambda + \phi_1^R} \right]$,

where:

BTCCE = welfare benefit of trade creation and consumption effect;

t_0 = base period tariff;

$\lambda = P_c/P_w$ as before; and

ϕ_1^R = the share of imports coming from ROW in the terminal period.

The derivation of equation (4) may be seen by referring to figure 1. In the graph, welfare gains from trade creation and consumption effect (TCCE) are the triangles, A + B. These in turn are equal to:

(4a) $A + B = (1/2)\ [P_w\,(1 + t_0) - P_c]\ [Q_1^M - Q_0^M]$

     $= (1/2)\ [1 + t_0 - \lambda]\ P_w\ [Q_1^M - Q_0^M]$.

The final term in (4a) is the quantity change of total imports from what their lower level would have been without integration; however, our measure TCCE is in value terms, not quantity. To restate (4a) in terms of TCCE a "price" is necessary for converting value to quantity. That price is the weighted average terminal price of the imported good, $\phi_1^R\,P_w + (1 - \phi_1^R)\,P_c$.

Thus (4a) may be written:

(4b) $A + B = (1/2)\ [1 + t_0 - \lambda]\ P_w \left[\dfrac{\text{TCCE}}{\phi_1^R\,P_w + (1 - \phi_1^R)\,P_c} \right]$,

yielding the equation (4) used for calculating welfare benefits of the "trade creation and consumption effect." Note that when complete specification in imports from the partner occurs, (4) becomes:

$\text{BTCCE} = \dfrac{1}{2} \left[\dfrac{1 + t_0 - \lambda}{\lambda} \right] \text{TCCE}$

which equals:

$(1/2) \left[\dfrac{P_w\,(1 + t_0) - P_c}{P_c} \right] \text{TCCE}$.

This last expression is intuitively more clear than (4) as it states the welfare benefit in terms of the proportional excess of the original price to the consumer $[(P_w\,(1 + t_0)]$ over the terminal price, P_c.

C.   Trade Suppression and External Trade Augmentation

Negative trade diversion is registered when the propensity to import from rest of world rises rather than falls $(\eta_1^R > \eta_0^R)$ after integration.

488

This occurrence can only be meaningful as a result of integration if, in moving to the new common external tariff, the country lowers its tariff facing ROW. In that event, the propensity to import from ROW could have increased, although this fact would imply very limited substitutability in demand between the ROW good and the same good from Common Market partners (or very inelastic partner supply)--since the tariff facing the latter will have fallen to zero. With demand substitutability and elastic partner supply, partner goods would have replaced ROW supply, lowering η^R.

In the opposite case--where the tariff rises as the country moves to the common external tariff--a rise in the propensity to import from ROW can only be due to structural shifts unrelated to the integration.

The treatment of negative trade diversion therefore follows these steps:

(i) If the tariff facing ROW rose ($t_1 > t_0$), the observed "negative trade diversion" is considered nongermane, and the trade diversion estimate is forced to zero.

(ii) If the tariff declined ($t_1 < t_0$), negative trade diversion is accepted as economically meaningful and is called "external trade augmentation" (ETA). For purposes of calculation, TD (trade diversion) is forced to zero, and the absolute value of the negative trade diversion is recorded as ETA.

Similarly, trade creation is registered as negative if the total import propensity declines rather than rises as expected with the opening of free trade among partners. Once again economic meaningfulness of this occurrence hinges on the change in tariff. If the country raised its tariff in moving to the common external tariff ($t_1 > t_0$), a shrinkage in the total import propensity is meaningful: the trade-depressing effect of raising the tariff on imports from ROW has swamped the liberalizing effect of freeing entry for partner goods. This result again implies limited demand substitutability between partner and ROW good, or limited partner supply elasticity (otherwise total import propensity would have risen due to newly free partner entry, regardless of the rise in tariff facing ROW).

If the tariff fell in the move to the common external tariff ($t_1 < t_0$), negative trade creation must represent structural shifts nongermane to integration. The total import propensity would have to have risen considering integration effects alone, since the tariff will have fallen for ROW goods and have terminated completely for partner goods.

For purposes of the calculations, when negative trade creation is recorded, the variable "trade creation and consumption effect" (TCCE) is forced to zero. If the tariff rose, then "trade suppression" is set equal to the absolute value of the negative measure of TCCE. If the tariff fell, no trade suppression is recorded. Thus, in the economically meaningful case of "negative trade creation," the economic phenomenon involved--the suppression of trade with ROW due to a rise in tariff--is specifically recorded.

Once "external trade augmentation" and "trade suppression" are measured, their corresponding welfare effects can be calculated. These two effects are the standard welfare impacts of tariff changes. To examine trade suppression, consider figure 2. The original tariff is t_n; the final tariff is t_m; and imports are suppressed from M_n to M_m. The welfare cost of this change is A + B, with A representing increased domestic resource costs for obtaining an amount of the good formerly imported, and B representing the shrinkage of consumer surplus. The welfare gain from external trade augmentation may be seen by reversing the process: original tariff is t_m, terminal tariff is t_n, and external trade augmentation is the growth in imports from M_m to M_n. The formal measures of these effects are stated below.

A final adjustment required is that when negative trade diversion is registered, the initial estimate of trade creation must be adjusted downward by the absolute value of this estimate, and when negative trade creation is found, trade diversion must be adjusted downward by the absolute value of that trade creation estimate. Consider negative trade diversion. The observed rise in propensity to import from ROW means that there will be a component in the total import propensity rise which is not attributable to trade creation through new importation from the partner. Indeed, this component is already captured in "external trade augmentation"--increased importation from ROW--so to leave the component in the trade creation estimate will double count the effect. The narrow measure of trade creation should be limited to increased propensity to import from partner. This contraction will be made appropriately by deducting from the initial estimate of trade creation (TCCE) the absolute value of the negative trade diversion estimate.[3]

Similarly, when trade creation is negative, the economic phenomenon of suppressing imports from ROW is captured in the "trade suppression" measure. To avoid double counting, the measure of trade diversion must therefore be collapsed to refer only to the rise in the propensity to import from partners. (If total import propensity falls due to trade suppression, but importation from partners remains unchanged, it is not meaningful to say trade has been "diverted" from ROW to partner supply.) This objective is achieved if the absolute value of trade creation is subtracted from trade diversion.[4]

The above reasons for reducing one of the basic variables (trade diversion or creation) by the absolute amount of the other when the other is negative pertain to the "germane" cases--where tariff shifts cause the negative effects observed. In the "nongermane structural shift" cases (negative trade diversion or creation unexplained by tariff change), the correction remains the same. Here the logic is that since negative effects is nongermane, it should be removed from all the integration effects being measured. This removal requires the same adjustments just described.[5]

The adjustments for negative trade diversion and creation may be summarized as follows, where the asterisk refers to the measure after adjustment:

(5)   If   TD $<$ 0:

(5a)   TD* = 0,

(5b)   TCCE* = TCCE - $\left| TD \right|$.

(5c)   If $t_0 > t_1$:   ETA = $\left| TD \right|$.

(5d)   If $t_0 \leq t_1$:   ETA = 0.

(6)   If TCCE $<$ 0:

(6a)   TCCE* = 0,

(6b)   TD* = TD - $\left| TCCE \right|$.

(6c)   If $t_0 \geq t_1$:   TS = 0.

(6d)   If $t_0 < t_1$:   TS = $\left| TCCE \right|$,

where ETA = external trade augmentation and TS = trade suppression.

The welfare benefit of external trade augmentation is:

(7)   BETA = (1/2) ETA $(t_0 - t_1)$.

This evaluation of the benefit may be seen to equal triangles A + B in figure 2, considering that

(7a)   A + B = $\frac{1}{2}[P_w(1 + t_m) - P_w(1 + t_n)]$ $[M_n - M_m]$.

Since $t_0 = t_m$ and $t_1 = t_n$ in the case of external trade augmentation, and since the value of increased importation, ETA, from ROW is merely the world price (P_w) times the increased quantity $[M_n - M_M]$, we may write:

(7b)   A + B = $\frac{1}{2}(t_m - t_n)$ P_w $[M_n - M_m]$ = (1/2)$(t_0 - t_1)$ ETA,

yielding the final form in equation (7) for benefits from external trade augmentation.

By identical reasoning, except with a reversal in the direction of tariff change, the welfare cost of trade suppression is:

(8)   CTS = (1/2)$(t_1 - t_0)$ TS.

To recapitulate, equations (1) through (8) show, for each product of sector of each country, trade diversion and trade creation-consumption magnitude resulting from integration, their corresponding welfare effects, and the appropriate adjustments for all these measures when negative trade diversion and creation are encountered. We may now turn to measurement of the less traditional effects, those involving opportunity cost of labor, economies of scale, and foreign exchange scarcity.

D.   Nontraditional Static Welfare Effects

When one country in the Common Market increases its imports from another partner due to integration, the second partner will increase production to fill this new export demand. For the individual partner "i," the export expansion (in a given product sector) equals:

$$(9) \qquad \text{DELTX}_i = \sum_j \Phi^c_{ij} \ [\ \text{TD}_j + \text{TCCE}_j],$$

where Φ^c_{ij} is country i's share in partner j's imports of the good from Common Market suppliers. (TD and TCCE refer to the adjusted values TD*, TCCE* whenever TD < 0 or TCCE < 0.)

Equation (9) states that country i will increase its exports to partners in an amount equal to the sum over all partners of its participation in each partner's imports from the Common Market, multiplied by that partner's increase in Common Market imports attributable to integration. This increase in imports from the Common Market is merely trade diversion plus trade creation-consumption effect. That is, when one country frees trade for its partners, it increases its total imports from them by an amount divisible into two parts: an increment due to switching supplier source from ROW to partners (trade diversion); and an increment due to reduction of its home production plus expansion of its consumption of the good (trade creation-consumption effect).

Given the estimate of increased exportation to partners and the other integration effect measures, the change in production attributable to integration may be estimated. The positive effects on production stem from: (i) expanded exports to partners (DELTX); (ii) trade suppression-- in which ROW supply is curtailed, requiring increased domestic output unless consumption declines. Negative effects on production can arise from: (i) the "trade creation" domestic-output reduction component of the trade creation-consumption effect; (ii) that portion of external trade augmentation which is absorbed by domestic output reduction rather than by increased domestic consumption.

Denominating the positive output effect as DQ for a given country and product sector:

$$(10) \qquad \text{DQ} = \text{DELTX} + \text{Min} \begin{cases} \text{TS} \\ \text{TS} - (C_0 - C_1) \end{cases} \text{subject to } C_0 > C_1$$

where:

   Min = the minimum of;

   C_1 = terminal consumption; and

   C_0 = base period consumption.

In equation (10), DELTX and TS constitute the impetus to domestic production. However, if trade suppression has reduced domestic consumption

$(C_0 > C_1)$, then the contribution of trade suppression (TS) to domestic output stimulus must be reduced by the amount of this reduction in consumption.

There is insufficient information to give a precise estimate of the output depressing effects of trade creation and external trade augmentation. Referring to figure 1, the calculations above for trade creation-consumption effect identify the total increase in imports, $Q_1^M - Q_0^M$, but but not the division of this increase between domestic output reduction (ab) and consumption expansion (cd). The same observation applies to external trade augmentation (figure 2). If domestic output is quite inelastic as in SS^i of figure 3, then increased imports will be due solely to a consumption effect.

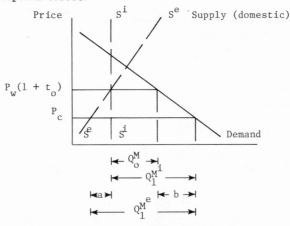

Figure C-3

If domestic supply is more elastic, as in SS^e, the increase in imports $(Q_1^{Me} - Q_0^M)$ will contain both a domestic output reduction component (a) and a consumption expansion component (b).

In the absence of supply elasticity information, it is possible to examine directly whether output has declined. A measure of output decline attributable to integration is thus:

(11)
$$ QDM = Min \left\{ \frac{Q_0 - Q_1}{ETA + TCCE} \right\}, $$

subject to $QDN \geq 0$,

where:

QDN is the measured decline in output due to integration,

Q_0 is output in the base year, and

Q_1 is the terminal year.

Thus, if domestic output declines in a section, that decline is attributed to integration up to a maximum of ETA + TCCE, the largest possible production declines due to integration (with no consumption-expansion effect and solely domestic output reducing "trade creation"). If output rose, however, no production reducing effect from integration is assigned whatever.[6]

1. Labor Opportunity Cost

Increased domestic output attributable to integration generates the following welfare gains from the standpoint of labor opportunity cost:

$$(12) \qquad BOC = DQ \quad (1 - \frac{w^*}{w}) \quad \left[\frac{WB}{Q_G} \right] \quad ,$$

where:

BOC = benefit of labor opportunity cost effect;

w = wage rate of unskilled labor in the sector;

w^* = shadow price of unskilled labor for the country;

WB = wage bill for unskilled labor in the sector; and

Q_G = gross output value for the sector.

Given the high underemployment rates found in the F.A.O. study cited in chapter 3, it might be reasonable to argue that rural workers could be withdrawn at zero social cost. The calculations here use a more conservative concept. The shadow price of labor is estimated as:

$$(13) \qquad W^* = W_R (1 - U_R),$$

where:

W_R = rural wage rate, and

U_R = rural underemployment rate.

The calculation of (13) assumes that if a worker remained in the rural sector, the probability of his obtaining full-time work at the rural wage would be $(1 - U_R)$. Multiplying this probability by the rural wage gives the "expected" rural wage earnings of the worker, which provides an upper-bound estimate of the shadow price of unskilled labor.

2. Economies of Scale

The next welfare effect of expanded output concerns economies of scale. When a sector has production characteristics with returns to scale, output increases by a greater percentage than do the inputs required. Consider a sector with output gains of $(1 + r)$ percent for every proportional increase of all factors and inputs by 1 percent. (In terms of the production function, $(1 + r)$ is the sum of the elasticities.)

Then for a given increase of gross output ΔQ, there is a windfall gain equivalent to $\Delta Q \left[\dfrac{r}{(1 + r)} \right]$. [7] Finally, since the production economies of scale refer to value added, the net welfare gain from an expansion output put ΔQ is $\left(\dfrac{1}{1 + r} \right) \Delta Q \left[\dfrac{VA}{Q_G} \right]$, where the final term is the ratio of value added (VA) to gross output value.

Estimates of economies of scale based on the 1968 industrial survey in Central America are presented in appendix I. The scale coefficients "r" from those estimates are utilized in the benefit costs measures of chapter 3. The benefit from economies of scale due to increased output attributable to integration is, for each sector and country:

(14) $BES = DQ \ (\Psi) \left(\dfrac{r}{1 + r} \right)$,

where:

Ψ = the value added / gross output ratio for the sector, and

r = the returns to scale coefficient.

Just as increased output generates labor opportunity cost and scale welfare gains, decreased output attributable to integration causes corresponding costs. Considering equations (11), (12), and (14), these costs are:

(15) $COC = QDN \ ^{(1 \ - \ \frac{w*}{w})} \left[\dfrac{WB}{Q_G} \right]$,

(16) $CES = QDN \ (\Psi) \left[\dfrac{r}{1 + r} \right]$,

where all variables are as before.

3.   Foreign Exchange Savings

As discussed in chapter 3, an important effect of integration among developing countries is that, by economizing on foreign exchange, it can provide a welfare benefit when the opportunity cost of foreign exchange exceeds the market exchange rate. This benefit will be:

(17) $BFE = [f* - 1](DELTX + TS - TCCE - ETA)$,

where f* is the ratio of the shadow price of foreign exchange to the market exchange rate. The elements in the second expression in parentheses represent the net impact of integration on the country's trade balance in the sector in question. Increased exports to partners appear as DELTX; import substitution through higher tariffs appears as a saving of foreign exchange of TS (trade suppression); and increased imports appear as TCCE (trade creation and consumption effect) and ETA (external trade augmentation).

The determination of the shadow price of foreign exchange as used in chapter 3 draws upon an econometric model (see appendix J) and upon two tariff-based approaches to the question. The first of these, the Harberger method, involves a formula considering the average tariff weighted by each product's share in imports times its price elasticity of import demand; and a similar average of export subsidy rates weighted by the share in exports and price elasticity of foreign demand.[8]   However, where all import elasticities are assumed to be equal (in the absence of information about specific elasiticties), and export subsidies do not exist, the shadow price premium on foreign exchange collapses to merely the import value weighted average tariff rate.

The other tariff-based approach, advocated by Bacha and Taylor,[9] asks what the equilibrium exchange rate would be in the absence of all tariffs and export subsidies. Whereas the Harberger approach concerns an "ex-ante marginal" scarcity price for foreign exchange, accepting the current structure of protection, the Bacha-Taylor approach represents an "ex-post average" concept, one which tends to give a lower shadow price.[10] Because the protective structure cannot in practice be assumed away, the ex-ante marginal approach is more relevant and is preferred in chapter 3.

As noted in chapter 3, the shadow pricing of foreign exchange raises the possibility that trade diversion will cause a benefit and trade creation a cost, rather than the reverse (as in the conventional analysis). That is, trade diversion causes an increased trade balance for the Common Market as a whole, and will result in a welfare gain as long as the scarcity price of foreign exchange exceeds the market price by greater proportion than that by which the cost of Common Market supply exceeds the world price. Trade creation will cause a welfare loss if

$$[f^* - 1] > (\tfrac{1}{2}) \left[\frac{1 + t_0 - \lambda}{(1 - \phi_1^R) + \phi_1^R} \right] \quad ,$$

from (4) and (17). Trade suppression will cause a welfare gain instead of a loss if

$$[f^* - 1] > (\tfrac{1}{2}) (t_1 - t_0).$$

And external trade augmentation will cause a welfare loss instead of a gain if

$$[f^* - 1] > \tfrac{1}{2} [t_0 - t_1].$$

E.   Intermediate Demand Effects

The direct effects of integration will cause indirect effects working through input-output relationships. These indirect effects may be measured as follows. The basic increase in output for each sector attributable to the direct effects of integration was identified in the previous section as $DQ_j - QDN_j$. Naming this net increase in demand for each sector's good as ΔQ_j, the induced intermediate demand for a given sector "i" will be:

(18) $\Delta INT_i = \sum_j a_{ij} \Delta Q_j$,

where:

ΔINT_i = increase in demand for intermediate use of goods from sector i, and

a_{ij} = input-output coefficient stating the fraction of section j's gross output value which is required as intermediate input value from sector i.

The increased intermediate use of good i will come from two sources: increased domestic output (which may be called ΔQ_i^{INT}) and increased imports (denominated as ΔM_i^{INT}). Moreover, of the increased import of intermediate good i, a portion will be supplied by partners in the common market, $\Delta M_i^{INT,C}$.

The terminal period import propensities used in the estimates of the previous section may also be used to obtain these indirect import effects. Thus:

(19) $\Delta M_i^{INT} = \Delta INT_i \ \mu_{1i}^T$,

where μ_{1i}^T = terminal period total import propensity (imports as a function of apparent consumption) for sector i.

(20) $\Delta M_i^{INT,C} = \Delta INT_i \ \mu_{1i}^P$,

where μ_{1i}^P = terminal propensity to import from Common Market partners in sector i.

The remaining trade effect is increase of intermediate goods exports to partners. Considering the induced exports to the k partners of product sector i in one country j, this effect will be:

(21) $\Delta X_{ij}^{INT} = \sum_k \phi_{jki} \ \Delta M_{ki}^{INT,C}$,

where:

ΔX_{ij}^{INT} = increased exports of good i by country j for intermediate use by partners,

ϕ_{jki} = share of country j in partner k's imports of sector i goods from Common Market, and

$\Delta M_{ki}^{INT,C}$ = increase in intermediate goods imports from Common Market by partner k, good i.

Finally, knowing the increase in intermediate demand (domestic and for export to partners) and the increase in imports to fill this demand, the increase in domestic output to provide intermediate demand for good i will be the difference between the two:

(22) $\quad \Delta Q_i^{INT} = \Delta INT_i - \Delta M_i^{INT} + \Delta X_i^{INT}$.

These output and trade effects of induced intermediate demand may then be translated into welfare effects, employing the three major welfare influences examined above: opportunity cost of labor, economies of scale, and savings of foreign exchange. (Note that the traditional trade creation and diversion benefits and costs do not apply, since they presume price changes, and the induced intermediate demand effects occur due to demand shifts at constant import price.) In a manner analogous to the calculation of the corresponding welfare effects in equations (12), (14), and (17) above, the welfare effects for intermediate demand for a given sector in a given country are:

(23) $\quad BOC^{INT} = \Delta Q^{INT} \left[1 - \dfrac{w^*}{w} \right] \left[\dfrac{WB}{Q_G} \right]$,

where BOC^{INT} = "labor opportunity cost" benefit deriving from expansion of output to provide additional intermediate demand;

(24) $\quad BES^{INT} = \Delta Q^{INT} (\Psi) \left[\dfrac{r}{1 + r} \right]$,

where BES^{INT} = economies of scale welfare gain associated with expansion of output to provide induced intermediate demand; and

(25) $\quad BFE^{INT} = [f^* - 1] (\Delta X^{INT} - \Delta M^{INT})$,

where BFE^{INT} = welfare gain (loss) from increased (decreased) net foreign exchange availability due to increased exports of intermediate goods to partners minus increased imports of intermediate goods for home use.

F. Structural Change

As discussed in chapter 3, an attempt is made to calculate the impact of integration on the structure of the economy by comparing the sectoral composition of output with the pattern that would be expected on the basis of cross-country regression analysis. Referring to table C-16 below, the test for Central America considered as a single unit (that is, a "country" with approximately 15 million inhabitants) does show a significant increase in manufacturing share over time above that explained merely by population and GDP. The coefficient "α" of .003 indicates that by the end of the twelve-year integration period examined, the share of manufacturing rose by 3.6 percent of GDP above what would have been expected from cross-country standards (that is, .003 x 12 = .036). A similar result is found for Guatemala, but the results for the remaining countries are not statistically significant, except for Nicaragua which shows a significant negative coefficient for the time variable--which is offset by a positive coefficient on the 1969-71 dummy variable (included to adjust for the impact of the war). Therefore, although the approach using cross-country patterns does suggest that Central America as a whole and Guatemala in particular experienced structural transformation toward manufacturing industry due to economic integration, the results using this approach are generally inconclusive.[11]

G.   Welfare Gains from Industrialization under Risk Aversion

Chapter 3 of volume I identifies the structural changes caused by integration by examining directly the sectoral composition of increased output attributed to integration. This section develops the methodology used to obtain the corresponding estimates of welfare benefits from structural change.

Advocates of industrialization in developing countries have emphasized the secularly declining terms of trade for raw materials exports as a justification for transforming the economy away from traditional agricultural exports toward industrial activity.[12] The empirical basis for this presumed deterioration has long been in doubt,[13] and currently appears all the more dubious in light of new concerns about raw materials scarcity as well as the recent revival of interest in the theory of rising real prices of nonrenewable resources.

In contrast, recent studies of industrialization in developing countries have tended to criticize apparently uneconomic and excessive industrialization in many countries.[14] By implication the new emphasis on return to free market pricing and static comparative advantages causes the state of the art concerning policy on industrialization to revert to that of the early 1950s when Viner[15] advised the developing countries to concentrate on their raw material exports and eschew costly industrialization, despite the fact that such a reversion would contradict the impressive empirical evidence provided by Chenery and others on the changing patterns of comparative advantage toward industry during the course of development.

The purpose of this section is to explore one reason for according a preference to industry in sectoral choice in development planning: risk aversion. Two important additional reasons--divergence between future and present comparative advantage, and external economies of scale in the industrial park--are not considered here.

The severe cyclical fluctuations of the economy dependent on raw material exports (especially those heavily reliant on single products) are well documented.[16] However, there has been no explicit formulation of the welfare costs of specializing in activities subject to such fluctuations as opposed to industrial activities with less fluctuation. Yet under reasonable assumptions of utility function and degree of fluctuation by activity, such welfare costs may be quantified. In essence, the welfare cost of concentrating in a risky activity may be measured by the difference between a higher level of income in this activity and a lower level of income in a less risky activity which would yield the same level of expected utility, due to risk aversion.

Consider a risk-averse developing country with logarithmic utility function:

(26) $U = \log Y$

where utility, Y, equals income. Suppose, with the same resources, one activity will produce average income, Y_1, and a less risky activity will produce a lower average income, Y_2. The first activity has a windfall gain or loss of $\pm\sigma_1$, with probability of .5 for positive or negative σ_1; the second activity has the corresponding $\pm\sigma_2$, again with equal probability.

As shown in figure 4, the expected utility from the second activity may exceed that from the first activity despite the fact that $Y_1 > Y_2$.

Thus:

(27a) $\quad E(U_1) = .5 \log (Y_1 + \sigma_1) + .5 \log (Y_1 - \sigma_1),$

(27b) $\quad E(U_2) = .5 \log (Y_2 + \sigma_2) + .5 \log (Y_2 - \sigma_2),$

and $E(U_1)$ may fall short of $E(U_2)$ even though $Y_2 < Y_1$ if $\sigma_1 > \sigma_2$ by a sufficient magnitude.

Quantification of the welfare gain through industrialization may be explored by considering the amount by which Y_1 in traditional agricultural exports must exceed Y_2 from industrial production in order to generate identical utility, when the risk factor σ_1 exceeds σ_2. First the absolute deviation, σ, may be respecified as a fraction of income,

$$\delta_1 = \sigma_1/Y_1 \text{ and } \delta_2 = \sigma_2/Y_2.$$

Then to answer the question posed, we may find Y_1 and Y_2 such that:

(28) $\quad .5 \log [Y_1(1 + \delta_1)] + .5 \log [Y_1(1 - \delta_1)] =$

$\quad\quad .5 \log [Y_2(1 + \delta_2)] + .5 \log [Y_2(1 - \delta_2)].$

Simplifying,

(29) $\quad \log [Y_1/Y_2] = 1/2 \left[\log [\dfrac{1 + \delta_2}{1 + \delta_1}] + \log [\dfrac{1 - \delta_2}{1 - \delta_1}] \right].$

Table C-1 shows illustrative combinations of Y_1/Y_2, δ_1, and δ_2 which satisfy equation (29). For example, if $\delta_1 = .3$ while $\delta_2 = .05$ (a 30 percent windfall gain or loss may be expected in the first activity but only a 5 percent gain or loss in activity two), $Y_1/Y_2 = 1.05$, meaning that income generated in activity two need be only 95 percent that generated in the first activity to yield the same utility.

Structural transformation of the economy away from traditional agricultural exports toward industry thus confers a welfare gain if the fluctuation expected from the latter is less than that from the former ($\delta_I < \delta_{AE}$, where subscripts I and AE refer to industry and traditional raw materials exports, respectively). Specifically, suppose that the economy has the following shares:

$$\Phi_I, \Phi_{AE}, \Phi_{AC}, \Phi_S,$$

where Φ = share, and subscripts "AC" and "S" refer to agriculture for home consumption and the services sector, respectively. Considering the

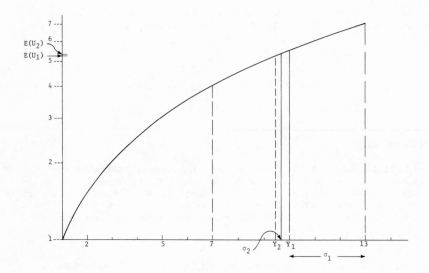

Figure C-4

Table C-1. Ratio of Income in Two Activities for Constant Utility
under Divergent Risk

Proportional Risk Factors (δ)		Y_1/Y_2
Activity 1	Activity 2	
.50	0	1.155
.30	.05	1.048
.30	.10	1.045
.228	.139	1.038
.20	.05	1.020
.20	.10	1.013

"tradables" subset of the economy,[17] Φ_I + Φ_{AE}, the weighted average risk
risk factor is $\bar{\delta} = \dfrac{(\Phi_I \delta_I) + (\Phi_{AE} \delta_{AE})}{\Phi_I + \Phi_{AE}}$. The shift from raw materials

exports toward industrial output lowers $\bar{\delta}$ as long as $\delta_I < \delta_{AE}$. By estimating δ_I and δ_{AE}, the welfare gain associated with any shift in
$\Phi_I/(\Phi_I + \Phi_{AE})$ may be measured by consulting the corresponding ratio of
Y_1 to Y_2 from a table such as table C-1, as the weighted risk factor $\bar{\delta}$
falls from δ_1 to δ_2.

Thus, if before industrialization Φ_I = .05, Φ_{AE} = .4, δ_I = .05,
δ_{AE} = .25, then $\delta_1 = \dfrac{.05 (.05) + .4 (.25)}{.45}$ = .228. After an industrialization effort, suppose Φ_I = .20, Φ_{AE} = .25, and δ_I and δ_{AE} remain
unchanged. Then $\delta_2 = \dfrac{.2 (.05) + .25 (.25)}{.45}$ = .139. The weighted average risk
factor in the tradables sector has fallen from .228 to .139. Employing
equation (29), Y_1/Y_2 (where δ_1 = .228 and δ_2 = .139) will be 1.038,
meaning that if observed output is as high after transformation as before,
real utility will have increased by an amount equivalent to 3.8 percent.
By applying this percentage gain to the terminal output value in the
tradables subsector, the estimate of the welfare gain from structural
transformation is obtained.

One qualification of this method is that it assumes resources are
equally productive in industry and agriculture. If instead the industrial output is less efficient than that for agricultural output, say
with a ratio β of total (shadow priced) factor content per unit of value
added in industry versus a ratio of 1 in agriculture ($\beta > 1$), then the
condition for the transformation toward industry to confer a welfare
gain is that $\beta < (Y_1/Y_2)$ (i.e., referring to equation (29)).

A second qualification is that a country capable of diversified
raw materials exports rather than having a monoculture may be able to obtain a low δ_{AE} by producing export goods with low correlation in cyclical
swings.[18]

A final qualification is that if industrialization itself requires a new reliance on imported inputs in the developing country, then the risk factor δ_I may not be appreciably lower than that for traditional agricultural exports, δ_{AE}, because fluctuation on the side of input cost replaces fluctuation on the side of export demand (and fluctuation due to climatic conditions).

H. Investment Effect

Chapter 3 sets forth the dynamic welfare gains obtained from the stimulus to investment provided by economic integration. The algebraic formulation of this effect is as follows:

(i) Let I_F be increased foreign investment and I_D increased domestic investment attributable to integration.

(ii) Let "B" be the incremental capital-output ratio showing the extra capital required per unit of value added.

(iii) Let w^* and w be the shadow price and market wage of unskilled labor, respectively, and Ω be the share of the wage bill for unskilled labor in value added. Then for extra foreign investment the annual welfare gain is:

$$(30) \qquad W_F^{INV} = \left[\frac{\Delta I_F}{B}\right] \Omega [1 - \frac{w^*}{w}] .$$

That is, the foreign investment ΔI_F produces an annual value added stream of $\Delta I_F/B$, of which the portion Ω is wage bill; and of this total wage bill, the portion $1 - \frac{w^*}{w}$ is a welfare gain due to the excess of wage (w) over labor's social opportunity cost (w^*).

I. Data

The nature and sources of data used in the study are described in general terms in chapter 3, volume I. The following discussion provides further technical details on the data.

The level of aggregation at which the study's estimates are conducted is the three-digit CIIU (International Standard Industrial Classification) level for industry, in addition to six major agricultural categories and one mining sector. The industrial data represent twenty-seven sectors (since three of the 29 sectors at three-digit CIIU detail had to be collapsed into one sector to harmonize trade and production data).[19] The trade and tariff data require aggregation from the approximately 1,500 tariff line items (NAUCA seven- or nine-digit categories; note that NAUCA is the Standard International Trade Classification).

The import propensities of equation (26) require: (i) aggregation of tariff line import data into three-digit CIIU categories, based on the standard CIIU-NAUCA correspondence between categories; and (ii) calculation of apparent consumption (C) at the three-digit CIIU level. For

this calculation, imports are added to gross output, and exports are subtracted. Data for gross output by industrial sector are from special
tabulations supplied to SIECA by the Central Banks of the CACM countries.

For the agricultural sectors, trade data are from special tabulations provided by the SIECA statistics division.[20] Data on gross production are from the F.A.O. study.[21]

The calculation of the welfare cost of trade diversion (equation (3))
requires the estimation of the parameter λ , Common Market supplier price
divided by world price, at the three-digit CIIU or major agricultural
product level. This parameter is calculated as follows:

(31) $\qquad \lambda_j = \sum_{k\epsilon j} \phi_k^{MC} \delta_k$,

where λ_j is the ratio of Common Market supplier price to world market
price for sector j; k refers to the most detailed NAUCA category level,
and $k\epsilon j$ refers to all NAUCA categories "k" which compose the particular
aggregative sector j in question; ϕ_k^{MC} is the share of commodity k in
total Common Market imports (including intraregional) for the aggregative sector j in question, and,

(32) $\qquad \delta_k = (P_c/P_w)_k$,

subject to:

$$1 \leq \delta_k \leq [1 + t_k^1]$$

where $(P_c/P_w)_k$ is the ratio of the unit value of imports from Common
Market suppliers (P_c) to the unit value of imports from the Rest of
World (P_w) for commodity k (where both of these unit values refer to
CACM-wide import values divided by import quantities, in kilograms);
and t_k^1 is the terminal common external tariff for commodity k.

The two-step procedure of equations (31) and (32) avoids measuring
a single "aggregate unit value" at the three-digit CIIU level, which
would involve serious problems of heterogeneity due to the high level
of aggregation. The lower-bound restriction placed on equation (32)
means that when unit value of the imported good from Common Market suppliers is below that for ROW (the rest of the world), the relative
price ratio δ_k is forced to unity. The logic here is that there is no
reason for the partner good to have a lower price than the world market
good--otherwise protection against the ROW good would not be needed--so
that any observed case with lower CACM supply price must represent lower
quality for the CACM-produced good, requiring an estimate placing the
CACM supply price equal to the world price (at a minimum) for goods of
equal quality. The upper-bound restriction means that at a maximum a
CACM-supplied good will be priced at the world price plus the tariff
rate for the commodity (otherwise the good could not compete with world
supply); if a price for the CACM good is observed to be higher than
this level, there must be quality difference or commodity composition
difference (even at the detailed seven- or nine-digit NAUCA level)
between CACM supply and ROW supply, and only the maximum relative price
$1 + t_k^1$ is allowed.

In the calculation of partner price relative to world market price, a single CACM-wide price is used for supply from partners and a single world price is used for imports into the whole Common Market. This procedure provides a more reliable estimate of the relative price than would the use of separate estimates for each Central American country, since variation in quality or product of the partner good versus that from ROW may be substantial at the level of each individual Central American country, but it tends to be averaged out in data for the Common Market as a whole. However, a result of this approach is that the analysis does not capture any possible differences among Central American countries with regard to excess price paid for goods supplied by the partners rather than by ROW. For example, if the CACM good imported into Honduras exceeds the price of the world market good by 20 percent while for the same category the excess is only 10 percent for CACM goods entering Guatemala, there will be a different degree of excess cost--and welfare loss from trade diversion--for the two countries. Such differences might arise in products for which transportation within the CACM is particularly costly relative to product price. In general, however, the price of the Common Market supply relative to world supply should be similar among the CACM members.

For the calculations referring to terminal year 1968, the relative price data used are from special SIECA computations of CACM-wide unit values of imports from the Common Market and from ROW. These data refer to 1970, but there should not have been major changes in the relative price relationships between 1968 and 1970. For the second terminal year, 1972, the average unit price of imports from CACM suppliers on the one hand and from ROW on the other were calculated from detailed trade data at the tariff line level.[22] The relative price for 1972 is calculated using data for the CACM of four only, excluding Honduras.

With respect to data on tariffs, chapter 3 discusses the sources of information for protection at the tariff-line level, including data on tariff exemptions granted under programs of fiscal incentives. The detailed data are aggregated to obtain tariff rates at the broader industrial categories for which the analysis of chapter 3 is carried out (three digits of the International Standard Industrial Classification). The aggregation procedure is as follows:

$$(33) \qquad t_{ij}^0 = \sum_{k \in j} \theta_{ik} \, t_{ik}^0$$

where, for country i, t_{ij}^0 is the tariff level in the base period at the desired aggregate level j; $k \in j$ means detailed category k is a member of aggregate category j; t_{ik}^0 is the seven-digit NAUCA estimate just described, and θ_{ik} is the share of item k in the total of import value for country i in aggregate sector j, referring to imports from ROW alone.

For the terminal period the tariff for an aggregated sector j is calculated as follows:

$$(34) \qquad t_j^1 = \sum_{k \in j} \theta_k^{CM} \, t_k^1$$

where t_j^1 is the terminal aggregate tariff rate; $k \varepsilon j$ indicates that detailed category k is a member of aggregate category j; t_k is the detailed terminal tariff rate (available from the statistics division of SIECA) referring to ROW goods; and θ_k^{CM} is the share of sector k in total import value into CACM from the rest of world for aggregate sector j.

J. Statistical Tables

The remainder of this appendix reports further statistical tables that accompany the text of chapter 3.

Table C-2. Data Sources

Variable	Index Range	Definition	Data Source
Q_{ij}	$i = 1,5$ $j = 1,34$	Gross output, country i, sector j; sector j; 27 three-digit CIIU industrial sectors; 6 agricultural, 1 mining sector	Industry: special tabulations, Central Banks. Agriculture: SIECA-S and F.A.O. study.
X_{ij}	$i = 1,5$ $j = 1,34$	Total exports, country i, sector j	SIECA-S.
M_{ij}^T	$i = 1,5$ $j = 1,34$	Total imports, country i, sector j	SIECA-S.
M_{ikj}	$i = 1,5$ $k = 1,6$ $j = 1,34$	Detailed imports into country i, in sector j, from source k (each CACM country, and ROW)	SIECA-S.
λ_j	$j = 1,34$	P_c/P_w for sector j, where P_c is Common Market supply price and P_w is world market price	Computed from trade data, unit values: SIECA-S.
t_{ij}^0	$i = 1,5$ $j = 1,34$	Ad valorem equivalent tariff rate, 1958, country i, sector j	Country tariff books.
t_j^1	$j = 1,34$	1968 CACM common external tariff ad valorem equivalent, sector j; excludes San Jose Protocol surcharge	SIECA-S.
w_{ij}	$i = 1,5$ $j = 1,34$	Wage rate for unskilled labor, country i, sector j	Industry: SIECA-C68. Agriculture: F.A.O. study.

Table C-2 (continued)

Variable	Index Range	Description	Data Source
w_i^*	$i = 1,5$	Shadow price of unskilled labor, country i	See text.
$\left[WB/Q_{Gij}\right]$	$i = 1,5$ $j = 1,34$	Share of unskilled labor wage bill in gross output value, country i, sector j	Industry: SIECA-C68. Agriculture: F.A.O. study.
r_{ij}	$i = 1,5$ $j = 1,34$	Returns to scale parameter	Calculated from SIECA-C68 for industry. Assumed 0 for agriculture.
$\bar{t}$	---	Overall weighted average ad valorem tariff rate, CACM common external tariff, 1968	Calculated from SIECA-S tariff data.

NOTES: SIECA-S: Statistics Division, SIECA.

F.A.O. Study: Grupo Asesor de la F.A.O. para la Integración Económica Centroamericana (GAFICA), "Plan Perspectivo Para el Desarrollo y la Integración de la Agricultura Centroamericana," mimeographed (Guatemala City: GAFICA, 1972).

SIECA-C68: Industrial Census of 1968, SIECA data file.

Country Tariff Books: Republica de Guatemala, Arancel de Aduanas (NAUCA): Republica de Guatemala, 1959 (Guatemala: Unión Tipografica, 1959); Republica de El Salvador, Diario Oficial 182 (15), 23 Enero 1959; Republica de Honduras, Arancel de Aduanas (Tegucigalpa: Ariston, 1958); Republica de Costa Rica, Ministerio de Economia y Hacienda, Arancel de Aduanas, Ley no. 1738 de 31 de Marzo de 1954 (San José: Imprenta Nacional, 1954); and unpublished SIECA study for Nicaragua.

Table C-3. Common Market Supply Price Relative to World Price, 1970

CIIU Category		Unadjusted P_c/P_w	Constrained P_c/P_w
WHT	Wheat	.888	1.000
CRN	Corn	.803	1.000
RIC	Rice	.358	1.000
BNS	Beans	.692	1.000
FRN	Fruits, nuts	.137	1.000
VEG	Vegetables	.304	1.000
290	Mining, nonmetallic	1.597	1.597
311	Food products	1.050	1.123
312	Food products, diverse	.639	1.030
313	Beverages	.602	1.001
314	Tobacco	.451	1.006
321	Textiles	.966	1.063
322	Clothing	.952	1.108
323	Leather products	.659	1.026
324	Shoes	.792	1.000
331	Wood products	.732	1.048
332	Furniture	.921	1.000
341	Paper	1.865	1.371
342	Printing	.829	1.009
351	Industrial chemicals	1.277	1.072
352	Other chemical products	.637	1.014
353	Petroleum refineries	1.380	1.018
354	Petroleum derivative products	2.961	1.403
355	Rubber products	1.149	1.158
356	Plastic products	.427	1.000
361	Ceramics	.803	1.008
362	Glass products	1.144	1.070
369	Other nonmetallic minerals	2.463	1.041
371	Basic steel and iron	1.304	1.096[a]
372	Basic metals, nonferrous	1.262	1.159
381	Metal products excluding machinery and equipment	1.100	1.036
382	Machinery and equipment, non-electrical	.837	1.016
383	Electric machinery and equipment	1.095	1.095
384	Transport materials	.841	1.021
385	Technical instruments	1.369	1.100
390	Other manufactures	.958	1.136

[a]Using adjusted tariffs: 1.081.

SOURCE: See text.

Table C-4. Common Market Supply Price Relative to World Price,
Industrial Sectors, 1972

CIIU Category	Unadjusted P_C/P_W	Constrained P_C/P_W	
		with legal tariff	with adjusted tariff
311	1.154	1.142	1.056
312	.765	1.128	1.064
313	.555	1.008	1.007
314	.440	1.008	1.008
321	.894	1.059	1.015
322	1.007	1.279	1.052
323	.586	1.018	1.004
324	.371	1.001	1.000
331	.679	1.016	1.002
332	1.008	1.148	1.114
341	1.256	1.303	1.030
342	1.107	1.014	1.014
351	1.364	1.113	1.034
352	.729	1.019	1.017
353	1.029	1.031	1.016
354	2.499	1.528	1.051
355	1.010	1.096	1.090
356	.389	1.000	1.000
361	.638	1.011	1.001
362	.900	1.075	1.036
369	.711	1.050	1.036
371	1.335	1.097	1.025
372	1.313	1.282	1.023
381	.853	1.063	1.040
382	.910	1.025	1.013
383	1.125	1.099	1.051
384	.867	1.049	1.029
385	1.627	1.118	1.070
390	1.095	1.128	1.092

510

Table C-5. Legal Tariff Rates in Central America, 1958 and 1968
(percent)

	1958					1968
Category	Guatemala	El Salvador	Honduras	Nicaragua	Costa Rica	CACM
WHT	24.0	0.0	20.9	12.0	2.0	0.0
CRN	147.0	50.2	210.7	38.1	34.1	98.5
RIC	76.0	33.8	95.4	180.7	79.2	45.2
BNS	41.0	21.6	60.0	67.0	27.2	41.9
FRN	77.0	41.8	53.2	44.6	103.4	85.2
VEG	47.4	19.3	62.2	46.9	76.7	23.6
290	9.4	18.0	289.0	51.5	79.0	86.7
311	61.8	24.3	70.1	47.6	55.5	55.1
312	78.8	30.0	26.0	55.0	23.6	53.2
313	216.7	58.1	148.0	251.1	357.7	232.7
314	95.5	73.3	69.1	145.5	193.3	165.3
321	66.8	24.9	44.1	59.3	84.4	57.1
322	114.9	26.8	49.7	68.8	55.0	124.3
323	51.6	16.9	15.6	21.6	31.8	38.3
324	65.3	36.9	64.3	96.9	69.3	31.9
331	337.4	11.8	56.3	77.2	80.4	58.5
332	75.1	21.8	35.6	39.2	89.2	120.6
341	24.4	14.5	24.3	40.2	48.9	50.4
342	37.1	0.0	60.4	40.3	47.0	38.8
351	10.5	5.9	10.4	10.5	16.8	17.6
352	23.6	24.2	25.3	25.0	24.1	30.3
353	263.8	156.3	140.3	53.0	254.2	5.4
354	19.7	12.4	16.8	54.1	53.0	40.3
355	11.2	18.9	11.1	14.3	18.0	36.0
356	36.7	0.0	26.8	183.1	40.0	94.0
361	372.5	40.6	55.6	77.5	245.4	62.3
362	76.6	40.7	18.1	29.0	37.6	29.0
369	26.8	13.1	38.8	25.7	40.9	25.9
371	9.7	11.1	12.3	17.4	27.4	17.8
372	11.5	18.0	14.4	22.3	15.0	19.3
381	18.4	15.7	14.5	24.4	21.4	26.3
382	5.6	5.1	0.0	0.0	14.4	9.0
383	22.8	8.7	15.0	21.1	21.0	22.3
384	21.9	12.3	4.9	31.4	36.0	6.6
385	20.7	12.4	16.9	22.4	27.2	19.7
390	47.0	6.8	25.8	16.3	47.0	58.1

Table C-6. Tariff Rates in Central America, Adjusted for Exemptions, 1958
(percent)

Category	Guatemala	El Salvador	Honduras	Nicaragua[a]	Costa Rica
WHT	24.0	0.0	20.9	12.0	2.0
CRN	147.0	50.2	210.7	38.1	34.1
RIC	76.0	33.8	95.4	180.7	79.2
BNS	41.0	21.6	60.0	67.0	27.2
FRN	77.0	41.8	53.2	44.6	103.4
VEG	47.4	19.3	62.2	46.9	76.7
290	9.4	18.0	289.0	51.5	79.0
311	59.2	0.0	13.3	34.4	41.9
312	75.6	24.7	26.0	50.9	23.6
313	185.5	13.2	148.0	156.9	317.2
314	95.5	73.3	69.1	145.5	193.3
321	59.0	24.9	40.9	47.3	83.9
322	93.2	6.2	38.2	57.5	51.6
323	49.0	4.9	5.6	21.4	31.8
324	27.5	0.0	48.9	0.0	0.0
331	314.9	4.8	56.3	77.2	80.4
332	75.1	21.8	35.6	39.2	89.2
341	20.6	0.0	15.9	21.5	46.4
342	37.1	0.0	60.4	35.8	47.0
351	8.0	0.0	9.4	5.9	13.9
352	21.5	9.0	20.9	21.4	22.2
353	252.1	24.0	140.3	0.0	251.3
354	19.0	2.4	16.8	15.0	52.2
355	8.6	0.0	8.1	9.8	16.5
356	27.5	0.0	26.8	106.5	30.4
361	372.5	40.6	55.6	77.5	245.4
362	70.6	0.0	18.1	11.1	37.1
369	15.8	0.0	29.6	7.4	30.0
371	9.3	1.4	12.1	2.5	23.8
372	10.2	5.7	14.4	13.1	14.5
381	14.0	0.0	13.8	10.7	7.3
382	3.7	0.0	0.0	0.0	11.6
383	19.5	6.9	15.0	0.0	18.3
384	19.6	7.8	3.8	0.0	30.0
385	16.8	6.4	16.9	15.8	22.3
390	44.4	0.0	24.6	12.5	44.2

[a]Based on 1958 legal rate and application of 1968 ratio of adjusted to legal tariff.

SOURCE: Calculated from legal tariff rates using tariff exemptions as reported in IMF study. See text.

512

Table C-7. Tariff Rates in Central America, Adjusted for Exemptions, 1968
(percent)

Category	Guatemala	El Salvador	Honduras[a]	Nicaragua	Costa Rica
WHT	0.0	0.0	0.0	0.0	0.0
CRN	98.5	98.5	98.5	98.5	98.5
RIC	45.2	45.2	45.2	45.2	45.2
BNS	41.9	41.9	41.9	41.9	41.9
FRN	85.2	85.2	85.2	85.2	85.2
VEG	23.6	23.6	23.6	23.6	23.6
290	86.7	86.7	86.7	86.7	86.7
311	28.8	43.3	10.4	39.8	40.3
312	42.4	51.4	53.2	49.2	42.3
313	139.6	178.5	232.7	145.5	200.1
314	165.3	165.3	165.3	165.3	165.3
321	49.7	51.2	53.0	45.5	43.1
322	26.3	124.3	95.5	103.8	118.6
323	37.9	38.3	13.7	38.0	38.1
324	29.8	31.9	24.3	0.0	0.0
331	58.5	58.2	58.5	58.5	58.5
332	120.6	120.6	120.6	120.6	120.6
341	45.6	39.2	33.0	27.0	0.0
342	33.8	38.6	38.8	34.5	30.6
351	10.2	12.6	15.9	9.9	6.2
352	25.8	29.1	25.0	25.9	24.3
353	3.2	0.0	5.4	0.0	4.1
354	5.3	14.8	40.3	11.2	29.3
355	32.7	35.9	26.3	24.8	20.2
356	50.8	77.8	94.0	54.7	49.4
361	62.3	62.3	62.3	62.3	62.3
362	21.1	16.1	29.0	11.1	20.9
369	19.9	24.1	19.8	7.5	22.8
371	5.7	13.6	17.5	2.6	8.2
372	3.4	0.0	19.3	11.3	6.7
381	16.2	21.8	25.0	11.5	16.5
382	5.8	5.7	9.0	4.7	3.7
383	13.6	13.2	22.3	0.0	0.0
384	2.2	5.3	5.1	0.0	0.0
385	15.7	13.8	19.7	13.9	15.0
390	44.3	58.0	55.4	44.7	51.5

[a]Based on 1968 legal tariff rate and application of 1958 ratio of adjusted to legal tariff.

SOURCE: Calculated from legal tariff rates using tariff exemptions as reported in IMF study. See text.

Table C-8. Legal Tariff Rates in Central America, Industrial Sectors, 1972
(percent)

Sector	Guatemala	El Salvador	Honduras	Nicaragua	Costa Rica
311	47.2	38.2	50.3	54.7	69.0
312	90.1	55.1	37.1	55.3	55.5
313	174.0	120.7	142.9	188.7	176.1
314	238.0	221.1	226.1	202.3	214.0
321	32.6	39.7	70.6	64.2	44.3
322	105.9	102.5	101.7	208.9	71.8
323	48.1	51.2	65.4	69.3	46.8
324	245.6	219.2	80.0	140.8	170.5
331	50.9	51.2	71.2	124.8	77.6
332	82.9	87.2	112.1	84.8	208.5
341	48.7	32.1	71.3	46.1	43.9
342	9.6	7.7	15.0	28.0	11.0
351	20.5	16.1	16.8	22.7	19.8
352	21.0	19.2	18.2	20.9	22.8
353	37.8	75.5	49.9	55.0	47.5
354	57.8	57.8	35.1	33.4	36.8
355	28.5	31.5	78.2	29.9	28.9
356	60.7	70.9	69.0	64.9	90.7
361	80.4	45.2	43.5	70.0	67.7
362	36.9	29.8	29.6	33.6	30.4
369	25.8	21.2	26.1	27.8	23.8
371	15.5	15.4	21.2	19.6	15.4
372	11.7	26.6	24.2	11.0	22.2
381	31.5	30.6	28.0	32.9	33.2
382	11.0	11.6	10.8	12.1	13.3
383	31.5	34.6	34.1	46.9	30.7
384	14.2	23.3	17.5	39.6	24.2
385	25.5	24.3	24.3	23.3	21.7
390	65.2	62.0	49.2	51.3	12.5

Table C-9. Tariff Rates in Central America, Adjusted for Exemptions,
Industrial Sectors, 1972
(percent)

Sector	Guatemala	El Salvador	Honduras	Nicaragua	Costa Rica
311	8.7	13.9	22.7	15.2	19.7
312	18.2	27.7	19.7	24.8	19.3
313	32.6	48.7	98.9	42.6	49.0
314	8.7	142.5	141.6	7.8	164.2
321	12.9	17.6	40.6	32.2	16.2
322	30.7	51.6	18.5	16.0	51.4
323	25.8	22.7	37.5	22.4	30.1
324	41.1	21.3	35.3	14.8	68.0
331	18.0	11.1	18.4	11.7	28.8
332	18.9	61.6	66.8	11.3	24.7
341	5.0	7.3	3.0	8.1	3.1
342	4.8	5.0	5.7	8.3	4.7
351	4.6	4.3	4.4	3.9	3.2
352	11.5	15.7	8.9	10.8	9.8
353	15.5	44.5	9.7	29.1	7.1
354	6.2	2.7	19.4	11.3	9.7
355	18.6	18.9	7.6	13.6	14.1
356	20.7	20.8	22.9	22.2	14.6
361	50.2	33.0	24.1	36.0	50.0
362	21.1	14.0	18.9	14.9	17.0
369	10.6	11.3	13.5	8.6	10.3
371	3.7	4.7	7.5	3.5	2.9
372	2.6	1.6	8.5	1.6	1.6
381	18.0	17.5	14.8	14.3	13.8
382	4.8	5.1	5.0	5.3	5.0
383	15.9	15.0	18.0	13.2	8.5
384	8.6	16.4	5.2	14.9	7.9
385	14.4	13.7	24.3	10.7	11.1
390	38.0	40.8	36.9	28.6	7.7

Table C-10. Integration Effects Due to Induced Industrial Demand for Intermediate
Goods, Legal Tariff Basis, 1968 and 1972
(1,000 $CA)

		1968				
		Guatemala	El Salvador	Honduras	Nicaragua	Costa Rica
Basic Effects						
Intermediate Demand	I	46,230	26,950	10,955	9,092	16,779
	A	9,232	6,189	1,435	2,853	4,095
Imports	I	23,000	17,244	7,368	5,200	11,218
	A	3,840	2,103	285	730	1,373
Exports	I	4,083	5,074	842	1,420	1,835
	A	152	141	411	86	35
Output	I	27,313	14,780	4,429	5,313	7,396
	A	5,544	4,227	1,561	2,210	2,758
Foreign Exchange Savings	I	-18,917	-12,170	-6,526	-3,779	-9,383
	A	-3,688	-1,962	126	-644	-1,338
Welfare Effects						
Labor	I	1,668	778	154	202	199
	A	865	700	201	146	160
Economies of Scale	I	343	102	23	70	52
	A	0	0	0	0	0
Foreign Exchange Savings	I	-4,729	-3,042	-1,632	-945	-2,346
at $f^* = 1.25$	A	-922	-491	32	-161	-335
Total	I	-2,718	-2,162	-1,455	-673	-2,095
	A	-57	209	233	-15	-175
	I & A	-2,775	-1,953	-1,222	-688	-2,270

(continued on next page)

Table C-10 (Continued)

	1972			
	Guatemala	El Salvador	Nicaragua	Costa Rica
Basic Effects				
Intermediate Demand	60,904	42,260	24,994	27,621
	9,776	6,980	12,146	8,875
Imports	31,901	23,055	11,005	17,306
	3,818	1,919	7,226	3,987
Exports	6,395	7,342	3,544	3,503
	210	264	223	79
Output	35,398	26,547	17,533	13,818
	6,167	5,325	5,143	4,966
Foreign Exchange Savings	-25,506	-15,713	-7,461	-13,803
	-3,608	-1,655	-7,003	-3,908
Welfare Effects				
Labor	2,175	1,466	598	368
	962	881	339	288
Economies of Scale	487	132	195	104
	0	0	0	0
Foreign Exchange Savings at $f* = 1.25$	-6,376	-3,928	-1,865	-3,451
	-902	-414	-1,751	-977
Total	-3,714	-2,330	-1,072	-2,979
	60	467	-1,412	-689
	-3,654	-1,863	-2,484	-3,668

NOTES: I = Industrial intermediate goods (CIIU 311-390); A - agricultural and mineral intermediate goods (CIIU 111, 121, 122, 220, 230). See text for explanation of variables.

Table C-11. Integration Effects Due to Induced Industrial Demand for Intermediate
Goods, Adjusted Tariff Basis, 1968 and 1972
(1,000 $CA)

		1968				
		Guatemala	El Salvador	Honduras	Nicaragua	Costa Rica
Basic Effects						
Intermediate Demand	I	44,120	26,950	10,955	8,686	14,419
	A	9,232	6,189	1,435	2,853	4,095
Imports	I	21,561	17,244	7,368	4,885	9,585
	A	3,840	2,103	285	730	1,373
Exports	I	3,993	4,774	811	1,379	1,782
	A	152	141	411	86	35
Output	I	26,551	14,479	4,399	5,180	6,616
	A	5,544	4,227	1,561	2,210	2,758
Foreign Exchange Savings	I	-17,569	-12,470	-6,557	-3,506	-7,803
	A	-3,688	-1,962	126	-644	-1,338
Welfare Effects						
Labor	I	1,612	763	153	199	180
	A	865	700	201	146	160
Economies of Scale	I	343	102	23	70	52
	A	0	0	0	0	0
Foreign Exchange Savings	I	-4,392	-3,118	-1,639	-877	-1,951
at f* = 1.25	A	-922	-491	32	-161	-335
Total	I	-2,437	-2,253	-1,463	-608	-1,719
	A	-57	209	233	-15	-175
	I + A	-2,494	-2,044	-1,230	-623	-1,894

(continued on next page)

Table C-11 (Continued)

| | 1972 | | | |
	Guatemala	El Salvador	Nicaragua	Costa Rica
Basic Effects				
Intermediate Demand	50,550	42,695	22,428	18,339
	9,487	6,175	10,670	3,915
Imports	24,221	23,795	9,592	11,549
	3,799	1,919	7,011	1,675
Exports	5,565	5,450	3,071	3,108
	143	169	85	57
Output	31,894	24,350	15,907	9,898
	5,831	4,424	3,745	2,297
Foreign Exchange Savings	-18,656	-18,345	-6,521	-8,441
	-3,656	-1,750	-6,926	-1,618
Welfare Effects				
Labor	1,977	1,310	540	285
	910	732	247	133
Economies of Scale	477	154	176	76
	0	0	0	0
Foreign Exchange Savings at $f^* = 1.25$	-4,664	-4,586	-1,630	-2,110
	-914	-438	-1,732	-404
Total	-2,210	-3,122	-914	-1,749
	-4	294	-1,485	-271
	-2,214	-2,828	-2,399	-2,020

NOTES: I = Industrial intermediate goods (CIIU 311-390); A = agricultural and mineral intermediate goods (CIIU 111, 121, 122, 220, 230). See text for explanation of variables.

519

Table C-12. Economies of Scale Parameters for Industrial
Sectors with Scale Coefficients Significantly
Different from Zero

Sector	Returns to Scale Parameters[a]	Regression Coefficients[b] α	β	γ	$\bar{R}^2$
311	.1533	See appendix D, table 11[c]			
313	.2578	See appendix D, table 11[c]			
314	.3166	-2.29 (-1.37)	+.2659 (1.81)	+.3166 (2.17)	.532
322	.1878	See appendix D, table 11[c]			
331	.0800	-.069 (.17)	+.1539 (4.03)	+.0800 (1.96)	.868
355	.1403	-.363 (.43)	+.1233 (1.73)	+.1403 (1.72)	.087
361, 362	.3096	-2.596 (-1.68)	+.1903 (1.23)	+.3096 (2.03)	.370
369	.0780	.063 (.16)	+.2172 (6.76)	+.0780 (2.01)	.358
371, 372, 381[d]	.0324 (Guatemala, El Salvador) .0918 (Honduras) .0664 (Nicaragua) .0213 (Costa Rica) .1076	-.156 (-.23)	+.2950 (2.99)	+.1076 (1.66)	.188

[a]Equals sum of factor elasticities less unity.
[b]Regression form: $\frac{Q}{L} = \alpha + \beta(\ln\frac{K}{L}) + \gamma \ln L$ where Q is value added, L labor, and ln refers to the natural logarithm.
K is capital. "T" statistics in parentheses.
[c]Estimated in chapter 4. Regression form:

$$\frac{Q}{L} = \alpha + \beta(\ln\frac{K}{L}) + \delta(\ln\frac{K}{L})^2 + \gamma \ln L$$

[d]A combined scale parameter for the joint sector 371, 372, 381 is based on estimate for subsector 3813, combined with zero returns to scale for other subsectors, weighting by shares of subsectors in value added in each country.

SOURCE: Calculated from 1968 industrial census.

Table C-13. Changes in Output Attributable to Integration, Industrial Sectors
(in 1,000 Central American pesos)

Sector	Guatemala (1972)			El Salvador (1972)			Honduras (1968)		
	Direct	Indirect	Total	Direct	Indirect	Total	Direct	Indirect	Total
311	8,799	2,778	11,577	4,025	1,554	5,579	1,933	486	2,419
312	4,043	147	4,190	4,090	207	4,297	433	57	490
313	76	13	89	1,434	157	1,591	103	12	115
314	1,455	493	1,948	4	1	5	52	17	69
321	18,825	7,329	26,154	32,898	9,470	42,368	2,972	394	3,366
322	1,172	0	1,172	8,159	0	8,159	1,358	0	1,358
323	518	700	1,218	1,733	1,004	2,737	847	175	1,022
324	2,676	37	2,713	2,914	40	2,954	-517	1	-516
331	931	166	1,097	41	38	79	415	13	428
332	268	18	286	2,524	25	2,549	11	1	12
341	10,708	3,195	13,903	8,195	2,315	10,510	10,418	2,590	13,003
342	462	42	504	1,385	23	1,408	118	12	130
351	1,508	-249	1,259	16,712	4,500	21,262	455	101	556
352	15,291	1,708	16,999	7,447	2,104	9,551	4,431	486	4,917
353	151	254	405	1,003	715	1,718	40	10	50
354	104	1	105	222	3	225	0	0	0
355	8,349	49	8,398	2,921	30	2,951	635	-2	633
356	881	1,004	1,885	5,638	536	6,174	1,331	55	1,386
361	0	-13	-13	257	26	283	0	0	0
362	5,115	1,049	6,164	52	35	87	6	0	6
369	337	90	427	1,191	94	1,285	790	55	845
371	0	0	0	0	0	0	0	0	0
372	0	0	0	0	0	0	0	0	0
381	62,181	16,047	78,228	13,613	2,893	16,506	297	-39	258
382	9,787	32	9,819	2,378	6	2,384	282	0	282
383	6,965	399	7,364	9,142	541	9,683	293	2	295
384	438	3	441	11,581	45	11,626	60	0	60
385	419	6	425	59	0	59	2	0	2
390	22,384	101	22,485	9,921	134	10,055	326	4	330

Table C-13 (Continued)

Sector	Nicaragua (1972)			Costa Rica (1972)		
	Direct	Indirect	Total	Direct	Indirect	Total
311	12,158	1,609	13,767	13,781	2,195	15,976
312	207	61	268	1,983	64	2,047
313	2	1	3	0	1	1
314	28	9	37	102	34	136
321	5,002	1,161	6,163	4,539	1,787	6,326
322	109	0	109	4,513	0	4,513
323	1,783	876	2,659	497	245	742
324	1,132	14	1,146	405	5	410
331	1,530	98	1,628	1,061	89	1,150
332	695	10	705	102	41	143
341	3,594	810	4,404	1,215	564	1,779
342	85	9	94	385	19	404
351	8,527	3,059	11,586	6,250	2,209	8,459
352	3,162	722	3,884	5,783	1,690	7,473
353	15,188	5,798	20,986	2	103	105
354	3	0	3	187	6	193
355	1,837	9	1,846	6,814	19	6,833
356	934	89	1,023	3,084	236	3,320
361	0	45	45	0	48	48
362	53	13	66	8	108	116
369	2,104	162	2,266	87	31	118
371	0	0	0	0	0	0
372	0	0	0	0	0	0
381	15,242	2,815	18,057	21,958	3,508	25,466
382	1,105	1	1,106	1,548	12	1,560
383	3,982	155	4,137	15,774	806	16,580
384	52	0	52	15	0	15
385	3	0	3	70	0	70
390	125	7	132	465	-5	460

Table C-14. Changes in Output Attributable to Integration, Primary Sectors
(Legal Tariff Bases), 1968
(in 1,000 CA pesos)

Sector	Guatemala			El Salvador			Honduras		
	Direct	Indirect	Total	Direct	Indirect	Total	Direct	Indirect	Total
Foodstuffs									
Wheat	0			45			-1,117		
Corn	5			541			700		
Rice	504			3,771			484		
Beans	95			191			2,538		
Fruits, nuts	289			452			477		
Vegetables	679			42			15		
Total	1,572	3,774	5,346	5,042	2,194	7,236	3,097	768	3,865
Mining	80	0	80	453	0	453	172	0	172
Cotton	n.a.	1,572	1,527	n.a.	1,873	1,873	n.a.	287	287
Wood extract	n.a.	91	91	n.a.	18	18	n.a.	96	96
Total	1,652	5,392	7,044	5,495	4,085	9,580	3,269	1,151	4,420

Table C-14 (Continued)

Sector	Nicaragua			Costa Rica		
	Direct	Indirect	Total	Direct	Indirect	Total
Foodstuffs						
Wheat	0			0		
Corn	125			0		
Rice	192			204		
Beans	932			-1,080		
Fruits, nuts	-84			239		
Vegetables	1			139		
Total	1,166	1,807	2,973	-498	1,588	1,090
Mining	480	0	480	7	0	7
Cotton	n.a.	164	164	n.a.	400	400
Wood extract	n.a.	153	153	n.a.	177	177
Total	1,646	2,124	3,770	-491	2,165	1,674

Table C-15. Annual Average Percentage Deviation from Trend[a]
of Export Value: Four Basic Export Crops, 1966-73
(percent)

	Bananas	Sugar	Coffee	Cotton
Guatemala	13.23	22.18	14.75	17.68
El Salvador	-	33.06	6.19	21.04
Honduras	4.81	37.13	8.10	426.15
Nicaragua	59.20	11.99	11.48	17.48
Costa Rica	6.73	16.85	8.84	-

[a]A regression of the following form was calculated:

$$E_t = \alpha + \beta_t$$

where E_t is export value in year t and t is "time" (with value from 1 for 1966 to 8 for 1973). The actual export value was then compared to predicted value, and the residual taken as a percentage of predicted value. Then the single average of the absolute value of these annual percentage deviations from trend was computed.

SOURCE: Calculated from SIECA, VI Compendio Estadístico Centroamericano, 1975 (Guatemala City: SIECA, 1975), pp. 278-82.

Table C-16. Results of Regression of Residual of
Manufacturing Share in GDP from Expected
Value Based on Cross-Country Patterns,
Central America, 1960-71

Country	Regression Parameters[a]			R^2
	Constant	α	β	
		(time)	(1969-71 dummy)	
Guatemala[b]	-.0742	+.0025 (2.40)	-.0121 (-1.47)	.401
El Salvador[b]	-.0023	+.0016 (1.20)	-.0009 (-.08)	.250
Honduras[b]	-.0038	+.001 (.13)	+.0104 (1.27)	.325
Nicaragua[c]	.0026	-.0020 (-2.61)	+.0102 (1.63)	.440
Costa Rica[c]	.0169	-.0011 (-1.10)	-.0024 (-.25)	.236
Central America[c]	-.0809	+.003 (3.39)	-.0084 (-1.20)	.635

[a] Regression: $R = C + \alpha t + \beta D$, where R is the residual, actual share of
manufacturing value added in GDP minus expected share (see notes b and c);
C is the constant; t is time (t = 1 for 1960 to 12 for 1971); D is a dummy
variable equal to zero for 1960-68, and 1 for 1969-71.
[b] Cross-country equation used:
$V = -.457 + .122 \ln Y - .003 (\ln Y)^2 + .066 \ln N - .008 (\ln Y)^2 + .261F$,
where V is share of manufacturing value added in GDP; Y is per capita
GDP in 1964 U.S. dollars; N is population in millions; ln is the
natural logarithm; F is the net capital inflow, estimated as the excess
of imports over exports as a fraction of GDP plus imports less exports
(the latter being a measure of total domestic supply). Source: Hollis
B. Chenery and Moises Syrquin, Patterns of Development, 1950-70 (London:
Oxford University Press, 1974), table S17.
[c] Cross-country equation used: $V = -.403 + .149 \ln Y - .006 (\ln Y)^2 +$
$.046 \ln N - .005 (\ln N)^2 + .216F + .006 T_1 - .002 T_2 - .01 T_3$. Source:
Ibid., table 21. Variables are the same as in note b except that
T_1, T_2, and T_3 are subperiod time dummy variables.
[d] The figures in parentheses are "t" statistics.

SOURCE: Ivan Garcia Marenco, Estimaciones Preliminares de las Trans-
formaciones Estructurales por Efecto de la Integración
Económica Centroamericana, Proyecto SIECA/Brookings, SIECA
75/PES/IE/19, 2a Versión (Guatemala City: SIECA, 1975,
processed).

526

Appendix C

NOTES

1. At any given quantity the demand curve shows the price consumers would be willing to pay. As there would always be some consumers willing to pay a higher price if scarcity were greater (i.e., at a point upward to the left on the demand curve), those consumers enjoy a windfall gain or "consumer surplus" when the market clears at a lower unit price and higher quantity.

2. The least efficient producer has supply cost equal to the price at market equilibrium, but the inframarginal producers (those who would have been "at the margin" at a point further down to the left along the supply curve) have lower unit cost. The excess of price over unit cost (i.e., over the supply curve) for these more efficient producers is "producers' surplus."

3. More specifically, with η = import propensity, T = total, R = ROW, P = partner, 0 = base year, 1 = terminal year, equation (2) measures trade creation as (i) $TCCE = (\eta_1^T - \eta_0^T) C_1$. But when $\eta_1^R > \eta_0^R$, we are already including the expansion of imports from ROW in the separate measure ETA. TCCE must therefore be collapsed to capture only the increased importation from partners.

Since:

(ii) $\eta^T = \eta^P = \eta^R$,

(iii) $TCCE = \left[(\eta_1^P + \eta_1^R) - (\eta_0^P = + \eta_0^R)\right] C_1 = (\eta_1^P - \eta_0^P)C_1 + (\eta_1^R - \eta_0^R)C_2$.

Limiting TCCE to the import effect vis-a-vis partners means limiting it to the first term, $(\eta_1^P - \eta_0^P) C_1$. This may be accomplished by subtracting from TCCE the absolute value $|TD|$, since from (1), that value will equal $(\eta_1^R - \eta_0^R)C_1$ when $\eta_1^R > \eta_0^R$.

4. That is, we desire to reduce TD from $(\eta_0^R - \eta_1^R)C_1$ to $(\eta_1^P - \eta_0^P)C_1$.

Since:

$\eta^R + \eta^P = \eta^T$,

we may rewrite (1) as:

(1) $TD = \left[(\eta_0^T - \eta_0^P) - (\eta_1^T - \eta_1^P)\right] C_1 = (\eta_1^P - \eta_0^P)C_1 + (\eta_0^T - \eta_1^T)C_1$.

Limiting TD to $[\eta_1^P - \eta_0^P]C_1$ will therefore be achieved by subtracting from TD the absolute value of TCCE, which will equal $(\eta_0^T - \eta_1^T)C_1$ when $\eta_1^T > \eta_0^T$.

5. For example, suppose η^R rose for nongermane reasons $(t_1 > t_0)$. The negative trade diversion implies overstatement of trade creation. That portion of observed trade creation $(\eta_1^T - \eta_0^T)C_1$ attributable to ROW imports should be removed as nongermane, and we are back to collapsing TCCE to $(\eta_1^P - \eta_0^P)C_1$ as shown above.

6. It is also possible to conduct sensitivity analysis by assigning varying proportional ETA and TCCE to output reduction versus consumption expansion.

7. That is, $\dfrac{\Delta Q}{Q_0} = (1 + r)\left[\dfrac{\Delta I}{I_0}\right]$, where I is all inputs, Δ means change, and 0 is base period. The required percentage change in inputs for an observed $\dfrac{\Delta Q}{Q_0}$ is thus $\left[\dfrac{\Delta Q}{Q_0}\right]/(1 + r)$. Therefore, of the full increase in output, ΔQ, we may say the fraction $\left(\dfrac{1}{1 + r}\right)$ is purchased at the cost of increased inputs. The remaining fraction, $\left[1 - \left(\dfrac{1}{1 + r}\right)\right]$, is gained free due to economies of scale. Therefore the windfall gain is the fraction

$$\left[1 - \left(\frac{1}{1 + r}\right)\right] \quad \text{or} \quad \left[\frac{r}{1 + r}\right] \quad \text{of the total output change.}$$

8. Thus, $\quad f^* = \dfrac{-\sum\limits_i \tau_i u_i \eta_i + \sum\limits_j \phi_j v_j \varepsilon_j}{-\sum\limits_i u_i \eta_i + \sum\limits_j v_j \varepsilon_j}$,

where τ_i is $1 + t_i$ and t_i is the tariff on product i; u_i is the share of good i in imports; η_i is the price elasticity of import demand for good i; ϕ_j is unity plus the export subsidy rate for good j; v_j is the share of good j in exports; and ε_j is the price elasticity of foreign demand for good j. See Edmar Bacha and Lance Taylor, "Foreign Exchange Shadow Prices: A Critical Review of Current Theories," Quarterly Journal of Economics 85(2) (May 1971), p. 206.

9. Bacha and Taylor, "Foreign Exchange Shadow Prices."

10. The Bacha-Taylor measure is:

$$F^* = F\ (1 + \bar{t})^{1/(1 - q)},$$

where:

F^* = shadow exchange rate,

F_0 = market exchange rate,

$\bar{t}$ = average ad valorem tariff level,

$q = D\ (1 + \eta_x)\varepsilon_x\ (\varepsilon_m - \eta_m)/(1 + \varepsilon_m)\ \eta_m(\ \eta_x - \varepsilon_x)$

528

D = ratio of export value to import value,

η = price elasticity of demand, subscripts x for exports and m for imports, and

ξ = price elasticity of supply, subscripts x for exports and m for imports.

If foreign supply and demand are infinitely elastic (small country case), and if trade is initially in balance (D = 1), the equation simplifies to:

$$F^* = F_0 (1 + \bar{t})^{\eta_m/(\xi_x + \eta_m)}.$$

Since the formulation uses a positively signed elasticity of demand η_m, the exponent on $(1 + \bar{t})$ must be less than unity (but positive), so that the Bacha-Taylor result gives a shadow exchange rate lower than that of the Harberger approach (which instead equals the market rate plus the tariff, in the simple case described here).

11. In addition to the lack of statistical significance for most of the tests, there is a problem of simultaneity. The normal industry share is computed using per capita income as an explanatory variable, but to the extent that economic integration raises income through its welfare effects, the variable for per capita income will already contain some of the influence of integration. Therefore, the ceteris paribus or control value for industrial share will be overstated, leaving an understatement of the net impact of integration on industrial share as measured by the difference between the actual figure and the control figure.

An interesting phenomenon implied by the regression results, although not directly relevant to the test for structural transformation, is the result indicated by the constant terms. These terms, reported in table C-16, indicate that Guatemala, El Salvador, and Honduras had lower shares of manufacturing in GDP than cross-country norms would suggest (with the shortfall ranging from 7.4 percent of GDP in Guatemala to 0.38 percent in Honduras), while Nicaragua and Costa Rica had higher than expected shares (by 2.26 percent and 1.69 percent of GDP, respectively). The region as a whole had a larger shortfall: its share of manufacturing was 8.1 percent below the cross-country norm, meaning that, under standard patterns, a country the size of Central America as a whole would have been expected to have a share of manufacturing in GDP of approximately 24.7 percent instead of the actual 16.6 percent for Central America (in the middle years of the period, 1965-67). (Calculated from SIECA, VI Compendio Estadístico, pp. 376, 358.) However, it would be wrong to conclude that true integration would therefore raise the region's manufacturing share by this 8 percent, because members--especially Guatemala-- also had shortfalls from the norm even as individual countries, so the shortfall for the region was not due solely to the fact that it was not integrated into a single country.

12. Raul Prebisch, "Commercial Policy in the Underdeveloped Countries," American Economic Review 49 (May 1959), pp. 251-73.

13. See, for example, T. Morgan, "The Long-Run Terms of Trade between Agriculture and Manufacturing," Economic Development and Cultural Change 8 (October 1959), pp. 1-23.

14. I. M. D. Little, Tibor Scitovsky, and Maurice Scott, Industry and Trade in Some Developing Countries: A Comparative Study (London: Oxford University Press, 1970).

15. Jacob Viner, International Trade and Economic Development (Glencoe, Ill.: Free Press, 1952); Hollis Chenery and Moises Syrquin, Patterns of Development 1950-1970 (London: Oxford University Press, 1975).

16. See, for example, Henry C. Wallich, "Stabilization of Proceeds from Raw Material Exports," in H. S. Ellis and H. C. Wallich, eds., Economic Development for Latin America (New York: St. Martin's Press, 1961); Clark W. Reynolds, "Domestic Consequences of Export Instability," American Economic Review 53 (May 1963): 93-102. There is, however, an inconclusive body of literature on whether export fluctuation is actually greater in developing countries than in industrial countries, and on whether greater fluctuation in exports and growth rates is associated with a greater degree of concentration in raw materials exports. A. I. MacBean, Export Instability and Economic Development (Cambridge, Mass.: Harvard University Press, 1966); Guy F. Erb and S. Schiavo-Campo, "Export Instability, Level of Development and Economic Size of Less Developed Countries," Oxford Bulletin of Economics and Statistics 31 (May 1969): 263-83; Benton F. Massell, "Export Instability and Economic Structure," American Economic Review 60 (September 1970): 618-30.

17. Since industrial goods are obtained either by direct production or by export of traditional agricultural goods.

18. However, recent experience in the international economy has been that a broad front of commodities has risen in price and then subsequently backed off. The relatively recent joint movement of industrial countries through their domestic business cycles appears to be primarily responsible. If this pattern continues, diversification across a set of raw materials exports would not appear to promise as much risk reduction as in the past, when individual commodity cycles were more important relative to broad cycles in industrial consuming countries.

19. Sectors 371 (basic iron and steel), 372 (nonferrous basic metals), and 381 (production of metal products except machinery and equipment) are treated as one sector.

20. These data are the "PATYEB" agricultural trade data series.

21. GAFICA, Plan Perspectivo. Note that the base year for agricultural products is 1960 rather than 1958, and the terminal year is 1970 rather than 1968.

22. These data are published in SIECA, Anuario Estadístico Centroamericano de Comercio Exterior, 1972.

The Demand for Industrial Labor: Methodology and Supplementary Tables

Charles R. Frank, Jr.,
Max A. Soto, and
Carlos A. Sevilla

A. Introduction

This appendix develops the formal methodology underlying chapter 4 of this book. In addition, after a brief discussion of possible biases in the empirical estimations, the appendix reports additional statistical findings omitted from the main chapter.

B. Elasticity of Substitution

Beginning with the CES production function, output may be expressed as a function of capital and labor inputs in the following way:

(1) $\qquad V = \gamma [\delta K^{-\rho} + (1 - \delta)L^{-\rho}]^{-h/\rho}$,

where V is production, K is the input of physical capital (such as machinery, structures, and equipment), and L is the labor input.

The parameter γ represents technological efficiency; δ is the distribution parameter which characterizes the degree to which technology is intensive in capital; h represents the degree of homogeneity of the production function, or the degree in which technology is characterized by constant, increasing or decreasing returns to scale; and ρ is the substitution parameter.[1] The CES function meets the neoclassical requirements that the marginal products of factors be positive and diminishing. Furthermore, this function permits the characterization of the degree of returns to scale.[2]

Using the CES production function, text equation (1), maximum profits will be achieved where marginal productivity of labor is equal to the real wage, or:[3]

$$\frac{\delta V}{\delta L} = \gamma^{-\rho/h} (1 - \delta)L^{-(1+\rho)} hV^{(h+\rho)/h} = \frac{w}{p} \quad .$$

532

For the case of constant returns ($h = 1$), this expression simplifies to:

$$\gamma^{-\rho}(1 - \delta)L^{-(1 + \rho)} V^{(1+\rho)} = \frac{w}{p}$$

where w is the nominal wage and p, the price of the product. By reorganizing and taking logarithms, we obtain:

$$\ln \frac{V}{L} = \frac{1}{(1 + \rho)} \ln \frac{\gamma\rho}{(1 - \delta)} + \frac{1}{(1 + \rho)} \ln \frac{w}{p} .$$

For purposes of statistical estimation, this form becomes:

(2) $$\ln \frac{V}{L} = a_0 + b_1 \ln \frac{w}{p} + u_1 ,$$

which expresses average labor productivity as a function of the real wage and a stochastic term, u_1. Note that coefficient b_1 is an estimate of the elasticity of substitution, which is the parameter in which we are interested.[4]

Equation (2) may be interpreted as a labor absorption function of manpower in which technology is characterized by constant returns to scale. Therefore, the coefficient b_1 represents the percentage change in employment that should result from a 1 percent change in real wages, holding constant the production level.[5]

Nevertheless, there is no reason to expect production to remain constant when there is a change in the real wage rate. A reduction in real wages could bring about an increase both in the use of labor and in the level of production, for a given amount of capital. Consequently the elasticity of substitution would be different from the elasticity of employment with regard to wages, as discussed above. The latter would be comprised of a substitution as well as an output effect. Assuming capital is constant, equation (2) may be expressed as a labor demand function in which the demand for labor depends on output, V, and the real wage, w/p. Then taking the derivative of this function with respect to labor, the resulting elasticity is:

(3) $$\frac{dL}{L} = \frac{\sigma}{(1 - se_L)} \frac{d(w/p)}{w/p},$$

where $s = (h + \rho)h$, and $e_L = (dV/dL)(L/V)$ is the employment elasticity of production. In accordance with (3), the elasticity of the demand for labor, $\sigma/(1 - se_L)$, is generally greater than the elasticity of substitution. For the case of constant returns to scale, the expression simplifies to:[6]

(4) $$\frac{dL}{L} = \frac{\sigma}{\phi_k} \frac{d(w/p)}{w/p},$$

where ϕ_k is the share of capital in value added.

To recapitulate, to this point we have stated the elasticity of substitution, parameter b_2 in equation (2), as well as the associated elasticity of demand for labor, equation (3), with both based on the optimal choice of labor in response to changes in the real wage rate, given a CES production function, equation (1).

It should be noted that the estimation equations outlined above assume that capital stock remains constant and, therefore, the price of capital does not affect the factor proportions decision. The model may then be restated to incorporate changes in both capital stock and labor in response to the relative prices of capital and labor.

In this case, with variable capital and variable cost of capital, if management maximizes profits it will equate the ratio of the marginal productivities of the factors of production (the marginal rate of substitution) to the ratio of the prices of the factors. That is:

$$\frac{\delta V/\delta L}{\delta V/\delta K} = \frac{f_L}{f_K} = \frac{1-\delta}{\delta} \left(\frac{L}{K}\right)^{-(1+\rho)} = \frac{c}{w} ,$$

where c is the cost of capital, and f_L, f_K are the marginal productivities of labor and capital, respectively. By reorganizing and using logarithms we obtain:

$$\ln (L/K) = -\frac{1}{(1+\rho)} \ln \frac{\delta}{(1-\delta)} - \frac{1}{(1+\rho)} \ln \frac{c}{w} ,$$

or for purposes of statistical estimation,

(5) $\ln (L/K = a_1 + b_2 \ln \frac{c}{w} + u_2 ,$

where u_2 is a random error term, with zero expected value and constant variance. With (5) it is possible to determine the demand for labor relative to demand for capital, the labor-capital ratio, as a function of the relative price of the two factors. In order to determine the absolute demand of labor, the scale of production and the amount of capital associated with it must be known first. Note that b_2 may be interpreted as an estimate of the "long-run" elasticity of substitution since both capital and labor adjust to changes in relative prices.

C.   Technological Change

In order to incorporate technological change into the analysis it is desirable to work with efficiency units of each factor rather than physical units. The production function may then be expressed as follows:

(6) $$V(t) = \left[\delta \, [e^{\lambda_K t} \, K(t)]^{-\rho} + (1-\delta) \, [e^{\lambda_L t} \, L(t)]^{-\rho}\right]^{-h/\rho} ,$$

where λ_K and λ_L are the capital-augmenting and labor-augmenting rates of technical change, respectively, while $K(t)$ and $L(t)$ represent the physical quantities of those factors, and $e^{\lambda_K t} \, K(t)$ and $e^{\lambda_L t} \, L(t)$ refer to units of efficiency.

The intensity of technological change, $R(t)$, may then be defined as the proportional rate of growth of output when capital, $K(t)$, and labor, $L(t)$, are held constant. That is,

$$R(t) = \frac{\partial V(t)}{\partial t} \cdot \frac{1}{V(t)}$$

Differentiating equation (6) with respect to time, and dividing by $V(t)$, we have:

$$R(t) = \left[\frac{h(1-\delta)(e^{\lambda_L t} L)^{-\rho}}{(1-\delta)(e^{\lambda_L t} L)^{-\rho} + (e^{\lambda_K t} K)^{-\rho}} \right] \lambda_L$$

$$+ \left[\frac{h (e^{\lambda_K t} K)^{-\rho}}{(1-\delta)(e^{\lambda_L t} L)^{-\rho} + (e^{\lambda_K t} K)^{-\rho}} \right] \lambda_K ,$$

$$= \left[\frac{\partial V}{\partial L} \frac{L}{V} \right] \lambda_L + \left[\frac{\partial V}{\partial K} \frac{K}{V} \right] \lambda_K ,$$

which may be expressed as:

(7)
$$R(t) = \frac{\partial V(t)}{\partial t} \frac{1}{V(t)} = \alpha_1 \lambda_L + \alpha_2 \lambda_K$$

This equation shows the intensity of technological change as a weighted average of the rates of growth of capital- and labor-augmenting technological change. The weights (α_1 and α_2) are the elasticities of production with regard to each input. Note that these elasticities contain the parameter h; consequently this measure of intensity incorporates the effect of the economies of scale in production.

The bias of technological change is defined as the proportional growth rate of the marginal rate of substitution (that is, of the ratio of marginal products of the two factors). This definition flows naturally from the concept of neutrality in technological change according to Hicks[7] in which the change is neutral when there occurs no change in factor proportions so long as the factor price ratio remains constant. In terms of equation (6) the bias against the use of labor $B(t)$, would be given by:

$$B(t) = \frac{d[\ln(f_K / f_L)]}{dt} = \frac{1}{f_K} \frac{\partial f_K}{\partial t} - \frac{1}{f_L} \frac{\partial f_L}{\partial t} ,$$

where f_K and f_L express the marginal productivity of K and L respectively. Therefore:

(8)
$$B(t) = \frac{1-\sigma}{\sigma} (\lambda_L - \lambda_K)$$

This last expression establishes that the bias of technological change is a function of the elasticity of substitution as well as of the difference between the rates of labor- and capital-augmenting technological change. It should be noted that when the factors of production have unitary elasticity of substitution ($\sigma = 1$, and a 1 percent change in the factor price ratio causes a 1 percent change in the ratio of factors used) or when the rates of technological change corresponding to K and L are the same ($\lambda_K = \lambda_L$), there would be no bias (B = 0) and, as a result, technological change would be neutral. The most interesting cases occur when the elasticity of substitution differs from unity. In the expected case in which the elasticity of substitution is less than 1, then $\lambda_L < \lambda_K$ would imply a labor-intensive technological change (capital-saving change), whereas $\lambda_L > \lambda_{Kg}$ would result in capital-intensive technical change (labor-saving change).

The foregoing provides a theoretical framework for analysis of technological change. To estimate the bias, equation (5) is modified to include a variable for change over time. Thus:

(9) $\qquad \ln(L/K) = a_2 + b_3 \ln (c/w) + dt + u_3,$

where: $\quad a_2 = -\sigma \ln[\delta/(1-\delta)],$

$\qquad\quad b_3 = \sigma,$ and

$\qquad\quad d = (1-\sigma)(\lambda_K - \lambda_L).$

Note that coefficient of t (time) is equal to the negative of B(t) multiplied by σ. Therefore, if $\sigma < 1$, a positive coefficient "d" would indicate that the technological change would have been capital-saving, while a negative coefficient "d" would confirm the hypothesis that the technological innovation in developing countries is biased against the labor factor.

To determine the intensity of technological change, it is necessary to know the elasticity of output with respect to each one of the inputs, as well as the rates of factor-augmenting technical change for both inputs. An approximation of those elasticities may be obtained from information on the share of each factor in value added, under the assumption of constant returns to scale. On the other hand, estimation of the derived short-run labor demand function, using equation (6) provides an estimate of λ_L, which can be used in turn to obtain λ_K by means of equation (8).[9]

D. Economies of Scale

Economies of scale can be estimated either by using the results obtained in the derived demand function for labor, or by estimating the production function directly. In the first case, the estimated equation would be:

(11) $\qquad \ln L = a_3 + b_5 \ln w + c_2 \ln V + u_5,$

in which

$$h = \frac{1 + b_5}{c_2 + b_5} \, .$$

In this formulation returns to scale are decreasing, constant, or increasing if h is less than, equal to, or more than unity. In practice, this equation presents several problems, making it difficult to obtain reliable estimates of the scale parameter, h. Among them is the bias introduced by errors in the measurement of variables V and w,[10] the possibility that the underlying production function will not be homothetic,[11] and the unstable nature of the relationship between h and coefficients b_5 and c_2 (due to division by the difference between the latter two parameters). The first two difficulties tend to produce overestimates of economies of scale, while the third makes h extremely sensitive when b approaches unity or when b_5 and c_2 are similar in magnitude.

The second method of estimation used in this study is the Kmenta approximation to the CES function. If one begins with equation (1) and applies a Taylor series expansion around $\rho = 0$, disregarding terms of quadratic and higher orders, the result is:[12]

(12) $\ln (V/L) = \ln \gamma + (h - 1) \ln L + h \delta \ln(K/L)$

$$- \frac{1}{2} \rho h \delta (1 - \delta)[\ln(K/L)]^2 + u_6,$$

or, for estimation purposes,

(13) $\ln (V/L) = a + h_1 \ln L = g_3 \ln(K/L) + g_4 [\ln(K/L)]^2 + u_6 \, .$

Unlike the method used in equation (11), the Kmenta approximation provides a direct estimate of parameter h_2 for which tests of statistical significance can be conducted. Other advantages of this procedure are that it requires no assumptions regarding the market structure, and that it provides a direct test of whether or not the production function is Cobb-Douglas. In addition, equation (13) produces estimates of h which are highly reliable.[13] The relevant hypotheses would then be whether the coefficient h_1 is less than, equal to, or larger than zero, which would indicate decreasing, constant, or increasing returns to scale.

Implicit in the above analysis is the supposition that economies of scale are constant at any level of production. In other words, if economies of scale are identified in a certain industrial activity, then all of the firms comprising this activity--whether they are large or small--will present the same degree of returns to scale. Due to the importance that industrial development policies and employment policies attach to the size structure of firms, it is of interest to examine what happens to economies of scale as the size of the industrial plant is expanded. This question may be investigated by estimating the function (13) for groups of firms of different sizes, or by estimating a function that relaxes the assumption of homotheticity. For the latter purpose, the "trans-log" function may be employed.[14] The estimating form of this function is:[15]

(14) $\ln V = a_5 + h_2 \ln L + z_1 \ln K + k_1 (\ln L)^2$

$+ m_1 (\ln K)^2 + n_1 \ln L \ln K + u_7.$

In order that the function be homothetic, it is necessary that $k_1 = m_1 = -1/2\ n_1$, which may be tested using the estimation results of equation (13) and the trans-log function presented here,[16] which has the characteristics that both the elasticities of the inputs as well as the economies of scale are variable.

E. Employment Effects of Integration

Starting from the labor demand function relating employment to the wage rate and value added, and replacing value added by gross output,[17] we obtain:

$\ln L = a + b \ln w + c \ln Q + dt,$

which expresses labor demand as a function of the wage rate, of gross production, and of time. Taking the derivative of this equation with respect to time,

$$\frac{d\,L}{L} = b\,\frac{dw}{w} + c\,\frac{d\,Q}{Q} + d\,(dt)\ ,$$

where L, w, Q, and t are employment, wage, output, and time, respectively, and where each term when preceded by "d" refers to the "change in" the variable in question.

The last equation allows for the estimation of the percentage change in employment resulting from a percentage change in any one of the other variables, holding the remaining variables constant. This procedure then, incorporates not only the effect on labor absorption of changes in the wage rate but also those effects stemming from changes in the level of production and from technical change which alters factor productivities. Since what is wanted is the effect of integration on labor demand, the relevant changes in the above explanatory variables to be considered are those due to integration, and not historical changes.

On the other hand, since technical change could be estimated only for Guatemala due to data limitations in the other countries, and given the difficulty in determining how much of that change was due to integration, the effect of technical change was included only for total manufacturing to give an idea of its possible magnitude. With these changes, the above formula reduces to

$$d\,L = c \left(\frac{d\,Q}{Q} \right) L\ ,$$

which expresses the change in employment as a function of the change in output attributable to integration. The coefficient c represents the labor elasticity of output or the percentage change in employment that will result from a 1 percent change in output. A modification to the above procedure was used for a few particular cases.[18]

Our second alternative assumes that in the above labor demand function there are constant returns to scale and the elasticity of demand for labor with respect to the size of output is unity. This variant is necessary because of the limited reliability of the implied parameter for returns to scale in this estimating form, as discussed above. In this second variant, employment attributable to integration is estimated by:

$$dL = (dQ/Q) L.$$

The third alternative applies the inverse of average labor productivity to the change in output to estimate the change in employment:

$$dL = (dQ)(L/Q).$$

F. Notes on Estimation Forms

It should be noted that, unlike the original equations of this appendix, the estimating equations used do not deflate the wage rate by the price of the product, and they express the value added as a value term rather than a physical quantity. For purposes of exposition the methodology here assumes a single physical product, but in practice it is impossible to state a product price because product mix varies across firms, even when they are separated into finely divided product categories.[19]

For the analysis of the elasticity of substitution, in addition to the estimates of forms "a" and "e" in table 1 of chapter 4, which correspond to equations explicitly mentioned in this appendix, results are obtained for form "b"--which assume that it is the quantities and not the prices that are exogenous. In this case the elasticity of substitution becomes $1/b_1$, where b_1 is the regression coefficient in "ln(V/L)." It can be shown that the estimate of the elasticity of substitution from form "b," which we may name σ', will always be larger (in absolute value) than that from form "a" (σ).[20] Maddala and Kadane[21] postulate that form "b" provides better estimates of the elasticity of substitution than form "a." However, to date there appear to be no empirical estimates for this form except those by Berndt. The remaining equations of table 1 have been discussed in chapter 4.

G. Estimation of the Cost of Capital

The estimation of capital cost presents conceptual and empirical difficulties. At the conceptual level, there are frequently confusions between the cost of possessing a unit of capital, on the one hand, and the unit value of capital services, on the other. Moreover there are problems in distinguishing between the accounting definition of capital cost and more appropriate economic definitions. At the practical level even greater obstacles beset efforts at quantification, especially when disaggregated estimates are desired. Nevertheless, the cost of capital is one of the critical variables for determining the factor proportions used and, thus, the demand for labor, the main concern here. This appendix presents a methodology for estimating the cost of capital which attempts to overcome these difficulties.

The first efforts of quantification of cost of capital considered it equal to the rate of interest; subsequently the influence of the depreciation rate of physical capital was included.[22] More recent studies recognize that the estimation of capital cost is more complex and incorporates other elements previously ignored, such as the effect of taxes, capital gains, and policies concerning accelerated depreciation.[23] The following discussion derives the cost of capital, understood as the cost of possessing a unit of capital for a specific period. Definitions of terms used are noted below:

x_1 = profits reinvested in fixed assets,

x_2 = profits reinvested in financial assets,

x_3 = profits distributed to shareholders,

x_4 = borrowed capital invested in fixed assets,

p = $(x_1 + x_2 + x_3)$ = total profits; p is a constant given in the previous period,

y = $[x_1 + x_4]/q$ = total investment in fixed assets,

$f(y)$ = return to capital invested in fixed assets, including capital costs but excluding labor costs,

q = price of capital goods,

δ = rate of replacement of fixed assets,

d = rate of depreciation for tax purposes,

dq = change in the price of capital goods,

r = interest rate on borrowed capital,

u_1 = income tax rate,

u_2 = tax rate on capital gains,

u_3 = tax rate on profits reinvested in fixed assets,

u_4 = tax rate on profits reinvested in financial assets,

u_5 = tax rate on distributed profits,

w_1 = proportion of depreciation cost not subject to tax,

w_2 = proportion of profits reinvested in fixed assets not subject to tax,

w_3 = proportion of profits reinvested in fixed assets deductible for tax purposes,

w_4 = proportion of profits reinvested in financial assets deductible from taxable income,

w_5 = proportion of distributed profits deductible from taxable income,

m = rate of maintenance costs for fixed assets, and

r^* = rate of return on financial assets.

Taxable income, Y_p, may be defined as return to fixed assets less cost of capital, or,

$$Y_p = f(y) - w_1[d][q]y - w_2 r x_4 - mqy.$$

The return to investment in fixed assets after tax, E_p^*, may be defined as:

$$E_p^* = f(y) - \delta qy - mqy - rx_4 + [dq]y - u_1 Y_p - u_2 [dq]y.$$

That is, E_p^* is the return on fixed assets net of the costs of capital (for replacement, maintenance, and interest), plus the capital gains, minus the tax on income and on capital gains. Similarly, the return to financial assets after taxes, E_f^*, is defined as:

$$E_f^* = r^* x_2 - u_1 r^* x_2 .$$

It should be noted, however, that in addition to taxes payable on profits in the present period, there exist taxes on profits from the previous period which depend on investment decisions made in the present period. This is the case for taxes which vary with the use of profits. To incorporate this element, we define T, the tax on profits from the previous period, as:

$$T = (p - w_3 x_1 - w_4 x_2 - w_5 x_3)u_1 + (1 - w_3)x_1 u_3 + (1 - w_4)x_2 u_4$$
$$+ (1 - w_5)x_3 u_5 .$$

The first term within parentheses on the right-hand side takes into account the general tax rate, u_1, payable on profits net of special exemptions, and the remaining terms refer to specific taxes corresponding to the utilization of reinvested profits in fixed assets, financial assets, or the distribution of profits.

We may now define the profit function, net both of taxes for the present period and for taxes of the previous period dependent on current investment decisions, as:

$$\Psi = E_p^* + E_f^* + g(x_3) - T,$$

where $g(x_3)$ is the utility function of the shareholders with respect to distributed profits, expressed in monetary terms.

The problem of optimization may be formulated, then, in the following way:

$$\text{maximize } \Psi = \Psi (x_1, x_2, x_3, x_4)$$

subject to the restrictions,

$$x_1 + x_2 + x_3 = p,$$

$$x_1, x_2, x_3, x_4 \geqq 0.$$

This formulation falls within the classic problems of optimization, which may be resolved using Lagrangian analysis. The function is, in this case:

$$\Psi^* = \Psi + \lambda [p - (x_1 + x_2 + x_3)].$$

The first order conditions for Ψ^* are:

$$\frac{\partial \Psi^*}{\partial x_1} = \frac{1}{q} f'(y) (1 - u_1) - (\delta - u_1 w_1 d) - m(1 - u_1) + \frac{dq}{q}(1-u_1)$$

$$+ (w_3 u_1 - u_3 + w_3 u_3) - \lambda \leq 0 ,$$

$$\frac{\partial \Psi^*}{\partial x_2} = r^*(1 - u_1) + (w_4 u_1 - u_4 + w_4 u_4) - \lambda \leq 0 ,$$

$$\frac{\partial \Psi^*}{\partial x_3} = g'(x_3) + (w_5 u_1 - u_5 + w_5 u_5) - \lambda \leq 0 ,$$

$$\frac{\partial \Psi^*}{\partial x_4} = \frac{1}{q} f'(y)(1 - u_1) - (\delta - u_1 w_1 d) - m(1 - u_1) + \frac{dq}{q}(1 - u_2)$$

$$- r(1 - u_1 w_2) \leq 0 ,$$

$$\frac{\partial \Psi^*}{\partial \lambda} = p - (x_1 + x_2 + x_3) = 0 ,$$

$$\sum_{j=1}^{3} \frac{\partial \Psi^*}{\partial \Psi x_j} x_j^* = 0 ,$$

$$\lambda^* [p - (x_1 + x_2 + x_3)] = 0 ,$$

where x_j^* and λ^* represent the values of x_j and λ at the optimum, Ψ^*. Note that the inequalities are due to the restriction imposed on x_1, x_2, and x_3 of non-negativity.

Six possible cases may be distinguished[24] in which there will be investment in fixed assets and for which there is a vector x^* and a λ^* satisfying the necessary conditions for optimality stated above. The six cases are numbered below:

1. $x_4 > 0$; $x_1 = 0$; $x_2 = 0$; $x_3 = p$;

2. $x_4 > 0$; $x_1 = 0$; $x_2 = p$; $x_3 = 0$;

3. $x_4 > 0$; $x = p$; $x_2 = 0$; $x_3 = 0$;

4. $x_4 = 0$; $x_1 = p$; $x_2 = 0$; $x_3 = 0$;

5. $x_4 = 0$; $x_1 > 0$; $x_2 > 0$; $x_3 = 0$;

6. $x_4 = 0$; $x_1 > 0$; $x_2 = 0$; $x_3 > 0$.

In the first three cases the firm obtains at least part of its financing from outside sources; in the last three cases, all investment is financed from internal funds.

Using the first order conditions of these six cases the following expressions may be derived for the cost of capital:[25]

(A)
$$c_{K1} = \frac{q}{(1 - u_1)} \left[(\delta - u_1 w_1 d) + m(1 - u_1) - \frac{dq}{q} (1 - u_2) + r(1 - u_1 w_2) \right] ,$$

(B)
$$c_{K2} = \frac{q}{(1 - u_1)} \left[(\delta - u_1 w_1 d) + m(1 - u_1) - \frac{dq}{q} (1 - u_1) - (w_3 u_1 - u_3 = w_3 u_3) + \lambda \right] ,$$

(C)
$$c_{K3} = \frac{q}{(1 - u_1)} \left[(\delta - u_1 w_1 d) + m(1 - u_1) - \frac{dq}{q} (1 - u_2) - (w_3 u_1 - u_3 + w_3 u_3) = r^* (1 - u_1) + (w_4 u_1 - u_4 - w_4 u_4) \right] ,$$

(D)
$$c_{K4} = \frac{q}{(1 - u_1)} \left[(\delta - u_1 w_1 d) + m(1 - u_1) - \frac{dq}{q} (1 - u_2) - (w_3 u_1 - u_3 + w_3 u_3) + g'(X_3) + (w_5 u_1 - u_5 + w_5 u_5) \right] .$$

Expression (A) corresponds to the first three cases, while the remaining three correspond to cases 4, 5, and 6, respectively.

The sources of financing for manufacturing investment in Central America have received very little study. Nevertheless, in this study we consider expression (A) to be sufficient, in the sense that the firms in the region finance at least a portion of their investments in fixed assets with funds from outside the firm.[26]

Note that capital gains are explicitly incorporated into this analysis. Nevertheless, their appropriate treatment remains controversial within the neoclassical theory of the firm. There are basically two alternative viewpoints: one considers capital gains as influencing the cost of capital and, therefore, the level of capital intensity in factor combinations; the other considers them merely transitory.[27]

If we accept the latter approach, then equation (A) reduces to:

$$f'(y) = \frac{q}{(1 - u_1)} \left[(\delta - u_1 w_1 d) + m(1 - u_1) + r(1 - u_1 w_2) \right].$$

We know of no attempt to test these two hypotheses for Central America. It is very likely, however, that capital gains are considered as transitory because of the practical difficulties of making periodic revaluations of assets necessary for purposes of calculating the rate of return to capital after taxes.

This model assumes, furthermore, that the fixed assets have a constant annual replacement rate, δ. It should be noted, however, that the replacement rate in reality is a function of time and that the rate of utilization may in fact be greater or smaller than that assumed. In this case the cost of capital used here would underestimate or overestimate the true cost, respectively.

In Central America, the value of depreciation of assets and the payment of interest are deductible in full for purposes of calculating taxable income. That is, $w_1 = w_2 = 1$. Moreover, given the difficulties of estimating maintenance costs, these may be considered to be insignificant ($m = 0$) without substantially altering the results. Therefore, the following formula results:

$$C_K = \frac{q}{(1 - u_1)} \left[(\delta - u_1 d) + r(1 - u_1) \right].$$

It is this formulation of the cost of capital which is used in this study.

H.   The Form of the Production Function: Empirical Results

As noted in chapter 4, it is of interest to verify whether the production function which characterizes industrial production in Central America is homothetic or not. By homothetic it is meant the marginal rate of substitution (the ratio of labor's to capital's marginal product) does not change with production, when the capital-labor ratio is held constant.

It is important to test the homotheticity assumption for several practical reasons. First, if homotheticity does not hold, the effect of general relative price policies could be diminished or even neutralized by the differential impact that these policies would have on firms of different sizes. Second, a nonhomothetic production function would make it possible to increase the efficiency of factor utilization in manufacturing through changes in the size structure of firms. Third, homotheticity is a necessary condition for estimating the bias of technological change by means of the methodology outlined in chapter 4, because changes in the marginal rate of substitution, holding relative prices constant, could be an indication either of biased technical change or nonhomotheticity. Similarly, testing for homotheticity could help explain the existing wide differences in capital-labor ratios across firms, since these differences could be due either to nonhomotheticity or to the existence of segmented factor markets for firms of different sizes.[28]

The empirical testing for homotheticity was done using two different procedures. The first was to fit equations "a" and "g" of table 1, chapter 4, to different size classes of firms within selected four-digit industries at the regional level.[29] Given the properties of the production functions implicit in these equations, changes in the marginal rate of substitution for a given capital-labor ratio--and therefore nonhomotheticity-- would be detected by differences in the estimated elasticities of substitution between size classes through equation "a," or by differences in the economies of scale parameter of equation "g" among size categories.

Table D-13 presents the results. It is seen that the value of the elasticity of substitution (parameter b) of equation "a" (which appears in the table as "functional form 1") does in fact differ among size classes of firms. The predominant pattern is a lower elasticity of substitution for medium-size establishments than for small or large establishments. On the other hand, the estimates for economies of scale (h) with equation "g" (functional form 3) indicate just the opposite pattern: larger economies of scale for medium-size establishments. Thus, whereas the elasticity of substitution by size classes presents a "u" shaped pattern, the economies of scale accommodate better to an inverted "u" pattern.[30] Nevertheless, statistical testing does not support this "apparent" pattern. Homogeneity tests showed significant differences among size classes in only half of the cases for equation "a" and in less than one-fourth of the cases for equation "g."

From this it can be concluded that even though estimation of a production function for different size classes of establishments suggests the existence of a nonhomothetic production function in Central America at the industry level, the homotheticity assumption cannot be rejected on statistical grounds.

The second procedure to test for homotheticity is to estimate a nonhomothetic production function for different industries. By comparing the results of fitting this function with those of a restricted homothetic function, it can be determined whether or not eliminating the restriction is worthwhile in a statistical sense and, hence, if the nonhomothetic version performs better than the homothetic one, as discussed above.

The nonhomothetic "trans-logarithmic" function (equation "h" of table 1 in chapter 4) was fitted for three-digit industries within each country,[31] and the results were compared with those of equation "g" (Kmenta approximation to the CES production function). In only two of sixty-eight cases for the four countries was homotheticity rejected.[32]

It can thus be concluded that there is insufficient empirical evidence to reject the traditional and convenient assumption of homotheticity for the production function of firms belonging to relatively homogeneous industrial groups. Therefore, both the argument for differential relative price measures applied to size classes of firms and the explanation of large differentials in factor proportions across firms should be based on segmented factor markets and not on the existence of nonhomothetic production functions for Central America. Furthermore, the above conclusion validates the analysis done below on the bias of technical change, for the reason explained before.

On the other hand, working with establishment data for industry as a whole and not for industrial groups, other interesting results are obtained. At this level, homotheticity is rejected in each country and consequently variable economies of scale result.[33] The resulting economies of scale (h_2) functions for each country and for the region are:

Honduras	h_2	$= 0.972 + 0.117 \ln k,$
Nicaragua	h_2	$= 0.995 + 0.025 \ln k - 0.102 \ln L,$
Costa Rica	h_2	$= 0.853 + 0.119 \ln L - 0.014 \ln k,$ and
Central America	h_2	$= 1.045 + 0.009 \ln k - 0.109 \ln L.$

In Honduras economies of scale depend exclusively on the scale of production, since production is a function of the stock of capital (K). In this case economies of scale increase by increasing the size of firms. For Nicaragua and the region as a whole, economies of scale are a function, in addition, of the capital-labor ratio. That is, for a given firm size, larger economies of scale can be attained in the more capital-intensive firms. Finally, for Costa Rica, as usual, the opposite is obtained: larger economies of scale for less-capital-intensive firms of a given size. For illustrative purposes, table D-16 presents economies of scale values for the average small, medium, and large establishment of each country.

It is interesting to note the differences between countries. In Honduras and Costa Rica, one begins with decreasing returns to scale for the small firms and ends with increasing returns for the large firms. In Nicaragua, as well as for the region, just the opposite happens. It can also be seen from the table that capital intensity (K/L) always increases with increases in the average size of firms.

These results may be compatible with those obtained in the previous section if one considers that small- and medium-size establishments predominate in each of the four countries. As a result, constant returns to scale are obtained for Nicaragua and Honduras, increasing returns for Guatemala, and decreasing returns for Costa Rica.

Finally, with the exception of Honduras, the determinant variable for economies of scale is the employment level. The coefficient of $\ln L$ is generally ten times as large as that of $\ln K$.

Summarizing this section, homotheticity of the production function cannot be rejected at the industry level, on the basis of the evidence here presented. For industry as a whole, however, a nonhomothetic production function with variable economies of scale is accepted. The latter results have to be interpreted with caution, given the strong assumptions implicit in the estimation. Notwithstanding, the results so obtained illustrate the effects of the size of firms and of production techniques on economies of scale.

I. Possible Biases in Estimates of the Elasticity of Substitution

The estimates presented in this study of the elasticity of substitution are subject to possible biases. These are primarily related to certain implicit assumptions underlying the model used. The purpose of this section is to examine how changes in these assumptions would affect the estimates obtained. The assumptions examined below concern the structure for the product and factors markets, and the homogeneity of the labor factor.

In the case of perfect competition in the product and labor markets, the first-order condition for profit maximization is:

$$f_L = \frac{1 + 1/e_L}{1 + 1/e} \; \frac{w}{p} \; ,$$

where e_L is the elasticity of supply for labor, e is the elasticity of product demand with respect to price, and f_L is the marginal productivity of labor in physical terms. If either e_L or e differs among industrial sectors but is constant for the establishments within each sector, then we obtain the expression:

$$\ln \frac{pV}{L} = \sigma \ln \left[\frac{\gamma'^{\rho}/h}{h(1 - \delta)} \; \frac{(1 + \frac{1}{e_L})}{(1 + \frac{1}{e})} \right] + \sigma \ln w + (1 - \sigma) \ln p$$
$$+ \frac{1-\sigma}{h} (h - 1) \ln V .$$

As may be seen, in this case the assumption of perfect competition ($e_L = e = \infty$) only affects the constant, not the estimate of σ . Thus, if physical productivity of labor differs from the real salary by a constant, or even if the deviation is variable but uncorrelated with the salary, the estimation of σ by means of regressing the logarithm of value added per worker on the wage will be unbiased. Note also that the same conclusion holds if the degree of imperfection is equal in the two markets ($e_L = e$).

Carrying the argument further, if it is postulated that each firm confronts its own demand curve for its product while the salary is exogenously given (that is, $e_L = \infty$), then the correct expression would be:

$$\ln \frac{pV}{L} = \sigma \ln \frac{\gamma^{\rho}/h}{h(1 - \delta)} + \sigma \ln \frac{1}{(1 + \frac{1}{e})} + \sigma \ln w$$
$$+ (1 - \sigma) \ln p + \frac{1-\sigma}{h} (h - 1) \; \ln V .$$

In this case, the omission of the second term on the right-hand side would introduce a bias in the estimate of σ . The expected value of $\hat{\sigma}$ would be:

$$E(\hat{\sigma}) = \sigma + p_1\sigma ,$$

where p_1 is the coefficient of ln w in the auxiliary regression between $\ln \frac{1}{(1 + (1/e))}$ and the independent variables included. If the excluded term is interpreted as a measure of the degree of monopoly existing, it may be expected that this measure will be correlated positively with the wage rate, from which, given that $\sigma > 0$ the bias in this case will be upwards and $\hat{\sigma}$ will be overestimated.

The equivalent case of different degrees of monopsony can be analyzed similarly. If for each firm the value of the marginal labor product differs from the observed wage rate by the factor $1 + \frac{1}{e_{Li}}$, then the relevant variable for profit maximizing factor determination is the wage rate adjusted by that factor, which gives the marginal cost of labor. However, since only unadjusted wage rates are observed, there is an error in measurement bias involved in the estimation of the elasticity of substitution. Thus, if the correct equation is

$$\ln \left(\frac{pV}{L}\right)_i = \alpha + \sigma \ln \left[\left(1 + \frac{1}{e_{Li}}\right) \frac{w_i}{p}\right] + u_i ,$$

for the case of perfect competition in the product market and constant returns to scale, but one estimates the equation

$$\ln \left(\frac{pV}{L}\right)_i = \alpha' + \sigma' \ln \left(\frac{w_i}{p}\right) + u_i' ,$$

then the expected value of $\hat{\sigma}'$ would be given by

$$E(\hat{\sigma}') = p_2\sigma .$$

The estimate of $\hat{\sigma}$ will be biased upward or downward if p_2, the coefficient of $\ln(w_i/p)$ in the auxiliary regression of the correct variable on the observed one, is greater or smaller than unity. Given that the marginal changes in the correct variable for changes in the observed wage are equal to the adjustment factor, and that $e_L > 0$ (since it characterizes the supply of labor curve), it can be expected that $p_2 > 1$. Therefore, the estimate of the elasticity of substitution will be biased upward.

It must be noted, however, that in Central America the situation is usually one in which a small group of large firms coexist with a large number of small enterprises, in each industrial sector. In these circumstances it is unlikely that industry operates under completely oligopolistic conditions. Instead, it is possible that the large firms exercise partial oligopoly power, in which they coordinate their actions but take into account the competitive behavior of the small firms.[34]

In this situation it is possible that the number of small firms will be insufficient to reduce the price to the cost level of the large firms, or that the small firms will confront cost functions which are progressively unfavorable, or that there exists product differentiation between the large and small firms. The coexistence can also exist for political or institutional reasons, under which it is politically inadvisable for the large firms to eliminate the small ones. In any case, the important point is that the price will be given, from the standpoint of the small firms, and they will produce that quantity at which their marginal cost equals the price. Considering the fact that these small firms constitute the bulk of the observations of the statistical sample used for the estimations of this study, the assumptions of the model concerning market structure may be reasonably valid.

Another issue concerns the fact that, in the absence of an adequate price deflator, the estimates are carried out under the assumption that product price does not vary among firms within the same industrial sector. If the price is not uniform, and if it is correlated with the wage, then the estimator of σ will be biased toward unity. In this case, the omission of the variable p introduces the following bias:

$$E\,(\hat{\sigma}) \;=\; \sigma \;+\; p_2\;(1-\sigma)\;,$$

where p_2 is the coefficient of the regression between ln p and ln w. Given that $\sigma < 1$, if $p_2 > 0$ then $\hat{\sigma}$ will be overestimated.

Finally, it may be demonstrated that the assumption that there do not exist differences in the quality of labor will bias the estimates of σ toward unity. Suppose that the true variable for representing the input of labor is qL, where q is a factor which corrects for differences in quality of labor and L is the total number of persons occupied. In this case, the first order conditions result in the estimating equation:

$$\ln \frac{V}{L} \;=\; a \;+\; \ln w \;+\; (1-\sigma)\;\ln q \;+\; u_8\;.$$

If, when estimating this equation, the final term "ln q" is ignored, then:

$$E\,(\hat{\sigma}) \;=\; \sigma \;+\; p_1\;(1-\sigma)\;,$$

where p_1 is the coefficient of the auxiliary regression between ln q and ln w. Given that the wage rate is likely to be positively correlated with the quality of labor, $\hat{\sigma}$ will be biased toward unity, with the direction of the bias depending on whether σ is less than or greater than unity.

In sum, there exist various conditions of imperfect competition, both in the product market and in the factor market, which are compatible with the model used. However, other considerations introduce biases in the opposite direction from those related to the problem of market imperfection. In the absence of information on the relative magnitudes of these opposing biases, it is impossible to conclude whether the estimates obtained here are on balance biased in one direction or the other.

J.   Statistical Tables

The remainder of this appendix presents statistical tables that accompany the main study, chapter 4 of this book.

Table D-1. Central America: Estimates of the Cost of Capital[a] at the Level of Four-Digit
CIU Industries, 1968
(percentages)

CIU[b]	Guatemala	El Salvador	Honduras	Nicaragua	Costa Rica	Simple Average	Standard Deviation	Coefficient of Variation
3111	15.17	14.12	9.89	14.02	12.90	13.22	2.03	0.15
3112	15.68	14.64	19.09	15.09	14.11	15.72	1.97	0.13
3113	15.31	14.34	14.62	--.--	13.92	14.55	0.58	0.04
3114	--.--	--.--	14.40	15.46	14.02	14.63	0.75	0.05
3115	13.32	12.42	12.86	13.25	11.95	12.76	0.58	0.05
3116	13.16	12.47	13.25	13.22	12.23	12.87	0.49	0.04
3117	14.48	14.02	15.09	14.58	13.73	14.38	0.53	0.04
3118	13.21	12.62	12.14	13.17	12.70	12.77	0.44	0.03
3119	15.30	14.91	15.00	15.44	14.02	14.93	0.55	0.04
3121	14.36	14.03	14.71	13.43	14.22	14.15	0.47	0.03
3122	12.61	12.03	12.49	13.06	12.36	12.51	0.38	0.03
3131	15.11	13.45	14.92	15.16	15.43	14.81	0.78	0.05
3132	14.71	13.79	15.85	--.--	14.19	14.64	0.89	0.06
3133	14.48	13.84	12.75	14.59	--.--	13.92	0.84	0.06
3134	14.45	14.04	15.29	15.27	14.08	14.63	0.62	0.04
3140	14.44	13.19	14.33	--.--	13.13	13.79	0.69	0.05
3211	15.25	14.40	14.78	13.35	13.84	14.32	0.75	0.05
3212	16.91	16.75	17.81	--.--	16.61	17.02	0.54	0.03
3213	17.32	16.42	16.79	16.88	16.71	16.82	0.33	0.02
3215	17.03	16.55	16.39	17.89	17.50	17.07	0.63	0.04
3220	17.30	16.66	16.39	15.65	15.22	16.24	0.82	0.05
3231	15.13	15.01	--.--	15.64	15.41	15.30	0.28	0.02
3232	--.--	--.--	15.08	--.--	--.--	--.--	--.--	--.--
3233	15.81	15.42	14.82	15.60	12.53	14.84	1.34	0.09
3240	16.90	15.81	15.76	16.14	14.60	15.84	0.83	0.05
3311	21.57	21.28	22.38	22.30	21.77	21.86	0.47	0.02
3312	17.22	16.59	17.21	--.--	16.27	16.82	0.47	0.03
3319	17.51	16.38	15.44	16.10	17.00	16.49	0.80	0.05
3320	16.85	16.20	15.04	15.99	14.49	15.71	0.94	0.06
3411	14.04	13.24	--.--	--.--	13.64	13.64	0.40	0.03
3412	14.20	14.02	14.62	15.94	14.12	14.58	0.79	0.05

Table D-1 (Continued)

CIIU[b]	Guatemala	El Salvador	Honduras	Nicaragua	Costa Rica	Simple Average	Standard Deviation	Coefficient of Variation
3419	15.32	14.63	--	14.98	14.73	14.92	0.31	0.02
3420	16.58	15.60	15.58	16.04	16.12	15.98	0.41	0.03
3511	15.51	15.11	15.47	16.32	14.99	15.48	0.52	0.03
3512	15.65	15.20	--	12.70	14.89	14.61	1.31	0.09
3521	15.01	14.35	14.79	--	13.15	14.33	0.83	0.09
3522	14.70	14.11	14.89	13.68	13.65	14.21	0.57	0.04
3523	16.29	15.52	16.16	14.94	14.99	15.58	0.63	0.04
3529	15.71	14.40	15.09	--	13.46	14.67	0.97	0.07
3530	16.90	16.20	16.84	--	--	16.65	0.39	0.02
3540	16.28	15.51	--	--	--	15.90	0.54	0.03
3551	14.45	13.62	14.37	--	13.04	13.87	0.67	0.05
3559	14.32	14.09	14.29	13.71	12.74	13.83	0.66	0.05
3560	16.76	15.75	16.45	15.75	15.30	16.00	0.59	0.04
3610	14.92	13.75	--	13.03	13.88	13.90	0.78	0.06
3620	13.68	12.73	13.42	--	12.25	12.89	0.73	0.06
3691	12.72	12.74	12.45	13.41	12.57	12.97	0.41	0.03
3692	12.72	12.58	13.89	12.80	11.86	12.78	0.37	0.03
3699	14.22	13.39	--	14.05	13.68	13.85	0.32	0.02
3710	13.50	12.43	--	--	12.33	12.75	0.65	0.05
3720	14.38	13.52	--	--	13.43	13.78	0.52	0.04
3811	14.48	13.85	14.97	14.97	15.43	14.68	0.68	0.05
3812	15.32	14.23	14.99	15.07	13.84	14.69	0.62	0.04
3813	14.32	14.03	20.99	14.79	13.77	14.38	0.51	0.04
3819	14.50	14.33	--	14.98	14.89	15.94	2.84	0.15
3821	14.84	15.42	--	--	--	15.13	0.41	0.03
3822	15.40	15.41	14.14	15.06	13.58	14.86	0.87	0.06
3824	13.81	13.63	14.63	--	--	13.86	0.26	0.02
3829	15.41	14.74	--	16.12	13.24	14.83	1.07	0.07
3831	15.26	14.24	--	--	--	14.75	0.72	0.05
3832	17.61	16.54	--	--	--	16.46	1.20	0.07
3833	15.40	15.41	--	15.22	--	15.41	0.07	0.00
3839	14.35	14.14	13.90	15.26	14.63	14.46	0.52	0.04
3841	16.28	15.42	--	--	--	15.85	0.61	0.04

(continued on next page)

Table D-1 (Continued)

CIIU[b]	Guatemala	El Salvador	Honduras	Nicaragua	Costa Rica	Simple Average	Standard Deviation	Coefficient of Variation
3843	15.06	14.28	---	---	---	14.67	0.55	0.04
3844	14.70	13.94	---	---	---	14.32	0.54	0.04
3845	14.72	13.85	---	---	---	14.29	0.62	0.04
3851	16.15	15.41	---	14.77	---	15.44	0.69	0.04
3852	13.93	13.94	14.06	---	---	13.98	0.07	0.01
3901	16.15	15.41	13.39	13.90	---	14.71	1.29	0.09
3909	15.59	14.91	14.53	15.27	13.08	14.68	0.98	0.07
Simple average	15.24	14.59	15.07	14.98	14.22	14.81		
Standard deviation	1.44	1.44	2.04	1.60	1.67	1.42		
Coefficient of variation	0.09	0.10	0.14	0.11	0.12	0.10		

[a]Formula: $c_k = \frac{q}{(1-u_1)} (-u_1 d) + rq$ (see section G of this appendix).

[b]See appendix J for descriptions.

SOURCE: (i) "q": to obtain the prices of capital goods (q), information from the Anuario de Comercio Exterior Centroamericano (SIECA, annual issues) was used to estimate indices of prices for machinery; the Boletín Estadístico del Banco de Guatemala (October–November 1973) provided indices of prices of construction materials; the Central American Industrial Survey of 1969 was used to determine the relative shares of buildings, machinery, and equipment in fixed assets; and SIECA sources provided information on the adjusted tariff on imports, defined as the ad valorem equivalent of import tariff adjusted for exemptions.

(ii) " ": the rate of replacement of fixed assets ( ) is calculated on the basis of estimates of the useful life of different capital goods that appear in: ADR System, Federal Tax Guide Reports, Code Sec. 167. The composition of fixed assets is obtained from the Central American Industrial Survey of 1969.

Table D-1 (Continued)

SOURCE: (Continued)

(iii) "d": the rate of depreciation of fixed assets (d) is estimated as a weighted average of depreciation on buildings, machinery, and equipment based on the depreciation rates allowed under the respective national income tax laws.

(iv) "r": The rate of interest on loans of the banking system (r) is obtained as follows: Guatemala--average rates of interest on new loans, for each industrial activity receiving loans in 1968 (Superintendencia de Bancos de Guatemala); El Salvador and Honduras-- simple average of the minimum and maximum rates charged by the commercial banks in each country; Nicaragua and Costa Rica--the single rate charged by the commercial banks in each country to the industrial sector (Consejo Monetario Centroamericano: ' Boletin Estadistico No. 5, 1968).

(v) "u_1": the tax rate on income (u_1) is estimated as follows: Guatemala--based on data of the Central American Industrial Survey of 1969 and the income tax law; El Salvador, Honduras, Nicaragua, and Costa Rica--an intermediate rate was established on the basis of rates registered in Guatemala and Costa Rica according to information supplied by the central income tax authorities (Direccion General de Impuestos) for each country.

Table D-2. Central America:[a] Labor Demand Functions, 1968, at the Establishment Level by Four-Digit CIIU Categories

CIIU[b]	Number of Observations	Functional Form 1 ln(V/L) = a + b (ln w)			Functional Form 2 ln L = a + b (ln w) + c (ln V)					Functional Form 3 ln w = a + b [ln (V/L)]		
		a	b	R²	a	b	c	R²	h	a	1/b	R²
3111	40	1.4066	0.9734c	0.2868	-0.9925	-0.4050d,e	0.6282c,e	0.8069	2.6658	4.2996	3.3941c,e	0.2868
3112	64	2.0076	0.8478d	0.1850	-1.9177	0.0051e	0.4556c,e	0.6140	2.1949	4.7857	4.5834c,e	0.1850
3113	26	1.2231	1.0031c	0.2970	-1.7144	-0.1166	0.5136c,e	0.7064	1.9470	4.2791	3.3768c,e	0.2970
3114	11	9.0050	-0.1498	0.0066	-2.1880	0.2259f	0.4017d,e	0.4709	2.4894	6.7912	-22.845c,e	0.0066
3115	13	4.1361	0.5774	0.2604	-2.0084	-0.3305f	0.6827c,f	0.7667	1.4648	3.4418	2.2175c,f	0.2604
3116	142	4.8419	0.5235c,e	0.1394	-0.9659	-0.2014d,e	0.4624c,e	0.4460	3.0598	4.2275	3.7542c,e	0.1394
3117	294	3.0154	0.6534c,e	0.1983	-0.8849	-0.3853c,e	0.5911c,e	0.5577	2.9869	4.3058	3.2957c,e	0.1983
3118	33	4.0833	0.6445c	0.2645	0.5798	-0.4783c,e	0.5465c,e	0.5266	7.6496	3.4088	2.4369c,e	0.2645
3119	40	2.5159	0.7603c	0.3127	-1.6674	-0.4077d,e	0.7015c,e	0.7493	2.0160	3.3736	2.4316c,e	0.3127
3121	93	3.3774	0.6601c,f	0.1540	-1.3011	-0.1901e	0.4910c,e	0.5523	2.0367	4.7377	4.2867c,e	0.1540
3122	22	-0.7997	1.3703c	0.3005	-1.1717	-0.3863	0.5648c,e	0.6558	n.a.	4.9081	4.5593c,e	0.3005
3131	27	9.0832	0.0950e	0.0042	-5.6858	0.1760e	0.5919c,e	0.6979	1.6895	6.1489	22.7946c,e	0.0042
3132	9	-0.9023	1.4696	0.4414	0.4813	-0.2723	0.3537d,e	0.6646	n.a.	3.7588	3.3293c,e	0.4414
3133	6	0.3907	1.2094	0.6426	3.4717	-0.7207c	0.4573c,e	0.9696	-2.0604	2.5421	1.8819c,e	0.6426
3134	36	-2.2963	1.5422c	0.3829	-0.8844	-0.2802e	0.5220c,e	0.7614	1.9157	4.6372	4.0277c,e	0.3829
3140	27	0.7540	0.9993c	0.6181	-0.3419	-0.3478c,e	0.5490c,e	0.9143	3.2416	1.7375	1.6168c,e	0.6181
3211	57	3.5799	0.5962c,f	0.1978	-1.2390	-0.2772d,e	0.6198c,e	0.7463	2.1097	4.0032	3.0151c,e	0.1978
3212	23	-2.2497	1.1692d	0.1846	-3.4538	0.3662e	0.3747c,e	0.5290	2.6688	5.2910	6.3335c,e	0.1846
3213	82	5.3552	0.2987d,e	0.0634	-3.2349	-0.1160e	0.6854c,e	0.7907	1.4500	4.9079	4.7119c,e	0.0634
3215	16	3.2622	0.7574c	0.6054	-2.3088	-0.5390	0.7915c	n.a.	n.a.	-0.3238	1.2510c	0.6054
3220	160	2.9471	0.6663c,e	0.1795	-1.7208	-0.2726c,e	0.6307c,e	0.7322	2.0313	4.3792	3.7122c,e	0.1795
3231	33	3.3389	0.6273c	0.2203	-2.2254	-0.0152e	0.4959c,e	0.6986	2.0165	3.7627	2.8471c,e	0.2203
3232	11	-3.0038	1.6159d	0.5281	0.3029	-0.7309	0.6927c	0.6081	n.a.	4.0308	3.0604c,e	0.5281
3233	23	4.5139	0.4276e	0.1315	-0.6113	-0.0706e	0.3448c,e	n.a.	2.9002	4.1807	3.2522c,e	0.1315
3240	128	4.6591	0.3815c,e	0.1079	-2.8764	-0.1145e	0.6392c,e	0.6592	1.5645	4.3553	3.5362c,e	0.1079
3311	155	2.6722	0.6924c,e	0.2408	-0.5418	0.4307c,e	0.6270c,e	0.6400	2.9002	3.9492	2.8760c,e	0.2408
3312	9	-6.3863	1.9677	0.2801	4.3582	-0.8757	0.4338c,e	0.7529	n.a.	5.6500	7.0269c,e	0.2801
3319	21	-1.4925	1.3971c	0.3416	1.1411	-0.6168	0.5312c,e	0.6997	n.a.	4.4523	4.0898c,e	0.3416

Table D-2   (Continued)

CIIU[b]	Number of Observations	Functional Form 1 $\ln\left(\frac{V}{L}\right) = a + b\,(\ln w)$ a	b	R^2	Functional Form 2 $\ln L = a + b\,(\ln w) + c\,(\ln V)$ a	b	c	R^2	h	Functional Form 3 $\ln w = a + b\left[\ln\left(\frac{V}{L}\right)\right]$ a	1/b	R^2
3320	95	3.8588	0.5385[c,e]	0.2775	-2.3402	-0.3710[c,e]	0.7351[c,e]	0.6619	1.7275	2.8441	1.9402[c,e]	0.2775
3412	23	7.6636	0.0335[e]	0.0010	-3.4959	0.0228[e]	0.6025[c,e]	n.a.	1.6598	6.2672	33.9905[c,e]	0.0010
3419	13	2.4230	0.8746	0.2972	0.8887	-0.2375	0.3158[e]	0.1455	n.a.	3.8314	2.9424[c,e]	0.2972
3420	141	3.1747	0.6478[c,e]	0.1428	-2.1266	-0.2022[e]	0.6031[c,f]	0.5796	1.6581	5.0558	4.5368[c,e]	0.1428
3511	24	-3.6983	1.6846[c,f]	0.6663	1.2585	-0.6675	0.5725[c,f]	0.5236	n.a.	3.6973	3.5280[c,e]	0.6663
3512	11	-2.7194	1.7445[d]	0.4886	7.0740	-1.0681[c]	0.2522[c,e]	0.8154	0.0835	4.4426	3.5700[c,e]	0.4886
3521	9	5.8816	0.3885	0.0600	-3.8164	0.2165[e]	0.4516[c,e]	0.7769	2.2143	5.4718	6.5172[c,e]	0.0600
3522	46	3.8401	0.6933[c]	0.1442	-1.2989	-0.0035[e]	0.3617[c,e]	0.4072	2.7647	5.0235	4.8075[c]	0.1442
3523	63	3.7092	0.6803[c]	0.1340	0.0489	-0.3645[d,e]	0.4657[c,e]	0.4840	6.2796	5.2437	5.0751[c,e]	0.1340
3529	19	0.9031	1.0999[d]	0.3180	-1.1055	-0.5107	0.6539[c,f]	0.6487	n.a.	4.0717	3.4594[c,e]	0.3180
3551	19	3.5578	0.7335	0.1978	-1.8800	-0.0888[e]	0.4693[c,e]	0.6815	2.1308	4.3637	3.7076[c,e]	0.1978
3559	18	0.6835	1.0835[c]	0.5222	-0.2976	-0.5639[d]	0.6420[c,e]	n.a.	5.5839	2.8747	2.0751[c,e]	0.5222
3560	51	3.0289	0.7496[c]	0.2387	-1.0420	-0.4270[d,e]	0.6304[c,e]	0.6290	2.8171	4.1490	3.1397[c,e]	0.2387
3610	10	-2.5063	1.5013[c]	0.8025	1.8686	-0.6832[d]	0.5482[c,e]	0.8248	-2.3467	2.5724	1.8707[c,e]	0.8025
3620	9	2.2929	0.8128[c]	0.8016	-1.2190	-0.6431[c,f]	0.7953[c,e]	0.9380	-2.3449	-0.9799	1.0142[c]	0.8016
3791	27	4.6892	0.4135[f]	0.1310	-3.8478	-0.0740[e]	0.7085[c,e]	0.9036	1.4114	4.1307	3.1564[c,e]	0.1310
3692	13	-1.8618	1.3700[c]	0.7799	1.2304	-0.7844[c]	0.6985[c,e]	0.8964	-2.5099	2.5280	1.7569[c,e]	0.7799
3699	93	3.8282	0.5486[c,e]	0.1469	-1.5406	0.2732[c,e]	0.5968[c,e]	0.7581	2.2460	4.5061	3.7333[c]	0.1447
3710	8	3.3301	0.7069[d]	0.5181	-2.8286	-0.6122	0.9047[c]	0.8831	n.a.	0.7357	1.8646[c]	0.5131
3720	7	5.4262	0.3029[f]	0.2044	-2.5159	-0.2981[e]	0.7013[c]	0.9074	1.4259	-1.1406	1.0000[c]	0.0044
3811	32	-4.7275	1.8042	0.6216	-0.8763	-0.4480	0.6410	0.9813	n.a.	4.2505	2.9826[c,e]	0.6216
3812	54	2.6210	0.7545[c]	0.2385	-1.6702	-0.3609[f]	0.6593[c,e]	0.6360	1.5168	4.1647	3.1631[c,e]	0.2385
3813	45	1.5088	0.9396[c]	0.3376	-0.7396	-0.3665[d,e]	0.5718[c,e]	0.7053	3.0857	3.8218	2.7839[c,e]	0.3376
3819	12	5.8629	0.3155[e]	0.0463	-4.1494	-0.1328[e]	0.7339[c,e]	0.6647	1.3626	5.4621	6.8194[c,e]	0.0463
3822	9	6.6640	0.8690[c]	0.5396	-2.4687	-0.1475	0.5991	0.7183	n.a.	2.0946	1.6103[c]	0.5396
3824	13	6.4213	0.1513	0.0199	-4.0501	-0.1187	0.7498	0.4816	n.a.	5.7898	7.6260[c,f]	0.0199
3829	8	0.4900	0.1565	0.2482	1.6587	-0.4732	0.4017[c,f]	0.5041	n.a.	4.8568	4.2566[c,e]	0.2482
3831		1.9774	0.7850	0.3200	0.4487	-0.2356	0.3405[f]	n.a.	n.a.	3.5259	2.4528[c]	0.3290

(continued on next page)

Table D-2 (Continued)

CIIU[b]	Number of Observations	Functional Form 1 $\ln\left(\frac{V}{L}\right) = a + b\,(\ln w)$			Functional Form 2 $\ln L = a + b\,(\ln w) + c\,(\ln V)$				Functional Form 3 $\ln w = a + b\,[\ln\left(\frac{V}{L}\right)]$			
		a	b	R^2	a	b	c	R^2	h	a	1/b	R^2
3832	12	0.0568	1.2299[d]	0.4272	3.3718	-1.0209[d]	0.5910[c,e]	0.7726	0.0486	3.9779	2.8789[c,e]	0.4272
3833	6	17.6409	-1.5251	0.1567	-4.7982	0.2442	0.5694	0.4147	n.a.	7.3704	9.7371[c,e]	0.1567
3839	21	2.5280	0.8560[d]	0.2011	-1.7511	-0.0932[e]	0.4665[c,e]	0.6112	2.1436	4.7435	4.2580[c,e]	0.2011
3843	16	4.5364	0.5210	0.0626	3.9492	-0.5491	0.2094[e]	0.3612	n.a.	5.6157	8.3209[c,e]	0.0626
3901	14	10.0429	-0.3908	0.0344	-2.1542	0.1547[e]	0.3464[e]	0.4604	2.8868	7.3346	-11.3469[c,e]	0.0344
3909	38	2.3704	0.7834[c]	0.2885	-0.9995	-0.2342[e]	0.5028[c,e]	0.6370	1.9889	3.7386	2.7157[c,e]	0.2835

n.a. = not available.

[a] Excludes El Salvador.
[b] See appendix J for description of categories.
[c] and [d] Significantly different from zero at 1 percent and 5 percent level, respectively.
[e] and [f] Significantly different from unity at 1 percent and 5 percent level, respectively.

SOURCE: Calculated from the Central American Industrial Survey of 1969.

Table D-3. Principal Results of Labor Absorption Functions: Estimates at the Establishment Level by Four-Digit CIIU Industry Groups, by Country (Functional Form 1)[a]

CIIU[b]	Guatemala		Honduras		Nicaragua		Costa Rica	
	b	R^2	b	R^2	b	R^2	b	R^2
3111	0.8948	0.2118	1.1219[c]	0.4377	1.5574[c]	0.6282	-0.9836	0.3143
3112	0.7417[d]	0.2184	1.4168[d]	0.7625	2.6793	0.4829	-1.2891	0.1361
3113	0.7563	0.2297	n.a.	n.a.	n.a.	n.a.	1.6986[d]	0.4941
3116	0.5488	0.1606	1.9281[c]	0.7128	0.4757[c,f]	0.1528	0.6910[d]	0.1602
3117	0.6543[d,f]	0.2403	0.9208[d]	0.3217	0.0286[f]	0.0004	0.7036[d,e]	0.2001
3118	-0.3412[f]	0.1594	n.a.	n.a.	n.a.	n.a.	0.9426	0.1483
3119	0.5848[d,e]	0.3371	n.a.	n.a.	0.5971	0.2433	1.5943[c]	0.3844
3121	0.5744[c]	0.1194	0.9621[c]	0.2990	n.a.	n.a.	-0.1463	0.0037
3122	1.4586	0.2364	n.a.	n.a.	n.a.	n.a.	n.a.	n.a.
3131	-0.4101	0.0494	0.3523	0.0427	n.a.	n.a.	n.a.	n.a.
3132	1.6425	0.5068	n.a.	n.a.	n.a.	n.a.	0.5801	0.1116
3134	2.0827	0.3521	n.a.	n.a.	1.3713[c]	0.4389	n.a.	n.a.
3140	1.4829[d,e]	0.7285	0.8090	0.4834	n.a.	n.a.	0.4925	0.0584
3211	0.5448[c,e]	0.1501	n.a.	n.a.	0.2320	0.0570	-1.4444[e]	0.3552
3212	1.3682	0.1656	n.a.	n.a.	n.a.	n.a.	0.1669	0.0352
3213	0.3028[c,f]	0.0672	n.a.	n.a.	n.a.	n.a.	n.a.	n.a.
3215	0.7464	0.6005	n.a.	n.a.	n.a.	n.a.	0.2598[f]	0.0342
3220	0.5303[c,e]	0.1229	0.7027[d]	0.1588	0.7574[d]	0.4180	0.0592[e]	0.0071
3231	0.1263	0.0067	n.a.	n.a.	1.1229[d]	0.8660	n.a.	n.a.
3232	n.a.	n.a.	1.5942[c]	0.5718	n.a.	n.a.	1.0875[c]	0.5803
3233	-0.0104[e]	0.0001	n.a.	n.a.	0.3091[d,f]	0.2092	0.3453[e]	0.0831
3240	0.2885[f]	0.0368	0.4933[d,f]	0.5274	1.0224[d]	0.4743	0.9951[c]	0.2370
3311	0.2744	0.0447	0.8931[d]	0.4685	n.a.	n.a.	n.a.	n.a.
3319	3.1443	0.5226	0.6600	0.1788	0.8759[d]	0.5724	0.9207[d]	0.5540
3320	0.1276[f]	0.0283	0.7709[d]	0.3759	n.a.	n.a.	n.a.	n.a.
3412	-0.0641[e]	0.0073	n.a.	n.a.	n.a.	n.a.	n.a.	n.a.
3419	n.a.	n.a.	n.a.	n.a.	0.1621	0.0515	0.6322	0.1690
3420	0.4588[f]	0.0950	1.1612[d]	0.2253	0.6057	0.1249	n.a.	n.a.
3511	1.3938[d]	0.5004	n.a.	n.a.	1.5175	0.4368	n.a.	n.a.
3512	n.a.	n.a.	n.a.	n.a.	1.1794	0.1152	n.a.	n.a.
3522	0.7674	0.1434	1.0644[c]	0.3782	0.0706	0.0016	0.3746	0.0662
3523	0.8805[d]	0.4269	-0.2701[e]	0.0698	n.a.	n.a.	0.4524	0.0217
3529	2.1430	0.6336	n.a.	n.a.	n.a.	n.a.	n.a.	n.a.
3551	0.3362	0.0549	n.a.	n.a.	n.a.	n.a.	n.a.	n.a.

(continued on next page)

Table D-3 (Continued)

CIIU[b]	Guatemala b	Guatemala R^2	Honduras b	Honduras R^2	Nicaragua b	Nicaragua R^2	Costa Rica b	Costa Rica R^2
3559	1.0314	0.3582	n.a.	n.a.	n.a.	n.a.	n.a.	n.a.
3560	0.3681[e]	0.0992	0.7305	0.0260	1.5411[d]	0.6471	1.2028[c]	0.4418
3610	1.2814[d]	0.8940	n.a.	n.a.	n.a.	n.a.	n.a.	n.a.
3620	0.8043[d]	0.8348	n.a.	n.a.	n.a.	n.a.	0.2535	0.0228
3691	0.1826[e]	0.1168	n.a.	n.a.	n.a.	n.a.	n.a.	n.a.
3692	1.4519[d]	0.8630	0.9673[d]	0.4332	-0.4436[c]	0.0615	n.a.	n.a.
3699	0.3083[f]	0.0565	n.a.	n.a.	n.a.	n.a.	n.a.	n.a.
3710	0.5800	0.0565	1.0439	0.3101	n.a.	n.a.	0.9090	0.4885
3812	0.2068[e]	0.0205	2.1128[c]	0.3614	1.2212[c]	0.6846	0.6459	0.4258
3813	0.4570[e]	0.1510	n.a.	n.a.	n.a.	n.a.	0.0100[f]	0.0001
3819	0.7162	0.1606	n.a.	n.a.	n.a.	n.a.	n.a.	n.a.
3821	-0.0947	0.0020	n.a.	n.a.	n.a.	n.a.	0.8072	0.3046
3822	n.a.	n.a.	n.a.	n.a.	n.a.	n.a.	n.a.	n.a.
3824	0.1860	0.0386	n.a.	n.a.	n.a.	n.a.	0.1000	0.0028
3829	n.a.	n.a.	n.a.	n.a.	n.a.	n.a.	n.a.	n.a.
3831	0.7881	0.1069	n.a.	n.a.	n.a.	n.a.	n.a.	n.a.
3832	0.9693	0.5825	n.a.	n.a.	n.a.	n.a.	0.0446	0.0005
3839	1.1485	0.3785	n.a.	n.a.	n.a.	n.a.	n.a.	n.a.
3843	0.3174	0.0288	n.a.	n.a.	n.a.	n.a.	n.a.	n.a.
3901	-0.6039	0.0957	n.a.	n.a.	1.2212[c]	0.6846	n.a.	n.a.
3909	0.5286	0.0870	1.3848	0.4508	n.a.	n.a.	0.4064	0.2391

[a] $\ln(\frac{V}{L}) = a + b \ln (w)$. Results are reported here only for the substitution parameter "b" and for the multiple regression coefficient, "R^2." Complete results, including corresponding country estimates for Functional Form 2, appear in Charles R. Frank, Jr., Max A. Soto, and Carlos A. Sevilla, Desempleo y Subempleo en Centroamerica, SIECA: Estudios Proyecto SIECA/Brookings, Tomo III (Guatemala City: SIECA, 1977), Cuadro 3 - Cuadro 6, Apendice 5.

[b] See appendix J for a description of categories.

[c] and [d] Different from zero at the 5 percent and 1 percent level, respectively.

[e] and [f] Different from unity at the 5 percent and 1 percent level, respectively.

SOURCE: Calculated from the Central American Industrial Survey of 1969.

559

Table D-4. Guatemala: Elasticity of Substitution, Economies of Scale, and Some Technical Relationships of the Manufacturing Sector at the Establishment Level by Three-Digit CIIU Industries, 1968

CIIU[a]	Description	Elasticity of Substitution (b)	Economies of Scale (h)	K/L[b]	V/K[b]	V/L[b]	Average[c] Remuneration	Percentage of Manufacturing Employment
b = 0								
323		0.0976[g]	0.1037[g]	2,212	0.937	2,073	667	1.23
332		-0.1276[g]	-0.0528[g]	1,227	1.519	1,865	848	1.64
324		0.2885[g]	0.1010[g]	560	2.248	1,261	697	3.43
356		0.3681[f]	-0.0693[g]	2,505	1.392	3,488	1,050	1.79
331		0.3762[g]	0.3269[d,g]	1,299	1.150	1,494	488	4.43
								12.58
0 < b < 1								
321		0.4299[e,g]	0.1327[g]	2,980	0.885	2,638	733	21.62
342		0.4588[d,g]	0.0962[g]	1,658	1.682	2,791	965	4.37
322		0.5303[d,f]	0.4481[e,g]	604	2.667	1,612	639	2.60
381		0.6168[e,f]	0.1671[g]	2,060	1.309	2,698	791	5.43
369		0.6249[e,f]	0.1631[g]	2,295	1.481	3,400	937	5.25
311		0.6285[e,g]	0.2098[e,g]	4,312	1.002	4,323	827	21.93
								61.20
b = 1								
312		0.6529[e]	0.3170[d,g]	3,462	1.145	3,965	817	3.53
352		0.8915[e]	0.2908[g]	6,249	1.645	10,286	1,150	3.79
361/362		1.0849[e]	-0.2786					1.82
383		1.0959[e]	0.5114[d,h]	1,584	4.759	7,540	1,041	1.64
313		1.4079[d]	0.2025[g]	5,086	2.663	13,549	987	3.29
								14.07
b > 1								
314		1.4829[e,f]		2,903	3.437	9,981	1,000	2.22
351		1.7588[e,f]	-0.3725	4,832	0.630	3,044	1,041	0.87
								3.09

(continued on next page)

Table D-4 (Continued)

CIU[a] Description	Elasticity of Substitution (b)	Economies of Scale (h)	K/L[b]	V/K[b]	V/L[b]	Average[c] Remuneration	Percentage of Manufacturing Employment
b (Inconclusive)							
390	0.2360	-0.0194[g]	1,616	1.340	2,166	629	0.91
341	0.2385	0.3231[f]	4,641	0.898	4,169	681	2.19
384	0.4699	-0.4948	2,382	1.499	3,572	531	0.97
355	0.5256	0.5104[e,f]	5,561	2.029	11,288	1,003	2.09
371	0.5800	n.a.	8,235	0.395	3,255	675	1.38
382	0.6158	0.1359[g]	1,756	1.203	2,113	999	0.84
							8.38

[a]See appendix J for descriptions of categories.
[b]Definitions: V = value added; L = production workers; and K = fixed assets at beginning of period.
[c]Includes wages, salaries, and other payments to production workers.
[d]and[e]Significantly different from zero at 5 percent and 1 percent level, respectively.
[f],[g]and[h]Significantly different from unity at 5 percent, 1 percent, and 10 percent level, respectively.

SOURCE: Calculated from the Central American Industrial Survey of 1969.

Table D-5. Honduras: Elasticity of Substitution, Economies of Scale, and Some Technical Relationships of the Manufacturing Sector at the Establishment Level by Three-Digit CIIU Industries, 1968

CIIU[a] Description	Elasticity of Substitution (b)	Economies of Scale (h)	K/L[b]	V/K[b]	V/L[b]	Average[c] Remuneration	Percentage of Manufacturing Employment
0 < b < 1							
324	0.4933[e,g]	-0.0473[g]	463	2.364	1,095	678	1.38
b = 1							
322	0.7027[e]	0.0767[g]	740	1.693	1,254	639	9.89
332	0.7709[e]	-0.0483[g]	602	1.906	1,148	831	3.01
331	0.8238[e]	0.0269[g]	1,330	1.222	1,626	765	21.87
321	0.8774[e]	n.a.	7,111	0.480	3,416	1,193	4.83
352	0.9212[e]	-0.1333[g]	3,963	1.134	4,497	868	5.21
312	0.9275[d]	0.0923[g]	8,862	0.478	4,244	1,145	1.93
313	0.9940[e]	0.1530[f]	17,690	2.582	45,682	1,247	2.79
369	1.1138[e]	0.0056[g]	5,461	0.690	3,770	996	6.67
311	1.1199[e]	0.0475[g]	10,391	0.494	5,138	988	19.36
342	1.1612[e]	0.2229[g]	2,526	0.725	1,831	1,113	5.80
381	1.2743[d]	0.0838[g]	2,207	4.175	9,215	936	4.93
323	1.4324[e]	0.0677	3,101	0.755	2,343	872	1.34
							87.63
b (Inconclusive)							
356	0.7305	n.a.	5,409	0.826	4,469	695	2.10
390	0.7432	0.0369	1,433	1.352	1,938	949	0.71
314	0.8090	n.a.	8,735	1.420	12,408	1,484	2.00
355	0.8734	n.a.	3,545	1.478	5,242	823	1.65
							6.46

[a] See appendix J for descriptions of categories.
[b] Definitions: V = value added; L = production workers; and K = fixed assets at beginning of period.
[c] Includes wages, salaries, and other payments to production workers.
[d] and [e] Significantly different from zero at 5 percent and 1 percent level, respectively.
[f] and [g] Significantly different from unity at 5 percent and 1 percent level, respectively.

SOURCE: Calculated from the Central American Industrial Survey of 1969.

Table D-6. Nicaragua: Elasticity of Substitution, Economies of Scale, and Some Technical Relationships of the Manufacturing Sector at the Establishment Level by Three-Digit CIIU Industries, 1968

CIIU[a] Description	Elasticity of Substitution (b)	Economies of Scale (h)	K/L[b]	V/K[b]	V/L[b]	Average[c] Remuneration	Percentage of Manufacturing Employment
b = 0							
369	-0.0980[g]	-0.2360[f,h]	9,883	0.503	4,972	1,131	4.83
321	-0.0430[h]	-0.1380[h]	6,508	0.307	2,000	892	18.21
							23.04
0 < b < 1							
324	0.3091[e,h]	0.0571[h]	934	3.009	2,811	903	5.04
311	0.4758[e,h]	0.0084[h]	6,457	1.156	7,468	972	26.93
							31.97
312	0.7207[d]	0.1320[h]	4,678	1.378	6,449	1,120	2.15
322	0.7574[e]	0.1293[h]	852	2.110	1,798	807	6.29
332	0.8759[e]	0.2506[g]	852	3.058	2,607	943	1.83
331	0.9664[e]	0.0749[h]	2,274	1.732	3,940	961	6.21
							16.48
b = 1							
390	1.0034[e]	0.2254	6,990	0.657	4,596	1,114	1.05
323	1.1306[e]	n.a.	2,842	1.445	4,108	1,145	1.70
356	1.5411[e]	-0.3879[h]	4,767	1.054	5,026	944	2.71
313	1.5712[e]	0.1679[h]	7,589	1.679	12,749	1,196	5.88
							11.34
b (Inconclusive)							
352	0.2703	-0.0416[h]	3,920	1.734	6,801	922	4.04
341	0.3967	-0.2499[g]	4,854	1.281	6,223	1,125	1.44
342	0.6057	-0.0426[h]	3,180	1.517	4,827	1,483	2.74
381	0.6523	-0.1281[h]	7,421	0.779	5,782	1,583	5.73
351	0.6946	-0.9181	31,742	0.500	15,894	1,781	1.28
							15.23

[a]See appendix J for descriptions of categories.
[b]Definitions: V = value added; L = production workers; K = fixed assets at beginning of period.
[c]Includes wages, salaries, and other payments to production workers.
[d,e,f]Significantly different from zero at 5 percent and 1 percent level, respectively.
[g,h]Significantly different from unity at 5 percent and 1 percent level, respectively.

SOURCE: Calculated from the Central American Industrial Survey of 1969.

Table D-7. Costa Rica: Elasticity of Substitution, Economies of Scale, and Some Technical Relationships of the Manufacturing Sector at the Establishment Level by Three-Digit CIIU Industries, 1968

CIIU[a] Description	Elasticity of Substitution (b)	Economies of Scale (h)	K/L[b]	V/K[b]	V/L[b]	Average[c] Remuneration	Percentage of Manufacturing Employment
b = 0							
321	0.2461[f]	-0.1731[g]	3,648	0.500	1,826	847	12.39
322	0.2598[g]	-0.0845[g]	945	2.224	2,103	609	10.81
381	0.3189[g]	-0.0195[g]	2,916	1.149	3,352	941	4.60
369	0.3399[f]	-0.0159[g]	3,921	0.807	3,166	860	3.69
324	0.3453[f]	-0.1391[g]	1,456	1.078	1,570	789	3.47
323	0.4158[f]	-0.3447[g]	1,833	1.427	2,617	913	1.11
							36.07
0 < b < 1							
311	0.6538[e,g]	-0.0346[g]	3,687	0.898	3,313	819	28.36
b = 1							
332	0.9707[e]	-0.3669[d,g]	1,165	1.796	2,094	1,033	2.60
331	1.0289[e]	-0.3174[g]	1,549	0.799	1,238	834	3.43
356	1.2028[d]	-0.2135[g]	4,365	0.758	3,312	962	1.88
355	1.2099[d]	n.a.	15,290	0.635	9,715	1,847	1.12
							9.03
b (Inconclusive)							
383	0.2277	-0.0483[f]	3,119	1.475	4,603	955	3.29
312	0.2431	-0.5827[d,h]	3,863	1.029	3,976	1,208	1.34
341	0.2763	0.2077[g]	4,691	0.841	3,947	1,003	1.95
382	0.3653	-0.3832[f]	1,621	1.474	2,390	955	2.54
352	0.3744	-0.5953[d,h]	3,529	10.554	37,256	1,100	3.36
390	0.4064	n.a.	1,167	2.222	2,594	822	0.65
342	0.6322	0.8006[g]	1,341	3.707	2,289	1,017	5.42
313	1.0667	0.7086[e]	4,165	5.308	22,113	916	1.95
351	2.5674	n.a.	2,382	11.789	28,091	898	1.01
							21.51

[a] See appendix J for descriptions of categories.

[b] Definitions: V = value added; L = production workers; K = fixed assets at beginning of period.

[c] Includes wages, salaries, and other payments to production workers.

[d,e] Significantly different from zero at 5 percent and 1 percent level, respectively.

[f,g,h] Significantly different from unity at 5 percent, 1 percent, and 10 percent level, respectively.

SOURCE: Calculated from the Central American Industrial Survey of 1969.

Table D-8. Elasticity of Substitution for 1965, 1968, and 1971 by Three-Digit
CIIU Industrial Categories, Estimated at the Establishment Level

CIIU[a]	1965	1968	1971	Constant Capital Model[b]	Variable Capital Model[c]
311	$0.6810^{e,f}$	$0.6285^{e,g}$	0.8677^{e}	$0.6952^{d,f}$	$0.3908^{d,f}$
312	1.3927^{e}	0.6529^{e}	2.5022^{e}	1.0157^{d}	0.6133^{d}
313	1.6607^{e}	1.4079^{d}	1.1628^{e}	1.2628^{d}	0.9405^{d}
314	$1.7333^{e,f}$	$1.4829^{e,f}$	1.1353^{e}	1.4642^{f}	1.6813^{d}
322	$0.5378^{d,f}$	$0.5303^{d,f}$	0.0164^{g}	0.6925^{d}	$0.4795^{d,f}$
331	1.0994^{e}	0.3762^{g}	1.0090^{e}	0.7370^{d}	1.1408^{d}
332	1.3424^{d}	0.1276^{g}	-0.3962	0.5626^{d}	0.0763_{f}
341	1.0360^{e}	0.2385	1.1085	0.7864^{d}	0.6155
342	0.6738^{d}	$0.4588^{d,g}$	1.6695	$0.6136^{d,f}$	$0.3568^{d,f}$
351	0.6256	$1.7588^{e,f}$	1.5934	1.4592	0.9924
352	1.0489^{e}	0.8915^{e}	$1.6521^{e,f}$	0.9314^{d}	0.8698^{d}
355	1.5740^{d}	0.5256	0.4069	0.9909^{d}	0.9551^{d}
356	0.7437	0.3681^{f}	0.6793	0.7618^{d}	0.3049^{f}
362	0.5378	0.8044^{e}	1.4194^{e}	0.7947^{d}	0.6217
369	1.2926^{e}	$0.6249^{e,f}$	1.1382^{e}	0.9843^{d}	0.8844^{d}
381	1.2595^{e}	$0.6168^{e,f}$	1.0058^{d}	0.7704^{d}	0.8995^{d}
382	0.7108	0.6158	0.9770^{d}	0.7304^{d}	0.3450
383	2.4237	1.0959	n.a.	1.2413^{d}	0.4234
384	-0.7459^{f}	0.4699	-0.1294	0.7600^{d}	0.3774
390	-0.0699	0.2360	2.0887	0.0889^{f}	0.7743

[a]See appendix J for descriptions of categories.
[b]Equation (2a) of chapter 4.
[c]Equation "f," table 1, chapter 4.
[d,e]Significantly different from zero at the 5 percent and 10 percent level,
respectively.
[f,g]Significantly different from unity at the 5 percent and 10 percent level,
respectively.

SOURCE: Calculated from the Central American Industrial Survey of 1969.

Table D-9. Estimates of the Elasticity of Substitution and
of Economies of Scale: Four Functional Forms for
Each Country, with Observations at the
Aggregate Levels of Four and
Three Digits, 1968

Functional Form 1

$$\ln V/L = a + b(\ln w)$$

Country	Digits	b	R^2
Guatemala	4	$1.6717^{c,e}$	0.2776
Guatemala	3	1.3366^{c}	0.4426
Honduras	4	1.1787^{c}	0.5408
Honduras	3	$1.9212^{c,f}$	0.7536
Nicaragua	4	n.a.	n.a.
Nicaragua	3	1.8372^{c}	0.4660
Costa Rica	4	1.2584^{c}	0.1633
Costa Rica	3	1.2622^{d}	0.1139

Functional Form 2

$$\ln L = a + b(\ln w) + c(\ln V)$$

Country	b	c	h	R^2
Guatemala	-1.0066^{c}	$0.6284^{c,f}$	0.0175	0.7089
Guatemala	-1.3765^{c}	$0.7827^{c,f}$	0.6341	0.8966
Honduras	-0.8888^{c}	$0.7468^{c,f}$	-0.7831	0.6942
Honduras	$-1.6677^{c,e}$	$0.8114^{c,e}$	0.7798	0.8419
Nicaragua	-1.1033^{c}	0.9211^{c}	0.5670	0.8486
Nicaragua	-1.7884^{c}	0.9499^{c}	0.9402	0.8726
Costa Rica	-1.1167^{c}	$0.8313^{c,f}$	0.4088	0.7563
Costa Rica	-1.5787^{b}	0.7539^{c}	0.7016	0.6769

(continued on next page)

Table D-9 (Continued)

Functional Form 3

$$\ln (v/L) = a + h(\ln L) + g_3 \ln (K/L) + g_4 (\ln K/L)^2$$

Country	Digits	h	g_3	g_4	R^2
Guatemala	4	0.1129^f	-0.0261	0.0282^f	0.1313
Guatemala	3	0.0433^f	1.1488	-0.0300^f	0.5319
Honduras	4	-0.0151^f	-0.8874	$0.0923^{c,f}$	0.7368
Honduras	3	0.0673^f	-0.3679	0.0647^f	0.8064
Nicaragua	4	-0.0697^f	0.2370	0.0076^f	0.3613
Nicaragua	3	-0.1427^f	-0.3555	0.0406^f	0.2700
Costa Rica	4	$-0.1753^{b,f}$	-0.6933^b	$0.0802^{c,f}$	0.2914
Costa Rica	3	$-0.2210^{d,f}$	0.6389	-0.0092	0.3118

Functional Form 4

$$\ln V = a + h(\ln L) + l(\ln K) + k(\ln L)^2 + m(\ln K)^2 + n([\ln L][\ln K])$$

Country	h	i	k	m	n	R^2	No. of Obser-vations	Homo-thetic Hypoth-esis[a]
Guatemala	0.7155	-0.1078	-0.7040	0.0303	0.0753	0.6872	67	*
Guatemala	2.5198	-0.2021	-4.3432	0.1641	0.0235	0.9043	27	*
Honduras	1.9014^b	0.1342	0.3524	0.0784^b	-0.2204^c	0.8694	50	*
Honduras	2.2607^b	-0.0135	-0.7002	0.0760	-0.1260	0.9023	22	*
Nicaragua	1.0981	-0.1491	0.1647	-0.0065	0.0712	0.8708	46	*
Nicaragua	2.5536	-0.3184	-4.2061	0.1366	0.1155	0.8732	21	*
Costa Rica	2.0028^b	0.1956	-0.7391^b	0.1062^c	-0.2900^d	0.7924	63	*
Costa Rica	0.4488	-0.1239	0.0506	-0.0033	0.0928	0.6813	25	*

[a] These tests are calculated at the 5 percent level of significance.
* = homotheticity rejected.
[b,c,d] Significantly different from zero at the 5 percent, 1 percent, and 10 percent level, respectively.
[e,f] Significantly different from unity at the 5 percent and 1 percent level, respectively.

SOURCE: Calculated from the Central American Industrial Survey of 1969.

Table D-10. Labor Absorption Functions with Aggregate
Observations at the Level of Three-Digit CIIU
for the Manufacturing Sector, Selected
Countries and Years

Country	Year	Functional Form 1 $\ln (V/L) = a + b (\ln w)$		
		a	b	R^2
Guatemala	1958	-1.4620	1.3609^a	0.3642
Guatemala	1965	-4.2539	$1.7381^{b,c}$	0.6498
Guatemala	1968			
El Salvador	1961	3.6428	0.6179^a	0.0631
Honduras	1966	-3.9059	1.6959^b	0.1724
Honduras	1968			
Nicaragua	1964	-0.5042	1.2679^b	0.3234
Nicaragua	1968			
Costa Rica	1958	-0.2181	1.1877^b	0.2908
Costa Rica	1964	-2.4895	1.4363^b	0.3391
Costa Rica	1968			

NOTE: Except for 1968, the years correspond to the
dates of the industrial censuses in the respective countries.

[a,b]Significantly different from zero at the 5 percent
and 1 percent level, respectively.
[c,d]Significantly different from unity at the 5 percent
and 1 percent level, respectively.

(continued on next page)

Table D-10 (Continued)

Functional Form 2

$$\ln L = a + b (\ln w) + c (\ln V)$$

Country	Year	a	b	c	R^2	h
Guatemala	1958	2.6459	-1.2496^a	0.8649^b	0.8267	0.6488
Guatemala	1965	5.3973	-1.4949^b	0.8105^b	0.8538	0.7231
Guatemala	1968					
El Salvador	1961	-0.8889	-0.7183^b	$0.8517^{b,c}$	0.8683	2.1117
Honduras	1966	5.8662	-1.5640^b	0.7984^b	0.5734	0.7367
Honduras	1968					
Nicaragua	1964	1.7550	-1.2293^b	0.8940^b	0.8625	0.6839
Nicaragua	1968					
Costa Rica	1958	1.3292	-1.0824^b	0.8772^b	0.7181	0.4016
Costa Rica	1964	3.1873	-1.3404^b	0.9074^b	0.8118	0.7861
Costa Rica	1968					

SOURCE: Calculated from industrial censuses and from the Central American Industrial Survey of 1969.

Table D-11. Central America: Kmenta Approximation and
Trans-log Function of the Establishment Level by
Three-Digit CIIU Categories

$$\ln(V/L) = a + h \ln L + g_3 \ln(K/L) + g_4 (\ln K/L)^2$$

CIIU[a]	a	h	g_3	g_4	R^2
311	6.0028	0.1533[d,g]	0.1050	0.0080[g]	0.1531
312	9.1378	0.0929[g]	-0.8759[e]	0.0838[c,g]	0.2155
313	7.6301	0.2578[e,g]	-0.3927	0.0516[e,g]	0.3356
314	19.2239	0.2460[f]	-4.1982	0.3291[f]	0.6758
321	5.1355	0.0911[g]	0.3384	-0.0114[g]	0.0769
322	5.7535	0.1878[d,g]	0.2915	-0.0235[g]	0.0684
323	6.7532	0.1504[g]	-0.1181	0.0210[g]	0.1376
324	7.9123	-0.0219[g]	-0.3523	0.0365[e,g]	0.0270
331	9.0787	0.0722[g]	-1.0155[d]	0.0977[d,g]	0.1887
332	8.4023	-0.1505[e,g]	-0.3433	0.0403[g]	0.0953
341	7.0157	-0.0289[g]	-0.2906	0.0513[g]	0.3480
342	11.5626	0.1138[g]	-1.5193[c]	0.1229[c,g]	0.1665
351	7.8984	-0.5621[e]	0.1316	0.0172[g]	0.2093
352	7.0050	-0.0589[g]	-0.0165	0.0248	0.1999
355	13.5804	0.3897[c,g]	-1.8814[c]	0.1303[c,g]	0.3964
356	2.3904	-0.0858[g]	1.1599	-0.0519[g]	0.1740
361/362	1.6032	-0.1653[f]	1.2508	-0.0535[g]	0.4307
369	5.7004	0.0785[g]	0.0499	0.0226[g]	0.4518
381	5.2811	0.0351[g]	0.3444	-0.0020[g]	0.2079
382					
383	5.4423	0.2193[g]	0.4034	-0.0209[g]	0.0560
384	5.7851	-0.2825[f]	0.1740	0.0288[g]	0.2530
390	5.0688	0.2053[g]	0.3653	-0.0120[g]	0.1693

(continued on next page)

Table D-11 (Continued)

$$\ln V = a + h \ln L + 1 \ln K + k (\ln L)^2 + m (\ln K)^2 + n[(\ln L)(\ln K)]$$

CIIU[a]	a	h	l	k	m	n	R^2	No. of Observations	Homotheticity Hypothesis Rejected[b]
311	9.1151	0.4230[e]	-0.2464[d]	-0.3610[d]	0.0073	0.1750[d]	0.6003	586	*
312	8.3594	2.3722[c]	0.3220[c]	-0.8229	0.0986[d]	-0.3201[c]	0.6284	111	*
313	6.0092	2.7162[d]	0.1912	-0.3634	0.0720[c]	-0.2718	0.7013	77	*
314	19.1633	9.1796[e]	1.0120	-5.5166	0.5159[e]	-1.4294[e]	0.9229	11	*
321	4.2282	1.5693[c]	0.0823	0.2642	0.0103	-0.1036	0.6876	177	*
322	6.1178	1.2366[c]	-0.2234[c]	0.1006	-0.0278	0.1478	0.7372	152	*
323	6.7814	1.4902	-0.2346	-0.1860	0.0091	0.0734	0.6552	68	*
324	8.8792	1.0853[c]	-0.0568	-0.5072[e]	0.0335	0.0090	0.6627	116	*
331	10.3379	1.5502[d]	0.1180	-1.1108[d]	0.0964[d]	-0.1558[c]	0.6550	178	*
332	8.3239	1.3712	-0.0926	-0.3857	0.0348	-0.0207	0.6332	88	*
341	7.1983	0.6410	0.1510	-0.1243	0.0431	-0.1059	0.7489	40	*
342	12.4435	2.1615[c]	0.1794[e]	-1.5804[c]	0.1254	-0.2361[e]	0.6788	130	*
351	5.7216	2.3833	0.0169	0.0064	0.0460	-0.2176	0.2570	29	*
352	6.0383	2.2981[d]	-0.0694	-0.1423	0.0376	-0.1164	0.5922	130	*
355	12.7506	5.7715[d]	0.4674	-2.3787[d]	0.2018[d]	-0.6513[c]	0.7819	39	*
356	6.7424	-3.7896	-0.5798[e]	1.3655	-0.1409	0.6967[e]	0.6772	50	*
361/362	4.2110	-7.9438[c]	-1.9974[e]	3.2889[c]	-0.4589[c]	2.0435[c]	0.8494	15	*
369	5.9843	1.0604[c]	-0.0840	-0.0162	0.0178	0.0132	0.8447	122	*
381	5.9986	0.2627	0.0167	0.3213	-0.0090	0.0030	0.7019	130	*
382									
383	7.0929	1.2346	-0.1739	-0.0568	-0.0025	0.0850	0.5997	44	*
384	3.5151	2.2053	0.3242	0.2065	0.0675	-0.3763	0.3304	35	*
390	3.8637	1.9721	-0.5182	0.3253	-0.0282	0.1753	0.6264	49	*

[a]See appendix J for description.
[b]These tests are at the 5 percent level of significance.
[c,d,e]Significantly different from zero at the 5 percent, 1 percent, and 10 percent level, respectively.
[f,g]Significantly different from unity at the 5 percent and 1 percent level, respectively.

SOURCE: Calculated from the Central American Industrial Survey of 1969.

Table D-12. Economies of Scale by Country and Three-Digit CIIU Industrial Category, with Observations at the Establishment Level, 1968

CIIU[a]	Guatemala	Honduras	Nicaragua	Costa Rica	Average Simple	Average Weighted[b]	Central America[c]
311	0.2098[e,h]	0.0475[h]	0.0884[h]	-0.0346[h]	0.0778	0.0974	0.1533[e,h]
312	0.3170[d,h]	0.0923[h]	0.1320[h]	-0.5829[d,i]	-0.0104	0.1350	0.0929[h]
313	0.2025[h]	0.15309	0.1679[h]	0.7086[e]	0.3080	0.2598	0.2578[f,h]
321	0.1327[h]	--	-0.1380[h]	-0.1731[h]	-0.0595	0.0314	0.0911[h]
322	0.4481[e,h]	0.0767[h]	0.1293[h]	-0.0845[h]	0.1424	0.0622	0.1878[e,h]
323	0.1037[h]	0.0677	--	-0.3447[h]	-0.0578	-0.0454	0.1504[h]
324	0.1010[h]	-0.0473[h]	0.0571[h]	-0.1391[h]	-0.0071	0.0212	-0.0219[h]
331	0.3269[h]	0.0269[h]	0.0749[h]	-0.3174[h]	0.0278	0.0720	0.0722[h]
332	-0.0528[h]	-0.0483[h]	0.25069	-0.3669[d,h]	-0.0544	-0.0881	-0.1505[f,h]
341	0.3231[h]	--	-0.24999[h]	0.2077[h]	0.0936	0.1584	-0.0289[h]
342	0.0962[h]	0.2229[h]	-0.0426[h]	0.0806[h]	0.0893	0.0838	0.1138[h]
351	-0.3725	--	-0.9181	--	-0.6453	-0.8002	-0.5621[f]
352	0.2908[h]	-0.1339[h]	-0.0416[h]	-0.5953[d,i]	-0.1200	0.0404	-0.0589[h]
356	-0.0693[h]	--	-0.38799	-0.2135[h]	-0.2236	-0.2270	-0.0858[h]
369	0.1631[h]	0.0056[h]	-0.2360[f,h]	-0.0159[h]	-0.0208	0.0036	0.0785[h]
381	0.1671[h]	0.0838[h]	-0.1281[h]	-0.0195[h]	0.0517	0.0344	0.0351[h]
382	0.1359[h]	--	--	-0.38329	-0.1237	-0.2178	--
383	0.5114[i]	--	--	0.04839	0.2799	0.3119	0.2193[h]
390	-0.0194[h]	0.0369	0.2254	--	0.0810	0.0640	0.2053[h]

[a]See appendix J for description.
[b]Weighting factor: share of sector in total value added of the sector for the countries included in the average.
[c]Refers to the coefficient of the regression including all establishments of the four countries.
[d,e,f]Significantly different from zero at the 5 percent, 1 percent, and 10 percent level, respectively.
[g,h,i]Significantly different from unity at the 5 percent, 1 percent, and 10 percent level, respectively.

SOURCE: Calculated from the Central American Industrial Survey of 1969.

Table D-13. Central America: Estimates of the Elasticity of Substitution and of Economies of Scale by Size Class of Establishment, and Three Functional Forms, Selected Four-Digit CIIU Categories, with Observations at the Establishment Level, 1968

			Functional Form 1 $\ln L = a + b (\ln w)$			Functional Form 2 $\ln L = a + b (\ln w) + c (\ln v)$				
CIIU[a]	Size Class[b]	No. of Observations	a	b	R^2	a	b	c	R^2	h
3111	1-7	6	-2.1487	1.4777	0.4728	2.4768	-0.4301[f]	0.1989[g]	0.7574	-2.4651
	8-40	17	6.0108	0.2871[f]	0.0644	0.9761	-0.1428[g]	0.2766[c,g]	0.3007	3.6152
	>41	14	0.5161	1.1519[c]	0.3632	1.2015	-0.2306[f]	0.3922[c,g]	0.4959	2.5495
3112	1-7	21	5.6385	0.2305	0.0181	0.5608	0.1121[g]	0.0513[g]	0.2666	-14.5911
	8-40	30	2.3278	0.8029[c]	0.1512	2.8509	-0.1609[g]	0.1077[g]	0.1058	-15.7511
	>41	10	-2.0442	1.4989	0.1766	0.9337	0.0060	0.2654[g]	0.3817	n.a.
3116	1-7	27	8.1103	0.0280[g]	0.0004	1.5928	0.0093[g]	0.0029[g]	0.0020	-152.6441
	8-40	88	3.7430	0.6717[d,f]	0.2013	1.8355	-0.2272[d,g]	0.2305[d,g]	0.2426	235.6067
	>41	19	4.4638	0.6197[c]	0.2654	3.2347	-0.2499[g]	0.2049[g]	0.2003	-16.6647
3117	1-7	105	4.7998	0.3940[d,g]	0.0807	0.4471	0.0091[g]	0.1282[d,g]	0.1504	7.7997
	8-40	121	2.6551	0.7049[d,f]	0.2037	1.3549	-0.3119[d,g]	0.3367[d,g]	0.3578	27.7472
	>41	12	0.7102	0.9919[d]	0.5095	3.5325	-0.2373[g]	0.2029	0.1618	-22.1525
3121	1-7	37	-3.2533	1.6904[d]	0.6034	1.9160	-0.1757[g]	0.0840[g]	0.0738	-8.9862
	8-40	39	4.7427	0.4392[f]	0.0817	1.0288	-0.0487[g]	0.1873[d,g]	0.2364	5.3393
	>41	14	6.4000	0.2563[g]	0.1530	1.4540	-0.0241[g]	0.2388[g]	0.2640	4.5460
3213	1-7	18	3.7812	0.5187[c]	0.2301	-0.3673	0.3150[d,g]	-0.0076[g]	0.5613	2.2287
	8-40	38	5.6346	0.2391[g]	0.0479	0.1382	-0.0300[g]	0.2970[d,g]	0.3184	3.3673
3220	1-7	32	3.5368	0.5255[c]	0.1397	1.2538	0.0249[g]	0.0328[g]	0.0377	124.2153
	8-40	83	3.2781	0.6263[d,f]	0.1601	0.3244	-0.1662[g]	0.3472[d,g]	0.4680	2.8805
	>41	36	6.5033	0.1345[g]	0.0068	-0.8948	-0.0726[g]	0.4921[d,g]	0.5104	2.0322
3311	1-7	26	1.6172	0.8769[d]	0.4044	3.5176	-0.2757[d,g]	-0.0139[g]	0.4625	-2.5014
	8-40	78	5.3207	0.2559[g]	0.0143	0.3755	0.0487[g]	0.2227[d,g]	0.3327	4.4901
	>41	46	2.3579	0.7575[d,f]	0.6033	1.5577	-0.3390[d,g]	0.4334[d,g]	0.3698	7.0032

Table D-13 (Continued)

Functional Form 3

$$\ln (V/L) = a + h (\ln L) + g_3 \ln (K/L) + g_4 (\ln K/L)^2$$

CIU[a]	Size Class[b]	No. of Observations	a	h	g_3	g_4	R^2
3111	1-7	6	-98.0496	0.9862	25.8218	-1.6055	0.0731
	8-40	17	9.7424	0.0328	-0.6343	0.0493	0.0234
	>41	14	10.2748	0.1656	-1.2597	0.1137	0.1840
3112	1-7	21	-6.0399	0.2976	3.1126	-0.1871	0.3393
	8-40	30	-7.6865	-0.2782	4.2767	-0.2782	0.1161
	>41	10	2.5034	-0.0590	0.7197	0.0055	0.7327
3116	1-7	27	3.1979	-0.7091	1.5432	-0.9020	0.0469
	8-40	88	7.0125	-0.0160	0.0047	0.0170	0.1885
	>41	19	9.2412	-0.2798	-0.3558	0.0509	0.5452
3117	1-7	105	6.7618	0.2332	0.0110	0.0037	0.0149
	8-40	121	6.9700	-0.1247	0.0225	0.0120	0.1065
	>41	12	6.5184	-1.1933[e]	0.3441	0.0595	0.7863
3121	1-7	37	10.3436	-0.2636	-1.2263[e]	0.1189[c]	0.2852
	8-40	39	7.9060	0.1951	-0.4498	0.0442	0.0322
	>41	14	-11.2283	0.6089	4.0175	-0.2341	0.2613
3213	1-7	18	0.7106	0.4233	1.5602	-0.1047	0.0619
	8-40	38	5.7925	0.1634	0.0488	0.0114	0.0960
3220	1-7	32	-0.5692	0.1266	2.6614[d]	-0.2376[d]	0.3252
	8-40	83	7.7777	0.3810[c]	-0.6529	0.0620	0.0987
	>41	36	9.3122	-0.0072	-0.7662	0.0712	0.0386
3311	1-7	26	12.8290	-1.4299[e]	-1.1310	0.0944	0.4334
	8-40	78	8.2840	0.3977[e]	-0.9608[c]	0.0352[d]	0.1503
	>41	46	9.8835	-0.0032	-1.4927[d]	0.1580[d]	0.6044

(continued on next page)

Table D-13 (Continued)

CIIU[a]	Size Class[b]	No. of Observations	Functional Form 1 ln L = a + b (ln w)			Functional Form 2 ln L = a + b (ln w) + c (ln v)				
			a	b	R^2	a	b	c	R^2	h
3320	1-7	31	4.3817	0.4821[d,g]	0.3566	1.1848	0.0059[g]	0.0541[g]	0.0568	16.7759
	8-40	47	3.5902	0.5829[d,f]	0.2021	0.6141	-0.3449[d,g]	0.4317[d,g]	0.5259	7.5482
	>41	10	-6.4243	2.0096[d]	0.6877	6.6481	-1.5123[c]	0.6873[c]	0.5909	0.6209
3420	1-7	42	2.9467	0.6902[c]	0.1219	2.4449	-0.1277[g]	0.0062[g]	0.0811	-7.1833
	8-40	66	4.1678	0.5024[c,f]	0.0958	-0.3356	0.0359[g]	0.2748[d,g]	0.3975	3.6397
	>41	22	0.4287	1.0327[d]	0.5320	2.5373	-0.5589[d,g]	0.4813[d,g]	0.7707	-5.6795
3523	1-7	19	1.8770	0.8933[d]	0.4682	2.8453	-0.2526[d,g]	0.0477[g]	0.3930	3.6475
	8-40	28	10.0180	-0.2326[g]	0.0192	-2.2978	0.3354[g]	0.2603[d,g]	0.3624	3.8414
	>41	9	-25.1305	4.7469	0.3306	10.9370	-1.1244	0.10799	0.0967	n.a.
3699	1-7	19	0.6127	1.0300[c]	0.4528	0.8664	0.0396[g]	0.0648[g]	0.1204	38.0976
	8-40	51	4.1064	0.5025[c,f]	0.1250	0.5131	-0.1939[g]	0.3481[d,g]	0.4672	2.8727
	>41	13	7.4556	0.07739[g]	0.0071	2.3261	0.0448[g]	0.1912[g]	0.1282	6.5214
3813	1-7	14	1.1070	0.9762[c]	0.3350	1.5978	0.0433[g]	-0.0360[f]	0.0334	142.1431
	8-40	19	2.4962[c]	0.7968[c]	0.3420	2.3987	-0.3674[d,g]	0.2735[d,g]	0.5760	-6.7380
	>41	16	2.0891	0.8933[c]	0.2643	1.7086	0.1842[g]	0.1153[g]	0.3050	3.9535
3819	1-7	7	4.6552	0.5391	0.1040	1.8298	0.9786[c,f]	-0.7020	0.7219	0.0776
	8-40	28	6.0349	0.2907[f]	0.0415	-0.0924	-0.0560	0.3052[d]	0.3905	n.a.
	>41	11	4.3805	0.5135	0.1621	1.9920	-0.4932	0.4705[c,f]	0.6006	n.a.

Table D-13 (Continued)

Functional Form 3

$$\ln (V/L) = a + h (\ln L) + g_3 \ln (K/L) + g_4 (\ln K/L)^2$$

CIIU[a]	Size Class[b]	No. of Observations	a	h	g_3	g_4	R^2
3320	1-7	31	8.6408	-0.0623	-0.5088	0.0561	0.0857
	8-40	47	8.3276	0.0556	-0.4800	0.0517	0.0147
	>41	10	-9.0328	-0.4652	5.1350	-0.3570	0.4681
3420	1-7	42	15.0497	-1.0722[e]	-1.9968[e]	0.1611[c]	0.2701
	8-40	66	8.6208	0.4218[c]	-0.9524	0.0865[e]	0.2513
	>41	22	7.4447	0.5649	-0.8553	0.0715	0.1044
3523	1-7	19	9.7594	-0.7973	-0.5604	0.0498	0.7981
	8-40	28	4.5003	-0.0597	1.0221	-0.0626	0.0158
	>41	9	52.1163	-0.5391	-10.1807	0.6175	0.1008
3699	1-7	19	-2.6305	0.6237	2.2227	-0.1352	0.4880
	8-40	51	6.7262	0.1478	-0.2332	0.0407	0.2904
	>41	13	3.7967	-0.5159	1.4793	-0.0872	0.1960
3813	1-7	14	7.4797	1.7858	-1.7928	0.2033	0.7541
	8-40	19	0.2692	0.1704	1.6651	-0.0907	0.2499
	>41	16	7.3592	-0.8412	0.4041	0.0227	0.3360
3819	1-7	7	15.7789	-1.5348	-1.4077	0.0895	0.5748
	8-40	28	8.9840	0.2391	-0.6646	0.0553	0.1421
	>41	11	11.7094	-0.0319	-1.3834	0.1164	0.4853

[a] See appendix J for description.

[b] Number of production workers.

[c,d,e] Different from zero at the 5 percent, 1 percent, and 10 percent level, respectively.

[f,g] Different from unity at the 5 percent and 1 percent level, respectively.

SOURCE: Calculated from the Central American Industrial Survey of 1969.

Table D-14. Central America: Effect of Economic Integration on the Demand for Labor in the Manufacturing Sector During 1958-68 and 1958-72: Three Alternative Estimates

CIIU[b]	Guatemala Alt. 1	Guatemala Alt. 2	Guatemala Alt. 3	$L_{68}-L_{58}$	El Salvador Alt. 3	I. 1958 – 1968 Honduras Alt. 3	I. 1958 – 1968 Nicaragua Alt. 3
311	829	1,482	1,124	4,995	865	155	323
312	173	358	251	1,121	95	35	28
313	16	41	21	-582	49	3	1
314	41	71	74	422	-	3	-
321	1,170	2,179	3,965	5,069	3,025	478	425
322	360	671	398	-952	988	443	22
323	82	182	124	-190	203	143	129
324	595	1,063	836	188	-360	-258	201
331	89	179	155	-71	34	78	123
332	70	102	61	-274	596	4	97
341	337	561	795	769	740	329	282
342	120	206	130	632	273	46	11
351	26	40	70	394	578	82	115
352	179	395	967	1,080	676	480	447
353	-	-	-	187	-	-	-
354	-	-	-	30	-	-	-
355	283	569	1,130	852	122	91	100
356	-	-	-	893	-	105	124
361	-	-	-	127	70	-	-
362	282	349	513	540	19	-	-
369	94	156	122	613	239	124	73
371	-	-	-	577	-	-	-
372	-	-	-	93	-	-	-
381	1,075	1,816	3,170	1,816	3,126	24	363
382	94	197	2,610	197	289	90	45
383	141	266	430	652	1,045	56	28
384	6	41	24	282	50	-	-
385	-	6	2	210	-	1	1
390	68	166	180	248	176	89	28
	6,190	11,098	17,152	19,908	12,828	2,601	2,966

Table D-14 (Continued)

CIU[b]	Costa Rica				Total C.A.
	Alt. 1	Alt. 2	Alt. 3	$L_{68}-L_{58}$	Alt. 3
311	701	1,186	539	-5,910	3,006
312	38	193	114	-309	523
313	–	–	–	-220	74
314	–	1	1	-152	78
321	638	735	1,036	2,027	8,929
322	926	1,176	747	1,331	2,598
323	111	180	120	-18	719
324	11	16	27	834	446
331	136	338	288	-252	678
332	270	321	202	-199	960
341	31	48	21	442	2,167
342	62	76	68	475	528
351	2	59	81	271	926
352	28	89	294	619	2,864
353	–	–	–	–	–
354	–	–	–	–	–
355	90	141	435	156	1,878
356	–	–	–	500	229
361	–	–	–	59	70
362	–	13	5	30	537
369	51	72	42	398	600
371	–	–	–	120	–
372	–	–	–	104	–
381	1,213	1,521	1,867	1,521	8,550
382	127	243	167	730	3,201
383	227	467	562	1,308	2,121
384	–	57	16	249	90
385	–	–	–	–	4
390	-51	-69	294	-69	767
	4,611	6,863	6,926	4,048	43,543

(continued on next page)

Table D-14 (Continued)

| | Guatemala | | | | El Salvador | II. 1958-72 Honduras | Nicaragua |
CIU^b	Alt. 1	Alt. 2	Alt. 3	$L_{72}-L_{58}$	Alt. 3	Alt. 3	Alt. 1
311	995	1,778	1,152	12,420	587	532	730
312	201	416	253	1,068	359	18	23
313	5	12	6	-369	111	–	–
314	55	95	101	337	0	–	–
321	1,282	2,388	4,578	5,480	3,756	1,000	698
322	309	672	435	-493	1,695	–	355
323	84	187	124	-149	393	256	49
324	873	1,561	995	633	1,119	281	13
331	209	420	303	839	14	283	188
332	132	192	153	124	1,022	83	39
341	86	143	257	868	764	32	54
342	136	234	160	1,843	429	15	118
351	33	51	108	433	875	322	3
352	377	832	1,747	1,763	1,607	315	33
353	–	–	–	153	–	–	–
354	–	–	–	32	–	–	–
355	275	554	1,126	881	387	176	58
356	–	–	–	1,145	–	148	–
361	–	–	–	-9	0	–	–
362	274	338	905	594	6	–	–
363	56	93	76	1,316	357	272	31
371	–	–	–	1,001	–	–	–
372	–	–	–	73	–	–	–
381	1,322	2,232	3,800	2,232	4,570	1,656	1,213
382	108	227	4,124	227	169	97	381
383	214	405	677	1,012	1,272	224	267
384	27	188	49	474	1,025	–	–
385	–	8	14	210	–	1	–
390	65	160	144	171	359	21	-51
	7,118	3,186	21,287	34,309	21,075	5,702	4,202

a Alternative 1: $\frac{dQ}{Q_0}(L_1 - L_0)$. Alternative 2: $\frac{dQ}{Q_0}(L_1 - L_0)$. Alternative 3: $dQ \cdot \frac{L}{Q}$. See text for definitions.

b See appendix J for description.

c Assumes 1958-72 employment effect for Honduras was the same as that estimated for 1958-68.

Table D-14 (Continued)

CIU[b]	Costa Rica Alt. 2	Costa Rica Alt. 3	Total C.A.[c]
311	1,236	561	2,927
312	117	49	733
313	–	–	120
314	–	–	104
321	804	1,134	10,946
322	451	286	2,859
323	80	53	969
324	18	30	2,167
331	468	398	1,076
332	61	39	1,300
341	85	136	1,518
342	145	101	781
351	128	178	1,565
352	105	350	4,699
353	–	–	–
354	–	–	–
355	91	282	2,062
356	–	–	253
361	–	–	–
362	1	2	913
369	44	26	855
371	–	–	–
372	–	–	–
381	1,521	1,867	11,917
382	733	732	5,212
383	550	663	2,892
384	53	15	1,089
385	–	–	16
390	-69	294	906
	6,622	7,244	57,939

Calculated from chapter 3; from Central American Industrial Survey of 1969; and Industrial Censuses of: Guatemala, 1958; Costa Rica, 1957; El Salvador, 1956; and Guatemala, 1972.

Table D-15. Central America: Percentage Impact of Economic Integration on Manufacturing Employment

					1958–68						
	Guatemala			El Salvador	Honduras	Nicaragua	Costa Rica			Total C.A.
CIIU[a]	Alt. 1	Alt. 2	Alt. 3	Alt. 3	Alt. 3	Alt. 3	Alt. 1	Alt. 2	Alt. 3	Alt. 3
311	13.4	13.5	6.6	6.7	6.0	10.9	17.3	15.2	7.8	7.1
312	3.2	2.8	1.5	0.7	1.3	0.9	2.8	0.8	1.6	1.2
313	0.4	0.3	0.1	0.4	0.1	–	–	–	–	0.2
314	0.6	0.7	0.4	–	0.1	–	–	–	–	0.2
321	19.6	19.1	23.1	23.5	18.4	14.3	10.7	13.8	15.0	21.0
322	6.0	5.9	2.3	7.7	17.0	0.7	17.1	20.1	10.8	6.1
323	1.6	1.3	0.7	1.6	5.5	4.3	2.6	2.4	1.7	1.7
324	9.6	9.7	4.9	-2.8	-9.9	6.8	0.2	0.2	0.4	1.0
331	1.6	1.5	0.9	0.3	3.0	4.1	4.9	2.9	4.2	1.6
332	0.9	1.1	0.4	4.6	0.2	3.5	4.7	5.9	2.9	2.3
341	5.1	5.5	4.6	5.7	12.4	9.5	0.7	0.7	0.3	5.1
342	1.9	2.0	0.8	2.1	1.8	0.4	1.1	1.3	1.0	1.2
351	0.4	0.4	0.4	4.5	3.2	3.9	0.9	–	1.2	2.2
352	3.6	2.9	5.6	5.2	18.5	15.1	1.3	0.6	4.2	6.7
353	–	–	–	–	–	–	–	–	–	–
354	–	–	–	–	–	–	–	–	–	–
355	5.1	4.6	6.6	0.9	3.5	3.4	2.1	2.0	6.3	4.4
356	–	–	–	–	4.0	4.2	–	–	–	0.5
361	–	–	–	0.5	–	–	–	–	–	0.2
362	3.1	4.6	3.0	0.1	–	–	0.2	–	0.1	1.3
369	1.4	1.5	0.7	1.9	4.8	2.5	1.0	1.1	0.6	1.4
371	–	–	–	–	–	–	–	–	–	–
372	–	–	–	–	–	–	–	–	–	–
381	16.4	17.5	18.5	24.2	0.9	12.2	22.2	26.3	27.0	20.1
382	1.8	1.5	15.2	2.2	3.5	1.5	3.5	2.8	2.4	7.5
383	2.4	2.3	2.5	8.1	1.8	0.9	6.8	4.9	8.1	5.0
384	0.4	0.1	0.1	0.4	–	–	0.8	–	0.2	0.2
385	0.1	–	–	–	–	–	–	–	–	–
390	1.5	1.1	1.0	1.4	3.4	0.9	-1.0	-1.1	4.2	1.8
	100.0	100.0	100.0	100.0	100.0	100.0	100.0	100.0	100.0	100.0

Table D-15 (Continued)

	Guatemala			El Salvador	Honduras	Nicaragua	Costa Rica			Total C.A.
	Alt. 1	Alt. 2	Alt. 3	Alt. 3	Alt. 3[b]	Alt. 3	Alt. 1	Alt. 2	Alt. 3	Alt. 3
311	13.5	14.0	5.4	2.8	6.0	9.3	18.7	17.4	7.7	5.2
312	3.2	2.8	1.2	1.7	1.3	0.3	1.8	0.5	0.9	1.3
313	0.1	0.1	-	0.5	0.1	-	-	-	-	0.2
314	0.7	0.8	0.5	-	0.1	-	-	-	-	0.2
321	18.0	18.0	21.5	17.8	18.4	17.4	12.1	16.6	15.7	18.9
322	5.1	4.3	2.0	8.0	17.0	-	6.8	8.4	3.9	4.9
323	1.4	1.2	0.6	1.9	5.5	4.5	1.2	1.2	0.7	1.7
324	11.8	12.3	4.7	5.3	-9.9	4.9	0.3	0.3	0.4	3.7
331	3.2	2.9	1.4	0.1	3.3	4.9	7.1	4.5	5.5	1.9
332	1.5	1.9	0.7	4.8	0.2	1.4	0.9	0.9	0.5	2.2
341	1.1	1.2	1.2	3.6	12.6	0.6	2.2	1.3	1.9	2.6
342	1.8	1.9	0.8	2.0	1.8	0.3	1.9	2.8	1.8	1.3
351	0.4	0.5	0.5	4.2	3.2	5.6	1.6	0.1	2.5	2.7
352	6.3	5.3	8.2	8.6	18.5	5.5	-	0.8	4.9	8.1
353	-	-	-	-	-	-	-	-	-	-
354	-	-	-	-	-	-	-	-	-	-
355	4.2	3.9	5.3	1.8	3.5	3.1	1.4	1.4	3.9	3.6
356	-	-	-	-	4.0	2.6	-	-	-	0.4
361	-	-	-	-	-	-	-	-	-	-
362	2.6	3.8	4.3	1.7	4.8	4.7	0.7	0.7	0.4	1.6
369	0.7	0.8	0.4	-	-	-	-	-	-	1.5
371	-	-	-	-	-	-	-	-	-	-
372	16.9	18.6	17.9	21.7	0.9	28.9	23.0	28.9	25.8	20.6
381	1.7	1.5	19.4	0.8	3.5	1.7	11.1	9.1	10.1	9.0
382	3.1	3.0	3.2	6.0	1.8	3.9	8.3	6.4	9.2	5.0
383	1.4	0.4	0.2	4.9	-	-	0.8	-	0.2	1.9
384	0.1	-	0.1	-	-	-	-	-	-	-
385	1.2	0.9	0.7	1.7	3.4	0.4	-1.0	-1.2	4.1	1.6
390	100.0	100.0	100.0	100.0	100.0	100.0	100.0	100.0	100.0	100.0

1958-72

[a] See appendix J for description.
[b] Applies the same quanity estimated for 1958-68.

SOURCE: Appendix table D-14.

Table D-16. Variable Economies of Scale

Country	Small Firms K/L	h_2	Medium Firms K/L	h_2	Large Firms K/L	h_2
Guatemala	1,783	n.a.	2,150	n.a.	3,520	n.a.
Honduras	1,249	0.8384	2,578	1.0517	6,350	1.3561
Nicaragua	854	1.0629	3,916	1.0176	4,635	0.8793
Costa Rica	1,352	0.7579	2,110	0.8694	2,918	1.0447
Central America	1,464	1.1341	2,470	1.0253	4,106	0.8616

NOTE: K/L refers to the value (in CA$) of fixed assets (excluding land) per person employed.

Appendix D

NOTES

1. The relationship between ρ and the elasticity of substitution, σ, is

$$\left| \sigma \right| = 1/(1 + \rho).$$

The parameter ρ takes on values greater than or equal to -1. When ρ is -1, the elasticity of substitution is infinity; when it is 0, the elasticity of substitution is unitary; and when it is greater than 0, the elasticity of substitution is less than 1.

2. For the demonstration of these properties see M. Brown, On the Theory and Measurement of Technological Change (Cambridge: Cambridge University Press, 1968).

3. It is important to note that the solutions for choice of capital-labor combinations hold even if there is imperfect competition in the product market, as appears to be the case in Central America. (See appendix H.) The case of imperfect competition is discussed below.

4. That is, $b_1 = \dfrac{1}{1 + \rho}$, which is the absolute value of the elasticity of substitution.

5. This fact is more apparent when equation (2) is rewritten as:

(2a) $\ln L = a_0 - b_1 \ln (w/p) + \ln V + u_1.$

Here the demand for labor is a direct function of the real wage and the level of output. Note that in the more general case where returns to scale are not necessarily constant, the term "$\ln V$" is preceded by a coefficient related to the degree of returns to scale.

6. When $h = 1$, $(dV/dL)(L/V)$ is equal to the share of wages in value added and therefore the denominator of (3) reduces to $(1 - \phi_L)$ where ϕ_L represents labor share.

7. J. Hicks, The Theory of Wages (London: Macmillan & Co., 1932).

8. On the other hand, if $\sigma > 1$, then $\lambda_L > \lambda_K$ leads to a bias against capital and $\lambda_L < \lambda_K$ to a bias against labor.

9. The estimated equation in this case would be:

(10) $\ln L = a + b_4 \ln(w/p) + c_1 \ln V + d_2 t + u_4,$

where $d_2 = (1 - \sigma) \lambda_L$. It should be noted that in a strict sense it is statistically impossible to distinguish between this equation and that which would be obtained from a production function with neutral technological changes, according to Hicks. Consequently, unless a priori information is available about which model is the most appropriate to be used, interpretation of the coefficient on t could be ambiguous.

584

10. Errors of measurement on the independent variables will introduce a downward bias in coefficients c_2 and b_5, resulting in an overestimate of h.

11. It can be shown that if the production function is heterothetic--
so that the shape of the isoquants depends on the level of production--an
estimating equation would be reached that was statistically identical to
(4), which hampers the interpretation of coefficient c_2. See V. Mukerji,
"A Generalized SMAC Function with Constant Ratios of Elasticities of Substitution," Review of Economic Studies 30(3) (1963).

12. See J. Kmenta, "On Estimation of the CES Production Function,"
International Economic Review 8(2) (June 1967).

13. See G. S. Maddala and J. B. Kadane, "Estimation of Returns to
Scale and the Elasticity of Substitution," Econometrica 35(3-4) (July-
October 1967).

14. This function, which is nothing more than a second-degree poly-
nomial in the logarithms of inputs, has been called the transcendental-
logarithmic function or "trans-log" by Jorgenson et al., "Conjugate Duality
and the Transcendental Logarithmic Functions," unpublished. It was used
by Z. Griliches and V. Ringstad, Economies of Scale and the Form of the
Production Function (Amsterdam: North-Holland, 1971).

15. For a review of the derivation of the trans-log function from
the Kmenta approximation, see SIECA/Brookings, Desempleo y Subempleo en
Centroamérica, vol. 3, appendix 1, (Guatemala City: SIECA, 1977).

16. That is, it is attempted to determine whether the restriction imposed on the coefficients of the quadratic term in equation (3) is valid.
This is done by verifying whether the unrestricted trans-log function produces statistically significant improvement in the explanatory power
obtained.

17. Notice that the substitution of V with Q affects only the constant term but not the other parameters if it is assumed that value added
represents a fixed proportion of gross production.

18. This was done for those industries in which there was no production in 1958 or where it was very small; in this case, extremely large
percentage increases were possible. For these particular industries,
the formula was modified to

$$d L = \frac{d Q}{Q_F - Q_I} \left(L_F - L_I \right)$$

where F and I refer to the final and initial year of the period under consideration. In other words, it is assumed that the change in employment
is in direct proportion to the ratio of the change in production due to
integration to the total change in production.

19. As a result the estimation model deals with marginal value product of labor in relation to value of the wage, rather than with marginal
physical product in relation to the physical product equivalent of the
wage (that is, the formulation in equation (2) of chapter 4). The two

alternative forms should yield identical results for the key parameters referring to substitution, scale, and technological change. In the specific case of the consumption estimates of the elasticity of substitution, the only change is in the constant term. In cross-section data the product price should not vary across observations for identical goods, so that price p is a constant. Rewriting equation (2) of chapter 4 in value terms, $\ln(V^*/L) = a^* + b \ln w$. Then $V^* = Vp$ and, because $\ln(V/L) = a + b \ln(w/p)$ or,

$$(V/L) = e^a(w/p)^b = e^a p^{-b} w^b,$$

we may write

$$(Vp)/L = e^a p^{1-b} w^b$$

so that $\ln(V^*/L) = a + (1-b) \ln p + b \ln w$. Thus, the parameter b remains unchanged in the value formulation but the constant changes so that $a^* = a + (1-b) \ln p$.

20. Because of the following relationship: $\sigma_1/\sigma_1' = R^2 = R^{2'}$, and because R^2, the multiple regression coefficient of determination, will always be less than unity (because less than 100 percent of variation is explained). See E. Berndt, "Reconciling Alternative Estimates of the Elasticity of Substitution," mimeographed (August 1973).

21. G. S. Maddala and J. B. Kadane, "Some Notes on the Estimation of the CES Production Function," Review of Economics and Statistics (August 1966): pp. 340-44.

22. See for example C. Clague, "Capital-Labor Substitution in Manufacturing in Underdeveloped Countries," Econometrica 37(3) (July 1969).

23. See L. R. Christensen and D. W. Jorgenson, "The Measurement of U.S. Real Capital Input, 1929-67," Review of Income and Wealth series 15 (December 1969); D. W. Jorgenson and C. D. Siebert, "Optimal Capital Accumlation and Corporate Investment Behavior," Journal of Political Economy 76 (November-December 1968): pp. 1123-51; and J. Williamson, "Capital Accumulation, Labor-Saving and Labor Absorption," mimeographed (Social Systems Research Institute, University of Wisconsin, June 1969).

24. In the remaining eight cases there is no investment in fixed assets or else no unique value of λ which satisfies the necessary conditions for an optimal Ψ^*.

25. See Charles R. Frank, Jr., "Notes on Formulation of Cost of Capital Variable," mimeographed, 1974; and M. Soto and C. Sevilla, "Metodologia para Estimar el Costo del Capital en el Sector Manufacturero Centroamericano," mimeographed, 1974.

26. Note also that it is impossible to determine the cost of capital in the equations (B) and (D), unless $f^1(y)$ and $g^1(x_3)$ are known.

27. See, for example, D. Jorgenson and C. Siebert, "Optimal Capital Accumulation," and J. Williamson, "Capital Accumulation, Labor Saving, and Labor Absorption Once More," Quarterly Journal of Economics 85 (1971).

28. From a theoretical point of view, homotheticity is also a necessary and sufficient condition for the cost function to factor into a production function and a homogeneous function of factor prices. This makes
it possible to study economies of scale using cost data, deflated by factor prices. On this see R. Shephard, Theory of Cost and Production Functions (Princeton: Princeton University Press, 1970).

29. The criterion for "size" is the number of production workers.
Small establishments are those with seven workers or less; medium-size
establishments are those with more than seven but no more than forty workers; and large establishments are those having forty-one workers or more.
Industries were selected according to the number of observations they had,
in order to count with enough degrees of freedom for the estimation.
Pooled firm observations of the four countries were used for each industry.

30. It is interesting that similar patterns were found in a study
for Chile. P. Meller, "Production Functions for Industrial Establishments of Different Sizes: The Chilean Case," Annals of Economic and Social Measurement 4(4) (1975).

31. In estimating the trans-log function, variables $\ln K$ and $\ln L$ were
transformed and expressed as deviations from their respective geometric
means to eliminate the effect of units of measurement on the estimated coefficients. Evaluation of the resulting variable elasticity of substitution functions, presented below, was thus done using the transformed value
of the variables.

32. SIECA/Brookings, Desempleo y Subempleo en Centroamérica, vol. 3,
appendix 5, (Guatemala City: SIECA, 1977), tables 16-19. It is interesting that the same result is obtained working with aggregate data, as shown
in table D-8.

33. This result should not be surprising, given the very heterogeneous nature of the units in the sample. In fact, these estimates assume
the same production function for all firms in the industrial sector, a
questionable assumption.

34. W. Fellner, Oligopoly.

A Model of Employment and Labor Shares in an Export Economy with Import-Substituting Industrialization

Clark W. Reynolds

A. A Model of Employment and Labor Shares in an Export Economy with Import-Substituting Industrialization

1. The Simple Model of a Pure Export Economy

The Central American experience provides an ideal prototype of agricultural export economies which have throughout their history depended substantially on their geographic and climatic conditions to provide an exportable "surplus" of commodities demanded in foreign markets. Initially dyestuffs constituted the basis for trade, after the conquest of the isthmus by Europeans, since the quantity of exportable minerals was minimal. The Colonial system was largely designed to facilitate the use of indigenous labor to produce commodities such as cochineal (animal dye) and indigo (vegetable dye), and the extent to which land and labor were required to produce them influenced the participation of the local population in the value of the exports. The following model is an attempt to formalize the manner in which the use of labor and land in such an economy determines the level and distribution of value shares. One of the most important elements of the model is the way in which the alternatives open to local labor affect its ability to participate in export rental income and hence its share of total income and product in the economy. Some practical political and social considerations, taken from the literature on the social history of Central America, will be introduced in order to

---

NOTE: This model makes use of the concept of a "wage profile" for a developing country as first presented in Richard C. Webb, Government Policy and the Distribution of Income in Peru, 1963-1973, Harvard Economic Studies, vol. 147 (Cambridge, Mass.: Harvard University Press, 1977). The diagrams are based on conventional trade modeling of partial equilibrium gains from trade for a single commodity, applied to the gains from labor service flows between sectors and regions. An earlier model of this type to analyze the distributional consequences of migration under conventional neoclassical assumptions appears in R. A. Berry and R. Soligo, "Some Welfare Aspects of International Migration," Journal of Political Economy, Sept.-October, 1969, pp. 778-794.

suggest why certain paths of participation obtained in some parts of the region which were quite different from those in others; both paths are quite consistent with the underlying economic model once these additional political—economic dimensions have been added.

Before the Conquest, the peoples of Central America enjoyed a variety of cultures which from an economic viewpoint had gone well beyond the level of subsistence. The basic support of life, as reflected in the philosophy and religion of the region, was maiz. This subsistence crop was cultivated much as it is today in highland Mesoamerica, in small hillocks (milpas) formed by hand, together with squash and beans which provide nutritional balance as well as a ground cover and root network which prevents erosion and maximum water supply for the corn. Rain and corn determined whether or not these cultures could accumulate, and since the bounty of nature came in cycles, so did their belief system accommodate the rise and fall of high civilizations as the will of the gods. The priestly system linked its teachings to the orderly movement of the stars, using a rather complex astronomical and mathematical basis, to provide an ideological foundation for society. Trade flourished between what is now Mexico, to the north, and the commercial centers of Central America. Cocoa beans were the means of exchange, and a wide variety of goods were traded including basic food-stuffs, cloth, ceramics, shells, feathers, and highly worked jewelry and artifacts of great value. Although accumulation in the form of knowledge (in codices, pictograms, glyphs, carved stellae), artifacts, and the build-ing of roads and great pyramids, temples, and dwellings was ubiquitous to the region, by the sixteenth century many previous centers of high culture had fallen into decay. The reasons for the decline are still unclear but must be related partly to the declining yields in agriculture after centuries of cultivation to support burgeoning urban populations in the ceremonial centers.

Accumulation based on the bounty of nature, hard work, and consis-tent belief and social discipline was always endangered by threatening tribes, such as the Aztecs who in Mexico used their warrior skills to overthrow and expropriate the great civilization of the Valley of Tehua-can. It was resentment by other tribes against these incursions by the Aztecs that facilitated the conquest of Mexico by Cortez. In a sense, the indigenous population of Central America also exchanged one set of external threats for another, and found themselves overcome and domi-nated by Europeans. The difference between the Aztec and Spanish invaders was, perhaps, the relatively greater gulf between the host culture and that of the Europeans. The Colonial system imposed on Central America, despite its many common elements with the precolombian cultures, was fundamentally different in terms of its system of beliefs, economic values, mode of production of exportable commodities, and conditions of life for the indigenous population. The model which is presented here for an ex-port economy reflects the new mode of production, in highly simplified form, and can be used to illustrate how the Colonial system could be used to transform native labor into rental income for the colonizers. The model can also be used to show how postindependence development of these export economies occurred and why some countries pursued quite different social and economic courses than did others. There is no attempt here to oversimplify an exceedingly complex history of these countries but rather to extract the basic elements essential to understanding the relationship between value and distribution in the export sector.

Figure E-1 illustrates the relationship between labor utilization (horizontal axes) and output (vertical axis) in the form of increments to output for each additional man-year employed in the respective sectors of economic activity. In order to simplify the analysis the economy has been divided into two main sectors, subsistence agriculture (producing for home consumption and for the domestic market) and the "export sector" which could be producing any of a variety of traditional exports of the Central American region, from cochineal and indigo to coffee, sugar, hardwoods, cattle, cotton, to minerals. The labor productivity curves (kc and ln, respectively) are drawn so that the activities or productive units with the highest output per worker are placed closest to the vertical axis. Both sectors show increases in employment moving from the vertical axis to the left in the northwest quadrant, and to the right in the northeast quadrant, respectively. In figure E-1 the stock of capital and land is given so that the labor productivity curves register increases in output as labor is increased due to the addition of labor to other inputs in fixed supply, but the curve is not precisely the same as the "marginal productivity of labor" because it is drawn from observed behavior of the units, and those with the highest output per worker may not be deriving this higher productivity from labor alone but from better quality land, more capital intensity, or other factors. Moreover labor includes other variable inputs which complement its use. What is shown by the diagram is a realistic presentation of how the respective sectoral productivity functions will appear when labor is drawn on one axis and increments to output on the other.

Because of the nature of the diagram, the labor productivity curves provide an envelope of value added in the sector, expressed in relation to labor utilized. The integral of the curves therefore equals the value added of the sector, up to the point of total sectoral employment. Within this envelope, a second curve can be drawn which represents the payments to labor within the sector. The integral of the labor income curve equals total wages and other labor income. While it is certain that in fact labor income levels will vary, probably in proportion to value per worker in the respective units, to simplify the presentation the wage is made identical for all labor in the respective sectors. At the outset the wage in the subsistence sector is Og per man-year and the wage-bill is Ogcb, while the share of income accruing to owners of land and other inputs is gkc.

In the first model, the total labor supply of the economy is assumed to be inelastic with respect to wages and equivalent to Ob + Oq = Oa + Op. In the absence of the export sector, this entire amount of labor would have to find productive employment in the subsistence sector, far to the left of point b, presumably at a level of productivity which would barely cover the cost of survival (this of course depends on the slope of the curve ec, which in turn will depend upon the supply of arable land). Of course if technology were introduced which would shift up the labor productivity curve, then the wages of labor (or their payments in whatever form) would be likely to rise, provided that the demand for labor were competitive. The land tenure system will determine the extent to which workers share in the rental income of the subsistence sector. If land is distributed in proportion to available labor time, then the income of the respective workers will be equal to their respective portions (segments) of the integral under the labor productivity curve. Those with the most productive units (to the right) will have higher incomes than those with poorer land, less capital, or fewer complementary inputs. It can be seen that in a pure subsistence economy, the distribution of income will tend to favor rental income and hence will favor the landholders, and this will be more skewed the more uneven the quality of land, given the size distribution of land units.

With the advent of the export potential, there is the introduction of a new sector. If exports are land-using (agricultural products), then the competition for land use will drive up land rents and shift the productivity curve to the right in the subsistence sector. Land will be drawn into the export sector where it can earn much higher rents. This will tend to depress labor earnings in the subsistence sector, leading to a migration of workers to the export sector. (For those who are landowners and are able to produce competitively in the export sector, they will shift from subsistence to export crops—from the northwest to northeast quadrant.)

Figure E-1 has been drawn with the labor productivity curves reflecting the shift of crop land, plus the investment essential for normal levels of export production. What remains is to determine what the respective outputs will be for the two sectors, and that depends on the migration of labor between the two sectors. If migration is relatively free and there are no barriers to exit or entry, then the pattern is likely to be that of a "gravity model of migration" in which labor moves from low to higher wage activities until wages are relatively equal, given a differential for the net cost of migration, dislocation, undesirability of export activities, and related factors. (The degree of uncertainty of employment in the export sector is also likely to determine the degree of migration, in combination with the degree of risk aversion of the workers in the job market.) In figure E-1 the amount of differential in the pure migration case is negligible, with workers in both sectors earning about Of wages per man-year after migration. The amount of employment in the two sectors is respectively Oa and Op. Note that the distribution of income has favored the labor share slightly in the subsistence sector, but in the export sector rental income is by far the dominant share (fln) compared with labor income Ofnp.

Obviously the gravity model is ideal for the landowners in the export sector, who wish to obtain labor at the lowest possible wage relative to its product. Wage laborers who are landless will find it more costly to rent land on which to support their families with subsistence cultivation. They may find themselves worse off, as a result, despite the rise in real wages. In principle they should be able to earn more on rented land, in direct proportion to its rental price, but the absolute rise in land rentals, plus inadequate access to credit for working capital (including advance payments on rent) and imperfect entry of smallholders into the export sector, will tend to discourage their participation. This will be particularly true if there are economies of scale in cultivation of the export crops. This phenomenon is observed in Central America at the present time, as commercial crop production for export has driven up land rents, particularly in the coastal regions of Guatemala, El Salvador, and Costa Rica, causing smallholders and rentiers as well as sharecroppers to be forced into the wage labor market because they are unable to pay high cash rents for land previously used for subsistence cultivation. In order to support themselves and their families, they are forced to have wives and children work as field hands on the commercial farms. The conditions of health, nutrition, and the adverse effects on

591

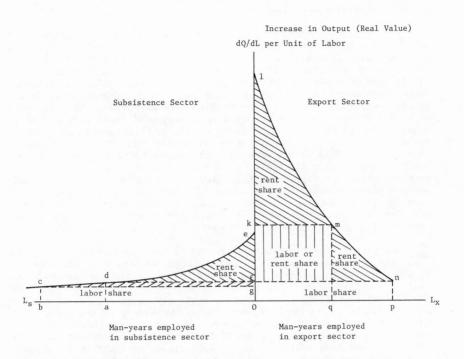

Figure E-1. Employment and Labor Shares in an Export Economy

the family unit are extremely detrimental to their welfare, despite some evidence of rising real wages for day labor.

An alternative model of labor adjustment to the export sector takes into consideration the possibility that labor may be adverse to migration or those which initially move to the export sector may erect barriers to further entry and thus restrict the supply of labor, forcing up wages. (It is also possible that employers will, for social or political reasons, or to raise worker productivity, increase wages in the export sector voluntarily above those that would obtain with free migration.) This is shown in figure E-1 for the case where the total supply of labor only partially adjusts, so that Ob of labor remains in the subsistence sector, and Oq moves to the export sector, with the resulting differential in wages of Ok - Og = gk. This is the case that currently obtains in the case of the large banana company plantations in Honduras and elsewhere. Wages on the company estate are well above those outside (including all benefits) and workers queue in order to have access to the company jobs. (One alleged cause of the recent expulsion of Salvadorians from Honduras was the favorable treatment that the former had from banana company employers at the expense of potential jobs for Hondurans.)

The broader the distribution of land in the export sector, the more equal the distribution of rural income, since workers will also benefit from the rental income from export crops. In this respect farm families will be indifferent as to the prevailing wage levels, since they will earn the whole integral under the labor productivity curve regardless, to the extent that they work the land themselves. The history of the coffee culture in Central America can be understood in terms of figure E-1. The northern countries (Guatemala and El Salvador) had an abundant supply of laborers drawn from smallholdings in subsistence agriculture in the highlands which were used on the coffee estates as wage laborers. The cultivation of coffee in these countries, with social and political systems accustomed to labor exploitation since Colonial times, enforced by police and the courts, resulted in a high concentration of economic rents in the hands of the landowners (many of whom were foreign, and particularly German settlers of the nineteenth century and emergent "middle-class" Guatemalan families). In Costa Rica, on the other hand, the land was more widely distributed and labor was relatively scarce, so that the coffee cultivation in that country generated rents which accrued to a broad segment of the rural smallholders. There it was not possible to exploit labor from the indigenous population, which was minimal by the nineteenth century, unlike the conditions in Guatemala and El Salvador. (It should be noted that in our model the real value of export output reflects physical production times the farm-gate price. Concentration at the stages of processing, marketing, and distribution abroad could still permit scarcity rents to be earned over and above the rents described under the labor productivity curves in the diagram. To the extent that such processing or marketing monopolies existed, as was the case for Costa Rican coffee, the domestic value of production included additional rents which should be added to the integral under the curve and which benefited a small number of families.)

We see therefore that the level of wages in an export economy and the distribution of labor income has much to do with the conditions which prevail in the labor market, _ceteris_ _paribus_, such that two countries facing

the same foreign demand, and with similar quality land but different conditions of labor supply or different tenure conditions could end up with
entirely different wage levels and distributions of labor income. The
cases of Guatemala and Costa Rica are polar opposites in the case of coffee
(though the concentration of land rents in the former is somewhat matched
by the concentration of processing rents in the latter). Moreover political
and social conditions may lead to segmentation of the labor market protecting workers in high productivity sectors from competition and allowing wages
to be bargained up in those sectors at the expense of workers in lower productivity sectors. We illustrate in the text how the profiles of labor
income in Central America reflect such segmentation. In this case the
average productivity of labor in the high productivity sectors is distortedly high because it arises from failure of markets to adjust. By the same
token the productivity levels in the low-income sectors are distortedly low
because workers there are not given a chance to move to better paying jobs.
Segmentation appears to have distorted productivity levels in Central American countries during the Common Market period, particularly with respect
to the modern industrial sector and export agriculture. The result is lower
total output and income than would have obtained under a gravity adjustment
system of migration, though the consequences for income distribution are
complex, as we may see from figure E-1. The segmentation result reduces
the rent share in the export sector in favor of the advantaged workers there.
However it lowers the wage share in the subsistence sector. The net effect is probably to increase middle-class incomes at the expense of the
very poor and the very rich.

2.   The Model of an Export Economy with Industrialization

In the case of Central America, the traditional export economies were
abruptly transformed in recent years into economies with growing industrial
and commercial sectors, particularly as a result of the incentives of the
Common Market. While this growth was highly uneven among the five countries, as is shown elsewhere in the SIECA/Brookings volume, it nevertheless had an important impact on the labor market. Indeed had not the supply of labor grown so rapidly during the period 1960 to the present, there
are strong reasons to suppose that the combined labor demand increases of
export agriculture and the urban sector would have faced severe bottlenecks
by now, and wages even for skilled labor would have risen sharply (see
text). However, the supply of labor increases resulting from demographic
acceleration in prior years and growing female participation rates had the
effect of shifting outward the number of man-year equivalents of labor time
available, amounting to a horizontal shift in the diagrams of figures E-1
and E-2. We now present the case of an export economy with expanding incentives for industrial production (see figure E-2).

Rising duties on imports of final goods from the rest of the world,
especially for those countries which initially had freer trade together
with the virtual elimination of duties on manufacturers produced within
the region, provided new incentives for industrialization in Central America. (Imports of intermediate goods from the rest of the world were frequently awarded reductions in duties, since they were used as inputs for
local manufacturing.) The net effect was to lower the terms of trade for
traditional exports (by making imports more expensive), hence reducing the
real value per unit of labor (shifting down the envelope described by the

594

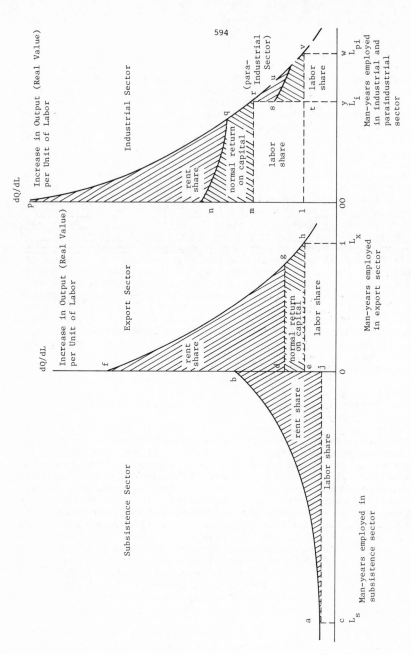

Figure E-2. Employment and Labor Shares in an Export
Economy with Industrialization

labor productivity curve in the export sector). On the other hand manufacturing for the region suddenly became much more attractive as the relative price of domestically produced goods was permitted to rise (higher external barriers), the cost of intermediate imports fell (lower external barriers), and demand expanded due to the elimination of regional customs barriers.

In figure E-2 this is illustrated by the high labor productivity curve for the new industrial sector. (It should be noted that this concept of "productivity" includes value distortions due to different degrees of effective protection among the three sectors. In terms of world relative prices, the curve for the subsistence sector should probably be higher, that of the industrial sector lower, and that of the export sector no doubt higher.) The curve is higher for the industrial sector in part because of the degree of capital intensity of manufacturing, since our curve includes returns to all factors including a normal return on capital, plus quasirents (which include excess profits due to monopoly, patent rights, and other factors which limit competition). In figure E-2 the normal return on capital (normal return represents the capital stock times the current social discount rate plus depreciation) is specifically included for both the export and industrial sectors. In the industrial sector it is assumed that labor productivity is proportional to capital intensity, so the curve for normal return on capital is downward sloping. In addition to the industrial sector per se, we also include a para-industrial subsector which represents those many activities which do not appear in the industrial production or employment data but which represent the ancillary production of component parts, piecework (as in the textile industry), services to industry, and all other activities which are normally classified in the "informal sector" but which in fact are directly linked to manufacturing. Many of these activities are located in urban homes and shops and use a considerable amount of capital (sewing and weaving machines, tools and dies, painting and other equipment), and this is taken into consideration in the diagram.

The steep downward slope of the labor productivity curve for the industrial sector reflects the fact that manufacturing is highly capital intensive in the region (as in most developing countries which follow the Western industrial modes of production), with relatively little elasticity of substitution of capital for labor. Of course this is a blessing in disguise for those workers fortunate enough to find employment in the modern industrial sector, since if barriers to entry can be assured, the position of the workers is suitable for bargaining up wages above the levels prevailing elsewhere, and even above levels in the export sector (except where the labor market is highly segmented in that sector as well, as occurs in the case of mining enclaves and specialized agricultural activities where much capital and infrastructure are invested).

The effect of the advent of industrial opportunities in the export economy is to attract labor away from the export sector through higher wages (and nonwage benefits) and better working conditions in the urban sector. Here again the initial supply conditions prevailing in the subsistence and export sectors will influence the attractiveness of investment in industry. A given labor productivity curve will allow a larger surplus of economic rents (excess profits) for new investors the lower is the labor share of value added (ceteris paribus). The labor share will be lower the lower are the alternative earnings of labor in the subsistence and export sector. Of course segmentation in the export sector will tend to increase the supply of labor to the industrial sector, ceteris paribus. (It should be noted that the height of the labor productivity curve will be influenced by the degree of skills of the work force as well as their propensities to work intensively, since the height depends upon the stock of physical and human capital employed, but the latter is dependent on the amount of labor employed as well as the degree of skill of the average worker.) It is not surprising then that the two economies in the region with abundant low-wage labor (Guatemala and El Salvador) drawn from a large subsistence agriculture sector have been most attractive to new investors in manufacturing.

The model allows for segmentation in the industrial sector by providing for a wage of 00m in the industrial sector vis-à-vis a wage of 0e in the export sector (also segmented) and 0j in the subsistence sector. This corresponds to the experience of all of the Central American countries and results in a highly skewed wage-bill leading to a very uneven distribution of labor income within each country and also among the five. Nevertheless the share of profits and rents in the manufacturing sector, as a portion of value added, is immense according to our data (see the text). The para-industrial sector facilitates this concentration of income in the hands of the owners of manufacturing companies by providing piecework and other inputs at wage levels well below those prevailing in the segmented industrial firms. (Of course if segmentation did not occur, there would be less apparent dualism between the industrial and para-industrial sector.) From the viewpoint of jobs created by manufacturing, however, the para-industrial sector permits far greater labor participation in industrial growth than would be possible with the highly segmented labor market in the modern firms (see figure E-2).

3.   Conclusions from the Model

The model illustrates how income distribution (by factor shares) is determined by the structure of production, among subsistence cultivation, exports, and import-substituting industrialization. It can be used to accommodate the effects of alternative institutional conditions prevailing in the labor market which influence the movement of workers from the subsistence to the export and industrial sectors. These alternative conditions of labor supply (given investment and cultivation opportunities) are sure to determine the level and distribution of wages. The model shows why it is not unusual to find the wage distribution highly skewed among the three sectors, especially where the labor market is segmented, with barriers to entry to prevent job competition from taking place. In Central America the segmentation occurs not only on the basis of historical priorities (first come, first served) but also on racial and class grounds. Hence workers are often prevented from competing for jobs with higher wages for reasons independent of their actual or potential productivity. A major implication of this approach is that policies to permit significant growth in productivity of labor per se (however potentially labor-using the technology) do not assure that these gains will be fully achieved or passed on in the form of maximum potential employment. Moreover the size distribution of income among wage and salary earners does not necessarily reflect the ex ante derived demand for labor resulting from the structure of final demand.

While this model does not go into the process whereby the segmentation of the labor market takes place, the text of the study gives many examples in which the "struggle for shares" has occurred in Central American history including those during the Common Market period. To further understand this process, detailed analysis of submarkets is required, including an examination of the evolution of such institutions as labor unions, cooperatives, labor legislation, and property relations including land tenure, access to credit, and protection of property rights of smallholders and investors. Historically work on "institutional economics" has tended to be ad hoc in its scope and policy relevance.

It is hoped that the present analysis will facilitate the relationship of individual case studies of economic institutions in the labor market to more general macro-modeling of employment and distribution. By defining the dimensions within which the distributive shares may lie, under alternative institutional conditions, the model exemplifies the way in which more conventional economic analytical techniques can be broadened to accommodate some of the most pressing issues of our time. In this respect the great insights of those involved in the study of social history and the struggle for shares can be combined with the "scientific techniques" of positive economics to provide policy suggestions that are realistic in terms of the economic dimensions of policy space. Of course such models are at best only tools and cannot provide the political will or humanitarian concern on which their implementation must ultimately depend.

B. Supplementary Tables

Table E-1. Value Added, by Economic Sectors
(millions of Central American pesos
in current prices)

Country	Total Gross Domestic Product	Agriculture	Mining	Industry	Construction	Energy
1960						
Central America	2,733.9	804.0	15.1	373.6	80.7	25.1
Guatemala	1,043.8	294.6	1.9	133.1	20.8	7.0
El Salvador	568.0	179.9	1.0	82.7	18.8	6.5
Honduras	345.4	128.6	5.4	43.0	13.2	2.1
Nicaragua	359.1	99.6	6.4	43.3	8.3	4.4
Costa Rica	417.6	101.5	0.4	71.5	19.6	5.1
1968						
Central America	4,679.0	1,304.6	28.0	788.6	142.1	62.8
Guatemala	1,610.6	444.5	1.6	257.7	32.2	16.1
El Salvador	916.7	241.1	1.2	179.2	22.7	14.0
Honduras	645.0	249.2	14.8	83.6	30.3	7.6
Nicaragua	742.9	188.0	9.7	120.9	22.2	13.0
Costa Rica	763.8	181.8	0.7	147.2	34.7	12.1
1971						
Central America	5,785.0	1,558.0	26.6	993.6	187.0	83.4
Guatemala	2,000.9	552.3	2.0	318.1	34.0	20.0
El Salvador	1,072.5	290.4	1.8	206.2	31.3	16.8
Honduras	741.2	261.3	15.5	99.0	40.5	9.7
Nicaragua	924.4	223.9	6.4	170.8	27.0	18.1
Costa Rica	1,046.0	230.1	0.9	199.5	54.2	18.8

599

Table E-1 (Continued)

	Transportation	Commerce	Banking, Real Estate	Services	Activities Not Itemized
1960					
Central America	130.9	640.2	271.7	193.5	199.1
Guatemala	42.3	310.5	105.5	65.0	63.1
El Salvador	26.6	127.0	40.6	45.9	39.2
Honduras	26.0	47.6	34.3	17.3	27.9
Nicaragua	20.1	78.9	42.0	27.1	29.0
Costa Rica	15.9	76.2	49.3	38.2	39.9
1968					
Central America	217.5	1,026.2	410.6	317.7	380.9
Guatemala	62.8	457.4	149.8	87.0	101.5
El Salvador	45.5	215.9	54.5	68.0	74.6
Honduras	41.4	88.5	61.0	18.6	50.0
Nicaragua	37.0	145.4	64.4	62.9	79.4
Costa Rica	30.8	119.0	80.9	81.2	75.4
1971					
Central America	276.2	1,271.4	501.2	411.2	476.4
Guatemala	86.0	580.3	174.1	110.0	124.1
El Salvador	53.4	232.5	63.9	85.5	90.7
Honduras	47.2	98.6	82.3	22.9	64.2
Nicaragua	47.0	184.8	76.1	72.4	97.9
Costa Rica	42.6	175.2	104.8	120.4	99.5

SOURCE: Prepared by the Development Division of SIECA based on figures supplies by the Central Banks. Figures for the year 1968 were interpolated from the data for 1960 and 1971 based on a compound rate of growth formula.

Table E-2. Labor Income Share of Value Added, by Economic Sector
(millions of Central American pesos in current prices)

Country	Total	Agriculture	Mining	Industry	Construction	Energy	Transportation	Commerce	Services
1960									
Central America	1,204.9	377.7	6.0	201.7	65.0	10.3	72.8	190.4	281.0
Guatemala	424.6	125.9	1.0	77.0	17.1	2.6	25.2	81.1	94.7
El Salvador	242.4	77.2	0.2	48.0	15.4	2.3	15.7	33.0	50.3
Honduras	150.9	55.3	0.9	24.9	10.8	1.2	7.0	19.0	31.8
Nicaragua	176.8	63.1	3.6	27.6	6.8	1.6	11.9	23.0	39.2
Costa Rica	210.2	56.2	-	24.2	14.9	2.6	13.0	34.3	65.0
1968									
Central America	2,053.9	554.1	10.7	443.1	115.9	44.6	120.1	352.9	412.5
Guatemala	674.4	175.5	1.2	155.7	29.7	14.0	36.7	146.8	114.8
El Salvador	395.8	94.0	0.8	107.5	18.8	12.2	26.4	69.1	67.0
Honduras	261.1	92.2	2.2	50.2	25.1	2.5	16.6	28.3	44.0
Nicaragua	379.5	120.7	6.5	78.4	18.4	11.3	21.5	52.4	70.3
Costa Rica	343.1	71.7	-	51.3	23.9	4.6	18.9	56.3	116.4
1971									
Central America	2,487.4	664.4	9.5	531.9	155.0	54.7	140.7	405.7	525.5
Guatemala	748.8	192.6	1.2	178.3	29.7	15.6	40.8	163.1	127.5
El Salvador	441.5	98.7	1.1	125.8	28.8	13.8	26.7	67.4	79.2
Honduras	306.4	98.8	3.2	44.7	37.2	3.3	21.4	38.6	59.2
Nicaragua	475.9	169.7	4.0	104.2	24.8	14.8	23.5	53.6	81.3
Costa Rica	514.8	104.6	-	78.9	34.5	7.2	28.3	83.0	178.3

SOURCE: Reports of the Central Banks and calculations by SIECA staff for this study:
1. Bank of Guatemala "National Accounts," 1968, pp. 21–22.
2. Central Bank of Nicaragua, Economic Indicators, 1975.
3. Central Bank of Costa Rica, "National Accounts," 1972.
4. Central Bank of Honduras and SIECA office, Tegucigalpa.
Labor income estimates used here include wages and salaries and nonwage benefits.

Table E-3. Cost of Capital Share of Value Added, by Economic Sector
(millions of Central American pesos in current prices)

Country	Total	Agri-cul-ture	Mining	Indus-try	Con-struc-tion	Energy	Trans-porta-tion	Com-merce
1960								
Central America	207.0	80.3	–	59.4	5.4	2.0	12.8	47.1
Guatemala	86.6	32.4	–	24.0	1.3	0.3	3.8	24.8
El Salvador	48.7	19.8	–	14.9	1.1	0.3	2.4	10.2
Honduras	28.9	14.2	–	7.7	0.8	0.1	2.3	3.8
Nicaragua	27.6	11.0	–	7.8	0.5	0.2	1.8	6.3
Costa Rica	15.2	2.9	–	5.0	1.7	1.1	2.5	2.0
1968								
Central America		105.4	0.5	171.9	9.2	5.7	25.7	76.5
Guatemala	150.9	40.1	–	64.4	1.9	1.0	6.9	36.6
El Salvador	91.0	21.7	–	44.8	1.4	0.8	5.0	17.3
Honduras	57.8	22.4	0.5	20.9	1.8	0.5	4.6	7.1
Nicaragua	64.9	16.9	–	30.2	1.3	0.8	4.1	11.6
Costa Rica	30.3	4.3	–	11.6	2.8	2.6	5.1	3.9
1971								
Central America	489.6	139.3	0.5	215.8	11.8	12.8	33.3	76.1
Guatemala	188.8	55.2	–	79.5	2.0	2.0	9.5	40.6
El Salvador	106.4	29.0	–	51.6	1.9	1.7	5.9	16.3
Honduras	66.9	26.1	0.5	24.8	2.4	1.0	5.2	6.9
Nicaragua	79.8	22.4	–	42.7	1.6	1.0	5.2	6.9
Costa Rica	47.7	6.6	–	17.2	3.9	7.1	7.5	5.4

SOURCE: Calculations prepared by SIECA staff for this study. Direct sources were available only for Guatemala and Costa Rica. For Guatemala: Bank of Guatemala, "National Accounts," Department of Economic Studies, tables 1.6 and 1.6A, pp. 22-23, Guatemala, 1968. For Costa Rica: Central Bank of Costa Rica and SIECA office, correspondence, 1976. For countries other than Costa Rica, the cost of capital as a share of value added in Guatemala was applied to the value added by sector. Hence these figures should be regarded as extremely tentative, offering only general orders of magnitude. The concept "cost of capital," as discussed in the text, represents a normal return to capital sufficient to provide incentive and motivate and maintain physical investment in plant, equipment, and inventories. The sectoral shares for Guatemala were:

Guatemala
(Cost of Capital as Percent of Value Added)

Year	Agriculture	Industry	Construction	Energy	Transport	Commerce
1960	13	18	6	3	7	8
1971	10	25	6	10	11	8

Table E-4. Economic Rent Share of Value Added, by Economic Sector
(millions of Central American pesos in current prices)

Country	Total	Agriculture	Mining	Industry	Construction	Energy	Transportation	Commerce
1960								
Central America	1,322.0	346.0	9.1	112.5	10.3	12.8	45.3	407.7
Guatemala	532.6	136.3	.9	32.0	2.4	4.1	13.3	204.6
El Salvador	276.9	82.9	.8	19.8	2.3	3.9	8.5	83.8
Honduras	165.6	59.1	4.5	30.2	1.6	.8	16.7	24.8
Nicaragua	154.7	25.5	2.8	12.9	1.0	2.6	6.4	49.6
Costa Rica	192.2	42.4	–	42.3	3.0	1.4	0.4	39.9
1968								
Central America	2,230.2	645.1	17.3	173.6	17.0	12.5	71.7	596.8
Guatemala	785.3	228.9	0.4	37.6	0.6	1.1	19.2	274.0
El Salvador	429.9	125.4	0.4	26.9	2.5	1.0	14.1	129.5
Honduras	326.1	134.6	12.6	12.5	3.4	4.0	20.2	53.1
Nicaragua	298.5	50.4	3.2	12.3	2.5	.9	12.4	81.4
Costa Rica	309.4	105.1	–	84.3	8.0	4.8	6.8	58.8
1971								
Central America	2,808.0	754.3	17.1	245.3	2.2	15.9	98.2	789.6
Guatemala	1,063.3	304.5	.8	60.3	2.3	2.4	35.7	376.6
El Salvador	524.6	162.7	.7	28.8	0.6	1.3	20.8	148.8
Honduras	367.9	136.4	12.3	29.5	.4	5.4	20.6	53.1
Nicaragua	368.7	31.8	2.4	23.9	.4	2.3	18.3	127.3
Costa Rica	483.5	118.9	–	103.4	15.8	4.5	6.8	86.8

SOURCE: Calculated for this study as a residual after deducting the wage share and cost of capital from value added by sector. (See tables 1, 2, and 3.)

Table E-5. Value Added Per Worker
(Central American pesos in
current prices)

Country	Agriculture	Mining	Industry	Construction	Energy	Transportation	Commerce	Services
1960								
Central America								
Guatemala	353	1,056	977	625	4,661	1,505	4,207	476
El Salvador	397	–	859	635	4,333	1,705	2,720	477
Honduras	339	3,375	975	1,168	1,909	3,377	1,770	249
Nicaragua	574	2,462	1,220	487	1,692	1,489	2,294	350
Costa Rica	582	444	1,838	1,101	1,594	1,272	2,367	654
1968								
Central America								
Guatemala	478	727	1,458	682	6,708	1,864	4,658	494
El Salvador	484	–	947	522	7,000	1,487	3,020	466
Honduras	498	6,435	1,370	1,894	2,533	3,185	2,229	205
Nicaragua	813	2,622	2,389	1,279	5,909	2,517	3,816	783
Costa Rica	918	583	3,073	1,382	2,161	1,987	2,662	1,032
1971								
Central America								
Guatemala	558	833	1,553	589	6,061	2,281	5,219	569
El Salvador	545	–	1,032	1,020	8,000	1,739	3,243	556
Honduras	686	6,200	1,429	2,225	2,366	3,168	2,211	229
Nicaragua	977	1,178	3,212	1,330	6,033	2,781	4,761	892
Costa Rica	1,108	692	3,844	1,895	2,725	2,536	3,469	1,367

SOURCE: These figures by sector and country were calculated from tables 1 and 7.

Table E-6. Output Per Worker in Manufacturing Industries
(Central American pesos in current prices)

CIIU	Guatemala			El Salvador		
	1958	1968	1972	1956	1968	1972
311	4,946	11,548	10,334	183	11,548	10,334
312	5,866	10,941	13,475	9,301	10,941	13,475
313	6,112	18,986	18,143	7,623	18,986	18,143
314	15,272	14,080	13,604	20,940	14,080	13,604
321	2,495	5,486	5,728	19,136	5,486	5,428
322	1,744	4,138	3,638	1,218	4,138	368
323	2,770	5,352	5,622	3,198	5,352	5,623
324	1,714	2,645	3,666	1,541	2,645	3,666
331	2,215	2,893	3,924	1,793	2,893	3,924
332	1,399	3,249	2,095	1,661	3,249	2,095
341	4,735	9,647	19,859	1,580	9,647	19,859
342	1,978	4,286	3,802	2,670	4,286	3,802
351	393	8,267	27,430	1,328	8,267	27,430
352	4,792	14,073	12,711	5,319	14,073	12,711
353	-	105,656	176,675	-	105,656	176,675
354	-	8,466	3,572	-	8,466	3,572
355	2,679	13,482	12,149	2,968	13,482	12,149
356	-	5,384	95,094	-	5,383	5,094
361	467	2,120	1,030	2,968	2,120	1,031
362	2,808	7,469	8,492	7,638	7,469	8,462
369	3,640	5,703	5,274	1,405	5,703	5,274
371	1,326	12,330	16,241	1,576	12,330	16,241
372	-	2,692	3,702	-	2,696	3,702
381	1,757	6,014	449	1,241	6,014	4,449
382	2,032	3,561	2,209	1,167	3,561	2,209
383	3,012	11,731	11,208	3,167	11,731	11,208
384	2,332	5,627	15,427	3,597	5,627	15,427
385	256	6,346	3,912	-	6,346	3,912
390	3,406	2,969	4,139	1,892	2,967	4,139

Table E-6 (Continued)

CIIU	Honduras 1968	Nicaragua 1968	Costa Rica 1958	Costa Rica 1968
311	12,466	16,310	4,017	13,678
312	12,253	11,661	8,870	21,202
313	32,096	15,116	11,076	18,302
314	18,960	–	14,639	28,469
321	6,212	3,994	2,877	5,127
322	3,066	3,239	1,883	4,046
323	5,921	6,963	2,474	4,989
324	2,002	4,033	22,746	4,307
331	5,353	5,406	2,267	3,059
332	2,701	3,371	1,668	3,635
341	31,649	10,856	3,908	13,924
342	2,557	5,583	3,648	3,246
351	5,562	26,466	18,757	44,112
352	9,238	10,052	4,401	28,663
353	256,228	–	–	–
354	–	–	–	–
355	7,002	10,435	3,393	14,072
356	12,700	6,319	–	10,032
361	–	9,243	155	8,010
362	–	–	2,012	8,143
369	6,344	7,741	1,980	4,770
371	–	–	–	24,669
372	–	–	–	16,248
381	12,255	9,205	1,605	6,720
382	3,118	11,426	1,447	2,781
383	5,185	17,812	932	9,520
384	–	–	281	1,710
385	2,793	3,504	–	–
390	3,654	6,013	437	5,898

SOURCES: 1. For code: CIIU, Revision 2.
2. For figures: Study of Projected Employment, SIECA/ Brookings, Max A. Soto and W. R. Cline.

Table E-7. Labor Employed, by Sector of Economic Activity
(thousands of worker-years)

Country	Agriculture	Mining	Industry	Construction	Energy
1960					
Central America	2,013.6	6.9	351.3	109.2	9.9
Guatemala	834.6	1.8	136.2	33.3	1.5
El Salvador	452.1	-	96.3	29.6	1.5
Honduras	379.1	1.6	44.1	11.3	1.1
Nicaragua	173.4	2.6	35.8	17.2	2.6
Costa Rica	174.4	0.9	38.9	17.8	3.2
1968					
Central America	2,358.1	9.4	525.4	150.0	15.2
Guatemala	930.7	2.2	176.7	47.7	2.4
El Salvador	497.7	-	189.2	43.5	2.0
Honduras	500.4	2.3	61.0	16.0	3.0
Nicaragua	231.2	3.7	50.6	18.2	2.2
Costa Rica	198.1	1.2	47.9	25.1	5.6
1971					
Central America	2,467.6	9.8	579.0	155.5	19.4
Guatemala	952.1	2.4	204.8	57.7	3.3
El Salvador	533.1	-	199.9	30.7	2.1
Honduras	538.2	2.5	69.3	18.2	4.1
Nicaragua	236.5	3.6	53.1	20.3	3.0
Costa Rica	207.7	1.3	51.9	28.6	6.9

Table E-7 (Continued)

Country	Commerce	Transportation	Services	Activities Not Specified
1960				
Central America	214.0	77.4	438.2	47.6
Guatemala	73.8	28.1	136.7	8.1
El Salvador	46.7	15.6	96.3	3.0
Honduras	26.9	7.7	69.4	26.0
Nicaragua	34.4	13.5	77.4	10.5
Costa Rica	32.2	12.5	58.4	-
1968				
Central America	292.2	107.5	571.8	62.2
Guatemala	98.2	33.7	176.0	19.3
El Salvador	71.5	30.6	146.0	3.1
Honduras	39.7	13.0	90.8	36.6
Nicaragua	38.1	14.7	80.3	3.2
Costa Rica	44.7	15.5	78.7	-
1971				
Central America	321.6	117.0	630.6	75.0
Guatemala	111.2	37.7	193.5	30.2
El Salvador	71.7	30.7	153.8	3.1
Honduras	44.6	14.9	99.9	33.8
Nicaragua	43.6	16.9	95.2	7.9
Costa Rica	50.5	16.8	88.1	-

SOURCE: Based on reports of the Ministries of Labor for each Central American country as well as decennial census figures and interpolations as prepared by the SIECA staff.

Industrial Comparative Advantage: Supplementary Tables

William R. Cline
Alan I. Rapoport

Table F-1. Comparative Advantage Rankings by Industrial Sector,
Central America

	Rankings[a]						Composite Rank[b]	
Sector	R1	R2	R3	R4	R5	R6	C1	C2
3111	21	54	66	61	73	67	72	73
3112	29	45	22	53	19	50	34	36
3113	12	55	65	64	67	68	70	71
3114	26	58	72	67	72	70	75	75
3115	18	7	63	10	60	18	17	20
3116	23	37	62	55	41	61	59	62
3117	70	23	7	24	59	29	32	35
3118	19	14	69	29	74	51	51	60
3119	37	27	53	33	62	43	50	55
3121	28	30	42	34	66	47	47	57
3122	16	22	46	38	40	41	26	32
3131	4	74	74	74	18	75	68	68
3132	5	75	68	75	29	74	69	69
3133	3	65	73	69	9	72	62	63
3134	15	59	41	62	45	65	61	66
3140	6	68	71	70	71	71	74	74
3211	50	8	59	11	34	39	25	29
3212	55	21	40	21	57	37	43	45
3213	65	40	38	32	35	55	53	58
3214	54	1	27	2	31	4	5	4
3215	64	12	56	19	30	45	39	40
3219	51	32	28	3	64	27	28	31
3220	74	66	18	56	52	26	64	50
3231	47	33	23	37	58	42	44	48
3232	63	10	36	12	39	22	19	18
3233	72	60	9	45	51	31	55	47
3240	73	63	15	44	48	23	54	44
3311	58	50	58	39	75	64	73	72
3312	75	47	30	13	69	60	65	67
3319	71	3	8	5	68	6	10	13
3320	68	64	11	47	54	34	58	53
3411	32	19	55	36	21	57	35	41
3412	36	13	57	25	42	48	37	43
3419	39	31	31	42	28	21	21	17
3420	49	26	17	17	36	5	7	8
3511	27	4	45	7	26	7	4	3
3512	2	72	64	73	43	52	67	64
3521	7	69	32	63	37	46	49	49
3522	9	44	39	52	49	11	27	21
3523	14	67	33	60	50	3	40	23
3529	44	41	19	40	55	9	30	22
3530	1	5	75	9	53	10	9	12
3540	17	39	6	15	16	2	2	1
3551	8	34	48	49	44	38	36	38
3559	22	49	37	59	24	62	48	54

(continued on next page)

Table F-1 (Continued)

Sector	Rankings[a]						Composite Rank[b]	
	R1	R2	R3	R4	R5	R6	C1	C2
3560	35	29	34	30	47	32	29	30
3610	34	24	54	43	13	59	41	42
3620	24	20	50	41	33	30	24	26
3691	57	9	51	20	8	20	12	10
3692	11	16	70	28	63	25	33	34
3699	48	43	43	48	27	36	46	39
3710	30	15	67	23	22	53	31	37
3720	56	18	52	22	65	16	42	33
3811	31	6	21	8	38	8	3	5
3812	46	56	26	54	56	35	57	51
3813	25	57	61	65	20	63	63	61
3819	43	11	35	16	32	28	13	15
3821	53	25	10	27	7	54	16	28
3822	69	36	13	18	11	14	11	9
3823	66	38	49	31	3	58	45	46
3824	62	42	29	6	10	19	14	11
3825	38	51	4	51	15	24	20	19
3829	61	48	24	50	25	17	38	24
3831	42	71	25	71	17	73	66	65
3832	20	70	47	68	23	56	60	59
3833	52	35	12	26	14	12	8	7
3839	13	73	60	72	46	69	71	70
3841	10	61	5	66	1	49	22	27
3843	40	52	44	58	4	66	52	52
3844	41	46	16	46	2	44	23	25
3845	59	53	3	1	5	15	6	6
3851	67	2	1	4	6	1	1	1
3852	33	28	20	35	12	40	15	16
3901	45	62	2	57	70	33	56	56
3909	60	17	14	14	61	13	18	19

[a]Rankings:
  R1 = unskilled labor/value added;
  R2 = value added/capital;
  R3 = value added/skilled labor;
  R4 = rate of return;
  R5 = (exports - imports)/(exports + imports); and
  R6 = (total factor productivity, Central America)/(total factor productivity, U.S.).
[b]Composite rank:
  C1 = simple average of individual rankings; and
  C2 = weighted average of individual rankings. One-ninth for each of R1, R2, R3, R4; two-ninths, R5; one-third, R6.

NOTE: Rankings are from 1 for lowest comparative advantage to 75 for highest comparative advantage.

613

Table F-2. Factor Intensity by Industrial Sector, Central America
(excluding El Salvador), 1968

Sector	Capital/Value Added	Skilled Workers/ $1,000 Value Added	Unskilled Workers/ $1,000 Value Added
3111	0.4610	0.0240	0.1220
3112	0.5720	0.0690	0.1610
3113	0.4430	0.0250	0.0910
3114	0.4410	0.0150	0.1380
3115	1.4330	0.0260	0.1100
3116	0.6740	0.0290	0.1310
3117	0.8190	0.1050	0.4090
3118	1.0980	0.0200	0.1160
3119	0.7880	0.0390	0.2040
3121	0.7580	0.0490	0.1420
3122	0.8230	0.0440	0.1060
3131	0.2360	0.0140	0.0290
3132	0.1610	0.0210	0.0420
3133	0.3910	0.0150	0.0220
3134	0.4280	0.0490	0.1050
3140	0.3010	0.0170	0.0470
3211	1.3120	0.0350	0.2880
3212	0.8260	0.0520	0.3100
3213	0.6590	0.0540	0.3470
3214	2.3960	0.0650	0.3010
3215	1.1250	0.0380	0.3300
3219	0.7380	0.0640	0.2880
3220	0.3860	0.0720	0.4700
3231	0.7300	0.0690	0.2740
3232	1.1490	0.0540	0.3230
3233	0.4220	0.0990	0.4270
3240	0.4090	0.0800	0.4410
3311	0.5040	0.0350	0.3120
3312	0.5370	0.0630	0.5440
3319	2.2130	0.1010	0.4270
3320	0.3970	0.0940	0.3750
3411	0.8830	0.0380	0.1680
3412	1.1130	0.0370	0.2010
3419	0.7560	0.0620	0.2050
3420	0.8080	0.0740	0.2880
3511	1.9290	0.0470	0.1400
3512	0.2670	0.0260	0.0190
3521	0.3000	0.0620	0.0480
3522	0.5960	0.0530	0.0590
3523	0.3620	0.0620	0.1240
3529	0.6510	0.0690	0.2450
3530	1.8130	0.0060	0.0090
3540	0.6630	0.1060	0.1060

(continued on next page)

Table F-2 (Continued)

Sector	Capital/Value Added	Skilled Workers/ $1,000 Value Added	Unskilled Workers/ $1,000 Value Added
3551	0.7110	0.0420	0.0480
3559	0.5080	0.0540	0.1300
3560	0.7670	0.0570	0.1860
3610	0.8150	0.0380	0.1860
3620	0.8700	0.0400	0.1330
3691	1.1570	0.0400	0.3110
3692	1.0760	0.0190	0.0850
3699	0.6220	0.0480	0.2770
3710	1.0870	0.0230	0.1610
3720	0.9310	0.0400	0.3110
3811	1.4990	0.0690	0.1630
3812	0.4410	0.0660	0.2660
3813	0.4410	0.0320	0.1350
3819	1.1350	0.0560	0.2260
3821	0.8150	0.0960	0.2950
3822	0.6790	0.0920	0.3830
3823	0.6720	0.0420	0.3520
3824	0.6360	0.0630	0.3210
3825	0.4960	0.1170	0.2040
3829	0.5280	0.0670	0.3200
3831	0.2770	0.0660	0.2200
3832	0.2900	0.0430	0.1210
3833	0.7010	0.0930	0.2910
3839	0.2600	0.0330	0.0910
3841	0.4100	0.1150	0.0810
3843	0.4940	0.0470	0.2080
3844	0.5580	0.0780	0.2090
3845	0.4730	0.1390	0.3150
3851	2.2800	0.2000	0.3550
3852	0.7850	0.0690	0.1810
3901	0.4100	0.1810	0.2510
3909	0.9500	0.0820	0.3150

SOURCE: Calculated from 1968 industrial census, Central America.

Table F-3. Rate of Return to Capital and Foreign Trade
Performance Indicator by Industrial Sector,
Central America

Sector	Rate of Return[a]	$\dfrac{\text{Exports} - \text{Imports}}{\text{Exports} + \text{Imports}}$ [b]
3111	1.4864	0.9563
3112	0.9967	-0.9868
3113	1.5449	0.0938
3114	1.7954	0.8708
3115	0.4008	-0.3374
3116	1.0752	-0.8925
3117	0.5410	-0.4259
3118	0.6453	0.9684
3119	0.6804	-0.1583
3121	0.6958	0.0658
3122	0.7502	-0.8943
3131	3.3392	-0.9874
3132	4.9215	-0.9540
3133	2.1085	-0.9962
3134	1.4941	-0.8683
3140	2.4402	0.5065
3211	0.4174	-0.9213
3212	0.4944	-0.5362
3213	0.6782	-0.9208
3214	0.0457	-0.9367
3215	0.4758	-0.9475
3219	0.0549	-0.1336
3220	1.1115	-0.6591
3231	0.7487	-0.4581
3232	0.4503	-0.8957
3233	0.8890	-0.7468
3240	0.8495	-0.8386
3311	0.7553	0.9785
3312	0.4542	0.2364
3319	0.2123	0.1447
3320	0.8953	-0.6061
3411	0.7469	-0.9831
3412	0.5768	-0.8840
3419	0.8090	-0.9565
3420	0.4745	-0.9197
3511	0.2556	-0.9683
3512	3.1257	-0.8736
3521	1.5216	-0.9072
3522	0.9945	-0.8171
3523	1.4027	-0.8023
3529	0.7836	-0.6009
3530	0.4004	-0.6113
3540	0.4643	-0.9917

(continued on next page)

616

Table F-3 (Continued)

Sector	Rate of Return[a]	Exports - Imports[b] / Exports + Imports
3551	0.9366	-0.8690
3559	1.3659	-0.9750
3560	0.6498	-0.8428
3610	0.8391	-0.9943
3620	0.8001	-0.9263
3691	0.4866	-0.9962
3692	0.6269	-0.1509
3699	0.8959	-0.9624
3710	0.5139	-0.9821
3720	0.5034	0.0409
3811	0.3083	-0.9010
3812	1.0338	-0.5366
3813	1.5663	-0.9839
3819	0.4694	-0.9361
3821	0.6095	-0.9980
3822	0.4750	-0.9954
3823	0.6693	-0.9991
3824	0.2536	-0.9960
3825	0.9397	-0.9930
3829	0.9386	-0.9689
3831	2.4991	-0.9891
3832	1.8491	-0.9818
3833	0.5958	-0.9932
3839	2.7006	-0.8556
3841	1.7792	-0.9997
3843	1.3061	-0.9985
3844	0.8942	-0.9995
3845	-0.0798	-0.9982
3851	0.1205	-0.9980
3852	0.7265	-0.9948
3901	1.2898	0.4603
3909	0.4550	-0.3151

[a]Average for Central America excluding El Salvador.
[b]Refers to trade with the rest of the world; excludes intraregional trade.

SOURCE: Rate of return calculated from 1968 industrial census. Trade indicator calculated from detailed trade data provided by SIECA Statistics Division. Trade data refer to 1970-72 annual averages.

Table F-4. Total Factor Productivity by Industrial Sector,
Central America and the United States

	A	B	C
Sector	Central America	United States	= A/B (Rank)
3111	5.92	n.a.	3.33^a (67)
3112	3.78	n.a.	2.12^a (49)
3113	6.27	n.a.	3.52^a (68)
3114	6.86	n.a.	3.85^a (70)
3115	2.67	n.a.	1.50^a (16)
3116	4.59	n.a.	2.58^a (61)
3117	3.08	n.a.	1.73^a (28)
3118	3.82	n.a.	2.15^a (51)
3119	3.54	n.a.	1.99^a (43)
3121	3.71	n.a.	2.08^a (46)
3122	3.52	n.a.	1.98^a (41)
3131	11.65	n.a.	6.54^a (75)
3132	9.92	n.a.	5.57^a (74)
3133	7.73	n.a.	4.34^a (72)
3134	5.47	n.a.	3.07^a (65)
3140	7.38	n.a.	4.15^a (71)
3211	2.94	1.51	1.95 (39)
3212	3.15	n.a.	1.90^b (37)
3213	3.65	n.a.	2.20^b (55)
3214	1.45	n.a.	0.87^b (4)
3215	3.07	1.48	2.07 (45)
3219	3.39	2.00	1.70 (26)
3220	3.20	1.88	1.70 (27)
3231	3.39	1.71	1.98 (42)
3232	2.74	n.a.	1.58^b (21)
3233	3.17	1.75	1.81 (31)
3240	2.87	1.78	1.61 (23)
3311	4.87	1.68	2.90 (64)
3312	3.41	1.40	2.44 (60)
3319	1.68	1.78	0.94 (6)
3320	3.22	1.73	1.86 (33)
3411	3.68	1.62	2.26 (57)
3412	3.30	1.57	2.10 (48)
3419	3.11	1.96	1.58 (22)
3420	2.68	3.00	0.89 (5)
3511	2.00	2.11	0.94 (7)
3512	6.78	3.14	2.16 (52)
3521	4.69	2.25	2.08 (47)
3522	3.60	2.74	1.31 (11)
3523	3.72	4.70	0.79 (3)
3529	2.58	2.44	1.05 (9)
3530	3.03	n.a.	1.19^c (10)
3540	1.94	n.a.	0.76^c (2)

(continued on next page)

Table F-4 (Continued)

Sector	A Central America	B United States	C = A/B (Rank)
3551	3.87	2.00	1.94 (38)
3559	4.45	1.65	2.70 (62)
3560	3.35	1.84	1.82 (32)
3610	3.56	1.55	2.29 (59)
3620	3.21	1.83	1.79 (30)
3691	2.66	1.72	1.55 (19)
3692	3.57	1.61	1.65 (24)
3699	4.03	1.88	1.89 (36)
3710	3.79	1.75	2.17 (53)
3720	3.34	2.22	1.50 (17)
3811	1.98	1.93	1.02 (8)
3812	3.58	n.a.	1.87[b] (35)
3813	5.64	2.02	2.80 (63)
3819	2.87	1.66	1.73 (29)
3821	3.95	1.80	2.19 (54)
3822	2.57	1.86	1.38 (13)
3823	3.47	1.53	2.26 (58)
3824	2.66	1.72	1.55 (20)
3825	3.67	2.26	1.65 (25)
3829	2.83	1.88	1.50 (18)
3831	7.49	1.69	4.44 (73)
3832	3.24	1.47	2.21 (56)
3833	2.79	2.11	1.32 (12)
3839	6.40	1.54	3.55 (69)
3841	3.71	n.a.	2.12[b] (50)
3843	5.52	n.a.	3.15[b] (66)
3844	3.75	1.83	2.05 (44)
3845	2.04	1.42	1.44 (15)
3851	1.22	1.68	0.73 (1)
3852	3.29	n.a.	1.96[b] (40)
3901	3.31	n.a.	1.86[a] (34)
3909	2.46	n.a.	1.38[a] (14)

[a] Calculated using overall median total factor productivity ratio for the United States (1.78).

[b] Calculated using unweighted average of total factor productivity ratios for other sectors within the same three-digit category for which direct estimates are given in column B.

[c] Calculated using unweighted average of total factor productivity ratios for other sectors within the same two-digit category for which direct estimates are given in column B.

NOTE: n.a. -- not available.

Table F-5. Spearman Rank Correlation Coefficients Between Pairs of
Indicators of Comparative Advantage

I. Static Indicators[a]

	R1	R2	R3	R4	R5	R6
R1		-0.248^b	-0.571^b	-0.516^b	-0.024	-0.352^b
R2			-0.006	0.816^b	-0.022	0.493^b
R3				0.277^b	0.222^c	0.540^b
R4					0.003	0.664^b
R5						0.002

II. Dynamic Indicators[d]

	F1	F2	F3
F1		0.225	0.229^c
F2			0.582^b

III. Composite Indicators

	Static (C2)[e]
Dynamic (FC)[f]	-0.365^b

[a]Static indicators:
R1 = unskilled labor/value added;
R2 = value added/capital;
R3 = value added/skilled labor;
R4 = rate of return;
R5 = (exports - imports)/(exports + imports); and
R6 = (total factor productivity, Central America)/(total factor
    productivity, U.S.).
[b]Significant at the 1 percent level.
[c]Significant at the 5 percent level.
[d]Dynamic indicators:
F1 = export growth rate;
F2 = growth elasticities; and
F3 = control country comparison.
[e]See table F-1.
[f]See table F-6.

Table F-6. Rankings of Industrial Sectors by Prospective Future
Increase in Comparative Advantage, Central America

Sector	F1 Export Growth	F2 Growth Elasticities	F3 Control Country Comparison	FC Composite[a]
3111	46	17.5	14	27
3112	49	17.5	14	32
3113	40	17.5	14	23
3114	30	17.5	14	17
3115	23	17.5	14	11
3116	43	17.5	14	26
3117	41	17.5	14	24
3118	33	17.5	14	20
3119	16	17.5	14	7
3121	22	17.5	14	10
3122	26	17.5	14	14
3131	62	17.5	22.5	50
3132	11	17.5	22.5	6
3133	4	17.5	22.5	3
3134	1	17.5	22.5	2
3140	55	17.5	25	46
3211	45	3.5	38.5	37
3212	34	3.5	38.5	22
3213	53	3.5	38.5	44
3214	44	3.5	38.5	33
3215	9	3.5	38.5	5
3219	65	3.5	38.5	52
3220	28	26.5	1	13
3231	31	8	34	21
3232	8	8	34	4
3233	13	8	34	8
3240	42	26.5	20	34
3311	29	31.5	3	18
3312	48	31.5	3	35
3319	51	31.5	3	39
3320	24	31.5	7	15
3411	59	70	55	65
3412	17	70	55	49
3419	50	70	55	62
3420	39	48	42	51
3511	38	44.5	57.5	53
3512	25	44.5	57.5	45
3521	73	44.5	44.5	64
3522	58	44.5	44.5	57
3523	32	44.5	44.5	47
3529	21	44.5	44.5	36
3530	19	44.5	47	31
3540	63	44.5	74	66

Table F-6 (Continued)

Sector	F1 Export Growth	F2 Growth Elasticities	F3 Control Country Comparison	FC Composite[a]
3551	52	49.5	48.5	56
3559	54	49.5	48.5	58
3560	36	44.5	8	28
3610	10	36	70	30
3620	66	36	59	63
3691	64	36	27	55
3692	6	36	27	9
3699	37	36	27	40
3710	56	28.5	71	60
3720	20	28.5	n.a.	19
3811	60	59.5	30.5	59
3812	18	59.5	30.5	29
3813	27	59.5	30.5	42
3819	47	59.5	30.5	54
3821	70	59.5	62.5	72
3822	12	59.5	62.5	43
3823	67	59.5	62.5	69
3824	72	59.5	62.5	73
3825	68	59.5	62.5	70
3829	74	59.5	62.5	74
3831	2	59.5	51.5	25
3832	57	59.5	51.5	61
3833	71	59.5	51.5	68
3839	75	59.5	51.5	71
3841	3	59.5	67.5	38
3843	61	59.5	67.5	67
3844	7	59.5	67.5	41
3845	14	59.5	67.5	48
3851	69	n.a.	72.5	75
3852	15	n.a.	72.5	16
3901	5	n.a.	5.5	1
3909	35	n.a.	5.5	12

[a]Based on weighted average of rankings F1, F2, and F3. Weights: F1, 50 percent; F2, 25 percent; F3, 25 percent.

NOTE: Rankings are from 1 for lowest prospective increase in comparative advantage to 75 for highest prospective increase.

Table F-7. Annual Average Growth Rates of Total Exports by Industrial
Sector, Central America, 1963-65 to 1970-72

Sector	Growth Rate in Percent (rank)	1970-72 Average Annual Exports ($1,000)
3111	23.83 (50)	87,574
3112	25.65 (53)	3,590
3113	17.96 (44)	6,340
3114	13.53 (34)	20,194
3115	9.82 (26)	17,725
3116	18.65 (47)	4,378
3117	18.25 (45)	2,546
3118	14.37 (37)	54,074
3119	5.93 (19)	3,099
3121	9.52 (25)	10,155
3122	11.17 (30)	1,467
3131	42.72 (66)	245
3132	1.11 (14)	441
3133	-10.41 (4)	10
3134	-29.54 (1)	2
3140	33.41 (59)	2,625
3211	21.69 (49)	37,629
3212	15.99 (38)	6,206
3213	28.27 (57)	14,903
3214	19.39 (48)	173
3215	-3.02 (9)	242
3219	116.34 (71)	3,650
3220	12.28 (32)	7,986
3231	13.61 (35)	2,582
3232	-3.59 (8)	5
3233	4.30 (16)	530
3240	18.46 (46)	8,671
3311	12.70 (33)	29,520
3312	24.10 (52)	372
3319	27.39 (55)	970
3320	10.30 (27)	1,943
3411	38.91 (63)	3,378
3412	6.02 (20)	4,906
3419	26.82 (54)	2,477
3420	17.85 (43)	2,946
3511	17.17 (42)	7,803
3512	10.64 (28)	13,874
3513	106.44 (70)	5,703
3515	0.0 (13)	0
3521	726.65[a] (81)	2,599
3522	38.47 (62)	19,231
3523	14.29 (36)	12,973
3529	7.93 (24)	5,844
3530	6.63 (22)	7,099
3532	0.0 (11)	0

Table F-7 (Continued)

Sector	Growth Rate in Percent (rank)	1970-72 Average Annual Exports ($1,000)
3540	69.47 (68)	384
3551	28.15 (56)	7,436
3559	28.98 (58)	1,362
3560	16.18 (40)	7,329
3610	-1.19 (10)	21
3620	134.88 (72)	5,458
3691	79.89 (69)	697
3692	-6.85 (6)	981
3699	16.22 (41)	1,794
3710	34.39 (60)	9,583
3720	7.27 (23)	15,983
3811	41.76 (64)	2,628
3812	6.19 (21)	1,131
3813	11.33 (31)	1,116
3819	23.84 (51)	7,922
3821	420.69 (78)	103
3822	2.45 (15)	165
3823	329.67 (73)	27
3824	536.88[a] (80)	420
3825	336.06[a] (74)	30
3829	778.31[a] (82)	3,971
3831	-19.18 (2)	520
3832	35.57 (61)	3,701
3833	508.60 (79)	305
3839	923.14 (83)	11,547
3841	-10.61 (3)	28
3842	10.77 (29)	4
3843	42.23 (65)	964
3844	-5.65 (7)	25
3845	4.59 (17)	6
3849	359.99[a] (75)	43
3851	377.45[a] (76)	56
3852	5.03 (18)	49
3853	48.39 (67)	2
3901	-6.86 (5)	3,700
3902	389.52[a] (77)	67
3903	0 (12)	0
3909	16.06 (39)	13,231

[a]Base period exports are zero. Growth rate calculated assuming base of one dollar.

Table F-8. Sectoral Growth Elasticities, Cross-Country

Sector	ISIC[a]	ISIC Revised[b]	Elasticity[c]	Rank[d]
Food, beverages, tobacco	20-22	311-12, 313, 314	0.862	3
Textiles	23	321	0.814	1
Clothing, footwear	24	322, 324	1.116	4
Wood products	25-26	331, 332	1.179	6
Paper, paper products	27	341	1.822	12
Printing, publishing	28	342	1.451	9
Leather products	29	323	0.840	2
Rubber products	30	355	1.456	10
Chemicals, petroleum, and coal goods	31-32	351, 352, 353, 354, 356	1.370	8
Nonmetallic mineral products	33	361, 362, 369	1.250	7
Basic metals	34	371, 372	1.146	5
Metal products	35-38	381, 382, 383, 384	1.705	11

[a]International Standard Industrial Classification. United Nations, International Standard Industrial Classification of All Economic Activities, Statistical Papers, Series M, No. 4, Rev. 2 (New York: United Nations, 1968).
[b]Ibid.
[c]Elasticity of value added per capita with respect to income per capita. Simple average of two alternative estimates for each sector (one based on "small, primary" countries and the other on "small, manufacturing" countries).
[d]From 1 for lowest elasticity to 12 for highest elasticity.

SOURCE: Calculated from H. Chenery and L. Taylor, "Development Patterns: Among Countries and Over Time," Review of Economics and Statistics 50(4) (November 1968): p. 407.

Table F-9. Sectoral Shares in Value Added, Manufacturing Industry
Excluding Nonferrous Metals (372), Central America,
Chile, Colombia, and Peru
(percentage)

Sector	A Central America	B Chile[a]	C Colombia[b]	D Peru[c]	E Average[d]	F = E/A (rank)	
311-12	29.81	14.96	13.66	23.62	17.41	0.58	(6)
313	11.44	4.84	13.77	8.15	8.92	0.78	(8)
314	4.11	4.04	3.38	2.55	3.32	0.81	(9)
321	8.27	11.06	16.35	9.65	12.35	1.49	(13)
322	6.20	2.59	3.25	1.93	2.59	0.42	(1)
323	.84	1.14	.89	.66	.90	1.07	(12)
324	2.64	2.85	.69	1.26	1.60	0.61	(7)
331	3.25	2.02	1.01	1.21	1.41	0.43	(2)
332	1.89	.63	.66	1.59	.96	0.51	(4)
341	1.34	3.39	3.12	2.04	2.85	2.13	(19)
342	2.20	4.26	2.82	3.06	3.38	1.54	(14)
351	1.34	2.24	3.31	4.41	3.32	2.48	(20)
352	4.10	5.28	7.57	6.27	6.37	1.55	(15)
353	2.86	2.77	3.84	6.85	4.49	1.57	(16)
354	.03	.11	.03	1.83	.66	22.00	(27)
355	1.30	2.53	2.12	1.88	2.18	1.68	(17)
356	2.18	1.59	1.39	.48	1.15	0.53	(5)
361	.18	.63	.53	.77	.64	3.56	(24)
362	.62	1.03	.97	2.83	1.61	2.60	(21)
369	3.10	2.16	3.90	1.73	2.60	0.84	(10)
371	.87	7.14	2.72	2.25	4.04	4.64	(25)
381	4.08	5.21	4.39	3.03	4.21	1.03	(11)
382	1.05	4.11	2.88	2.52	3.17	3.02	(22)
383	1.95	5.30	2.51	2.87	3.56	1.83	(18)
384	1.41	7.47	2.63	4.17	4.76	3.38	(23)
385	.03	.16	.25	.04	.15	5.00	(26)
390	2.85	.47	1.34	2.31	1.37	0.48	(3)
	100.00	100.00	100.00	100.00	100.00		

[a]1970-72 average.
[b]1970-72 average.
[c]1968-70 average.
[d]Simple average, columns B, C, D.

SOURCES: Column A, SIECA, for 1972. Column B: Calculated from United
Nations, The Growth of World Industry, 1973 Edition, vol. I
(New York: United Nations, 1975).

Table F-10. Tax and Tariff Incentives by Industrial Sector,
Central America (Excluding El Salvador)

Sector	Effective Rate of Protection[a]	Fraction of Income Tax Exempted	Proportionate Contribution of Incentive to After-Tax Profits		
			Effective Protection	Tax Exemption	Total
3111	0.0446	0.8965	0.06616	0.33495	0.40111
3112	0.2658	0.8436	0.39313	0.26532	0.65845
3113	0.6717	0.9934	0.61054	0.38310	0.99363
3114	1.8827	0.8754	0.85932	0.26384	1.12315
3115	-0.0493	0.5328	-0.09822	0.21130	0.11307
3116	8.5864	0.5518	1.44140	0.17970	1.62111
3117	12.3945	0.6309	2.32811	0.12663	2.45474
3118	0.1736	0.4767	0.22568	0.21054	0.43622
3119	1.2551	0.9386	1.12675	0.32574	1.45250
3121	0.3804	0.3216	0.56923	0.11231	0.68154
3122	0.0994	0.9473	0.15880	0.21715	0.37594
3131	0.8540	0.4058	1.89009	0.23195	2.12204
3132	1.0011	0.8188	0.69473	0.34893	1.04366
3133	0.2355	0.0275	0.37182	0.01612	0.38794
3134	0.4813	0.4256	0.78765	0.14366	0.93131
3140	1.0195	0.6293	1.50918	0.29931	1.80849
3211	0.1897	0.7464	0.35081	0.30325	0.65406
3212	0.4922	0.3337	0.87789	0.14375	1.02164
3213	1.0898	0.8810	1.24211	0.28104	1.52315
3214	1.6240	1.0000	9.90095	0.32178	10.22273
3215	0.1126	0.7414	0.20816	0.20311	0.41128
3219	0.5066	1.0000	9.68992	0.19503	9.88495
3222	0.7892	0.7896	1.10357	0.20823	1.31179
3231	0.2212	0.6482	0.36414	0.14026	0.50441
3232	-0.0224	0.9172	-0.04870	0.15572	0.10701
3233	0.5674	0.8942	1.02802	0.13200	1.16002
3240	0.9004	0.8163	1.52455	0.18935	1.71392
3311	0.2992	0.4084	0.66004	0.10044	0.76049
3312	0.1477	0.9804	0.60899	0.13088	0.73987
3319	0.3396	0.0784	0.58662	0.01286	0.59969
3320	0.7392	0.2928	1.32028	0.07332	1.39360
3411	0.0307	0.9938	0.05217	0.42043	0.47260
3412	0.1706	0.8411	0.24188	0.27153	0.51341
3419	0.2904	0.6467	0.39163	0.15228	0.54391
3420	0.0693	0.6123	0.18417	0.16551	0.34967
3511	0.0342	0.4945	0.08964	0.13692	0.22656
3512	0.0509	0.9812	0.06044	0.34164	0.40208
3521	0.2756	0.7550	0.50669	0.25681	0.76350
3522	0.0863	0.8365	0.14013	0.31007	0.45019
3523	1.1696	0.9691	1.14551	0.28132	1.42683
3529	0.2036	0.4829	0.44424	0.08705	0.53129
3530	0.1102	0.0000	0.14139	0.00000	0.14139

Table F-10 (Continued)

Sector	Effective Rate of Protection[a]	Fraction of Income Tax Exempted	Proportionate Contribution of Incentive to After-Tax Profits		
			Effective Protection	Tax Exemption	Total
3540	0.0363	0.0000	0.15575	0.00000	0.15575
3551	0.2740	0.9049	0.34366	0.38532	0.72898
3559	0.1681	0.9281	0.22003	0.35858	0.57861
3560	0.3606	0.8663	0.56734	0.22075	0.78810
3610	0.7282	0.8196	0.63351	0.20329	0.83679
3620	0.2666	0.9928	0.32978	0.44591	0.77568
3691	0.1225	0.8643	0.20695	0.26294	0.46989
3692	0.1591	0.6148	0.22111	0.27880	0.49991
3699	0.1004	0.3727	0.17646	0.11359	0.29005
3710	0.0409	1.0000	0.07793	0.37356	0.45150
3720	0.0440	0.9233	0.29968	0.10115	0.40083
3811	0.2727	1.0000	0.49360	0.21617	0.70976
3812	0.3192	0.4697	0.57397	0.11542	0.68939
3813	0.0597	0.9580	0.08455	0.32068	0.40523
3819	0.3319	0.9318	0.50606	0.24711	0.75318
3821	0.1250	0.0000	0.25753	0.00000	0.25753
3822	0.0673	0.9703	0.20794	0.18046	0.38840
3823	0.0096	1.0000	0.02308	0.17890	0.20198
3824	0.0119	0.0313	0.08674	0.01281	0.09954
3825	0.2996	1.0000	0.54632	0.17619	0.72252
3829	0.1103	0.9138	0.21252	0.18830	0.40081
3831	0.0183	0.9954	0.02740	0.34004	0.36744
3832	0.1963	1.0000	0.34410	0.29261	0.63672
3833	1.0588	0.9680	1.27957	0.25793	1.53751
3839	0.3062	0.9773	0.34714	0.38033	0.72747
3841	0.0510	1.0000	0.06920	0.17939	0.24859
3843	0.2163	0.9352	0.28329	0.30381	0.58712
3844	0.4123	0.9954	0.63985	0.25216	0.89201
3845	0.0011	0.1182	0.00000	0.00000	0.00000
3851	0.0982	0.0000	0.41925	0.00000	0.41925
3852	0.3910	0.0512	0.52649	0.00984	0.53633
3901	0.1038	0.0527	0.19099	0.00916	0.20016
3909	0.5884	0.6888	0.95448	0.12312	1.07759

[a]Taking into account the effect of tariff exonerations on final product and intermediate inputs.

Table F-11. Rankings of Industrial Sectors by Degree of
Incentives Received, Central America

Sector	Tax Incentive	Effective Tariff Protection Incentive[a]	Total Incentive
3111	65	8	20
3112	52	40	41
3113	72	53	57
3114	51	59	61
3115	41	1	4
3116	32	69	69
3117	19	73	73
3118	40	27	25
3119	64	64	66
3121	15	49	42
3122	43	17	15
3131	45	72	72
3132	68	57	59
3133	10	38	16
3134	24	58	56
3140	58	70	71
3211	59	36	40
3212	25	60	58
3213	55	66	67
3214	63	75	75
3215	37	23	23
3219	36	74	74
3220	39	63	63
3231	23	37	31
3232	27	2	3
3233	21	62	62
3240	35	71	70
3311	13	56	50
3312	20	52	48
3319	9	51	38
3320	11	68	64
3411	74	6	29
3412	53	28	32
3419	26	39	35
3420	28	19	13
3511	22	13	9
3512	67	7	21

Table F-11 (Continued)

Sector	Tax Incentive	Effective Tariff Protection Incentive[a]	Total Incentive
3521	48	45	51
3522	61	14	26
3523	56	65	65
3529	12	42	33
3530	3	15	5
3540	2	16	6
3551	73	33	47
3559	69	25	36
3560	44	48	53
3610	38	54	54
3620	75	32	52
3691	50	21	28
3692	54	26	30
3699	16	18	12
3710	70	10	27
3720	14	31	19
3811	42	43	44
3812	17	50	43
3813	62	11	22
3819	46	44	49
3821	5	29	11
3822	33	22	17
3823	30	4	8
3824	8	12	2
3825	29	47	45
3829	34	24	18
3831	66	5	14
3832	57	34	39
3833	49	67	68
3839	71	35	46
3841	31	9	10
3843	60	30	37
3844	47	55	55
3845	4	3	1
3851	1	41	24
3852	7	46	34
3901	6	20	7
3909	18	61	60

NOTE: Sector rankings are from 1 for lowest incentive to 75 for highest incentive.

[a]Including effect of exonerations from tariffs on final and intermediate goods.

Table F-12. Classification of Industrial Sectors by Factor Intensity
and Scale Economies, Central America

Sector	A Unskilled Labor Intensive	B Capital Intensive	C Skilled Labor Intensive	D Scale Economies
3111	N	N	N	Y
3112	N	N	Y	Y
3113	N	N	N	Y
3114	N	N	N	Y
3115	N	Y	N	Y
3116	N	Y	N	Y
3117	Y	Y	Y	Y
3118	N	Y	N	Y
3119	N	Y	N	Y
3121	N	Y	N	N
3122	N	Y	N	N
3131	N	N	N	Y
3132	N	N	N	Y
3133	N	N	N	Y
3134	N	N	N	Y
3140	N	N	N	Y
3211	Y	Y	N	N
3212	Y	Y	N	N
3213	Y	N	N	N
3214	Y	Y	Y	N
3215	Y	Y	N	N
3219	Y	Y	Y	N
3220	Y	N	Y	Y
3231	Y	Y	Y	N
3232	Y	Y	Y	N
3233	Y	N	Y	N
3240	Y	N	Y	N
3311	Y	N	N	Y
3312	Y	N	Y	Y
3319	Y	Y	Y	Y
3320	Y	N	Y	N
3411	N	Y	N	N
3412	N	Y	N	N
3419	Y	Y	Y	N
3420	Y	Y	Y	N
3511	N	Y	N	N
3512	N	N	N	N
3521	N	N	Y	N
3522	N	N	N	N
3523	N	N	Y	N

Table F-12 (Continued)

Sector	A Unskilled Labor Intensive	B Capital Intensive	C Skilled Labor Intensive	D Scale Economies
3529	Y	N	Y	N
3530	N	Y	N	N
3540	N	N	Y	N
3551	N	Y	N	Y
3559	N	N	Y	Y
3560	N	Y	Y	Y
3610	N	Y	N	Y
3620	N	Y	N	Y
3691	Y	Y	N	Y
3692	N	Y	N	Y
3699	Y	N	N	Y
3710	N	Y	N	Y
3720	Y	Y	N	Y
3811	N	Y	Y	Y
3812	Y	N	Y	Y
3813	N	N	N	Y
3819	Y	Y	Y	Y
3821	Y	Y	Y	N
3822	Y	Y	Y	N
3823	Y	N	N	N
3824	Y	N	Y	N
3825	Y	N	Y	N
3829	Y	N	Y	N
3831	Y	N	Y	N
3832	N	N	N	N
3833	Y	Y	Y	N
3839	N	N	N	N
3841	N	N	Y	N
3843	Y	N	N	N
3844	Y	N	Y	N
3845	Y	N	Y	N
3851	Y	Y	Y	N
3852	N	Y	Y	N
3901	Y	N	Y	N
3909	Y	Y	Y	N

NOTE: Y = affirmative (sector is intensive in factor indicated, or has economies of scale).
N = negative (opposite case).

Table F-13. Rankings of Central American Countries by Intraregional Comparative Advantage, by Industrial Sector: Unskilled Labor and Capital Intensity Bases

Sector	Unskilled Labor Intensity					Capital Intensity				
	Guatemala	El Salvador	Honduras	Nicaragua	Costa Rica	Guatemala	El Salvador	Honduras	Nicaragua	Costa Rica
3111	3	1	2	4	5	3	4	5	2	1
3112	3	1	2	4	5	3	4	5	2	1
3113	3	1	2	4	5	3	4	5	2	1
3114	3	1	2	4	5	3	4	5	2	1
3115	3	1	2	4	5	3	2	1	4	5
3116	3	1	2	4	5	3	2	1	4	5
3117	3	5	4	2	1	3	2	1	4	5
3118	3	1	2	4	5	3	2	1	4	5
3119	3	1	2	4	5	3	2	1	4	5
3121	3	1	2	4	5	3	2	1	4	5
3122	3	1	2	4	5	3	4	5	2	1
3131	3	1	2	4	5	3	4	5	2	1
3132	3	1	2	4	5	3	4	5	2	1
3133	3	1	2	4	5	3	4	5	2	1
3134	3	1	2	4	5	3	2	1	4	5
3140	3	1	2	4	5	3	2	1	4	5
3211	3	5	4	2	1	3	4	5	2	1
3212	3	5	4	2	1	3	2	1	4	5
3213	3	5	4	2	1	3	2	1	4	5
3214	3	5	4	2	1	3	2	1	4	5
3215	3	5	4	2	1	3	2	1	4	5
3219	3	5	4	2	1	3	2	1	4	5
3220	3	5	4	2	1	3	4	5	2	1
3231	3	5	4	2	1	3	2	1	4	5
3232	3	5	4	2	1	3	2	1	4	5
3233	3	5	4	2	1	3	4	5	2	1
3244	3	5	4	2	1	3	4	5	2	1
3311	3	5	4	2	1	3	4	5	2	1
3312	3	5	4	2	1	3	4	5	2	1
3319	3	5	4	2	1	3	4	5	2	1
3320	3	5	4	2	1	3	4	5	2	1

Table F-13 (Continued)

Sector	Unskilled Labor Intensity					Capital Intensity				
	Guatemala	El Salvador	Honduras	Nicaragua	Costa Rica	Guatemala	El Salvador	Honduras	Nicaragua	Costa Rica
3411	3	1	2	4	5	3	2	1	4	5
3412	3	1	2	4	5	3	2	1	4	5
3419	3	5	4	2	1	3	2	1	4	5
3420	3	5	4	2	1	3	2	1	4	5
3511	3	1	2	4	5	3	2	1	4	5
3512	3	1	2	4	5	3	4	5	2	1
3521	3	1	2	4	5	3	4	5	2	1
3522	3	1	2	4	5	3	4	5	2	1
3523	3	1	2	4	5	3	4	5	2	1
3529	3	5	4	2	1	3	4	5	2	1
3530	3	1	2	4	5	3	2	1	4	5
3540	3	1	2	4	5	3	4	5	2	1
3551	3	1	2	4	5	3	2	1	4	5
3559	3	1	2	4	5	3	4	5	2	1
3560	3	1	2	4	5	3	2	1	4	5
3610	3	1	2	4	5	3	2	1	4	5
3620	3	5	4	2	1	3	2	1	4	5
3691	3	1	4	2	5	3	2	1	4	5
3692	3	5	2	4	1	3	4	5	2	1
3699	3	5	4	2	1	3	2	1	4	5
3710	3	1	2	4	5	3	2	1	4	5
3720	3	5	4	2	1	3	2	1	4	5
3811	3	1	2	4	5	3	2	1	4	5
3812	3	5	4	2	1	3	4	5	2	1
3813	3	1	2	4	5	3	4	5	2	1
3819	3	5	4	2	1	3	2	1	4	5
3821	3	5	4	2	1	3	2	1	4	5
3822	3	5	4	2	1	3	2	1	4	5
3823	3	5	4	2	1	3	4	5	2	1
3824	3	5	4	2	1	3	4	5	2	1
3825	3	5	4	2	1	3	4	5	2	1
3829	3	5	4	2	1	3	4	5	2	1

(continued on next page)

Table F-13 (Continued)

Sector	Unskilled Labor Intensity					Capital Intensity				
	Guatemala	El Salvador	Honduras	Nicaragua	Costa Rica	Guatemala	El Salvador	Honduras	Nicaragua	Costa Rica
3831	3	5	4	2	1	3	4	5	2	1
3832	3	1	2	4	5	3	4	5	2	1
3833	3	5	4	2	1	3	2	1	4	5
3839	3	1	2	4	5	3	4	5	2	1
3841	3	5	2	4	5	3	4	5	2	1
3843	3	5	4	2	1	3	4	5	2	1
3844	3	5	4	2	1	3	4	5	2	1
3845	3	5	4	2	1	3	4	5	2	1
3851	3	1	2	4	1	3	2	1	4	5
3852	3	1	2	4	5	3	2	1	4	5
3901	3	5	4	2	1	3	4	5	2	1
3909	3	5	4	2	1	3	2	1	4	5

NOTE: Rankings are from 1 for lowest comparative advantage within region to 5 for highest.

Table F-14. Rankings of Central American Countries by Intraregional Comparative Advantage, by Industrial Sector: Skilled Labor Intensity and Economies of Scale Bases

Sector	Skilled Labor Intensity					Economies of Scale				
	Guatemala	El Salvador	Honduras	Nicaragua	Costa Rica	Guatemala	El Salvador	Honduras	Nicaragua	Costa Rica
3111	5	2	4	3	1	5	3	1	2	4
3112	1	4	2	3	5	5	3	1	2	4
3113	5	2	4	3	1	5	3	1	2	4
3114	5	2	4	3	1	5	3	1	2	4
3115	5	2	4	3	1	5	3	1	2	4
3116	5	2	4	3	5	5	3	1	2	4
3117	1	4	2	3	1	5	3	1	2	4
3118	5	2	4	3	1	5	3	5	2	2
3119	5	2	4	3	1	5	3	5	4	2
3121	5	2	4	3	1	1	3	1	4	4
3122	5	2	4	3	1	1	3	1	2	2
3131	5	2	4	3	1	5	3	1	2	4
3132	5	2	4	3	1	5	3	1	2	4
3133	5	2	4	3	1	5	3	1	2	4
3134	5	2	4	3	1	5	3	1	2	4
3140	5	2	4	3	1	1	3	5	2	2
3211	5	2	4	3	1	1	3	5	4	2
3212	5	2	4	3	1	1	3	5	4	2
3213	5	2	4	3	1	1	3	5	4	2
3214	1	4	2	3	5	1	3	5	4	2
3215	5	2	4	3	1	1	3	5	4	2
3219	1	4	2	3	5	1	3	1	4	4
3220	1	4	2	3	5	5	3	5	2	2
3231	1	4	2	3	5	1	3	5	4	2
3232	1	4	2	3	5	1	3	5	4	2
3233	1	4	2	3	5	1	3	5	4	2
3242	1	4	2	3	5	1	3	5	4	2
3311	5	2	4	3	1	5	3	1	2	4
3312	1	4	2	3	5	5	3	1	2	4
3319	5	4	2	3	5	1	3	5	4	2
3320	1	4	2	3	5	1	3	5	4	2

(continued on next page)

Table F-14 (Continued)

Sector	Skilled Labor Intensity					Economies of Scale				
	Guatemala	El Salvador	Honduras	Nicaragua	Costa Rica	Guatemala	El Salvador	Honduras	Nicaragua	Costa Rica
3411	5	2	4	3	1	1	3	5	4	2
3412	5	2	4	3	1	1	3	5	4	2
3419	1	4	2	3	5	1	3	5	4	2
3420	1	4	2	3	5	1	3	5	4	2
3511	5	2	4	3	1	1	3	5	4	2
3512	5	2	4	3	1	1	3	5	4	2
3521	1	4	2	3	5	1	3	5	4	2
3522	5	2	4	3	1	1	3	5	4	2
3523	1	4	2	3	5	1	3	5	4	2
3529	5	2	4	3	1	1	3	5	4	2
3530	1	4	2	3	5	1	3	5	4	2
3540	5	2	4	3	1	5	3	1	4	4
3551	5	4	2	3	5	5	3	1	2	4
3559	1	4	2	3	5	5	3	1	2	4
3560	5	2	2	3	5	5	3	1	2	4
3610	5	2	4	3	1	5	3	1	2	4
3620	5	2	4	3	1	5	3	1	2	4
3691	5	2	4	3	1	5	3	1	2	4
3692	5	2	4	3	1	5	3	1	2	4
3699	5	2	4	3	1	5	3	1	2	4
3710	5	2	4	3	1	5	3	1	2	4
3720	5	2	4	3	1	5	3	1	2	4
3811	1	4	2	3	5	5	3	1	2	4
3812	1	4	2	3	5	5	3	1	2	4
3813	5	2	4	3	1	5	3	1	2	4
3819	1	4	2	3	5	5	3	1	2	4
3821	1	4	2	3	5	1	3	5	4	2
3822	1	4	2	3	5	1	3	5	4	2
3823	5	2	4	3	1	1	3	5	4	2
3824	1	4	2	3	5	1	3	5	4	2
3825	1	4	2	3	5	1	3	5	4	2
3829	1	4	2	3	5	1	3	5	4	2

Table F-14 (Continued)

Sector	Skilled Labor Intensity					Economies of Scale				
	Guatemala	El Salvador	Honduras	Nicaragua	Costa Rica	Guatemala	El Salvador	Honduras	Nicaragua	Costa Rica
3831	1	4	2	3	5	1	3	5	4	2
3832	5	2	4	3	1	1	3	5	4	2
3833	1	4	2	3	5	1	3	5	4	2
3839	5	2	4	3	1	1	3	5	4	2
3841	1	4	2	3	5	1	3	5	4	2
3843	5	2	4	3	1	1	3	5	4	2
3844	1	4	2	3	5	1	3	5	4	2
3845	1	4	2	3	5	1	3	5	4	2
3851	1	4	2	3	5	1	3	5	4	2
3852	1	4	2	3	5	1	3	5	4	2
3901	1	4	2	3	5	1	3	5	4	2
3909	1	4	2	3	5	1	3	5	4	2

NOTE: Rankings are from 1 for lowest comparative advantage to 5 for highest.

Table F-15. Rankings of Central American Countries by Comparative
Advantage: Intraregional Trade Performance Basis[a]

Sector	Guatemala	El Salvador	Honduras	Nicaragua	Costa Rica
3111	5	2	1	4	3
3112	3	2	1	5	4
3113	5	3	1	2	4
3114	2	3	1	4	5
3115	2	4	3	5	1
3116	4	3	1	5	2
3117	2	3	1	5	4
3118	5	1	4	3	2
3119	5	3	2	1	4
3121	5	3	1	2	4
3122	5	1	2	3	4
3131	1	5	4	3	2
3132	5	4	1	2	3
3133	5	2	1	3	4
3134	4	2	3	5	1
3140	5	2	3	4	1
3211	4	5	1	3	2
3212	4	5	1	3	2
3213	5	4	1	2	3
3214	4	3	2	1	5
3215	2	5	4	1	3
3219	2	5	1	4	3
3220	2	5	4	1	3
3231	3	1	4	5	2
3232	5	2	3,5	3,5	1
3233	4	5	1	2	5
3240	5	4	1	3	2
3311	4	1	2	5	3
3312	3	2	5	4	1
3319	4	2	3	1	5
3320	2	5	1	4	3
3411	5	4	3	1	2
3412	4	5	3	1	2
3419	3	4	2	1	5
3420	4	5	2	1	3
3511	2	1	4	5	3
3512	3	4	1	2	5
3521	5	2	1	4	3
3522	5	3	1	2	4
3523	5	3	4	2	1
3529	5	1	2	4	3
3530	3	5	2	4	1
3540	3	4	2	1	5
3551	5	1	2	3	4
3559	4	2	3	5	1
3560	3	5	1	2	4

Table F-15 (Continued)

Sector	Guatemala	El Salvador	Honduras	Nicaragua	Costa Rica
3610	5	1	4	3	2
3620	5	4	1	3	2
3691	4	2	1	5	3
3692	4	3	2	5	1
3699	4	2	1	5	3
3710	4	3	1	2	5
3720	1	5	2	4	3
3811	3	5	1	4	2
3812	3	4	1	2	5
3813	3	4	1	5	2
3819	3	2	1	4	5
3821	5	2	3	1	4
3822	4	1	2	3	5
3823	3	2	4	1	5
3824	5	1	2	3	4
3825	5	1	3	2	4
3829	2	4	1	3	5
3831	4	1	2	3	5
3832	3	4	1	2	5
3833	5	4	1	2	3
3839	5	4	1	2	3
3841	3	4	1	2	5
3843	5	3	4	2	1
3844	5	2	1	3	4
3845	5	2	4	3	1
3851	4	2	3	1	5
3852	3	5	2	1	1
3901	2	3	5	4	1
3909	3	5	2	1	4

[a](Exports - imports)/(exports + imports), referring to intraregional trade only.

SOURCE: Calculated from detailed trade data (1970-72 annual averages) provided by SIECA Statistics Division.

Table F-16. Rankings of Central American Countries by Intraregional
Comparative Advantage, by Industrial Sector:
Linear Programming Basis

Sector	Guatemala	El Salvador[a]	Honduras	Nicaragua	Costa Rica
3111	4	1	0	0	0
3112	0	1	0	4	0
3113	4	1	0	0	0
3114	0	1	0	4	0
3115	0	1	0	4	0
3116	0	1	4	0	0
3117	0	1	0	4	0
3118	2	1	0	2	0
3119	0	1	0	0	4
3121	0	1	0	0	4
3122	0	1	0	4	0
3131	0	1	0	0	4
3132	4	1	0	0	0
3133	0	1	4	0	0
3134	4	1	0	0	0
3140	0	1	0	0	4
3211	4	1	0	0	0
3212	4	1	0	0	0
3213	0	1	3	1	0
3214	4	1	0	0	0
3215	0	1	0	0	4
3219	0	1	0	0	4
3220	0	1	0	0	4
3231	0	1	0	4	0
3232	0	1	0	0	4
3233	4	1	0	0	0
3240	0	1	0	4	0
3311	0	1	4	0	0
3312	0	1	0	0	4
3319	0	1	0	0	4
3320	0	1	0	4	0
3411	4	1	0	0	0
3412	0	1	0	0	4
3419	0	1	0	4	0
3420	4	1	0	0	0
3511	0	1	0	0	4
3512	0	1	0	0	4
3521	0	1	4	0	0
3522	4	1	0	0	0
3523	1	1	0	3	0
3529	0	1	4	0	0
3530	0	1	4	0	0
3540	4	1	0	0	0
3551	4	1	0	0	0
3559	0	1	0	4	0

641

Table F-16 (Continued)

Sector	Guatemala	El Salvador[a]	Honduras	Nicaragua	Costa Rica
3560	0	1	4	0	0
3610	0	1	0	0	4
3620	4	1	0	0	0
3691	0	1	0	4	0
3692	4	1	0	0	0
3699	4	1	0	0	0
3710	0	1	0	0	4
3720	0	1	0	0	4
3811	0	1	0	0	4
3812	0	1	0	0	4
3813	0	1	4	0	0
3819	0	1	0	0	4
3821	0	1	0	0	0
3822	0	1	0	0	4
3823	0	1	0	0	4
3824	4	1	0	0	0
3825	4	1	0	0	0
3829	0	1	0	4	0
3831	0	1	0	0	4
3832	0	1	0	4	0
3833	4	1	0	0	0
3839	4	1	0	0	0
3841	4	1	0	0	0
3843	0	1	0	0	4
3844	0	1	0	0	4
3845	4	1	0	0	0
3851	0	1	0	4	0
3852	4	1	0	0	0
3901	0	1	0	4	0
3909	0	1	0	0	4

[a]El Salvador is excluded from the linear programming analysis. It is assigned in each sector the "expected score" of one, based on a one-fifth probability of achieving the full possible score of five if it had been included in the linear programming analysis.

Table F-17. Rankings of Central American Countries by Intraregional Comparative Advantage: Total Factor Productivity and Rate-of-Return Bases

Sector	Total Factor Productivity					Rate of Return				
	Guatemala	El Salvador	Honduras	Nicaragua	Costa Rica	Guatemala	El Salvador	Honduras	Nicaragua	Costa Rica
3111	4.5	4.5	3	2	1	4.5	4.5	2	3	1
3112	1.5	1.5	3	5	4	1.5	1.5	3	4	5
3113	4.5	4.5	3	2	1	3.5	3.5	2	5	1
3114	4.5	4.5	2	3	1	4.5	4.5	1	3	2
3115	3.5	3.5	5	5	1	3.5	3.5	5	5	2
3116	2.5	2.5	1	4	1	2.5	2.5	1	4	1
3117	3.5	3.5	1	5	2	2.5	2.5	1	5	4
3118	4.5	4.5	1	3	2	4.5	4.5	1	3	2
3119	4.5	4.5	1	2	3	4.5	4.5	1	2	3
3121	4.5	4.5	3	2	3	4.5	4.5	3	2	3
3122	1.5	1.5	1	5	4	1.5	1.5	1	4	5
3131	2.5	2.5	1	4	5	2.5	2.5	2	5	4
3132	4.5	4.5	3	1	2	4.5	4.5	5	1	3
3133	3.5	3.5	5	2	1	2.5	2.5	1	4	1
3134	4.5	4.5	1	3	2	3.5	3.5	2	5	4
3140	3.5	3.5	2	1	5	4.5	4.5	3	1	5
3211	4.5	4.5	3	2	1	4.5	4.5	3	2	1
3212	4.5	4.5	3	3	2	2.5	2.5	1	1	2
3213	4.5	4.5	2	1	1	3.5	3.5	5	5	4
3214	4.5	4.5	1.5	1.5	3	3.5	3.5	1.5	1.5	5
3215	3.5	3.5	2	1	5	2.5	2.5	4	1	5
3219	2.5	2.5	2.5	2.5	5	2.5	2.5	2.5	2.5	5
3220	4.5	4.5	1	3	2	3.5	3.5	2	1	5
3231	2.5	2.5	1	4	5	2.5	2.5	1	5	4
3232	2	2	4	2	5	2	2	4	2	5
3233	4.5	4.5	5	4	3	3.5	3.5	1	5	2
3240	2.5	2.5	5	4	1	2.5	2.5	4	5	1
3311	2.5	2.5	5	4	3	3.5	3.5	2	5	1
3312	4.5	4.5	2	1	3	3.5	3.5	2	1	5
3319	4.5	4.5	1	2	3	4.5	4.5	1	2	3
3320	3.5	3.5	1	5	2	3.5	3.5	1	5	2

Table F-17 (Continued)

Sector	Total Factor Productivity					Rate of Return				
	Guatemala	El Salvador	Honduras	Nicaragua	Costa Rica	Guatemala	El Salvador	Honduras	Nicaragua	Costa Rica
3411	4.5	4.5	1.5	1.5	3	4.5	4.5	1.5	1.5	3
3412	4.5	4.5	3	2	1	4.5	4.5	1	3	2
3419	2.5	2.5	1	5	4	2.5	2.5	1	5	4
3420	4.5	4.5	5	3	4	3.5	3.5	5	5	2
3511	4.5	4.5	5	1	2	3.5	3.5	1	2	1
3512	3.5	3.5	1	2	5	4.5	3.5	3	2	5
3521	4.5	4.5	3	1	2	4.5	4.5	1	1	2
3522	4.5	4.5	1	2	3	4.5	4.5	1	3	2
3523	4.5	4.5	3	1	2	4.5	4.5	1	3	2
3529	4.5	4.5	2	3	1	4.5	4.5	5	3	2
3530	3.5	3.5	5	1.5	1.5	3.5	3.5	2	1.5	1.5
3540	4.5	4.5	2	2	2	4.5	4.5	5	2	2
3551	3.5	3.5	5	1	2	3.5	3.5	1	1	2
3559	4.5	4.5	1	3	2	4.5	4.5	2	3	2
3560	3.5	3.5	5	2	1	4.5	4.5	2	4	1
3610	2.5	2.5	1.5	4	5	2.5	2.5	1.5	4	5
3620	4.5	4.5	1.5	1.5	3	4.5	4.5	1.5	1.5	3
3691	2.5	2.5	1	5	4	2.5	2.5	1	4	5
3692	4.5	4.5	3	2	1	4.5	4.5	3	1	2
3699	4.5	4.5	3	1	5	4.5	4.5	2	3	3
3710	3.5	3.5	1.5	1.5	5	3.5	3.5	1.5	1.5	5
3720	3.5	3.5	1.5	1.5	5	4.5	4.5	1.5	1.5	3
3811	3.5	3.5	1	2	5	3.5	3.5	1	2	5
3812	2.5	2.5	5	1	4	1.5	1.5	5	3	4
3813	3.5	3.5	5	2	1	2.5	2.5	5	1	4
3819	4.5	4.5	2	1	3	4.5	4.5	1	2	3
3821	4.5	4.5	2	2	2	4.5	4.5	2	2	2
3822	4.5	4.5	1	3	2	3.5	3.5	1	5	2
3823	2.5	2.5	2.5	2.5	5	2.5	2.5	2.5	2.5	5
3824	4.5	4.5	2	1	3	3.5	3.5	2	1	5
3825	2.5	2.5	2.5	2.5	5	2.5	2.5	2.5	2.5	5
3829	3.5	3.5	2	5	1	3.5	3.5	2	5	1

(continued on next page)

Table F-17 (Continued)

Sector	Total Factor Productivity					Rate of Return				
	Guatemala	El Salvador	Honduras	Nicaragua	Costa Rica	Guatemala	El Salvador	Honduras	Nicaragua	Costa Rica
3831	3.5	3.5	1.5	1.5	5	3.5	3.5	1.5	1.5	5
3832	4.5	4.5	1	2	3	3.5	3.5	1	5	2
3833	4.5	4.5	1.5	1.5	3	4.5	4.5	1.5	1.5	3
3839	4.5	4.5	2	3	1	4.5	4.5	2	3	1
3841	4.5	4.5	2	2	2	4.5	4.5	2	2	2
3843	3.5	3.5	1.5	1.5	3	4.5	4.5	1.5	1.5	3
3844	4.5	4.5	1.5	1.5	5	3.5	3.5	1.5	1.5	5
3845	4.5	4.5	1.5	1.5	3	4.5	4.5	1.5	1.5	3
3851	4.5	3.5	3	3	1.5	3.5	3.5	3	5	1.5
3852	4.5	4.5	2	1.5	1.5	4.5	4.5	3	1.5	1.5
3901	3.5	3.5	2	5	1	3.5	3.5	2	5	1
3909	4.5	4.5	3	1	2	4.5	4.5	2	1	3

NOTES: Rankings are from 1 for lowest comparative advantage to 5 for highest.
Direct data unavailable for El Salvador. It is assumed that indicators for El Salvador
are identical to those for Guatemala, and a "tied" ranking is assigned to them jointly.

Table F-18. Rankings of Central American Countries by Intraregional
Comparative Advantage: Industrial Sectors,
Producer Price Basis

Sector	Guatemala	El Salvador	Honduras	Nicaragua	Costa Rica
3111	3	5	4	1	2
3112	1	4	5	2	3
3114	2	4	3	1	5
3115	3	5	1	4	2
3116	5	4	3	1	2
3117	5	3	4	1	2
3118	4	2.5	1	2.5	5
3121	1	4	3	2	5
3134	1.5	3	4	5	1.5
3140	2	5	4	1	3
3211	1	2	5	4	3
3220	3	4	5	1	2
3240	4	5	2	1	3
3320	5	4	1	2	3
3420	5	1	3	2	4
3523	4	1	3	5	2
3529	4	1.5	1.5	4	4
3559	5	2	3	1	4
3812	5	3	2	4	1
3839	1	2.5	5	4	2.5
3901	3	4	2	1	5
3909	5	4	1	3	2

NOTE: Rankings are from 1 for lowest comparative advantage (highest
price) to 5 for highest comparative advantage (lowest price).

Table F-19. Producer Price Comparisons Among Central American
Countries: Selected Industrial Sectors
(Guatemala = 1.000)

Sector	N	Guatemala	El Salvador	Honduras	Nicaragua	Costa Rica
3111	6	1.000	0.607	0.655	1.165	1.027
3112	5	1.000	0.804	0.756	0.996	0.907
3114	1	1.000	0.640	0.860	1.870	0.220
3115	1	1.000	0.610	1.100	0.980	1.050
3116	2	1.000	1.107	1.366	1.927	1.652
3117	4	1.000	1.115	1.010	1.324	1.214
3118	1	1.000	1.120	1.310	1.120	0.940
3121	1	1.000	0.650	0.780	0.860	0.630
3134	2	1.000	0.670	0.500	0.330	1.000
3140	2	1.000	0.397	0.558	1.333	0.834
3211	2	1.000	0.962	0.369	0.713	0.901
3220	8	1.000	0.966	0.871	1.636	1.451
3240	3	1.000	0.941	1.155	1.797	1.103
3320	3	1.000	1.033	3.326	1.246	1.215
3420	2	1.000	1.723	1.171	1.348	1.118
3523	1	1.000	2.500	1.500	0.750	2.250
3529	1	1.000	2.000	2.000	1.000	1.000
3559	1	1.000	1.920	1.380	2.150	1.170
3612	1	1.000	3.580	7.050	3.080	8.450
3839	1	1.000	0.780	0.520	0.710	0.780
3901	1	1.000	0.470	1.140	1.300	0.330
3909	1	1.000	1.400	4.000	2.250	3.350

NOTES: N = number of items within sector on which index is based.
Within-sector weights based on weights of SIECA/Brookings
consumer price study (appendix A).
Prices as of November 1973.
Producer price comparisons unavailable for omitted sectors.

A Model of Agricultural Production: Equations and Supplementary Tables

Carlo Cappi, Lehman Fletcher, Roger Norton,
Carlos Pomareda, and Molly Wainer

A. MOCA Equations

The 271 structural equations of MOCA are set out fully in algebraic form in this appendix. A number of strictly accounting equations are not shown here; they were included in the linear programming models but they could have been replaced as well by a report-writing subroutine. Further details on the model, including derivations of all numerical coefficients, are given in a large mimeo notebook entitled "A Spatial Equilibrium Model for the Central American Agricultural Sector."

The reader will notice that there are a number of instances in which equations could be substituted out to reduce the rank of the linear programming matrix. However, from the viewpoints of efficient matrix generator design and flexibility of model specification,[1] it was preferable to generate the model in the form shown here.

According to the notational convention adopted, capital Roman letters represent variables and right-hand side values, and Greek letters and small Roman letters indicate parameters. Each set of equations is given a brief title and, in most cases, a verbal description of each term is given in brackets after the algebraic statement. Following the title, the equation's FORTRAN name, as used in the numerical computer version, is given. When there are two symbolic names separated by a semicolon, the second one refers to the corresponding generic equation used in the schematic tableau which is discussed in the text. The number of individual equations within each matrix equation is given to the right of the equation statement.

A table containing descriptions of all the symbols precedes the equations.

---

[1] "Flexibility" here means ease of varying the model's structure to test differing hypotheses. This is an important attribute for an applied model.

All of the equations are written in inequality form. Obviously, many of them will be binding in any solution, and hence those equations could have been written as strict equalities. However, writing them as inequalities reduces the computer time associated with each solution, for it eliminates the need to pass through phase I of the simplex algorithm, and by judicious use of signs we can be sure that restrictions will be binding when exact equalities are desired.

For readers interested in implementing sector models, it may be of interest to note that writing the algebra of this appendix was not the initial step in preparing the model's computer version. The initial step was to design a symbolic nomenclature for columns and rows, assigning certain fields to country indices, others to product indices, and so forth. This convention is not readily apparent in the FORTRAN equation names quoted below, because empty-field designations are ignored. Nevertheless, for structuring the model and for writing its matrix generator, it was immensely helpful to have notations established from the beginning.

It was evident beforehand that the entities which would need special fields were countries, farm size groups, products, inputs, and demand function segments. Also, special symbols were used for accounting balances (B) and restrictions (R). Product symbols (two characters) and all other abbreviations were decided upon at the outset, and then the equations were developed in layers, beginning with farm size class-specific equations and then moving to national and then regional balances and restrictions.

Table G-1. Notation for the MOCA Equations

Symbol	Description	Superscripts, Subscripts
I. Variables:		
FOB_r	Country contribution to the overall objective function	r = Country G = Guatemala E = El Salvador H = Honduras N = Nicaragua C = Costa Rica
$D_{j,g,r}$	Demand curve interpolation weight variable (segment choice variable); see Duloy and Norton [8]	j = final (processed) product[2] g = demand curve segment index
$XR_{j,r}$	Extraregional exports	
$MR_{j,r}$	Imports of agricultural goods from outside the region	
$SMF_{h,r}$	Input of farmers' labor, own their own farms	h = farm size class (= 1, 2, 3)
$SMC_{h,r}$	Input of labor by landless laborers	
SMI_r	Labor of small farmers (class 1) on the largest farms (class 3)	
$SIN_{h,r}$	Value of purchased inputs, excluding labor	
TR_r	Total processing costs for agricultural goods	
TP_r	Transportation costs associated with international trade in agricultural products	
TA_r	Total tariffs on agricultural imports from outside the region	

---

[2] A few products go directly to final use, and thus they are counted both as farm-gate products (raw materials) and final products.

Table G-1 (Continued)

Symbol	Description	Superscripts, Subscripts
T_j^{rs}	Volume of intraregional trade flowing from (to) country r to (from) country s, good j ($T_j^{rs} \geq 0$)	s = country
$Q_{i,h,r}$	Quantity (in tons) of raw agricultural product delivered to the processing industry	i = farm-gate product
$D_{j,r}$	Final sales activity for goods whose prices are fixed	
$\overline{S1}_r$	Total annual labor available (in man-years) from size class 1 farmers	
$\overline{S2}_r$	Total annual labor available (in man-years) from size class 2 farmers	
$\overline{S9}_r$	Total annual labor available (in man-years) from landless laborers	
$P_{i,h,r}$	Hectares planted in product i	
$\overline{T}_{h,r}$	Total arable land (in hectares), farm size class h	
$\overline{ML}_{j,r}$	Quota on imports from other countries of the region	

II. Parameters:

$\omega_{j,g,r}$	Area under the domestic demand function	j = final product g = demand curve segment index r = country
p_j^e	Price for extraregional exports	
p_j^m	Price for imports from outside the region	

651

Table G-1 (Continued)

Symbol	Description	Superscripts, Subscripts
$\tilde{w}_r$	Reservation wage: valuation of the farmer's own time	
w_r	Market wage $[\tilde{w}_r \leq w_r]$	
τ_j^{rs}	Unit transportation cost between countries r and s for shipments of good j	s = country
ϕ_j^m	Unit domestic transportation costs associated with the import of good j from outside the region	m = imports
ϕ_j^e	Unit domestic transportation costs associated with the export of good j to countries outside the region	e = exports
$a_{j,r}$	Unit tariff rate on imports from outside the region	
$c_{i,r}$	Unit processing costs, unprocessed good i	i = farm-gate product
$\mu_{i,r}^j$	Unit output of final good j from the processing of farm-gate product i	
$\theta_{j,g,r}$	Cumulative quantity sold at segment g of the demand curve for product j	
$y_{i,h,r}$	Yield (in kg/ha)	
$\lambda_{i,h,r}$	Field labor requirements, in man-days per hectare	
$n_{i,h,r}$	Purchased input requirements, in \$CA per hectare	

The equations of MOCA are shown below; notations for the equations are in table A-1.

Number of
Constraints

1. Aggregate objective function [FOB]

$$\sum_{r} FOB_r \rightarrow max \qquad (1)$$

2. Country-level contributions to the objective function [rFOB]

$$\sum_{j,g} \omega_{j,g,r} D_{j,g,r} + \sum_{j} p_j^e XR_{j,r} - \sum_{j} p_j^m MR_{j,r}$$

$$-\sum_{h=1,2} \tilde{w}_r SMF_{h,r} - \sum_{h} w_r SMC_{h,r} - w_r SMI_r$$

$$-\sum_{h} SIN_{h,r} - TR_r - TP_r - TA_r - FOB_r \cdot \geq 0 \qquad (5)$$

$$\left[\begin{array}{l}\text{Area under the domestic}\\\text{demand functions for}\\\text{processed and other}\\\text{final agricultural goods}\end{array}\right] + \left[\begin{array}{l}\text{Gross revenue from}\\\text{extraregional export sales}\end{array}\right]$$

$$- \left[\begin{array}{l}\text{c.i.f. costs of imports}\\\text{from outside the region}\end{array}\right] - \left[\begin{array}{l}\text{Reservation wage x farmers}\\\text{labor on their own farms,}\\\text{farm size groups 1 and 2}\end{array}\right]$$

$$- \left[\begin{array}{l}\text{Market wage cost of}\\\text{hiring landless labor}\end{array}\right] - \left[\begin{array}{l}\text{Market wage cost of small-}\\\text{holders (size class 1)}\\\text{working on size 3 farms}\end{array}\right]$$

$$- \left[\begin{array}{l}\text{Total purchased input}\\\text{costs, excluding}\\\text{labor}\end{array}\right] - \left[\begin{array}{l}\text{Product processing}\\\text{costs}\end{array}\right] - \left[\begin{array}{l}\text{Product trans-}\\\text{port costs}\end{array}\right]$$

$$- \left[\begin{array}{l}\text{Tariffs on imports}\\\text{from outside the}\\\text{region}\end{array}\right] - \left[\begin{array}{l}\text{Total contribution to}\\\text{the objective function}\\\text{from country r}\end{array}\right] \geq 0$$

3. Transport costs accounting rows [rRTPRI]

$$- TP_r + \sum_{j,s} \tau_j^{rs} \; T_j^{rs} + \sum_j \phi_j^m \; MR_{j,r}$$

$$+ \sum_j \phi_j^e \; XR_{j,r} \le 0 \qquad\qquad (5)$$

$$- \begin{bmatrix} \text{product total transport} \\ \text{costs, country } r \end{bmatrix} + \begin{bmatrix} \text{intraregional transport} \\ \text{costs associated with} \\ \text{shipments to (from) coun-} \\ \text{try s from country } r, \\ \text{product } j \end{bmatrix}$$

$$+ \begin{bmatrix} \text{transport costs associated} \\ \text{with imports from outside} \\ \text{the region} \end{bmatrix} + \begin{bmatrix} \text{transport costs asso-} \\ \text{ciated with extra-} \\ \text{regional exports} \end{bmatrix} \le 0$$

4. Tariff accounting row [rRTARI]

$$- TA_r + \sum_j a_{j,r} \; MR_{j,r} \le 0 \qquad\qquad (5)$$

$$- \begin{bmatrix} \text{Total tariffs,} \\ \text{country } r \end{bmatrix} + \begin{bmatrix} \text{tariff rate times in-} \\ \text{puts from outside the} \\ \text{region} \end{bmatrix} \le 0$$

5. Processing costs accounting row [rRTRRI]

$$- TR_r + \sum_{i,h} c_{i,r} \; Q_{i,h,r} \le 0 \qquad\qquad (5)$$

$$- \begin{bmatrix} \text{total processing} \\ \text{costs, country } r \end{bmatrix} + \begin{bmatrix} \text{unit costs times} \\ \text{quantities processed,} \\ \text{raw goods } i \end{bmatrix} \le 0$$

6. Consumer-level commodity balances (endogenous-price products)
   [rBiBP; FB]

$$- \sum_h \mu_{i,r}^j \; Q_{i,h,r} + \sum_g \theta_{j,g,r} \; D_{j,g,r} - MR_{j,r}$$

$$+ XR_{j,r} + \sum_s T_j^{rs} \le 0 \qquad\qquad (64)$$

$-\begin{bmatrix} \text{net output of final good} \\ \text{j from the processing of} \\ \text{farm gate product j} \end{bmatrix} \quad + \quad \begin{bmatrix} \text{quantity demanded of} \\ \text{final good j, domes-} \\ \text{tic markets} \end{bmatrix}$

$-\begin{bmatrix} \text{imports from outside} \\ \text{the region} \end{bmatrix} + \begin{bmatrix} \text{extraregional} \\ \text{exports} \end{bmatrix} + \begin{bmatrix} \text{Net } (\stackrel{<}{>} 0) \text{ ex-} \\ \text{ports from} \\ \text{country r to} \\ \text{other countries} \\ \text{of the region} \end{bmatrix} \leq 0$

7. Consumer-level commodity balances (fixed price crops) [rBiBF; FB]

$$- \sum_h \mu^j_{i,r} \, Q_{i,h,r} + D_{j,r} - MR_{j,r} + XR_{j,r}$$

$$+ \sum_s T^{rs}_j \leq 0 \tag{20}$$

8. Convex combination constraints on the interpolation weight variables for the demand functions [rRiRC; C]

$$\sum_g D_{j,g,r} \leq 1.0 \tag{64}$$

9. Labor constraint for farmers of size class 1 (smallest farms) [r1RMO; R]

$$SMF_{1,r} + SMI_r \leq \overline{S1}_r \tag{5}$$

$\begin{bmatrix} \text{farmers' labor on} \\ \text{their own farms,} \\ \text{in man-years} \end{bmatrix} \quad + \quad \begin{bmatrix} \text{labor of class 1 farmers} \\ \text{on class 3 farms, in} \\ \text{man-years} \end{bmatrix}$

$\leq \begin{bmatrix} \text{total annual labor avail-} \\ \text{able (in man-years) from} \\ \text{class 1 farmers} \end{bmatrix}$

10. Labor constraint for farmers of size class 2 [r2RMO; R]

$$SMF_{2,r} \leq \overline{S2}_r \tag{5}$$

11. Labor constraint for landless laborers [r9RMO; R]

$$\sum_h SMC_{h,r} \leq \overline{S9}_r \tag{5}$$

12. Producer-level product balances [rhBiBP; PB]

$$- Y_{i,h,r}\ P_{i,r,h}\ +\ 1{,}000\ Q_{i,h,r}\ \leq\ 0 \tag{49}$$

$$\begin{bmatrix} \text{yield (in kg) per hectare} \\ \text{times hectares sown} \end{bmatrix} + \begin{bmatrix} \text{scale factor times quantity} \\ \text{produced (in tons) at the} \\ \text{farm level} \end{bmatrix}$$

13. Land constraints [rhBTI; R]

$$\sum_i P_{i,h,r}\ \leq\ \overline{T}_{h,r} \tag{5}$$

$$\begin{bmatrix} \text{total hectares planted} \\ \text{by farm size class} \end{bmatrix} \quad \leq \quad \begin{bmatrix} \text{total arable land by} \\ \text{farm size class} \end{bmatrix}$$

14. Labor input balances, farm size class 1 and 2 [rhBMO; IB]

$$\sum_i \lambda_{i,h,r}\ P_{i,h,r}\ -\ 280\ SMF_{h,r}\ -\ 280\ SMC_{h,r}\ \leq\ 0 \tag{10}$$

$$\begin{bmatrix} \text{labor requirements per} \\ \text{hectare, in man-days,} \\ \text{times hectares planted} \end{bmatrix} - \begin{bmatrix} \text{scale factor times farmers'} \\ \text{labor on their own farms,} \\ \text{in man-years} \end{bmatrix}$$

$$- \begin{bmatrix} \text{scale factor times use} \\ \text{of hired landless labor} \\ \text{in man-years} \end{bmatrix} \leq\ 0$$

15. Labor input balances, farm size class 3 [r3BMO; IB]

$$\sum_i \lambda_{i,3,r}\ P_{i,3,r}\ -\ 280\ SMI_r\ -\ 280\ SMC_{3,r}\ \leq\ 0 \tag{5}$$

$$\begin{bmatrix} \text{class 3 farms;} \\ \text{field labor} \\ \text{requirements} \end{bmatrix} - \begin{bmatrix} \text{use of class 1} \\ \text{farmers in their} \\ \text{off-season} \end{bmatrix} - \begin{bmatrix} \text{use of} \\ \text{landless} \\ \text{laborers} \end{bmatrix} \leq\ 0$$

16. Purchased input balances [rhBIN; IB]

$$\sum_i n_{i,h,r}\ P_{i,h,r}\ -\ 1{,}000\ SIN_{h,r}\ \leq\ 0 \tag{5}$$

$$
\begin{bmatrix} \text{input coefficient per} \\ \text{hectares times} \\ \text{hectares sown} \end{bmatrix} - \begin{bmatrix} \text{scale factor times total} \\ \text{value of purchased inputs,} \\ \text{excluding labor} \end{bmatrix} \leq 0
$$

17. Intraregional trade restrictions [rRiIM]

$$
- \sum_s T_j^{rs} \leq \overline{ML}_{j,r} \tag{13}
$$

$$
\begin{bmatrix} \text{Total net imports of good} \\ \text{j from other countries in} \\ \text{the region} \end{bmatrix} \leq \begin{bmatrix} \text{regional import restric-} \\ \text{tion, good j, country r} \end{bmatrix}
$$

B. Supplementary Tables

Table G-2. Comparison of the MOCA Prices with Actual Prices,
Costa Rica, 1970 (in CA$/kg)

Consumer Prices				Producer Prices			
Commodity	Observed	MOCA	Deviation	Commodity	Observed	MOCA	Deviation
Maize	.132	.126	.006	Maize	.090	.084	.006
Sorghum	.100	.071	.029	Rice	.149	.080	.069
Beans	.335	.369	-.034	Sorghum	.083	.056	.027
Banano (export)	.078	.047	.031	Wheat	n.a.	n.a.	n.a.
Banano (domestic)	.090	.114	-.024	Beans	.226	.258	-.032
Guineo	.100	.080	.020	Banano (export)	.050	.022	.028
Plantain	.100	.105	-.005	Banano (domestic)	.016	.035	-.019
Coffee	1.130	.938	.192	Guineo	.034	.020	.014
Rice	.303	.189	.114	Plantain	.022	.026	-.004
Wheat flour	.350	.331	.019	Sugar cane	.009	.005	.004
Sugar	.160	.107	.053	Coffee	.550	.360	.190
Lump molasses	.200	.161	.039	Cotton	.193	.189	.004
Vegetable oil	.740	.688	.052				
Cotton fiber	.570	.572	-.002				
Bran	.073	.073	.000				
Molasses	.073	.073	.000				
Cottonseed cake	.073	.073	.000				
Average absolute deviation			.036	Average absolute deviation			.036
Percentage absolute deviation			13.409	Percentage absolute deviation			27.991

NOTE: n.a. = not applicable because not produced.

Table G-3. Comparison of the MOCA Prices with Actual Prices,
El Salvador, 1970 (in CA$/kg)

Consumer Prices				Producer Prices			
Commodity	Observed	MOCA	Deviation	Commodity	Observed	MOCA	Deviation
Maize	.091	.069	.022	Maize	.070	.049	.021
Sorghum	.080	.063	.017	Rice	.126	.041	.085
Beans	.363	.255	.108	Sorghum	.065	.049	.016
Banano (export)	n.a.	n.a.	n.a.	Wheat	n.a.	n.a.	n.a.
Banano (domestic)	.110	.089	.021	Beans	.197	0.94	.103
Guineo	.110	.174	-.064	Banano (export)	n.a.	n.a.	n.a
Plantain	.110	.095	.015	Banano (domestic)	.034	.016	.018
Coffee	1.180	.961	.219	Guineo	n.a.	n.a.	n.a.
Rice	.284	.150	.134	Plantain	.021	.009	.012
Wheat flour	.460	.435	.025	Sugar cane	.008	.003	.005
Sugar	.200	.147	.053	Coffee	.450	.235	.215
Lump molasses	.140	.088	.052	Cotton	.196	.146	.050
Vegetable oil	.510	.655	-.145				
Cotton fiber	.580	.405	.175				
Bran	.058	.058	.000				
Molasses	.058	.058	.000				
Cottonseed cake	.058	.058	.000				
Average absolute deviation			.066	Average absolute deviation			.058
Percentage absolute deviation			23.869	Percentage absolute deviation			44.986

NOTE: n.a. = not applicable because not produced.

Table G-4. Comparison of the MOCA Prices with Actual Prices,
Guatemala, 1970 (in CA$/kg)

Consumer Prices				Producer Prices			
Commodity	Observed	MOCA	Deviation	Commodity	Observed	MOCA	Deviation
Maize	.115	.095	.020	Maize	.066	.047	.019
Sorghum	.100	.060	.040	Rice	.095	.043	.052
Beans	.297	.196	.101	Sorghum	.078	.040	.038
Banano (export)	n.a.	n.a.	n.a.	Wheat	.165	.043	.122
Banano (domestic)	.130	.131	-.001	Beans	.187	.090	.097
Guineo	.180	.164	.016	Banano (export)	.050	.014	.036
Plantain	.180	.181	-.001	Banano (domestic)	.016	.017	-.001
Coffee	1.650	1.509	.141	Guineo	.016	.008	.008
Rice	.295	.214	.081	Plantain	.016	.017	-.001
Wheat flour	.360	.189	.171	Sugar cane	.008	.002	.006
Sugar	.150	.080	.070	Coffee	.450	.311	.139
Lump molasses	.220	.139	.081	Cotton	.170	.128	.042
Vegetable oil	.920	.674	.246				
Cotton fiber	.550	.485	.065				
Bran	.055	.055	.000				
Molasses	.055	.055	.000				
Cottonseed cake	.055	.055	.000				
Average absolute deviation			.065	Average absolute deviation			.047
Percentage absolute deviation			19.457	Percentage absolute deviation			42.587

NOTE: n.a. = not applicable because not produced.

Table G-5. Comparison of the MOCA Prices with Actual Prices,
Honduras, 1970 (in CA$/kg)

Consumer Prices				Producer Prices			
Commodity	Observed	MOCA	Deviation	Commodity	Observed	MOCA	Deviation
Maize	.083	.057	.026	Maize	.078	.049	.029
Sorghum	.080	.062	.018	Rice	.127	.059	.067
Beans	.234	.150	.084	Sorghum	.064	.047	.017
Banano (export)	.180	.132	.048	Wheat	.147	.073	.074
Banano (domestic)	n.a.	n.a.	n.a.	Beans	.174	.094	.080
Guineo	.180	.158	.022	Banano (export)	.040	.013	.027
Plantain	.180	.157	.023	Banano (domestic)	n.a.	n.a.	n.a.
Coffee	.860	.653	.207	Guineo	.028	.009	.018
Rice	.228	.113	.115	Plantain	.028	.008	.020
Wheat flour	.340	.235	.105	Sugar cane	.006	.005	.001
Sugar	.190	.175	.015	Coffee	.400	.197	.203
Lump molasses	.220	.189	.031	Cotton	.213	.097	.116
Vegetable oil	.630	.698	-.066				
Cotton fiber	.550	.203	.347				
Bran	.048	.048	.000				
Molasses	.048	.048	.000				
Cottonseed cake	.048	.048	.000				
Average absolute deviation			.069	Average absolute deviation			.059
Percentage absolute deviation			27.000	Percentage absolute deviation			50.012

NOTE: n.a. = not applicable because not produced.

Table G-6. Comparison of the MOCA Prices with Actual Prices, Nicaragua, 1970 (in CA$/kg)

Consumer Prices				Produce Prices			
Commodity	Observed	MOCA	Deviation	Commodity	Observed	MOCA	Deviation
Maize	.121	.130	-.009	Maize	.073	.081	-.008
Sorghum	.100	.058	.042	Rice	.135	.044	.091
Beans	.310	.185	.125	Sorghum	.079	.042	.037
Banano (export)	.150	.143	.007	Wheat	n.a.	n.a.	n.a.
Banano (domestic)	n.a.	n.a.	n.a.	Beans	.210	.090	.120
Guineo	.110	.049	.061	Banano (export)	.020	.023	-.003
Plantain	.110	.097	.013	Banano (domestic)	n.a.	n.a.	n.a.
Coffee	1.450	1.338	.112	Guineo	.045	.015	.030
Rice	.265	.101	.164	Plantain	.022	.010	.011
Wheat flour	.430	.453	-.023	Sugar cane	.005	.003	.002
Sugar	.210	.186	.024	Coffee	.450	.340	.110
Lump molasses	.150	.105	.045	Cotton	.193	.136	.059
Vegetable oil	.670	.634	.036				
Cotton fiber	.530	.369	.161				
Bran	.060	.060	.000				
Molasses	.060	.060	.000				
Cottonseed cake	.060	.060	.000				
Average absolute deviation			.051	Average absolute deviation			.047
Percentage absolute deviation			17.151	Percentage absolute deviation			38.360

NOTE: n.a. = not applicable because not produced.

Industrial Structure in Central America

Alan I. Rapoport

A. Introduction

The main objective of this brief analysis is to measure the existing degree of industrial concentration in Central America under two different assumptions, viewing Central America as (i) a completely integrated region and (ii) five individual countries.

There is quite a wide variety of measurements and bases which are utilized in studies of industrial concentration. The simple concentration ratio is a measure of the share of an arbitrary number of the largest firms or plants in an industry. This measure suffers from severe limitations in that it completely ignores both distributional differences among the firms which are chosen for the ratio and also the remainder of firms present in the industry. The Gini coefficient, a measure based on the Lorenz curve frequency distribution, looks at the relative shares of all the firms in an industry. This measure also has serious limitations in that it does not distinguish between the case where a small number of firms equally share the market and the one where a large number of firms equally share the market. The Herfindahl index, which is defined as the sum of the squares of the market shares, does a better job than the preceding two measures in that it takes into account both the number of firms and the distribution of firms within the market.[1]

The choice of the variable to be used in the measure of concentration chosen is quite important. Production, sales, employment, value added, capital stock, and asset value can all be used for measuring market shares. Production and sales can both lead to problems of double counting in the presence of vertically integrated firms which classify their products separately at different stages of production. Employment will tend to give greater weight to firms in an industry which uses more labor-intensive technologies, whereas measures of capital stock will achieve exactly the opposite results. There are also serious measurement problems relating to the valuation of assets and of capital stock. Value added might be the best measure to use but in many cases may be one of the most difficult to obtain.

This study will first consider each country in its entirety as a single closed market and will analyze four-digit International Standard Industrial Classification (CIIU) categories, as these are the most disaggregated industrial groupings for which the information necessary to undertake the appropriate measurements is available. The data to be

664

utilized were collected by SIECA from the most current industrial census available for each country.[2] Since the most accessible data for the five countries were in the form of total value of production at the firm level, this was the basis chosen for the analysis rather than value added.

In the Central American manufacturing sector, seventy-eight four-digit CIIU categories were represented, with Guatemala having industrial production in the largest number of sectors (seventy-six) and Honduras, the smallest (fifty-five).

B. Analysis

It can be seen readily from table H-1 below that the economies of the five Central American countries have quite highly concentrated industrial sectors. There are 320 manufacturing sectors represented in the five countries of Central America and, in 160 of these, one firm is responsible for more than 50 percent of the production of that sector.

Table H-1. Summary Concentration Statistics

Country	Number of Sectors	CONC4>90%	CONC4<50%	CONC1>50%
Guatemala	76	35	5	34
El Salvador	65	43	3	36
Honduras	55	37	5	28
Nicaragua	59	38	0	29
Costa Rica	65	37	6	33
Total	320	190	19	160

NOTE: CONCn is the share of the n largest firms in a given sector measured via the value of production.

In order to look at the region as a single entity and to compare that situation with the individual country alternative, two types of concentration measures have to be developed. First, direct concentration measures for the "single entity" region must be calculated. This is done by grouping each of the seventy-eight manufacturing sectors which appear in the region. Each sector now contains a number of firms equal to the sum of the number of firms in that sector in each country. Herfindahl indices and four firm-concentration ratios can then be calculated for each sector in the region. These results can either be compared to each country separately or to some type of average concentration measures for the countries of the region. Since interest lies in comparison of the region as a single entity with the region as five distinct countries, the latter would be a more fruitful comparison. Consequently, average concentration measures are now computed for each sector by taking a weighted average of the existing concentration measures, where the weights are the shares of each country's production in the region's total for that sector. This is done for both the Herfindahl index and the four firm-concentration ratios. Table H-2 depicts the Herfindahl and four firm-concentration ratios, both for the region and for the average of the individual countries.

It is clear that concentration drops markedly when the region is thought of as a single unified market. The relevant question, then, is whether one can conclude from these measures that integration has had a major impact in reducing industrial concentration; and, similarly, whether further or fuller integration would lead to still greater competition in the region.

Unfortunately, it can be inferred that only under certain assumptions does union diminish concentration. This analysis must be qualified by a number of factors. Several studies have shown, not surprisingly, that concentration is inversely related to market size. Consequently, it is rather obvious that the Central American economy viewed as a unique entity would be subject to a much less concentrated industrial structure than any of the average of its component countries. There are several other valid criticisms which could be made about the comparisons which were undertaken. A question which could be raised is whether the industrial structure resulting from the union of the five countries would be anything similar to the single country structure. There are probably many reasons to argue that it would not.

Nevertheless, the Central American Common Market has been in existence since around 1960 and, though it has not evolved into a complete economic union, many of the changes in structure may have already occurred before the late 1960s and early 1970s, which is the basic time period of this study.

There are two more serious criticisms that might be made of these comparisons. Both relate to the definition of a market. Even if Central America were a single entity, could one expect that its total area would define a single market for any given product grouping? Transport facilities within the Central American region are probably inferior to transport facilities from outside the region, though one might argue that the system between the major markets in each of the five countries is probably superior to the network within each country. This is not a very simple question to answer. Another serious criticism which could be made is that the comparison is not fully contained in that it completely ignores external imports in the case of the region as an entity and ignores all imports when looking at the individual countries. If there exist strong external sources of supply of products being analyzed, then a study of industrial structure which ignores these sources will not be a good guide to industrial performance.

The strong degree of concentration exhibited in table H-1, though, would lead one to believe that there might be a rather strong and small economic industrial bloc which would be rather interested in restricting at least extraregional competition, if not all external competition. Thus, it is quite feasible to believe that the existing industrial structure

Table H-2. Regional Concentration Comparison

Sector	No. of Firms	Countries Represented	WHERF[a]	HERFT[b]	WHERF/HERFT	WCONC4[c]	CONC4T[d]	WCONC4/CONC4T
3111	66	5	0.272	0.076	3.578	0.850	0.464	1.833
3112	73	5	0.373	0.070	4.307	0.767	0.429	1.788
3113	37	5	0.333	0.112	2.973	0.884	0.578	1.527
3114	23	3	0.278	0.088	3.159	0.882	0.450	1.959
3115	35	5	0.351	0.089	3.950	0.945	0.505	1.870
3116	158	5	0.118	0.023	5.021	0.493	0.193	2.572
3117	340	5	0.495	0.020	4.686	0.452	0.235	1.923
3118	66	5	0.167	0.036	4.670	0.653	0.248	2.537
3119	60	5	0.222	0.064	3.139	0.927	0.444	2.285
3121	126	5	0.372	0.138	2.699	0.711	0.503	1.415
3122	29	5	0.340	0.084	4.071	0.920	0.478	1.924
3131	52	5	0.372	0.078	4.783	0.818	0.444	1.844
3132	12	5	0.424	0.248	1.714	0.991	0.827	1.199
3133	6	4	0.896	0.253	3.540	1.000	0.937	1.067
3134	43	5	0.341	0.092	3.706	0.941	0.503	1.569
3140	36	5	0.698	0.141	4.947	0.992	0.652	1.521
3211	123	5	0.232	0.108	2.140	0.723	0.503	1.437
3212	38	4	0.302	0.140	2.166	0.849	0.626	1.357
3213	20	4	0.330	0.093	3.544	0.880	0.533	1.654
3214	3	2	0.999	0.787	1.269	1.000	1.000	1.000
3215	21	5	0.515	0.161	3.193	0.875	0.713	1.226
3219	1	1	1.000	1.000	1.000	1.000	1.000	1.000
3222	227	5	0.063	0.013	4.948	0.387	0.125	3.104
3231	22	2	0.186	0.091	2.032	0.744	0.516	1.441
3232	47	4	0.369	0.105	3.503	0.883	0.652	1.354
3233	37	5	0.297	0.085	3.504	0.787	0.402	1.057
3240	81	5	0.400	0.127	3.149	0.795	0.576	1.380
3311	191	5	0.086	0.029	2.925	0.485	0.278	1.749
3312	10	4	0.577	0.235	2.458	0.988	0.798	1.250
3319	48	5	0.352	0.157	2.242	0.893	0.590	1.514
3320	119	5	0.123	0.025	4.869	0.594	0.199	2.985

Table H-2 (Continued)

Sector	No. of Firms	Countries Represented	WHERF[a]	HERFT[b]	$\dfrac{\text{WHERF}}{\text{HERFT}}$	WCONC4[c]	CONC4T[d]	$\dfrac{\text{WCONC4}}{\text{CONC4T}}$
3411	30	4	0.432	0.124	3.478	0.933	0.665	1.403
3412	34	5	0.364	0.100	3.637	0.924	0.546	1.693
3419	9	2	0.530	0.277	1.911	0.998	0.875	1.150
3420	147	5	0.124	0.028	4.430	0.590	0.242	2.444
3511	20	5	0.614	0.199	3.089	0.974	0.826	1.179
3512	32	4	0.287	0.083	3.446	0.870	0.482	1.796
3521	18	5	0.498	0.098	5.095	0.968	0.523	1.851
3522	62	5	0.126	0.062	3.893	0.573	0.254	2.258
3523	51	5	0.230	0.042	4.820	0.714	0.316	2.255
3529	72	5	0.194	0.050	3.858	0.782	0.342	2.285
3530	11	5	0.872	0.234	3.733	1.000	0.929	1.276
3540	1	1	1.000	1.000	1.000	1.000	1.000	1.272
3551	32	5	0.656	0.344	1.904	0.962	0.799	1.204
3559	16	5	0.643	0.204	3.157	0.991	0.753	1.316
3560	93	5	0.146	0.030	4.932	0.607	0.229	2.656
3610	17	5	0.426	0.278	1.533	0.970	0.867	1.119
3620	17	4	0.801	0.437	1.833	0.994	0.910	1.093
3691	46	5	0.723	0.633	1.142	0.942	0.885	1.064
3692	13	5	0.919	0.235	3.913	1.000	0.882	1.134
3699	138	5	0.372	0.127	2.923	0.805	0.546	1.474
3710	32	4	0.274	0.077	3.557	0.859	0.445	1.929
3720	12	3	0.812	0.494	1.644	0.990	0.923	1.073
3811	35	5	0.427	0.144	2.974	0.943	0.682	1.392
3812	59	5	0.283	0.067	4.255	0.843	0.429	1.957
3813	78	5	0.236	0.087	2.723	0.788	0.491	1.602
3819	55	5	0.327	0.072	4.573	0.868	0.442	1.964
3822	22	4	0.301	0.074	4.043	0.753	0.428	1.763
3823	6	3	0.701	0.263	3.004	1.000	0.938	1.066
3824	5	2	0.590	0.367	1.608	1.000	0.950	1.053
3825	4	2	0.613	0.540	1.134	1.000	1.000	1.000
3829	34	4	0.373	0.142	2.634	0.932	0.662	1.408

(continued on next page)

Table H-2 (Continued)

Sector	No. of Firms	Countries Represented	WHERF[a]	HERFT[b]	$\dfrac{\text{WHERF}}{\text{HERFT}}$	WCONC4[c]	CONC4T[d]	$\dfrac{\text{WCONC4}}{\text{CONC4T}}$
3831	9	2	0.286	0.259	1.105	0.942	0.927	1.239
3832	25	5	0.347	0.072	4.824	0.963	0.400	2.408
3833	7	3	0.931	0.435	2.140	1.000	0.973	1.027
3839	39	5	0.564	0.206	2.741	0.962	0.736	1.306
3841	6	3	0.891	0.770	1.156	1.000	0.992	1.208
3843	44	3	0.437	0.268	1.632	0.900	0.703	1.283
3844	10	4	0.530	0.197	2.692	0.984	0.765	1.286
3849	4	1	0.392	0.392	1.000	1.000	1.000	1.000
3851	9	3	0.662	0.313	2.115	0.929	0.866	1.073
3852	7	3	0.460	0.165	2.793	1.000	0.704	1.420
3853	1	1	1.000	1.000	1.000	1.000	1.000	1.000
3901	28	4	0.312	0.100	3.130	0.837	0.557	1.503
3902	2	2	1.000	0.621	1.611	1.000	1.000	1.000
3903	2	2	1.000	0.545	1.834	1.000	1.000	1.000
3909	65	5	0.182	0.044	4.187	0.713	0.320	2.227

[a] Weighted Herfindahl index.
[b] Total Herfindahl index for region.
[c] Weighted concentration ratio.
[d] Concentration ratio for region.

might be a good guide to potential economic performance if not to actual economic performance of the market, especially in countries like those of Central America where governmental policies are usually influenced rather markedly by industrial groups.

Although very little work has been done on international comparisons of industrial structure, there are several interesting comparisons of industrial concentration which might be made with respect to Central America.

A study by White (1974)[3] looks at concentration in Pakistan and in one section compares industrial concentration for several specific indus- tries in Pakistan with that of similar industries in the United States. All the comparisons are done in terms of four firm-concentration indices, and it is quite illuminating to compare Central American sectors which can be matched with corresponding sectors in the White study. Table H-3 compares the United States, Pakistani, and Central American concentration ratios for twelve sectors. Both the Central American average concentration measure and the regional concentration measure are included. The results demonstrate that in many cases a single market in Central America leads to concentration moving closer to that of the United States and away from that of Pakistan, which is much more concentrated.[4]

Table H-3. Pakistan, United States, Central America: Comparison of Four Firm-Concentration Ratios

Industry Description	CIIU	Pakistan	U.S.	Central America WCNC[a]	CNCT[b]
Knitting	3211	10	15	72	50
Cigarettes	3140	92	81	99	65
Paper	3411	100	26	93	67
Tires and tubes	3551	97	71	96	80
Cement	3692	86	28	100	88
Petroleum refining	3530	100	32	100	93
Shoes	3240	41	27	79	58
Cosmetics	3523	46	36	71	31
Distilleries	3131	82	52	82	44
Wheat and grain milling	3116	14	37	49	19
Tanning	3231	30	20	74	52
Fertilizers	3512	100	33	87	48

[a] Weighted concentration ratio for average country in region.

[b] Concentration ratio for region as "single entity."

Various studies (for example, White [1974] have noted that the U.S. weighted average for the firm-concentration ratio for all manufacturing has been around 40 percent for the decade of the 1960s. The similar Central American ratio would be 48 percent if the region were a single market compared to a 78 percent average for the five countries taken individually. Scherer (1971)[5] claims that 40 percent is about the point where potential oligopoly becomes important. Therefore the Central American industrial structure might seem quite concentrated whether or not it is considered a single market. Yet, it is quite obvious that overall concentration is much worse in the case of five separate markets and much closer to overall U.S. concentration in the former case.

Another quite interesting comparison could be made between U.S. concentration ratios for industry groups at the two-digit SIC level and for Central American two- and three-digit CIIU industries. There are twenty two-digit SIC industries classified in the United States to which can be matched all but one (section 356, plastic products) of the three-digit CIIU sectors in Central America. Table H-4 shows the average of weighted four firm-concentration ratios calculated for Central America. Once again, it is quite clearly demonstrated that a single Central American market would have industrial concentration which is much more similar to that of the United States than would five separate markets.

C.   Conclusion

In sum, these measures show extremely high industrial concentration for each Central American country considered separately. They show quite a bit lower overall concentration, more comparable with that in the United States, if the region is considered as a single unit. The impact of the formation of the Central American Common Market was probably to transform market structure from the former situation to one part way along the path--but not all the way--to the latter (considering the caveats pointed out above). As a result, two conclusions emerge: (i) the Common Market very probably made an important contribution toward reducing monopoly and oligopoly power in Central America (through widening competition to include supply from partner countries) but (ii) even so, a substantial degree of imperfect competition still remains in the region.

671

Table H-4. United States and Central America: Sectoral Comparison of
Four Firm-Concentration Ratios

	U.S. SIC	CIIU	1954 U.S. Average Concentration	WCNC[a]	CNCT[b]
Food and related products	20	311 312,313	33.8	75.4	41.5
Tobacco manufactures	21	314	73.4	99.2	65.2
Textile mill manufactures	22	321	26.5	74.5	52.3
Apparel and related products	23	322	13.0	38.7	12.5
Lumber and wood products	24	331	10.8	52.6	31.0
Furniture and fixtures	25	332	20.3	59.4	19.9
Pulp, paper and products	26	341	24.8	93.3	60.5
Printing and publishing	27	342	17.7	59.0	24.2
Chemicals and products	28	351,352	48.6	79.3	45.2
Petroleum and coal products	29	353,354	36.6	100.0	92.9
Rubber products	30	355	54.1	97.2	78.3
Leather and leather products	31	324	26.4	80.1	56.7
Stone, clay and glass products	32	36	46.4	91.5	75.6
Primary metal products	33	37	49.5	86.5	46.8
Fabricated metal products	34	381	26.1	85.7	51.1
Machinery, except electrical	35	382	33.2	91.5	66.7
Electrical machines	36	383	48.2	96.4	62.5
Transportation equipment	37	384	58.7	93.0	76.0
Instruments and related products	38	385	47.4	94.3	83.8
Miscellaneous manufactures	39	39	16.1	73.5	36.4

[a] Weighted concentration ratio for average country in region.

[b] Concentration ratio for region as "single entity."

Appendix H

NOTES

1. In fact, the reciprocal of the Herfindahl index is a quite use-ful summary measure because it depicts the number of equal-sized firms which would generate the given Herfindahl index. See M. A. Adelman, "Comment on the 'H' Concentration Measure as a Numbers Equivalent," Re-view of Economics and Statistics 51 (1969): pp. 99-101.

2. Guatemala (1972), Nicaragua (1972), El Salvador (1972), Costa Rica (1968), Honduras (1971).

3. Lawrence J. White, Industrial Concentration and Economic Power in Pakistan (Princeton: Princeton University Press, 1974).

4. Compared to Pakistan, consideration of the countries individual-ly finds Central American industry substantially more concentrated (sev-en sectors of higher concentration than Pakistan, two lower, three the same), whereas considering the region as a single market, Central America shows less industrial concentration than Pakistan (four sectors higher, seven sectors lower, one sector the same).

5. F. M. Scherer, Industrial Market Structure and Economic Perfor-mance (Chicago: Rand McNally, 1971).

Economies of Scale Parameters for Central American Manufacturing Industry

Robert G. Williams

This appendix presents alternative estimates of economies of scale in Central American manufacturing industry which, together with the estimates reported in chapter 5, form the basis for the returns to scale parameters used in the cost-benefit study (chapter 3).

A. Form of the Production Function

The unconstrained version of the Cobb-Douglas production function is used for the estimates of this appendix. That is:

(1) $\qquad V/L = e^A [K/L]^\alpha L^{(\alpha + \beta - 1)}$,

or, in logarithmic form,

(2) $\qquad \ln(V/L) = A + \alpha \ln[K/L] + (\alpha + \beta - 1) \ln L$,

where V is value added, K is capital, and L is labor.

This form has the following properties: (i) it is linear in its logarithms (unlike the CES production function); (ii) the estimates of α and $[\alpha + \beta - 1]$ are independent of the units of measurement of K and L (unlike the CES); (iii) it provides a direct estimate of the scale parameter ($\alpha + \beta - 1$), or "r" as used in chapter 3; and (iv) it provides a direct test of the statistical significance of the scale parameter, in the form of a t-test.

The results from this form supplement those obtained in chapter 5 based on the Kmenta approximation of the CES production function, with the estimating form:

$\qquad \ln (Q/L) = \alpha + \beta \ln (K/L) + \Omega [\ln(K/L)]^2 + \gamma (\ln L)$.

The data source is the industrial census survey of 1968, taken for each Central American country except El Salvador. These data cover all firms with two or more workers, giving a total of 2,501 firms.

From the raw data, the three variables, value added (VA), value of the stock of capital (K), and the total wage labor bill (L) were derived. A brief description of the rationale behind the three variables and the principles used in their derivation follows:

(i) Value Added. Instead of gross output, 1968 value added by each firm was calculated. The dependent variable in production function analysis should be value added rather than gross output, to avoid bias in the estimates due to the intrinsic collinearity between intermediate inputs and output in industrial processes. Sixteen of the variables from the raw data were used in generating VA, and the process consisted of subtracting all raw materials and intermediate inputs used during the period from outputs produced during the period. In measuring output, inventories at the beginning and end of the period were taken into account. Since all value figures were denominated in local currencies, VA, after it was calculated, was converted into Central American pesos (that is, U.S. dollars), using free market exchange rates when several exchange rates existed. The same conversion was used on the K and L values.[1]

(ii) Capital. The capital stock variable draws upon twenty-four of the original variables. Average capital stock during the period is computed on the basis of the value of buildings, machinery, vehicles, and office machines at the beginning of the period adjusted for acquisitions and depreciation during the period. A figure for value of land was excluded from the capital stock.[2]

(iii) Labor. The total labor bill paid was calculated.[3] Included were social insurance payments, salaries, and payments to third persons outside of the firm. A value for family labor input was imputed at the average wage for unskilled labor, since only the number of family members employed was given in the survey.

B.   Procedure and Results

Because of the problem of aggregation in estimating production functions, estimates were first conducted at the four-digit CIIU level, to minimize heterogeneity problems. To overcome the problem of insufficient sample size, data were pooled across countries. However, in several cases estimates conducted at the three-digit level (that is, more aggregated) provided superior statistical results (particularly with regard to significance of the scale parameter). In these cases, in the absence of strong evidence contradicting the appropriateness of aggregating, the three-digit results were used in preference to the four-digit results.

The results of the scale parameter estimates (r) for the four-digit industrial groupings are shown in table I-1. Also included are the t-ratios and the accepted values of r at the 5 percent and 2.5 percent significance levels. The corresponding estimates at the three-digit level are shown in table I-2.

There is one serious drawback resulting from use of the Cobb-Douglas form. If the elasticity of substitution between capital and labor (σ) differs significantly from 1, which is assumed in deriving the

Table I-1. Four-Digit Industrial Returns to Scale[a]

Industry Grouping	r	t	Degrees of Freedom (n - 3)	Critical Value "t" (5% level)	Critical Value "t" (10% level)
3111	.01081	.1765	35		
3112	.10486	1.5765	60		(1.671)
3113	.17629	1.6493	23		(1.714)
3114/115	-.16415	-1.6216	23		(1.714)
3116	-.12306	-2.3574	140	1.960	
3117	.00029	.0056	240		
3118	-.00683	- .6731	30		
3119	.14270	2.1829	33	2.036	
3121	.04742	.8899	87		
3122	.14146	1.1835	19		
3131/132/133	.03135	.3438	39		
3134	.25525	3.8678	32	2.038	
3140	.31664	2.1704	9		1.833
3211	.04753	.7772	68		
3212	.02352	.1247	19		
3213	.07657	1.4513	79		
3214/215	-.01612	-1.4953	15		
3220	.97801	1.4046	164		
3231/232	-.01293	- .1620	44		
3233/240	-.15666	-3.4832	137	1.960	
3311	-.05345	1.1999	160		
3312/319	.13572	1.1154	27		
3320	-.03076	- .5933	89		
3412/419	-.08307	- .8766	33		
3420	-.03918	- .9499	142		
3511/512	-.01067	- .0772	26		
3521/529	-.07649	.8895	24		
3522	-.07257	- .9957	44		
3523	-.05775	-1.0108	55		
3551/559	.14029	1.7209	36		(1.689)
3560	.00962	.1321	48		
3610/620	.30962	2.0300	14		1.761
3691/692	.09722	2.0295	35		1.692
3699	.08990	.5717	85		(1.665)
3710/720/811	.11281	- .0888	18		
3812	-.08143	- .8663	28		
3813	.10757	1.6601	52		(1.677)
3819	-.10138	-1.3232	44		
3822	-.09699	- .7474	10		
3823/824/829	-.02136	.2024	28		
3831/832/833/839	.14653	1.3187	45		
3841/843/844/845	-.09879	- .9204	39		
3851/852/901	-.27118	-1.6084	18		(1.734)

[a]Estimating form: $\ln(V/L) = A + \alpha \ln(K/L) + r \ln(L)$.

Table I-2. Three-Digit Industrial Returns to Scale[a]

Industry Grouping	r	t	Degrees of Freedom (n - 3)	Critical Value "t" (10% level)
311	.06029	2.6516	605	1.645
312	.06458	1.3461	109	
313	.13587	2.0019	74	1.671
314	.31664	2.1704	9	1.833
321	.02598	.7265	192	
322	.07801	1.4046	164	
323	-.00324	- .0457	66	
324	-.16713	-3.5297	115	1.658
331	.08001	1.9557	190	1.645
332	-.03076	- .5933	89	
341	-.03775	- .4747	38	
342	-.03918	- .9499	142	
351	-.01067	- .0772	26	
352	-.01421	- .3506	129	
355	.14029	1.7209	36	1.689
356	.00962	.1321	48	
361/62	.30962	2.0300	14	1.761
369	.07797	2.0053	123	1.658
371/72/81	.03181	.8120	151	
382	-.00128	- .0157	47	
383	.14653	1.3187	45	
384	-.09879	- .9204	39	
385	-.43729	-1.3895	5	
390	-.06802	- .6745	48	

[a]Estimating form: $\ln(V/L) = A + \alpha \ln(K/L) + r \ln(L)$.

Table I-3. Bias in Estimated Returns to Scale

$\hat{a}_3$	$\hat{a}_2$	σ	Direction of Bias in Parameter $\hat{r}$ (from (2))
Not sig.	Not sig.	1.0	None
$\neq 0$	Not sig.	?	Unknown
>0	>0	>1	Downward
>0	<0	<1	Upward
<0	>0	<1	Upward
<0	<0	>1	Downward

Table I-4. Test for Difference of Elasticity of Substitution from Unity[a] (Four-Digit Industries)

Industry Grouping	t of a_3	Degrees of Freedom (n - 4)	Critical Level of "t" (10% level)	t of a_2	Direction of r(1) Bias
3111	.381	34			None
3112	- .090	59			None
3113	.150	22			None
3114/115	.286	22			None
3116	1.090	139			None
3117	1.140	239			None
3118	5.920	29	1.699	1.648	Unknown
3119	- .390	32			None
3121	2.538	86	1.665	3.557	Downward
3122	1.731	18	1.734	- .832	Unknown
3131/132/133	- .941	38			None
3134	.232	31			None
3140	2.115	8	1.860	2.814	Downward
3211	2.381	67	1.670	3.351	Downward
3212	- .357	18			None
3213	2.254	78	1.666	3.871	Downward
3214/215	-1.458	14			None
3220	.670	163			None
3231/232	.893	43			None
3233/240	3.392	136	1.645	5.014	Downward
3311	2.697	159	1.645	4.929	Downward
3312/319	.642	26			None
3320	3.494	88	1.665	4.533	Downward
3412/419	2.562	32	1.695	4.520	Downward
3420	-1.433	141			None
3511/512	- .924	25			None
3521/529	- .681	23			None
3522	- .418	43			None
3523	1.689	54	1.675	6.799	Downward
3551/559	1.481	35			None
3560	.788	47			None
3610/620	- .031	13			None
3691/92	3.138	34	1.695	5.690	Downward
3699	.903	84			None
3710/720/811	1.181	17			None
3812	- .048	27			None
3813	.854	51			None
3819	2.490	43	1.683	2.055	Downward
3822	- .498	9			None
3823/824/829	7.447	27	1.703	2.060	Downward
3831/832/833/839	- .992	44			None
3841/843/844/845	2.808	38	1.685	6.166	Downward
3851/852/901	- .235	17			None

[a]Estimating form: $\ln(V/L) = A + a_1 \ln(L) + a_2 \ln(K/L) + a_3 [\ln(K/L)]^2$.

Cobb-Douglas form, the scale parameter will be biased. To check on the direction of bias resulting from a violation of the $\sigma = 1$ assumption, the CES log-linear approximate form,

$$(3) \quad \ln \left[\frac{VA}{L} \right] = a + a_1 \ln L + a_2 \ln \left[\frac{K}{L} \right] a_3 \ln \left[\frac{K}{L} \right]^2,$$

was used since it allows σ to differ from 1, and provides an indirect test of whether σ is greater than or less than 1. The implications of the estimates, $\hat{a}_2$ and $\hat{a}_3$, on the value of σ and the bias resulting from using the Cobb-Douglas estimates are shown in table I-3.

Table I-4 contains the results at the four-digit level of the test (3) on whether the $\sigma = 1$ assumption is violated. In the majority of the cases (twenty-eight out of forty-three), the Cobb-Douglas assumption that $\sigma = 1$ cannot be rejected. In only one case was the bias determined to be upward, and in twelve instances the bias was downward. Our results from using the Cobb-Douglas form can be considered as unbiased in most cases, and on balance, conservative (low) in the remainder of the cases. Results at the three-digit level shown in table I-5 show the same general pattern.

C.   Conclusion

The general finding of the estimates of this appendix is that a majority of sectors show constant returns to scale. This result is similar to that found in the alternative scale estimates of chapter 5. However, the conclusion is subject to doubt because of the strong reasons for expecting increasing returns to scale in small, developing economies just reaching market sizes where advantages of larger scale production should be materializing. Moreover, the tests reported in tables I-4 and I-5 suggest that in several cases the estimates of returns to scale here are downward biased, but in no case are they upward biased.

To select the final scale parameters for use in chapter 3 analyzing the benefits and costs of integration, the results of chapter 5 as well as those here are taken into account. Because of the likelihood that scale estimates are downward rather than upward biased, the procedure adopted is to choose, for each sector, that estimate (of the available alternatives) which is: (i) statistically significant, (ii) positive (rejecting decreasing returns to scale out of hand), and (iii) the highest among the alternative estimates obtained.[4] Table I-6 presents these final selections of returns to scale estimates and indicates which set of estimates provided the basis for the parameter chosen.

Table I-5. Test of Difference of Elasticity of Substitution
from Unity[a] (Three-Digit Industries)

Industry Grouping	t of $\hat{a}_3$	Degrees of Freedom (n - 4)	Critical Level of "t" (5% level)	t of $\hat{a}_2$	Direction of r(1) Bias[b]
311	3.0407	604	1.645	14.038	Downward
312	2.8299	108	1.658	3.7984	Downward
313	-0.0709	73			None
314	2.1149	8	1.860	2.8139	Downward
321	2.8770	191	1.645	6.6647	Downward
322	0.6705	163			None
323	1.7920	65	1.671	3.3183	Downward
324	3.0996	114	1.658	4.6179	Downward
331	1.7617	189	1.645	4.3943	Downward
332	3.4938	88	1.664	4.5326	Downward
341	2.7982	37	1.684	4.9918	Downward
342	-1.4326	141			None
351	-0.9244	25			None
352	0.8603	128			None
355	1.4806	35			None
356	0.7883	47			None
361/62	-0.0306	13			None
369	2.5902	122	1.658	7.3164	Downward
371/72/81	2.2908	150	1.645	5.7533	Downward
382	2.0033	46	1.684	3.3981	Downward
383	-0.9919	44			None
384	2.8083	38	1.684	6.1658	Downward
385	-1.2573	4			None
390	0.4692	47			None

[a]Estimating form: $\ln(V/L) = A + a_1 \ln(L) + a_2 \ln(K/L) + a_3 [\ln(K/L)]^2$.
[b]See table I-4.

Table I-6. Returns to Scale Estimates Used in Cost-Benefit Study
(Chapter 3)

Sector	Returns to Scale Parameter	Estimating Source[a]
311	.1533	A
313	.2578	A
314	.3166	B
322	.1878	A
331	.080	B
355	.1403	B
361	.3096	B
362	.3096	B
369	.078	B
371, 372, 381[b]		
Guatemala	.0324	C
El Salvador	.0324	C
Honduras	.0918	C
Nicaragua	.0664	C
Costa Rica	.0213	
Others[c]	0	No significant returns to scale found in A, B, or C.

NOTES: a. A: table D-11, appendix D.
        B: three-digit CIIU estimates of this appendix.
            See table I-2.
        C: based on four-digit CIIU estimates of this
            appendix (table I-1).

        b. Note that estimate varies with the country. Obtained apply-
            ing individual country weighting (based on four-digit sectoral
            value added) to the four-digit results in order to aggregate
            results to the three-digit level.

        c. Includes sectors 312, 321, 323, 324, 332, 341, 342, 351, 352,
            353, 354, 356, 382, 383, 384, 385, 390.

Appendix I

NOTES

1. The following exchange rates were used: Guatemala, 1 quetzal/ Central American peso ($CA); Honduras, 2 lempiras/$CA; Nicaragua, 7.05 cordobas/$CA; Costa Rica, 7.35 colones/$CA.

2. Rental payments for land were subtracted from value added; rent was not imputed for owned land and subtracted from VA under the assumption that inframarginal units held yield zero return.

3. This implies that the sum of salaries paid during the year equals the quantity of labor used as input. A worker who receives $500 for a year's labor contributes one-third the labor input of a worker receiving $1,500 for a year's work.

4. Note that the estimates using the first of two approaches in chapter 5--those based on the regression of the logarithm of labor on the logarithm of wage and the logarithm of value added--are completely excluded in this process. As discussed in chapter 5, those estimates are biased upward by extremely large amounts. Furthermore, they have no direct test for statistical significance.

Calculation of the Shadow Price of Foreign Exchange Based on the Central American Econometric Model

Gabriel Siri

For a developing country a unit of foreign exchange usually represents a greater value than the corresponding sum of local currency converted at the exchange rate. This appendix formulates a methodology for estimating the scarcity price of "hard" foreign exchange for open developing economies such as those in Central America.

The method of estimating the "shadow price" of foreign exchange presented here refers to economies which maintain the stability of their currencies through internal measures (deflationary) more than through external measures (tariff barriers, export subsidies, devaluations of currency), or through the use of international liquidity (reserves, external loans).[1]

The methods commonly used for calculating the scarcity premium of foreign exchange over the exchange rate assume that the economies counteract external deficits with changes in the exchange rate or in the tariff levels. Through these types of artificial alterations in the prices of imports and exports, a deficit country can promote an overvaluation of its exchange rate that is adequate for reestablishing equilibrium in its commercial balance.[2]

However, the Central American economies have not followed the normal pattern of reaction to external deficits. As these economies are open to the exterior for reasons of size, location, and geographical configuration, they have traditionally tended to restrict global demand in the face of a drop in exports, reducing their imports through monetary and fiscal policies directed toward decreasing global demand, particularly consumption. At the same time, the governments of the region have maintained their exchange rates practically unaltered during the past three decades and have set relatively low tariffs (especially when exonerations are considered) compared, for example, with most of the South American countries. As a a result, the "overvaluation" of their official exchange rates, in the sense of excess above the rate that would prevail in the absence of protection, has been rather low. Nevertheless, their scarcity price of foreign exchange, in the sense of the increment in domestic product made possible per unit of extra foreign exchange available, can be quite high, considering the fact that such increases permit a relaxation of the fiscal and monetary restrictions on the economies.

The formation of the Common Market led to the accentuation of the pattern described above because the integration agreements established a common external tariff that has been relatively rigid for all member countries (ruling out or limiting temporary adjustment by changes in tariffs). At the same time, the integration agreements imposed restrictions on unilateral changes in exchange rates.

The pattern of internal adjustment of the economies has been especially painful because of the difficulty in increasing exports in the short run and the growing dependence of the countries on foreign exchange for their economic development. The exports of each of the Central American countries to the rest of the world are concentrated in a few agricultural commodities. When there is a substantial decline in external demand for one of these commodities, it becomes extremely difficult to find alternative markets for other products which the country is capable of exporting. Limitations on the demand side are complemented by rigidities on the supply side, considering the high cost of abandoning the cultivation of permanent crops such as coffee and bananas.

At the same time, dependence on imports from outside the region has become more critical for the Central American countries during the last decade. Economic growth of the countries requires expansion of capital stock, and practically all machinery and equipment are imported. Moreover, the Central American economy imports more and more raw materials from outside the area, especially as inputs for industrial production. Finally, petroleum imports have acquired a dominant position in very recent years.

It is worth noting that during the last decade the countries have resisted continuing the traditional pattern of internal adjustment. In the first place the governments have placed greater emphasis on external measures, for example, by raising the level of the common external tariff. (See the "Protocol of San José, Emergency Measures for the Balance of Payments Defense," 1968.) At the same time, the economies have resorted more to external financing. The total of short- and long-term foreign loans rose from $112 million in 1969 to $559 million in 1974.

In addition, the governments have opted for internal measures other than deflation in defense of the balance of payments. They have attempted, with varying degrees of success, the following policy alternatives:

      (i) Import substitution of manufactured products (one of the principal objectives of the process of integration).

      (ii) More recently, increases in agricultural production oriented toward achieving self-sufficiency in basic grains.

      (iii) The achievement of a certain degree of independence of fiscal revenues from the foreign sector, making feasible the adoption of anticyclical programs for public investment.

In open economies such as in Central America, it is appropriate to approach the problem through the estimation of changes in the GDP which may occur in the face of a decline in exports, using an econometric model that can simulate the patterns of behavior characteristic of the economies under balance of payments deficit situations. The scarcity price for foreign exchange estimated in this first stage of the calculation understates the total effect, over the longer term, of the reduction of exports because it is not possible for a country to maintain indefinitely the deficit that appears in the commercial balance. The maintenance of a state of external equilibrium for the economy implies a decrease in imports of a magnitude similar to that of the initial decline in exports. Once again, an econometric model may be used to simulate the anticipated economic process by manipulating the variables for monetary and fiscal policy until the required reduction in imports is achieved. The shadow price or scarcity price of foreign exchange may be derived from the effect on GDP caused by a decrease in exports, plus the effect induced by the parallel reduction in imports.

To carry out a first effort at the application of this method, this appendix uses the Central American econometric model developed in the Special Studies Unit within SIECA. This model is a macroeconomic model basically oriented toward demand (with special emphasis on commerce within and outside the area) which includes, however, a production function that establishes a limit on the supply side (see table J-1).

Through a process of dynamic simulation,[3] the model has been used to estimate the effect of a decrease in the value of exports on the GDP of one Central American country (El Salvador),[4] both in the year in which the reduction of exports occurs and in following years. Taking into account the fact that the effects die out rapidly, the estimates here examine only the first three years subsequent to each impact. The process is repeated for each of the years for the period 1963-69 (see table J-2). The exercise is limited to examining the direct effect of a reduction in exports, without considering the additional effect that would result from a parallel induced reduction in imports.[5]

The results indicate that, on the average, a decline in exports by one value unit provokes a reduction of 1.6 units in the present discounted value of the stream of GDP. It may therefore be concluded that, on the basis of the econometric model, the shadow price of foreign exchange from exports, in the Central American case, is on the order of 60 percent above the exchange rate. Note that this estimate is probably conservative because the simulation exercise does not include the effect on GDP of a reduction in imports necessary to reestablish external balance.

The model reflects reality in that it indicates that the negative impact on GDP from a reduction in exports varies from year to year, diminishing in boom periods (during which the supply constraint is in effect), especially when the boom is attributable to export expansion. In these years the model indicates that small reductions in exports have virtually no effect on GDP, and even larger impacts have limited effects.

The analysis implicitly presupposes that the increments in GDP resulting from increases in exports constitute real increases in production and income for the community. The analysis ignores the effects of disequilibria in other markets that might restrict the attainable production and income and likewise ignores other components of economic welfare that are not included in measurements of GDP. For example, the distortions in the capital and labor markets existing in the Central American

Table J-1. Structure of the Central American Econometric Model
Utilized to Estimate the Shadow Price

---

1   Private consumption = f(disposable income, total private
          credit).

2   Government consumption = f(total taxes, credit to the
          government).

3   Private investment = f(growth of GDP, total private credit,
          private investment in the prior year).

4   Capital stock = f(distributed lag of total investment).

5   GDP demand = private consumption + government consumption
          + private investment + government investment + exports
          - imports.

6   Potential GDP = f(capital stock, labor force).

7   GDP = minimum of (potential GDP, GDP demand).

8   GNP = GDP - net factor income to the exterior.

9   Depreciation = f(capital stock).

10   Direct taxes = f(GNP).

11   Indirect taxes = f(private consumption).

12   Disposable income = GNP - total taxes - subsidies -
          depreciation.

13   Manufacturing prices = f(world prices of manufactures plus
          tariffs, unutilized capacity of industrial sector).

14   Agricultural prices = f(world agricultural prices plus
          tariffs, domestic agricultural production).

15   Implicit price of GDP = f(manufacturing prices, food prices,
          fuel prices).

16-18   Central American imports (three sectors) = f(variables of
          total demand, Common Market).

19-22   Imports from rest of world (four sectors) = f(total demand
          variables).

23-25   Central American exports (three sectors) = f(variables of
          total demand of the other Central American countries).

26   Sight deposits = f(disposable income).

Table J-1 (Continued)

---

27   Time deposits = f(disposable income).

28   Mortgage bonds = f(disposable income, change in domestic
              prices).

29   Commercial bank reserves = f(legal reserves on sight
              deposits + legal reserves on time deposits).

30   Private credit of commercial banks = sight deposits +
              time deposits + mortgage bonds + central bank credit -
              commercial bank reserves + other accounts.

31   Total private credit = private credit of commercial banks
              + private credit of the Central Bank.

---

economies make the estimated increases in the GDP smaller than they would
have been if resources had been distributed in optimum form.

At the same time, foreign trade provides tariff and, indirectly,
other fiscal revenues, which are difficult for a government to substitute.
Therefore, since the marginal utility of the fiscal revenue, from the
viewpoint of the community, is greater than the marginal utility of personal income, increases in exports can produce increases in welfare that
are greater than the increment in the GDP. Similarly, given that increases
in income affect its pattern of distribution, it is probable that gains
in income do not coincide with gains in economic welfare.

In sum, the shadow price of foreign exchange estimated in this study
may be overestimated or underestimated because of imperfections in the
markets of goods and of factors of production, and because of discrepancies between the value of the GDP given in the national accounts and the
economic welfare of a country.[6] It is believed, however, that the proposed methodology, applied to the Central American case, captures the
more relevant aspects of the problem, and the results obtained are an
acceptable approximation of the shadow price of foreign exchange.

Table J-2. Decrease in GDP in Millions of Dollars as Result of a Reduction of $20 Million in Exports, and Estimated Shadow Price of Exports (Based on the Simulation of the Central American Econometric Model)[a]

Year of Export Drop	Years Following the Original Impact										Present Discounted Value of GDP Losses (at 15% discount rate)	Estimated Shadow Price of Exports
	1963	1964	1965	1966	1967	1968	1969	1970	1971	1972		
1963	-29	- 9	- 8	- 7							-48	2.41
1964		-21	- 6	- 5	- 1						-31	1.54
1965			-20	- 6	- 2	- 0					-27	1.33
1966				-22	-11	- 4	- 1				-35	1.75
1967					-27	-13	- 7	- 1			-44	2.20
1968						-26	-16	- 5	0		-43	2.17
1969							- 2	0	0	0	- 2	0.10
Average values:											-33	1.64

[a] For example, the impact on value of GDP for 1966 of a reduction of $20 million in exports in the same year is $22 million. This reduction in 1966 GDP causes a reduction of $11 million in the GDP of the next year. The effect repeats itself in a similar manner in following years, reaching practically zero in 1970. The present discounted value of the stream of losses of GDP, discounted at 15 percent annually, is $37 million. Dividing this value by the initial export decline of $20 million, the resulting "shadow price" of export earnings for this particular year is 1.75.

Appendix J

NOTES

1. See R. N. Cooper, "The Relevance of International Liquidity to Developed Countries," American Economic Review 58 (May 1968). A less formal treatment of the theme is given in R. Nurkse, "Conditions of International Monetary Equilibrium," in H. S. Ellis and L. Metzler, eds. Readings in the Theory of International Trade (Philadelphia: Blakiston, 1950). Also see comments on the problem in B. Balassa and D. M. Schydlowsky, "Effective Tariffs, Domestic Cost of Foreign Exchange, and the Equilibrium Exchange Rate," Journal of Political Economy 76 (May/June 1968).

2. For a good survey of the principal approaches used to address the problem, see E. Bacha and L. Taylor, "Foreign Exchange Shadow Prices: A Critical Review of Current Theories," Quarterly Journal of Economics (May 1971).

3. In order to cope with nonlinearities, the Gauss-Seidel iterative simulation method is used to obtain the solution.

4. To approximate more closely the conditions found in Central America, it is assumed that the export decline (exogenously imposed in the model) corresponds to a decrease in the prices of export products (for example, coffee, cotton, and so on). Therefore it is not necessary to introduce restrictions on the global production function of the model.

5. The short-run behavior of the commercial balance depends largely on the specification of the lag structure of the group of equations that make up the external sector of the model. Given this sensitivity, the simulation results have been interpreted with the utmost caution, and it has appeared preferable to postpone this second stage of the analysis until improvements are achieved in the underlying model.

6. These ideas are based on the following works of Daniel Schydlowsky: "Methodology for the Empirical Estimation of Shadow Prices," Discussion paper series no. 2 (Center for Latin American Development Studies, Boston University, April 1973); "Project Evaluation in Economies in General Disequilibrium: An Application of Second Best Analysis," Discussion paper series no. 1 (Center for Latin American Development Studies, Boston University, March 1973).

Effective Protection Rates in Central America

Alan I. Rapoport

The main objective of this appendix is to analyze the effective rates of protection prevailing in the Central American manufacturing sector at the four-digit CIIU level. Effective protection is commonly defined as some measure of the excess of value added permitted in a given production process, owing to the presence of protection on both the final product of the process and the tradable input going into the production process itself, over the amount of value added that would be permitted if the product and its tradable inputs were not at all protected. Another and a bit more analytical way of looking at this is to think of the effective rate of protection of a given process as the arithmetical difference between value added at domestic prices and value added at world prices divided by value added at world prices.

There are many controversies among economists about the theory of effective protection, relating either to its measurement or directly to the concept itself. Since measurement of effective protection is basically a comparison between two situations--one hypothetical and one existing--two types of production information are needed for its calculation. Value added at both world and domestic prices are necessary. In all empirical studies of effective protection one of these is always derived from the other, that is, the starting point is either a world or efficient production process or the existing domestic production process.

Some empirical studies utilize domestic input-output data or domestic cost-of-production data and thus begin with all of the relevant measures in terms of domestic currency value. This information is then combined with tariff information on both final product and tradable inputs to calculate these same domestic measures in terms of world prices. This is basically the approach that will be followed here.

Many other empirical studies begin with some form of input-output or cost of production data which serves as a proxy for the existing domestic production process. These studies usually use either an input-output table of a country that is considered similar to the country being analyzed or some type of average production process combining information from many countries. Hence, these studies begin with world prices and use tariff information to create production parameters at domestic prices.

Conceptually, the above two methods differ in that they use quite different production processes as a base from which to measure effective rates of protection, and thus it is quite easy to see that they can lead to quite different results. The important fact to be emphasized is that effective protection can only be defined in relation to a given production process. Both methods usually implicitly assume fixed proportions between tradable inputs and value added, and in some cases even among the individual components of value added.

Once one chooses a method for calculating effective protection, problems of measurement begin to develop. The basic data necessary for calculating effective rates of protection are production coefficients and nominal rates of protection on final products and intermediate inputs. Detailed data at the product level would be the most useful, but in most cases, data can only be obtained at the firm or sectoral level. The key is to have the production and tariff information consistent. If the production coefficients are for a given product grouping, the tariff rate should be some average applicable to that grouping. Measurement problems usually boil down to data collection and proper aggregation techniques.

Once the breakdown of production between value added and intermediate inputs has been determined, the protection being received by the inputs in the production process must be calculated. Intermediate inputs may be traded or nontraded goods. The prices of the former are usually determined by world prices and tariffs. The prices of the latter are determined more by domestic forces. For those inputs being imported, protection is usually the nominal tariff, or in cases where there exist other trade restrictions, it is the equivalent nominal tariff. Domestically produced traded inputs are usually quite a bit harder to deal with. In this case, the actual protection is the difference between the domestic price of the inputs and the world price (provided quality is identical).

A great variety of methods have been concocted to handle nontraded inputs. The two most widely known are probably the Corden and the Balassa methods. The Corden method begins with the assumption that inputs are produced by combining traded inputs and factor inputs (moving back vertically) and thus some fraction of their value should be included in value added, with the remainder included with traded inputs. The Balassa method assumes nontraded inputs can be supplied at constant costs and that there is no effect on their prices. Hence, they are then treated in the analysis like any other traded input but considered to have a zero tariff. This appendix uses a modified Corden method and includes all nontraded inputs and services in value added. The available data do not allow their separation in any other manner. Using the Balassa method would tend to overestimate the actual effective protection being received by a given sector.

Another important question relating to effective protection measurement is, What components of value added can actually be protected? Value added usually consists of the returns to the services of capital and labor. Unfortunately (for many analyses), capital and labor are not homogeneous categories. There are different types of capital and different types of labor. It can be argued that in certain cases the returns to capital and to certain skill levels of labor are internationally rather than domestically determined, and that when this is in fact the case these services cannot be protected and it is thus useless to speak of an effective rate of protection pertaining to them. Unfortunately,

once again, one's information does not always permit making these distinctions, especially in the case of labor. The case of capital can also be
clouded by the presence of monopoly or oligopoly considerations which may
allow some of the protection to take the form of excess profits.

Another problem that frequently arises is that existing market values
of factors--labor, capital, foreign exchange--do not always reflect their
true scarcity values. Some empirical studies, therefore, have tried to
calculate a corrected effective protection; that is, they have tried to
correct for distortions between the private and social cost of one or
several scarce factors. Section A will present the framework and methodology for the empirical analysis.

The following set of variables is utilized in calculating effective
rates of protection in this appendix:

Variable	Definition
GVP	Gross value of production
VA	Value added
RM	Intermediate inputs
t	Nominal tariff rate on final products
t*	Nominal tariff rate on intermediate products
e	Effective rate of protection
w	World
d	Domestic

The following three equations are nothing more than depictions of the
definitions of the three concepts of protection that are being dealt with
in this appendix:

(1) $GVP_d = GVP_w (1 + t)$,

(2) $VA_d = VA_w (1 + e)$, and

(3) $RM_d = RM_w (1 + t*)$.

From these initial relationships (equations) and other defined relationships between the variables, a formula can be derived for the effective
rate of protection that uses the information available relative to tariffs and industrial production coefficients. The subsequent set of
equations traces through the calculation of effective protection from the
underlying relationships between the variables:

(4) $GVP_d - RM_d = VA_d$,

(5) $VA_w (1 + e) = VA_d$,

(6) $VA_w = GVP_w - RM_w$,

(7) $VA_w = \dfrac{GVP_d}{1 + t} - \dfrac{RM_d}{1 + t*}$

(8)
$$\frac{VA_d}{1 + e} = \frac{GVP_d}{1 + t} \quad \frac{-RM_d}{1 + t^*} ,$$

(9)
$$VA_d = (1 + e) \left(\frac{GVP_d}{1 + t} \quad \frac{-RM_d}{1 + t^*} \right) ,$$

(10)
$$GVP_d - RM_d = \left[\frac{GVP_{d'} (1 + t^*) - RM_d (1 + t)}{(1 + t)(1 + t^*)} \right] (1 + e),$$

(11)
$$e = \frac{(GVP_d - RM_d)(1 + t)(1 + t^*)}{GVP_d (1 + t^*) - RM_d (1 + t)} - 1,$$

(12)
$$e = \frac{(GVP_d - RM_d)(1 + t)(1 + t^*) - GVP_d (1 + t^*) + RM_d (1 + t)}{GVP (1 + t^*) - RM_d (1 + t)},$$

(13)
$$e = \frac{GVP_d (1 + t^*) t - RM_d (1 + t)(t^*)}{GVP_d (1 + t^*) - RM_d (1 + t)} .$$

A. Data

The data used for these calculations are basically of three types--industrial production data, input-output data, and tariff and trade data. The production data are created from the 1968 industrial census for Central America (excluding El Salvador). The original data consist of ninety-five variables measured in domestic currencies. The description of these variables can be found in this section (table K-9), and the appropriate exchange rates for their conversion are in section B. The observations are at the individual firm level, with 2,760 firms covered.

A slightly modified set of variables had to be created from the original variables in order to proceed with the effective protective calculations. These modified variables are value added, gross value of production, and intermediate inputs. Section B gives the relationship between the latter variables and the original variables in the survey. It should be noted that the new set of data does not include all of the original observations. Observations for which value added, capital stock, or the total wage bill were negative or zero were discarded.

Since the effective protection was to be calculated at the four-digit CIIU level rather than at the firm level, the data had to be aggregated over these sectors. The results show the following industry sectoral breakdown within the four countries represented in the survey:

Country	No. of Sectors
Guatemala	71
Honduras	51
Nicaragua	49
Costa Rica	67

There are 238 manufacturing sectors represented in the four countries and 75 distinct sectors in the region as a whole.

Once the production (or technical coefficients) had been determined from the census results, nominal rates of protection then had to be determined at the sectoral level for both the output of that sector and the inputs entering the production process for that sector.

Nominal tariff rates for final products are first determined at the seven- and nine-digit NAUCA (tariff-line) levels and then calculated at the sectoral level by weighting these tariffs by extraregional imports of each product in the sector. Two types of nominal tariffs were used—legal tariffs and adjusted tariffs. The legal tariffs were calculated by combining the specific and ad valorem tariffs which were present in the books (to the ad valorem was added the 30 percent San José Protocol tariff in cases where applicable). Since the specific tariff was usually in the form of dollars per kilo, some kind of price had to be chosen in order to convert into percentage terms. A unit price was calculated for each relevant NAUCA category by dividing value of rest-of-world inputs by quantity. A different unit price was calculated for each country. Adjusted tariffs were treated as actual tariff collections divided by import value.

It should be noted that the import weighting procedure used to obtain sectoral tariffs gives zero weights to products which are not imported and thus gives zero weights to prohibitive tariffs and very low weights to very restrictive tariffs, that is, those that do a good job of impeding imports. To obtain a truly accurate picture of the protection being received by particular sectors including any nontariff barriers, one would have to be able to measure price differentials between the imported and domestic substitute good. Consumption weights would probably be preferable to import weights in calculating tariffs at the sectoral level—especially if price differentials were utilized rather than pure tariffs as measures of product protection.

The next major step in the analysis is to calculate intermediate rates of protection, that is, the amount of protection on the intermediate inputs being used in the production process being analyzed (sectoral production process). The main source of data for these calculations was the 1971 industrial survey of Guatemala. For each manufacturing sector purchases of material inputs were classified by sector. An average rate of protection on inputs could then be calculated for each sector by multiplying the tariff rate for a particular input by the proportion of that input in total input purchases. Since this input-output type of information was only available for Guatemala, the same weights were used in calculating the intermediate rates of protection for the other countries, except of course the tariff rates were changed. This procedure was carried out for both legal and adjusted tariffs.

Once the nominal protection at the final and intermediate level had been determined it was quite easy to apply equation (13) and calculate the effective rates of protection for each sector in each country. It was also decided to estimate effective rates of protection for El Salvador since this country is an integral part of Central America. Since tariff information was already available for El Salvador, nominal final and intermediate rates could be determined in the same manner as they were for the other countries. No production information being available for El Salvador, it was decided to use the production information of Guatemala as a proxy. This seemed to be quite a realistic solution to the problem since it is agreed by most experts that these two countries have the most similar industrial structures in Central America.

Before analyzing the results, some explanation of how to interpret the effective protection measure used in the study would be helpful. The arithmetic measure in its simplest form is

$$\frac{(VA_d - VA_w)}{VA_w}.$$

This measure can take on both positive and negative values. Positive values always denote positive effective protection. Negative values may or may not denote negative protection; this depends on whether the numerator or denominator causes the expression to be negative. The numerator will be negative when the inputs used in the production process are given greater absolute protection than the output. In this case, the production process is actually receiving negative protection. The denominator VA_w can also be negative—a case of domestic value added being negative when measured at world prices. This is not negative protection but actually is a case where there is quite heavy positive protection. In cases where value added at world prices is very small, there will be heavy protection. There is actually little difference among cases where VA_w is small and positive and those where it is small and negative. Both cases will lead to very large figures for effective protection, the sign being quite irrelevant.

In the calculations of adjusted effective protection there were never any cases where VA_w was negative. Therefore, all negative values correspond to actual negative protection. On the other hand, in the case of legal protection, there were several cases where VA_w proved to be negative, and large negative numbers resulted which were not signs of negative protection but of high positive protection. In tables K-1 and K-2 legal and adjusted effective rates of protection are presented for all sectors in the five countries. Negative rates resulting from negative value added will be differentiated from those which result from actual negative protection. There are only five cases among the 238 observations for which this occurs. Five cases of rather high adjusted effective rates of protection (arbitrarily defined as greater than 900 percent) also occur. In the subsequent analysis these extreme values will be left out because of the sensitivity of the measures being studied to those extreme cases.

Table K-1. Legal Effective Rates of Protection

Sector	Guatemala	El Salvador	Honduras	Nicaragua	Costa Rica
3111	1.1366	0.6416	3.9973	0.3560	0.3538
3112	0.3023	0.5519	0.2688	0.1662	1.2145
3113	2.5445	3.0620	2.8993	1.9258	-9.1138[a]
3114	1.9604	2.0146	3.2622	1.6934	-49.8767[a]
3115	0.3895	0.4979	0.9716	0.4101	3.8222
3116	3.5237	15.2783	1.4991	0.7584	2.1137
3117	1.5659	3.4798	12.1209	1.7725	-69.8488[a]
3118	0.7094	1.0635	0.6108	1.3479	1.2930
3119	1.9143	2.1878	3.3016	3.2027	1.9301
3121	1.9905	1.3352	0.5199	0.7458	12.7377
3122	0.0563	-0.0067	-0.1994	-0.0287	-0.0999
3131	3.6148	3.1887	3.0292	2.7070	4.0116
3132	2.5883	2.6983	8.6678	--	39.9681
3133	0.2621	0.2745	0.3186	0.5108	--
3134	0.5074	0.4016	0.7043	0.6053	0.5809
3140	2.6104	2.4236	2.5875	--	2.3442
3211	0.2924	0.4701	0.7650	0.6002	0.4688
3212	0.7508	0.8287	1.6786	--	0.9740
3213	3.0604	2.3224	1.8057	2.6599	3.0084
3214	5.4920	3.4306	--	--	3.8212
3215	0.5252	0.4242	0.3416	0.3235	0.4367
3219	--	--	--	--	1.4063
3220	18.2282	9.4313	3.8309	26.8381	1.8064
3231	0.5549	0.1501	--	-0.0907	0.1038
3232	--	--	12.6691	--	1.1186
3233	0.7421	0.4359	0.4807	0.6592	0.5992
3240	-15.3023[a]	12.5231	0.7538	1.7770	-15.3661
3311	1.0814	0.2147	1.6856	6.5137	3.1454
3312	0.3370	2.4829	1.3283	--	0.3798
3319	0.5943	0.7596	0.7506	1.1204	1.1508
3320	2.8160	3.2805	17.0772	1.2236	-12.1528[a]
3411	0.5674	0.3494	--	--	0.4970
3412	0.1343	0.1868	-0.4956	0.4874	0.3647
3419	0.2710	0.3877	--	0.3123	0.0248
3420	0.0290	0.0346	0.0679	0.2812	0.0346
3511	0.2734	0.2316	0.2508	0.2332	0.2620
3512	-0.0826	-0.1791	--	-0.0090	0.0054
3521	0.5412	0.4759	0.6587	--	0.5078
3522	0.0824	0.1059	-0.0475	0.1198	0.0679
3523	2.4260	1.4076	5.3199	2.3451	2.0075
3529	1.1380	0.7716	0.6419	0.5183	1.6967
3530	0.2901	0.7882	0.5055	--	--
3540	1.0428	0.5869	--	--	--
3551	0.4036	0.5189	1.1713	--	0.3110
3559	0.2469	0.2646	0.2688	0.2642	0.2667
3560	0.9957	1.1515	1.5531	0.7139	3.8431
3610	1.3995	0.6221	--	1.0858	2.5879

(continued on next page)

Table K-1 (Continued)

Sector	Guatemala	El Salvador	Honduras	Nicaragua	Costa Rica
3620	0.4488	0.3607	--	--	0.6596
3691	0.1753	0.2024	0.8025	0.3908	0.4672
3692	0.3534	0.3293	0.3554	0.4240	0.3865
3699	0.2742	0.1804	0.2004	0.3027	0.2446
3710	0.1774	0.1766	--	--	0.1933
3720	0.1896	0.4586	--	--	0.8702
3811	0.3344	0.3258	--	0.3507	0.4012
3812	1.7742	1.3190	1.3119	1.2018	0.8116
3813	0.3261	0.4631	0.4202	0.3085	0.8101
3819	0.7129	0.6278	0.4763	0.6124	0.4897
3821	0.1936	0.2125	--	--	--
3822	0.0530	0.0566	--	0.0545	0.0299
3823	--	--	--	--	0.0630
3824	0.0714	0.0611	-0.0130	--	0.0685
3825	--	--	--	--	0.4662
3829	0.1838	0.2089	0.1881	0.1713	0.4002
3831	0.1544	0.1648	--	--	0.1491
3832	0.6198	0.5947	--	1.4128	0.8589
3833	0.4839	0.5053	--	--	1.2469
3839	0.5069	0.4943	0.6129	0.4038	0.4934
3841	0.2227	0.1318	--	--	--
3843	0.4526	0.3963	--	--	0.6017
3844	1.6000	1.9191	--	--	2.2520
3845	0.1211	0.1211	--	--	0.1927
3851	0.2692	0.2778	--	0.3051	--
3852	0.7467	0.7164	0.6826	--	--
3901	0.6370	0.7267	0.7360	-0.0352	--
3909	1.0821	0.9086	0.9289	0.9571	-0.0273

[a]Cases where value added at world prices is negative.

699

Table K-2. Adjusted Effective Rates of Protection

Sector	Guatemala	El Salvador	Honduras	Nicaragua	Costa Rica
3111	-0.0923	0.1780	0.7712	-0.1003	-0.0812
3112	0.0684	0.3810	0.2179	0.1075	0.5272
3113	0.4650	1.8662	1.9193	0.5918	0.4413
3114	1.0516	1.0451	2.0663	1.2120	4.6175
3115	-0.0584	-0.0309	0.0400	-0.0777	-0.0913
3116	-0.0220	-0.0308	0.19887	0.6418	22.2395[a]
3117	0.3603	53.2904[a]	11.9754[a]	0.9294	28.7988[a]
3118	-0.0461	0.0175	0.1541	0.4567	0.0989
3119	0.7709	0.8393	2.0354	0.7565	1.6791
3121	0.2753	0.7552	0.3728	0.3608	0.8645
3122	0.2563	-0.0415	-0.0952	0.1106	-0.2001
3131	0.3800	0.8976	2.0521	0.5861	0.7396
3132	0.8713	1.5474	5.1965	--	6.5944
3133	0.2404	0.2281	0.2561	0.1930	--
3134	0.6480	0.4258	0.5001	0.3064	0.6201
3141	0.0940	1.5572	1.6121	--	1.7959
3211	0.0927	0.1624	0.4487	0.3169	0.1463
3212	0.2500	0.6279	0.2342	--	0.8095
3213	1.0423	1.8437	1.1021	1.4893	0.9300
3214	1.5439	1.5308	--	--	1.6384
3215	0.0978	0.3095	-0.0476	0.0650	0.3608
3219	--	--	--	--	0.5066
3220	0.7795	1.1860	0.1925	0.1819	1.3645
3231	0.4895	-0.3403	--	0.0713	0.0813
3232	--	--	-0.0457	--	0.7048
3233	0.3960	0.2626	1.9139	0.3526	0.5735
3240	0.7690	0.1960	0.7129	0.1854	2.5185
3311	-0.0308	0.0016	0.4094	0.1598	0.4587
3312	0.2316	10.3919[a]	0.0090	--	0.0665
3319	0.4136	0.1824	0.4675	0.1133	0.5163
3320	0.3553	1.7599	2.7482	0.1424	0.4701
3411	0.0309	0.0564	--	--	0.0202
3412	0.1308	0.0859	0.3425	0.0257	0.0811
3419	0.3356	0.3042	--	0.2877	0.2897
3420	0.0564	0.0514	0.0735	0.0954	0.0664
3511	0.0306	0.0429	0.0507	0.0303	0.0414
3512	0.2766	-0.0099	--	0.0808	0.0188
3521	0.2699	0.2899	0.3684	--	0.2188
3522	0.0987	0.0901	-0.0145	0.1043	0.0820
3523	0.5787	0.6772	4.9438	0.6511	0.5679
3529	0.3898	1.0968	0.1670	0.1318	0.2888
3530	0.1356	0.4624	0.0983	--	--
3540	0.0363	-0.1248	--	--	--
3551	0.3476	0.4089	0.0552	--	0.1928
3559	0.1818	0.1474	0.1422	0.1190	0.1769
3560	0.3262	0.3175	0.4565	0.3124	0.3517
3610	0.7778	0.4348	--	0.5030	1.4721

(continued on next page)

Table K-2 (Continued)

Sector	Guatemala	El Salvador	Honduras	Nicaragua	Costa Rica
3620	0.2607	0.1560	--	--	0.4610
3691	0.0460	0.1946	0.3335	0.1549	0.0981
3692	0.1395	0.1710	0.2322	0.0905	0.1544
3699	0.0972	0.1236	0.1047	0.1013	0.1132
3710	0.0424	0.0544	--	--	0.0358
3720	0.0407	0.0247	--	--	0.0449
3811	0.2647	0.2533	--	0.2602	0.3618
3812	0.2161	0.6651	0.6016	0.1762	0.2827
3813	0.0405	0.0135	0.0578	0.0777	0.0485
3819	0.4376	0.4967	0.3364	0.2745	0.2253
3821	0.1250	0.1514	--	--	--
3822	0.0249	0.0643	--	0.0593	0.0696
3823	--	--	--	--	0.0096
3824	0.0182	0.0156	-0.0255	--	0.0156
3825	--	--	--	--	0.2996
3829	0.1038	0.1015	0.1146	0.0732	0.1348
3831	0.0220	0.0818	--	--	0.0170
3832	0.2825	0.1851	--	0.1894	0.1301
3833	0.3229	0.3709	--	--	1.0996
3839	0.3171	0.3563	0.2774	0.2324	0.3095
3841	0.0510	0.0174	--	--	--
3843	0.3490	0.2973	--	--	0.1461
3844	0.5136	1.0009	--	--	0.2460
3845	0.0087	0.0058	--	--	0.0002
3851	0.1143	0.1105	--	0.0963	--
3852	0.3894	0.3802	0.3929	--	--
3901	0.4593	0.3495	0.4596	-0.0382	--
3909	0.6307	0.6753	0.9119	0.7945	0.1212

[a]Cases of extremely high effective protection--greater than 900 percent.

The remainder of this appendix will analyze both the adjusted and the legal rates of protection. The major emphasis will be on the former as they are the actual rates in existence and thus those which affect the economic system. On the other hand, it is important to keep in mind when discussing policy decisions that the legal rates, if in effect, would lead to a protectionist system quite distinct from the current one.

Tables K-3 and K-4 attempt to offer a clearer picture of the effective and nominal protection within the Central American manufacturing sector. Two distinct methods for segmenting the manufacturing sector have been used in order to analyze the protection on different classes of industry. The first, used by Max Soto and Carlos Sevilla, classifies all four-digit CIIU categories either as traditional (I) or dynamic sectors.[1] See table K-5. The second method separates all sectors into three categories—traditional (II), intermediate products, and metal-mechanic products. This method was used in the industrial section of the SIECA decade study.[2]

Tables K-3 and K-4 clearly demonstrate that the traditional sector has been receiving much more protection than the dynamic sector in all of the Central American countries except Guatemala. Comparing the intermediate and metal-mechanic sectors—both likely to be dynamic sectors—it appears that the protection is similar among all the countries except Honduras. Honduras has a rather high rate of effective protection in its intermediate goods sector relative to the metal-mechanic one, which seems to be due to a high differential between the nominal rates in the two sectors. It is interesting though that the adjusted nominal tariff rates on both final and intermediate products do not differ that much from those of the other countries in the region, which seems to suggest that Honduran technology must not be very value added intensive in producing intermediate-type goods.

The rates of protection in tables K-3 and K-4 were calculated by weighting the four-digit CIIU rates by the value added of that sector. The omitted observations for both the legal and the adjusted rates were all in the traditional sector. The result of the omissions was to arrive at slightly lower rates than otherwise, that is, actual legal and adjusted protection would have been somewhat higher if these extreme cases were still included in the averaging process.

The material in table K-6 is taken from Little, Scitovsky, and Scott.[3] It is probably quite safe to assume that their classifications of consumption goods, intermediates, and capital goods correspond to the traditional, intermediate, and metal-mechanic sectors of the preceding analysis. Comparing the results for all manufactures in table K-6 with the adjusted effective rates of table K-4, only three of the seven countries represented have rates lower than any of the Central American countries. There are four countries which have rates from two to five times higher than the highest Central American effective rate. Legal rates are much more in line with the countries having high effective rates of protection. Without the presence of the differentials between the legal and adjusted rates of protection, Central America would have an extremely highly protected manufacturing sector. The actual rates seem quite moderate compared with those of many other countries.

Table K-3. Effective and Nominal Protection at Legal Rates

Sector	Guatemala	El Salvador	Honduras	Nicaragua	Costa Rica
Legal Rates of Effective Protection					
Dynamic	57.25	51.06	80.91	62.20	73.80
Traditional I	170.40	214.36	169.53	185.25	225.99
Traditional II	174.00	219.09	174.81	186.70	231.09
Intermediate	55.16	48.07	81.34	63.47	77.10
Metal-mechanic	56.81	54.64	50.40	56.17	61.77
Total Sector	131.45	158.11	140.35	154.11	164.43
Nominal Final Protection					
Dynamic	35.52	36.77	45.15	38.75	36.87
Traditional I	92.65	88.16	90.90	87.69	126.70
Traditional II	94.03	89.76	92.29	88.06	128.86
Intermediate	35.73	36.50	46.26	39.52	38.03
Metal-mechanic	34.11	34.12	37.74	37.69	35.20
Total Sector	72.98	70.46	75.84	75.30	90.35
Intermediate Protection					
Dynamic	18.17	21.92	26.23	19.67	18.44
Traditional I	54.40	45.78	54.15	55.16	75.97
Traditional II	54.42	46.11	53.58	55.07	76.70
Intermediate	21.05	24.29	31.32	21.79	22.54
Metal-mechanic	13.70	14.08	18.54	18.55	12.74
Total Sector	41.93	37.56	44.96	46.18	52.69

Table K-4.   Effective and Nominal Protection: Adjusted Rates

Sector	Guatemala	El Salvador	Honduras	Nicaragua	Costa Rica
Adjusted Rates of Effective Protection					
Dynamic	23.76	27.90	42.41	20.64	20.48
Traditional I	23.57	59.75	64.00	34.59	84.53
Traditional II	24.23	61.30	64.85	35.05	86.31
Intermediate	21.56	25.49	49.90	21.68	20.00
Metal-mechanic	26.77	30.40	13.03	14.74	21.14
Total Sector	23.64	48.78	56.89	31.06	58.61
Nominal Final Protection					
Dynamic	16.29	20.23	14.97	13.17	12.08
Traditional I	17.65	39.11	45.88	26.78	54.98
Traditional II	18.15	40.07	46.89	27.02	56.29
Intermediate	15.34	19.88	15.69	13.87	12.09
Metal-mechanic	15.99	16.89	9.43	10.30	11.30
Total Sector	17.18	32.61	35.70	23.34	37.63
Intermediate Protection					
Dynamic	6.70	10.57	6.50	3.75	4.19
Traditional I	10.01	19.24	25.75	15.32	29.48
Traditional II	10.18	19.53	26.27	15.40	30.19
Intermediate	6.93	11.89	6.13	3.64	4.76
Metal-mechanic	4.97	4.25	6.82	4.32	2.69
Total Sector	8.87	16.25	19.41	12.39	19.25

Table K-5.   Segmentation of Four-Digit CIIU Sector

Sector	Soto Sevilla	SIECA Decade	Sector	Soto Sevilla	SIECA Decade
3111	T	T	3523	D	I
3112	T	T	3533	D	I
3113	T	T	3529	D	I
3114	T	T	3530	D	I
3115	T	T	3540	D	I
3116	T	T	3551	D	I
3117	T	T	3559	D	I
3118	T	T	3560	D	I
3119	T	T	3610	D	I
3121	T	T	3620	D	I
3122	T	T	3691	D	I
3131	T	T	3692	D	I
3132	T	T	3699	D	I
3133	T	T	3710	D	I
3134	T	T	3720	D	I
3140	T	T	3811	D	M
3211	T	T	3812	D	M
3212	T	T	3813	D	M
3213	T	T	3819	D	M
3214	T	T	3821	D	M
3215	T	T	3822	D	M
3219	T	T	3823	D	M
3220	T	T	3824	D	M
3231	T	T	3825	D	M
3232	T	T	3829	D	M
3233	T	T	3831	D	M
3240	T	T	3832	D	I
3311	T	T	3833	D	I
3312	T	T	3839	D	M
3319	T	T	3841	D	M
3411	T	T	3843	D	M
3412	T	I	3844	D	M
3419	T	I	3845	D	M
3420	T	I	3851	D	M
3511	T	T	3852	D	M
3512	D	I	3901	D	M
3521	D	I	3909	D	M
3522	D	I			

NOTE: T = Traditional, D = Dynamic, I = Intermediate, M = Metal-mechanic.

Table K-6. Rates of Effective Protection in Selected Countries

Goods	Argentina	Brazil	Mexico	India	Pakistan	Philippines	Taiwan
Consumption	164	230	22	NA	883	94	NA
Intermediates	167	68	34	NA	88	65	NA
Capital	133	31	55	NA	155	80	NA
All sectors	162	118	27	313	271	49	33

Another interesting way to analyze the effective protection in Central America is to study the distribution of the highest and lowest rates within specific sectors among the five countries. There are seventy-five sectors represented within the data. In three of these (3219, 3823, and 3825) Costa Rica is the only country appearing to exhibit any production. For the seventy-two remaining sectors, table K-7 below depicts the number of sectors in which each of the five Central American countries has the highest effective tariff in the region, and the number in which each has the lowest effective tariff in the region.

Utilizing legal rates, it is obvious that Costa Rica is the most highly protected country in terms of numbers of industries and that El Salvador is the least protected. But, when adjusted rates are chosen for the comparison, though Costa Rica seems to retain its position, that

Table K-7. Country Distribution of Highest and Lowest Rates of Effective Protection: Central America, 72 Sectors

Country	Adjusted Rates		Legal Rates	
	High	Low	High	Low
Guatemala	14	15	16	18-1/2
El Salvador	15	14	7	19-1/2
Honduras	19	8	13	9
Nicaragua	4	21	11	16
Costa Rica	20	14	25	9

position is not as clear-cut as before. It is now Nicaragua rather than El Salvador that exhibits the lowest number of maximum rates and the highest number of minimum rates.

The next section of this appendix analyzes effective and nominal rates of protection in order to discern any clear-cut relationship between these two measures of protection. Little, Scitovsky, and Scott[4] claim "there is normally a good correlation between the two measures. But effective protection for manufactures is usually higher than nominal protection: and in particular cases, the two can diverge quite sharply." This claim seems to be borne out in table K-8 below.

Some rather interesting results arise from table K-8. One thing that stands out is the difference between the relationships for legal rates and for adjusted rates. The correlation coefficients, the t-statistics and the R^2s are all much higher when analyzing the adjusted rates. It seems that adjusted nominal rates are much better predictors

Table K-8. Results of Regressions of Effective Rate of Protection on Nominal Rates (ERP = a (NRP) + b)

Country	a^a		R^2
Legal Rates			
Guatemala	2.1281	(4.3755)	.2197
El Salvador	2.8141	(5.5301)	.3134
Honduras	2.7221	(5.9702)	.4261
Nicaragua	3.9636	(4.9231)	.3402
Costa Rica	4.3252	(4.3580)	.2435
Region	3.1403	(10.568)	.2733
Adjusted Rates			
Guatemala	1.7967	(19.463)	.8478
El Salvador	1.6774	(14.240)	.7517
Honduras	2.0950	(7.3052)	.5265
Nicaragua	1.6800	(19.983)	.8947
Costa Rica	2.4686	(10.851)	.6662
Region	2.0688	(22.388)	.6279

[a]"t-statistic" in parentheses. Critical level of "t" ranges from 3.3 to 3.6.

rates are of legal effec-
might be that intermediate
ce on legal effective protec-
nse that there is probably much
ate rates than among the adjusted
ow from the fact that exonerations
percentage terms and, in the extreme
ations on imported inputs, there would
l intermediate rates as they would all be

effecti   ndertaken of the relation between nominal and
                              tection.   Spearman rank correlation coefficients
were meas.   th legal and adjusted rates.   The coefficient for
the legal r.   equal to .8206 and for the adjusted rates, to .9534,
both signific.   at a 99 percent level.   Another strong presumption can
thus be made that, especially among actual tariffs, the nominal rates
are good guides to the effective rates, at least in terms of rankings.
But it should also be emphasized that effective protection is usually
much higher than nominal protection and that it would take considerable
cuts in the nominal rates to achieve large changes in the effective rates.

The original data for this appendix consist of ninety-five variables
measured in domestic currencies.   See table K-9 for a description of
these variables.

B.   Conversion and Calculation of New Variables

1.   Exchange Rates for Conversion

Guatemala = 1 quetzal / 1 Central American peso.
Honduras = 2 lempiras / 1 Central American peso.
Nicaragua = 7.05 cordobas / 1 Central American peso.
Costa Rica = 7.35 colones / 1 Central American peso.

2.   Calculated Variables

Value added = 77 + 79 - 78 + 80 + 82 - 81 + 83 + 84 + 85 - 38 + 40 - 39.
Gross value of production = 77 + 79 - 78 + 80 + 82 - 81 + 83 + 84 + 85.
Intermediate inputs = 38 - 40 + 39.

The value added concept utilized for this appendix is a gross type
of value added in that it includes such things as net expenditure on
electrical energy, rental payments, third party payments, advertising
expenditures, and insurance premiums.   This choice of concept is made
rather arbitrarily and a more net type of value added could also have
been used.   The author prefers the former concept because of a greater
confidence in the more aggregated figures than in the individual components.   This method essentially corresponds to using a modified Corden
method in the treatment of nontraded goods and services.   All of these
are lumped into value added and it is assumed that they can be benefited
by protection as well as capital and labor.

Variable No.	Description

A — <u>Datos Generales</u>

1	Código del país
2	Número de boleta
3	Clasificación industrial
4	Ano de iniciación
5	Clasificación ley
6	Organización jurídica
7	Provincia o departamento
8	Cantón o municipio

B — <u>Personal Ocupado y Remuneraciones</u> (31-8-68)

B1 — <u>Propietarios y familiares</u>

9	Promedio
10	Personal masculino
11	Personal femenino

B2 — <u>Personal administrativo</u>

12	Promedio
13	Personal masculino
14	Personal femenino
15	Sueldos pagados
16	Cuotas seguros sociales

B3 — <u>Técnicos de producción</u>

17	Promedio
18	Personal masculino
19	Personal femenino
20	Sueldos pagados
21	Cuotas seguros sociales

B4 — <u>Obreros calificados</u>

22	Promedio
23	Personal masculino
24	Personal femenino
25	Sueldos pagados
26	Cuotas seguros sociales

B5 —

27	Promedio
28	Personal masculino
29	Personal femenino
30	Sueldos pagados
31	Cuotas seguros sociales

Table K-9 (Continued)

Variable No.	Description
	C - Energía Eléctrica
32	Energía eléctrica comprada (en KWH)
33	Valor de energía eléctrica comprada
34	Energía eléctrica generada (en KWH)
35	Energía eléctrica vendida (en KWH)
36	Valor de energía eléctrica vendida
37	Energía eléctrica consumida
	D - Compra y Existencia de Materiales
38	Valor total de materias primas compradas
39	Valor de existencias (inicio período)
40	Valor de existencias (final período)
	D1 - Envases y empaques
41	Valor total compras
42	Valor existencias (inicio período)
43	Valor existencias (final período)
	D2 - Combustibles y lubricantes
44	Valor total compras
45	Valor existencias (inicio período)
46	Valor existencias (final período)
	D3 - Otros materiales
47	Valor total compras
48	Valor existencias (inicio período)
49	Valor existencias (final período)
	E - Valor Activo Fijo y Depreciaciones
	E1 - Terrenos, edificios, y otras construcciones
50	Valor inventario inicial de terrenos
51	Adquisiciones en el período (terrenos)
52	Ventas y retiros en el período (terrenos)
53	Valor inventario inicial de edif. y otras construcciones
54	Depreciación acumulada al iniciar el período (edif. y constr.)
55	Adquisiciones de bienes nuevos
56	Adquisiciones de bienes usados
57	Ventas y retiros en el período (edif. y otras constr.)
58	Depreciaciones en el período

Table K-9 (Continued)

Variable No.	Description
	E2 - Maquinarias y equipo de producción
59	Valor inventario inicial
60	Depreciación acumulada al iniciar el período
61	Adquisiciones de bienes nuevos
62	Adquisiciones de bienes usados
63	Ventas y retiros en el período
64	Depreciaciones en el período
	E3 - Vehículos y equipos de transporte
65	Valor inventario inicial
66	Depreciación acumulada al iniciar el período
67	Adquisiciones de bienes nuevos
68	Adquisiciones de bienes usados
69	Ventas y retiros en el período
70	Depreciaciones en el período
	E4 - Mobiliario, equipo de oficina, y otros
71	Valor inventario inicial
72	Depreciación acumulada al iniciar el período
73	Adquisiciones de bienes nuevos
74	Adquisiciones de bienes usados
75	Ventas y retiros en el período
76	Depreciaciones en el período
	F - Venta y Existencia de Productos
	F1 - Productos elaborados
77	Valor total ventas
78	Valor existencias (inicio período)
79	Valor existencias (final período)
	F2 - Productos en proceso de elaboración
80	Valor ventas
81	Valor existencias (inicio período)
82	Valor existencias (final período)
	G - Otros Ingresos
83	Por trabajos y servicios a terceros
84	Valor venta artículos sin transformación
85	Otros
	H - Gastos Generales
86	Pagos por arrendamientos de terrenos y edificios
87	Alquileres de maquinarias y equipos
88	Intereses pagados

711

Table K-9 (Continued)

Variable No.	Description
89	Impuestos sobre producción
90	Otros impuestos
91	Seguros del establecimiento y sus activos fijos
92	Gastos de propaganda
93	Sumas pagadas a terceros por trabajos de caracter industrial
94	Sumas pagadas a terceros por servicios profesionales
95	Otros gastos

Appendix K

NOTES

1. "The Demand for Manufacturing Labor: Empirical Results" by Max A. Soto and Carlos A. Sevilla. Chapter 5 in 1st vol. SIECA/Brookings ed. by Cline and Enrique Delgado.

2. "El Desarrollo Integrado de Centroamerica en la Presente Decada" (Guatemala: SIECA, 1972).

3. I. M. D. Little, T. Scitovsky, and M. Scott, <u>Industry and Trade in Some Developing Countries</u> (New York: Oxford University Press, 1970), p. 174.

4. Ibid., p. 169.